Notable Asian Americans

Notable
Asian
Americans

Helen Zia and
Susan B. Gall, Editors

Foreword by George Takei

An International Thomson Publishing Company

NEW YORK • LONDON • BONN • BOSTON • DETROIT • MADRID
MELBOURNE • MEXICO CITY • PARIS • SINGAPORE • TOKYO
TORONTO • WASHINGTON • ALBANY NY • BELMONT CA • CINCINNATI OH

Notable Asian Americans was produced by
Eastword Publications Development, Inc., Cleveland, Ohio

Gale Research Inc. Staff

Allison McNeill, *Developmental Editor*
Lawrence W. Baker, *Managing Editor*
Paulette Petrimoulx, *Copyeditor*

Mary Beth Trimper, *Production Director*
Evi Seoud, *Assistant Production Manager*
Mary Kelley, *Production Associate*

Cynthia Baldwin, *Product Design Manager*
Barbara J. Yarrow, *Graphic Services Supervisor*
Somberg Design, *Cover Design*
Willie Mathis, *Camera Operator*

Library of Congress Cataloging-in-Publication Data

Notable Asian Americans/Helen Zia and Susan B. Gall, editors–1st ed.
468 p. cm.
Includes bibliographical references and index.
ISBN 0-8103-9623-8
1. Asian Americans–Biography. I. Zia, Helen. II. Gall, Susan B.
E184.06N67 1994
920'.009295073'–dc20 94–33638
CIP

Contents

Highlights

Notable Asian Americans is a reference source designed to meet the burgeoning need for information on this fast-growing ethnic group in the United States. This work contains 250 biographical sketches of noteworthy Asian Americans, both living and deceased, from all fields of endeavor. Included are:

- Hiroaki "Rocky" Aoki, Entrepreneur

- March Fong Eu, Politician, ambassador

- Lance Ito, Judge

- Brandon Lee, Actor

- Greg Louganis, Olympic diver

- Yo-Yo Ma, Cellist

- Syngman Rhee, Political activist

- Amy Tan, Writer

- Tritia Toyota, Television journalist

- Chien-Shiung Wu, Physicist

Sketches are signed by the writers and, whenever possible, include information gathered from interviews—conducted especially for *Notable Asian Americans*—with the listees themselves, lending unique information and personal insights to the sketch. Other special features include:

- Over 220 photographs of listees

- Comprehensive subject index listing important people, places, terms, and organizations mentioned in the text

- Occupation and ethnicity indexes allowing greater access to listees

- Guest foreword by television and movie actor George Takei

Foreword

In my role as Sulu in the television series *Star Trek*, I served on the Starship *Enterprise* with two men who had foreign accents—Pavel Checkov and Montgomery Scott; I worked beside an African woman named Uhura, an Iowa-born captain named James Kirk, and even a pointy-eared alien named Mr. Spock.

We had no glass ceilings with Star Fleet. From helmsman of the *Enterprise*, I became the captain of the U.S.S. *Excelsior*. In microcosm, the Star Fleet represents an American ideal, in its diversity and its strengths. We were able to tap many different talents and viewpoints to take on a common challenge. We had confidence in our abilities, innovativeness and creativity. Indeed, life on the *Enterprise* and the *Excelsior* is vibrant and engaging because of its pluralism. *Star Trek* is a life-affirming, optimistic view of our future. It is science fiction.

The United States is a unique experiment in pluralism. We say that pluralism is our strength and we have struggled to build a nation of people from many diverse backgrounds on the fundamental ideals of justice, opportunity and human dignity, but in real life these ideals have often been in collision, with prejudice and racism serving to undermine our pluralism. Asian Americans are no strangers to such biases. In my parents' generation, World War II brought a presidential executive order that suspended the Constitution and the principle of due process for Japanese Americans, cancelled our citizenship and any form of individual justice.

Today these biases exist in large part because, historically, Asian Americans have been defined by others. Our story has been told for us by non-Asians. Whether by benign Asiaphiles like Pearl Buck or "yellow journalists" like William Randolph Hearst, we have often been characterized by others loving us or hating us. In the movies and on stage, we have held subordinate roles and have been told what to say and how to behave by non-Asian writers and directors. Whether by novelists or journalists, by academics, artists or politicians, the image of Asians in America has repeatedly been shaped, molded, and formed for us by non-Asians. The result is the stereotyping by which we are perceived in much of America.

Any opportunity to look at the real lives of Asian Americans is an opportunity to break those stereotyped images that have been shaped for us. It is essential to shatter such rigid molds and define ourselves in America so that open dialogue and a free flow of ideas can truly exist in this pluralistic society.

Notable Asian Americans offers an opportunity to understand the Asian American. By using this book as a means to understanding our pluralism and the fundamental ideals of our society, the social science fiction of *Star Trek* can become a reality. If I may paraphrase a greeting from *Star Trek*, gain strength from diversity, live long, and prosper.

George Takei

Introduction

Of the many forces that have motivated me as a writer and an activist, one of the most significant has been the need to understand what it means to be Asian American. The eldest daughter of very traditional Chinese immigrants, I often felt that I was straddling two worlds—one Asian, the other American—with neither representing the reality of my life. But growing up in New Jersey in the 1950s, it was hard to construct an Asian American sensibility when I never saw people who looked like me in the images of the world around me.

It wasn't for lack of searching that I failed to find those role models. When I was a young girl, I devoured books about historic figures and what life was like for them when they were kids. Frank W. Woolworth, Clara Barton, Babe Ruth, Virginia Dare, Thomas Edison, Knute Rockne—even the briefest of biographies made their lives seem so real. My imagination would spin with endless possibilities, of life abroad as a foreign correspondent, or an explorer of undersea worlds—or distant galaxies.

Yet when it came to thinking about my own true-life prospects, I couldn't make the connection. It never occurred to me that I, a young Asian American girl, could ever become an astronaut, a pioneer, an entrepreneur, or a correspondent. None of the people I read about or saw on screen had almond-shaped eyes or skin color like mine; they didn't get stared at because they looked different or cursed at to "go back where [they] came from"—the way I often did.

In a thousand different ways I and other Asian Americans were also told that our Asianness was non-existent. During the civil rights movement in the 1960s, I remember talking with my high school classmates about the urban uprisings taking place across the United States, when an African American girlfriend turned to me and said, "Helen, you've got to decide whether you're black or white."

Even today, this attitude is still too common. As recently as 1992, following the civil disturbances in Los Angeles after the Rodney King verdicts, report after report considered the issue to be solely black and white—despite the well-documented impact on Asian Americans in L.A.

Looking back, I now know why my dreams were so limited. In the popular consciousness of America, people of Asian descent are not black, not white, not really American. Where can Asian American young people go to learn about people who look like themselves who are accomplishing noteworthy deeds? The absence of such role models is a vast empty space in a young person's imagination; how can a child reach for a star that she or he has never seen?

I can think of no good reason for the empty space to exist. Of the millions of Asian Americans who have blazed their own distinctive paths, there are innumerable wonderful stories to tell. Many are in *Notable Asian Americans*. Readers will find accounts of rich and varied ethnic backgrounds and career paths—American dreams realized from a wide range of starting points.

Notable Asian Americans was compiled with the help of dozens of people. Editorial advisors assisted with the nomination and selection of profilees, gifted writers and journalists from all over the country contributed the profiles, many of which are based on personal interviews. Management of the entire project was undertaken by the dedicated staff of Eastword Publications, led by the unflappable Susan Gall. From first nominations to final edit, the effort took more than two years.

As with any book of this type it is unfortunate that more notables could not be included. There are certainly many extraordinary individuals missing from this edition in spite of the care that went into soliciting nominations. A list of candidates for the next edition of *Notable Asian Americans* is already being compiled, and the editors invite your comments.

I am proud to be associated with this first edition of *Notable Asian Americans*. It gives me a very special feeling to know that an Asian American child in New Jersey is likely to read this book and think that she or he might one day be an astronaut like Eugene Trinh, a pioneer like Urvashi Vaid, an entrepreneur like Josie Natori, or a foreign correspondent like James Hattori. This book is a giant step toward filling those vast empty spaces with vibrant, inspiring stories of real-life Asian Americans so that every star, no matter how bright or how far, seems within reach.

Helen Zia

Acknowledgments

Many people helped in the preparation of *Notable Asian Americans*. Our advisors and writers were creative and supportive, embracing the project with enthusiasm from the start. In addition, there are several individuals who contributed special expertise and effort to make the work a reality: Our editors at Gale Research were Amy Marcaccio, who developed the concept, and Allison McNeill, whose expert advice and patient attention to detail proved invaluable. Paulette Petrimoulx and Betty King, copyeditor and proofreader respectively, added considerably to the consistency and accuracy of the profiles. Deb Rutti, graphic artist and typesetter, applied her considerable skills to produce the final pages under a tight deadline. But above all, appreciation is due to the Asian Americans profiled in this work. Their willingness to reflect on details of their lives—sometimes painful to recall—guarantees depth and perspective to the profiles and a rewarding experience for the users of this work.

Please send comments and suggestions to:

The Editors

Notable Asian Americans

Gale Research Inc.

835 Penobscot Bldg.

Detroit, MI 48226

800-347-GALE

Entrants

Occupation Index

Ethnicity Index

About the Editors

Helen Zia is a contributing editor to *Ms.* magazine, the nation's leading feminist publication, where she was formerly executive editor. She has been an activist for social justice for most of her life on issues ranging from civil rights and peace to women's equality and countering hate violence.

A second-generation Chinese American who grew up with her sister and four brothers in New Jersey, Zia began working in her parent's floral novelty business when she was five years old. She is a graduate of Princeton University's Woodrow Wilson School of Public and International Affairs, where she was a Woodrow Wilson Scholar and a member of the university's first graduating class of women.

Zia has been recognized for her work as a investigative reporter and magazine editor, receiving writing awards from the Asian American Journalists Association, the National Women's Political Caucus, the American Society of Business Press Editors, the Detroit Press Club, and the Jesse Neal Award.

As an activist, Zia has been involved in the Asian anti-violence movement; her work on the Asian American landmark civil rights case is documented in the Academy Award-nominated film, *Who Killed Vincent Chin?* She is one of the founders of Detroit-based American Citizens for Justice, the first organization in the United States to counter anti-Asian violence, and she is a member of the National Network Against Anti-Asian Violence. Zia lives with her life partner, Lia Shigemura, in the San Francisco Bay Area, where she is editor-in-chief of a multimedia publishing company. Among her many activities, she particularly enjoys discussing contemporary issues with Asian American young people.

Susan Gall is partner with her husband Timothy Gall in Eastword Publications Development, Inc., specializing in the development of reference books and electronic media. In addition to *Notable Asian Americans*, Eastword has produced two other works concerning this rapidly growing segment of the U.S. population—*Statistical Record of Asian Americans* (1993), and *Asian American Almanac* (1995). All three are published by Gale Research Inc. Gall holds a master's in business administration from Case Western Reserve University's Weatherhead School of Management. Prior to forming Eastword, she worked for over ten years developing training programs and educational materials for an arboretum, a large professional society, and for a New York-based publisher of technical training programs.

Editorial Advisors

The following individuals contributed to the development of *Notable Asian Americans* in many ways—from reviewing the list of nominees, to suggesting individuals to be profiled, to helping our researchers and writers locate profilees for interviews. *Notable Asian Americans* could not have been prepared without their insights and suggestions.

Benjamin Aranda
American Bar Association

Valerie Chow Bush
Asian American Journalists Association

Lillian Gonzalez-Pardo
American Women's Medical Association

Daniel K. Inouye
U.S. Senator

Le Xuan Khoa
Southeast Asian Resource Action Center

Lillian Kimura
Japanese American Citizens League

Daphne Kwok
Organization of Chinese Americans

Kamla Motihar, Librarian
Andrew W. Mellon Foundation

Irene Natividad
National Commission on Working Women

Shazia Rafi
Parliamentarians for Global Action

Linda Sherry
Asian Week

Jeff Yang
A. *Magazine*

Melinda Yee
U.S. Department of Commerce

Affiliations listed were those in effect at the time of involvement with the project.

Contributors

Valerie Chow Bush

Samuel R. Cacas

Steven Chin

Shamita Das DasGupta

Ferdinand M. de Leon

Marilyn Eppich

Susan Gall

Himanee Gupta

Jim Henry

Terry Hong

Susan Ketchum

Nan Kim

Mary Anne Klasen

Melanie Mavrides

Nancy Moore

Kim Moy

Felicia Paik

Natasha Rafi

Shazia Rafi

Margaret Simon

Anne Standley

Visi Tilak

Cindy Washabaugh

Grace Wong

Amy Wu

Douglas Wu

Helen Zia

Photo Credits

The photos used in *Notable Asian Americans* came from the following sources:

Cover photos (clockwise from center), **courtesy of Josie Cruz Natori; courtesy of Christine Choy; courtesy of ICM Artists, Ltd.; courtesy of Daniel K. Inouye.**

Courtesy of Daniel Akaka: page 1; **Photograph by Frank Ockenfels 3,** ©1993 Sony Music, courtesy of Columbia Records: page 3; **Courtesy of Benihana:** page 5; **Courtesy of George Aratani:** page 6; **Courtesy of George R. Ariyoshi:** page 8; **Courtesy of Simon and Schuster:** page 10; **AP/Wide World Photos:** page 11; **Photo by Liane Enkelis Photography, courtesy of Kavelle Bajaj:** page 13; **Courtesy of Atlanta Ballet:** page 15; **Courtesy of Lynda Barry:** page 18; **Courtesy of Julia Chang Bloch:** page 19; **Filipino American National Historical Society Collection, used by permission:** page 21; **Photograph by Ackerman Photography, courtesy of Phyllis J. Campbell:** page 23; **AP/Wide World Photos:** page 25; **Courtesy of M. Casto:** page 26; **Photograph by C.W. Monaghan, courtesy of Benjamin J. Cayetano:** page 27; **Courtesy of Dia Cha:** page 29; **Courtesy John Cha:** page 31; **Photograph by Mariana Romo-Carmona, courtesy of June Chan:** page 32; **Courtesy of Chandrasekhar Subrahmanyan:** page 34; **Photograph by Russ Adams Productions, courtesy of Michael Chang:** page 35; **Photograph by Christian Steiner, courtesy of Sarah Chang:** page 37; **Courtesy of Elaine Chao:** page 39; **Courtesy of Stephen Chao:** page 41; **Reuters/Bettman:** page 43; **Courtesy of William Shao Chen:** page 45; **Courtesy of Dr. Joy Cherian:** page 46; **Photograph by ILM, courtesy of Doug Chiang:** page 48; **Photograph by NASA, courtesy of Leroy Chiao:** page 49; **Courtesy of Corky Lee:** page 51; **Courtesy of Margaret Cho:** page 53; **Courtesy of Ping Chong:** page 55; **Courtesy of Rachelle B. Chong:** page 57; **Courtesy of Vernon Chong:** page 58; **Courtesy of Deepak Chopra:** page 59; **Photograph by Mark America, courtesy of Christine Choy:** page 61; **Courtesy of Herbert Y.C. Choy:** page 64; **Photo by Tony Esparza, courtesy of CBS Inc.:** page 66; **Courtesy of Eugene Chung:** page 67; **Courtesy of Lilia Clemente:** page 69; **International Swimming Hall of Fame:** page 71; **Courtesy of Dinesh D'Souza:** page 73; **Courtesy of Phoebe Eng:** page 74; **Photograph by Harry, courtesy of March Fong Eu:** page 76; **Courtesy of *Asian Week*:** page 78; **Courtesy of Hiram Fong:** page 79; **Courtesy of Matthew Fong:** page 81; **Courtesy of IMG Artists:** page 83; **Courtesy of John Liu Fugh:** page 84; **AP/Wide World Photos:** page 86; **Courtesy of Lillian Gonzalez-Pardo:** page 89; **Photo by Hideo Yoshida, courtesy Philip Kan Gotanda:** page 91; **Courtesy of Wendy Lee Gramm:** page 92; **Photograph by Max Hirshfeld, courtesy of Emil Guillermo:** page 94; **Photograph by Joe Berger, courtesy of McKinsey & Company, Inc.:** page 95; **Photograph by Paul I. Tanedo, courtesy of Maria Haley:** page 97; **Courtesy of Ross Harano:** page 99; **Courtesy of Sumi Haru:** page 101; **Courtesy of Lon Hatamiya:** page 103; **Courtesy of James Hattori:** page 105; **UPI/Bettmann:** page 106; **Courtesy of *A. Magazine*:** page 108; **Courtesy of Le Ly Hayslip:** page 109; **Courtesy of Irene Hirano:** page 111; **Courtesy of David Ho:** page 113; **Courtesy of Reginald Ho:** page 115; **Courtesy of Florence Hongo:** page 117; **Photograph by Susan Gilbert, courtesy of Jeanne Wakatsuki Houston:** page 119; **Courtesy of David Henry Hwang:** page 123; **Courtesy of Daniel K. Inouye:** page 127; **Courtesy of Seattle Mariners:** page 129; **AP/Wide World Photos:** page 131; **AP/Wide World Photos:** page 133; **Photograph © Mark Richards, courtesy of Knopf:** page 135; **Courtesy of H.W. Pak:** page 136; **AP/Wide World:** page 140; **Photograph © Joyce Ravid, courtesy of Viking:** page 142; **International Swimming Hall of Fame:** page 144; **© 1990 Capital Cities/ABC, Inc., used with permission:** page 146; **Courtesy of Joyce Kennard:** page 148; **AP/Wide World Photos:** page 151; **Courtesy of Andrew Kim:** page 152; **Courtesy of Elaine H. Kim:** page 154; **Courtesy of Jay Kim:** page 156; **Courtesy of Ki Ho Him:** page 157; **Courtesy of San Francisco Giants:** page 159; **Courtesy of Lillian Kimura:** page 162; **Courtesy of Harry H.L. Kitano:** page 167; **Courtesy of Harold Koh:** page 168; **AP/Wide World Photos:** page 169; **Courtesy K.V. Kumar:** page 173; **Courtesy of Paul Kuroda:** page 174; **Courtesy of Cheryl A. Lau:** page 177; **Courtesy of Fred Lau:** page 179; **Courtesy of Good Machine:** page 181; **Photo by Robert Zuckerman, courtesy of *A. Magazine*:** page 182; **Photo by Columbia Pictures Industries, courtesy of *A. Magazine*:** page 185; **Courtesy of Carol F. Lee:** page 188; **Courtesy of Christopher Lee:** page 189; **Photograph © Norman Studios, courtesy of Knopf:** page 192; **Courtesy of K.W. Lee:** page 195; **Photograph by Marty Umans:** page 197; **Courtesy of Ronald D. Lee:** page 199; **Courtesy of Roosevelt University Library:** page 200; **Courtesy of Sammy Lee:** page 202; **Archive Photos:** page 204; **AP/Wide World Photos:** page 205; **Courtesy of Channing Liem:** page 209; **AP/Wide World Photos:**

page 210; **Photo by Ascherman, courtesy of The Cleveland Orchestra:** page 212; **Courtesy of Gary Locke:** page 214; **Photo by Robert McEwan, courtesy Lone Dragon Productions, Inc.:** page 216; **Photo by Bachrach, courtesy of Ivy Books:** page 219; **Courtesy of Greg Louganis:** page 221; **Photo by Amy Cheng, courtesy of Knopf:** page 223; **Photo by Elsonz Alexandre, courtesy of Elwood Lui:** page 225; **Photograph by J. Henry Fair, courtesy of ICM Artists, Ltd.:** page 227; **Courtesy of Mako:** page 231; **Courtesy of Beckie Masaki:** page 233; **Courtesy of Tom Matano:** page 236; **Courtesy of Prema Mathai-Davis:** page 237; **Courtesy of Robert T. Matsui:** page 239; **UPI/Bettman:** page 241; **Courtesy of Nobu McCarthy:** page 242; **Courtesy of Ruthann Lum McCunn:** page 245; **Courtesy of Ajai Singh "Sonny" Mehta:** page 247; **AP/Wide World Photos:** page 249; **Courtesy of Zubin Mehta:** page 251; **Courtesy of Merchant Ivory Productions:** page 253; **Photograph by Satoru Ishikawa, courtesy of The Midori Foundation:** page 255; **Photograph by Joan Chen, courtesy of Pantheon Books:** page 257; **Courtesy of Dale Minami:** page 258; **Courtesy of Norman Mineta:** page 259; **Courtesy of Patsy Mink:** page 261; **Photograph by George T. Kruse, courtesy of Janice Mirikitani:** page 263; **Courtesy of the Morikami Museumand Japanese Gardens:** page 265; **Academy of Motion Picture Arts and Sciences:** page 267; **Courtesy of William C. W. Mow:** page 269; **Photograph © Jerry Bauer, courtesy of Knopf:** page 271; **Photograph by Christian Steiner, courtesy of Columbia Artists Management Inc.:** page 273; **Courtesy of Perez Production Ltd.:** page 275; **Courtesy of Don Nakanishi:** page 277; **Photograph by Corky Lee, courtesy of Phil Tajitsu Nash:** page 279; **Photograph by Michael Geissinger, courtesy of Irene Natividad:** page 281; **Courtesy of Josie Cruz Natori:** page 283; **Courtesy of Haing S. Ngor:** page 285; **Courtesy of Sean Nguyen:** page 287; **AP/Wide World Photos:** page 290; **Courtesy of Gyo Obata:** page 292; **Photograph by Frank Wolfe, LBJ Library Collection:** page 297; **Courtesy of Steven Okazaki:** page 299; **Courtesy of Ayub Ommaya:** page 301; **Courtesy of NASA:** page 303; **AP/Wide World Photos:** page 305; **Photograph by Larry's Photography, courtesy of George Ow, Jr.:** page 309; **Photography by Christian Steiner, courtesy of Seiji Ozawa:** page 311; **Photograph by Ingbet Gruttner, courtesy of Ieoh Ming Pei:** page 313; **Courtesy of Arati Prabhakar:** page 317; **AP/Wide World Photos:** page 319; **Courtesy of Beulah Quo:** page 322; **Courtesy of AST Research:** page 324; **Courtesy of Jhoon Rhee:** page 326; **UPI/Bettmann:** page 328; **Courtesy of Patricia Saiki:** page 331; **Courtesy of Richard Sakakida:** page 335; **AP/Wide World Photos:** page 336; **Courtesy of Scott Sassa:** page 337; **AP/Wide World Photos:** page 339; **Courtesy of Allen Say:** page 341; **Courtesy of San Diego Chargers:** page 342; **Photograph by Aradhana Seth, courtesy of HarperCollins:** page 343; **Photo by Wah Lui, Yuen Lui Studio, courtesy of Bright Sheng:** page 345; **Courtesy of Milkweed Editions:** page 348; **Courtesy of The White House:** page 350; **Courtesy of Pitambar (Peter) Somani:** page 352; **Photo by John Eddy, courtesy of Cathy Song:** page 354; **Photograph by Kevin Leong, courtesy of Anna Sui:** page 357; **Photograph by Corky Lee, courtesy of Betty Lee Sung:** page 359; **Courtesy of Bob Suzuki:** page 361; **Photograph by Travis Photography, courtesy of Shirin Tahir-Kheli:** page 363; **Photo by Carol Takaki, courtesy of Ronald Takaki:** page 365; **AP/Wide World Photos:** page 367; **Courtesy of Paramount Pictures:** page 369; **Courtesy of G.P.Putnam's Sons:** page 371; **Courtesy of Thomas Tang:** page 373; **Photograph by Ajay Malik, courtesy of Arcade Publishing:** page 374; **Photograph by John Blaustein, courtesy of Chang-Lin Tien:** page 376; **AP/Wide World Photos:** page 378; **Courtesy of Charles D. Toy:** page 381; **AP/Wide World Photos:** page 383; **Photograph by NASA, courtesy of Eugene Trinh:** page 384; **AP/Wide World Photos:** page 385; **Photograph by Deborah Storms, courtesy of the estate of Yoshiko Uchida:** page 387; **Courtesy of Huynh Cong Ut:** page 389; **Photograph by Patsy Lynch:** page 390; **Photograph by Eric Lachica, courtesy of David M. Valderrama:** page 392; **Photograph by Trung Doan, courtesy of Simon and Schuster:** page 395; **Courtesy of John David Waihee, III:** page 397; **Courtesy of Wang Laboratories:** page 399; **Courtesy of Charles B. Wang:** page 401; **Courtesy of Charles Pei Wang:** page 403; **Photograph by NASA, courtesy of Taylor Wang:** page 405; **Courtesy of Vera Wang:** page 406; **AP/Wide World Photos:** page 409; **Courtesy of Michi Weglyn:** page 411; **Academy of Motion Picture Arts and Sciences:** page 415; **Courtesy of Touchstone Picture & Television:** page 417; **Courtesy of Flossie Wong-Staal:** page 419; **Courtesy of S.B. Woo:** page 420; **AP/Wide World Photos:** page 421; **AP/Wide World Photos:** page 423; **Photograph by Taro Yamasaki, courtesy of the photographer:** page 428; **Archive Photos:** page 429; **AP/Wide World Photos:** page 432; **Photograph by Sue Klemens Photography, courtesy of Melinda C. Yee:** page 434; **Photograph by K. Yep, courtesy of Laurence Yep:** page 435; **Courtesy of Shirley Young:** page 437; **Photograph © David Weintraub, courtesy of Connie Young Yu:** page 439; **Courtesy of Diane Yu:** page 441; **Courtesy of Eleanor N. Yu:** page 443; **Photograph by Danny Feld, courtesy of Columbia Pictures:** page 445.

Notable
Asian
Americans

A

Daniel K. Akaka

(1924–)

Politician, educator

While other politicians grandstand to win votes and impress colleagues, Senator Daniel K. Akaka is a quiet presence in Congress. Keeping a low profile is his trademark. But while the slight man with the salt-and-pepper hair quietly shuns the spotlight in Washington's beltway, he has not gone unnoticed. As the U.S. Senate's first native Hawaiian ever to serve and the only currently sitting native Hawaiian and Chinese American member of Congress, he has been successful with a sharp focus: to preserve and bolster Hawaii's interests. So intensely devoted is he to his native land that in 1990 he delayed accepting an appointment to the U.S. Senate after serving in the U.S. House of Representatives for fourteen years, until he could ensure that several projects in Hawaii would advance by the House Appropriation's Committee.

His reserved nature is rooted in the "spirit of Aloha," as Akaka calls it. "I am not a born politician," he said in an interview with Melanie J. Mavrides. "People tell me I have to be feisty to get my way in Congress. But that's not my style. I use my Hawaiian abilities and the spirit of Aloha that brings people together."

Island Roots

Akaka's gift for bringing people together was inherited from his mother and father, he told Mavrides. Born in Honolulu on September 11, 1924, Daniel K. Akaka was the youngest of eight children in a deeply religious family that managed to live in a cramped, two-bedroom house. His father had attained a third-grade education and worked in a machine shop that molded steel pots used to boil sugar cane. "My big goal as a boy was to work at Pearl Harbor. But I somehow never made it there," he said.

As early as he can remember, Akaka says he began to understand that Hawaii's future hinged on a better-trained workforce. Despite his parents' lack of education, they had insisted that their children get a good education in order to have more options outside of the hard-labor jobs most natives were forced to take on sugar and coffee plantations.

Daniel K. Akaka

At his parents' urging, Akaka decided he would go to school and obtain advanced degrees. He enrolled in the Hamehameha School for Boys, a private school from which he graduated in 1942. He began looking for work to earn money for college. He became a welder with the Hawaiian Electric Company before joining the U.S. Army Corps of Engineers as a welder-mechanic. By 1945, the nation was at war and he was stationed with the Army Corps in Saipan and Tinian. After the war, he enrolled at the University of Hawaii to fulfill his dream of becoming a teacher. He obtained a bachelor's degree in education in 1953, a certificate to teach secondary education the following year, and a master's in education in 1966.

From his parents, Akaka said, he learned about community service, which laid the foundation for his political career. "My parents believed in feeding and helping others," he recalled to Mavrides. "My mother would yell to our visitors, 'Hele Mai E Ai,' which means 'Come in and eat.'"

Leader in Education

It wasn't long before Akaka became known as a rising star on the state's education front. He had extensive teaching experience, having worked in rural and urban schools and, later, in a military school. Akaka was even a school principal for a time. At an education convention in 1963, Akaka got his first taste of politics. It was his first year as a school principal and he had been chosen as a delegate to the National Convention of the Department of Elementary School Principals, which was held in Hawaii that year.

Determined to spread good will and the "Aloha spirit" on Hawaii's behalf, Akaka arrived at the convention with a truckload of flower leis and macadamia nuts. But his hospitality didn't end there. "They needed some impromptu entertainment so I ended up singing "Blue Hawaii" before 6,000 delegates," he said, laughing. By this time, Akaka's public exposure as an educational leader was building. Before the national convention had adjourned, he was approached to run for the National Board of Directors.

In 1968, Akaka was named program specialist for the state Department of Education. Six years later, Democratic gubernatorial candidate George R. Ariyoshi had tapped him as his choice for lieutenant governor. Although Akaka lost in the Democratic primary, Ariyoshi won his bid for governor and appointed Akaka as his special assistant for human resources.

Politics and the Future

In 1976, Akaka decided to run for U.S. representative. He took eighty percent of the vote and has won by substantial margins in every election since. Akaka served nearly seven terms in the U.S. House of Representatives before he was appointed in 1990 to fill the senate seat left vacant after the death of Senator Spark M. Matsunaga. In both his House and Senate positions, Akaka earned a reputation for being a liberal Democrat. In 1984, the House Democratic leadership was one vote shy on a crucial roll call to block President Ronald Reagan's request for production of the MX missile, a controversial weapons system. Akaka's last-minute vote was critical for the anti-MX forces victory, several observers say. And later in the Senate, Akaka vigorously spoke out and voted against the confirmation of Clarence Thomas, who was viewed as a conservative candidate for Supreme Court Justice.

Formidable opposition doesn't phase Akaka. After joining the Senate ranks, he successfully fought an effort by Democratic Senator Bill Bradley of New Jersey to cut federal sugar subsidies by two cents per pound, a threatening proposition to Hawaii's sugar cane growers. His motion to table Bradley's amendment to the 1990 farm bill passed by a 54–44 vote. Tiny compared to Bradley, a lanky, former pro basketball player, Akaka joked afterward: "I'm only 5-feet-7, but I slam-dunked him."

Akaka believes that Hawaii faces numerous social and environmental problems today. As a vacation destination, the state relies on tourism to stay afloat but must bear the negative impact on its environment, he told Mavrides. About seventy percent of all endangered species covered by federal law are located in Hawaii, Akaka noted, adding, "We need to take precautions." Nature has also wreaked havoc in Hawaii. After Hurricane Iniki ripped through the islands in September of 1992 leaving chaos in its wake, Akaka successfully lobbied the Federal Emergency Management Agency to establish a Hawaiian field office.

Akaka is also concerned with setting history straight. He worked to get a congressional joint resolution signed in 1993 that formally apologized to Hawaiians for the 1893 overthrow of the islands' native government. In this vein, Akaka worked to establish the Kahoolawe Island Conveyance Commission. Kahoolawe, located southwest of Maui, was recently returned to the people of Hawaii after it had long been used as a military practice site. He also got bills signed into law to commend civilians who acted heroically in the aftermath of Pearl Harbor.

Overcoming the barriers of racial discrimination and his impoverished roots are the things that Akaka most likes to reflect on. He frequently talks to native Hawaiian groups, urging people to get involved in community service. He's not afraid to brag about the accomplishments of his own family; he has been married to Mary Mildred Chong since 1948, and the couple has four children and fourteen grandchildren. Several family members work in the social services in Hawaii.

Speaking before a group of lawyers in Honolulu recently, Akaka urged native Hawaiians to considered running for public office. "You are our strength," he told members of the National Asian Pacific American Bar Association. "You are our hope. Your skills and commitment provide the tools we need to change what is wrong today and build what is right for tomorrow. You do indeed hold the keys to power... the power to help. All I ask is that you never let anger and fear and hurt displace the pureness of your hearts as the force that drives your search for it or your use of it. Mahalo! (Thank you). Aloha!"

Sources:

Books

Congressional Quarterly's Politics in America: 1994, the 103rd Congress. Washington, DC: Congressional Quarterly, Inc., 1994.

Other

Akaka, Daniel, telephone interview with Melanie J. Mavrides, June 23, 1994.

Akaka, Daniel, professional resume and press releases supplied by Bob Ogawa, press officer, 1994.

—Sketch by Melanie J. Mavrides

Toshiko Akiyoshi
(1929–)
Jazz pianist, band leader, composer, arranger

Toshiko Akiyoshi

The first time jazz legend Oscar Peterson heard Toshiko Akiyoshi play in 1953, he referred to her as the greatest female jazz pianist he had ever heard. Twenty years later, Akiyoshi would have her own band, the seventeen-piece Toshiko Akiyoshi Jazz Orchestra. The group would eventually garner twelve Grammy nominations and earn for its founder the Best Arranger title and the Best Big Jazz Band award in the 1978 *Down Beat* Readers' Poll, making Akiyoshi the first woman in jazz history to be so honored. For four consecutive years Akiyoshi and the band were again named Best Arranger and Best Big Jazz Band by *Down Beat*. In 1992, Akiyoshi and the band celebrated Akiyoshi's thirty-fifth year in the United States recording *Toshiko Akiyoshi Live at Carnegie Hall,* their first album for Columbia Records.

Born in Manchuria, China, on December 18, 1929, Toshiko Akiyoshi was the last of four daughters. Growing up in China, she first considered a career in medicine: "My father always wanted me to go to medical school .... I suppose he was disappointed he never had a son, and for some reason he thought I would be the one to accomplish something," she said in a 1992 press release.

Akiyoshi's family returned to Japan in 1946 and settled in the resort town of Beppu. Although she had been classically trained, she found a job playing piano in one of the many dance halls set up for the numerous post-World War II occupation soldiers who populated the region. The music she played was not exactly jazz, but eventually, she met a young man who introduced her to Teddy Wilson's recording of "Sweet Lorraine" as well as other jazz greats via his 78 r.p.m. record collection. The young Akiyoshi was convinced she had found her musical medium.

Restless in her small town, Akiyoshi moved to Tokyo where there was an active jazz scene. By 1952, she had her own group. This was an exciting time in Japanese jazz. Many American giants were touring Japan, and often they would stop by the clubs and play with local musicians, inlcuding Akiyoshi. She was spotted by Oscar Peterson during Norman Granz's 1953 "Jazz at the Philharmonic" tour of Japan who told Granz that Akiyoshi was the greatest female jazz pianist he had ever heard. This led to her first recording, accompanied by Peterson's own rhythm section.

An American Life

In 1956, Akiyoshi arrived in the United States to study at the prestigious Berklee College of Music, in Boston, Massachusetts. Graduating in 1959, she played in numerous clubs in major cities throughout the United States where she encountered both racial and gender prejudice. She recalled that people were amazed to see an Asian woman playing jazz.

After years of performing as a solo artist and with small groups, Akiyoshi moved to Los Angeles in 1973 and with the help of saxophone player Lew Tabackin, who had become her husband, formed what she then referred to as a "rehearsal band." The modest band she founded soon evolved into the Toshiko Akiyoshi Jazz Orchestra and their first recording, *Kogun,* is recognized as one of the best-selling big band jazz albums in history. In addition to the dozen albums the group has recorded, including *Tales of a Courtesan, Wishing Peace, Farewell to Mingus, European Memoirs,* and *Insights,* the orchestra has received twelve Grammy nominations along with three nominations for Akiyoshi for Best Arranger. *Down Beat* magazine has recognized both Akiyoshi and the band with top honors, and other major jazz polls in the United States and abroad have also been in concurrence. Akiyoshi has also received two silver and two gold awards from one of Japan's leading music publications, *Swing Journal.*

Throughout Akiyoshi's recordings, the majority of the music tends to be her own. Her compositions often deal with social themes and reflect her Asian background, as well. For example, the title cut from her *Tales of a Courtesan* album expresses the unpleasant life of an Asian courtesan, caught between a superficial life of luxury and the reality of virtual slavery. Today, Akiyoshi's big band compositions are considered standard textbook study among jazz students at music schools across the country.

In 1982, Akiyoshi's career was the subject of *Jazz is My Native Language,* a documentary portrait of her move from Los Angeles to New York. Akiyoshi recalled in a 1993 interview with *Down Beat* magazine the differences she noticed in her players following the move: "New York is harder, much harder than Los Angeles, simply because life is hard here. I had forgotten how hard people are here. Los Angeles people have a certain camaraderie, much more than they have here [in New York]." In spite of the hardships, the band adjusted quickly, making their Carnegie Hall debut as part of the Kool Jazz Festival one year later in 1983.

Since the move, Akiyoshi has continued to perform with her band, as well as in a quintet or trio setting, traveling all over the world, including the United States, Europe, Asia, South America, and Africa. Her more than three-decade career is testament to her tenacity and talent. After making her most recent album, Toshiko Akiyoshi Live at Carnegie Hall, she remarked in *Down Beat,* "Basically, I am very proud of the fact that I actually survived as a jazz musician. Because I think even American musicians, born here—even for those musicians it's very difficult."

Sources:

Periodicals

Seidel, Mitchell. "The Perils of Toshiko," *Down Beat,* vol. 60, no. 2, February 1993, pp. 30–32.
Stephen, Lynnéa Y. "Toshiko Akiyoshi: Jazzing It Up at Carnegie Hall," *Ms.,* May–June 1993, p. 82.

—Sketch by Terry Hong

Hiroaki "Rocky" Aoki

(1938–)

Entrepreneur

Rocky Aoki is the founder of Benihana restaurants, a chain of very popular Japanese-style eateries now located in the United States, Canada, Mexico, England, South Korea, Japan, Australia, and Thailand. He is also well known as a world-class sportsman, participating primarily in long-distance road rallies, speedboat racing, and ballooning. He has also become a noted philanthropist and fund-raiser for international art exchanges and environmental causes.

Hiroaki Aoki was born on October 9, 1938, in Tokyo, Japan, the first child of Yunosuke and Katsu Aoki. His parents were fairly well off and were owners of a popular jazz, coffee, and tea shop called Ellington, after the legendary American jazz musician Duke Ellington. Ellington was a popular night spot in Tokyo until Japan and the United States entered into a state of war after the Japanese bombing of Pearl Harbor in 1941, when Rocky was three years old. The Aokis spent the first two years of the war in Tokyo, but by 1944 the American bombing forced them to flee to Rocky's mother's home town in the rural province of Gumma. After the war the family returned to the nearly destroyed Tokyo and started a restaurant called Benihana, a Japanese word that can be translated as either red flower or saffron.

Aoki was educated at Keio, an exclusive private high school, after which he attended Keio University. He was a gifted student, if a bit wild at times, and was very popular among his fellow students. He was also a talented athlete, competing in track and field, karate, and, most successfully, wrestling. He became the captain of the Keio team and one of Japan's top wrestlers at the age of nineteen. In 1959 he toured America as an alternate on Japan's Olympic team and was undefeated in his weight class. He was intrigued with the United States and he decided to try to get a scholarship to study there.

Coming to the United States

In 1960 Aoki arrived in the United States, where he had been offered wrestling scholarships from a few colleges. He lived in New York City while deciding where he should go. (While in New York he roomed with an old family friend from Japan, Seiji Ozawa, who is today conductor and music director of the Boston Symphony Orchestra.) He first enrolled in Springfield College in Massachusetts but quickly transferred to C.W. Post College in Long Island, New York. There, Aoki ran into trouble for fighting, a problem that had dogged him since his middle school days in Tokyo, and he was thrown out of the college. He then enrolled in New York City Community College, (NYCCC) where he earned an associate's degree in management in 1963.

Benihana in America

Aoki had wanted for some time to open a restaurant and had set aside $10,000 from part-time jobs. In 1963, after he had graduated from NYCCC, he was offered some prime restaurant space in midtown Manhattan for very little rent by the owner of a Chinese restaurant who couldn't make his restaurant succeed. Aoki enlisted the help of his well-to-do parents who helped him secure a loan, and in May of

Hiroaki "Rocky" Aoki

1964 the first American Benihana restaurant opened. What made the restaurant unique was the way food was prepared. The menu featured steak, chicken, and seafood prepared on a *teppanyaki* (Japanese for steel top) grill around which guests were seated, so that they could watch as skilled chefs prepared their food with dramatic flair.

The first restaurant took a while to catch on and Aoki showed considerable persistence through the first half-year, during which they did very little business. Soon, however, word got around about the unique little restaurant, and then Benihana got a glowing review from the food critic for the *New York Herald Tribune*. Aoki's wife, Chizuru, whom he had known for years and married that year, remembered the early days at the first Benihana for Jack McCallum in his biography of Aoki, *Making It in America: The Life and Times of Rocky Aoki, Benihana's Pioneer*. She said she mostly remembers Aoki "running around like a chicken with his head cut off. He spent a lot of time going around and seeing other restaurants to see what made the so successful. He never talked about the restaurant failing. He believed in his idea even when it looked like it would fail for sure. His energy was completely focused."

On May 15, 1966, the second Benihana opened on Manhattan's East Side. The restaurants had become huge successes among the fashionable set in New York. Aoki had celebrities as regular customers, including Sean Connery, Lawrence Welk, Angie Dickinson, and Burt Bacharach. In 1968 the first Benihana opened in Chicago.

In May of 1969, Aoki expanded to the West Coast where he opened Benihana San Francisco.

The Emergence of the Aoki Flamboyance

Aoki had spent the early years of Benihana's rise living frugally, giving everything to the restaurant. By the early seventies, however, Aoki had become a very wealthy man and he began to live like one, at times investing in big splashy business opportunities that netted him notoriety, but generally lost money. He backed a Broadway play starring Joan Rivers that flopped; he opened Club Genesis, a posh Manhattan club that went out of business after one year; he promoted a boxing match in Japan for his long-time friend Muhammad Ali that attracted a lot of publicity but earned him almost no money.

He also gave himself lots of leisure time and in 1974 he became the world champion leisure class backgammon player. He started collecting expensive automobiles, mostly sports and racing cars. Reflecting on his rapid rise in fame and the money that accompanied it, Aoki is the first to admit he handled it rather poorly, wasted a lot of money, and behaved rather foolishly. He told McCallum: "When I first started making money, my personal life got poorer. I don't mean financially. I just mean poorer. I bought a nice house, yes, but that was it. I didn't put furniture in it. Then, suddenly, I changed my life. I started buying clothes, Rolls Royces, Cadillacs, anything. And I kept my family poor. I didn't want to put money into them. I wanted to put it where it would show."

Aoki continued his flamboyant lifestyle throughout the seventies and early eighties. He became a champion powerboat racer and was nearly killed in accident in 1979. He piloted a helium gas balloon across the Pacific in November 1981. In 1987 he won the first Milan-Moscow Road Rally, driving the 1300 miles from Italy to Red Square in a 1959 Rolls Royce Silver Wraith. In the 1990s, Aoki has settled a bit and devoted his time and money to more socially responsible ventures. Recently he was recognized by the United Nations' Environmental Program Directorate for his sponsorship of the *New York Times* environmental supplement "Imagine." He has also established a Green Arts Program promoting international understanding through arts exchanges. In 1993, Aoki sponsored environmental art exhibitions in Japan, the United States, and England highlighting the work of prominent, environmentally concerned Japanese artists.

Sources:

McCallum, Jack. *Making It in America: The Life and Times of Rocky Aoki, Benihana's Pioneer*. New York: Dodd, Mead & Company, 1985.

—Sketch by Jim Henry

George Aratani
(1917–)
Business leader

George Aratani

George Aratani is the founder and chairman emeritus of Mikasa Corporation, one of the largest privately owned international firms. In an interview with Visi R. Tilak, he described his childhood curiosity about business: "As a child, watching my father work, I was very interested and would constantly ask questions. One thing I was very curious about . . . was why people from the Midwest and East Coast wanted to buy produce from the West Coast? Why didn't they grow the same things there? My father would very patiently answer my questions and that's how I found out that . . . the climatic conditions in those areas was very different from the West and they could not grow this produce there. Ever since I was a little child, I started learning about the intricacies of business and marketing from these little experiences I had with my dad."

George Aratani was born in Gardena, California, south of Los Angeles, on May 22, 1917. His family moved to the San Fernando Valley when he was very young, and it was there that he attended kindergarten. The family moved again, to Guadalupe, a small town ten miles west of Santa Maria, where they finally settled down. "I was the only child and consequently I was very close to both my father and my mother. When I was in high school I was very much interested in what my father was doing. He was into large-scale agricultural produce business. He had about four thousand to five thousand acres in the Santa Maria Valley. I found that very interesting, especially during my high school years, and I used to tag along with him whenever I could," Aratani told Tilak.

The more Aratani learned about his father's business, the more he enjoyed it. The elder Aratani was not only growing different types of produce, he was also in the wholesale industrial market in Los Angeles. In addition, he dehydrated chili peppers, handling all stages from growing the chili peppers to dehydrating and selling the finished product. As head of a fully integrated agricultural venture, Aratani's father had business interests that extended to chemical fertilizers, hog farming, and produce distribution.

"During summers I worked for my father in the assembly line at the shipping division. Packing produce in crates with crushed ice to keep it fresh, wrapping it in oil paper, putting on the lids and loading them into freight cars, then covering the crates with crushed ice and sealing the freight car were all the different tasks that I did," recounted Aratani. He found business fascinating:

"Watching my father's business motivated me to get more involved in business. I wanted to be a businessman like my father."

Study in Japan

Aratani graduated from Santa Maria High School in 1935. "I was all ready to go to Stanford when my parents told me that being a Japanese American I should know more about Japanese culture, language, and traditions. They sent me to Japan to study. I went back since I was their only child and they were begging me to do so. However, instead of going to school, my father had hired a live-in private tutor to stay with me and my grandmother. I received very intensive coaching in Japanese language and culture. There were no weekends, no leisure—all the waking hours were spent studying. I achieved high school level Japanese in ten months," he recalled.

At the end of these ten months Aratani took an entrance exam to attend Keio University in Tokyo, but was not able to get into the economics department as he had desired. Instead, he entered the political science department. He had completed three years of college at Keio University when his father became ill. Because air travel was not widely available at that time, Aratani had to endure a two-week ocean voyage on his return to the United States. Aratani's father was in a sanitarium and still recuperating when he came back. "At that time, for the first time in our lives, we were able to converse in fluent Japanese. He was very impressed and happy. He told me I had stayed in Japan long enough," said Aratani.

Stanford University accepted Aratani's transcript from Keio University, and he entered Stanford as a junior in 1940. But Aratani was not able to complete his schooling; after his first term at Stanford, his father died. Aratani followed the advice of family and friends and quit school to take care of his father's business empire.

Internment

In 1941, World War II broke out. There were rumors that the Japanese aliens who were working for Aratani's company would be deported to Japan. Aratani warned the alien Japanese working for him to be prepared to be removed to concentration camps. At that point President Franklin D. Roosevelt issued Executive Order 9066, allowing the military to forcibly relocate everyone of Japanese descent, even native-born U. S. citizens. "It [the internment] came as a big surprise to us. We [Japanese Americans and resident aliens] were taken to camp with two suitcases," recalled Aratani.

Because of the size of Aratani's company, it was very difficult to dispose of it on short notice, so the whole business was put into a trust. "After we were put in camp in Arizona, the trustees decided that they could not continue due to rising anti-Japanese sentiments. We had no choice but to sell," remembered Aratani, describing this as one of the most difficult decisions in his life.

The war ended in 1945, but Aratani had no business to return to. "I had to start from scratch again after the war was over. Since my return from Japan in 1940, everything had happened so quickly that I did not have enough time to learn much about my father's business other than what I had learned as a child. Without experience there was no way I could get back into the farming business. So I decided to get into something else. Because I studied in Japan, I knew the Japanese mentality and the way things worked in Japan.

"I feel that the fact that you are an ethnic minority means you have to do more work in order to prove yourself. Overall, you have to put in more concentrated effort in what you do," said Aratani, who is a Buddhist. "During my parents' time they did not have the opportunity to become naturalized citizens. Europeans could but the Asians couldn't. The fact that they put me in a concentration camp even though I was American by birth was a big disappointment to me. After all, this was my country."

Imports Launch Mikasa

In 1947 Aratani decided to try foreign trade with Japan. Because this was a totally new venture for him, he decided to go to Japan and study the situation. It took a few years for Aratani to decide what business to pursue. "By 1949 I

knew what I wanted to do. I reactivated one of our old companies, All Star Trading Company, and renamed it American Commercial Incorporated." Around 1950, this seed from Aratani's father's empire began to grow into what would become Mikasa Corporation.

The origins of the company name can be traced to a mountain range in the Nara district in Japan. Its three peaks were called Mikasa—*Mi* meaning the number three in Japanese and *Kasa* meaning umbrella; therefore *Mikasa* means three umbrellas. The former Japanese emperor's younger brother was also called Prince Mikasa. Aratani said, "I picked this as our brand name because I wanted a Japanese name which is easy to pronounce."

Mikasa was officially started in 1950. "Even though the company was called American Commercial Incorporated, the brand name was Mikasa, therefore we were doing business as Mikasa. I was importing dinnerware from Japan and marketing it in America. By 1960, Mikasa was well established, especially since I opened an office in New York. More than one-half of the population lives on the East Coast and more people means a bigger market," said Aratani.

One day a friend talked to Aratani about hi-fidelity. Aratani confessed, "I had no idea what he was talking about then. I knew it was something to do with sound. He was talking about mono and hi-fi stereo systems. I studied more about it. Through a unique invention, radio sounds will be transmitted by air through two signals rather than one signal: mono versus stereo, where you need two speakers. Beginning in 1960, transmitting radio stations converted to the stereo mode. The receiving sets also had to be stereo to get the stereophonic effect. With that you had the best seats in the house. I said, 'Wow this is really terrific.' To me this was the best invention since automatic transmission in cars."

The business-wise Aratani latched on to the idea and launched a second company. "I decided to get into this business. I met with a manufacturer in Japan and made arrangements for this company to manufacture the equipment under the Kenwood name. Kenwood was a wholly-owned subsidiary of Mikasa. I was to be doing marketing and distribution. This company started in 1961. . . . The more you sell, the more working capital you need. I thought of going public [with Mikasa], but decided against it because of the danger of takeovers. I offered to sell the Kenwood distribution company to the manufacturer in Japan and they agreed to accept my offer on one condition: that [I] continue on as chairman of the Kenwood company."

Before the war Aratani had met his future wife, Sakaye Inouye, in Los Angeles. They were married in 1944 and have two daughters: Donna and Linda. Talking about the secret of his business savvy, Aratani commented, "My father told me the secret of his success which to this day is my guiding motto—if you want to succeed in business, you have to work very hard. There are only twenty-four hours in a day and there is a limit to what you can do in twenty four hours. In order for your company to grow you have to surround yourself with qualified people and take good care of them and make them feel like they are part of the company. The best way to do that is to let them buy into the company so they feel responsible for the company and are personally involved."

Sources:

Aratani, George, telephone interview with Visi R. Tilak, June 10, 1994.

Mikasa Corporation. "George Aratani." Biographical information and press releases, 1994.

—Sketch by Visi R. Tilak

George R. Ariyoshi
(1926–)
Politician, attorney

George R. Ariyoshi

In 1974 George Riyochi Ariyoshi became the first American of Japanese descent to be elected governor of a state. The state was Hawaii, and Ariyoshi served in that post for three terms, until 1986. His tenure was marked by a time of rapid growth for the state, mostly in tourism. One of Ariyoshi's consistent legislative concerns throughout his political career was Hawaii's economic development. He wanted to ensure that the state's natural beauty was not destroyed by greedy overdevelopment, and that what economic development there was benefited as many people as possible, rather than just a few landowners.

George Ariyoshi was born on March 12, 1926, in Honolulu, to Japanese immigrants to the Hawaiian Islands, which were not yet part of the United States. His father, Ryozo Ariyoshi, had been a sumo wrestler in Japan and worked in Hawaii as a stevedore and, later, as the proprietor of a dry cleaning shop. His mother, Mitsue [Yoshikawa] Ariyoshi was from Kumamoto, Japan. The Ariyoshis encouraged their son to achieve all that he could with his education, and they were very supportive when he decided, at quite a young age, to become a lawyer.

Ariyoshi's political career began when he was elected class president his senior year in high school. After graduation in 1944, he entered the army and served as an interpreter for the U.S. Military Intelligence Service in occupied Japan after World War II. Following his service, he returned to Hawaii and enrolled for a brief time in the University of Hawaii before transferring to Michigan State University, where he earned a bachelor's degree in history and political science in 1949. He continued his studies in Michigan and in 1952 earned his J.D. from the University of Michigan Law School. In 1953 Ariyoshi returned to his homeland and set up private practice in Honolulu as a criminal lawyer.

Politics

One year after Ariyoshi had returned to Hawaii, the chairman of the Hawaiian Democratic party, John A. Burns, urged him to run for a seat in Hawaii's territorial house of representatives. Ariyoshi won that race and at the end of his term in 1958 he ran for a seat in the other house, the territorial senate, which he won as well. In 1959 Hawaii was admitted into the United States, and Ariyoshi continued his successful career as a state senator. He was named chairman of the powerful Ways and Means Committee in 1964, became the senate majority leader in 1965, and majority floor leader in 1969. During this time he continued to practice law and in 1968 was elected vice president of the Hawaii Bar Association and then president in 1969.

Meanwhile Burns had become governor of the state, and in 1970 he invited Ariyoshi to run as his lieutenant governor. They won the election with 55 percent of the vote. The Burns/Ariyoshi administration was one characterized by brisk economic growth, especially in tourism, and by a desire to expand Hawaii's international role, reaching out especially to the countries of Asia and the Pacific Rim, a remarkably farsighted policy.

In 1973 Burns became ill with cancer and in October he turned the day-to-day management of the state over to his lieutenant governor. Less than one year later, Ariyoshi announced that he would seek the Democratic nomination for governor in the October 1974 primary. It was at this point that Ariyoshi began to modify some of his views on development. He began to push for greater investment in areas other than tourism, such as agriculture, to diversify the state's economy. He was elected governor and spent his first term dealing with problems such as the global recession's effects on Hawaii, years of overdevelopment, and a state population explosion resulting from an influx of immigrants from Asia and mainland America.

Preferred Growth

In 1977 Ariyoshi appointed a panel of forty experts from various fields to a Growth Management Task Force to initiate legislative proposals that would stimulate economic growth without the usual drawbacks such as environmental loss and immigration increases. In other initiatives, Ariyoshi made a bid for multinational corporations to use Hawaii as a base of operations when dealing with Pacific Rim countries; attempted to ease congestion on Oahu; and worked to reduce the state's dependence on imports. He was in the forefront nationally in promoting environmental technologies such as ocean thermal energy conversion and the development of aquaculture. He also supported a controversial measure, the Hawaiian Land Reform Act of 1967, which granted the state the right to redistribute land ownership from huge private estates to the tenants of the land.

Ariyoshi's bid for reelection in 1978 was hotly contested by the mayor of Honolulu, Frank Fasi, who bitterly opposed many of the governor's policies. Ariyoshi defeated him in the Democratic primary by the slimmest of margins and then won the general election in another close vote. It is widely thought that his policy of preferred growth won him both elections. In 1982 Ariyoshi began his campaign for his third term in office. The constitution of the state limited executives to three terms, so it would be his last if he could win the election. Again he faced strong opposition in his party's primary, and in the general election he faced Frank Fasi, who had entered the race this time as an independent. He managed to win both elections and served out his final term as governor until 1986.

During his tenure as governor and since, Ariyoshi received many awards and honors, including honorary law degrees from the University of the Philippines at Quezon City and the University of Guam at Agana. He served as chairman of the Western Governor's Conference in 1977 and 1978, and was president of the Pacific Basin Development Council in 1980 and 1981. In 1984 he was elected as the first chairman of the newly formed Western Governors' Association, an organization of the chief executives of sixteen western states and three Pacific territories. In

his entire political career, from 1954 until 1986, Ariyoshi never lost an election. Today he is a busy man, sitting on many boards, chairing cultural institutions, managing several lucrative real estate holdings, and practicing law.

Ariyoshi married Jean Miya Hayashi in February of 1955. They have three children: Lynne Miye, born in 1957; Todd Ryozo, born in 1959; and Donn Ryoji, born in 1961.

Sources:

The office of George R. Ariyoshi, Watanabe, Ing & Kawashima, Attorneys at Law, Honolulu, Hawaii. *Current Biography Yearbook.* New York: H.W. Wilson, 1985.

—Sketch by Jim Henry

Jose Aruego
(1932–)
Author, illustrator

Jose Aruego is a graphic artist and award-winning children's book illustrator and author. He has illustrated more than sixty books, several of which he himself has written. He is also a fine cartoonist with work appearing in prominent magazines such as the *New Yorker* and the *Saturday Evening Post.*

Jose Espiritu Aruego was born on August 9, 1932, in Manila, the Philippines. His father, Jose Maminta Aruego, was a prominent legal scholar and practicing attorney. As a young child, Aruego was interested in drawing, and spent a great deal of time pursuing his art. In their 1992 children's book, *Famous Asian Americans,* authors Janet Nomura Morey and Wendy Dunn quote Aruego as saying, "If I am good at drawing, people notice me."

Despite his interest in art and drawing, it was understood in the Aruego family that Jose would study law. He first attended the University of the Philippines, where he earned his bachelor's degree in 1953. He then went on to law school at the same university and earned his degree in 1955. He had trouble maintaining an interest in law, however, and only just barely passed the bar exam. Aruego's law career was short and undistinguished. He tried one case, which he lost, and decided to leave the profession.

Aruego left the Philippines to study art and graphic design at the Parsons School of Design in New York City. In 1959 he graduated from Parsons with a certificate in

Jose Aruego

graphic arts and advertising. He then began working for various New York City design firms, advertising agencies, and magazines. During this time he also was commissioned to paint a large mural of New York City for a wall at the International House, a large dormitory for students at the various colleges, universities, and seminaries on New York's Upper West Side. In 1961 he married Ariane Dewey, an artist.

In the early sixties Aruego began submitting cartoons for publication, and his work began appearing in such distinguished magazines as the *New Yorker,* the *Saturday Evening Post,* and *Look.* He also began work on his first book, which he both wrote and illustrated. Entitled *The King and His Friend,* it was published in 1969 by Scribners. In 1970 he illustrated *Whose Mouse Are You?* by Robert Kraus, a writer with whom Aruego would work a lot. It was honored as a Notable Book by the American Library Association. Also that year, Aruego wrote and illustrated *Juan and the Asuangs: A Tale of Philippine Ghosts and Spirits,* which was named an outstanding picture book of the year by the *New York Times.* In 1972 he wrote and illustrated a book with his wife entitled *A Crocodile's Tale.* Although the couple divorced the following year, they continue to collaborate.

In 1976, Aruego was chosen as the Outstanding Filipino Abroad in the Arts, an award granted by the Philippine government. He told Dunn and Morey of his experiences going home to receive the award: "It was nice being recognized in my new profession. Lots of lawyer classmates and professors were proud of me that I made it as an illustrator. I changed professions and changed to what is successful."

The Nature of His Work

Aruego often incorporates Philippine folk tales into his writing and uses tropical or jungle motifs in his illustrations. His books are generally comical, with endearing, eccentric animal characters. He told Dunn and Morey: "I have written mostly animal stories. The ideas must have humor. They must take off from something funny. If they are serious, I cannot get my juices working. Kids like to be happy and my books give them the opportunity."

In recent years, Aruego has given up drawing cartoons, the work that first sustained him as an independent artist, devoting himself exclusively to writing and illustrating. Discussing his career and what he sees as his major accomplishments, Aruego told Dunn and Morey, "I take particular pride in two books done nearly twenty years ago that are still around and still popular." The books he referring to are *Leo the Late Bloomer* and *Whose Mouse Are You?,* both of which he illustrated and Kraus wrote.

Sources:

Morey, Janet Nomura, and Wendy Dunn. *Famous Asian Americans,* New York: Cobblehill Books, 1992.
Simon and Schuster. "Jose Aruego." Publicity and press release, New York, 1994.

—Sketch by Jim Henry

Salevaa Atisanoe "Konishki"
(1964–)
Sumo wrestler

Salevaa Atisanoe, who uses the name Konishki professionally, is a champion in the vehemently archaic and tradition-bound world of Japanese sumo wrestling. In 1987 he became the first foreigner to reach the rank of *ozeki* (champion) and has since stirred a considerable amount of controversy among sumo purists who insist that a foreigner, even one as accomplished as Konishki, should never be allowed to attain the ceremonial title of *yokozuna* (grand champion). In the two-hundred-fifty-year history of modern sumo wrestling, only sixty-two wrestlers have been so elevated by Sumo Kyokai, the sports ruling body.

Salevaa Fuauli Atisanoe was born on the island of Oahu, Hawaii, in 1964, the eighth of nine children. His parents were native Samoans who'd left the island in 1959, determined to provide their children with more opportunities than life in Samoa offered. On Oahu, the Atisanoes lived in a Samoan community with only very basic accommodations. Everyone in the family slept in a common room on mats and showered outside. Salevaa's father had been a religious leader in Samoa and he established a church in Hawaii.

By the age of eleven, Sale (pronounced like Sally), as he was known, weighed 180 pounds. At Honolulu's University Laboratory High he played noseguard on the football team and was a champion weight lifter—he could bench press 550 pounds and squat powerlift 600. Late in his senior year in high school, Sale was on the beach cutting class when he was spotted by a scout who had been sent to Hawaii by sumo coach Kuhualua to recruit wrestlers. Kuhualua had become a legendary figure in Hawaii in the early 1970s when he became the first non-Japanese sumo wrestler to win a *basho* (tournament). The scout encouraged Sale to meet with Kuhualua when he visited the islands. At first Sale was not interested in sumo. He knew nothing about the peculiar Japanese sport. Kuhualua, however, met with Sale and was able to persuade him to come to Tokyo with him and give it a try. In 1982, at 380 pounds, Sale left Hawaii for Japan to train at the Takasago stable in Tokyo.

Life as a *Sumotori*

As a *sumotori* (apprentice) in a Tokyo sumo stable, life was difficult for Sale, who by now had taken the name Konishki from his stable boss. (He was named for a grand champion from the nineteenth century.) As a sumotori, Konishki was ritually abused and attacked, which is part of the initiation into the sport. Writing in *Sports Illustrated* in 1992, Franz Lidz described this initiation period: "Stablemasters spat at him, threw salt water into his mouth and whacked him in the knees with bamboo canes. One night an older wrestler stumbled in drunk and knee-dropped the sleeping Konishki on the head." The duties of sumotori, Lidz continued, included "bathing and feeding his tormentors, sponging the sweat off them, running errands for them. . . . The only way to get freedom from these indignities was to fight up the rankings until he was privileged to use beginners as his servants."

As a competitor, Konishki became one of the fastest rising sumos in modern history. He made it into the top of sumo's six divisions after only eight tournaments, which set a record. In 1984 he finished second in the prestigious Emperor's Cup tournament. It was then that the controversy surrounding Konishki's ethnic heritage began. While he is racially a Pacific Islander, he is by nationality an American—a Westerner, something that is unforgivable to purists. He has also been criticized for not being built like a classic sumo—he weighs 170 pounds more than the average sumo—and for relying on his bulk rather

Salevaa Atisanoe "Konishki"

than the grace, strategy, and skill traditionally employed by sumos. A movement sprung up among fans of the sport to ban Konishki from competition.

Konishki became the center of tremendous media attention in Japan in the 1980s and he started receiving hate mail and death threats. Newspapers demanded that tournaments be canceled if Konishki participated, and one commentator compared Konishki's arrival in Japan with that of Commodore Perry's fleet, which arrived in Japan in the nineteenth century, forcibly opening the country to Western trade and, some would say, exploitation. All the negative press hurt Konishki's performance in the ring. He had a couple of bad years, but then in 1987 he made it to the level of *ozeki*. And then in 1989 he won his first tournament, the Kyushi *basho*.

Sumomania

In recent years Konishki has been a perennial force on the sumo circuit, and he has become an immensely popular cultural icon in Japan. He still has his detractors among the purists but, generally, the people of Japan love him. Lidz reported that "old women and young children rub him for good luck like some giant Buddha. Teenage girls swoon at the sight of his huge haunches. Konishki masks line the shelves of Tokyo toy stores." Konishki commented on his status is Japan in the same article, saying, "I'm treated like royalty, I'm a walking god."

Konishki's private life has also become fodder for Japan's tabloid press. He told Lidz, "Journalism in Japan is a rat race, and journalists are a bunch of rats." Konishki created an international incident in 1992 when he allegedly complained to a reporter for *Nihon Keizai Shimbum,* Japan's leading financial newspaper, that the reason he had not been elevated to the level of *yokozuna* was racism. He also allegedly told a reporter for the *New York Times* that if he were Japanese he would certainly be a *yokozuna.* In the furor that followed his remarks, Japan's prime minister, foreign minister, and the American ambassador to Japan all had their say. Konishki ultimately denied both reports after being reprimanded by sumo's ruling authority.

When he was married in Tokyo in February of 1992 to a former fashion model named Sumika, there were one thousand guests in attendance, including politicians and some of the country's richest businessmen. A television network paid nearly half a million dollars to broadcast the event, which pre-empted the winter olympics for two hours. "In no other sport do you get this kind of attention," Konishki told *Sports Illustrated.*

In discussing his plans for the future, Konishki told Lidz, "I'd like to be a sumo as long as I can. If I last another five, six, or seven years, I'll be happy. But I'm not really into what's after sumo yet. I don't even think about tomorrow. That just slows me down. I never take two days at a time, just one day. My way."

Sources:

"The Fat's in the Fire." *People Weekly,* May 11, 1992, p. 47.

Lidz, Franz. "Meat Bomb." *Sports Illustrated*, vol. 76, no. 19, May 18, 1992, p. 68.

—Sketch by Jim Henry

B

Kavelle R. Bajaj
(1950–)
Entrepreneur

Moving to a new country halfway across the globe, taking care of a family, and creating a successful new business are not easy feats. Accomplishing even one of these tasks is laudable for any individual. Kavelle Bajaj did all three. Having immigrated to the United States from India in 1974 as a young bride, she raised two sons, started her own computer company, and within a decade, had built it into a flourishing enterprise.

Brainstorming

In 1985, while sitting around the dinner table with her husband and two children, Kavelle Bajaj expressed her desire to do something useful outside the home. However, when it came to adhering to a single goal she had a poor track record. "I used to get bored easily and would quickly give up projects I started," Bajaj told Shamita Das Dasgupta in an interview. Aware of his wife's mercurial nature, her husband, Ken, challenged her. To prove her mettle, Bajaj borrowed $5,000 from him to start a computer business. Once she declared her intentions, Bajaj was propelled into completely unknown territory. She had no experience in establishing an organization and knew nothing about computers. "But I knew I could never work for anyone. It is not in my character," Bajaj declared. With this limited seed money she launched I-Net, a computer firm that provides all services for computer-based networking. Even though she knew little about the subject, her instincts told her that personal computers were the wave of the future. "In business, timing is everything," mused Bajaj. "I was there at the right time, in the right kind of business. Everything clicked." In 1994, I-Net's revenues were over $200 million. It had grown into a company with two thousand employees working in thirty-eight different locations in twenty-two states. "With I-Net, I was determined to see the business through. It was a challenge."

Nothing in Bajaj's early childhood training prepared her for the entrepreneurial life. She was born Kavelle

Kavelle R. Bajaj

Maker in India on June 15, 1950. Her mother, Agya Kaur, was a home maker. Her father, Daljit Singh, was an entrepreneur in the truest sense of the word. By the time he was fifteen or sixteen, Daljit had left home to make something of his life. Rather than joining his father's construction business, Singh formed a separate construction company. His work took him to remote districts of India. Bajaj and her two siblings traveled with their parents.

Bajaj was educated in Bihar and New Delhi, India, where she received her bachelor of science degree from Delhi University. Although they encouraged education, her parents brought up their daughters within strict gender guidelines. Bajaj learned early that a woman's role was that of care-taker of the family, but she did not accept the restrictions of this role easily. "I was a free spirit—independent, headstrong, and stubborn as a child. I did whatever I set my mind to. I gave my parents quite a few gray hairs," Bajaj confessed laughingly. In 1973, her marriage was arranged with Ken Bajaj. "The environment I was brought up in basically groomed girls for marriage and nothing else," she said. Soon after the wedding, the couple immigrated to the United States. She enrolled in a university to pursue a master's degree in nutrition, but quickly gave it up. "Working in the basement of a hospital was not for me," Bajaj explained. "I wanted it all—the plush office, the decision-making power, the independence."

Bajaj started I-Net as a minority-owned business receiving contracts from government programs. Due to Bajaj's dedication to excellence and the exemplary services I-Net offered to customers, the company soon took wing. Its growth was rapid and phenomenal. In 1994, *Federal Computer Week* ranked I-Net among the country's top ten small businesses that deal with information technology. In 1993, Bajaj was one of six women selected to receive the prestigious Women of Enterprise award from Avon Company and the U.S. Small Business Administration. In the same year, I-Net was also recognized by *Government Computer News* as one of the top ten minority businesses in the same year. In addition, Bajaj won the coveted Entrepreneur of the Year award, given jointly by *Ernst & Young, Inc.* magazine and Merril Lynch, in the woman-owned business category. Numerous other awards have honored I-Net and its owner for their successes.

Defining Success

Yet, Bajaj says that she does not subscribe to the conventional idea of success and failure. "Success and failure can be measured only by one's self. We set a goal and try to reach it. Reaching it is the only success." She furthermore does not believe in external barriers. "Obstacles are self-imposed. We can't blame outside sources for our failures," she said. As an Asian Indian woman working in unfamiliar surroundings, Bajaj's hurdles were generally personal. She had to surmount the teachings of a traditional family that regarded women's responsibilities as primarily confined to the domestic arena. And she added, "I had to get over the cultural differences and the shyness. I had to learn to bring a balance between work and family." The journey was indeed difficult, but Bajaj learned readily. She cannot recall how she overcame her conservative background and natural reticence. "I just did it," she said. Bajaj firmly believes that along with a strong focus on objectives, contextually suitable behavior is the key to achieving a balance in life. "One must achieve a balance between work and home, and give full attention to each at the appropriate time," Bajaj asserted. Her husband and children understood her struggles and supported her endeavors. In 1988, Ken Bajaj joined I-Net as the executive vice-president. In 1994, her two young sons were also preparing to join their mother's company in the future.

Once Bajaj had started her business she found many teachers. "I have learned a little from not only mainstream entrepreneurs, but minority enterprises." Her role models are successful Asian American businessmen. She holds a

special respect for Ross Perot, whose business philosophy she finds intriguing. And Bajaj particularly recognized working mothers all over the world. "These supermoms are my heroes," she proclaimed.

Being a mother and caring for her sons are high on Bajaj's list of priorities. "They come first," she stated. At the same time she feels adults tend to underestimate children's resilience. "Children need to have total and around-the-clock access to you. Communication is vital. That is what leads to their feeling secure in a parent's love," Bajaj said candidly. "I talk to my children. I tell them that I may not be the perfect mother, but I am the only mother they have. We must do the best by each other." Her pride in her children is further reflected in her feelings about the next generation of Asian Indians. She believes that the key to the future lies with the younger population. However, she does not always agree with the way these future leaders are being brought up. Bajaj takes exception to the emphasis Asian Indian immigrants place on their children's academic achievements. She urges the community to open additional doors for children and expose them to other areas such as the arts, business, and athletics.

Bajaj is quite aware of the success Asian Indian immigrants have carved for themselves in their new country. However, she feels that the cultural-linguistic divisions within the community weakens its political influence. "A unified voice will actually be a louder voice," she maintains. Bajaj's goal is to organize a national resource center for Asian Indian women which would provide relevant information at the governmental, industrial, and political levels. She believes that such a center would help improve images of Asian Indian women by disseminating accurate information about them. Ultimately, this could lead to providing training for Asian Indian women in various occupational fields. Bajaj has already committed some of her precious time to the realization of this dream.

Sources:

Periodicals

"A Network Hit." *Working Woman.* May 1994, p. 49.

Other

Bajaj, Kavelle R., telephone interview with Shamita Das Dasgupta, June 20, 1994.

———. Personal profile produced by Bajaj, June 1994.

—Sketch by Shamita Das Dasgupta, Ph.D

Maniya Barredo
(1951–)
Dancer

In a way Maniya Barredo's life is not unlike one of the fairy tales she might have danced before adoring crowds. But unlike the classical ballets (like *Giselle* or *Romeo and Juliet*) that are closest to her heart, in Barredo's story the ending is anything but tragic: the young girl with the big dreams in a distant, impoverished land grows up, perseveres against all odds and expectations in a strange and foreign country, and makes her wishes come true. "When I left the Philippines, everyone told me I'd never make it: my friends, my teacher, my family," she recalled in an interview with Ferdinand M. de Leon. "I said, 'Well, we'll see.' I believed in who I was and that with hard work, I could do just about anything."

Dreams of Dancing

On November 19, 1951, Josephine Carmen Barredo was born in Manila, Philippines. She was the fourth child of Eugenio and Grizelda Barredo, who both played important roles in shaping their daughter's future, but for very different reasons.

Barredo's father, a practical businessman whose family owned Mabar Trucking Company, saw no future for Barredo in dancing, and he pushed his daughter to concentrate on school. His resistance, however, only strengthened her determination to pursue dance. Her mother, a former dancer who married at age fifteen and then had nine children, one after the other, channeled her own ambitions through her daughter. "I wouldn't be where I am if it were not for her dreams for me," Barredo told the *Atlanta Journal and Constitution* in 1986. "Somehow when I came along she just knew I should dance in her place. I never thought otherwise and I never said no to her. She sees in me the fulfillment of her dreams."

Barredo began dancing when she was four years old. Later she took ballet lessons with her aunt, Julie Borromeo, one of Manila's best-known ballet teachers. In finding a vehicle for her dreams, Grizelda had a willing collaborator. "When I was seven I knew I wanted to be a dancer," Barredo told de Leon. "I sang and took up the piano and acted, but the minute I went to ballet I knew this was what I wanted. It was my best way of reaching people and it made me very happy. It still does."

By the time she was nine years old, she had her own children's TV show and was contributing money toward her siblings' educations. When she was fourteen, Barredo joined Hariraya Dance Company, quickly becoming the

Maniya Barredo

darling of the troupe. She was chosen by one of the Bolshoi's teachers, then on loan in Manila, to train for the La Fille Mal Garde, a ballet the instructor was mounting for the famed ballet company.

New York and Joffrey

But when Barredo was eighteen, according to *Sunburst* magazine, a Philippine publication, Barredo announced that she intended to get married. Her teacher and her mother pleaded with her to return to dancing, but she was unswayed. Her mother then talked to former first lady Imelda Marcos, who convinced Barredo that she owed it to herself and to her country to be a great ballerina.

Barredo left the Philippines and flew to New York City. Once there, she learned she had received a scholarship for the American Ballet Center, the official school of New York's Joffrey Ballet. Robert Joffrey took a liking to her and christened her Maniya Barredo. "He said a ballerina couldn't possibly make it with a name like Josephine, which is my real name, much less Honey [her nickname]," Barredo told *Sunburst.*

Being given a new name by Joffrey was an honor bestowed only on a few dancers, some of whom—like Paul Sutherland and Trignette Singleton—had gone on to greater fame and acclaim. Among younger dancers, being renamed by Joffrey came to be regarded as a sign of good luck.

In New York, Barredo relied not on luck but on hard work. She trained daily from nine in the morning to seven at night for two years. Her teachers included Ann Parsons, Leon Damielin, and Patricia Wilde. She was also tutored by William Griffith. While she was still training, Barredo also toured with Joffrey II and later joined Joffrey I.

When auditions for the National Ballet of Washington were announced, Joffrey sent six of its students but not Barredo. She went to the auditions anyway and found sixty other girls in competition—all tall, white, and long-limbed.

"I was nervous that at the sight of my tan, five-feet-flat height, and 83 pounds, I would be eliminated without a trial," Barredo told *Sunburst*. "I made it to the final five after all kinds of tests, developé, attitudé, steps that weren't exactly my forté. Imagine my joy when the final test was to be pirouettes. The girl before me told the pianist to go faster, but only lasted sixteen pirouettes. So when my turn came, I had no choice but to tell the pianist to go even faster."

Barredo, who has counted pirouettes among her strengths, completed thirty-two fouettes, a quick whipping movement of the raised leg often accompanied by continuous turning on the supporting leg. She was accepted at once, but eventually turned down the National Ballet contract in favor of a J.D. Rockefeller Fund Fellowship in Ballet, which she was awarded the same month.

"I wanted to be a professional at once, but Mr. Joffrey and Mr. Griffith advised me to perfect my training first," Barredo told *Sunburst*. "I had a special problem being a Filipina in the US. Being short and dark, I couldn't possibly get into any company as a member of the corps. I would stick out like a sore thumb. I had to come in immediately as a soloist or not at all."

Professional Career

Barredo got her wish. In May 1972, she gave a solo dance concert at Carnegie Hall, the first such solo concert given by a Filipina in the United States. In the fall of 1973, she joined Montreal's Les Grand Ballets Canadiens, one of the three major ballet companies in Canada, becoming its youngest principal dancer. She toured Canada and spent a month's residence with the Paris Opera Theater Ballet in France. It was at Les Grands Ballet that she met Mannie Rowe, a principal dancer, whom she married. In September 1975, the couple traveled to the Philippines to dance *Time out of Mind* and *Romeo and Juliet,* a piece that Les Grand Ballets Canadiens' choreographer, Brian Macdonald, presented them as a wedding gift.

In 1976, Barredo represented Canada in the International Dance Festival in Cuba. Later that year, she left Les Grand Ballets Canadiens, taking a large pay cut to join the Atlanta Ballet, then a civic ballet company with a small $800,000 budget. She explained she had fallen in love with the city and was eager to escape Canadian winters. She also wanted to do more classical roles.

"It was a gamble, but dancers are artists and they do what they do for the art," she told the *Atlanta Journal and Constitution* in 1986. The gamble paid off and in the next decade, the Atlanta Ballet blossomed into a fully professional company and increased its budget to more that $3 million. Over the years, other companies, including the American Ballet Theater and the Joffrey Ballet wooed Barredo, but she stayed.

She did, however, continue performing as a guest performer around the world. In 1979, Dame Margot Fonteyn invited her to join the "Stars of the World Ballet" tour where she was the only dancer not aligned with a New York or European company. Aside from serving as prima ballerina for the Atlanta Ballet, Barredo also became its coach in 1983. In early 1986, she was divorced from Mannie Rowe, who was then ballet master of the Atlanta Ballet, but their friendship and professional union continued.

"Someone asked me recently if I stayed because I wanted to be a big fish in a little pond," Barredo said in the 1986 *Atlanta Journal and Constitution* interview. "That's not it at all. An artist is not rated by where she works. It doesn't make me any less of a dancer to dance here. I believe in the Atlanta Ballet . . . . Having been with the Joffrey, I have seen the pitfalls of a big New York company. Here I have room to grow without the pressures of all the politics. I have found my little corner in this hemisphere."

Classical Roles

Barredo also got her wish to do more classical roles. Today, she is most widely known for her classical repertoire, including the title roles in *Giselle, Sleeping Beauty, Romeo and Juliet, Swan Lake, La Sylphide* and *Coppelia.* Her interpretations of the Sugar Plum Fairy in the *Nutcracker* and the new roles she has taken on, including Karen in Thor Sutowski's *The Red Shoes* and Titania in Dennis Nahat's *A Midsummer Night's Dream,* were widely praised. Of George Balanchine's masterworks, among her favorites are *Serenade, Concerto Barocco, Allegro Brillante, The Four Temperaments,* and *Stars and Stripes.*

As a coach, she has a reputation for being demanding. "Not everyone is going to like me. Being a prima means a lot of responsibility, especially toward the younger kids who are just coming up in the company," she told the *Atlanta Journal and Constitution.* "I'm headstrong. I speak my mind and I'm a workaholic and sometimes people resent that. The greatest pain I carry is that I expect people to do more than they think they can. It's hard for me not to push them. I've always believed you have to put 200 percent into rehearsal so you give 100 percent on stage. It's hard for me to stop caring."

In January 1994, Barredo danced her farewell performance in Manila, performing Giselle at the Cultural Center of the Philippines. When she finished, she received a fifteen-minute standing ovation. She said in May 1994 that she planned to dance for the Atlanta Ballet another year, and then concentrate on coaching, giving lectures, and writing an autobiography. Barredo, who now lives in suburban Atlanta with her second husband, L. Patterson Thompson III, and their five dogs, eventually plans to open her own ballet school. She faces her future away from performing with equanimity.

"It was such a good marriage, a good friend," Barredo told de Leon. "But there will be no sadness. I've gotten more than I ever dreamed I could attain. I'm excited about the next stage and I hope I do as well with the next forty years of my life."

Sources:

Periodicals

Smith, Helen C. "Maniya Barredo Celebrates 10 Years in Atlanta." *Atlanta Journal and Constitution,* November 2, 1986, p. 1J.
Viana, Francis. "Honey Barredo." *Sunburst,* pp. 46–47.

Other

Atlanta Ballet. "Maniya Barredo." Press releases and biographical materials, 1994.
Barredo, Maniya, telephone interview with Ferdinand M. de Leon, May 5, 1994.

—Sketch by Ferdinand M. de Leon

Lynda Barry
(1956–)
Cartoonist, playwright

Cartoonist Lynda Barry first recognized the value of her artistic talents in second grade when one day she drew an orange grove to illustrate the letter O. The popular girls in school liked her drawing and for a few days, the drawing elevated her status. Up until then, Barry had been interested in insects and had thought of being a vet, she told *Mirabella* magazine in 1991. But with her newfound popularity, she knew she had found her calling. "It turned out to be a good thing, but I chose it so I could be better-liked," Barry said. "I can remember all the brain action behind it."

It's a quintessentially Barry story—one that captures all the tugs and pulls and social maneuverings of childhood. It's a story, in short, that could have come straight out of her popular "Ernie Pook's Comeek," which every week, in more than sixty alternative publications throughout the United States and Canada (and even a few in Russia and Hungary), gives grown-ups her insightful explorations of childhood.

"My feeling is that our problems as adults have their root systems in childhood," Barry said in a 1993 interview with *Now,* a weekly Toronto publication. "It's much easier to sort out and make a clear picture of a problem by setting it in childhood. . . . It's the most soulful time of life. It's one of the last great awake times in human existence."

Childhood Interest in Art

Barry's own childhood was less than perfect. She was born in Seattle, and grew up in a working-class neighborhood that was predominantly black and Asian. Her Filipino mother worked as a hospital janitor and her Irish-Norwegian father worked as a meatcutter at a supermarket. They had met in the military and settled in Seattle to be near her mother's family. When she was fourteen her father left the family, leaving her mother to support her and her two brothers.

Once she discovered art, Barry often turned to her drawings to cope with the turbulence of her home life. In a 1992 *Elle* article, Barry said her grammar school teacher often sent her off with a pad and pencil when she had one of her frequent emotional "flipouts." "Drawing was a calming thing," she said. Even when she was a child, Barry recalled, she liked to watch and study how people spoke and what they said, then wrote down her observations in her notes.

Barry studied fine arts at Evergreen State College in Washington, where she became friends with other cartoonists, including Matt Groening (who would go on to create "The Simpsons"). She never considered a career in cartooning until one day, after breaking up with her boyfriend, she found herself doodling a strip where the men were like cactuses, smoking cigarettes and trying to get women to sleep with them. A friend at the University of Washington liked her drawings and published them in his school paper.

But it was from artists in other mediums that Barry drew her inspiration. "I've been more influenced by artists like Toulouse-Lautrec and writers like Raymond Carver than I have by cartoonists," Barry said in the *Elle* magazine interview. "But I did read underground cartoonist R. Crumb in the sixties. I was impressed with the variety of people he put in his work, more than with his storylines—he drew real people instead of superheroes."

She was also inspired by an art professor who encouraged students to tell the story of their lives. Barry got her big break as a cartoonist a few years after graduation when

Lynda Barry

the *Chicago Reader,* an alternative weekly, began running her strip. It soon caught the attention of other alternative weeklies, including the *Village Voice,* and led to syndication.

"Ernie Pook's Comeek"

In 1977, the strip evolved into "Ernie Pook's Comeek," which she named after her little brother's turtles. The four-panel serial strip, drawn in a scratchy child-like style, follows the adventures of Arna, Arnold, Freddie, Maybonne, and Marlys, a group of children growing up in the sixties. Although the strip is set in a specific time and place, the emotions she delves into and the themes she explores are universal. "Her success is pinned to her ability to revisit childhood, objectifying it for adults who see themselves in her characters—alone in their confusion, naked in their vulnerability, and hilarious in their clumsy honesty," wrote Margot Mifflin in *Elle.* A *Mirabella* writer said of her strips: "The comic often illuminates small, telling truths that stick to the heart like burrs."

Over the years, Barry has collected her works into books. In 1994 she released her eighth, *It's So Magic.* While the early books chronicled innocent rites of passage, like bad haircuts and a shared first smoke, her most recent collections have tackled more serious subjects. Her 1992 collection, *My Perfect Life,* for instance, takes on issues like race, sex, alcoholism, and religion. Barry's name is often grouped with other leading innovators who have radically redefined cartoon art in recent years,

straying from traditional formats and themes to deal with serious issues.

Novelist and Playwright

In 1988, Barry published her first novel, *The Good Times Are Killing Me,* which later won the Washington State Governor Writer's Award. She developed the story into a play, which was originally staged off-Broadway in 1991 and later had successful runs throughout the country and in Canada. Set in the mid-60s, the play is about the friendship between two twelve-year-old girls, Edna, who's white and Bonna, who's black. "The play is a love story," Barry said in *Now.* "That's what making friends is, falling in love. Everybody's felt it when you make a new friend. And it's really dynamic. You're thinking about them all the time."

Barry has also tried out other artistic mediums over the years. In 1990, she became a commentator for National Public Radio's "Morning Edition." Prior to that she wrote a strip on gender relations for *Esquire* magazine, and for several years she wrote a fiction column for the progressive political magazine *Mother Jones.* When Barry lived in Chicago, she and her friend cartoonist Heather McAdams put on a performance based on their ten-year correspondence, complete with music and dancing. Her paintings have been featured in several exhibits.

Barry, who now lives in Minneapolis, recently released a CD, *The Lynda Barry Experience,* featuring her readings of her short stories. She also completed her first television special, "Grandma's Way-Out Party," which was aired on KCTS in Minneapolis. She is now working on her second novel, *Cruddy.*

Barry, however, says she remains loyal to her first love: cartooning. "It's my favorite thing," she said. "A comic strip doesn't take that long to do, and I only do one a week. I do it right before it's due. I sit down until I hear the first line and then I just write it and draw it right there on the paper. It's like the live performance of a writer. It's the closest you can get to being live."

Sources:

Periodicals

Hollett, Micahel. "Lynda Barry: Fearless Cartoonist's Razor-Sharp Recollections Explode on Stage." *Now,* April 8–14, 1993.

Mifflin, Margot. "A Not So Perfect Life: The Anxious Humor of Lynda Barry." *Elle,* April 1992.

Oppenheimer, Judy. "Lynda Barry Outstrips Them All." *Mirabella,* April 1991.

Other

Barry, Lynda. "Biography," May 1994.

—Sketch by Ferdinand M. deLeon

Julia Chang Bloch
(1942–)
International businessperson, diplomat

Julia Chang Bloch

Julia Chang Bloch came to national prominence in 1989 when then-president George Bush named her ambassador to Nepal, making her, remarkably, the first Asian American ambassador in the history of the United States diplomatic corps. In 1993, she left public service to become group executive vice-president and head of corporate relations for BankAmerica Corporation. As such, she is responsible for BankAmerica's governmental, media, public policy, and internal and external communications programs.

Julia Chang Bloch was born in China in 1942. She came to the United States at age nine and earned a bachelor's degree in communications and public policy from the University of California at Berkeley in 1964. Later that year Chang Bloch joined the Peace Corps and served for two years in Sabah, Malaysia, where she taught English as a second language in a Chinese middle school. She returned to the United States and enrolled in Harvard University where she earned a master's degree in government and East Asia regional studies in 1967.

Also in 1967, Chang Bloch took a position as a training officer in the Peace Corps. In this position she planned, developed, and conducted training programs, specializing in cross-cultural training for volunteers interested in working in the East Asia and Pacific region. She was also responsible for monitoring Peace Corps contracts in host countries and providing all sorts of technical assistance in the areas of program design and training techniques. She also served on the volunteer selection board that picked candidates for overseas service.

In 1968 Chang Bloch took another job in the Peace Corps hierarchy when she became an evaluation officer. In this position Chang Bloch worked further in the design of evaluation methods for training programs of volunteers, and then used her new evaluation framework in assessing the effectiveness of various programs in Asia and Central America.

Politics

In 1971 Chang Bloch moved from administrative to legislative work when she became a congressional staffer for the Senate Select Committee on Nutrition and Human Needs. In 1976 she was elevated to the position of chief minority counsel of the same committee. In these positions Chang Bloch directed legislative activities in twelve functional areas. Her responsibilities included developing legislative proposals; writing briefing papers, speeches,

and reports for various members of the committee; managing the budget of her staff; and serving as spokesperson for the ranking minority member of the committee.

In 1977 Chang Bloch was named deputy director of the Office of African Affairs of the International Communication Agency. As such she assisted the director in developing and directing U.S. public diplomacy policies for sub-Saharan Africa, administering a $20 million budget and a staff of more than five hundred. This position required coordination of policy with the National Security Council, the State Department, and the Agency for International Development (AID) on all public diplomacy policy involving U.S. African policy.

In 1980 Chang Bloch was awarded a one-semester fellowship to the Institute of Politics at the Kennedy School of Government at Harvard University in Cambridge, Massachusetts. She conducted a study on American foreign policy and domestic politics. After her fellowship, Chang Bloch became a special assistant to the administrator of the AID. As such she reviewed and reported on the refugee resettlement and assistance programs in the war- and famine-decimated country of Somalia. She also was responsible for coordinating with the State Department in determining AID responsibilities for refugee programs.

In 1981, Chang Bloch became assistant administrator of the Food for Peace and Voluntary Assistance Bureau, an agency within the AID. The first Asian American to be a presidential appointee and confirmed by the Senate, she administered the world's largest food aid program, with a budget of over $2 billion serving populations in eighty countries. It was during Chang Bloch's tenure that AID and Food for Peace administered one of the most complex and costly famine relief efforts in history, during which three million tons of food was delivered to an estimated forty million people throughout Africa in 1984 and 1985. She was also responsible for directing food aid policy and allocations with the National Security Council, the Office of Management and Budget, and the departments of state, agriculture, treasury, and commerce. She also managed the $250 million biennial pledge to the World Food Program, headed numerous delegations to hunger conferences sponsored by the United Nations, supervised a $70 million grants portfolio to assist the American Schools and Hospitals Abroad program, and coordinated the Agency's relationship with nearly two hundred private and voluntary organizations.

In 1987 Chang Bloch moved from Food for Peace to become assistant administrator of the Asia and Near East Bureau of AID. In this position she administered a regional bureau spanning sixteen time zones with a staff of more than two thousand and a $3.8 billion program—the largest in the agency—providing assistance to more than twenty-six countries. Working in this vast a geographic area, Chang Bloch managed programs meant to serve a huge array of interests. There were purely humanitarian programs, programs in countries that were considered vital to U.S. strategic global interests, and programs in countries that were vital for their economic dynamism. She worked closely in this position with the World Bank, the International Monetary Fund, and other international donors, especially the Japanese.

In 1988, Chang Bloch returned to the academic setting when she became an associate in the U.S.-Japan Relations Program at Harvard's Center for International Affairs. Here she conducted research and seminars on Japanese American relations, with a particular focus on foreign aid. Based on her studies she wrote a paper on U.S.-Japan aid cooperation, an abstract of which was published in *Yen for Development*, a book published by the Council on Foreign Relations.

Ambassador to Nepal

In 1989, Chang Bloch was named U.S. Ambassador to Nepal by President George Bush. During her tenure in Nepal the country was wracked by a popular uprising that brought about the first democratically elected government in more than 30 years in the Himalayan kingdom. Chang Bloch was responsible for articulating the United States' position during this tumultuous time and lending diplomatic assistance to the process of democratization, always a tenuous transition. In this process, Chang Bloch initiated and directed the Democratic Program Initiative in support of the consolidation of democracy in Nepal.

In 1993, Chang Bloch retired from public service to become a group executive vice-president for corporate relations at BankAmerica. In her second career, she hopes her lifetime experience in public service will bring a new dimension to her corporate responsibilities.

Chang Bloch has received many awards during her career. Among these are the International Award of Honor from the Narcotic Enforcement Officers Association (1992), the Woman of the Year Award from the Organization of Chinese American Woman (1987), an honorary doctorate of Human Letters from Northeastern University (1986), and the Hubert H. Humphrey Award for International Service (1979). Chang Bloch says of her achievements: "Only in this country can a first generation American become an ambassador and go on to a major corporate executive position in one lifetime."

Sources:

BankAmerica Corporation. "Julia Chang Bloch." Internal Document (Resume). San Francisco, California, 1994.
Bloch, Julia Chang. Written interview with Jim Henry, June 1994.

—Sketch by Jim Henry

Carlos Bulosan
(1911–1956)
Writer, poet

For decades after Carlos Bulosan's death, his works languished in obscurity and his extraordinary achievements were virtually forgotten. But in his short life, Bulosan rose from an impoverished childhood in colonial Philippines to become a celebrated man of letters in the United States, despite the deeply entrenched racial barriers of the day. His books and poems bore unsparing witness to the racism and hardships Filipinos encountered in their adopted home. While America failed to live up to his dreams, Bulosan continued to lay claim to his vision for the land that rejected him and his countrymen. "America is not a land of one race or one class of men," Bulosan wrote in his autobiography, *America Is in the Heart*. "We are all Americans that have toiled and suffered and know oppression and defeat, from the first Indian that offered peace in Manhattan to the last Filipino peapickers. . . . America is a prophecy of a new society of men: of a system that knows no sorrow or strife or suffering." The book, when rediscovered by another generation of Asian Americans in the late 1960s and 1970s, would later become an instant classic in the emerging canon of Asian American literature.

Poverty and Flight

Although there is conflicting information on the exact date of Bulosan's birth, Susan Evangelista, author of *Carlos Bulosan and His Poetry: A Biography and Anthology*, believes he was born on November 2, 1911, in Binalonan, Philippines. Bulosan's parents were peasants who eked out a living from the land. In his autobiography, Bulosan described his father's losing battle to keep the small parcel of land that supported their large family, and the setbacks that continually dashed any hopes for improving their lives. In his vivid portrayal of his family's poverty, Bulosan captured the forces that ultimately drove him—just as it had thousands of others—to seek a better life abroad.

After striking out on his own and saving enough money for his passage, Bulosan left Manila aboard a ship bound for Seattle. He never returned to the Philippines. During the harrowing transoceanic crossing, an epidemic of meningitis broke out and several of the Filipino passengers, who were confined to the steerage section, became ill or died. When Bulosan arrived July 1, 1930, the United States was a country deeply mired in the Great Depression. With unemployment high and competition for the few available jobs intense, immigrants who were drawn by promises of opportunity instead encountered increasing resentment and racism. Those who were too new to know their rights were often exploited. With no money or family in Seattle, Bulosan was quickly recruited to work in the Alaskan fish canneries. After a season of hard labor, his total earnings, after the questionable deductions, were only thirteen dollars.

Once back from Alaska, Bulosan started working his way south, toward California, where two of his brothers lived. Along the way, he found occasional work as a field hand or crop picker, and came to know the marginalized world of the Filipino immigrants. Ostracized by the mainstream, Filipino men (few women immigrated) created their own rough-and-tumble bachelor societies.

Racism

On the West Coast, they were often the target of racial violence. While working in an eastern Washington orchard, Bulosan and other Filipino workers were driven out by a group of white men, their bunkhouse set on fire. At a pool hall in Los Angeles, Bulosan saw two policemen gun down a Filipino. In California, racist laws made it illegal for Filipinos to marry white women, and cars with Filipino men were routinely stopped by patrol cars and searched. "I came to know afterward that in many ways it was a crime to be a Filipino in California," Bulosan wrote in his autobiography. "I came to know that the public streets were not free to my people."

In California, Bulosan became involved in an effort to organize independent unions—a reaction to the wage cuts,

Carlos Bulosan

unemployment, and the exploitation of the Depression and a protest against the drive to exclude Filipinos from unions in the early 1930s, noted Carey McWilliams in his introduction of *America Is in the Heart*. McWilliams, who was the editor the *Nation* magazine, knew Bulosan. The organizing effort led to the formation of anew international union known as UCAPAWA, United Cannery and Packing House Workers of America, representing fish cannery workers in Seattle and packing house workers in Salinas, California—often the same workers at different times of the year.

An older brother helped Bulosan find enough work to keep them alive. McWilliams described Bulosan as sickly. Because of a limp, the kinds of jobs open to him were limited, although he did manage to get work now and then, mostly as a dishwasher. McWilliams quoted John Fante, the novelist and screenwriter who was also a friend of Bulosan's, who described him as a poet-saint, having "an exquisite face, almost facially beautiful, with gleaming teeth and lovely brown eyes, shy, generous terribly poor, terribly exiled in California."

Reading and Writing

To pass time during the periods when he was not well enough to work or when he was unable to find jobs, he spent long hours at the Los Angeles Public Library, where he read everything from children's books to Freudian psychology, said Evangelista. When he left the Philippines, he had only three years of formal education and spoke little

English. Although he hadn't written much before coming to the United States, once he discovered writing, he never stopped. Bulosan sold his first story while he was working in a fish cannery in San Pedro.

In 1934, Bulosan published *The New Tide*, a bimonthly radical literary magazine that brought him into contact with several prominent writers, including William Carlos Williams, William Saroyan, and Richard Wright. He also met and befriended Harriet Monroe, editor of the prestigious magazine *Poetry*, who published and championed his work. At other times, Bulosan was involved in writing more political news, working for the *Philippine Commonwealth Times* and at least two other newspapers in the Stockton-Salinas areas that focused on the problems of the Filipino workers, according to Evangelista.

In 1936 Bulosan, suffering from tuberculosis, was taken to the Los Angeles County hospital where he underwent three operations for a lesion in his right lung. He spent two years in the hospital, mostly in the convalescent ward. Bulosan used his long stay in the hospital to develop his education by reading voraciously and constantly writing. "Writing is a pleasure and a passion to me. I seem to be babbling with multitudinous ideas, but my body is weak and tired," Bulosan wrote at the time. "I locked myself in the room, unplugged the phone, pulled down the shades and shut out the whole damned world. I knew enough of it to carry me for a lifetime of writing."

With the end of the Depression and the start of World War II, during which the Philippines and the United States were allies in the fight against Japan, the status of Filipinos in the United States began to change slightly. It was during this time that Bulosan began to receive wider acceptance as a writer, noted Evangelista. In 1942 he wrote two thin volumes of poetry, *Letter from America* and *Chorus for America*. That year he was included in *Who's Who in America*. The following year he published *The Voice of Bataan*, written in memory of the soldiers who died there. That same year, the *Saturday Evening Post* published four articles on the four freedoms—freedom of speech, freedom to worship, freedom from want, freedom from fear—and Bulosan was chosen to write the section on freedom from want. In 1944, Bulosan published *The Laughter of My Father*, which became an instant wartime success. The book was translated into several European languages and was transmitted worldwide over wartime radio. The following year, Harcourt, Brace and Company asked him to write what would become his most enduring work, his autobiography, *America Is in the Heart*. When it was published in 1946, the book was a critical success.

McWilliams, in his introduction to the reprinted edition nearly three decades later, called it a social classic: "It reflects the collective life experience of thousands of Filipino immigrants who were attracted to this country by its legendary promises of a better life or who were recruited for employment here." The *Saturday Review of Literature* said of the book: "People interested in driving from America the scourge of intolerance should read Mr. Bulosan's autobiography. They should read it that they may draw from the anger it will arouse in them the determination to bring to an end the vicious nonsense of racism."

Political Repercussion

In the conservative postwar climate, Bulosan's star started to face. His left-wing politics and involvement in union activities were at odds with the fervent anticommunism of the McCarthy era. But Bulosan became increasingly involved with UCAPAWA. In 1950, he was hired to edit the union's highly political yearbook. The repercussions for his political stand were severe. Bulosan believed that he was blacklisted in Hollywood and was unable to find work there because of his political beliefs, according to Evangelista. His friend, John Fante, reportedly said that he was barred from working at MGM studios simply because of his association with Bulosan.

Bulosan's health progressively worsened in the early 1950s. He spent his final years in Seattle, and was hospitalized for part of that time. When he died of tuberculosis and malnutrition, union leader Chris Mensalvas, a close friend of Bulosan's, wrote this obituary, as quoted in Evangelista's book: "Carlos Bulosan, 30 years old (sic), died 11 September 1956, Seattle. Birthplace: Philippines; Address: Unknown; Occupation: Writer; Hobby: Famous for his jungle salad served during Foreign-Born Committee dinners. Estate: One typewriter, a twenty-year old suit, unfinished manuscripts, worn out sock; Finances: Zero; Beneficiary: His people."

For two decades after his death, Bulosan and his works were largely forgotten. But a generation of young Asian Americans hungry to reclaim their lost history and heroes rediscovered him. *America Is in the Heart* was reprinted by the University of Washington Press in 1973 and it has since become a fixture in Asian American studies programs at universities across the county.

Sources:

Bulosan, Carlos. *America Is in the Heart*. 1943; reprinted with introduction by Carey McWilliams, Seattle and London: University of Washington Press, 1973.

Evangelista, Susan. *Carlos Bulosan and His Poetry: A Biography and Anthology*. Seattle: University of Washington Press, 1985.

—Sketch by Ferdinand de Leon

C

Phyllis Jean Takisaki Campbell
(1951–)
Banker

In twenty short years, Phyllis Campbell rose through banking's ranks from a management trainee fresh out of college to become the president and chief executive officer of the U.S. Bank of Washington in Spokane, one of Washington State's leading financial institutions. During this period, she served as branch manager and then senior vice-president and manager of all Spokane branches of Old National Bank. In 1987, after the acquisition of Old National Bank by U.S. Bank of Washington, Campbell was promoted to senior vice-president and area manager for eastern Washington. In 1989, she became executive vice-president and manager of the Distribution Group for U.S. Bank of Washington, and in 1992, was tapped to lead the Seattle-King County area. Today as president and chief executive officer, Campbell is responsible for the leadership and management of all U.S. Bank of Washington retail and business banking in the state, including three area banks representing over 160 branches.

Born on July 25, 1951, in Spokane, Phyllis Jean Takasaki was the oldest of five children born to Marion Takisaki, a medical technologist, and Raymond J. Takisaki, a merchant who owned and operated his own dry cleaning business. Although poor, her family was close. "When we were growing up, we all helped in the family business," she recalled in an interview with Nancy Moore. "My mother worked and maintained a career throughout her whole life, even raising five children. She was a real role model for me as a strong woman, a person in her own right. My sister and brothers and I took care of each other and occasionally, a lady in the neighborhood would come in to help. Back in those days neighborhoods were safer places. My brothers and sisters and I are still very close today." Although vacations and travel were not a regular part of their lifestyle, local family outings and picnics were. "I remember one family trip to Disneyland where the seven of us all piled into the old Rambler sedan. My sister was under the dashboard and off we went," she laughed.

Phyllis Jean Takisaki Campbell

Campbell's grandfather, who immigrated from Japan and settled in Seattle, was a merchant who owned a grocery store. His ethics of hard work and community service were instilled in her whole family. "My grandfather always said that this country had afforded him great opportunities, and he taught us that we had a responsibility to give back to people what had been given to us," she explained. Her family's experiences during World War II, in which her father served in the army, did nothing to change her grandfather's convictions. "During the war, my grandfather and my uncle and aunt were forced to liquidate the business and were interned in North Dakota, but even after that my grandfather never spoke ill of the government." In his mind, the government's apology and restitution payments to Japanese Americans who were interned were taken as proof of the nation's resolve never to let a similar experience happen again.

Growing up, Campbell always had an inclination toward business, business management, and leadership. Working in the family business in high school, she learned she enjoyed accounting and dealing with people. "But I did not want to stay in the family business," she explained, "because I wanted something larger with corporate finance and corporate structure." Determined to pursue her goals, Campbell worked her way through Washington State University, where she received a bachelor's degree in business administration and later a master's in the Executive Marketing Program. She is also a graduate of the University of Washington's Pacific Coast Banking School and Stanford University's Marketing Management Program. She was awarded an honorary doctorate from Whitworth College.

Campbell's life has not been without its hurdles. After establishing herself as a successful professional in the banking industry, she was faced with a personally devastating crisis when she was diagnosed with cancer at age thirty-two. "Having cancer at such a young age was a lot to assimilate," she admitted. "I underwent radiation therapy and won the battle, but it forced me to reassess my life and rethink where I was going. Now I try to live each day to the fullest and I want to be a role model in giving back to others just like my grandfather was for me."

Today Campbell lives with her husband, a civil engineer in suburban Seattle, where she serves as vice-chair of the Greater Seattle Chamber of Commerce, vice-president of the Board of Regents at Washington State University, and chair of the Association of Washington Business. She is also a member of the board of the Washington Roundtable and Puget Power and Light. In 1992, for her civic service, Campbell received the Puget Sound Matrix Table's Woman of Achievement Award.

One of her favorite charitable causes is "Success by Six," a program that emphasizes the need to help young children get ready to learn. "Our children are our future, and their education is the key. But we will determine the world our children will live in. For this reason I am working to give something back to young people," Campbell declared.

Campbell views her Japanese American heritage as "two sides of the coin." As a result of her background and the trials her family experienced during the war, she is proud of her heritage, but views it and the qualities that are a product of it as a responsibility. "In my life I have always tried to stand out in positive, not negative ways," Campbell added. "I'm proud of the attributes I can bring to business, civic roles, and other life experiences. Living each day to the fullest and taking advantage of each page as it is turned is my goal."

Sources:

Campbell, Phyllis, telephone interview with Nancy Moore, June 27, 1994.

U.S. Bank of Washington. "Phyllis Campbell." Executive profile. Seattle, Washington, June 1994

-Sketch by Nancy Moore

Tia Carrere
(1969–)
Actress

In 1992, Tia Carrere scored major roles in two Hollywood productions, and she hasn't paused for a break since. In the box-office success *Wayne's World,* she played Cassandra, a heavy-metal rock and roller and girlfriend of the main character, played by Mike Myers. In *Rising Sun,* a thriller based on the best-selling novel by Michael Crichton, she played a computer hacker and love interest of star Sean Connery. Her next roles were in *Quick,* in which she portrayed a police officer on the trail of drug smugglers, and in *Wayne's World II,* in which she reprised her role as Cassandra. By late 1993, she was promoting her career as a singer with the release of her solo album. Although she contributed two cuts to the *Wayne's World* platinum sound track album, the heavy-metal sound she created for the film is not her solo style. In an interview with Tom Green for *Cosmopolitan,* she described her music as "exotic, grooving, organic pop—a little bit dancy."

Carrere was born Althea Janairo in 1969 in Hawaii, but she has always used her childhood nickname, Tia. Of primarily Filipino descent, Carrere is the oldest in a family that includes sisters Alesaundra and AudraLee. Carrere told *People* in 1992, "My upbringing in Hawaii taught me that family is the most important thing." She changed her last name to Carrere when she became an actress, aiming for a more exotic image.

In November 1992, Carrere married Elie Samaha, a Lebanon-born entrepreneur and owner of a trendy nightclub in Los Angeles, Roxbury, where the two met in 1990. Commenting about adjustments to domestic life, Carrere quipped to *People:* "My grandmother always said, 'Tia, one day you are going to be married; you have to learn how to cook.' But I got lucky, I married a restaurateur." They were married in a rainswept ceremony near Honolulu where Carrere grew up.

Lucky Breaks

With an apparent knack for being in the right place at the right time, Carrere has received several breaks along the way that have boosted her career. When she had just graduated from a Catholic girls' school in Hawaii at the age of seventeen, she was spotted at a Honolulu grocery store by a movie producer's mother, which led to a major role in the beach movie *Aloha Summer.* Following this she moved to Los Angeles where she continued to perform in films, including *Harley Davidson and the Marlboro Man,* and *Showdown in Little Tokyo.* Carrere had paid her acting dues on the television soap opera "General Hospital." Her role

Tia Carrere

as Jade, a nursing student, was reasonably successful. However, influenced by her then-boyfriend and manager, she sued the soap to get out of her contract. When his promise of a more lucrative acting contract never materialized, Carrere realized her mistake and ended their professional and personal relationship. "I was stupid. I let it happen," recollected a wiser Carrere to Tom Green in *Cosmopolitan.* She canceled the lawsuit and "General Hospital" took her back for six more months. In spite of her blossoming acting career, Carrere's real interest was her singing career. Ironically, she happened to be at the office of a record company executive, Mo Ostin when word came through that Paramount Pictures was looking for an Asian rock-n-roller—which led to her landing her star-making role in *Wayne's World.*

Assigning Priorities

Carrere has always dreamed of having children and plans to have a large family, but for now she and Samaha have hectic careers that require long separations. They are rarely home and nights run late. Carrere lives with her husband and their pet Akita, Dante, in their house in the Hollywood Hills which features a deck with a Japanese hot tub and a panoramic view, where Carrere goes to meditate and work on her songs. About her future, Carrere emphasizes the priority she assigns to her singing career, saying that although she looks forward to a sustained career in films, her current emphasis is on her music.

Sources:

Green, Tom. "Tia Carrere." *Cosmopolitan,* August 1993, p. 102.
Levitt, Shelley. "Tying the Not!" *People,* December 7, 1992, p. 162.

—*Sketch by Visi R. Tilak*

Maryles V. Casto

Businessperson

Founder, owner, and manager of Casto Travel, the largest privately owned corporate travel agency in northern California, Maryles Casto believes that "there is no such thing as *can't.*" She told *Notable Asian Americans,* "I admire people who work hard to make a difference, and those who are willing to change, if necessary, in order to achieve their goals." Casto has demonstrated both qualities since she established Casto Travel more than twenty years ago in 1973. Drawing from her experience as a flight attendant, manager of in-flight service for Phillipine Airlines, and manager of a major travel agency in the San Jose area, Casto has built her business on dedication to customer service and pride.

Born in San Carlos City in the Philippines, Maryles Casto grew up in a close, caring Catholic family of seven children where mutual support was a primary value. "Family was the most important aspect in our lives," recalled Casto, who followed the professional path of her older sister, a flight attendant. Even her career choice was made in part because it permitted visits with her family each year. Although she attended school in a different province, her family lived in San Carlos during her whole childhood. Both her parents were strong role models. Her mother's motto, "There is no such thing as *can't,*" has served as a guiding force in her life. Her father preached the personal values of pride and integrity which, he claimed, were important because they couldn't be bought, and, if lost, could never be replaced no matter how much money you might have.

As a young person, Casto interacted with a variety of people. The experiences she had sensitized her to different types of individuals and their needs, which has been an asset in her career. She believes strongly in personal growth through continued learning in life and in the power of prayer as a source of strength. She moved to the United States in 1964 with her husband. Although the couple divorced in 1989, she maintains friendships with both her ex-husband and her eighteen-year-old son, Marc.

Maryles V. Casto

Entrepreneur

With a partner and an initial investment of fifteen-hundred dollars, Casto launched a travel agency. In 1973, she bought out her partner and renamed the agency Casto Travel, which, as of 1994, was the largest privately held travel agency in Northern California.

Casto feels her Asian upbringing has made her a service-oriented person and has taught her to be able to anticipate the needs of others before they are expressed. These have given her a reputation in the travel industry for her "personal touch."

Believing in the ethic of service to others, Casto is committed to a variety of community causes. She is a member of the board of the National Council of Christians and Jews, the Phillipine Foundation, the San Jose Cleveland Ballet, the Silicon Valley Global Trading Center, Capital Circle, the Committee of 200 (a global organization of leading business women), San Jose Airport Travel Agent Advisory, the San Jose Sharks/Leadership Council, The International Alliance, The Lincoln Club, United States Pan Asian American Chamber of Commerce, Women's Forum West, and Women's Forum of Washington, D.C.

For her achievement in the travel industry, Casto was named Woman of the Year in 1985 by the San Francisco Chamber of Commerce. In the same year, Casto Travel joined the "Savvy 60" list of top businesses owned by

women. After being the first woman to receive the Asian Pacific American Heritage award from former President George Bush in 1992 and the second woman to be inducted into the Santa Clara County Junior Achievement Business Hall of Fame in 1993, Casto was appointed in 1993 by Governor Pete Wilson to the California Council to promote business ownership by women.

In 1994, the Asian U.S. Pan Asian American Chamber of Commerce, an organization representing approximately eighteen hundred professionals, awarded Casto and five others its Excellence 2000 awards.

Sources:

Periodicals

"Six Outstanding Asian Americans Honored at Excellence 2000 Event." *Asian Week*, vol. 15, no. 44, May 29, 1994, p. 10.

Other

Casto, Maryles V., written interview with Helen Zia, June 1994.
Casto Travel. "Maryles V. Casto." Biographical profile, 1994.

—Sketch by Nancy Moore

Benjamin J. Cayetano
(1939–)
Politician

Despite the rhetoric of the American dream, individuals who rise from what many consider the dregs of society to top political leadership spots are few and far between. One person who did is Benjamin J. Cayetano, Hawaii's lieutenant governor and the nation's highest elected Filipino American. He's often listed as one of Hawaii's most effective legislators. And, with Governor John D. Waihee set to retire in 1994, Cayetano has all but formally announced his plans to seek the state's top elected position. A product of a tough blue-collar Honolulu district, a child who was forced to become an adult much too soon, Cayetano has indeed beat the odds and attained the American dream.

He grew up the son of a Filipino immigrant who worked as a waiter and often left the task of child-rearing to others. As a teenager, Cayetano sought comfort in the rough-and-tumble world of pool halls, fist fights, and fast cars. He once spent a night in jail, and he barely graduated from high school. Although he dreamed of becoming a lawyer, he was told to consider a profession more suitable to his circumstances. Cayetano ignored the advice and became a successful attorney. Known for his intensity and outspokenness, he has become one of Hawaii's most well-known political fixtures since his career began in the early 1970s.

Difficult Childhood

Benjamin Cayetano was born November 14, 1939, in Honolulu, in a neighborhood known as Kalihi, a tough industrial area not known for the lush greenery or peaceful waterfalls that are typically associated with Hawaii. His father, Bonifacio, and his mother, Eleanor, divorced when he was six. He and his younger brother, Kenneth, stayed with their father after the divorce. Bonifacio, in an effort to care for the boys, worked a split shift as a waiter. This allowed him to come home to cook dinner for his sons, but forced him to work late hours. On Saturdays, Bonifacio would take his sons with him to work. "Sometimes, they sleep on the kitchen floor. Sometime on the beach," Bonifacio told *Honolulu* magazine in 1979. "The Hawaiian beach boys take care of them. Take them for rides in the canoes." An early photograph of Cayetano shows him with his younger brother. Both stare straight ahead, their lips clamped together, a tough, intense look in their eyes. "I don't remember hardship," he said in an interview with *Rice* magazine. "But if you've never tasted steak, you never know what you're missing."

Cayetano recalls growing up in Hawaii, before statehood, playing with a mixed group of Hawaiian, Chinese, Japanese, and Filipino children. No *haoles,* or whites, were part of that group. A sharp-minded child, he initially did well in school. But a lack of role models and encouragement swiftly began to take its toll. By junior high school he was branded as something of a troublemaker. "I got into smoking, fighting. In those days, that was considered delinquent," he told Himanee Gupta.

At one point, he was sent to live with his mother, a fiercely independent woman who after the divorce had moved to a more rural area with her second husband. She tried to get her son into line by sending him to church and trying to supervise him more closely. But the trouble continued. After a fist fight, he wound up in jail. His mother bailed him out. His girlfriend, Lorraine Gueco, now his wife, remembers thinking he'd never amount to anything.

In the eighth grade, Cayetano had written a book report about Clarence Darrow, the attorney who defended the theories of scientific evolution during the Scopes Trial. Darrow's own troubled background and his persuasive arguments inspired Cayetano to consider a career in law, but his mother urged him to consider something more realistic.

Barely making it through high school, Cayetano graduated in 1958 and married Gueco. The prospect of

Benjamin J. Cayetano

supporting a wife, and soon, three children, seemed to straighten him out. He began working in a junkyard, packing metal. He then became an electrician's apprentice after which he worked as a truck driver. Then, after passing a state civil service examination, he began working on state highway crews. Cayetano then figured he'd make a good draftsman, so he took a required exam and passed it with high scores. He applied for a couple of jobs and didn't get any of them. He began to feel that stronger discriminatory forces were at work. A Japanese American was responsible for hiring; another Japanese American got the job. He developed a big chip on his shoulder, packed up his family, and moved to Los Angeles. "I said, 'I'm never coming back to his place unless I come back as something,'" he recalled in his interview with *Rice* magazine.

Fortune smiled on Cayetano in Los Angeles. For the first time, he saw whites—who had run everything in Hawaii—doing the same kinds of manual labor jobs he was accustomed to holding. It helped him realize that hard work and education could make a difference. He enrolled in a junior college, worked in the afternoons and then took his wife to Los Angeles Airport in the evenings where she worked as a waitress. Junior college led to admission at UCLA, and later to law school at the Loyola University School of Law. While his wife worked, Cayetano fed his children and studied. He'd pick her up at midnight and snatch a few hours sleep before beginning the day's cycle over again. This continued for seven years.

Return to Hawaii

Cayetano finally earned his law degree in 1971. He decided then that it was time to return to Hawaii. "This was the height of the civil rights movement," he recalled in an interview with Derek Ferrar in *Honolulu Weekly* in 1993. "I saw what was happening throughout the country. I worked near where the Watts riots took place. The white folks, the black folks, the Chicanos … I went out and bought a gun! I was afraid and I used to carry that thing in my glove compartment."

Back home in Honolulu, he landed a job with a mixed ethnic law firm. In 1972, an influential politician, then-governor John A. Burns, tapped Cayetano as an appointee to the Hawaii Housing Authority. The move was made strictly on the grounds of diversity. When Cayetano thanked Burns for the appointment, Burns told Cayetano that there weren't many Filipinos from the rough Kalihi area who go on to become attorneys. Indeed, Cayetano has said he is the only attorney in his high school graduating class of nine hundred students. But Burns' remark didn't bother him as it might have a few years earlier. Instead, he believed that Burns was trying to give all ethnic groups a piece of Hawaii's action.

The appointment plunged Cayetano into politics. He ran for the state house of representatives in 1974, while living in a Honolulu suburb dominated by Japanese American voters. He defeated a popular incumbent, who happened to be Japanese American. This helped him erase the painful feeling of the past of being passed over for a job in favor of another Japanese American. He served two terms in the state house and two terms in the state senate, before running successfully for lieutenant governor in 1986. He was reelected to a second term in 1990.

In 1994, Cayetano was a candidate for governor. He is known for defending Japanese investments in Hawaii and for promoting equal opportunities for minorities. As a state politician, he's led a fight for education reform and helped put into effect an After-School Plus (A+) Program, the nation's first state-funded after-school program for working families. The program is aimed at helping connect children of working parents with teachers and high school and college students who organize homework, games, and special sessions for kids. He sees the state's educational system as a means of keeping Hawaii from becoming a state of "room maids and bell boys." "We've got to create the kind of high educational institutions that are needed to make this place something other than a tourist destination," he told *UCLA Magazine* in 1992.

As a candidate for governor, Cayetano described himself to *Honolulu Weekly* as "tough on the outside, soft on the inside . . . I think I'm a person who has great passion for the work I do. When you're an elected official, you're given a great privilege and a great burden. You need to feel a sense of urgency about what you do." He takes this sense of urgency with him, as he looks to the future.

Sources:

Periodicals

Boylan, Dan. "The Odds Against Ben Cayetano." *Honolulu,* April 1979.
Ferrar, Derek. "Cayetano." *Honolulu Weekly,* May 26, 1993.
Kobayashi, Ken. "On the Rise: Hawaii's Benjamin Cayetano." *Rice,* December/January 1989.
Soderburg, Wendy. "Overcoming Trouble in Paradise." *UCLA Magazine,* Fall 1992.

Other

Cayetano, Benjamin, telephone interview with Himanee Gupta, March 10, 1994.

—Sketch by Himanee Gupta

Dia Cha
(1962?–)
Community activist

"**I** was very young, about six or seven years of age when one of my relatives, a soldier, fell in love with a lady, so he forced her to marry him. In Hmong culture, if a man likes a woman he can force marriage on her. She, on the other hand, was in love with someone else. When she came home from the market one day, he grabbed her and took her to his house to marry her. For three days she tried to escape, she was watched closely. After three days she committed suicide." Dia Cha, relating her experiences in a telephone interview with Visi R. Tilak, is a Hmong refugee who immigrated to the United States when she was sixteen years old. She had already seen and experienced a lot of pain.

A Refugee Child Finds Herself

"I do not know when I was born. Nobody kept track. When we filled out the immigration forms my brother guessed my age. Since my older sister had to be eighteen years old to be qualified for immigration, they decided to make her eighteen years old and my age was decided at sixteen years. My legal birthday is May 1962, but everyday is my birthday," said Cha laughingly. She was born in a province of Laos called Sam Neou, very near the Vietnam border. Soon after Cha was born, the United States military intervention in Vietnam began to escalate. Her family moved all the time, never living in one place for more than two years. Cha is a member of the ethnic group the Hmong who live in the highlands of Laos, Thailand, Vietnam, and

China. It was the Hmong who supported the U. S. government's secret and illegal war in Laos during the war.

In 1972, Cha's father was lost. During the war, Laos was divided into two political sects: one was supported by the U. S. government and the other by China and the Soviet Union. "My father was a soldier for the American CIA. In 1972 he went to the battlefield and never came back. We don't know if he has been killed or what," Cha told Tilak. In 1975 Cha moved with her family to a refugee camp in Thailand and lived there for four and a half years.

Cha has two younger siblings, a brother and a sister, and three older, two brothers and a sister. After going through all this instability they became very close to each other. Each has influenced Cha in his or her own way. "Family ties were very strong, they still are. We have a caring relationship. When my father was lost we were still very young. We had a very hard time, but we all tried to look after each other," said Cha.

Cha was a very dedicated and obedient child. She did all the household cooking and cleaning chores, never complained, and constantly looked for a chance to learn new things. She believed in accepting advice from others, especially her elders. "When I was little I always wanted to go to school and my father would not let me go. I would always think, 'If I go to school I will study very hard and be very good,'" she recalled. A sensitive child, Cha was very distraught and upset about what had happened to her female relatives. At that very young age she started believing that women were not treated fairly. She felt that if she had an education she would not have to marry if she did not want to—she could be independent. "I really don't like the way Hmong men treat women, the way they force them. I started thinking about women's role in society and the many things that are not fair for women," said Cha. She appreciates the fact that her mother has always been supportive of her.

She never did go to school in Laos, because her father believed it was a waste for women to attend school. However, she took part-time classes when the family was in the refugee camp. "When we came to America I directly joined the ninth grade in high school without really having had any formal education before that. It was extremely difficult to learn a new language, a new culture. All through college I changed my major three times. It was all very difficult to adjust to," she said. In 1987 she took a course in anthropology and found it so fascinating that she finally changed her major to anthropology.

Professional Accomplishments

Cha holds a bachelor of arts in anthropology from Metropolitan State College, Denver, Colorado, and a master of arts in applied anthropology from Northern Arizona University in Flagstaff, Arizona. She currently works as the Asian Community Outreach Coordinator at the Mental

Dia Cha

Health Center of Boulder County in Colorado. Her job is to provide support service to Asian students in high school and middle school, and to serve as an intermediary between parents and faculty in the Boulder Valley Public Schools. As part of her job she also advocates and promotes cultural understanding among the diverse Asian groups in Boulder County.

"I basically do two things in my job. One is to give a lot of speech presentations to the community in order to address the different ethnic and culture needs. Secondly, I work with Asian middle and high school students and provide support group help and guidance. I encourage the students to talk a lot about prejudice, living in different cultures, intergenerational conflict," explained Cha who not very long ago faced all these problems herself.

Cha is also a department associate in the anthropology department of the Denver Museum of Natural History, where she offers consultation, organizes collection materials, conducts research, and interviews people to gather information for the Southeast Asian Tribal Collections Project. Cha has also worked with the United Nations Development Fund for Women as a project director in Thailand and Laos. Her job was to assess the needs, concerns and protection issues of Lao and Hmong refugee women repatriates in Laos and in the refugee camps in Thailand.

Among the other prestigious organizations that she has served are the Indochina Resource Action Center as a summer fellow, the U.S. National Park Service as a ethnographic field researcher, and the Department of Commerce, U.S. Census Bureau as a census enumerator. Cha has traveled widely in Europe, Russia, and Southeast Asia. She has published extensively and won many awards, including the TRIO Achievers Award and an award "Honoring Outstanding Refugee Women." She is also affiliated with several professional anthropological and Hmong organizations.

Cha has said she had several role models who inspired her along the way. "When I was little, there was this lady, she was a nurse, my mother's cousin. She was very well known in her field and very good at what she did. I always wanted to be like her, she is one of my role models. Most of my teachers and friends, especially those older than me, in school and college were also very helpful to me and they guided me in my professional life," said Cha.

Beliefs and Philosophy from Life Experiences

"When things are very difficult you have to learn to look at it as a challenge—it really helps shape your life. I really like to be at new places to do new things to get a taste of life," said Cha. "When I am done solving a problem I feel good about it. So when I have a new opportunity or challenge I don't try to get away. Instead, I try to face it."

Cha, whose religion is Roman Catholic, believes that sometimes people become very successful, whether monetarily or otherwise, and forget where they came from. "I will never abuse whatever I have when I become successful. When you eat food, you eat enough but you don't eat too much. Similarly, whatever you do you don't do too much of it," she declared. Cha feels that no matter how successful one is, one should always remember one's family history and where one comes from. To her, family is a major support and influence in everyone's life. "Sometimes you may be really angry and think that you don't care about anything, but you always have to think of your family and that will stop you from doing things you should not be doing," reflected Cha. She said she has always believed in her family and felt their support in all her endeavors.

Cha has carved a niche for herself and gained respect both professionally and in her personal life. She said, "My mother is a widow and illiterate. As a child I witnessed people looking down on her many times. I didn't want to be treated like her. I made sure that did not happen. I will always do my best and when things don't work out the way I want I have no regrets. I'll pick up where I left off and keep going."

Sources:

Cha, Dia, telephone interview with Visi R. Tilak.

—Sketch by Visi R. Tilak

Theresa Hak Kyung Cha
(1951–1982)
Artist, author

Best known for her 1982 book, *DICTÉE*, Theresa Hak Kyung Cha was a writer, experimental filmmaker, and performance and visual artist who expressed an acute sensitivity toward language and communication in all of her art. Cha immigrated from Korea to the United States in 1962 at age eleven, and as an artist she often drew from this experience of physical and linguistic displacement. Although Cha was murdered at age thirty-one by a stranger in New York City, she left behind a remarkable and extensive body of work. A 1993 retrospective exhibition at the Whitney Museum of American Art included experimental videos, concrete poetry, performance documentation, pages from some of her many journals, artists books, mixed media work, and a copy of *DICTÉE*, Cha's last completed work.

Early Life

Theresa Hak Kyung Cha was born in Pusan, Korea, on March 4, 1951. Her parents, two former schoolteachers, had fled their home outside of Seoul earlier that year to escape from advancing troops during the Korean War. Hak Kyung, later baptized Theresa, was the third of five children in the Cha family, which was forced to move residences more than a dozen times amidst the war's chaos in the early 1950s. When the fighting ended, the family returned to the Seoul area, where the young Cha attended Ewha University Elementary School and Toksoo Elementary School. After her father returned from a business trip abroad, he decided to move the family to the United States, first to Hawaii in 1962 and later to California in 1964. The Chas eventually settled in San Francisco, where Theresa and her older sister Elizabeth attended an all-girls Catholic school, the Convent of the Sacred Heart. As the only Asian Americans at the predominately white school, they had to adapt quickly to a new language and culture.

In high school, Theresa discovered a love of French, which she felt had an affinity to the Korean language and which strongly influenced her later work. Cha went on to study at the University of San Francisco but soon transferred to the University of California at Berkeley. There she worked with Bertrand Augst in the Comparative Literature Department, receiving both undergraduate and master's degrees, and studies with artists Jim Melchert while completing her master of fine arts degree. Cha continued her postgraduate work in Paris, where she studied with film theoreticians Christian Metz, Raymond Bellour, and Thierry Kuntzel. From this research, she compiled and edited an influential anthology of film theory entitled *Apparatus, Cinematographic Apparatus: Selected Writings*, which was published in 1980. Among Cha's literary influences were modernist writers who worked with language in self-conscious ways, including Samuel Beckett, James Joyce, Stephane Mallarme, Nathalie Sarraute, and Monique Wittig. Other sources of inspiration were Roland Barthes and Marguerite Yourcenar.

Multicultural Artist

In her work, Cha combined a sense of a Korean aesthetic with her knowledge of classical and modern Western literature, film theory, and fine arts. In the early seventies, Cha began doing work in multimedia and performance art. According to critic Susan Wolf, Cha became well-known in the San Francisco Bay area for her ability to express an emotive personal vision while also dealing with theoretical and psychological concepts. During her multimedia performances, Cha would often combine her slow and intense movements with projections of film, video, still images of slides, and her own soft and resonant voice, as she would utter words suggesting the passage of time or loss of memory and language over time—an experience said to evoke an almost hypnotic state. Cha also repeatedly explored the relationships between languages, at time alternating phrases in English, French, and Korean. In an article about Cha's work, Wolf writes: "Although separated from her native Korea as a child, Cha's sense of having a self formed in part by a past recalled only in fragments gave her broader ideas about the psychological aspects of remembrance. The Western concept of a unified self is also challenged by Cha's ideas of how memory shapes the self in complex, unconscious ways continually affecting us in a disparate but profound fashion."

Cha's exploration of memory continues in *DICTÉE*, which was released in 1982 just nine days before her death. In the book, divided into nine parts each attributed to one of the Nine Muses, Cha explores the relationship between memory and both personal and common history. Autobiographical in nature, *DICTÉE* incorporates Cha's descriptions of dreams, biographical prose about her mother, Korean history accounts, French translation exercises, and reinterpretations of Catholic ritual. Some passages are written in the voice of someone struggling to speak an unfamiliar language. The writing is interspersed with film stills, photographs, copies of a handwritten rough draft, brush calligraphy, anatomy diagrams, and found letters. Throughout, *DICTÉE* often calls upon the reader to engage her or his own imagination in an attempt to fill in the gaps, with words or images on the page giving rise to multiple narrative possibilities.

During her last years of life, Cha practiced tai-chi faithfully, beginning her exercises every morning at dawn. Her various forms of artwork reflect this same sort of sustained, controlled, yet lyrical movement. Drawing not only

Theresa Hak Kyung Cha

on French film theory and classical literature but also on personal memory, her work gestures toward rigorous philosophical concepts while pursuing an emotional, evocative vision. In a project proposal, the artist once attributed her experimental interest in language to the experience of having to learn English after immigrating as an adolescent. Cha wrote: "As a foreigner, learning a new language extended beyond its basic function of communication as it is generally for a native speaker, to a consciously imposed detachment that allowed analysis and experimentation with other relationships with language." The resulting artwork suggest the vulnerability exposed by loss and dislocation, in the apparent hope of stirring the viewer or reader to imagine beyond words.

Sources:

Cha, Theresa Hak Kyung. *DICTÉE*. New York: Tanam Press, 1982.

Kim, Nan. "Mujeres en el Arte: Diez Perfiles—Theresa Hak Kyung Cha." *Arte Internacional. Museo de Arte Moderno de Bogata, Colombia,* January-March, 1994, pp. 65–67.

———. "Other Things Found." in "Voices Stirring: An Anthology of Korean American Writing." *APA Journal,* Winter 1992, pp. 43–47.

Wolf, Susan. "Theresa Cha: Recalling Telling ReTelling." *Afterimage,* Summer 1986, pp. 11–13.

—Sketch by Nan Kim

June Chan
(1956–)
Lesbian activist

June Chan is the co-founder of Asian Lesbians of the East Coast (ALOEC), a political and cultural support group headquartered in New York City. Chan founded the group in 1983 when she noticed an absence of Asian lesbians among the politically active groups with which she was then involved. Today the group has about 150 members and offers support for Asian lesbians in the process of coming out to themselves, family, friends, and society at large, and networks nationally through an organization called the Asian Pacific Lesbian Network, and internationally through the Asian Lesbian Network.

June Chan was born on June 6, 1956, in lower Manhattan. Her father was a printer of Chinese and English language newspapers whose printing shop was in Chinatown. She was educated in the New York City public school system and attended the Bronx High School of Science where she cultivated her interest in science. She was especially interested in biology, and when she graduated in 1973 she enrolled in the City College of New York, where she majored in biology. She earned her bachelor's degree in 1977 and then immediately went on to graduate school at the State University of New York at Buffalo, earning a master's degree in biology. Today Chan works as a laboratory technician at Cornell Medical College in Manhattan where she conducts research in neurobiology. She lives in New York with her life partner Mariana Romo-Carmona, a writer and activist, and her son.

Chan first became politically active as an undergraduate at City College, which was then the site of massive student demonstrations against the introduction of tuition to the historically free City University of New York system. The tuition battle was fierce and resulted in a student occupation of the administration building. Despite the protests, tuition was instituted because of the severe economic crisis then being faced by the nearly bankrupt city of New York. Still, the battle excited Chan and demonstrated to her the power of political organizing. She also recalled a memory from her childhood in Chinatown when there were people who demonstrated against the racist attitudes of the tourists who would flock to her neighborhood, at times asking residents to pose for pictures with them.

After graduate school when Chan revealed her homosexuality to her family, which she described to Jim Henry as a positive experience in which she was supported by her mother, she became active in organizing politically in the women's movement. Her main area of concern was in reproductive rights, and she worked for the Committee

June Chan

for Abortion Rights and Against Sterilization Abuse, which fought to protect mainly non-English speaking women from unwanted sterilizations when they thought they were only getting abortions.

Asian Lesbians of the East Coast is Born

Chan noticed at this time that many of the organizations with whom she was working were predominantly white, and she began looking for ethnic lesbians with whom she could form a group. In 1983 she met Katherine Hall, a woman of mixed Asian descent, and together they formed Asian Lesbians of the East Coast, the first such organization of its kind. The idea behind the group was primarily to provide support and education for other Asian lesbians, and to empower themselves through political activism. They also hoped, Chan told Henry, "to make some inroads into the gay community, which at that time was very white and male. And also to work within the Asian community . . . to break stereotypes. There were so many stereotypes, in every direction we faced. We almost had to elbow our way to come out within the Asian community."

The organization began as a small discussion group, but within a year grew to include about eighty members. With one of its primary goals being the destruction of stereotypes, ALOEC began researching the history of Asian lesbians, and found some historically significant predecessors. Among these, Chan mentioned Chiu-Chin and Yosano Akiko, politically active Asian lesbians. ALOEC also researched the representation of lesbians among Hindu goddesses and in Hindu statuary.

ALOEC's next major organizing event was the 1989 march on Washington in which gay and lesbian groups from around the country descended on the nation's capital to demand civil rights and equal protection under the law. While working to organize a visible Asian presence at the march, Chan discovered a network of similar groups around the country and together they formed the Asian Pacific Lesbian Network (now known as the Asian Pacific Bi-Sexual Lesbian Network). This laid the groundwork to begin connecting with the Asian Lesbian Network in Asia, which has organized several lesbian conferences in various Asian countries.

On the political front, ALOEC was very critical of the representation of Asian women in the Broadway play *Miss Saigon,* and was active in the 1994 commemoration of the twenty-fifth anniversary of New York City's Stonewall Rebellion, a spontaneous riot in Greenwich Village in protest of police brutality and intimidation that is generally considered to mark the birth of the gay rights movement.

Chan described her role models as her mother and older sister, both of whom have been very supportive of her and who have given her strength and determination from an early age. Her mother was born in China and was a refugee from the Japanese invasion, surviving years of war and starvation. Chan found strength and inspiration in her mother's courage and perseverance. She said that she and her mother "have a very deep respect for one another . . . and I consider myself very lucky."

Sources:

Chan, June, telephone interview with Jim Henry, August 4, 1994.

—*Sketch by Jim Henry*

Subrahmanyan Chandrasekhar
(1910–)
Astrophysicist

Astrophysicist Subrahmanyan Chandrasekhar was awarded the Nobel Prize for physics in 1983, with William A. Fowler. Chandrasekhar's award-winning theory, completed some thirty years earlier, concerned the structure of white dwarfs, medium-sized stars that have spent all of their fuel and collapsed into dense, white-hot balls about the size of the Earth. His pioneering work would lay the theoretical groundwork for the eventual discovery of black holes.

Subrahmanyan Chandrasekhar was born on October 19, 1910, in Lahore, India (now Pakistan). His father was a distinguished musicologist and his uncle was the physicist Sir Chandrasekhar V. Raman, who was awarded the Nobel Prize in 1930. Subrahmanyan was very excited by his uncle's work and decided at a young age to study physics himself. He published his first paper, an analysis of the thermodynamics of the interior of stars, at the age of eighteen in the *Indian Journal of Physics*.

The Chandrasekhar Limit

After graduation from high school, Chandrasekhar studied theoretical physics at the University of Madras, where he was especially interested in the field of astrophysics and the pioneering work then being done by two British scientists, Sir Arthur Stanley Eddington and Ralph Howard Fowler. Chandrasekhar earned his bachelor's degree in 1930 and received a scholarship from the government of India to continue his studies at Cambridge University in England. At Cambridge, he concentrated his studies on the behavior of stars that have run out of fuel, or "died." Chandrasekhar believed that he had detected an error in the prevailing scientific literature about the way in which stars larger than the sun died. Contrary to the theory of the day, he believed that the tremendous gravitational force of large stars would prevent their stabilization into white dwarfs. Rather, the electrons in the star's gasses would move increasingly faster, approaching a state known as relativistic degeneracy, at which molecular matter is moving at speeds near the speed of light. Under these conditions, the young astrophysicist postulated, stars would not collapse into white dwarfs, but simply continue to collapse.

In 1932, Chandrasekhar published his first paper on the subject. The next year he received his Ph.D. from Cambridge, where he was offered a fellowship to continue his studies. By this time he had developed a complete theory detailing his new hypothesis, and he was invited by the Royal Astronomical Society to present his findings at their annual meeting. When Chandrasekhar presented his theory, however, it was not well received. The scientific establishment was less than eager to adopt a new theory that refuted the work of a prominent member, which Chandrasekhar's certainly did. It called into question the theories of Sir Arthur Stanley Eddington, perhaps the most respected English physicist of his time. After Chandrasekhar delivered his presentation, Eddington took the podium and ridiculed the young scientist's propositions, suggesting they were outlandish and, if taken to their logical conclusion, suggested the existence of tiny balls of energy so dense and with such a tremendous gravitational field that not even light would be able to escape. Time has proven Chandrasekhar correct in this instance, and today

Subrahmanyan Chandrasekhar

the point that separates stars that will collapse into white dwarfs and those that will collapse into black holes is called the Chandrasekhar Limit.

In *A Passion to Know* by John Tierney, Chandrasekhar discussed how differently his life could have been had Eddington not ridiculed his now proven hypotheses. "It's very difficult to speculate. Eddington would have made the whole area a very spectacular one to investigate, and many of the properties of black holes might have been discovered twenty or thirty years ahead of time. I can easily imagine that theoretical astronomy would have been very different....My position in science would have been radically altered as of that moment. Eddington's praise could make one famous in astronomy."

Coming to the United States

Being in a theoretical dispute with England's greatest astronomer left Chandrasekhar with few academic options in England and in 1937 he left for America, where he took a position as a research associate at the University of Chicago. In this position he continued his work on the deaths of stars and in 1939 published *An Introduction to the Study of Stellar Structures.* Largely ignored at the time of its publication, the book was recognized as a classic work only twenty years later.

In the next several years Chandrasekhar began studying various other aspects of astrophysics while being

promoted to an associate professor in 1942, professor in 1944, and, in 1947, just ten years after coming to Chicago, distinguished service professor of theoretical astrophysics. Throughout his career he has shown a remarkable ability to change areas of expertise. In 1942 he published his second book, *Principles of Stellar Dynamics,* which described the behavior and evolution of star clusters. Toward the middle of the 1940s Chandrasekhar began studying yet another field, the radiative transfer of energy in the interior of stars. He followed studies in this area with inquiries into the effects of magnetism in the universe, the stability of ellipsoidal figures of equilibrium, and the general theory of relativity and relativistic astrophysics. In the 1970s, Chandrasekhar returned to the first field he had studied—the creation of black holes—work the scientific community had finally come to validate. He has written several books, many of which are considered classics. Among them are: *Radiative Transfer* (1960), *Hydrodynamic and Hydromagnetic Stability* (1961), *Ellipsoidal Figures of Equilibrium* (1969), and *The Mathematical Theory of Black Holes* (1983).

Chandrasekhar has received many honors during his career, including the Nobel Prize in 1983. The announcement from the Swedish Academy stated: "Chandrasekhar's possibly best known achievement, accomplished when he was in his 20s, is the study of the structure of white dwarfs. Although many of these investigations are of older dates, they have through the great process of astronomy and space research in recent years gained renewed interest."

Chandrasekhar also holds twenty honorary degrees, holds membership in twenty-one learned societies, and is the recipient of the Gold Medal of the Royal Astronomical Society of London, the Rumford Medal of the American Academy of Arts and Sciences, the Royal Medal of the Royal Society of London, the National Medal of Science, and the Henry Draper Medal of the National Academy of Sciences.

As of mid-1994, Chandrasekhar had retired from the University of Chicago and was working on translating Isaac Newton's classic work *The Principia* into the language of modern mathematics.

Sources:

Books

Tierney, John. "Subrahmanyan Chandrasekhar: Quest for Order." In *A Passion to Know,* edited by Allen L. Hammond. New York: Charles Scribner's Sons, 1984.

Periodicals

"Nobel Prize to Chandrasekhar and Fowler for Astrophysics." *Physics Today,* January 1984, pp. 17–20.

—Sketch by Jim Henry

Michael Chang

(1972–)

Professional tennis player

Professional athletes, world leaders, celebrities, and other role models in our society often point to defining moments that shape their lives and catapult them to greatness. Michael Chang's defining moment occurred in June 1989, when he became the youngest male tennis player in the world to win a Grand Slam tournament and the first American man in thirty-four years to win the French Open. Chang went into the tournament ranked nineteenth in the world; by the end of 1989, he was ranked in the top five. He took the title after an astonishing semifinal win over the world's top-ranked player, Ivan Lendl, and a come-from-behind win over Stefan Edberg in the final round. His victory was hailed as an exciting breath of fresh air, which infused the sport with a much-needed lift. Through the 1980s, Americans had been lulled to sleep with what *Sports Illustrated* writer Curry Kirkpatrick described as the "humdrum excellence" of the world's top tennis players. Chang created a new level of excitement. And he was only seventeen.

Today, Chang is older, more seasoned, and perhaps slightly less sensational. But he remains a solid, well-established player on the U.S. professional circuit. He achieved his career-high world ranking of fourth in 1992, and was ranked seventh as of early 1994. Though his 1989 French Open probably will always be considered the tournament of his career, he generally takes at least one singles title every year. His winnings have paid him nearly $4.5 million since he turned pro at age sixteen. And in 1994, at age twenty-two, Chang still sees a full life before him. "You can always improve," he said in a biography by Pamela Dell. "There are still many things I haven't learned."

Michael Chang was born February 22, 1972, in a family that seemed to thrive on tennis. His parents, Joe and Betty, were research chemists who had followed Chinese nationalist leader Chiang Kai-Shek from mainland China to Taiwan in the 1960s. Both eventually emigrated to the United States and met on a blind date in New York City. Chang and his older brother, Carl, were born in Hoboken, New Jersey.

As a toddler, Chang remembers watching his father play tennis in local tournaments in St. Paul, Minnesota, where the family moved when he was two. Sensing that her son had an interest in the sport, Michael's mother suggested he try playing. At age six, he picked up a racquet for the first time. He and his brother Carl, who later played tennis for the University of California, got more than a little encouragement from their father.

Michael Chang

Joe Chang would spend hours coaching the two boys, Dell wrote in her biography, setting up matches between the two and suggesting pointers to improve their game. From this experience, Chang picked up a keen sense of competition. At age eight, he played his father. When his father won, Chang was so disappointed that he broke his racquet. Recognizing his competitive streak, his parents started to encourage him to enter matches.

From his parents, Chang also seemed to inherit a strong sense of spirituality. He would read the Bible frequently and later attributed his tennis victories to the grace of God. Though this occasionally drew hoots and boos from fans, he remained steadfast in his beliefs. "I know every time I bring Jesus up, everybody nods and gets sick of it," he told Kirkpatrick. "But it's the truth. He gets all the credit."

Sweeping the "Juniors"

As Chang's interest in tennis grew, the family moved to San Diego, partly so he could practice outdoors year round. His mother attributed this decision to a Chinese saying, *Mung mu san tien*, "a mother will move many times for her child." Shortly after moving to San Diego, he began to sweep up junior tournament titles. In 1984, at age twelve, he won the Junior Hard Court singles title of the United States Tennis Association (USTA). He also won a doubles' title in the Hard Courts with Marco Zuniga. One year later, he won the Fiesta Bowl 16s. The following year, 1986, his rise to the top of the juniors' rankings continued. Chang joined the U.S. Sunshine Cup team, the World Youth Cup team, and became the European Indoor 14s champion and a runner-up in the USTA's Boys' 16s. The year after, he won the USTA's junior championship, which gave him the chance to play in the U.S. Open, one of tennis' four grand-slam events. Though nobody expected much of him in the U.S. Open, he won a first-round match against Paul McNamee.

Early 1988—Turning Pro

Up to this point, Chang had played tennis purely for the joy of competition. He thrived on pressure, and he had developed a sort of gritty determination to win, at whatever price. But he didn't see tennis as a profession. His parents always stressed the importance of education and limited his playing to four days a week—if he got his homework done. Chang understood that school was important, but by age sixteen, he faced a dilemma. He'd gone as far as he could in the junior circuit. He needed to seek bigger challenges to improve his tennis skills. The next step would be to turn professional, but it would also mean dropping out of high school. He decided to choose tennis and managed to pass a final exam to receive a high school diploma. He turned pro in February 1988.

Suddenly, the pressure to excel intensified. Here was a teenager on the pro tennis circuit. Would he be a true champion, or another flash in the pan? Media attention began to focus on him; the pro circuit began to watch his progress. He met the challenge, displaying poise under pressure. Kirkpatrick wrote that Chang's skill was "based on anticipation, reflexes, speed—nobody has been quicker to the ball since Bjorn Borg [the Swedish champion who dominated the sport in the 1970s]—and defensive instincts that make an opponent feel as if he is slugging away at Chang's garage door." He also remained coolly contemplative and unemotional on the court, thinking through technique. He reached the quarterfinals of two major tournaments in 1988, and performed respectably at the U.S. Open.

The French Open

In Chang's biography, Dell describes the sensation that hit the Paris clay tennis courts in 1989 this way: "The tennis ball flies wild. It hits the net and bounces out of bounds. Thousands of fans jammed together in the stadium leap to their feet in sudden chaos—the opponent has double-faulted! The young American [Michael Chang] thrusts his arms in the air, triumphant!" Shortly afterward, Jose Higueras, a well-known tennis coach, said, "This is truly the most incredible match I've ever seen. Michael has the head of a champion."

Oddly enough, the sensational victory didn't come in the French Open finals but the fourth round, when Chang defeated Ivan Lendl, then the world's top-ranked player. Lendl, as expected, had won the first two sets and seemed ready to head for the final round. But Chang took the next two sets, setting the stage for a "David-and-Goliath" showdown professional tennis rarely sees. In the final set, Chang's legs cramped up so badly that he could barely move. He ran for water and bananas between breaks, but managed to keep himself in the game. He broke Lendl's serve three times, and Lendl broke Chang's serve twice. Then, with the set at 4-3, Chang lobbed an underhand serve, which distracted Lendl and caused the more seasoned player to lose his composure. Chang then tried to break Lendl's concentration by moving near the service box. As Lendl's serve failed to reach its goal, Chang fell to his knees in tears. He later admitted to *Sports Illustrated* that he was trying to break Lendl's concentration. "I would do anything to stay out there. It was that mental thing."

Despite the upset victory, Chang's maneuvers didn't exactly win public opinion. Many called his efforts to distract Lendl poor sportsmanship, and some sportswriters went so far as to wonder whether Chang's leg cramps were for real. Chang also became the victim of some blatant racism. One French journalist made reference to Chang's "vicious Oriental mind," while another newspaper ran a headline referring to Chang as "the Chink." A third referred to the Chinese American player as "our little slant eyes."

Nevertheless, Chang remained cool on court. His mother, who had left her job as a chemist to travel with him, fed him fortifying Chinese noodles in their hotel room, and Chang continued to concentrate on his game. Early on, he'd learned that the road to success contained no short cuts. He kept this philosophy in the back of his mind as he prepared for the French Open final again Stefan Edberg. Though Edberg was heavily favored, Chang walked away with the victory in five sets.

Setback

After winning the French Open, Chang's world ranking shot to fifth. He realized, as *Sports Illustrated* reported, that he'd probably played one of the biggest matches of his lifetime. Shortly after the match he said, "These two weeks are going to stay with me the rest of my life."

His attitude was good. Though 1989 gave his life its high point, it also produced a stunning low. Late in the year, after competing at Wimbledon and the U.S. Open, he fractured his hip during practice, an injury that put him out of circulation until mid-1990. Though he knew when he turned pro that injury was a risk he'd have to live with, he acknowledges that the broken hip discouraged him a great deal. Nevertheless, it also gave him time to put his life in perspective.

Sarah Chang

Still known as one of professional tennis' fastest players, Chang continues to relentlessly hammer away at his technique. But he also is learning to relax. Growing up in Minnesota, he developed a passion for fishing, which he pursues when he feels he needs a sense of peace. He calls the sport more complicated than tennis in some ways, because it requires more preparation. Though he held a total of fourteen singles titles as of early 1994, Chang claims one of his most cherished accomplishments is hooking an eight-pound carp after a tournament in Cincinnati.

Sources:

Books

Dell, Pamela. *Michael Chang*. Chicago: Childrens Press, 1992.

Periodicals

Kirkpatrick, Curry. "Giant Killers." *Sports Illustrated,* vol. 70, no. 26, June 1989, p. 34+.

Other

IBM/ATP Tour Media Information System. "Michael Chang." Player Biography, 1994.

—*Sketch by Himanee Gupta*

Sarah Chang
(1981–)
Violinist

In a mere eight years of playing the violin, child prodigy Sarah Chang has achieved what few musicians accomplish in a lifetime. At the age of eight, she accepted an invitation from internationally renowned conductor, Zubin Mehta to appear as a surprise guest soloist with the New York Philharmonic at Avery Fisher Hall. Her rendition of Paganini's Violin Concerto No. 1 earned her a standing ovation. In recent years, she has performed at the Presidential Gala Concert in South Korea and the Concert for Planet Earth at the Rio de Janeiro Earth Summit, as well as with the London Symphony Orchestra. Chang also has worked with numerous renowned conductors including James Levine, Gerard Schwarz, Pinchas Zukerman, James DePriest, Charles Dutoit, Sir Colin Davis, Lawrence Foster, and Herbert Blomstedt.

The Roots of Chang's Success

The daughter of Korean-born immigrants who came to the United States in 1979, Sarah Chang was born in Philadelphia in 1981. Her father, Dr. Min Soo Chang, is a violinist and her mother, Myoung, a pianist and composer. She began taking violin lessons from her father at age four. Though she longed to play his violin, he prevented her from doing so until the day he bought one more suited for her small fingers—a 1/16 size violin. "I think performing is part of me, and I really love what I'm doing," Sarah told *People Weekly.* Sarah found her calling when she was 4. "I always wanted to play my dad's violin," she said, "but he wouldn't let me touch it. Little kids have sticky fingers."

She began performing with local orchestras at age five and one year later began taking lessons from famed Juilliard School teacher Dorothy DeLay. After hearing Chang's audition, where she played the Mendelssohn concerto, Dorothy DeLay was impressed. She recalled to Jesse Frohman, ". . . she played the Mendelssohn concerto with real emotional involvement, and I said to myself, 'I have never seen or heard anything quite like it in my entire life.'"

Chang excelled in playing the bowed stringed instrument to such an extent that when famous conductor Zubin Mehta heard the eight-year-old play just a week before an engagement of the New York Philharmonic, he invited her to take the place of a scheduled performer who had canceled. Her performance drew nothing short of instant raves by concert impresarios and music critics from coast to coast. She was immediately on her way to stardom as a young musician.

Chang's Music Career Takes Off

Just weeks after her New York performance, Chang was invited by conductor Riccardo Muti to play with the Philadelphia Orchestra. Her 1991 hometown performance drew more unreserved critical esteem, as did subsequent performances with the California, Chicago, Pittsburgh, and Montreal symphonies. Of her Pittsburgh performance, a *Washington Post* critic wrote: "Nine-year old Sarah Chang mixed supple phrasing and mind-boggling technique in virtually tossing off Paganini's fiendish First Concerto. Chang plays with controlled abandon, never distorting her gorgeous tone or the music's structure and leaving plenty of room for her maturing lyric sense to shine." Her performance with the California Symphony—the result of impressing that orchestra's Barry Jekowsky with her skill at a party hosted by Gordon Getty in San Francisco—was called "formidable" and "dazzling" by the San Jose *Mercury News,* which noted that she performed "with an adult's poise, a virtuoso's touch." Her rendition of the Spanish-tinged melodies of Lalo's "Symphonie Espagnole" with the Chicago Symphony Orchestra in 1991 drew critical superlatives from a *Chicago Tribune* music critic who praised her "astonishing technical dexterity."

In 1992, Chang's performance at the Concert for Planet Earth was later released on compact disc by Sony Classical and broadcast worldwide, airing on PBS's "Great Performances" in the United States. In May of that year she became the youngest musician ever to receive the coveted Avery Fisher Career Grant. In her September Hollywood Bowl debut with the Los Angeles Philharmonic, Chang did a rendition of the Tchaikovsky Violin Concerto "with a prowess and vision rare at any age," according to the *Los Angeles Times.* In an October date with the London Symphony Orchestra, she again performed Tchaikovsky to the critical acclaim of the *London Times.* Also in 1992 Chang released her first album, "Debut," which features works by Prokofiev, Gershwin, Sarasate, and others. It quickly became a best seller on Billboard's classical chart.

Chang's busy schedule continued in 1993 with her subscription concert debut with the New York Philharmonic under music director Kurt Masur, return engagements with the Philadelphia Orchestra and the London Symphony, and debuts with the Montreal Symphony, Toronto Symphony, the New World Symphony of Miami, l'Orchestra National de France, Leipzig Gewandhaus Orchestra, the Monte Carlo Philharmonic, and Japan's NHK Symphony. And her second album, a recording of her first engagement with the London Symphony Orchestra, helped her win *Gramophone* magazine's 1993 Young Artist of the Year award. The *New York Times* also lauded Chang, calling her the "definitive violin prodigy of her genera-

tion, a child with the requisite dazzling technique but also considerable expressiveness."

Still a Work in Progress

Chang is often compared to Korean prodigy Midori because both are Asian and studied under the same Juilliard teacher. However, Chang's style is distinctive in that it indicates a brilliant technical command, a sharpness of attack, and a boldness of gesture that contrast with Midori's more elegant, seamless approach. Her teacher, Dorothy DeLay, commented about Chang's playing to Jesse Frohman: "I have compared her playing with records of other prodigies and I don't think anything quite like her has ever happened before. But one never knows what's going to happen in the next ten years. She might decide she wants to become a professional golfer, or who knows . . . "

Chang's life as a student and teenager have not been significantly altered by the demands of her career. Although she practices violin four hours a day and attends a full Saturday program at Juilliard that includes classes in solfege (exercises for the voice using the set of syllables—do, re, mi—to represent the tones of the scale), theory, ensemble, and chamber music, she still finds time to roller-skate and to watch her favorite television shows like "Full House," "Saved By The Bell," and Saturday morning cartoons. And she still manages to turn in her homework on time at Germantown Friends School (she faxes it in when she's traveling), where her favorite subjects are social studies and French.

Time for these typical schoolgirl pastimes are made possible because her Juilliard teacher and parents limit her to two concerts per month. But performing is as much a part of her life as slumber parties, as Chang noted in *People Weekly:* "I think performing is a part of me, and I really love what I'm doing." Concern about injuring her fingers keeps her from practicing gymnastics which she performed on television at the same early age she was learning to play the violin. And she continues to rack up major accomplishments in her still-fledgling career as a violinist. What comes next for the young prodigy from Philadelphia, Pennsylvania? Only time will tell.

Sources:

Frohman, Jesse. "String Fever." *Town & Country Monthly,* April 1994, p. 85.

"Philadelphia, There She Goes: Violin Prodigy Sarah Chang Has the World on Her Strings." *People Weekly,* Jan. 11, 1993, p. 88.

—Sketch by Samuel R. Cacas

Elaine Chao

Organization executive

The year is 1961. President John F. Kennedy has just created the Peace Corps. He speaks idealistically of creating world peace and promoting friendship, of encouraging American volunteers to learn how to work side by side with citizens of developing nations.

In one of those developing nations, Taiwan, eight-year-old Elaine Chao plays in the red earthen clay with her sisters, while her parents, James and Ruth, dream of a better future. James, at the time, was studying at St. John's University in Queens, New York. Later that year, Elaine, her mother, and sisters board a freighter from Taipei to join their father in America.

"It was a wonderful trip for a small child of eight," Chao told Geraldine Baum in a 1992 interview with the *Los Angeles Times,* shortly after then-president George Bush named her director of the Peace Corps. "My first port of call was Los Angeles. That's where I laid my first foot on America."

Peace Corps

Though Chao had never served as a Peace Corps volunteer, her appointment to head the agency in late 1991 seemed like a natural fit: an immigrant from a developing country heading an agency in the midst of transition. A Republican loyalist who'd campaigned for Bush, California governor Pete Wilson, and other Los Angeles-area Republicans, she represented a new, young and refreshing political face.

The limelight faded quickly, however. Chao lost her job as head of the Peace Corps when Bush lost his bid for re-election. But she had too many skills to disappear entirely. In mid-1992, she was named president of United Way of America, a job that has perhaps stretched her well-touted management skills and experience with nonprofits to the limit.

When Chao took over the job of United Way director, the agency was in turmoil. Former United Way president William Aramony had been pulling in a $390,000 annual salary. He had spent agency donations on first-class airline tickets and had hired a friend with questionable bank dealings as the agency's chief financial officer. As these disclosures became known, local United Way agencies began withholding dues. As the scandal hit the headlines, Aramony resigned under fire. United Way donations plummeted by $140 million between 1991 and 1992.

Elaine Chao

Chao's job was to reform the agency and help it regain credibility. Selected from a list of 600 candidates, she was praised for her integrity, honesty, and management skills. She did not seek the position, but after accepting the job, called it too good to pass up. "United Way of America is a challenge that I could not decline," she said in an August 1992 interview with the *Washington Post.*

Born in Taiwan, she emigrated to the United States with her mother and sisters in 1961. The family, rejoining her father, James, settled in Queens, New York. After her father completed college, he formed a shipping and trading business, Foremost Maritime Corporation, which today is well known in international shipping circles.

Chao remembers her father as hard-working and driven, a man who taught his daughters how to fix toilets and apply tar to driveways. He passed on conservative values, stressing the importance of hard work and education in achieving one's goals. As the shipping business prospered, the family moved from Queens to Long Island and eventually to an affluent New York City suburb in Westchester County.

Chao graduated from Mount Holyoke College and received her master's in business administration from the Harvard Business School. She also studied at such prestigious institutions as the Massachusetts Institute of Technology, Dartmouth College, and Columbia University. After completing her schooling, Chao began to climb the corporate ladder. With a background in international banking and finance, she worked from 1979 to 1983 as an international banker at Citicorp in New York. She was selected as a White House fellow to serve at the White House in 1983 and 1984, and joined BankAmerica Capital Markets Group in San Francisco as vice-president of syndications.

After moving to California, she got involved in Republican politics, campaigning for Bush, Wilson, and local politicians. She served as national chairman of Asian Americans for Bush/Quayle in 1988 and spoke briefly at the GOP convention.

Her work was rewarded with an appointment as deputy administrator of the Maritime Administration, which launched her on a slow but steady climb through federal government bureaucracy. After two years as deputy administrator, she became chairperson of the Federal Maritime Commission and then was appointed deputy secretary of the U.S. Department of Transportation. As she climbed the ranks, she gained a reputation as a confident, hard-working manager. She also gained insights into Washington D.C.'s inside political network.

Chao attended luncheons with Supreme Court justice Sandra Day O'Connor, dated various political insiders, and networked heavily. This networking, along with her hard work, made her the highest ranking Asian Pacific American woman in the executive branch in U.S. history.

But some of her stances occasionally infuriated other Asian Americans. For instance, she joined Bush in opposing the Civil Rights Act of 1991 because it promoted quotas, a concept she felt inhibited minorities' meritorious achievements.

Nevertheless, when first appointed Peace Corps director, she spoke of her immigrant roots with pride. At her swearing-in ceremony, she talked about playing with red earthen clay as a child because there were no other toys and of eating duck eggs because chicken eggs were unavailable. "These memories of living in a developing nation are part of who I am today and give me a profound understanding of the challenges of economic development," she said in a January 1992 interview with the *Los Angeles Times.*

The Peace Corps, at the time, was in the midst of transition. Bush wanted the organization to develop more specialized training for less-poor but highly needy emerging democracies, such as Hungary and Bulgaria. It also was fighting to overcome an image of arrogance that had been fostered through its thirty-year existence. Chao felt she could understand this arrogance well. "I still remember . . . how valuable tissue paper was and how rich Americans seemed because they would use it up and throw it away so easily," she said in a 1992 interview with *American Shipper* magazine. "It's an attitude thing, born

out of naturally acquired affluence. It's hard to explain, but it stays with you and you understand the feeling."

United Way Challenge

When she joined United Way, she approached the agency much as she approached the Peace Corps. Just as she visited nearly half of the agency's active volunteers worldwide, she spent much of her first year as United Way director visiting local affiliates from Maine to Oregon, trying to determine what they felt was missing. She felt strongly that making the national organization more sensitive to local needs would be a key to turning United Way around. "This is a redress that is badly needed and is long in coming," she said in a May 1993 interview with the *Christian Science Monitor.*

To restore public confidence in the agency, Chao started at a salary of $195,000, half the salary of her controversial predecessor. She imposed new travel and expense controls, and restructured programs to put more emphasis on training, field regulation, and service. Before she joined United Way, the agency had increased its board of directors from thirty to forty-seven members to include more local affiliate representatives. To directly serve local agencies, she established a member-services division.

Like most restructurings, the changes at United Way were painful. Nearly one-third of the agency's staff was let go, and its budget was cut by one-third. But Chao is slowly getting results. As of late 1993, most affiliates who had withheld dues had returned to the fold. And, although a difficult economy caused a slowdown in charitable contributions, Chao said her prognosis for 1994 was "cautious optimism."

Sources:

Periodicals

Baum, Geraldine. "An Insider Moves Up." *Los Angeles Times,* January 19, 1993.

Canna, Elizabeth. "Free Market Peace Corps." *American Shipper,* March 1992.

MacLachlan, Suzanne L. "United Way Hit by Weak Economy, Old Scandal and Competition." *Christian Science Monitor,* May 18, 1993.

Melillo, Wendy. "United Way Names New President." *Washington Post,* August 27, 1992.

Scala, Richard P. "Chao to head United Way of America." *Fund Raising Management,* October 1992.

Other

United Way. "Elaine Chao." Biographical materials, 1994.

—Sketch by Himanee Gupta

Stephen Chao
(1956–)
Television producer

Stephen Chao is the president of Q2, a new at-home television shopping channel. Prior to assuming this position, Chao was a programming executive with Fox Television, where he created such innovative, controversial shows as "America's Most Wanted," "Cops," and "Studs." Known for unconventional behavior as well as creativity and outspokenness, Chao will try to make a success of Q2, envisioned as a more upscale version of QVC, the incredibly successful home shopping channel.

Stephen Chao was born in Ann Arbor, Michigan, in 1956 to a middle-class family. His maternal grandfather had been a prominent political figure in China in the 1940s and 1950s, serving for a time as economic minister to the United States. Chao was eight years old when his parents' marriage ended in divorce, and he moved with his mother and siblings to New Hampshire. He was an excellent student and earned a scholarship to Exeter Academy, one of the finest private boarding schools in the country. From there he went on to Harvard, where he studied classics. He graduated *cum laude* in 1977.

The National Enquirer and the Movie Business

After graduation Chao took a job as a reporter for *The National Enquirer,* the notorious tabloid weekly often criticized for sensationalism. It was not a traditional avenue for Harvard graduates, but Chao relished the notoriety his position lent him and genuinely considered the *Enquirer* to be a serious and important social phenomenon worthy of understanding rather than dismissal. At the paper he covered such tabloid fare as celebrity fertility problems and funerals. He stayed with the paper for two years and then returned to Harvard for a master's degree in business administration.

After graduation, Chao became interested in the movie business. Describing his interest for *New York* magazine in 1993, he said, "I don't have a story where I creep into the theater and dream about the nickelodeons. But I remember seeing *Road Warrior* six times. It was, to me, totally original—visually, emotionally, countrily [sic], everything! I had no idea this could be done on film."

Chao tried unsuccessfully to sell himself to the major studios in Hollywood and was rejected by each of them. He ended up working in New York for the film producer Dino De Laurentis as a fund raiser, work he despised. He saw a chance to make it in Hollywood when he read that the international tabloid mogul Rupert Murdoch was

Stephen Chao

trying to buy a Hollywood studio. He eventually landed a job with the Murdoch News Service in the mergers and acquisitions department—not exactly what he was looking for, but a foot in the door. After two years he was given the opportunity to contribute creatively to Murdoch's newly established Fox Television network.

Fox Television

At Fox, Chao worked directly for Barry Diller, president of the network. His job was to develop innovative shows with low production costs. The network was up against formidable competition as the first broadcast network to challenge the domination of the big three of ABC, CBS, and NBC, which had dominated the airwaves for half a century. Chao's first efforts were often not very successful. These shows included "The Ron Reagan Show," a late night talk show patterned after daytime talk shows that featured as host the son of the former president; "Dr. Science," which *New York* magazine described as "a cross between 'Pee-Wee's Playhouse,' and 'Watch Wizard'"; and "King of the Mountain," a game show in which contestants attempted to climb a hill while being rained upon by papier-mâché boulders.

Chao finally launched a successful show with "America's Most Wanted," although at first, the show had a rough time gaining acceptance with the network. The program features dramatic recreations of violent crimes and then enlists the help of viewers in finding the criminals. At the time of its creation it was a brand-new concept. It was also very inexpensive to produce, costing about a third as much as an average prime-time drama.

His next show for the network was "Cops," in which a cameraman follows police officers on duty in some of the more violent neighborhoods of various cities around the country. The brutal realism of the show was often criticized as exploitative and morally disinterested in the ramifications of the brutality it displayed, seeming at times to revel in personal crises. In discussing these criticisms, Chao said in *New York* magazine, "That was the beauty [of "Cops"]—to me there isn't a lesson. We're just showing something that *is*. It's not coded with music and narration and writing and directing. It's just edited, in a really simple way. It's pure, and you derive your own lesson."

Chao's final successful show for Fox was "Studs," a late night game show of sorts in which generally beautiful young men and women discussed dating and sexual fantasies in shrouded language that was, by Chao's own admission, silly. Yet the show was incredibly successful, making $20 million a year. Murdoch, however, did not like the show's celebration of promiscuity, and he canceled the show despite its success.

Life after Fox

Chao was fired from Fox Television after he hired a male stripper to perform at a conference of television executives and other powerful men and women, including the former secretary of defense, Dick Cheney. Though Chao was widely known to be full of such antics, this was too much for Murdoch, who fired Chao on the spot. He then spent a year traveling with his family and considering the future. He worked briefly for Fox's movie division as a developer of ideas for films, a position that did not work out.

In 1993, Chao was hired by his old boss at Fox Television, Barry Diller, to run his new channel, Q2. Diller hopes Q2 will lure upscale retailers into the home shopping market, which has traditionally been seen as a haven for only low-end merchandise.

Chao's rise to success has been by a nontraditional path. Reflecting on it, he told *New York* magazine, "I believe in people and events. There's some whim and there's some events and atoms that happen—you can't look at it retrospectively."

Sources:

Smith, Chris. "Chao, Baby." *New York*, October 18, 1993, pp. 68–75.

Yang, Jeff. "Power Brokers." *A. Magazine*, vol. 2 no. 3, December 15, 1993, p. 25–34.

—*Sketch by Jim Henry*

Joan Chen
(1961–)
Actress

Actress Joan Chen, known as "China's Elizabeth Taylor" has won awards and acclaim for her work in China and the United States. She is best known in the United States for her role as the Empress Wan Jung in Bernardo Bertolucci's film *The Last Emperor* and for playing Josie Packard on the television series "Twin Peaks."

Chen was a star in China from the age of fourteen when she made her first film, *Youth*. Her second film, *Little Flower*, which she made at age eighteen, won her a Golden Rooster Award, the Chinese equivalent of an Oscar. She was then declared the "country's best-loved actress." Chen acted in three more films in China before moving to the United States in 1981. The work she has done in the U.S. includes episodes of "Miami Vice," "Tai-Pan," "The Blood of Others," "Turtle Beach," and "Deadlock." Her feature films include *Golden Gate, On Deadly Ground*, and *Heaven and Earth*.

The Roots of Chen's Success

Born Chen Chong on April 26, 1961, in Shanghai, Chen was the second of two children born to Chinese physicians. Because Chen's parents were intellectuals, they, like others, were sent to farms and factories to be re-educated by the workers in party doctrine during the Cultural Revolution. Chen's grandparents took care of her and her brother. Chen has described this time with her grandparents as fun for the two children, who were unaware of the greater significance of their stay away from their parents

At the age of fourteen, Chen was picked out of school by a local film studio to play a young guerrilla in a Shanghai movie. Although she had only two lines in the film, they were enough to draw her toward an acting career. Chen was delighted when she was later selected for a two-year acting class. However, upon her parents insistence, she continued regular schooling at home. Before she had completed the acting course, Chen was selected to star as a deaf mute in a film that was a great success in China. She was making eighteen dollars a month at the time, all of which she gave to her mother. After a few more parts in local films, Chen was a celebrity in China. People recognized her wherever she went. When she was not acting, Chen traveled throughout China. Chinese performers were sent to different places to gain an understanding of various professions and to interact with working people. As part of her training as an actress, she worked on the railway, where she said she learned acting, politics, and how to present herself in public in China.

The Journey Begins

Despite her stardom, Chen felt the need for a higher education. Her parents had already moved to the United States since her mother was in the first group of scientists sent to study in New York when China opened up in the late 1970s. Chen's parents thought it would be a good idea for her to join them. Chen said her mother would send her articles, and tapes of music by Elvis Presley. When Chen listened to "Love Me Tender" by Elvis Presley, she recalled being inspired to go to America. At the age of twenty, Chen left China for America with a one-way ticket, not knowing whether she would ever come back. "It was frightening," she said "but I wasn't too scared then. I was able to pick up English very fast, but I had no cultural references, no past, no history."

Chen attended a state university in New York, where she enrolled in premed courses, since her parents felt no one would offer her an acting role in America. But after a year, Chen moved to California State University and took up film studies. Two years into film school Chen started searching for acting jobs. She took the name "Joan" because it sounded like Chong. Her initial job search was not encouraging. "I had to start all over again," she told Bob Thomas. "Agents didn't want me. I had no photos, no film. They all said the same thing: 'Leave your photos and call me back.' I finally prepared a resume and found an agent who would take me."

The Drive to do Better

Chen's first roles were limited to playing the occasional Oriental woman in television series such as "Miami Vice" and similar productions. She got her break one day in an unusual manner as she was walking across the MGM parking lot. A voice called out from a limousine: "Did you know that Lana Turner was discovered in a drug store?" Chen was wondering who Lana Turner was when she discovered that the voice belonged to Dino De Laurentis, the film magnate. He was casting for the movie *Tai-Pan* based on James Clavell's novel. He invited Chen to audition and offered her the role.

The film meant a return to China where the authorities did not welcome Chen. They felt that her role as a concubine to a foreigner was a degrading one. "The homecoming hit me with mixed emotions," Chen told *Time.* "In some ways I accepted that it was no longer possible for me to visit the people, for I could no longer be one of them." Even her fans kept their distance.

Back in the United States Chen married an American, Jimmy Lau, and settled in Los Angeles. However, her marriage lasted only a short time. Her next professional break came when director Bernardo Bertolucci approached her and asked if she could introduce him to Chinese officials and filmmakers. Her initial contact with Bertolucci later led to the role of Wan Jung and worldwide recognition as

Joan Chen

The Last Emperor won the Academy Award for best picture in 1987. Soon after, Chen married Peter Jui, a cardiologist, and moved to San Francisco.

Chen's 1993 feature, *Heaven and Earth,* directed by Oliver Stone, was based on a pair of memoirs written by Vietnamese American Le Ly Hayslip. Chen played a mother of six who ages to seventy in the film. She suffered infections and leg burns while preparing for the role in Vietnam. This role is unlike her glamorous image in earlier films. According to Chen, the screen image is not representative of her own life. She lives a quiet life, enjoying reading and playing the piano.

Throughout her career and personal life, Chen has always maintained her Chinese identity. She has said that China is her home, and Los Angeles is her adopted home. Her media image in the United States has often forced her to encounter disapproval from her native home. An Asian edition of *Penthouse* magazine printed provocative photos of Chen that could damage her image in China. Chen was not happy about the exposure and said she did not know how the magazine obtained the pictures.

Chen keeps up with events in China and believes that she is now in a position to break stereotypes of Chinese people in American films by informing directors "about what really is Chinese." In 1994, she was pursuing a film about the Burmese activist Aung San Suu Kyi, the Nobel Peace Prize winner who is living under house arrest. Chen admires Suu Kyi's idealism and determination. Chen strongly believes, "We need an ideal . . . our lives should be subject to an ideal."

Sources:

Periodicals

Bruden, Martin. "China's Liz Taylor and the Foreign Devil." *New York Post,* September 1, 1986.

Carter, Gayle Jo, Monika Guttman and Richard Vega. "Joan Chen Moves 'Heaven and Earth.'" *USA Weekend,* December 24–26, 1993, p. 8.

Cohn, Lawrence. "Chinese Biopic Set as a Four-Way U.S. Coprod." *Variety,* December 17, 1990, p. 10.

"DeLaurentis Gets Oriented." *Newsweek,* August 11, 1986, p. 13.

Lurie, Rod. "On Deadly Ground." *Los Angeles Magazine,* February 1994, p. 110.

Morgan, Susan. "Joan Chen." *Interview,* August 1990, p. 80–83.

"People." *Time,* May 5, 1986, p. 71.

Thomas, Bob. "Beauty and the East." *Daily News,* September 4, 1986, p. 71.

—*Sketch by Natasha Rafi*

William Shao Chang Chen

(1939–)

Military officer

William Shao Chang Chen was the first Chinese American major general in the armed forces of the United States. He served more than thirty years in the army, rising steadily through the ranks. He eventually served as the commanding general of the U.S. Army Missile Command, where he was in charge of the management of all the army's missile systems, from development through procurement and support.

William Shao Chang Chen was born in Shanghai, China, on November 11, 1939. His American father, who was orphaned at age ten, had put himself through school and left the United States during the depression to work as a commercial pilot with an affiliate airline of Pan Am in China. While living there he met and married a Chinese woman with whom he would have two children. At the time of William's birth, China was at war with Japan, and when that war expanded to include the United States, the Chens left China for Canton, Ohio, where they had relatives. William's father joined the U.S. Army Air Corps and served in the China-Burma-India theater of operations.

The family stayed only briefly in Canton before moving to New York City, and then on to Washington, D.C., where William spent most of his childhood. He was educated in the public school system, except for the last two years of high school, which he spent at the Storm King School in Cornwall-on-Hudson, New York, about sixty miles north of New York City. He graduated from high school in 1956 at the age of sixteen. He then went to the University of Michigan in Ann Arbor, where he earned a bachelor's degree in engineering mathematics in 1960 and a master's degree in aeronautical and astronautical engineering in 1961.

The ROTC

Throughout his studies at college, Chen took army classes in the Reserve Officer Training Corps (ROTC). Because the war in Korea had just ended in stalemate and the cold war was raging, Chen believed that he would eventually have to serve in the military in some capacity. With an ROTC background, he reasoned, he would be able to serve as an officer. Chen had not at this point considered a career in the military.

Upon his graduation in 1961 he was offered a regular army commission as a first lieutenant, and he entered the service on what was ostensibly a three-year commitment. He found the work challenging, however, and he enjoyed much of what he was doing. He decided that a career in the military might be very interesting. His first assignment was at Fort Meade, Maryland, in army air defense during the Cuban Missile Crisis when American reconnaissance planes detected the deployment in Cuba of Soviet nuclear warheads capable of easily reaching the United States. Chen was a second lieutenant at the time, working with a team monitoring the air defense command post for the Washington-Baltimore area. In an interview with Jim Henry, Chen described this period as especially exciting. He recalled that the base was on heightened alert, monitoring all incoming flights from the coast, running drills, and manning the defense systems in twelve-hour shifts.

After this assignment, Chen was sent for what would be the first of several assignments at the Redstone Arsenal in Redstone, Alabama. Here he began what would become essentially his life's work in the military, the project management of weapons systems, especially missile systems. As such, he was involved in all phases of weapons systems management—engineering, production, testing, deployment, and support.

His first such assignment came in 1963, when he was the research and development project officer for the Nike Hercules surface-to-air missile. The goal of this project was to modify an existing system to make the missiles capable of shooting down tactical missiles. Chen was responsible for the entire program, something he remembered as being very exciting in that it was a tremendous amount of responsibility for a first lieutenant.

William Shao Chang Chen

In a later assignment in 1967, Chen's experience in the area of anti-missile systems was tapped when he was put in charge of developing requirements for new missile systems. He was specifically in charge of developing requirements for SAM-D, surface-to-air missile development, the predecessor system to today's patriot missile system used in the Gulf War of 1991. Chen followed the production of this system various times throughout his career. In 1972, when he was assigned to the Redstone Arsenal for the third time, he was the project manager of the SAM-D system.

Overseas Postings

Chen was first posted overseas in 1964 in Korea, where he served first as assistant chief and later chief of the missiles and weapons branch of the Eighth Army depot command. In 1966 he was sent as a captain for a tour of duty in Vietnam, where the United States was supporting South Vietnam in a war against North Vietnam. He served as an adviser to a South Vietnamese infantry division and was assigned as an ordnance and assistant logistics adviser. In this capacity he was responsible for the management of huge amounts of material that had to be deployed deep into the jungle. One mission, Chen told Henry, required him to open up a special forces camp, which involved moving a large convoy carrying supplies, equipment, and ammunition through the jungle. The entire convoy, about fifty trucks, then had to be airlifted on C-130 aircraft further into the jungle to continue its journey.

In 1973 Chen once again was stationed overseas, first in Thailand and then in Laos, where he served in a logistics and support capacity.

The Sergeant York

In 1984 the army called in Chen to help them with a missile system that was in political trouble. He was made project manager of the division air defense gun, also known as the Sergeant York. When Chen took over the project, it had failed to pass certain technical and operational tests. Congress, meanwhile, had stipulated that the system pass these tests before it would be funded further. The army was in a bind and needed a proven manager to move the system through this crucial test, which was reported on widely in the media, increasing the pressure for positive results. The test did not prove successful, however, and Chen briefed Secretary of Defense Caspar Weinberger—a rare privilege for a project manager—on the findings. Based on Chen's report, the secretary eventually recommended to scrap the system.

Chen told Henry that he thought the highly controversial system was doomed because of overly high expectations about its capabilities. He also mentioned that earlier in his career, in 1977, he had worked as an operations research analyst on the Sergeant York system, and according to an affordability analysis Chen had made at the time (largely ignored by his superiors), the system would eventually have the problems it actually did end up having. From this, Chen said, he learned that the special interests behind a system can often override careful analysis of its efficacy.

To Chen, the highlight of his career was his position as commanding general of the U.S. Army Missile Command at the Redstone Arsenal, a camp he had served at in various ranks throughout his career. Here he was responsible for the management of all the army's missile systems. He felt this posting was recognition by the military that he had excelled in the area he was most interested in.

In commenting on the impact of his heritage on his life and career, Chen told Henry that he believes it is incumbent upon Americans, nearly all of whom are descended from immigrants, to acknowledge the impact ethnic cultures have had on American society. More important, he said, is that "we go into and be a part of the mainstream of America, that we should tend to avoid being stereotyped, but be all you can be to be a part of the mainstream, even when that means diverting from what might be considered the traditional aspects of one's cultural heritage."

Chen is married and has two children, both boys. In September of 1993, he retired from the military after 33 years of service. He is now a division vice-president for Nicholls Research Corporation, a high technology engineering services company.

Sources:

Chen, William Shao Chang, telephone interview with Jim Henry, May 17, 1994.

United States Army. "William Shao Chang Chen." Biographical materials and press releases.

—Sketch by Jim Henry

Joy Cherian

(1942–)

Attorney, government relations consultant, scholar

Joy Cherian

Joy Cherian came to national prominence in his service as a commissioner on the federal government's Equal Employment Opportunity Commission from 1987 until 1993—a subcabinet-level presidential appointment. After leaving the commission, Cherian founded J. Cherian Consultants (JCC), a government relations firm that represents corporations interested in international trade in services and leads seminars and workshops dealing with U.S. equal employment opportunity issues. In addition, JCC provides senior advisors for all facets of international business development including introductory visits, analysis of regulations, acquisition of licenses, arrangement of joint venture partnerships. JCC's current clients include entrepreneurial ventures and large financial institutions.

Cherian was born in the city of Cochin in the southern state of Kerala in India on May 18, 1942. His father was a pioneer in the field of commercial photography. The family was Catholic, and Cherian was educated at parochial schools run by Carmelite and Jesuit priests. He was an excellent student in high school and was elected president both of the student government and of his class. He was also politically active and participated in anti-Communist demonstrations prior to the Communists coming to power in Kerala State, India. He spent his first year of college at the University of Madras, but then returned to his home state to complete his education. In 1963 he earned a bachelor of science degree from the University of Kerala, where two years later he also earned a law degree.

Cherian practiced law in India before coming to America in 1967 to study at the Catholic University of America in Washington, D.C. In 1970, he earned a master's degree in international law and four years later obtained his Ph.D., also in international law. In 1975 Cherian reworked his doctoral dissertation and published it as *Investment Contracts and Arbitration*, a reference book that is still widely used today and can be found in most law school libraries around the world. In 1978, he received his fifth university degree, a master of comparative law (American practice) from the George Washington University's National Law Center.

In 1973, while still working on his Ph.D., Cherian joined the legal department of the American Council of Life Insurance, the largest trade association of American life insurance companies. In that position, he traveled to various countries in Asia, Europe, and North America promoting international trade in services. In 1982 he was promoted to Director of International Insurance Law. Four years later he was awarded a certificate by the late Malcolm Baldrige, a former secretary of commerce, for outstanding services. He also served as a registered lobbyist for the life insurance industry, and as such played a substantial role in the enactment of several international trade bills and treaties affecting U.S. trade in services. In recognition of Cherian's initiatives on behalf of the insurance industry and his contributions to the establishment of an international insurance trade, the National Association of Insurance Commissioners (NAIC) appointed him to serve as an adviser to its Task Force on International Insurance Relations.

Aside from his professional activities, Cherian has been politically active in the Asian American community. In 1982 he founded the Indian American Forum for Political Education (IAFPE), a national nonprofit civic organization working with the executive and legislative branches of the federal government to help increase political awareness and participation among Americans of Asian Indian descent. And in 1986, Cherian was elected national chairman of the Asian American Voters Coalition (AAVC), an umbrella group representing more than a dozen national ethnic organizations.

The EEOC

President Ronald Reagan appointed Cherian to the U.S. Equal Employment Opportunity Commission (EEOC) in 1987. During his tenure with the commission, Cherian, the first Asian American to serve on the commission, championed many causes and published widely in law journals on the topic of equal opportunity. He was especially active in the area of national origin-based discrimination. As he told the *Washington Post* in 1991, "The issue [of national origin discrimination] is very serious. This is one of the areas where in the last 26 years after the enactment of the Civil Rights Act there is still not enough focus. Women's groups are concerned about sexual harassment, the AARP [American Association of Retired Persons] is concerned about age discrimination, the NAACP and others talk about race discrimination. Who talks about national origin?"

Discrimination on the basis of national origin takes the form of restricting recent immigrants' job status on the basis of their accent, their insistence on speaking their native language, or the way in which they dress, among other factors. Cherian became an outspoken critic of such discrimination and increased the EEOC's action in defense of those discriminated against. In 1987, the year Cherian joined the EEOC, there were 9,653 complaints of national origin discrimination filed with the commission—or 8.8 percent of the agency's caseload. In 1990 there were 11,688—or 11.1 percent.

Cherian also pursued several high profile cases, including Professor Rosalie Tung's claim against the University of Pennsylvania for denial of tenure, Dr. Alfred Bennun's claim against Rutgers University for denial of promotion, and the prosecution of La Rouche College in Pennsylvania for discrimination against Professor M. Sidky.

His advocacy for the protection of all Americans' civil rights abroad led to the highly unusual EEOC intervention in the Supreme Court case against Aramco (*EEOC v. Aramco*). While Congress was debating the Civil Rights Bill to override the Supreme Court's decision in Aramco, Cherian strongly promoted the need to protect American employees' rights, not only under Title VII of the Civil Rights Act, but also under the newly enacted Americans with Disabilities Act. The Civil Rights Act of 1991 now extends extraterritorial protection to all Americans under both these laws.

Returning to Private Life

In 1993, Cherian's term on the EEOC ended and he left government service to found J. Cherian Consultants, a Washington, D.C.-based government relations firm that offers a variety of services to its clients. Cherian has become especially successful as a consultant to international business and government in the area of establishing ethnic diversity within organizations. He holds seminars on topics such as diversity training, success with respect, the factual basis for assertions about workforce diversity, and harassment on the basis of race, color, and national origin, among many other related topics.

In addition to this work, Cherian has long been involved in the legal community. He chaired the American Bar Association's committee on international insurance and law from 1983 until 1987, and the committee on international employment law from 1988 until 1992. In June 1994, he conducted successful business seminars in several Japanese cities.

Cherian has written extensively throughout his career. In addition to his book, *Investment Contracts and Arbitration,* he has compiled and edited a law reference manual and has contributed articles to professional journals and popular magazines. He has also presented papers and spoken before organizations around the world, including the Kennedy School of Government at Harvard and the Center for Management Development and Organizational Research at the City University of New York. Cherian's published works have addressed a broad range of topics, including international investment arbitration, insurance business overseas, political participation among Asian Americans, appropriate affirmative action in the American workplace, transnational employment rights of U.S. citizens, and many other such concerns. As of 1994, Cherian was the legislative advisor to the Small Business Exporters Association (SBEA).

Sources:

Periodicals

Swoboda, Frank. "Foreign-Born, Too, Face 'Glass Ceiling' in Job Promotion," *Washington Post,* March 10, 1991, p. H2.

Other

Cherian, Joy, telephone interview with Jim Henry, May 10, 1994.

Joy Cherian Consultants, Inc. "Joy Cherian, Ph.D." Press release. Washington, D.C, 1994.

—Sketch by Jim Henry

Doug Chiang

(1962–)

Art and Special Effects Director

Doug Chiang is the art director and associate creative director at Industrial Light and Magic (ILM), the special effects company founded by filmmaker George Lucas. Chiang has been responsible for the creation and design of many special effects and movie sets, including the 1992 Oscar-winning *Death Becomes Her*. A substantial asset to the ILM team, Chiang has been a part of a number of successful Hollywood movies ranging from *Ghost* to *Terminator 2*, the latter utilizing imagery generated through computer graphics, one of Chiang's specialties. Chiang is also an accomplished painter, with his work exhibited nationally and in several publications.

Born in Taiwan in 1962, Doug Chiang was five when he and his family moved to the United States. His father, now a design engineer for Ford, had been studying engineering at the University of Alabama when the family was finally able to join him. Eventually the Chiangs settled in Westland, Michigan, where Chiang first started to cultivate his interest in film and what he saw as the unlimited potential of special effects.

Backyard Filmmaker

As a fifteen-year-old high school student, Chiang filmed his first short feature in his backyard. A year later, he made a second short film, *Gladiator*, using clay animation. The animated short landed him the grand prize in a statewide film festival for students. It was this same feature that caught the eye of John Prusak, a teacher at the William D. Ford Vocational/Technical center in Westland. Prusak taught a media production course at Ford and encouraged Chiang to enroll in the school and offered him a job as a teaching assistant.

The offer came at a good time for Chiang. His graduation from John Glenn High School had to be postponed until 1981 due to ulcer complications, and he was unsure where he was headed or what the future held. Prusak's offer seemed like the ideal solution. He joined the program, which gave students hands-on instruction in still photography and film and video production, including lighting, editing, sound, animation, and special effects. Prusak recognized Chiang's talent immediately. "Doug is the kind of student you get once in a lifetime. He'd get an idea in his head and you could see it coming through his fingertips," Prusak told the *Vocational Education Journal* in 1993.

Doug Chiang

Chiang transferred to the University of California at Los Angeles and graduated in 1986 with a bachelor's degree in fine arts. It was during this time that Chiang received top honors for *Mental Block*, his four-and-a-half-minute clay animation short, in the FOCUS Awards. FOCUS, a Nissan-sponsored college/university contest that enabled Chiang to participate in seminars and be exposed to production and design crews, was a wonderful experience for the budding film student.

After college Chiang quickly submersed himself in numerous free-lance projects, mostly commercials, and landed a job with Digital Productions in 1986. While working for Digital he was a design director for such productions as "Oprah Winfrey" and "Good Morning America." In 1987 he worked as a designer and key animator for CBS-TV's innovative and now-legendary children's show "Pee Wee's Playhouse."

Feature Films

Since joining ILM in 1988 Chiang has received both an Academy Award and a British Academy Award for his work. He has been a substantial part of the making of such films as *The Mask* (1994), *The Doors* (1991), *Terminator 2* (1991), *Ghost* (1990), and *Death Becomes Her* (1992), for which he won his Academy Award. He was also in charge of art direction for the 1994 box-office smash, *Forrest Gump*, starring Tom Hanks.

Leroy Chiao

Chiang has mastered the art of special effects. By implementing miniature models as well as other props, Chiang told Abby Warren in an interview that he uses a "mixture of stop-motion photography, multiple film exposures, animatronics and computer graphics . . . play(ing) visual tricks on the audience." As an art director, Chiang is responsible for a myriad of tasks in the production of a film. He typically handles everything from estimating the viability of a writer or director's vision of a scene—whether or not the technology exists to film what is envisioned—to set designs, special effects techniques, and even budgeting.

An example of Chiang's work was described in the *Vocational Education Journal:* "in . . . *Death Becomes Her,* audiences saw Meryl Streep's character walk and talk with her head twisted backward, after a fall downstairs breaks her neck. It looks impossibly real, but Streep's neck is a 3-D computer graphic with [her] real head imposed above it." This was an image Chiang created. Through this sort of unique artistry he is able to trick the audience into seeing the impossible, one of the most cherished aspects of contemporary filmmaking.

Chiang has already accomplished a great deal in his relatively short career. He shared his advice for anyone dreaming of a career in special effects and cinematic art design with Warren: "A well-rounded education and computer knowledge is a must."

Sources:

Periodicals

Dykman, Ann. "Oscar Winner Learned the Ropes in Vo-Tech School." *Vocational Education Journal,* October 1993, p. 16.
Gandel, Cathy. "Special Effects Magician." *Asia, Inc.* March 1994, pp. 58–59.
Industrial Light and Magic. "Doug Chiang," Professional resume. 1994.

Other

Chiang, Doug, telephone interview with Abby Warren, July 7, 1994.

—Sketch by Abby Warren

Leroy Chiao
(1960–)
Astronaut

In July of 1994, less than a month before his thirty-fourth birthday, Leroy Chiao fulfilled a lifelong dream when he took off on the space shuttle Columbia as a mission specialist. It was his first flight in space, something he has dreamed of doing from the time he was a child of seven watching the Gemini and Apollo missions of the sixties and early seventies.

Leroy Chiao was born on August 28, 1960, in Milwaukee, Wisconsin, to Tsu Tao and Cherry Chiao, but considers his home to be Danville, California, where his family moved when he was quite young. Education was highly valued in the Chiao household, as it is in most Chinese American families like his, Chiao told *Notable Asian Americans.* His father has a master's degree in chemical engineering and his mother holds a Ph.D. in material sciences and engineering. They both continually stressed to their children the importance of education in getting what you want from life. It was advice the young Chiao took to heart. He received a bachelor's of science degree in chemical engineering from the University of California at Berkeley in 1983.

Early Challenge

In an article for *College Digest,* Chiao reflected on the challenges of getting his undergraduate degree: "The philosophy at Berkeley is that they take more students than they plan to graduate, especially in the chemical engineering program. Only about 55 percent of the students who started actually graduated. My engineering friends and I hardly had time to do anything but study to just keep afloat." It was a grueling program, but one that taught Chiao some valuable lessons. "We learned to look things up for ourselves and to discover things on our own. This ability has become crucial to me in my career." In 1985 Chiao earned a master of science degree from the University of California at Santa Barbara, where he also received his doctorate in 1987.

Chiao's first job upon graduation was with Hexcel, a medium-sized material supplier to the aerospace industry. Here he was given the opportunity to work on a project in conjunction with NASA—bringing him a step closer to fulfilling his dream of becoming an astronaut—and the Jet Propulsion Laboratory developing materials for future space telescopes. From here Chiao moved to the Lawrence Livermore Laboratory, a government-funded research institution administered by the University of California and located on the Berkeley campus. He continued working in materials science and applied to the astronaut training program at NASA.

Soaring to New Heights

In an interview with Jim Henry, Chiao described the application process for the astronaut program. Of the many thousands of applications NASA receives over the course of two to three years, a final 2,500 are reviewed as worthy of serious consideration. Of these, 100 are interviewed, and 23 chosen. In other words, 1 percent of the serious applicants are chosen for the program. Chiao was selected and began training in 1990, becoming an astronaut in 1991.

As a mission specialist on the July 1994 Columbia launch, Chiao conducted life and material sciences experiments in the International Microgravity Laboratory II, or the Space Lab, as it is commonly known. This lab is a pressurized module within the cargo bay of the shuttle that offers the astronauts extra room in which to conduct their experiments. He was trained as one of two mission specialists who will go on any space walks outside the shuttle should some minor problems develop.

Chiao said his training for space flight was intensive, yet fun and very exciting. To practice weightlessness, he and his fellow astronauts were taken up in an Air Force KC135, a converted passenger airliner, where they replicated zero gravity by going into 20,000-foot free-falls. These typically lasted twenty to thirty seconds, during which time the astronauts floated freely in the specially designed cargo bay, just as if they were in outer space.

Chiao was able to fulfill his dream of becoming an astronaut through perseverance and, most importantly, through education. His parents' examples were not lost on the young man.

Sources:

Periodicals

Chiao, Leroy. "Your Rocket to the Stars." *The College Digest,* Special Edition, 1993-94, pp. 2–3.

Other

National Aeronautics and Space Administration, "Biographical Data," Houston, 1994.
Chiao, Leroy, written interview with Jim Henry, February 1994.
Chiao, Leroy, telephone interview with Jim Henry, March 2, 1994.

—Sketch by Jim Henry

Frank Chin
(1940–)
Writer

Frank Chin describes himself first and foremost as "a writer." In the biographical profile he provided after declining to be interviewed, he wrote, "I have written short fiction, plays, nonfiction, reviews, essays, and research pieces on Chinese and Japanese America. I have also written the backs of bubble gum cards, 'stupid' radio contests, documentary films on fishing and boxing, and hacked." His writing career is marked with milestones, including the distinction of being the first Asian American playwright produced on a New York stage—*The Chickencoop Chinaman* at American Place Theatre in 1972. A year later, Chin founded San Francisco's Asian American Theatre Workshop which evolved into the Asian American Theatre Company, one of the nation's foremost Asian American theatres. Together with Jeffery Paul Chan, Lawson Fusao Inada, and Shawn Wong, Chin also was responsible for creating what is widely considered the seminal text of Asian American literature, *Aiiieeeee! An Anthology of Asian American Writers,* published in 1974. Its follow-up companion, *The Big Aiiieeeee! An Anthology of Chinese American and Japanese American Literature,* was published in 1991.

In addition to his status as an established and respected writer, Chin is equally well known as a critic of Asian American literature. He and his three *Aiiieeeee!* editors have been dubbed "the gang of four," fighting in an Asian American literary war between what they describe in an introductory essay as "the real," with its "sources in the Asian fairy tale and the Confucian heroic tradition," and "the fake," with its "sources in Christian dogma and in

Western philosophy, history and literature," as represented by such Asian American writers as Maxine Hong Kingston, David Henry Hwang, and Amy Tan.

History of a Chinaman

Frank Chin was born in Berkeley, California, in 1940. In his biographical profile he described himself as a "fifth-generation Chinaman." In the past, particularly early in his career, Chin made a clear distinction between the use of "Chinaman" and the term "Chinese American" which for him was inscribed with a sense of complicit assimilation into the controlling white society. Chin wrote that he is "the son of a Chinese immigrant father and fourth-generation Chinatown mother whose father worked in the steward service of the Southern Pacific Railroad." Chin followed his grandfather's career on the railroad, first working "clerk jobs" around the Western Pacific Railway's Oakland Yard between 1962 and 1965. "Between tracks of standing and moving boxcars I did everything but get hurt, get lost and get scared," Chin recalled. He left the railroad for the University of California at Berkeley from which he graduated in 1966 with a degree in English. After a brief stint at the Iowa Writer's Workshop, Chin returned again to the tracks, becoming "the first Chinese-American brakeman on the Southern Pacific since Chinese built the Central Pacific over the Sierras."

In 1966 Chin moved to Seattle, Washington, working first for television station KING-TV where he filmed documentaries on the Seattle Repertory Theatre and the history of Seattle's Chinese New Year's celebration, and a film biography of former light heavyweight champion Archie Moore. Chin moved on to King Screen Productions, the film company owned by King Broadcasting Company, where he worked as a story editor and scriptwriter for "Sesame Street."

In 1972, Chin made theatre history as the first Asian American playwright to have work produced on a mainstream stage in New York. *The Chickencoop Chinaman* was mounted off-Broadway at The American Place Theatre. In this irreverent work, Chin introduces three unpredictable, often comic characters who defy generalizations of any kind and who challenge and satirize existing media stereotypes of Asian Americans. A hip and raunchy piece, a new generation of questioning Asian Americans found in Tam Lum an unlikely hero who, according to Chin in the play's cast list, has "a gift of gab and an open mouth, [a] multi-tongued word magician losing his way to the spell who trips to Pittsburgh to conjure with his childhood friend and research a figure in his documentary." After the play's opening to glowing reviews from such publications as the *New Yorker* and *Newsweek*, Chin wrote in "Backtalk," an article in The American Place Theatre's newsletter, "That this play is the first play by an Asian American to, in any sense, make it, that people should be surprised at our existence, is proof of the great success white racism has had with us. America might love us. But America's love is not good. It's racist love. I don't want it."

Frank Chin

Chin's next play, *The Year of the Dragon,* was mounted in 1974, again at The American Place Theatre. The play's theme is the disintegration of the Chinese American family: Pa Eng, the respected mayor of Chinatown, is dying; Ma Eng sings about Chinese slave girls; first son Fred Eng, head of Eng's Chinatown Tour 'n Travel hates himself for having built a business whose success demands that he assume a demeaning persona not unlike the humble, passive Charlie Chan; daughter Mattie chooses Boston and escapes Chinatown with a white husband; and young Johnny is little more than a hoodlum. On the whole, the play received generally good notices and went on to be filmed as a PBS production in 1975. Chin's other works for the theatre, though lesser known, include *Gee, Pop!, Chinatown Mortuary,* and *Oofty Goofty.*

A Writer's Legacy

An established playwright, Chin was encouraged by the American Conservatory Theatre (ACT), the San Francisco Bay Area's oldest and largest regional repertory theatre, to found the Asian American Theatre Workshop (AATW). With financial support and donated space from ACT, AATW began in 1973 as Chin's personal vision: "I founded the workshop as the only Asian American theatre that was conceived as a playwright's lab and not a showcase for yellows yearning to sell out to Hollywood. I failed. I was director of the workshop until 1977," wrote Chin in his biographical profile.

While Chin might be quick to dismiss his involvement with AATW, his achievement is undeniably long-lasting. According to Frank Abe, one of the original workshop members who is currently communications director for Seattle politician Gary Locke, AATW provided "both a theatrical and cultural experience." Abe explained, "Many of us did not have an Asian American consciousness at the time. Mine was strictly suburban Californian. Through the workshop, I came to understand and embrace the fact that Asian American was a unique sensibility with a unique history. Through the written word, the goal was to recover our history, that which had been lost, falsified and suppressed."

As AATW grew and evolved, the focus shifted from the writers to the actors until, as Abe described it, "the inmates took over the asylum." In frustration and disgust, Chin left AATW in mid-1977. After his departure, AATW continued as a theatre group, renaming itself a "Company." As an expanded group, the Asian American Theatre Company (AATC) flourished, attracting numerous Asian American writers, actors, directors, and designers. More than twenty years later, AATC is a stalwart part of the Asian American community.

In 1978, Chin's "theatrical sense combined with [his] scholarly nature and need to make things right" led to "Day of Remembrance," which he described as "ceremonial events that restored history and civility inside Japanese America, and between the Japanese Americans and Seattle and Portland." The events publicized the campaign to redress the constitutional grievances suffered by Americans of Japanese ancestry during World War II: "I put together groups of Japanese American leaders and activists to lead a return to the county fairgrounds outside of Seattle and Portland that had been converted into concentration camps for the Nikkei in 1942. The Day of Remembrance included participation by the National Guard, local politicians, a display of art and artifacts from the concentration camps, a huge potluck dinner and a couple thousand Japanese Americans in both cities," explained Chin.

Out of Theatre

Chin eventually abandoned all of the theatre world. He wrote with finality, "I am out of theatre. I will not work with any theatre, producer, writer, director, or actor who plays and lives the stereotype. So I write fiction, essays, and articles." Chin has "written extensively on Chinese and Japanese history, culture and literature, and presence in popular local news magazines, TV documentaries, and literary journals." His fiction includes *The Chinaman Pacific & Frisco R.R. Co.*, a collection of short stories published in 1988, and two novels, *Donald Duk*, published in 1991, and *Gunga Din Highway*, published in 1994.

In addition to writing, Chin has "taught Asian American history and ideas using storytelling, theatre and writing games, in four- to five-week long workshops" at Washington State University, Michigan State University, and in five Portland high schools.

In both his writing and teaching, Chin's goal is to expose and correct "the white racist characterization of Chinese fairy tales and childhood literature as teaching misogynistic ethics and despicable morals as fact." Chin's harshest criticisms are directed at best-selling authors Maxine Hong Kingston and Amy Tan and renowned playwright David Henry Hwang. As he explained in "Come All Ye Asian American Writers of the Real and the Fake" in *The Big Aiiieeeee*: "What seems to hold Asian American literature together is the popularity among whites of ... Kingston's *Woman Warrior*. . . Hwang's *F.O.B.* . . .and *M. Butterfly* . . . and Tan's *Joy Luck Club*. These works are held up before us as icons of our pride, symbols of our freedom from the icky-gooey evil of a Chinese culture where the written word for 'woman' and 'slave' are the same word (Kingston) and Chinese brutally tattoo messages on the back of women (Kingston and Hwang). . . . Kingston, Hwang, and Tan are the first writers of any race, and certainly the first writers of Asian ancestry, to so boldly fake the best-known works from the most universally known body of Asian literature and lore in history. And, to legitimize their faking, they have to fake all of Asian American history and literature, and argue that the immigrants who settled and established Chinese America lost touch with Chinese culture, and that a faulty memory combined with new experience produced new versions of these traditional stories. This version of history is their contribution to the stereotype." Chin and others argue that readers who know little about Chinese culture are being constantly misled about Chinese and Chinese Americans, which in turn feeds the stereotypes of a white racist America.

In answer, Chin has, "like the Cantonese and Chinese before me, wherever Chinese literature and language have been banned, taken to storytelling and the comic book as a tactic for making the real accessible in a hostile literary and learning atmosphere." One of his current ongoing projects is to condense and retell "the most popular stories and operas from the Chinese fairy tale and heroic tradition to fit sets of drawings from old Chinese comic books." Chin remains a crusader of "the real," acting as the voice of conscientiousness, welcomed or not, in the growing realm of Asian American literature.

Sources:

Books

Chin, Frank. *"The Chickencoop Chinaman" and "The Year of the Dragon"*: Two Plays by Frank Chin. Seattle: University of Washington Press, 1981.

Chin, Frank, Jeffery Chan, Lawson Inada, and Shawn Wong. *Aiiieeeee! An Anthology of Asian American Writers.* New York: Mentor, 1974.

————. *The Big Aiiieeeee! An Anthology of Chinese American and Japanese American Literature.* New York: Meridian, 1991.

Periodicals

Chin, Frank. "Backtalk." *News of The American Place Theatre,*
    vol. 4, no. 4, May 1972.
———. "Confessions of the Chinatown Cowboy." *Bulletin of
    Concerned Asian Scholars,* vol. 4, no. 3, Fall 1972, pp. 58–
    70.
———. "Don't Pent Us Up in Chinatown." *New York Times,*
    October 8, 1972.

Other

Chin, Frank. Biographical profile provided by Chin.

—*Sketch by Terry Hong*

Margaret Cho

Margaret Cho
(1968–)
Comedian

A second-generation comedian as well as a second-generation Korean American, Margaret Cho was barely into her twenties when she became known as the reigning Asian American funny woman. A child of the eighties, she's broken barriers and stereotypes by performing on such television shows as the "Bob Hope Special," "Evening at the Improv," "Arsenio Hall," and "Star Search." In 1994, Cho was the first Asian American to star in her own television show, "All-American Girl," a sitcom about a Korean American family. The comedy was designed by Cho with co-producer Gary Jacobs, a veteran writer and producer. Members of the cast agree that this is a period of expanding opportunity for Asian Americans in the performing arts.

Drive to Perform

Margaret Cho was born December 5, 1968, and raised in San Francisco. She derives much of her material from her upbringing in a liberal yet religious Korean American Family. "My father writes Korean books like *1,001 Jokes for Public Speakers,* real corny stuff," said Cho in a press release. As a child, her parents encouraged her to learn voice, dance, and piano, but stopped short of endorsing her venture into acting at age thirteen. Undaunted, Cho pursued her dream of becoming an actor, gaining admission to San Francisco's prestigious High School of Performing Arts and later enrolling in San Francisco State University's theatre department. She had hoped to continue her acting studies at Juilliard or Yale, but became frustrated by the limited roles available to Asian women. It was then that she turned to stand-up comedy at the suggestion of a friend.

"I wasn't sure I could make it as an actor because I didn't see any successful Asians," she told the *Daily Bruin.* "Stand-up is a way to acting but it's also its own art form. I've grown to love and respect comedy." Cho developed her comedy act at a club built, coincidentally, on top of her parents' bookstore, where she worked part time. On her breaks she would go upstairs and perform a set. Her parents were initially less than pleased that she quit college to perform in nightclubs. "Stand-up goes against any typical Asian aesthetic," she told the *Daily Bruin.* "It's too personal. You have to reveal yourself. It's not what a woman should do." But since Cho has gained broad popularity—as well as support from the Asian American community, her parents relented. "Now my mom says, 'That's my baby on TV!'"

Generational Humor

Cho's comedy routine pokes fun at her own generation. "Slacking off is the main art form of my generation, the only pleasure we have left," said Cho in a press release highlighting some of her work. "We have so many restrictions—no sex, no drugs—the only vice left was greed, but where did that take us? 'Just Say No' has become the 'Keep on Truckin'' of my generation." The press release reveals that Cho's ethnicity and gender are fair game as well. "Men look at me and think I'm going to walk on their backs or something. I tell them the only time I'll walk on your back is if there's something on the other side of you I want." Her jokes push sexual boundaries, drawing on gay themes—and her experiences working in an S/M shop.

Since 1991, when she became the West Coast division champion of the U.S. College Comedy competition that led to a billing with comic Jerry Seinfeld, Cho has accumulated numerous credits. She's appeared on MTV's "Half-Hour Comedy Hour," Lifetime's "Six Comics in Search of a Generation," and Fox's "Comic Strip Live." Cho portrayed a Brooklyn nurse in *Angie,* which starred Geena Davis. ("It was a small part," deadpanned Cho in her press release. "It's not exactly 'Thelma and Margaret.'") She's also starred in the film *The Doomed Generation* with Dustin Nguyen. When she was admitted to the Friar's Club, the exclusive comedy fraternity, even her father was won over.

For Cho, comedy offers an opportunity to spotlight Asian Americans. "'All American Girl' is basically about me and the people in my life," she told Gerard Lim. "It's the first show that sees Asian Americans as they really are. These days there are more extraterrestrials on shows than Asians—even if you include reruns of *Kung Fu,*" which, she noted, should be renamed "That Guy's Not Chinese." "I want to continue the trend *The Joy Luck Club* started. We're the first layer of generational culture. This is important because we are on the ground floor of things for the future of Asian Americans in this country. I want to be part of that."

Sources:

Periodicals

Lee, Elisa. "Margaret Cho Brings APA Twenty-Somethings to Television." *Asian Week,* November 19, 1993, p. 19.

Lim, Gerard. "What Makes the First Asian American Sitcom So Special? It's Cho's Show . . ." *Asian Week,* July 1, 1994, p. 1.

McNamara, Mary. "The New Feminist Comics." *Ms.,* January/February 1992, p. 23.

Polkinghorne, Rex. "Comic Cho Proves Laughter Can Sever Racial Stereotypes." *Daily Bruin,* February 22, 1994, p. 21.

Provenzano, Jim. "It's Cho Time." *Advocate,* July 1994, p. 54.

Other

Cho, Margaret. Press releases and biographical materials, summer 1994.

—Sketch by Helen Zia

Ping Chong
(1946–)
Artist

Ping Chong refers to what he does as "making works." The work he makes is found at the intersection of text, choreography, music, sounds, slides, and other visual designs—what he calls "interdisciplinary" or "contemporary" theatre. Chong has always used the metaphor of traveling to a foreign country to describe his work, "a foreign country where you might have unexpected experiences or see something you don't understand. But like visiting a foreign country, the more you see it, the more familiar it gets," he said in an interview with Terry Hong.

Since the late 1960s, Chong has been stretching the limits of theatre, originating more than twenty interdisciplinary performances and installations throughout the United States, Europe, and Asia. "What I'm doing is the exploration of a new syntax in theatre which reflects the changes in the contemporary world. . . . I chose not to do traditional Eurocentric theatre and so had to create my own syntax," he told Hong. "In that way, I'm very American—perhaps American in a truer sense because I'm influenced by *everything* this country is. I don't stop at just Europe."

Chong began his theatrical career as a member of Meredith Monk's The House Foundation, eventually collaborating with Monk on such major pieces as *The Travelogue Series* and *The Games.* He branched out on his own, gathering a group of artists to create *Lazarus,* his first independent theatre work in 1972. The group began as The Fiji Theatre Company, evolving into Ping Chong and Company. Since then, his "contemporary theatre" includes *Humboldt's Current* (1977 Obie Award), *Nuit Blanche, A.M./A.M.—The Articulated Man* (1982 Villager Award), *Nosferatu, Angels of Swedenborg, Kind Ness* (1988 USA Playwrights Award), *Brightness* (two 1990 Bessie awards), and his two latest, *Deshima and Undesirable Elements.*

During his flourishing career that has spanned almost a quarter of a century, the many honors Chong has received include a National Institute for Music Theatre Award, a 1992 Bessie Award for Sustained Achievement, five National Endowment for the Arts fellowships, as well as a Guggenheim fellowship.

A Completely Chinese Universe

Born in 1946, Ping Chong grew up speaking Chinese in New York's Chinatown in the 1950s. "Chinatown was a very different place then," he wrote in an article titled

"Who is 'The Other'?" for *Inside Arts* in 1993. "It was not a commercialized tourist center; it was very small, village-like and self-contained. So my immediate universe was completely Chinese. When I went outside of Chinatown, it was like going to someplace distant and exotic. I loved going out of Chinatown, because I knew there was a bigger world out there and I wanted to see it."

When Chong left Chinatown to study art at the Pratt Institute, he found himself immersed in this bigger world. "My social signals and certain kinds of values became alien. That was the beginning of trauma for me." he told Hong. "All through college I was very uncomfortable, I couldn't feel at home."

From Pratt, Chong went on to study filmmaking at the School of Visual Arts, but in the midst of his training, he decided he wanted to learn more about dance and signed up for a workshop with Meredith Monk, one of the first multi-media choreographers and composers. As a member of Monk's The House Foundation, Chong first performed in several of Monk's works; then between 1972 and 1976, he collaborated with her to create three works, *Paris, Chacon,* and *Venice/Milan.*

In working with Monk, Chong discovered the medium through which he could express himself. Influenced throughout his career by Monk, Chong also drew heavily on his non-Western past: "My background was . . . certainly not Western theatre. My first theatrical experience was the Chinese Opera [Chong's parents were Chinese Opera performers], which had an incredible impact on me. The pageantry, ritual and color are so antithetical to traditional Western drama. Because of this, I gravitated toward experimental theatre in the late sixties. Growing up in a culture like the Chinese, I was more involved in myth and ritual than realism. . . . I am the result of a culture that is 2,000 years old mixing with one that is 200 years old."

Collaborative Efforts

At the same time Chong was collaborating with Monk, he was also beginning to establish himself as an independent artist. Gathering a group of artists who would eventually evolve into The Fiji Theatre Company and later Ping Chong and Company, Chong debuted his first project, *Lazarus,* in 1972 at the Lee Nagrin Studio in New York City.

Over the next twenty-plus years, Chong has created more than twenty-five works for the stage. A few highlights of his vast body of works include *Kind Ness* (1986), a surreal comedy that follows the friendships of six characters from their elementary school days through their college years, including a gorilla named Buzz; *Elephant Memories* (1990), a wild investigation of a culture both archaic and futuristic, civilized and barbaric, humorous and frightening, like and unlike our own; *Deshima* (1993), a dance theatre work about Japan and the West from the sixteenth century to the present, combining such elements as Van

Ping Chong

Gogh's "Sunflowers," Javanese court dance, Jitterbug contests, and the internment of Japanese Americans during World War II; and *Undesirable Elements* (1993), an ongoing series of community-specific works that explore the effects of history, culture, and ethnicity on the lives of individuals in the context of their community.

Always unpredictable, Chong is currently making *Chinoiserie,* an exploration of the relationship between China and the West, and *A Feather on the Breath of God,* a work with puppets slotted to premiere at the 1996 Olympics in Atlanta.

Chong is the first to credit his actors and designers as integral to the creation of his works. Although Chong holds the ultimate authority, the creative process is a democratic one that revolves around gathering and distilling ideas with his performers during rehearsals. Each piece is entirely collaborative as Chong describes himself not so much as a "creator," but an "editor." *TheatreCrafts* magazine likened Chong's creative method to "a well-oiled jazz ensemble in which each player gets a turn displaying his virtuosity and originality, putting his own stamp on a piece of music while maintaining the work's coherence."

An American Artist

From the beginning of his long career, Chong has been both struggling with and celebrating the notion of being "the other" in a predominantly white, European society: "I always think of myself as an outsider," Chong wrote in

American Theatre. "I don't belong to the Asian community.
. . . I was not born in China and I have not lived in Chinatown for over twenty-five years. In the same way, I belong
to the American community, but how much do I belong to
Lincoln, Nebraska? I know nothing about that environment. I've been described as an 'East Coast, cutting-edge,
male expatriate artist.' I consider myself all and none of
the above: I'm a New Yorker, always outside of things."

Chong argues against the "ghettoization" by choice of
members of the Asian American community, citing that
only two of his many works have been directly related to
Asia. "I don't identify myself primarily as an Asian American artist. I don't know what that means," he said. "I'm
not going to allow myself to be ghettoized as an Asian
American artist. I'm an *American* artist."

As an American artist, Chong has performed all over
the country and beyond in Europe and Asia, taking his
audiences to alien places and cultures, not for the thrill of
novelty, but as a means to making these diverse audiences
think about the nature of their own surroundings. By
pointing out elements unfamiliar and alien, he confronts
the audience with the sense of otherness that each individual harbors, asking them to question that which is unfamiliar and alien about their own selves.

Sources:

Periodicals

Caroll, Noel. "A Select View of Earthlings." *The Drama
     Review,* vol. 27, no. 1, Spring 1983, pp. 72–81.
Chong, Ping. "Who is 'The Other'?" *Inside Arts,* Septem-
     ber 1993.
———. [no title] *American Theatre,* October 1991.
Downey, Roger. "Little Worlds." *Seattle Weekly,* Arts and Lei-
     sure section, April 21, 1993.
Feingold, Michael. "Getting in Dutch." *The Village Voice.*
     January 6-12, 1993.
Gussow, Mel. "A Performance Montage of East-West Trou-
     bles." *The New York Times,* [no other bibliographical
     data.]
Howard, Beth. "Ping Chong: Creating a Visual and Aural
     Feast." *TheatreCrafts,* March 1990, pp. 27–31+.
Osborn, M. Elizabeth. "The Divine Comedy of Ping
     Chong." *The Boston Sunday Globe.* May 5, 1991.
R., J. "Chong Show." *Vanity Fair,* vol. 55, no. 5, May 1992.
Sandler, Robert. "Practical Visionary: Ping Chong." *The-
     aterWeek.* January 30, 1989, pp. 26–33.
Unger, Miles. "Peaceful Setting, Unquiet Thoughts." *The
     Boston Sunday Globe.* May 5, 1991.
Westfall, Suzanne. "Invasion of a Cornfield." *American The-
     atre,* January 1993, pp. 10–11.

Other

Chong, Ping, interview with Terry Hong, March 10, 1994.

—Sketch by Terry Hong

Rachelle Blossom Chong
(1959–)
Attorney, Chairperson, Federal Communications Commission

Chong is one of five commissioners to sit on the Federal Communications Commission (FCC), a federal regulatory agency. She was nominated by President Bill
Clinton in April 1994 to fill one of the five commissioner
posts. Chong's nomination was confirmed by the Senate
on May 19, and four days later she was sworn in as one of
two Republican party members that by law must sit on the
commission.

Prior to being named to the commission, Chong was a
partner in the San Francisco-based law firm of Graham
and James, where she specialized in telecommunications
and served as head of the firm's policy-making committee.
She was an active member of the firm's international telecommunications practice group, made up of telecommunications lawyers in the United States, the Pacific Rim,
and Australia.

Rachelle Blossom Chong was born on June 22, 1959, in
Stockton, California, to second-generation Chinese Americans. She was educated at the University of California at
Berkeley where she majored in political science and journalism, graduating in 1981 as a Phi Beta Kappa member.
After graduating she enrolled in the Hastings College of
Law, where she served as editor in chief of *COMM/ENT,*
the school's communications and entertainment law journal. She earned her J.D. in 1984 and is licensed to practice
law in both California and the District of Columbia.

Following her graduation, Chong moved to Washington, D.C., where she went to work for the law firm of Kadison, Pfaelzer, Woodward, Quinn & Rossi. She
concentrated in communications law and often appeared
before the FCC on behalf of clients. Other areas of practice at Kadison, Pfaelzer included broadcast law, common
carrier regulations, and intellectual property matters.

In 1987 Chong left the nation's capital to work at Graham and James in San Francisco. Her first position was
with the public utilities group, where she focused on
issues related to the wireless communication industry. She
served as principal regulatory counsel to four Bay Area
cellular telephone carriers, including McCaw Cellular
Communications and Pacific Telesis, appearing as their
representative before the California Public Utilities Commission on a broad range of regulatory matters. She
defended her clients in complaint cases, served as an
advocate in public policy debates affecting the industry,
and prepared applications and compliance filings.

Rachelle B. Chong

The magazine *Television Digest* quotes colleagues of Chong as supporting her nomination without qualification. Congressman Robert Matsui of California stated: "Rachelle Chong will be a strong, independent voice on the FCC. She has built a career exploring the legalities of the ever-expanding field of communications and will be invaluable as the Commission prepares to tackle some of the most complex issues it has ever faced." James Troup, an attorney who worked with Chong at Kadison, Pfaelzer said of her: "I always found her work to be very thorough and accurate. . . . She'll make a good commissioner. . . . She has a good attention to detail which will serve her very well." He went on to assure critics that, despite her history of attachment to many large concerns which she will now regulate, she will be a fair voice. "She definitely . . . will make independent decisions. . . . I don't think she'll be influenced by politics, and that might be very refreshing."

Chong was chosen for the FCC spot after winning praise by Republican lawmakers in 1993. She had served from 1992 through 1994 as the commissioner of the Republican party's legal services trust fund commission in San Francisco, and was contacted by an administration official in September of 1993 who told her that the White House was looking for a female minority candidate with fifteen to twenty years experience in communications. Chong's ten years proved to be enough to serve on the commission which will become more and more important in coming years as the communications industry struggles to establish control of what is envisioned to be a huge new industry: information, telephone, and entertainment delivery and production.

Chong is married to Kirk Del Prete, a project director for Whalen & Company, a contracting and consulting firm working mostly in the fields of cellular and digital communications. Chong is heavily involved in professional activities and holds memberships in the governing committee of the American Bar Association's forum committee of communications law, the Federal Communications Bar Association, the American Bar Association, the California State Bar Association, the International Bar Association, the Asian American Bar Association, the California Conference of Public Utilities Counsel, the U.S. Pan Asian American Chamber of Commerce, and Women in Telecommunications. While working with Graham and James, Chong regularly supervised *pro bono* cases in the area of social security and California disability insurance.

Sources:

Periodicals

"Chong Gets Nod for GOP Seat at FCC," *Television Digest.* March 7, 1994, p. 2.

Other

Federal Communications Commission. "Rachelle B. Chong," Press release, Washington, D.C, 1994.

—Sketch by Jim Henry

Vernon Chong
(1933–)
Military surgeon

Major General Vernon Chong is the command surgeon at the headquarters of the Air Training Command and the commander of the Joint Military Medical Command at Randolph Air Force Base in Randolph, Texas. As such he is responsible for managing 7,500 personnel and overseeing health care—medical and dental—to various military hospitals in Texas.

Medicine and Military

Vernon Chong was born on November 13, 1933, in Fresno, California. He attended public schools and graduated from Fresno High School in 1951. He earned a bachelor of arts degree in basic medical sciences from Stanford University in 1955. He then enrolled in the Stanford

University School of Medicine, from which he graduated in 1958. Chong interned at the General Hospital of Fresno County, California, where he completed his internship in 1963.

Chong entered the air force in 1963. His first assignment was as chief of general surgery at the U.S. Air Force Hospital at Scott Air Force Base in Illinois. In June of 1965 he was transferred to the air force hospital at Tachikawa Air Base in Japan, where he served as a staff general surgeon and later, as director of intern and resident education for Japanese physicians.

In 1968, Chong returned to the United States and was assigned as a staff general surgeon and instructor for the surgical residency training program at the David Grant USAF Medical Center at Travis Air Force Base in California. From July 1970 to June 1974, he served at the Air Force Hospital of the U.S. Air Force Academy in Colorado. He worked as a staff general surgeon and then as chairman of the department of surgery before becoming director of hospital services. He also functioned as an adviser to cadets in the premedical program and was the team physician for the air force hockey team.

Chong became deputy commander and director of hospital services at the U.S. Air Force Regional Hospital at March Air Force Base in July 1974. Two years later, he returned to Travis Air Force Base in California and served as deputy commander and director of hospital services at the base's David Grant Medical Center. He became commander of that institution in 1978.

Command Posts

In November of 1981, Chong was assigned as commander of the Malcolm Grow Medical Center at Andrews Air Force Base in Maryland. In March of 1985 he became the command surgeon for the Military Airlift Command at Scott Air Force Base, and two years later was assigned as commander of the Willford Hall Medical Center at Lackland Air Force Base in Texas. He assumed his present position in May of 1990 overseeing health care activities at Fort Sam Houston, Lackland Air Force Base, and at clinics at Brooks, Kelly and Randolph Air Force bases, all in Texas.

Chong also participated in the manned space program as a member of the launch site recovery force, the team standing by to provide medical services that might be required for the crews of space flights. Chong was involved in the launch site recovery activity for all of the Apollo, Skylab, and Apollo-Soyuz manned missions.

He has served as a member of the board of regents of the National Library of Medicine and as an adviser to the board of regents of the Uniformed Services University of

Vernon Chong

Health Sciences. He is a fellow of the American College of Surgeons and a member of the Pan Pacific Surgical Association, the Association of Military Surgeons of the United States, the Aerospace Medical Association, the Society of Air Force Clinical Surgeons, the Society of Air Force Flight Surgeons, the Society of NASA Flight Surgeons, and the American College of Physician Executives. He is currently the Air Force representative to the board of governors of the American College of Surgeons.

Chong's military awards and decorations include the Distinguished Service Medal, the Legion of Merit with oak leaf cluster, the Meritorious Service Medal, the Air Force Commendation Medal, the Air Force Outstanding Unit Award with four oak leaf clusters, the Air Force Organizational Excellence Award, the Naval Unit Citation, the National Defense Service Medal, the Vietnam Service Medal with service star, the Air Force Overseas Ribbon, the Air Force Longevity Service Award Ribbon with five oak leaf clusters, and the Order of Merit (Brazil). Chong is married to the former Ann S. Kawana of Fresno, California. The couple has three children.

Sources:

United States Air Force. "Vernon Chong." Biographical information, July 1990.

—*Sketch by Jim Henry*

Deepak Chopra

(1946–)

Physician, author

The teachings of Deepak Chopra on the relationship between mind and body have had a major influence on health issues in America and around the world. In his several best selling books, the Indian-born American physician has offered to his readers a new way of looking at life, their bodies, and the concept of health. His most celebrated and perhaps most controversial contribution to the literature of alternative health theories is his assertion that what we understand as the process of aging is, in fact, not beyond our control. As he says in his internationally best selling book of 1993, *Ageless Body, Timeless Mind: The Quantum Alternative to Growing Old,* "Because the mind influences every cell in the body, human aging is actually fluid, changeable; it can speed up, slow down, stop for a time, and even reverse itself." It is statements like these that have gained Chopra international attention, including the scorn of certain segments of the medical establishment.

Deepak Chopra

Deepak Chopra was born in India to a prominent cardiologist. He studied medicine at the All India Institute of Medical Science, where he became interested in Western medicine. He left his home for the United States in 1970 and completed residencies in internal medicine and endocrinology. He went on to teaching posts at major medical institutions—Tufts University and Boston University schools of medicine—while establishing a very successful private practice. By the time he was thirty-five, Chopra had become chief of staff at New England Memorial Hospital.

The Doctor as Drug Dealer

Still, there was something disturbing to Chopra about the way medicine is traditionally practiced in the West. He especially disliked the reliance on medication. As he told *People* magazine in 1993, by 1980 he had begun to see himself as a "legalized drug pusher, dispensing antibiotics and sleeping pills" at what he considered an alarming rate. He began a search for alternatives and discovered one in the teachings of the Maharishi Mahesh Yogi, an Indian spiritualist who had gained a cult following in the late sixties and early seventies teaching Transcendental Meditation (or TM) to such celebrities as The Beatles.

Chopra began practicing TM fervently and within a couple of years he had the opportunity to meet the Maharishi. In Chopra the Maharishi saw a well-established American professional firmly ensconced in the medical establishment who could act as a conduit, a way to introduce ancient Eastern philosophies of medicine and lifestyle into American culture. The Maharishi asked Chopra

to help him bring Ayurveda medicine to America. Developed in India, Ayurvedic medicine, Chopra told *USA Today,* is "an ancient holistic system of medicine that takes into account all aspects of a patient's life and includes the environment, the body, the mind, and consciousness." In 1985 Chopra established the Ayurvedic Health Center for Stress Management and Behavioral Medicine in Lancaster, Massachusetts, where he began his practice of integrating the best aspects of Eastern and Western medicine. In this he has been wildly successful.

The Doctor as Healer

With his emphasis directed firmly toward holistic healing, Chopra began to achieve remarkable successes. In an era when books on healing and recovery are rampant, filling whole sections in most bookstores, his stand out. One reason is his traditional Western training and his impeccable credentials. He is seen as someone who knows firsthand what the limitations, excesses, and abuses of traditional medicine are. In describing these failings he told *USA Today* that "Eighty percent of all the drugs we use in Western medicine are 'optional' or of marginal benefit, which means that if we didn't use them, it wouldn't make a bit of difference to the person except to save money and prevent side effects."

These sorts of challenges resonated with a large segment of the American public who had become disillusioned with traditional medicine and what they perceived as uncaring, unsympathetic, and overpaid doctors. Chopra began writing books, giving speeches, and organizing seminars; he became a preacher for a new way of thinking about health and fitness. His first book, *Creating Health,* published in 1987, and his next, *Return of the Rishi: A Doctor's Search for the Ultimate Healer,* published in 1988, were both best sellers. They dealt with his holistic approach to health and wellness and established Chopra as one of the premiere writers in this field.

He continued writing prolifically in the early nineties, publishing *Perfect Health: The Complete Mind/Body Guide* in 1990 and *Unconditional Life: Discovering the Power to Fulfill Your Dreams* in 1991. And then in 1993 he published two books that would put him at the top of best seller lists and into the homes of Americans via talk shows like "The Oprah Winfrey Show." These books were *Creating Affluence: Wealth Consciousness in the Field of All Possibilities,* and the enormously successful best seller, *Ageless Body, Timeless Mind.* In the latter he presents his most radical thesis: that aging is not the inevitable deterioration of organs and mind that we have been traditionally taught to think of it as. Rather, it is a process that can be influenced, slowed down, and even reversed with the correct kinds of therapies, almost all of which are self-administered or self-taught. Put simply, Chopra says that getting rid of "toxic relations, emotions, [and] foods can influence your life span by thirty years." He teaches that applying a regimen of nutritional balance, meditation, and emotional clarity characterized by such factors as learning to easily and quickly express anger, for instance, can lead to increased lifespans of up to 120 years. And he claims these lives would not be spent wasting away in nursing homes like so many of the elderly today, but would be productive, creative lives.

Defending Himself

Chopra's ideas have caused controversy within the medical community. One of his first brushes with the American Medical Association came when he wrote an article describing the practice of Ayurvedic medicine for the *Journal of the AMA.* After it was published, the editors found out that he was the president of the American Association of Ayurvedic Medicine and had a financial relationship with a company that supplied some of the commonly prescribed herbs, including some mentioned in his article. Chopra dismissed these charges of conflict of interest as racially motivated.

Others in the medical community find fault with his claims that aging can be slowed or reversed, and that disease is always—or even in most cases—a result of behavior or thought patterns. In defending this last charge he described his thoughts on causality and personal responsibility in disease for *Psychology Today:* "You know, we are all participants in the whole process of illness. There are two levels of responsibility; one is individual, the other is shared. If I smoke cigarettes then I am to a great extent responsible for the carcinoma that is statistically more

likely to occur. But what about the innocent twelve-year-old with leukemia? That is where the level of collective responsibility comes in." In his view, what we see as tragic illness in innocents is really the culmination of generations of metabolizing negative emotions incorrectly, and that a longer view needs to be incorporated with an eye toward correcting our relationships with disease and illness for the benefit of generations to come.

In considering the long-term ramifications of his views on aging and the science he would like to see applied to it, Chopra told *Psychology Today* that he envisions a future in which "we will have a different perception of the elderly. We will begin to honor them, respect them and venerate them and love them and nourish them as we have never done before, because they will be, when this science reaches its ultimate expression, the caretakers of society. They will have the exquisite combination of wisdom and psychological youth."

Chopra and his teachings and writings have hit a resonant chord with people all over the world. His clients include such celebrities as George Harrison, Michael Jackson, and filmmaker David Lynch. His books have sold copies in the millions and have been translated into twenty-five languages. In 1992 Chopra was named to the National Institutes of Health's newly created board to study alternative medicine. He also sits on the Scientific Advisory Board of *Longevity* magazine. He continues to lecture around the world, making presentations to such auspicious organizations as the World Health Organization in Geneva, London's Royal Society of Medicine, and the United Nations. He also has lectured at the medical schools of Yale and Johns Hopkins, and at the Harvard School of Public Health and the National Institutes of Health. He is commonly featured in major newspapers and is a frequent guest on national television and radio programs.

Sources:

Books

Chopra, Deepak. *Ageless Body, Timeless Mind: The Quantum Alternative to Growing Old.* New York: Harmony Books, 1993.

Periodicals

Bromberg, Craig. "Doc of Ages: Deepak Chopra Offers a Fountain of Youth." *People Weekly,* November 15, 1993, pp. 169–170.
Mauro, James. "From Here and Now to Eternity: An Interview with Deepak Chopra." *Psychology Today,* November/December 1993, pp. 36–37.
Reynolds, Barbara. "Treat Whole Person, Not Just the Disease: An Interview with Deepak Chopra." *USA Today,* January 4, 1990.

—Sketch by Jim Henry

Christine Choy
(1954–)
Filmmaker

What began as a five-minute video to get support for a Chinese woman in Detroit seeking justice for the murder of her son evolved, five years later, into *Who Killed Vincent Chin?*, a full-length documentary that stunned the nation. On the eve of his wedding, Chin, a young American of Chinese descent was stalked and brutally beaten to death with a baseball bat by a man and and his stepson, two unemployed autoworkers who blamed the Japanese for the loss of their jobs and used Chin as a scapegoat because of his Asian features. The legal system failed Chin's survivors, as well as all American citizens, when his assailants received only probation and fines.

The film, nominated in 1989 for an Academy Award for best feature documentary, spotlighted the growing incidence of anti–Asian American violence throughout the United States. The film also brought into the limelight a team of talented Asian American women filmmakers, Christine Choy and Renee Tajima.

Who Killed Vincent Chin? is one of almost fifty films which Christine Choy has completed in her two-decade film career as producer, director, and cinematographer. She is, without question, a pioneer filmmaker, Asian American or otherwise, especially of documentaries. "I want to deal with real experiences, cultures and values, not usually addressed in the mainstream media. I want to do this with, and for, people who haven't often had their lives validated in films. Everyone has something important to say," Choy told Bianca Jagger (a former film student of Choy's) in *Interview* magazine in 1991.

In Search of the 'American Dream'

Born in Shanghai, China, on September 17, 1954 to a Korean father and a Mongolian mother, Christine Choy is a woman of many names. Her Chinese name was Tsui Ming Huei, while her Korean name was Che Myung Hae. She would later become Theresa Tsai, Chris Choy, Chai Ming Huei Christine Choy Siegel and finally Christine Choy. "I drive the frequent flyer programs crazy," she told Terry Hong with a laugh.

Choy's father, involved with the Korean independence movement against Japan, left China for Korea before Choy's birth. Choy's pregnant mother remained in Shanghai with Choy's older sister. The family would not be reunited with the father again until Choy was nine years old. "Since I didn't have my father, my mother's influence was quite a deal for me," Choy told *Interview*.

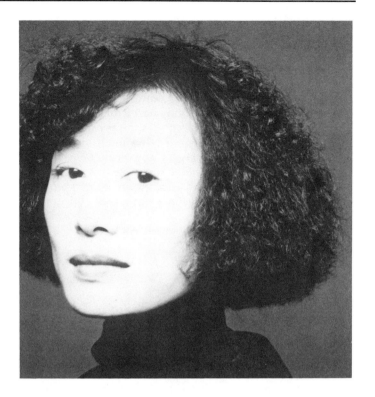

Christine Choy

Before the start of the 1965 Cultural Revolution, China experienced a large exodus among its foreign residents. Choy told Hong, "My mother wrote a letter to Chairman Mao and asked him for permission to leave so the family could be reunited." Granted permission, Choy left with her mother and sister for Hong Kong where they waited for a month for immigration papers into Korea. In 1962, the family was finally reunited in Seoul where Choy lived for four years. "The memories are not good ones," recalled Choy. "I remember the poverty. Korea was definitely third world. It was still recovering from the [Korean] War. The haves and have nots were very clear. American influences were everywhere—American GIs, American blue jeans, American gum, American movies. I felt that Korea was overly influenced by Americans. It seemed there were anti-American student demonstrations going on every other day. Nationalism hit hysteric proportions."

Unable to speak Korean, Choy went to a Chinese high school. "I was a foreigner again. Koreans did not accept me as Korean, and the Chinese knew my father was Korean, so they didn't quite accept me as Chinese. I learned both languages. It was an advantage, but at the time I felt pretty much alone," Choy told *Interview*.

Choy could not ignore the imported American pop culture, and she became hooked on American movies, with favorites that included John Wayne and *Gone With the Wind*. "I had a vision of America that everyone looked like Sandra Dee with Audrey Hepburn hair. Every family had two parents, two kids, two dogs, two cars. They always went to parties. I had no other references," said Choy. She even joined the Catholic Church because they sponsored Koreans going to the United States, especially students pursuing an American education. In 1967, at age fourteen, Choy arrived in New York City, alone, with only sixty dollars in her pocket. "I came in search of the American Dream that I had seen in the movies. I was on a full scholarship and I wanted to pursue studies in either space science or electrical engineering," Choy recalled to Hong. "I came to America being told I was a genius. I took the TOEFL [Test of English as a Foreign Language, required of foreign students for entrance into U.S. universities] and scored number two in all of Asia. Then upon arrival in the U.S., I went to the bottom of my class."

An American Education

Choy entered Manhattanville College of Sacred Heart in Purchase, New York, and was immediately renamed Theresa Tsai by the nuns. "Two terms later, I was told I was too dumb and that I had tuberculosis," Choy recalled. Chest x-rays that had been taken at the time of entry into the United States revealed a spot on Choy's lung. She was sent to Grasslands, a sanatorium hospital in Westchester County, New York. She told Hong: "That's where I realized that there are black people and Hispanic people in this country. We watched "I Love Lucy" and "General Hospital" all day. And I quickly became a TV addict."

Choy returned to Manhattanville where she eventually made a number of good friends with whom she still remains in contact. "But I still had no home, nowhere to go during the holidays. I used to work in the basement of the library mending books. I learned to smoke in that basement. The nuns didn't know what to do with me," she said with a laugh. In her second year, she was requested by the administration to transfer to another school. "My grades were too low. I told them I wanted to go to either Barnard or Columbia, even with those low grades, but I couldn't get in as a scholarship student." Instead, Choy was sent to Maryville College of Sacred Heart in Missouri. "I got all As and Bs in Missouri, but then I realized that I didn't want to be a scientist because I wanted to be an architect. I knew that would still please my parents—being an architect meant I could combine both art and science."

Choy applied and was accepted to the architecture program at Washington University in St. Louis. She quickly changed her name to Christine Choy. "I used only 'Chris' because I didn't want to necessarily be known as either male or female just through my name," she recalled. Washington University proved to be an affirming experience. "I really learned a lot there. I had this one professor who came up to me and said, 'Chris, you're very creative,' and that really gave me confidence. I had been a genius, then been put at the bottom level, and two and a half years later, someone was finally telling me that I was okay."

Choy did not stay in St. Louis very long. "I finished my B.S. and decided I didn't like Missouri anymore and applied to Princeton University. When I got there, I didn't have to go to any classes because with the protests going on against the bombings in Cambodia, everyone was too occupied and busy to study. We just protested," she remembered. Choy did not remain at Princeton very long, transferring to Columbia University in the urban planning department. "I wanted to be back in New York City. So many important organizations were starting up, especially in regard to Asian American issues and groups." While Choy was glad to be in New York, she was not satisfied with Columbia. "Going there was like a dream come true, but it just bored me to death. But I decided that I should at least finish the degree and then change my life."

While completing her master's in urban planning, Choy became involved with Newsreel, a film company she described to Hong as "anti-establishment, anti-Hollywood, anti-television, anti-movies, anti-intellectual." She began as an intern and "learned to make movies." Eventually, in 1974, Choy took over the organization and changed the name to Third World Newsreel, which she ran until 1983.

American Movies

Choy made her first film in 1974, called *Teach Our Children*. "I don't know where the negative is. It won a first prize, believe it or not, in the International Black Film Festival in Philadelphia. But I was told I could not go down to receive the prize because I was not black," she told *Interview*.

Over the next twenty-plus years, Choy has continued to make films on such controversial subjects as prison inmates, battered women, racial discrimination, drug addicts, and alcoholics. Her titles include *From Spikes to Spindles* (1976), *Inside Women Inside* (1978), *To Love, Honor, and Obey* (1980), *Bittersweet Survival* (1981), *Mississippi Triangle* (1982), *Namibia: Independence Now* (1984), *Permanent Wave* (1986), *Who Killed Vincent Chin?* (1989), *Monkey King Looks West* (1989), *The Best Hotel on Skid Row* (1990), *Homes Apart: The Two Koreas* (1991), *Jennifer's Jail* (1992), *Out in Silence* (1994), and *SA-I-GU* (1994).

"I like underdogs," she told *Interview*, regarding her subjects. "I like people who don't have a voice in the mass media. Like myself. Like many of us. Nobody cares about them, because they don't sell. They're not sexy enough." While Choy's subjects might not receive attention from the mass media, her films certainly do not go unnoticed. Critically acclaimed, Choy has been the recipient of numerous awards and fellowships, including a Peabody Award for Excellence in Broadcast Journalism, a Guggenheim Memorial Fellowship, a Mellon Fellowship, a Rockefeller Fellowship, and the American Film Institute's Woman's Director Fellowship.

While Choy has built a solid career in film, her life has not been without its difficult challenges. "I was on welfare from 1974 to 1978. I had two kids, no money, and working as a film editor while trying to make my own films. I was on unemployment. Eventually went through the entire welfare system," she recalled to Hong.

"I've also been busted twice," she said with a stifled laugh. "The first time, it was for jumping the New York subway turnstile when the fare went up. Everyone was doing it and I was the one that got caught. Then I got arrested for leafletting in front of a department store in New Jersey. I was told that it was a private sidewalk, so I was trespassing and then I was charged with resisting arrest. Both times, I spent the night in the precinct. I learned firsthand about the injustice and brutality inflicted by police and the lack of legal rights among common citizens." Not surprisingly, Choy's personal favorite among her own films is *Inside Women Inside*, a documentary about women in prison. "It's something I can really relate to—with women who are put in prison, who have no choice, who are faced with great shame. It's something I feel very close to."

In addition to filmmaking, Choy is also a teacher. "In 1988, I separated from my husband. *Vincent Chin* was taking so long to finish, and I just ran out of money. So I took a teaching job at Cornell University and commuted between New York City and Ithaca." After one term, Choy was offered a position at New York University's Tisch School of the Arts. Today, she is the chairperson of the graduate division of the Tisch School's Institute of Film and TV.

Bianca Jagger, former wife of Rolling Stone Mick Jagger, is one of Choy's former students. "By the time I came to be her pupil, I was having second thoughts about becoming a film director. But there is no turning back when you study with Christine Choy. She is an inspiration to all her students. For me it was not different. She was instrumental in helping me get my film project, *Nicaragua in Transition*, off the ground," wrote Jagger in the preface to her interview with Choy for *Interview*.

Teaching and nurturing potential filmmakers is certainly an important part of Choy's life, one she combines fluidly with her own filmmaking endeavors. She told *Interview*: "When I was in college, not a single . . . professor paid attention to me—with the exception of one, who died. Any creative work needs individual attention and encouragement. Each vision is different. Each student's personal experience is different. They need a separate, different guidance. In order to be a good professor, you must constantly update your own skills. That means you have to produce, you have to direct. . . . You have to be extremely knowledgeable. But the only way you become knowledgeable is by doing it, by practicing."

Practice and practicality aside, the most important advice Choy imparts to her students is emotional, as she told *Interview*. "Feel it! *Feel! Feel* feelings. Sadness, happiness, regrets. If you can feel how you live, you're able to understand what others are feeling."

Sources:

Periodicals

Jagger, Bianca. "Christine Choy," *Interview,* January 1991.

"Video Justice," *Esquire,* November 23, 1989.

Other

Choy, Christine, telephone interview with Terry Hong, July 29, 1994.

—Sketch by Terry Hong

Herbert Choy
(1916–)
Judge

Herbert Choy became the first Asian Pacific American to be named to a federal court when President Richard Nixon appointed him in 1971 to the U.S. Court of Appeals for the Ninth Circuit. This achievement is only one of many accomplishments that have marked a trailblazing career that started when he became the first lawyer of Korean descent to practice law in the United States.

Born in Kauai, Hawaii, the second of four children born to Korean immigrant parents, Herbert Choy was five when he and his family relocated to Honolulu. His father, Doo Wok Choy, a tailor, made the move so that he could pursue military contracts for uniforms. The elder Choy became the biggest military uniform supplier in Hawaii. Many prominent servicemen wore his uniforms, which were known as "Choy Tailor Mades."

Early Inspiration

Choy's interest in law took root when as a youngster, he observed a neighbor who was a lawyer at work. "I noticed my father going to seek advice from him, in connection with his business. I thought it was a wonderful way to serve people." Choy was shy and slightly introverted, however, and while his parents thought he would make a better doctor than a lawyer, they didn't discourage him. Instead, they emphasized the importance of education in general. "From the time I could understand language, they drummed that message into us," says Choy.

Choy attended grammar school at the Royal School, which once specialized in training the children of Hawaiian royalty for their future careers as leaders of the Hawaiian

Herbert Choy

kingdom. There he developed such a passion for reading his mother tried to encourage him to pursue other activities because he was such a bookworm. During his high school years he worked part time at the public library, but by then he had joined the Boy Scouts and had become interested in camping, hiking, and other sports that served to balance his enthusiasm for reading. Choy would later discover surfing, which became a lifetime passion until a serious accident forced him to give it up at age fifty-three.

Important Advice

Choy graduated from high school in 1934 and enrolled at the University of Hawaii. While at the university, Choy met up with Walter Short, the college's placement director and a family friend. When Choy was seeking a summer job to help pay for his schooling, Short offered some advice that Choy believes eventually helped him to succeed in his career. "He knew I wanted to be lawyer, and because of my shy nature, he said that I would have to learn how to stand up and talk and be understood," Choy said. So he joined the college debating team, the theater guild, and took singing lessons all in an effort to cultivate the verbal skills he would need as lawyer.

Choy went on to earn a law degree from Harvard, where he said he had to work extra hard to compete against many brilliant students who came from poor families and who were highly motivated. After graduating from law school in 1941, his legal ambitions were interrupted by

war. Choy entered the army shortly after Pearl Harbor, and was sent to the School of Military Government in Charlottesville, Virginia. There he met Helen Shular, a high school teacher, who became his wife in 1944.

Choy began his law career in 1946 after he returned from the service. He joined one of the first multiracial firms in the country, Fong and Miho, where he was made a partner in just six months. As a general practice lawyer, Choy handled thousands of cases ranging from criminal defense to corporate cases involving trusts and partnerships.

He left the practice in 1957 to serve as Attorney General of the Territory of Hawaii. After only one year in the post, however, Choy returned to his law firm at the prompting of his former law partner Hiram Fong, who wanted him back to handle an overflow of cases. Fong became a U.S. Senator when Hawaii achieved statehood and later played a key role in Choy's nomination to the court of appeals.

Court Career

Of his appointment to the court, Choy said: "It was a great honor to the first Asian federal judge, but it does not make me feel special. I feel a great responsibility to make a good judicial record for the sake of future judges of Asian ancestry, my state, and my family." In 1984, Choy was named senior judge of the court of appeals.

During his time on the court, Choy has taken a special interest in cases involving American Indian treaties, land, and fishing rights. "I think it is because I am of a minority group. American Indians were the former owners of all the land in our country. When what little they have left is encroached upon by others, naturally I have a great deal of sympathy for them." Choy made his sympathies clear in *Kale v. United States*, a case involving a soldier's homestead rights in conflict with Indian allotment rights. Although Choy and his colleagues ruled in favor of the Indians, their decision was appealed and later reversed.

Choy said he relies on his strong Christian faith as a powerful guiding force in his life. Raised as a Methodist, Choy described himself as a "nominal" Christian until 1976, when he and his wife attended a faith healing session in Waikiki led by the Reverend Joe Popell. Helen was suffering excruciating back pain as the result of a crushed disc, from which she had found no medical relief. She was invited to pray with Popell and the pain disappeared. Choy said that she "felt an inner peace she had never felt before."

The Choys have no children of their own, but have "adopted" dozens of law clerks that have served the judge over the years. "We have forty-eight children and twenty grandchildren. We keep in touch, and every five years we have a reunion."

Sources:

Periodicals

Kobayashi, Ken. "Herbert Choy, Hawaii's most retiring judge, retires." *Sunday Star-Bulletin & Advertiser*, December 16, 1984.
"Profile." *Los Angeles Daily Journal*, June 6, 1983.

Other

Choy, Herbert. Biographical information. January 1994.
———. telephone interview with Grace Wong, February 1994.

—*Sketch by Grace Wong*

Connie Chung
(1946–)
Television journalist

On June 1, 1993, Connie Chung became the co-anchor of the "CBS Evening News." She became the first Asian and only the second woman ever to be named to the coveted post of nightly news anchor at a major network, traditionally thought of as the pinnacle of broadcast journalism. In addition to her role as co-anchor, Chung hosts "Eye to Eye with Connie Chung," a popular prime-time television news magazine that highlights interviews with controversial newsmakers, a specialty of Chung's. She has become one of the most recognizable personalities in American culture, and one of the most sought-after and highly-paid broadcasters in contemporary media.

Constance Yu-hwa Chung was born on August 20, 1946, in suburban Washington, D.C., to Margaret Ma and William Ling Chung. Her father had been an intelligence officer in China's Nationalist Army who fled his war-torn homeland for the United States in 1944. Before the family left, five of his children, including all of his sons, were lost in the bloodshed. In 1946 Margaret gave birth to her tenth child, Connie, the only member of the family to be born in the United States. Male children are highly prized in traditional Chinese culture, and William was devastated that his wife had not given birth to a boy. The young Chung sensed her father's disappointment and partly attributes her aggressive drive for success to an innate desire to make up for being born female.

Chung earned a degree in journalism from the University of Maryland in 1969. Her first job was with WTTG-TV, an independent television station in the nation's capital.

She worked for a time as a copy person and as a secretary, waiting for an opportunity to advance to the news division. When a position opened up Chung was denied it on the grounds that she was essential where she was. Unwilling to accept this, she found a replacement for herself and reapplied, this time getting the job. She was made an assignment editor and then, in 1971, an on-the-air reporter.

Her first assignments were typical local news fare. She covered fires, murders, and airplane disasters. Later that year she secured a job at CBS's Washington bureau, aided in part by the Federal Communications Commission's timely mandate for stations to hire more minorities. In her early years with CBS, Chung covered stories such as the 1972 presidential campaign of George McGovern, anti-Vietnam War protests, and the presidency of Richard M. Nixon. In this capacity she traveled with the president to the Middle East and the Soviet Union. She did not, however, accompany him to China, although she used her fluency in Chinese to help in the preparation of stories related to this historic event.

Chung distinguished herself at CBS for her tenacity and aggressiveness in pursuing stories. When members of Nixon's reelection committee were arrested for illegal activities in 1972, marking the beginning of the Watergate scandal, she was only twenty-five. She threw herself into the story, hounding principal players in a way that was at the time unique. Reflecting on those days almost twenty years later for *Redbook* magazine, Chung said, "To me, Watergate was the story of the decade. It was the unraveling of the presidency, a textbook course in responsible reporting and a lesson in truth." She says she still vividly recalls those monumental days, especially the day "the House Judiciary Committee voted on the articles of impeachment. I can still hear the whispered 'yeas' and 'nays' and feel the tension." She has kept as mementos her press pass and all her notes.

Reporter to Anchor

In 1976 Chung moved to Los Angeles to become an anchor at the local CBS affiliate, KNXT (now KCBS). She began hosting three news broadcasts a day, and the station went from third to second place in ratings. In response her salary increased drastically and by 1983 she had become the highest paid local anchor in the country, receiving an estimated $600,000 annually. She also was the recipient of several honors, including local Emmy Awards in 1978 and 1980 and a citation from the Los Angeles Press Club for outstanding television reporting.

In the early eighties Chung began looking into a return to national reporting. She especially wanted to be in on the coverage of the approaching 1984 presidential election. In 1983 she took a drastic pay cut and moved to NBC where she worked as a correspondent and anchored shows such as the Saturday edition of "The NBC Nightly News," "NBC News at Sunrise," "NBC Digests," and several

Connie Chung

prime-time news specials. She also served as political analysis correspondent for the network.

Chung covered both major party conventions in 1984 and served as podium correspondent during the 1988 presidential campaign and political conventions. Her work at NBC catapulted Chung to celebrity status. She was seen as pleasant, warm, and engaging by television audiences who look for such characteristics in anchors. She began substituting for Jane Pauley on NBC's "Today Show" and in 1985 was named chief correspondent for NBC's fourteenth attempt at creating a prime-time news magazine. The show, "American Almanac" was co-hosted by longtime NBC anchor and correspondent Roger Mudd. Like all its predecessors at NBC, the show failed.

In 1986 Chung negotiated a new contract with NBC that allowed her to give up her duties at "NBC News at Sunrise" and called for her to sit in for Tom Brokaw on "The NBC Nightly News," her first stint on the prestigious network evening news. She was also given a new news magazine to anchor, "1986." This show failed quickly and Chung began working on a series of one-hour documentaries broadcast in prime time by NBC in the late eighties. These included "Life in the Fat Lane," an account of obesity and the national obsession with thinness; "Scared Sexless," a look at sexuality in the age of AIDS; "Stressed to Kill," an examination of the physical aspects of work-related stress; "Everybody's Doing It," a sometimes light-hearted look at aging; and "Guns, Guns, Guns," a report

on the massive amount of guns and their easy accessibility in the United States.

Return to CBS

In 1989 Chung announced that she would leave NBC for CBS when her current contract expired. The move, which had been preceded by a substantial bidding war for her services, ended months of speculation about where she would go. Her contract with CBS was reported to be worth $1.5 million annually. Her initial duties at CBS included hosting "West 57th," "The CBS Sunday Night News," and serving as the principal replacement for Dan Rather on "The CBS Evening News." After the failure of "West 57th" Chung began hosting "Saturday Night with Connie Chung," a one-hour news magazine CBS launched in 1989. The show was the first network news program to include dramatic recreations of news events, a staple of tabloid television, and was widely criticized for doing so. Some critics, however, believed that the format made for excellent television, although it lacked what is traditionally regarded as journalistic integrity. The show has since been canceled.

In the winter of 1991 Chung served as rotating anchor and contributing correspondent to CBS's coverage of the Persian Gulf War. In 1992 she co-anchored with Rather, "America on the Line," an experiment with interactive television which broadcasted viewer response to then-president George Bush's 1992 State of the Union address. And in 1993, she joined Rather as co-anchor of the "CBS Evening News," and was once again named anchor of a prime-time news magazine, "Eye to Eye with Connie Chung."

Controversial Promotion

CBS's decision to put Chung opposite Rather has been widely commented upon in the media. Critics of the move say it demeans the institution of network evening news broadcasts, while supporters argue that it elevates minorities and women to a traditionally male domain. As has been the case throughout her career, Chung has had very vocal detractors and supporters. And she has found some of the harsher criticisms painful. Recounting a story she did on the dangers of cosmetic silicone breast implants in women, Chung told *A. Magazine,* "FDA chairman David Kessler told me that he moved on the issue because of our story." She feels that her record as a journalist should stand on its own and she shouldn't have to defend her manner and professional disposition, which some critics have regarded as too fluffy and informal for serious consideration.

Awards

Chung has received numerous accolades for her work, including three National Emmy Awards (two of them for best interview/interviewer), a Peabody, a 1991 Ohio State Award, a 1991 National Headliner Award, two American Women in Radio and Television National Commendations, a 1991 Clarion Award, and in 1990 she was chosen as favorite interviewer by *U.S. News and World Report* in their annual "Best of America" survey.

On December 2, 1984, Chung married television journalist Maury Povich, then the host of Fox Television's tabloid program, "A Current Affair." In 1993 Povich began hosting "The Maury Povich Show," a syndicated day-time television talk show.

Sources:

Anderson, Kurt. "Does Connie Chung Matter?" *Time,* May 31, 1993.
Romano, Lois. "Stories that Changed their Lives. Connie Chung, Witness to Truth." *Redbook,* October 1991.
Yang, Jeff and Betty Wong. "Power Brokers." *A. Magazine,* December 15, 1993, pp/ 25–34.

—Sketch by Jim Henry

Eugene Y. Chung

Eugene Y. Chung
(1969–)
Football player

When Eugene Chung was growing up, he often wondered where the Asian athletes were when he turned on the television to watch professional sports. "How come there are no Korean guys playing basketball? How come they're not out there slamming the ball in the basket and tearing the rim down? How come they're not playing pro baseball and hitting that home run? What's going on with that?" Chung questioned. He saw African American, Hispanic, and Caucasian players, but not a single Asian face. It was not surprising since only two other Asian Americans had played professional football. When Chung joined the New England Patriots in 1992, he became the third Asian American and second Korean American to play professional football in the United States. An all-American player in college, Chung was also the first Asian American drafted in the first round.

Born Eugene Yon Chung on June 14, 1969, in Prince George's County, Maryland, Chung grew up in Northern Virginia, just outside of Washington, D.C. His father, Choon Chung, came to the United States in 1956, completely alone. A man of great ambition, the older Chung studied public administration at City College of New York, political science at Columbia University, and law at Yale University. He settled in the Washington area where he worked primarily as an attorney. Choon Chung taught his three sons that there were no limitations in life. "I told

them that this is their country," Choon said, "I told them they can do whatever they want to do. America is free."

Breaking Stereotypes

The young Chung took his father's words to heart. Athletic as a child, Chung was always trying to break the stereotype about Asians and athletic ability: "You always have your stereotypes about Asians. People say they're always small, they can't play sports, and if they do, it's tennis or golf or something like that," he said. At 6-foot-5 and 295 pounds, Chung is anything but small. His grizzly bear strength combined with superior agility from years of judo training make him an incredible athlete. And, at Oakton High School in Oakton, Virginia, Chung was an all-around athlete who never played tennis or golf. Instead, he began his football career and was selected All-District and All-Region after recording eighty-six tackles, eight sacks, and six fumble recoveries. He earned three letters in both football and track. He also competed in judo, winning the Virginia State Judo Championship in 1990.

As a freshman at Virginia Tech, Chung broke into the starting lineup seven games into the season. At the end of the 1990 season, he was voted the Best Offensive Lineman and was the only lineman to start every game. By the end of his college career, he was selected first team All-American and All-Big East. In the tiny college town of Blacksburg, Chung did not feel he was ever a target of racism: "I really didn't get hassled at all being a Korean here. I faced more prejudice being an athlete. There's that stereotype of a football player here. People think athletes get everything paid for, that [athletes] get [good]grades given to them; they get this, they get that. None of that's true. I just wish I could take a few people to class with me and show them what I go through. I'm sure they'd change their minds."

As Virginia Tech's most famous athlete since Buffalo Bills Pro Bowl defensive end Bruce Smith, Chung headed the National Football League (NFL) with a goal: "I think by having a chance to play in the NFL it's going to do a lot for the Korean community. I'd like to be somewhat of a spokesperson for that. Playing in the NFL, you're going to be in the limelight. I think by doing this it will let the people know back in Korea and in the United States to be aware that we are able to do this. We're not a meek people. The Korean American kids should know that Asians can do more than play Ping-Pong."

The Professional Experience

In 1992, Chung became the first Asian American drafted in the first round and the third Asian American to play in the NFL. However, his experience as an Asian American professional athlete is very different from his predecessors. The first Asian American, Walter Aichu, a 150-pound running back drop kicker for the Dayton Triangles in the 1927 and 1928 seasons, was listed in the player sheets as "Hawaiian–American–Caucasian." The all-encompassing label allowed Aichu to eat and travel with the team during a time of racial segregation. Korean American John Lee, a former kicker for the St. Louis Cardinals and Los Angeles Raiders who was selected in the second round of the 1986 National Football League draft, succumbed to rookie pressures and left the professional circuit after only two seasons. One of the most prolific kickers in NCAA history, he set a collegiate record for consistency in field goal attempts.

Considered a critical acquisition for the New England Patriots, Chung's rookie year began with professional difficulties and personal tragedy. By the opening of training camp in 1992, Chung had not agreed on a contract. The dispute gave him a late start. Just after he finally arrived in camp, Chung's father died. Losing his father was difficult for Chung who explained, "He wasn't just my father, he was my best friend."

Chung tried to continue training, but his late start took its toll. Bothered by nagging injuries, he was bounced to different positions on the line. During his rookie year, he played four different spots. For each new spot, he had to learn new moves and strategies. The year proved dismal not only for Chung but the rest of the team with a 2–14 season.

Things finally began turning around for Chung in 1993. Mending through both his physical and emotional injuries, Chung played with all the promise of a first-draft choice. Finally anchored in his position as right guard, he looked back at his first year as a true learning experience: "If anyone has to go through a situation like that, they're going to be a stronger person and they just gain from that year of experience and they know how to handle things as they come. I can say yes, it made me a stronger person."

Sources:

Periodicals:

Conroy, Steve. "Chung Strong on Rebound." *Boston Herald,* September 25, 1993.
Freeman, Mike. "For Chung, NFL Dream Has Special Glow." *The Washington Post,* April 15, 1992, pp. D1, D3.
Mannix, Kevin. "Pats Pick Their Spots." *Boston Herald,* April 27, 1992, Back Page and p. 74.
———."Vote of Confidence for Chung." *Boston Herald,* August 20, 1992.
May, Peter. "Chung is Starting to Feel Comfortable." *Boston Globe,* October 22, 1992.
Price, Terry. "Chung Now Ready to Give Pats His All." *Attleboro Sun Chronicle,* August 18, 1993, pp. 29, 32.

—Sketch by Terry Hong

Lilia C. Clemente
(1941–)
Business executive

Who is a little under five feet tall, manages approximately $450 million, and is a staunch believer in global investing? The answer is Lilia Clemente, chairperson, CEO, and founder of Clemente Capital, Inc. (CCI), a Wall Street investment company. The firm currently manages the First Philippine Fund and Clemente Global Growth Fund—two closed-end funds listed on the New York Stock Exchange—and the Clemente Korea Emerging Growth Fund listed on the London Stock Exchange. The secret of Clemente's success, as she so simply puts it, is the three G's: God, genes, and grunt work. This and good connections would explain the current success of the three funds. The Global Fund netted $54,920,000 since 1987, the First Philippine Fund has 8.98 million outstanding shares, and the Korea Emerging Growth Fund's NAV was up 21.48 percent during 1993.

An Iron Butterfly

Clemente is a busy woman, and has been described as an "iron butterfly"—a feminist who uses charm rather than abrasiveness to accomplish her goals. Another apt label for Clemente has been "Wonder Woman of Wall Street" because of the breakneck pace at which she works. Besides running the New York–based firm, she spends ten weeks a year looking for international investment opportunities and meeting with government officials, such as former Philippine president Corazon Aquino, with whom Clemente is friendly. Clemente is also chairperson of the Manila-based Asian Securities Industry Institute, which organizes region-wide research and training activities for professionals in the Asian securities industry, and of the Washington-based Philippine American Foundation. Critics would even find it hard to believe that the woman they sometimes call the "Philippine Tigress" started out with little more than her family background when she first came to America at age nineteen to study at the University of Chicago.

God, Genes, and Grunt Work

Lilia Clemente was born in Manila, Philippines, on February 21, 1941. An avowed feminist, Clemente must have gotten her strong will from her successful and headstrong parents, especially her mother. Her father, Jose Calderon, was a prominent Filipino lawyer who served on the boards of large mining companies and helped frame the 1973 and 1987 constitutions. He also served time in prison for opposing the policies of Ferdinand Marcos, then president of the Philippines. Clemente's mother, Belen Farbos Calderon, taught psychology at the University of Philippines, served as governor of Luzon province, became the first woman to hold a seat on the Manila Stock Exchange, and managed to have seven children as well. Clemente was the oldest and remembers thinking that women only had two career choices in life: business or politics. Even as a child Clemente was interested in finance. She recalled, "When I turned ten years old, my father said, 'Do you want a party with balloons and cake or do you want stock?' I picked stock." Clemente has always been known to take risks and try what is different, which may explain why her favorite memento is a framed quotation from a Robert Frost poem that hangs in her New York office: "Two roads diverged in a wood, and I— / I took the one less traveled by, / And that has made all the difference."

The Journey to America

Clemente left the Philippines in 1960 to attend the University of Chicago, where she earned a master's in economics and a doctorate. "I was like an orchid in a hothouse," she said of her pampered, early years in the Philippines. "Then I got to the jungle of Chicago." She was unique because she saw emerging foreign markets as having profit potential before most people saw it. "These days you hear a lot about globalization," she says. "I started thinking globally in 1969." That was the year the 28-year-old economist was hired by the Ford Foundation. Clemente was their first female investment manager and successfully moved $150 million of the $3 billion portfolio

Lilia C. Clemente

into investments overseas. There she became familiar with the Japanese market.

In 1976, at the age of thirty-five, Clemente rented offices on Park Avenue and started playing with $25,000 of her own capital. Clemente Capital started out very modestly, with one secretary and some secondhand furniture. An astute businesswoman, Clemente was determined to succeed on her own terms. "In business, they say a woman should think like a man, act like a lady, and work like a dog," Clemente asserted. "If I followed this advice, I would have ended up like some kind of mythical figure, with a man's head, a woman's torso, and a dog's feet. I said, 'I'd rather be myself, right!'"

The Start of Success

One of Clemente Capital's first successes was the launching of a mutual fund for Mitchell Hutchins Asset Management, a division of Wall Street's Paine Webber. By 1985 the Paine Webber Atlas Fund was top in the global funds, that year netting 66 percent of capital. In 1989, the firm launched two closed-ends funds. The first, Clemente Global Growth, invests in small- and medium-sized companies in the United States, Japan, and Germany and in blue chips in the Philippines, Thailand, and Mexico. The second, the $100 million First Philippine Fund, was created on the eve of 1989's coup attempt against the Aquino government. Clemente's sharp planning kept most of the fund in U.S. Treasury bonds, and its loss as a result of the government unrest was a minor 13 percent.

Clemente has earned respect as an intelligent risk taker and a global visionary in the investment world. In late 1992 she launched the Cathay Clemente (Holdings) LTD fund, which invests in new Chinese companies. She also established an office of the Asian Securities Institute in Beijing. Fu Fengxiang, chairman of Beijing's Securities Exchange Executive Council, is chairman of the Institute's board.

According to CCI Managing Director Thomas J. Prapas, Clemente's vision is powerful. "She has a particular ability for spotting the emerging markets—and she knows what she is talking about because she is from a developing country." Yet, almost paradoxically, Clemente views future trends with an eye toward the past. "I believe the faster the rate of change in the world, the more we need to have a firm grasp of our roots—not to cling to them but to assure continuity of things worth bringing into the future."

Besides the three major funds the firm currently runs are dozens of other bookings that have included the Tucker Anthony-sponsored Freedom Global Fund and Freedom Global Income Plus Fund, and the Sentinel Global Fund sponsored by a group of Canadian brokerage firms. One of their biggest clients was American Family Life Assurance of Columbus, Georgia, where Clemente managed about $1.6 billion of the company's Japanese reserves on a nondiscretionary basis. The investment income has risen at a rate of 25 percent.

Connections, Connections, Connections

The secret of Clemente's success is her ability to connect with people. Simply put, she's a people person. Her husband Leopoldo is the firm's managing director and chief investment officer. He and Clemente married in Manila before he received a master's in business administration from Northwestern University. The husband and wife team have been described as fire and ice—one an introvert and the other an extrovert, but both sharp business people. "The stuff Leo likes to do, I'm not so fond of," Clemente says. "He enjoys solitary pursuits like fishing. I am much more relationship-oriented, building up the networks, getting to know people."

A Butterfly in a World of Sharks

The husband and wife team have no children and have set up a fund to put promising Filipinos through college. Clemente has also written an autobiography entitled *Growing Up In World Street* published in 1990 by Japanese publisher Shufonotomo. Clemente Capital has come a long way from the modest office with one secretary and second-hand furniture. Clemente now oversees a staff representing ten countries and speaking eighteen languages. She remains an "iron butterfly" in a world of challenges as well as great opportunities.

Sources:

Periodicals

"Filipino First." *Asia, Inc.*, April 1993, p. 74.

Kraar, Louis. "Iron Butterflies." *Fortune* Special Report, 1991.

"Lilia Clemente: No Innocent Abroad." *Money*, January 1986.

MacDonald, Lawrence. "Philippine Fund Manager Builds Networks." *The Asian Wall Street Journal*, August 8, 1991.

———. "A Philippine Fund Manager's Recipe: Blend Connections With Global Outlook." *The Wall Street Journal*, August 16, 1991.

Maher, Tani. "Philippine Tigress." *Financial World*, September 6, 1988.

Phalon, Richard. "Family Portfolio." *Forbes*, September 7, 1987.

———. "The Japanese Connection." *Forbes*, April 3, 1989.

Platt, Adam. "Clemente Connects." *Global Custodian*, December 1992, p. 28.

"Wonder Woman of Wall Street." *Asiaweek*, August 10, 1990. p. 58.

Xiu, Li Ling. "Clemente's China Coup." *Window*, December 18, 1992, pp. 10–11.

Other

Clemente Capital, Inc. Fact sheets, biographical information. January 1994.

—Sketch by Amy Wu

D

Victoria Manolo Draves
(1924–)
Olympic diver

Vicki Manolo Draves is a former national champion diver and the winner of two Olympic gold medals. In the 1948 Olympic Games she became the first woman to win gold medals in both the ten-meter platform and three-meter springboard events. After her Olympic victory she performed in aquacades in Minnesota and Chicago and then toured Europe in an exhibition show with Buster Crabbe, the great Olympic swimmer and Hollywood film star.

Victoria Manolo was born on December 31, 1924, in San Francisco, California. Both her parents were immigrants, her father from the Philippines and her mother from England. While a student in high school, Manolo became interested in diving and swimming and used to practice in downtown San Francisco at the Fairmount Hotel and at the Crystal Bath Plunge, both of which had public pools with diving boards. Manolo was already a gifted diver and she caught the attention of Phil Patterson, a well-known coach of an amateur swimming and diving team.

After graduating from high school in 1938, Manolo briefly attended San Francisco State Junior College, but ultimately withdrew when World War II broke out. She then began competing in earnest on the amateur diving circuit. In 1941 Jack Lavery, who was associated with the Fairmount Swim Club, took an interest in Manolo (who was forced to compete under the name Taylor, her mother's maiden name, in an effort to disguise her Filipino heritage). Lavery sent a picture of her to Sammy Lee, then one of the finest divers in America. Lee saw in the picture that Manolo had a lot of potential and became interested in her career.

Sammy Lee as Mentor

In 1943 Lee, who by that time had become a national diving champion, saw Manolo compete for the first time. He told Jim Henry in an interview that he was stunned by

Victoria Manolo Draves

her natural abilities, especially the way she naturally straightened her back just prior to hitting the water—something Lee described as normally requiring a great deal of coaching. After watching her dive, Lee introduced himself and told her that she would become a champion diver.

Manolo's first national competition was in 1944 at the national championships in Shakemack, Indiana. That year's competition was fierce, and Manolo Draves placed in the top four in her two events, the ten-meter platform and the three-meter springboard. The following year Manolo continued diving at the same level of competition, and Lee, again taking an interest in her career, told her that she should consider finding a better, more consistent coach. He suggested Lyle Draves, who was coaching some of the world's best divers at that time at the Athens Swim Club in Oakland, California. In 1945 Manolo began working with Draves and at that year's national championships placed in the top four again.

In 1946 Manolo and Draves were married and at that year's national championships she won the ten-meter platform competition, her first national championship and the first time she had beat out her arch rival, Zoen Olsen.

A First for Women Olympians

In 1948 Manolo Draves qualified for the Olympics but just barely. At the qualifying meet she lost again to Olsen in both her events, but scored high enough to go to the Olympics. Lee told Henry that at that year's Olympics the rivalry between Olsen and Manolo Draves heated up when, over dinner prior to the competition, Olsen vowed to win the gold in both events. Lee said this spurred Manolo Draves on, and she won gold medals in both events, becoming the first woman to win both diving events at the same Olympics.

Manolo Draves was the darling of the 1948 Olympics, and when she returned to the United States, she was treated like a celebrity. There was talk of a movie career and in 1949 she was invited to the Philippines to be honored. She then appeared around the country in various aquacades and exhibitions. In 1952 she went to Europe and performed with Buster Crabbe's traveling aquacade.

Manolo Draves dropped out of international competition after the Olympics, however, and she and Lyle began raising their family of four children. She has been inducted into the International Swimming Hall of Fame in Fort Lauderdale, Florida.

Sources:

Lee, Sammy, telephone interview with Jim Henry, August 6, 1994.

Sessions (Manolo), Connie, telephone interview with Jim Henry August 1, 1994.

—*Sketch by Jim Henry*

Dinesh D'Souza
(1961–)
Author

Dinesh D'Souza first came to national prominence in 1987, at the age of twenty-six, when he was appointed to a position in the Reagan White House as an assistant to domestic policy chief Gary Bauer. In 1991 he published *Illiberal Education: The Politics of Race and Sex on Campus*, a critique of what he argued was the academically stifling atmosphere permeating political and artistic life on some of the major university campuses in the country. The book

became an instant sensation in academic and political circles, and catapulted the young man to national fame—even a sort of cult status in certain circles.

Dinesh D'Souza was born on April 25, 1961, in Bombay, India, into a family of Catholics, a minority religion in India. His father was an executive at Johnson and Johnson Pharmaceuticals, and his mother worked in the home. Dinesh was educated in private Jesuit schools that stressed a traditional, heavily Western, mostly British curriculum. In 1978, Dinesh came to the United States for his final year of high school. The trip was funded by the Rotary Club, and he spent a year living in Patagonia, a small town on the Mexico-Arizona border. As he told Charles Trueheart of the *Washington Post* in 1991, "It was like going back to eighth grade academically speaking, but I was really there for something different." What he came for was exposure to another culture.

The *Dartmouth Review*

D'Souza was expecting to return to India for college but he was persuaded to stay in the United States by a guidance counselor at the local high school. He enrolled at Dartmouth in 1979, where he immediately immersed himself in student activities such as writing for the campus newspaper, working with the international students association, and serving on the campus energy conservation committee. In his junior year, he began working on the *Dartmouth Review,* a newspaper not affiliated with the college, which opposed what its editors declared was the mindless liberalism exhibited in nearly all campus affairs, classrooms, and publications. The newspaper gained national attention for its sometimes outrageous editorials and its perceived insensitivity to minorities, whose presence on Ivy League campuses, the editors argued, was due to affirmative action and not to the academic credentials of the students, a situation they believed ran counter to the idea of schools for the intellectually elite. D'Souza became the *Review*'s third editor.

Although D'Souza insists that he brought a moderating influence to the *Review,* it was during his editorship that a controversial editorial known as the jive column was published. Written in a satire of African American dialect, the editorial took a position against affirmative action and caused such controversy that some of the paper's wealthy supporters—Dartmouth alumni sympathetic to the editor's right leanings—distanced themselves from it. D'Souza told Trueheart that it was "a satirical misfire, but I don't think its objective was racist."

A Writing Life

D'Souza graduated from Dartmouth in 1983 with a bachelor of arts degree. He then moved to Princeton, New Jersey, to become editor of *Prospect*, a magazine published by Princeton alumni. He also began contributing articles to magazines such as *National Review* and *Policy*

Dinesh D'Souza

Review, two conservative political journals closely allied ideologically with President Ronald Reagan and his conservative agenda.

In 1984 D'Souza published his first book, *Falwell: Before the Millennium,* a critical biography of Jerry Falwell, evangelist and political activist founder of the Moral Majority, a conservative movement dedicated to convincing morally conservative voters to support like-minded candidates. The book was widely criticized, even on the right, for not presenting a balanced view of Falwell. Writing in the *New York Times,* Marty Zupan asserted that "D'Souza might object that he is careful to note Falwell's failings. Indeed he does, and then he generally excuses them. . . . Meanwhile, Falwell's controversial positions are not discussed."

Two books followed in the next three years, during which time he had also moved to Washington, D.C., to work as an editor with the Heritage Foundation's journal, *Policy Review.* In 1986 he published *The Catholic Classics,* a two-volume series of interpretive essays on the ideas and writings of the great Catholic thinkers throughout time. And in 1987 he collaborated with Gregory Fossedal, a friend from Dartmouth, on the novel *My Dear Alex: Letters from the KGB,* a recasting of the C.S. Lewis novel *The Screwtape Letters,* a classic Catholic parable of evil's influence in the world.

Also in 1987, D'Souza took a job in the Reagan administration. His first position was as assistant to domestic pol-

icy chief Gary Bauer, where he distilled Reagan domestic policy for the Congress and the press. He described to Trueheart his job during the Bush-Quayle election campaign in 1988 as "director of Catholic votes." After the Republicans won, D'Souza met with President George Bush's chief of staff about the possibility of serving in the new administration. He told Trueheart: "There was a kind of obscene manhunt for minorities in the new administration, and I didn't want to go that route. I became quickly bored with debates on whether to appropriate an additional $38 million for Title X programs. I could not rouse much enthusiasm for this."

Illiberal Education

In 1991 D'Souza published *Illiberal Education: The Politics of Race and Sex on Campus.* Described by Diane Ravitch in the *Wall Street Journal* as a "conservative critique of the liberal policies of the past generation," the book became a bestseller and fueled ongoing national debates about political correctness, the role of the university in society, and the relevance of traditional studies in Western history, art, and literature in what is increasingly referred to as a multicultural society. D'Souza takes conservative positions on all these issues, arguing especially for the importance of retaining a core curriculum grounded in the Western tradition as the best way to educate students.

The fame D'Souza achieved with the success of his book made him a much-demanded lecturer and contributor to the nation's more prestigious op-ed pages. He has written extensively for the *Wall Street Journal,* the *New York Times,* the *Los Angeles Times,* the *Boston Globe,* and the *Washington Post.*

D'Souza told Trueheart that he intends to devote the coming years to figuring out "how, in an increasingly diverse society, fair rules can be established to arbitrate differences between majorities and minorities, immigrants and natives." Describing his own experiences as an immigrant citizen, he said, "Most stories of immigrants are: 'I came in rags, and now I employ hundreds.' Mine was an uncomfortable search for a congruence of values and principles. Was I really at home in the American system as constructed? I concluded ultimately that I was."

Sources:

Ravitch, Diane. "Race and Sex on Campus," *Wall Street Journal,* March 28, 1991.

Trueheart, Charles. "Big Man Off Campus, Author Dinesh D'Souza, Leading the Politically Incorrect Crusade." *Washington Post,* April 16, 1991, pp. B1, B4.

Zupan, Marty. Review of *Fallwell: Before the Millennium. New York Times Book Review,* December 30, 1984.

—Sketch by Jim Henry

E

Phoebe Eng
(1961–)
Publisher, attorney

In 1992 Phoebe Eng joined *A. Magazine* as publisher. *A. Magazine* is a quarterly national consumer magazine targeted at the Asian population in the United States. Eng serves as publisher and, until summer 1994, was chairman of the board of Metro East Publications, the company that owns and operates *A. Magazine*. Prior to joining the magazine at the age of thirty-two, Eng was a corporate and securities attorney with the international law firm of Coudert Brothers, based in New York City and Paris.

Phoebe Eng was born in Philadelphia, Pennsylvania, in 1961. Her father, an architect, had roots in Hong Kong, and her mother, a nursing supervisor, had roots in Taiwan. Both are second-generation immigrants. The family later moved to Brooklyn and then to Long Island, where Eng went to high school. In an interview with Jim Henry, Eng described her parents as typical Asian parents in that they encouraged her to succeed, to set her sights high, to take chances, and to speak up. She also had and continues to have the support of her sister, whom she describes as her best friend and confidante. For inspiration she looked to heroes like Eleanor Roosevelt; she admired what she saw as Roosevelt's spunk, creativity, and courage. She also cites as inspiring a number of Asian women attorneys she met in early adulthood.

Early Education

In 1979 Eng enrolled in the University of California at Berkeley where she earned a bachelor's degree in finance in 1983. From there she went on to New York University School of Law where she earned a J.D. in 1989. She worked as an corporate attorney in mergers and acquisitions, a segment of corporate law that is marked by aggressive financial maneuvering and high stakes profit taking. In this world she was often confronted with racial stereotyping. Eng told the *New York Times,* "I know that when they see me, as an Asian American woman, they question whether I can say anything of worth, whether I should get the coffee."

Phoebe Eng

Issues of race are of great concern to Eng. She told Henry: "There is a great deal of dishonesty in pretending race does not matter. I really believe that if you do not acknowledge color or background in social dynamics, be it individual or group-related, you're not acknowledging what's really going on." These deeply held beliefs ultimately led her from the lucrative world of international law to the financially uncertain world of publishing. In discussing her career decision, she told *Word One*: "I chose to do this because there were too many forces on Madison Avenue and in the news that weren't giving a voice to this ever-growing group [of Asian Americans]. Ownership and direction of this kind of medium must be controlled by the people who consume it; otherwise, it doesn't ring true. *A.* covers those who don't always get in mainstream publications."

A. Magazine is Born

A. Magazine first appeared in 1990, the creation of co-founders Jeff Yang, Amy Chu, Bill Yao, and Sandra Kim.

The first issue of the redesigned *A. Magazine* as a quarterly (it had existed previously in other forms) hit newsstands in July of 1992 with a modest circulation of 20,000, a slow start by industry standards. It was greeted with skepticism in some corners and envy in others. The magazine had a good look, was well written, and reached a well-to-do target audience—second- and third-generation Asian Americans in the eighteen to forty age bracket—an attractive audience for advertisers.

In describing the first issue, *Crain's New York Business* said it "is a bold mix of serious and flip articles. There are tough, hard-edged pieces: a feature on Asian American political activism, another on Asian studies programs at U.S. colleges. But there are also irreverent and witty articles, including a parody of hit television shows in which, for example, Homer Simpson is transformed into Homer Samsung." The magazine has continued in that vein, mixing hard news with profiles of Asians in the arts and business, for example. It also reports on the mainstream media and how it portrays, or avoids portraying, Asian Americans, calling attention to especially offensive stereotyping.

As of the beginning of 1994, *A. Magazine* had a readership of 80,000, up four hundred percent in two years, and the prospects are good that this upward trend will continue. As publisher, Eng deserves her share of the credit for the magazine's business success, but she is the first to say that a magazine depends on its editorial content; she credits the editorial direction given by editor-in-chief Jeff Yang. In 1993 Eng received the Arthur T. Vanderbilt Medal and the New York City Mayor's Innovator Award for outstanding young businesswoman of 1993. Eng has worked with Asia Watch (a human rights monitoring organization), the New York City Commission on Human Rights, and the Nature Conservancy. She also plans to use some of *A. Magazine*'s profits in various philanthropic endeavors. As she told Henry, "To treat the magazine as something that is strictly a revenue-producing vehicle would be irresponsible and egregious." Eng lives in Manhattan with her husband, Zubin Schroff, a British photographer.

Sources:

Periodicals

Hochwald, Lambeth. "A. Is for Asian-Americans." *Word One,* January 15, 1994.
Lee, Felicia R. "Publisher Sees Asian American Identity As Work in Progress." *New York Times,* October 10, 1993.
Mirabella, Allen. "Magazine's Aim: Asian-American Market." *Crain's New York Business,* vol. 8, no. 31, August 3–9, 1992.

Other

Eng, Phoebe, telephone interview with Jim Henry, March 1994.

—*Sketch by Jim Henry*

March Fong Eu
(1922–)
Politician, ambassador

In 1994, President Bill Clinton tapped March Fong Eu for the post of ambassador to Micronesia. This appointment, which came while she was serving her fifth term as California's secretary of state, capped a distinguished political career that has spanned more than four decades. Twenty years earlier Eu had made history when she became the first woman to serve in the state assembly. Eu has successfully met each challenge with characteristic determination and empathy, and in 1988 was named by *Ladies Home Journal* as one of America's 100 Most Important Women.

A Self-Made Success

Eu was born March Kong in the back room of a hand laundry in the small farming community of Oakdale, California, in 1922. A third-generation Californian, her ancestors originated in Guangton, China. As a young child, Eu moved to the small community of Richmond, California, where hers was the only family of Chinese ancestry. There she lived with three older siblings in the back of a laundry operated by her parents.

She chooses the term "self-made" to describe herself, citing a strong desire to help others in situations similar to her own as a motivating factor in her success. "My childhood was not unhappy, mind you," she told *Notable Asian Americans*. "But I wished that circumstances were different so that my parents would have had a better life than working seven days a week, morning, noon, and night, washing and ironing clothes."

After graduating from high school, Eu attended Salinas Junior College for one year, then completed a bachelor of science degree at the University of California at Berkeley. At Mills College in Oakland she received a master's in education, and completed her doctoral degree in education at Stanford University. Though Eu had been active in high school student government, she had otherwise shown little interest in politics. Initially, an interest in science led her to a career in health care, first as a dental hygienist and later as a professional health educator. After leaving this field to raise her two children, she began lobbying the legislature on educational issues. This interest led her to an elected post with the Alameda County Board of Education in 1956 where she completed three terms. In 1966, Eu was elected to the California Legislature, the first Asian-American assemblywoman in California history.

March Fong Eu

Smoothing the Wrinkles

After serving four terms in the legislature, Eu ran for secretary of state, winning the 1974 election with a record-setting three million votes. Her accomplishments while in office have been extensive in areas as varied as international trade and human rights. She reorganized and streamlined many policies and procedures. Particularly celebrated are her successes in simplifying and automating filing requirements and procedures in the Political Reform, Corporate, and Uniform Commercial Code Divisions. Hers is one of the few state offices that generates more revenue than is required to run it, partly due to these efforts such as these.

Additionally, Eu's voter reforms have impacted millions and include voter registration by mail, availability of bilingual ballots, and a voter outreach program that has become a national model. As an advocate to the elderly and handicapped, she has made voting sites and materials more accessible by creating a curbside voting program and by providing cassette tapes of state ballot pamphlets to the visually impaired.

It has been one of Eu's central missions as keeper of the California State Archives to create a safe and suitable home for these timeworn documents. In 1979 she established a traveling exhibit program in an effort to increase public awareness about these historical resources. After years of lobbying, she received the authority and the fund-ing to construct a secretary of state complex which will house a state-of-the-art archival facility. Construction began in June 1992, and projected completion is set for early 1995.

Eu is well known as an advocate to all citizens. She has made victims' rights and crime fighting a high priority. Her empathy is personal: In 1986 she was ambushed and attacked by an intruder in her home. She is also a strong supporter of women's rights and has authored bills related to improved child care facilities, fair pregnancy leave, and the creation of Information and Guidance Centers for Women. Many of her top aides are women. She often cites service to others as a cornerstone of her political philosophy, viewing government as "the servant, not the master." In her 1991 inaugural address as secretary of state, Eu stated, "This morning I renew my commitment to continuing to serve as California's unofficial ombudsman, making government responsive—making government work for all Californians."

Beyond Politics

While her list of accomplishments as a government official is extensive, her capabilities extend beyond this realm. She is also an artist of considerable skill. She discovered her hidden talent during a trip to Taiwan in 1988. To relieve the stress of an intensive Mandarin language program, she took up brush painting and calligraphy. Since that time she has exhibited her work at the Pacific Asia Museum in Pasedena. Serendipitously, she has also found that by satisfying a growing public demand for her art, she has created a source of capital to reduce her campaign debts.

Eu has been breaking racial and cultural barriers since the 1950s when she spoke out against racism within the dental profession as an American Dental Hygiene Association leader. As a person of Chinese heritage she believes it is important to prove to the larger culture that "whatever they could do, we could do." She recalled a conversation she had had with her high school bus driver who had asked of her career plans. She told him she was interested in chemistry.

"He replied that would be a very good field for me to go into because when I finished my studies I could go back and help my people in China," she told *Notable Asian Americans*. "That really hurt me . . . but that was the kind of era in which I grew up. The implication that I was not American was very disillusioning, however."

Forging Ahead

Since then Eu has integrated her Asian ancestry and her American experience in a life and career rich in service and achievements. The determination that ignited her drive as a youngster still fuels her ambition today. Her visions for the future include upgrading her department's technological capabilities, increasing computer security for voting and vote tabulation systems, and supervising completion of the Secretary of State/State Archives Complex. All are solidly grounded in her past accomplishments and in her resolution to serve. On June 24, 1992, at the ground-breaking ceremony for the Archives Complex, Eu addressed her constituents saying, "Generations to come will thank you . . . as I do today. Because this complex will not belong to the secretary of state or to the State Archives. It will belong to the people of California . . . and to the ages."

Sources:

Periodicals

Chan, Cecilia. "Asian Census Numbers Growing." *Merced County Sun-Star,* May 1, 1991.

Hirano, Steve. "March Fong Eu." *RICE,* November 1988.

Lyons, Steve. "March Fong Eu, Ed.D.: Breaking Barriers to Serve." *ACCESS,* July 1992.

Maxwell, Jacqueline. "Color March Fong Eu Successful." *Ledger Dispatch,* September 26, 1990.

Wong, Jerrye. "Friends and Supporters Clamoring for Eu Originals." *Asian Week,* May 24, 1991.

————. "Supporters Gather To Hear Eu Take Oath For Fifth Term." *Asian Week,* January 1, 1991.

Other

Office of the Secretary of State. "Eu Hosts Groundbreaking Ceremony for New Building." News release, California, June 24, 1992.

—Sketch by Cindy Washabaugh

F

John Ta-Chuan Fang
(1925–1992)
Journalist, Publisher

John T.C. Fang, founder and longtime editor of the nationally distributed weekly newspaper *Asian Week*, was a working journalist for more than forty years. Considered one of the leading pioneers in ethnic journalism, he is credited with bringing news of interest to Asian Americans to the Asian community, as well as to mainstream America.

John Ta-Chuan Fang was born in China in 1925. He was educated at the National Cheng Chi University in Nanking, China. A loyal follower of Nationalist leader Chiang Kai-shek, Fang fled mainland China when the Communists took power in 1949. He followed Nationalist leaders to Taiwan where they established a government in exile. In Taiwan he started his career as a translator, reporter, and associate editor of the *New Life Daily News*.

Chinatown Guides

Fang came to the United States in the early 1950s to do graduate work at the University of California at Berkeley. While there, he took a job as managing editor of the *Chinese Daily Post* in San Francisco. He continued this work throughout the 1950s and into the 1960s. He also became active in community affairs, and worked to establish relations between the Chinese community and the mainstream white community. In the early 1960s he published a series of booklets in English called the "Chinatown Handy Guides." These booklets focused on the customs and attractions of the Chinese communities in San Francisco, New York, Los Angeles, Chicago, and other cities with large concentrations of Chinese Americans, and were meant to help mainstream America understand the Chinese community.

In the late 1960s Fang saw the need for a quality printer that could publish ethnic newspapers and magazines in a variety of languages. He believed that California's burgeoning immigrant population would require its own native-language media. In response to this need he established Grant Printing in San Francisco's Chinatown. The

John Ta-Chuan Fang

company now prints about forty newspapers and magazines in Chinese, Korean, Vietnamese, Tagalog, Spanish, Russian, and other languages.

In the 1970s, Fang worked as publisher of *Young China Daily News,* a Chinese-language newspaper founded in San Francisco by Dr. Sun Yat-Sen in the days before the Republic of China was established in 1911. A great figure in Chinese history, Sun Yat-Sen had established the Kuomintang government in China after the fall of the Manchu dynasty. It was almost immediately torn apart by civil war, the world wars, and then another civil war in the 1940s against the Communists. He lived for many years in exile in the United States.

Asian Week Begins

In 1979, Fang established *Asian Week,* a weekly English-language newspaper covering Asian American news. In the years since its founding, *Asian Week* has come to be

Hiram Fong

president Dwight D. Eisenhower to promote interpersonal relationships between individuals in different countries throughout the world by organizing cultural exchanges and homestays for visiting students.

Sources:

Asian Week, "John Fang." Biographical sketch, 1992.

—Sketch by Jim Henry

Hiram Fong
(1907–)
Politician, attorney

Hiram Fong was the first American of Asian descent to be elected to the U.S. Senate when he was chosen as Hawaii's first senator in 1959. A Republican, Fong went on to serve Hawaii for three terms until retiring in 1977. Prior to becoming a senator, Fong had served in Hawaii's territorial legislature from 1938 to 1954, including four years as vice-speaker of the house of representatives, and six years as speaker. He was vice-president of the Hawaii State Constitutional Convention held in 1950, and was a longtime, ardent supporter of Hawaiian statehood.

Hiram Leong Fong was born in the Kalihi district of Honolulu, Hawaii, on October 1, 1907, the seventh of eleven children. Both his parents were immigrants from Kwangtung Province, China. His father, Lum, was an indentured laborer on a sugar cane plantation who had left China for Hawaii at age fifteen. His mother immigrated to Hawaii at age ten and worked as a maid.

A Childhood in Poverty

The family was poor, and the neighborhood they lived in was "rough and tumble," Fong told *Notable Asian Americans*. From the time he was four until he was seven, he worked on a plantation picking algorroba beans, which were sold as cattle feed. He was paid ten cents for each thirty-pound bag. From age seven to age ten he shined shoes and sold newspapers on the streets of Honolulu. Later he sold fish and crabs he caught, delivered poi, and caddied at a local golf course, where he was paid twenty-five cents for nine holes.

Fong graduated from McKinley High School in Honolulu and then went on to study at the University of Hawaii where he was the editor of the school newspaper, associate editor of the yearbook, adjutant of the ROTC, and was on the debating, volleyball, and rifle teams. (He competed at

recognized as the definitive paper of record in the Asian American community. The paper brought Asian Americans to the nations' attention in 1984 when it prepared a special edition focusing on issues of particular ethnic concern in the presidential campaign, and distributed copies to every delegate and alternate at both the Republican and Democratic National Conventions that year. The paper has championed Asian American causes in every major election campaign in the ensuing years, and has become mandatory reading on Capital Hill and in the White House. *Asian Week* is the recipient of three Eugene Block Journalism Awards from the San Francisco Human Rights Commission, a John Swett Award for journalism from the California Teachers' Association, as well as many other honors.

In addition to his work at *Asian Week* and with Grant Printing, Fang was the owner of the *San Francisco Independent,* a thrice-weekly newspaper with a circulation of 250,000 in San Francisco. The newspaper is run today by Fang's son, Ted, and has the largest home-delivery circulation in San Francisco. Fang also founded and owned *Chinese TV Guide* (circulation 20,000), *Mission Life,* a Spanish/English monthly newspaper, and *San Francisco Real Estate Express.* Fang married the former Florence Lee in 1960. The couple had three children.

In addition to his work in journalism, Fang served as president of the San Francisco chapter of People to People International, an organization founded by former the National Rifle Championships in 1929.) In 1930 he graduated with honors after only three years of study with a bachelor of arts degree.

Fong continued his education at Harvard, where he studied law. He had to leave school twice temporarily to save money to continue his studies, but in 1935 Fong earned his J.D. from Harvard, quite an accomplishment for the son of an indentured laborer, for a man who had worked to support himself since the age of four.

Returning to Hawaii

Returning to Hawaii, Fong formed the multi-ethnic law firm of Fong, Miho, Choy, and Robinson. He also began his career in public service by serving as the deputy attorney for the city and county of Honolulu, a post he held until 1938, when he was elected to the territorial legislature. He served in the legislature for fourteen years, all the while working for Hawaiian statehood. And in 1959, when the territory became the forty-ninth state, he was elected to the U.S. Senate as its first senator.

In the Senate, Fong worked hard for the people of his newly established state. He demanded that Hawaii get its fair share of federal funds for the Defense Department's national highway construction programs of the 1960s. The federal government reasoned that since Hawaii didn't have any roads connecting it to other states, it didn't qualify for funds. Fong challenged this thinking and acquired $50 million for highway construction between military installations. He also helped establish and then substantially increase funding for the University of Hawaii's East West Center, an internationally regarded think tank.

Fong also worked to improve civil rights. He passed legislation that provided for auditors at polling stations on the islands, so that indigenous peoples and immigrants would not be denied access to polls. He voted in favor of the Civil Rights Act of 1964, and was one of the instrumental architects of the sweeping immigration reforms passed in 1965. In an interview with Jim Henry, Fong said he was generally in favor of President Lyndon Johnson's sweeping social welfare legislation known as the Great Society programs. He characterized his own political beliefs as liberal when it came to social policy and as conservative when it came to the military and to fiscal policy, especially taxes.

Fong describes himself as having been generally "hawkish" on the Vietnam War; he believes that the war could have been won had the Democrats not blocked appropriations. A different course would have saved countless lives and alleviated the suffering of hundreds of thousands of people who ended up as refugees, he said.

During the Nixon administration, Fong worked closely with the Republican White House—the first of his Senate career—in the areas of minorities and hiring and helped to bring about several high-level minority appointments.

Since his retirement from the Senate in 1977, Fong has established himself as a very successful businessman. He founded and serves on the board of many corporations: Finance Enterprise, Finance Securities, Finance Investment, Finance Factors Building, Finance Insurance and Market City; Finance Factors and Grand Pacific Life Insurance Company; Finance Factors Foundation and Oceanview Cemetary; and Highway Construction Company. He is an honorary consultant to China Airlines and an honorary member of the board of directors of the Lincoln University Foundation. He established Senator Fong's Plantation and Gardens, a privately owned 725-acre estate open to tourists, which features landscaped gardens, tropical forests with more than seventy-five edible fruits and nuts, and a panoramic view of the Koolau Mountains and Kaneoho Bay.

Fong served in the U.S. Army Air Corps from 1942 to 1944, where he achieved the rank of major. He continued serving in the reserves for twenty years and currently holds the rank of retired colonel. He has eleven honorary degrees and dozens of other honors recognizing a lifetime of civic, political, and entrepreneurial leadership.

Fong married the former Ellyn Lo of Honolulu, and the couple has four children: Hiram, Jr., Rodney L., Merie-Ellen Gushie, and Marvin Allen. Fong believes that one should "aim high and work hard" to attain one's goals, and cites as his guiding principle the Golden Rule.

Sources:

Financial Factors, Ltd. "Biographical Sketch: Hiram Leong Fong." Promotional material. Honolulu, Hawaii, June 1, 1993.

Fong, Hiram, telephone phone interview with Jim Henry, April 4, 1994.

—Sketch by Jim Henry

Matthew K. Fong
(1953–)
Politician, attorney

Matthew Fong is the vice-chairman of California's State Board of Equalization, a statewide administrative entity that sets policy and manages a variety of tax programs—such as sales, gasoline, hazardous waste, and alcohol taxes—involving more than $36 billion annually. Prior to his appointment to the board, Fong practiced law with the international law firm of Sheppard, Mullin, Richter and Hampton.

Matthew Fong is a fourth-generation Californian of Chinese descent. His mother is March Fong Eu, a perennial participant in California politics who most recently served as secretary of state. She is currently U.S. ambassador to Micronesia. His father was a colonel in the United States Air Force (USAF). Matthew graduated from the United States Air Force Academy in Colorado Springs with a bachelor of science degree in 1975. Following graduation he served for five years in the air force, during which time he was awarded the USAF Meritorious Service Medal for exceptional management performance. Fong remains active in the reserves as a major and serves as a counselor to inner-city students as a USAF admissions liaison officer.

An Introduction to Politics

After leaving the air force, Fong managed his mother's third campaign for secretary of state. When she was reelected he remained with her as a staff member, working on, among other things, the California World Trade Commission. In this capacity he organized a highly successful trade mission to Asia. He also returned to school intending to become an international business lawyer. He earned a J.D. from Southwestern Law School and a master's in business administration from Pepperdine University toward this end.

Fong's first job as an attorney was with the international law firm of Sheppard, Mullin, Richter and Hampton in Los Angeles, where he specialized in transactional law. During his time with the law firm, Fong remained active in politics. He served as cochairman of the 1988 Bush/Quayle California campaign, as cochairman of the Pete Wilson for Senate campaign, and as a member of the executive board of the California Republican party. He also continued to be involved in community improvement and cultural organizations. He began working as a counselor to high school students interested in air force or ROTC scholarships, and he served on the board of the Los Angeles County Museum of Natural History.

The State Board of Equalization

In 1990, Fong ran for statewide office as the Republican candidate for state controller. He lost the election, but a year later when a seat opened up on the State Board of Equalization, Governor Pete Wilson named Fong to fill the vacancy. The board is a very powerful unit of government that oversees thirteen different tax programs that generate approximately a billion dollars a month. All state revenues fall under its jurisdiction except those raised by personal income taxes. And when a new tax is passed, or an existing one raised or lowered, the board makes the rules on applying it. So in one way or another, most Californians are directly affected by the actions of the board.

Fong's tenure on the board has been during perhaps the worst economic recession California has experienced since the Great Depression of the 1930s. Fong has been a staunch advocate of lowering taxes on manufacturing

Matthew K. Fong

and lessening the bureaucratic hold of governmental regulation in order to let businesses prosper in California. As he wrote in a 1992 op-ed article for the *Sacramento Bee:* "We need to realize that tax fairness is a vital protector of our jobs. If our tax system is seen as hostile to business, industry will simply relocate to a more hospitable environment."

This assertion has been proven correct in recent times more often than not. One year after he wrote his article, Intel, the giant microprocessing chip manufacturer decided to locate a new plant in New Mexico rather than pay the large California sales tax on new equipment. Fong has been actively working against such short-sighted tax policy since his appointment to the board. In his *Sacramento Bee* piece, he described his commitment as a member of the board as "ensur[ing] that California's taxpayers—individuals and businesses—are treated fairly by the tax system. Tax fairness is an important guarding of individual liberty. . . . Concern about tax fairness produced the Boston Tea Party."

Recent action Fong has taken on behalf of the board includes successfully completing negotiations among California's utility companies, the state, and its fifty-eight counties over property tax assessment methods that will save the state over one billion dollars. He also recently met with New York investment banking firms to discuss California's bond ratings and to get their perspectives on the economic prospects for California's future.

Fong is married to Paula Fong, an accountant. The couple has two children, Matthew II and Jade. Fong is a licensed flight instructor and commercial pilot, and is also licensed to fly gliders. He continues to be involved in community and cultural organizations, serving as a regent for Pepperdine University (which awarded him a Distinguished Alumnus Award in 1992), a regent for the Children's Hospital of Los Angeles, a member of the board of governors and the board of trustees of the Los Angeles County Museum of Natural History, and a member of the board of directors of the Young Executives Association. He also serves as one of three unpaid political leaders on Burger King's new diversity action council, which recently recommended to the fast food chain that it set aside funds to recruit and assist minority franchise owners and begin utilizing more minority vendors.

Fong believes wholeheartedly in the importance of public service, and that voters play an important role in the decisions that affect them. As he told the *Sacramento Bee*: "Our individual responsibility is to make sure that we are represented by elected officials who have the courage and the capacity to do what has to be done."

Sources:

Periodicals

Fong, Matthew K. "California Crisis a Golden Opportunity for Voters." *Sacramento Bee*, March 22, 1992.
————. "Unfair Taxes Are Hurting State Revenue by Killing Jobs," *Sacramento Bee*, October 4, 1992.
Lin, Sam Chu. "Matt Fong Scopes Asian Pacific American Economic Opportunities." *Asian Week*, February 4, 1994.

Other

Fong, Matthew K. Biographical materials provided by the State Board of Equalization. Sacramento, California.

—Sketch by Jim Henry

Haijing Fu
(1957–)
Opera singer

Haijing Fu is a rising star in the world of opera, an award-winning baritone who has performed with some of the world's great orchestras and opera companies including the Metropolitan Opera in New York, the Boston Symphony Orchestra, the Cleveland Orchestra, and Opera de Nice.

Haijing Fu was born on September 12, 1957, in Dalian, a resort city in northeastern China. His father was a doctor who practiced both Chinese and Western medicine. Fu was educated in the public school system and did not express any real interest in music until his later years of high school. His primary interest was in basketball; he was six feet tall, which is very tall in China, by the time he was twelve years old. It wasn't until a high school music teacher told him he should consider singing that he ever gave a career in music any serious consideration.

Music Career Begins

Fu graduated from high school in 1974 and enrolled in the Beijing Conservatory of Music, where he studied both traditional Chinese music and Western music. He stayed there for two years, but did not take a degree from the conservatory. At that time, the Chinese government required graduates from the Beijing Conservatory to work for the government for five years. Fu was not interested in making that long of a commitment, and he began planning to move to the West. Meanwhile, however, he had become a popular performer in China, appearing on television and radio concerts. He had also been on several tours in both Europe and North America with the Chinese National Opera.

Because of his popularity, it was difficult for Fu to leave the country. He was able to participate in a competition in London in 1984, where he placed second. There he met Phyllis Curtin, a competition judge and dean of the Boston University School of Arts, who soon thereafter offered him a scholarship to study in Boston. In 1986 Fu took her up on her offer. He told the authorities that his intention was to simply study in Boston, after which he would return. In an interview with Jim Henry, Fu said that it was only through this sort of deception that one could leave the country.

Fu enrolled in Boston University in 1986. He did not speak any English at the time, so he had to spend his mornings in English language classes and his afternoons at music school. In 1988, Fu won the Metropolitan Opera National Council Competition, which he describes as a major turning point in his career. After that, he signed with IMG Artists, one of the world's largest representatives of classical performers. He began performing outside of the school a year before he graduated with an artist's diploma (a degree in performance rather than academics) in 1989.

Fu performed early in his career with the Boston Symphony Orchestra. In 1989 he performed his first big roles with the Opera Company of Philadelphia in *Luisa Miller* and *Lucia* with Luciano Pavarotti. He sang the roles of Miller and Enrico, for which he had to audition for Pavarotti, who remembered Fu from a performance he had given in Beijing many years earlier.

Haijing Fu

Good Reviews

In 1990, Fu made his premiere at the Metropolitan Opera in *La Traviata*, where he was the first Chinese singer to perform a major role. *New York Times* reviewer Allan Kozinn was impressed: "Mr. Fu's portrayal of Germont had just about everything one looks for in the role. . . . Vocally, he seemed fully connected to the characterization, taking a stately approach to 'Pura siccome un angelo' and singing 'Di Provenza il mar' with touching tenderness and passion. His phrasing is thoughtful, often beautifully shaped and well projected. And he has a pleasing tone that is steady throughout his range."

Also in 1990, Fu made his European debut, singing the role of Renato in *Un Ballo in Maschera* at the Opera de Nice. Later that year he sang Marcello in *La Boheme* at the Mann Music Center with the Philadelphia Orchestra. In August of that year he performed at the Mondack Music Festival in the role of Ford in Verdi's *Falstaff*. Reviewing the performance in the *Boston Globe*, Anthony Tommasini said, "[Fu's] Ford was a dynamic portrayal, magnificently sung. His voice is burnished, his lyricism is supple and his diction is getting quite good."

In the 1992-93 season, Fu returned to the Metropolitan Opera to sing Enrico in *Lucia*, Germont in *La Traviata*, and Renato in *Un Ballo in Maschera*. He also sang Enrico with the Dallas Opera, and in May 1993 performed Beethoven's Ninth Symphony and Bruckner's *Te Deum*

with the Montreal Symphony, followed by a performance of Michele in *Il Tabarro* at the Spoleto Festival in Italy. During this season the *New York Times* called Fu a "strong and eloquent baritone, rich in the darker colors."

Fu has continued performing around the world, and generally receives excellent reviews wherever he does. He told Henry that it was at first very difficult to break into Western opera as a Chinese. There is not a tradition of Chinese singers in the West, and music directors were at first skeptical of the young man's ability to sing in Western languages. Fu has proven himself, though, over time.

As of mid-1994, Fu was working on rehearsals for a Metropolitan Opera of New York production of *Lucia*, for which he will sing the part of Enrico. Fu is married to Jin Chuan Wang, a former folk dancer whom he met while still in China. The couple has one child, a daughter, Xiao. Fu has been very happy with his education and career in the West, as opposed to what he would have been able to achieve in China. He especially appreciates the academic and artistic freedom and the range of roles and venues available.

Sources:

Periodicals

Kozinn, Allan. "Chinese Baritone's Debut." *New York Times,* December 18, 1990.
Ross, Alex. "Cast Changes in 'Lucia' and 'Eugene Onegin'." *New York Times,* December 23, 1992.
Tommasini, Anthony. "A Loving Performance of 'Falstaff'." *Boston Globe,* August 27, 1990.

Other

Fu, Haijing, telephone interview with Jim Henry, May 18, 1994.

—Sketch by Jim Henry

John Liu Fugh
(1934–)
Military

Major General John L. Fugh served in the U.S. Army for more than thirty years. He was the first Chinese American to attain general officer status in the military and served as judge advocate general of the army from 1991 until his retirement in 1993.

John Liu Fugh was born on September 12, 1934, in Beijing, China. In the midst of the civil war fought against the communist insurgency of Mao Zedong, the Fugh family fled the mainland for Hong Kong in 1948, one year before Mao's final victory. In Hong Kong the family received visas to come to the United States. They settled in the Washington, D.C. area, and John attended a public high school. After graduation he went to Georgetown University in Washington, D.C., where he studied at the school of foreign service. He graduated with a bachelor of science degree in international relations. In 1957, he became an American citizen and entered the George Washington University Law School. After graduation he was commissioned as an officer in the army's Judge Advocate General's Corps (JAG Corps).

Law and the Army

Fugh's first assignment after being trained at an infantry officer training school and the U.S. Army Judge Advocate General School, was as an assistant staff judge advocate at the Presidio of San Francisco, California. He held this position from 1961 until 1964. The office of the JAG Corps, where Fugh spent the entirety of his military career, consists of thousands of attorneys and legal professionals stationed all over the world representing the U.S. military's legal interests. Since this first assignment, Fugh has served four tours of duty in California, Europe, Vietnam, Taiwan, and Washington, D.C. He went on to graduate from the Army Command and General Staff College, the Army War College, and the Kennedy School of Government at Harvard.

In 1984 Fugh was promoted to brigadier general and became assistant judge advocate general for civil law. As such, he established a badly needed acquisition law for army contract attorneys. He also created the Procurement Fraud and Environmental Law divisions of the corps, and consolidated the administration of all army litigation functions at the Army Litigation Center.

Fugh was promoted to the judge advocate general (TJAG) in 1991. As such, he was legal adviser to the chief of staff of the army and the army staff, and served as the military legal adviser to the secretary of the army and the army secretariat. In this role, Fugh is credited with advancing the reputation of the corps and with increasing the army's role in dealing with growing environmental concerns. He also provided legal assistance to families of soldiers who served in the Persian Gulf War of 1991. He established a program for human rights training in developing countries, and he published the *War Crimes Report,* the first documentation of worldwide war crimes since the end of World War II. He successfully led the army through litigation involving its promotion policies, its homosexual exclusion policy, and its conscientious objector policy. He also established a legal support system to protect military doctors in malpractice suits and other matters.

John Liu Fugh

Accomplishment and Awards

In addition to these accomplishments, Fugh instituted policies and procedures in a number of areas that will have wide impact in the future. He invigorated the ethical standards for military lawyers, he upgraded the assignment criteria for appellate judges sitting on the U.S. Army Court of Military Review, he established a tenure review policy for the JAG corps to avoid stagnation in the higher ranks, and he created the army law placement service to assist legal personnel in the military in finding civilian work upon their discharge.

Among the many awards and commendations Fugh received in his more than thirty years of military service are the Defense Superior Service Medal, the Legion of Merit with oak leaf cluster, the Meritorious Service Medal with oak leaf cluster, the Air Medal, the Joint Service Commendation Medal, and the Army Commendation Medal with oak leaf cluster. At his retirement ceremonies in 1993 the chief of staff of the army awarded Fugh the Distinguished Service Medal. Fugh was selected as Man of the Year in 1994 by the Chinese American Planning Council of New York City, a major social service organization.

In January of 1994, Fugh joined the law firm of McGuire, Woods, Battle and Boothe as a partner in its Washington, D.C., offices. McGuire Woods is one of the country's largest law firms with more than 380 lawyers, and with offices in Alexandria, Baltimore, Charlottesville,

Norfolk, Richmond, Tysons Corner, Washington, D.C., Brussels, and Zurich. The firm deals in all aspects of legal practice in local, state, national, and international jurisdictions. Fugh is married to the former June Chung of Washington, D.C. They have two children, both of whom are attorneys.

Sources:

United States Army. "Major Fugh Retires." Press release. Washington, D.C., 1993.

—Sketch by Jim Henry

G

Roman Gabriel

(1940–)

Football player

Roman Gabriel was the quarterback for the Los Angeles Rams football team from 1962 until 1973. In his eleven seasons with the Rams he was chosen their most valuable player three times, he was named to the All-Pro team four times, was voted Most Valuable Player (MVP) of the 1969 Pro-Bowl game, and was named the National Football League's Most Valuable Player that year as well.

Roman Ildefonzo Gabriel, Jr., was born on August 5, 1940, in Wilmington, North Carolina. His father was a Filipino immigrant who supported the family as a cook for the Atlantic Coast Line Railroad. Gabriel attended New Hanover High School in Wilmington and excelled there in athletics. He was an All-State, All-American quarterback on the football team, an All-Conference baseball player, and a conference MVP in basketball.

Gabriel graduated from high school in 1958. He turned down an offer to play professional baseball with the New York Yankees to attend North Carolina State University on a football scholarship. He continued to play baseball and basketball but concentrated his efforts on football. When he was a sophomore, he led the nation in pass completions, throwing with a 60.4 percent accuracy. He continued to distinguish himself throughout his college career. In 1960 and 1961 he was named Athlete of the Year in the Atlantic Coast Conference, an All-American, and Football Player of the Year. He also was named a Scholastic All-American, received the Teague Award as Carolina's most outstanding amateur athlete, and was a two-time recipient of the Governor's Award. His career passing yardage was 2,951 yards, and as a junior and senior he accounted for more than 50 percent of his team's offensive yardage.

The Early Years with the Los Angeles Rams

When the National Football League (NFL) held the college draft in 1962, Gabriel was a highly sought-after player. Many coaches considered him to have been one of the greatest college passers of all time. He was drafted by the

Roman Gabriel

Los Angeles Rams and the Oakland Raiders, but ended up signing with the Rams. In his first two seasons, he was a backup quarterback and played infrequently. He started only four games and yet went on to be selected as quarterback of the NFL's All-Rookie Team and established an NFL record for allowing the fewest interceptions (two) in more than one hundred passing attempts. In spite of this impressive start, Gabriel was used only sparingly in the next three seasons. He spoke of the difficulty of his early years with the Rams in the *Peterson's Pro Football Annual 1970.* "The first year was one of the biggest hardships I had to overcome. Having a coach like Bob Waterfield, who was one of the finest players ever to play the game . . . but a kind of guy who was an introvert. . . . It was hard for me to express myself to him and his way of coaching wasn't to express his thoughts to the players. . . . So we really started off on the wrong foot right away. . . . I wasn't aware of just what to do with myself. I had an inner confidence in my ability, but not the confidence to go out and try to win new people."

In the next two seasons a new coach, Harland Svare, was brought in. The team had three quarterbacks at the time and the competition for playing time was intense. Gabriel started nine of fourteen games in the 1963 season, six of fourteen in 1964, and was down to four of fourteen in 1965, the year he suffered a severe knee injury. Also in 1965, the Rams drafted another quarterback, Tom Munson, who immediately became a starter. It began to look as if Gabriel's career was over before it had a chance to really start. Dr. Jules Rasinski, the Rams' team physician recalled for *Peterson's Pro Football Annual 1970* that other players faced with Gabriel's difficulties might have quit. "Munson was doing well and [Gabriel] had this knee injury. He had to spend hours on the 'knee machine,' working his leg up and down. . . . I used to marvel at the character that kept him there . . . the desire he had to play."

Starting Quarterback

Gabriel's determination paid off for him. Beginning in 1966, when the Rams hired George Allen as their new head coach, Gabriel became the starting quarterback. That year the Rams had their first winning season in years (8-6). That year Gabriel set a Rams' single season record with 217 completions in 397 attempts, passing for 2,540 yards. In 1967 the Rams finished with a record of 11-1-2 and made it to the NFC Championship game, which they lost to the Green Bay Packers. Gabriel again had a remarkable season, completing 196 of 371 passing attempts for 2,779 yards and setting another Rams single season record with 25 touchdown passes.

The 1968 season was an important one for Gabriel's development as a player. As he told *Peterson's Pro Football Annual 1970,* "I think I actually came alive as a professional quarterback, a leader, that year. Because we had so many people hurt, offensively, that season, I didn't only have to worry about the plays I was calling, but about the type of individuals who were going to fill the roles—and their condition. . . . Looking back now on '68, that's when I became a leader. I had the confidence of both myself and those around me." That year the team posted a 10-3-1 mark and Gabriel completed 184 of 366 passes for 2,364 yards and 19 touchdowns.

The 1969 season was Gabriel's and the Rams' best. The team finished with an 11-2-1 record and lost to the Minnesota Vikings in the Western Conference championship game. Gabriel tied his passing record of 217 completions and set a new record for attempts at 399. His passing totaled 2549 yards with 24 touchdowns. That year he was also awarded the NFL's Most Valuable Player Award—the Jim Thorpe Trophy—by the Associated Press, United Press International, the Columbus Touchdown Club, and the Maxwell Club of Philadelphia.

During the next three seasons Gabriel continued delivering outstanding performances. In 1970 he broke his own club record for passing attempts and maintained a completion record of over 50 percent, averaging 2,272 yards and 15 touchdowns per season.

Second Life as an Eagle

In 1973, after eleven seasons with the Rams, Gabriel was traded to the Philadelphia Eagles. It was thought that he was nearing retirement and the Rams needed a younger quarterback. In his first season with the Eagles, however, Gabriel set a personal record of 270 completions of 460 attempted passes for 3,219 yards and 23 touchdowns, numbers far exceeding even his MVP year with the Rams. In one season, Gabriel took the Eagles from being one of the worst offensive teams in the NFL to the league's second most powerful. For this he was named Comeback Player of the Year. Gabriel played well in 1974 and 1975, but injuries plagued him as he approached his mid-thirties, an old age for football players. In 1976 he underwent his fifth operation on his knee and played in only the last four games of the season. Gabriel retired from professional football after the 1977 season with 201 touchdown passes, 30 rushing touchdowns, 149 interceptions, and 2,366 completions in 4,498 attempts for 29,444 yards.

Since Retirement

Since retiring from the NFL, Gabriel has been active in coaching at the college and professional level. He was the quarterback coach of the Arizona Wranglers and offensive coordinator of the Boston Breakers, both of the short-lived World Football League, and head coach of the Raleigh-Durham (North Carolina) Skyhawks of the World League of American Football, another now-defunct challenger to the NFL. He also spent three seasons as head coach at the California Polytechnic Institute in Pomona. He has served as a sports analyst for CBS television and radio and has even done a little acting, appearing on such television shows as "Sheriff Lobo," "Wonder Woman," and "Ironside," and in the John Wayne film *The Undefeated*.

In recent years, Gabriel has returned to his home state of North Carolina where he is president and general manager of the Charlotte Knights Class AA baseball team. He is also active in the community as a board member of the Greater Carolinas Chapter for Multiple Sclerosis, the Center for the Blind in Phoenix, Arizona, and the Onslow County Charities in Jacksonville, North Carolina. He also has served as vice-president of the Carolinas Chapter of the National Football League's Alumni Association.

Sources:

Books

Baker, Hugh. "It Takes Six Years." In *Peterson's Pro Football Annual 1970.*

Other

Charlotte Knights Baseball Club. "Biography, Roman Gabriel." Press release. Charlotte, North Carolina.

Los Angeles Rams. "Roman Gabriel." Press release. Los Angeles, California.

Twentieth Century-Fox Film Corporation. "Biography of Roman Gabriel." Press release. Beverly Hills, California.

—Sketch by Jim Henry

Jorge M. Garcia
(1941–)
Heart surgeon

Jorge Garcia is one of the premier heart surgeons in the United States. The former chief of the cardiac surgery division at the Washington Hospital Center in Washington, D.C., was named in a poll of his peers to be the surgeon they would most want to operate on their heart. He has in recent years been working to bring the modern techniques of cardiovascular surgery to underdeveloped countries. He spends much of each year in Cairo, Egypt, China, and the Philippines, teaching local doctors to perform heart surgery.

Jorge Garcia was born in the city of Binan in Laguna Province, the Philippines, a small farming community about twenty-five miles south of Manila. His father was an agriculturist who rented parcels of land on which he grew cane and rice, providing his family with a modest standard of living. Garcia attended public schools for most of his schooling, but he finished his high school education at the Far Eastern University of Manila, a private school.

School Success

Garcia studied biology at the University of Santo Tomas in Manila. In an interview Garcia told Jim Henry that he studied medicine because that's what his mother told him to do, "and in those days we listened to our parents." While an undergraduate, Garcia played intramural basketball as a center. He said that he worked hard in college but found the time to enjoy himself too. Garcia earned his bachelor's degree in 1959 and entered medical school that year.

He was an excellent student, placing fifth on the national medical board examination in 1964. After graduation from medical school, Garcia became a resident at Santo Tomas University Hospital in Manila, where he was first exposed to the still relatively new procedure of open heart surgery, developed in 1962 in the United States. Garcia was fascinated with these operations and decided to pursue heart surgery as his specialty. Another factor influencing his decision was that the medical technology in the Philippines was lagging behind the developed world and he wanted to learn all he could about these operations and someday bring this knowledge to his home country. This sense of frustration for his homeland was brought about in part by Garcia's relationship with Dr. Ben Villemonte, the man who first brought open heart surgery to the Philippines, but who could perform such operations only on an extremely limited basis; the hospitals in Manila simply didn't have all the necessary ancillary technology.

In 1967 Garcia arrived in the United States to begin an internship at Washington Hospital Center in Washington, D.C. The techniques in heart surgery had advanced since his time in the Philippines and he was interested in learning them. Most notable among these was the coronary bypass, developed at the Cleveland Clinic in 1967. Garcia found the United States accommodating and doesn't recall ever feeling discriminated against. Instead, he believes the most challenging aspect of his immigration was catching up with all the new technology. He spent a lot of time studying in the library.

Training and Travel

Garcia's residency lasted seven years. He trained for five years to become a general surgeon and then spent an additional two years studying to become a certified thoracic and cardiovascular surgeon at the Cleveland Clinic. The clinic is one of the finest hospitals in the world, where much of the early work in heart surgery was pioneered. In 1974 Garcia became an attending physician, returning to the Washington Hospital Center. In 1978 he was named as chief of the cardiac surgery division of the hospital.

In 1988 Garcia began a regimen of international travels in which he teaches and performs heart surgery in underdeveloped countries. He began with a program initiated by the State Department that has since become privately financed with the Salam International Hospital in Cairo. He has in recent years become a trustee at this hospital's heart institute. Garcia also travels to the Xian Medical University in Xian City, China's oldest city. Garcia is an honorary professor chairman of the department of cardiac surgery at the university. In this program, Chinese students are trained in the latest techniques in the United States and then Garcia observes their practice back in China. He recently started a similar program in Fujian Province in southern China.

As for his homeland, Garcia started the Makati Heart Foundation to upgrade the quality of cardiac care in the Philippines, an ambition dating back to his medical school days. The foundation subsidizes the training of doctors and nurses in the field of cardiac surgery in the

United States for work at the Makati Medical Center in Manila. In 1991, this international work began taking too much of Garcia's time and he decided that in order to keep it up he would have to give up his position as chief of cardiac surgery at Washington Hospital. He resigned in 1991 and now travels nearly year round. He goes to the Philippines with special frequency, and on May 28, 1994, he performed the Philippines' first heart transplant.

Garcia said that the values his parents instilled him have been an enormous help to him through the years. He stated that Asians are, in general, hard-working, family-oriented people and that he has remained true to these values and has tried to pass them on to his children. When he is in the Philippines he visits his mother every Sunday, as do his four sisters; he considers the closeness of his family to have contributed greatly to his success.

Sources:

Garcia, Jorge M., telephone interview with Jim Henry, June 15, 1994.

—Sketch by Jim Henry

Lillian Gonzalez-Pardo, M.D.

Lillian Gonzalez-Pardo, M.D.

(1939–)

Physician

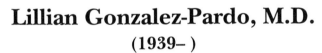

Lillian Gonzalez-Pardo was the first Asian American woman to serve as president of the American Medical Women's Association. A clinical professor of pediatrics and neurology at the University of Kansas Medical Center in Kansas City, Kansas, she has worked to promote better health care for women and children, both nationally and internationally.

Lillian Gonzalez was born on February 5, 1939, in Manila, Philippines. Her maternal grandmother's influence during her early childhood helped Lillian learn responsibility, organization, good manners, and proper conduct. Her parents, especially her father, a lawyer, encouraged her to pursue education as the means to higher achievement in life.

Following her father's advice, Lillian enrolled in the University of the Philippines in Quezon City. She graduated with an associate of arts in premed in 1957 and a doctor of medicine in 1962. In 1961 she served an internship at Philippines General Hospital in Manila, after which she received her certification from the Philippines Medical Board in May 1962.

She then traveled to the United States to begin her postgraduate training at the University of Kansas Medical Center (UKMC) in Kansas City, Kansas. Upon arriving in Kansas City to begin her residency, she met Dr. Manuel C. Pardo, whom she married a year later. From 1963 until 1967, Gonzalez-Pardo was a resident at UKMC, first in neurology, then in child psychiatry. In 1967, she was a fellow in pediatric neurology at Children's Mercy Hospital in Kansas City, Missouri. She subsequently returned to UKMC, where she was a fellow in developmental pediatrics from 1972 until 1973 and a resident in pediatrics in 1974.

Physician and Teacher

Returning to the Philippines, Gonzalez-Pardo became an instructor in medicine at the University of the Philippines College of Medicine in Manila from July of 1969 to April of 1971. She also was a consultant in neurology at three Manila hospitals, Philippines General Hospital, Metropolitan General Hospital, and Quezon Institute. She continued her teaching in 1975, when she became an assistant professor of pediatrics and neurology at the University of Kansas School of Medicine. From 1979 until 1981 she also worked as the medical director of the Children's Rehabilitation Unit/University Affiliated Facility at UKMC. In 1980 she was granted her American citizenship. She became a full clinical professor at UKMC in 1992. While continuing this position, she began work in 1994 on a master's degree in health services administration at the University of Kansas.

Apart from her teaching duties, Gonzalez-Pardo has also been active in many medical associations and community service projects. She has served on the board of directors for the Orton Society of Greater Kansas City, Marillac Center for Children, the Academy of Health Professionals, and the Epilepsy League of Greater Kansas City, which she also served as president in 1988. Beginning in 1984, she served for two years as president of the Filipino American Neurological Society of America. Out of all the medical organizations, however, her greatest dedication has been to the American Medical Women's Association (AMWA).

American Medical Women's Association

From 1979 on, Gonzalez-Pardo has held many positions at AMWA, on both the local and national levels. In 1992 she was national president, the first Asian American to serve as president in the history of the association. In her president's address before the 1992 Midwest Regional Conference of AMWA, she stated, "AMWA is committed to the development of an advanced women's health curriculum for physicians to provide improved and integrated health care to women patients." She called for the AMWA's involvement in the political and legislative arena, in public and professional education, and at global conferences. She advocated increased biomedical research for women, reproductive rights, and sharing resources with other countries to improve the health care of women and children worldwide.

Gonzalez-Pardo also used her term as AMWA president to promote cultural diversity, especially drawing attention to Asian Americans. She developed the Asian American Women Physicians Project, in cooperation with the Archives and Special Collection on Women in Medicine of the Medical College of Pennsylvania. The project was to identify, document, and develop educational materials about Asian American women physicians, both contemporary and historical.

Aside from the medical arena, Gonzalez-Pardo has been active in many community organizations. She has been a member of the Asian Council of Greater Kansas City, the Filipino Association of Greater Kansas City, the Advisory Group of the Kaw Valley Arts and Humanities Council, the International Women's Forum, the steering committee of the Mid-Continent Regional Educational Laboratory Project to encourage girls in science, engineering, and mathematics, and the National Research Councils' Committee on Women in Science and Engineering, among many other organizations.

For her dedication as a physician and a citizen, Gonzalez-Pardo has received several awards. She was named the Outstanding Alumnus of the University of the Philippines College of Medicine in 1991. The same year the University of the Philippines Alumni Association gave her the Outstanding Alumnus Community Service Award. And in May 1993, she was given the Excellence 2000 Award as Outstanding Asian American by the U.S. Pan Asian American Pacific Chamber of Commerce in Washington, D.C.

Gonzalez-Pardo and her husband, Manuel P. Pardo (faculty and staff psychiatrist at UKMC) have three children, Manuel, Jr., who is also a doctor, Lillie, and Patrick. They reside in Mission Hills, Kansas.

A role model both as a woman physician and an Asian American, Gonzalez-Pardo said at the close of her term as president of AMWA: "It is my hope that others like me will follow, that I have paved the way to promote the cultural diversity that this country needs to recognize. Be challenged, as I was, with these words from Eleanor Roosevelt, 'You must do the things you think you cannot do.'"

Sources:

Periodicals

Asian American and Pacific Islander Journal of Health, Winter 1994, vol. 2, no.1.

Journal of the American Medical Women's Association (JAMWA), vol. 47, May–June 1992, September–October 1992, and November–December 1994.

Other

Gonzalez-Pardo, Lillian, M.D. "The Heart of the Matter," Third Midwest Regional Conference on Women in Medicine.

Gonzalez-Pardo, Lillian G., M.D., professional resume, 1994.

—*Sketch by Susan Ketchum*

Philip Kan Gotanda
(1951–)
Playwright, filmmaker

"**I**t's the best of times, and the worst of times," said Philip Kan Gotanda, echoing the century-old words of British writer Charles Dickens. An acclaimed playwright whose works include *The Wash* and *Yankee Dawg You Die*, Gotanda is one of the few Asian Americans who is a clear presence in the cultural mainstream. In spite of his own success, Gotanda maintains that "Asian American artists and writers are marginalized now as much as we ever were. While I can get plays up in mainstream houses, San Francisco's Asian American Theater Center is struggling to stay afloat. Or, while *The New York Times* will run an article about me acknowledging my work as a known writer . . . I still walk

Philip Kan Gotanda

down the street and someone will yell out 'you #! gook.' I'm still a one-dimensional stereotype. In some ways, nothing has been resolved and that's something we as Asian Americans must all live with."

However, for Gotanda, living with such stereotyping does not hinder him from effecting change. In spite of what he calls the current "post-LA uprising era," a period defined by the worst anti-Asian sentiment and violence that Gotanda has ever experienced, he is convinced that "artistic expression by Asian Americans is here to stay. I sense the passion," he said. "There is a *need* to express ourselves. There are people literally trying to kill you out there, so you *must* answer that need to speak and be heard . . . to say 'hey, we're here, look at us, we're not going away and you're not going to make us disappear.' What we're doing as a community is to rethink, to reenvision who we are as Asian Americans, to figure out how we're all going to live together and still have our own community."

Elvis and Me

Born in Stockton, California, on December 17, 1951, Philip Kan Gotanda was the youngest in a family of three boys and a third-generation Japanese American descended on both sides from immigrants from Hiroshima, Japan. Gotanda said he had "a very good childhood" and he claimed that his role model was Elvis Presley. "I *really* liked him when I was growing up," he remarked with a chuckle.

In 1969, Gotanda began studying at the University of California at Santa Cruz, stayed for a couple of years and left. "It was just too isolated and too free form for me," he said. He traveled to Japan, then returned to California, this time to the University of California at Berkeley. He didn't stay long and moved on to the University of California at Santa Barbara where he earned a degree in Japanese art in 1974. He went on to law school and eventually found work as a legal aide in San Francisco.

Gotanda also began to write music. "But songs dealing with Asian American identity just weren't a commercial product," he recalled. He persisted, however, and completed a musical, *The Avocado Kid.* He sent the script to East West Players, the nation's first Asian American theatre, in Los Angeles. In 1980, his first production quickly became a reality and suddenly he found himself "writing for the theatre—by accident." Gradually, he moved away from musicals to plays. "I became more interested in the spoken word, in hearing characters talk," he explained.

The following year, Gotanda wrote *Song for a Nisei Fisherman,* a Japanese American family saga with autobiographical underpinnings, which was first produced at San Francisco's Asian American Theater Company. He followed with *The Dream of Kitamura,* a fantastical fairy-tale like work set in ancient Japan, which premiered in 1984, also at the Asian American Theater Company.

Gotanda earned national acclaim with his next play, *The Wash,* a poignant depiction of the troubled marriage of an older couple. First staged at San Francisco's Eureka Theatre in 1987, the play was made into a 1988 PBS American Playhouse film and in 1990 was staged by the Manhattan Theater Club in co-production with L.A.'s Mark Taper Forum.

Yankee Dawg You Die, which opened at the Berkeley Repertory Company in 1988, went on to New York's Playwrights Horizon in 1990. In the play, two actors face off, the elder who has survived in the industry by doing character parts and the younger who in the thralls of idealism still believes he will find substantial roles.

In 1992, Gotanda garnered "some of the best notices [he has] ever gotten" with *Fish Head Soup* which also premiered at the Berkeley Repertory Company. In this portrait of a Japanese American family, a long-lost son returns to his home, bringing with him the emotional baggage that his mother, father, brother and he himself must finally face.

Guggenheim, Rockefeller, National Endowment for the Arts and McNight fellowships interspersed throughout Gotanda's "accidental" career confirm his immense talent. His latest accolade comes from the prestigious Lila Wallace-*Reader's Digest* Fund in the form of a three-year grant that began in 1993 and will support his projects at East West Players.

Wendy Lee Gramm

Life after Writer's Block

Shortly after the premiere of *Fish Head Soup,* Gotanda reached an artistic impasse. For a time, he stopped writing plays altogether. In the meantime, he wrote, directed, and starred in a short film, *The Kiss.* A charming work about a downtrodden, harassed office worker who, during his lunch hour in a crowded restaurant quietly, heroically saves a person's life with a single kiss, *The Kiss* played at the 1993 Sundance, Berlin, Edinburgh, and Asian American film festivals to favorable reviews.

When Gotanda finally picked up his pen again, he wrote *Day Standing on Its Head*—in just two-and-a-half weeks. In the past, he said, he had always been "grinding out pieces," constantly caught in a cycle of writing, not writing, thinking and trying again. His method changed: "Sometimes you have to get out of the way of the writing and not worry so much about being in control. Writing *Day* was a process of just letting it come out of me, to put it out there and not worry if it's a bit rough-hewn," he said. The result is the story of law professor Harry Kitamura who, on the verge of middle-age, embarks on a dream-scape/nightmare journey toward his true self.

In addition, Gotanda is currently working on a new play, *The Ballad of Yachiyo,* "something [he's] been trying to write for years." Set on the Hawaiian island of Kauai, the play is based on the life of an older aunt who died tragically in the early 1900s.

Moreover, the success of his first film, *The Kiss,* has inspired Gotanda to a new feature-length endeavor: "It's about a man, similar to the guy in *The Kiss.* He works in an antique store, surrounded by old things. He discovers that he's dying, goes on a journey, and in the process, his life becomes transformed." Filming is tentatively scheduled to begin in summer 1994. In reference to the title, *Gioconda Smile,* Gotanda explained, "'Gioconda' was the original name of Mona Lisa, so the title of the film is encoded much in the same way as Mona Lisa's smile is encoded in the famous painting." A writer always, Gotanda continues to play word games, even on celluloid.

Source:

Gotanda, Philip Kan, telephone interviews with Terry Hong, October 10, 1993 and January 25, 1994.

—Sketch by Terry Hong

Wendy Lee Gramm
(1945–)
Economist, political appointee

Wendy Lee Gramm has achieved much in the areas of academics, government, and private industry. A former college professor, she is a member of the Chicago Mercantile Exchange's governing board and a board member of the Enron Corporation. Prior to that she served as chairperson of the United States government's Commodity Futures Trading Commission, where she was responsible for regulating the trade of commodities such as wheat, cattle and precious metals. As such she oversaw the activities of some 55,000 commodities traders, and presided over the turbulent days in the wake of the Wall Street market breaks in 1987 and 1989.

Wendy Lee was born on January 10, 1945, in the city of Wailaua, Hawaii, on the island of Oahu. Her parents always stressed the values of hard work and a good education, and she excelled in school like her parents had. Her father, Joshua Lee, had left the islands during the Great Depression to attend Tri-State College in Angola, Indiana. He worked a variety of part-time jobs while in college, and, according to Gramm, had once raced a dishwasher to prove that he was faster washing dishes in order to keep his job. After earning an engineering degree from Tri-State College, he returned to Hawaii and got a job with the sugar company harvesting sugar. He worked his way up through the company and became a vice president. Gramm's mother, Angeline, was a librarian.

Gramm read a lot while she was in grade school, but she didn't have a favorite subject until she was in the eighth grade in 1957. That year the Soviet Union made history when it launched an artificial satellite, Sputnik, into space and initiated a fierce competition with the United States to be first in space exploration. Along with the rest of America's students, these events led Gramm to become interested in math and science. When she earned a scholarship to Wellesley College, she decided to major in math, but later changed to economics because in that field she could use both her business and math skills. Though she was a good student she found time to participate in many extracurricular activities, and in 1966 she graduated from Wellesley with a bachelor's degree in economics.

A Career in Economics

Gramm started her career as an assistant professor of economics at Texas A&M University shortly after receiving her Ph.D. in economics from Northwestern University in 1971 at the age of twenty-five. For her dissertation at Northwestern Gramm studied women as part of the labor force. In an article in the *Wall Street Journal* she said: "The well-being of women is more dependent on economic growth and a strong economy than on taxpayer-funded programs for child care or parental leave." She believes that it is necessary to recruit and retain women workers in order to maintain a strong growth rate in the economy and that programs such as maternity and parental leave may actually be barriers to women who wish to work.

While on the faculty at Texas A&M Gramm met and married Phil Gramm, then a twenty-eight year old professor of economics. In 1976 her husband ran for the Senate as a Democrat and lost in the primaries to Lloyd Bentsen, who later became Secretary of Treasury in the administration of President Bill Clinton. In 1978 he ran for the House of Representatives and won. Gramm followed her husband to Washington and found a job at the Institute for Defense Analysis, where she said she had to wrestle with such questions as how many pounds of titanium there are in an F-14. In 1982 she began working for the Federal Trade Commission.

Her husband was reelected to the House of Representatives in 1980 and 1982 as a Democrat, but he changed his party affiliation from Democrat to Republican in 1983. Gramm also changed her party affiliation and began working for the Office of Management and Budget in 1984, where she worked on limiting the amount and scope of regulations issued by the government. That same year her husband was elected to the Senate.

Gramm was appointed to the Commodity Futures Trading Commission in February of 1988 by then-president George Bush. On January 20, 1993, the day President Clinton was inaugurated, she resigned from her post and became a board member of the Chicago Mercantile Exchange shortly thereafter.

The Gramms have two boys: Marshall Kenneth, who was born in 1973, and Jefferson Philip, who was born in 1975. When Gramm is not working she likes to exercise, play tennis, and spend time with her family on wilderness trips.

Sources:

Books

Morey, Janet Nomura and Wendy Dunn. *Famous Asian Americans.* New York: Cobble Hill Books. 1992.

Periodicals

Crawford, William B. Jr. "CFTC's Ex-Chief Joins Merc Board." *Chicago Tribune,* Section 3-3, February 18, 1994.

Gramm, Wendy L. "The Economy, A Women's Issue." *Wall Street Journal,* March 22, 1994, p. A14.

Hershey, Robert D. "Working Profile: Wendy Lee Gramm." *New York Times,* February 26, 1986.

—*Sketch by Douglas Wu*

Emil Guillermo

(1955–)

Humorist, broadcast journalist

Emil Guillermo is a radio and television journalist who came to national prominence as the weekend anchor of National Public Radio's news program "All Things Considered," which he hosted from 1989 until 1991. His commentaries and humorous essays became very popular with the show's audience and led to his column "Amok," which is published monthly in *Filipinas* magazine.

Guillermo was born on October 9, 1955, in San Francisco, California, to first-generation Filipino immigrants. His father was a fry cook who had immigrated to the United States in the 1920s. At that time, there were laws barring Filipinos from intermarrying, and with male Filipinos outnumbering females by a ratio of sixteen to one, many Filipinos were bachelors for at least three decades. Guillermo's father was in his fifties before he married one of the many Philippine immigrants who flocked to the United States after World War II. In an interview with Jim Henry, Guillermo recalled that his childhood was difficult, partly because his family was poor. Like all poor children, he said, it took him a while to realize he was poor. But then, he told Henry, "You start wondering why your friends aren't in the free lunch program."

Emil Guillermo

Ivy League Filipino

Guillermo was an excellent student, and after graduating high school in 1973 he won a scholarship to Harvard. He chose Harvard because his idol at the time, author Norman Mailer, had gone there. At Harvard he studied history and worked on the school's noted humor magazine, the *Harvard Lampoon,* which has launched the careers of several successful comedy writers who later wrote for popular television shows such as "Saturday Night Live," David Letterman's late-night talk shows, and "The Simpsons." He was also a disc jockey for the school's radio station and worked for a couple of commercial radio stations in Boston as well.

In 1975, two years into his education at Harvard, Guillermo went to Texas to work at KLOL radio in Houston. His role there, he told Henry, was as a "shock jock, in the pre-Howard Stern mold." He enjoyed the experience and got a lot of hate and fan mail, but he eventually returned to Harvard, where he graduated in 1977 after only three years of study.

One of the traditions of Harvard's graduation ceremony is the Ivy Oration, the speech the class humorist gives after the more serious graduation speeches. Usually given by the editor of the *Lampoon,* Guillermo won the honor after a schoolwide competition. Guillermo flew his parents out to Boston to hear him deliver his speech,

which was very well received, and he described the event as one of the high points of his life.

Broadcast Journalism

After graduation, Guillermo returned to San Francisco uncertain of what he wanted to do. He had often been encouraged to try his hand at stand-up comedy, and for a while, especially after the accolades his Ivy Oration brought him, he considered it. He visited some clubs and saw many of today's comics (like Robin Wiliams) who were just then starting out. Ultimately, though, the idea just didn't appeal to him. He didn't like the smoky environment, and the comics at times seemed too willing to do or say anything for a laugh.

He had always been interested in news so he tried his hand at television reporting. He didn't have any experience, but he was able to persuade a station in Salinas, California, to give him a chance as a reporter. They gave him a camera and sent him out to cover an antimilitary protest. If they liked his work he could have a job. If not he could keep the tape as an audition tape. He never heard from them again.

His first on-air job in television news was in 1979 at KOLO in Reno, Nevada, where he was a reporter, sportscaster, and backup anchor. In 1980 he went to KXAS in Dallas where he worked in his first major news-market. In Dallas he learned everything a television reporter needs to know. He covered crime, fires, disasters, and politics. He stayed in Dallas for about fourteen months and then was offered a job back in San Francisco at KRON.

He began at KRON in 1981 as a general assignment reporter and won a Spot News Award in 1982 for a story he did on a chemical spill in the Bay Area. In 1984 as an arts and entertainment critic, he reviewed films and concerts and other performances in the San Francisco area. When the station had a change of management in 1988, Guillermo left. As a leading Filipino in the media, he then started his own radio show called "Bay Area Filipino with Emil Guillermo." The show was a half-hour news and entertainment program which featured Guillermo's personal essays and was the only Filipino American broadcast in the continental United States. The show was well-sponsored and had a wide listening audience. He ended the show in 1989 when he was offered a position with National Public Radio (NPR).

Guillermo was the first Asian American anchor of a national radio program in the country. As the weekend anchor of NPR's popular news show, "All Things Considered," he conducted interviews with major newsmakers, did reporting for the daily broadcast, and produced long form pieces, commentaries, and essays. In 1991 the Asian American Journalists Association recognized him with a National Achievement Award, naming him best in radio.

In 1991, Guillermo left NPR and began hosting a talk show on a local Washington, D.C. radio station. He called his show "Amok in Washington: the Emil Guillermo Show" and described it to Henry as "a sort of anti-Rush Limbaugh." Guillermo continued honing his style of political commentary from an Asian perspective, and in 1992 he published his first column on the editorial page of *USA Today*. He also wrote in such publications as *Asian Week, Transpacific,* and the *San Francisco Bay Guardian,* for which he served as Washington correspondent.

Guillermo decided he wanted to experience politics firsthand, so from 1993 until spring of 1994, he served as press secretary to Norman Y. Mineta, California's fifteenth district representative in the U.S. Congress and the highest-ranking Asian American in the House. He enjoyed working in politics but ultimately missed the freedom he had had as a writer and journalist.

An Asian American Commentator

Because Guillermo is one of the very few Asian American humorists and commentators on the national scene, he considers it his task to help redefine the role of the Asian American in America. He thinks that perhaps the immigrant community from Asia has been too insulated and too private, both of which he considers aspects of Asian culture, which generally shuns publicity and narcissism. In his column, "Amok," which is run monthly in *Filipinas* magazine, he has used humor to discuss such issues as Asian under-representation in mainstream media, the Filipino tradition of eating dogs, Howard Stern's condescension to Filipinos, the success of CBS News anchor Connie Chung, and the 1992 cheating scandal involving the Little League baseball champions from the Philippines.

Guillermo wrote in one of his columns, "Going amok is . . . saying publicly what others won't, or what many Filipinos would leave unsaid." And on occasion, Guillermo has done just that. He tries to be constructive, though, and to make a point. He believes that it is the humorist's job in society to get people to think, even if it is sometimes about unpleasant things. The difference between the humorist and the comedian, he told Henry, is that "the comedian will say anything for a laugh; the humorist will say anything for a point."

Sources:

Periodicals

Guillermo, Emil. "The Connie Controversy," *Filipinas,* November, 1993, p. 24.

Other

Guillermo, Emil, telephone interview with Jim Henry, May 2, 1994.

—*Sketch by Jim Henry*

Rajat Gupta

Rajat Gupta

(1948–)

Business leader

In 1973, Rajat Gupta was just another job applicant without enough work experience on his resume when he submitted his first application to McKinsey and Company, the prestigious management consulting firm that he now heads. His application was rejected. Thriving on a combination of perseverance and luck, however, Gupta has propelled himself to the very top of McKinsey, becoming in March of 1994 the managing director and first non-Western to lead the giant firm. Founded in 1926, McKinsey has a worldwide professional staff of three thousand and in 1993 had revenue totaling $1.3 billion.

Born on December 12, 1948, in Calcutta, India, Rajat Gupta was the second of four children. When he was five years old, his family moved to New Delhi, where his father was an editor and active in India's independence movement and his mother was a Montessori teacher. Tragedy struck early as Gupta lost both his parents by the time he was eighteen.

Gupta worked to pay his way through college. He earned an undergraduate degree in mechanical engineering at the Indian Institute of Technology. It was there that he met his wife, Anita Mattoo, who was an electrical engineering major. Both were involved in drama as an extracurricular activity and they met at a rehearsal. At the time of his election to head McKinsey, the Guptas had four daughters.

In 1971, Gupta won a scholarship to attend the Harvard Business School. Harvard classmates remember Gupta as being exceptionally gifted and smart. One former roommate said in the *New York Times:* "Things came easily to Rajat. He reviewed cases very easily. Even if we had tests, he would study for a time and then sit down without fail every day to write a letter to his girlfriend."

In 1973, Gupta graduated from Harvard with a master's degree in business administration. He applied for a position at McKinsey, but was rejected due to a lack of work experience. A professor intervened and urged McKinsey to reconsider its decision. The company changed its mind.

Gupta joined McKinsey and in 1980 was made junior partner. One year later he was sent overseas to manage McKinsey's foothold in Scandinavia. In three years, the Scandinavian operations grew to one hundred consultants from the original twenty-five. He was head of McKinsey's Chicago office before being named managing director in 1994.

Since 1980, the firm has opened thirty-three offices, only six in the United States. More than half the senior partners—78 of 148—are now abroad, compared to 17 of 47 in 1980. Gupta's elevation as managing director signals that McKinsey's growth will continue to be overseas in emerging markets like the former Soviet republics, Eastern Europe, China, and India.

Gupta's colleagues say in some ways his approach to business is decidedly non-Western. One colleague who called Gupta's style a Tao approach to leading said in the *New York Times,* "If it feels right, he concludes it is the correct decision. If it doesn't, he reverses the decision and sleeps on it again."

Sources:

Byrne, John A. "A Global Citizen for a Global McKinsey." *Business Week,* April 11, 1994.

Pandya, Mukul. "Triumph of the Quiet Man at McKinsey and Co.," *New York Times,* May 22, 1994.

Sreenivasan, Sreenath. "Firmly at the Top," *India Today,* May 15, 1994.

—Sketch by Felicia Paik

H

Maria Luisa Mabilangan Haley

(1940–)

Political appointee, entrepreneur

In 1993, when Maria Haley entered the Oval Office of the White House as special assistant to President Bill Clinton and associate director of presidential personnel for econmics, commerce and trade, she felt her life had come full circle. Now as the highest-ranking Filipino American in the Clinton Administration, she stood where her father, Felipe Mabilangan, had stood sixty-five years ago, when, as a Filipino political science student at Syracuse University, he had testified before Congress appealing to them to grant his homeland independence. Reflecting on her life and career accomplishments, Haley believes her success boils down to four valuable lessons—flexibility, humility, hard work, and perseverance.

Born in Manila in the Philippines on November 14, 1940, three weeks before the bombing of Pearl Harbor, Maria Mabilangan, along with her brother and parents, spent the first five years of her life hiding from the Japanese in the mountains of Batangas and living at her parents' home in Santo Thomas, Batangas, during the occupation. From 1945 to 1950, Maria's family lived in Manila, where her father was an officer in the Philippine Foreign Service, and where she attended St. Paul's Convent. In 1950, she began her a childhood of traveling when her father became the first Philippine Consul General in New Delhi, India.

Raised in the traditional Philippine way by parents from the "old school," Mabilangan attended Senior Cambridge Convent of Jesus and Mary in New Delhi. Following a typical career diplomat path, her family traveled globally, living in Pakistan, France, Spain, with a short stay Laos. During this period, she attended the best finishing schools in Europe and Asia to train for the life of a diplomat's wife. Her brother received similar training and is today the Philippine Ambassador to China. In addition to speaking fluent Filipino, French, Spanish, and English, she studied art and humanities at the Ecole du Louvre as well as classical Indian dance.

Maria Luisa Mabilangan Haley

Entrepreneur and Businesswoman

In her early twenties, however, Mabilangan decided to change directions and develop a career. In 1964, pooling resources with good friend, Conchitina Sevilla, then one of the Philippine's most successful fashion models, she returned to Manila and opened the Karilagan Finishing School, the first of its kind in Southeast Asia. A year later, at age twenty-five, she took another major leap and, by a complete fluke, ended up joining a managerial training program at the Hilton International in Manila. "In an interview, the vice-president of the company asked me, 'Maria, can you type?' I said, 'No.' 'Can you take shorthand?' I said, 'No.' And he said, 'Never mind. We will make you a manager,'" Mabilangan recalled in a speech given at a leadership training conference sponsored by the Filipino American Women's Network in June 1994. Armed only with determination, flexibility, and humility, she began her training in Hong Kong and Tokyo and worked all shifts peeling potatoes, changing beds, and cleaning bathrooms—in short, learning to manage people and programs. In just two years, Mabilangan became the second female sales manager in an international hotel chain, a male-dominated business. For three years with the Manila Hilton, she traveled worldwide to develop new markets, negotiate tour, airline, and commercial contracts, and coordinate conferences and banquets.

In 1971, after marriage to an American lawyer from Little Rock, Arkansas, John Haley, and a subsequent move to the United States, Haley sought an opportunity to continue her career. For a year she worked as a travel agent and then, in 1974, accepted the position of general manager of the new resort division of Fairfield Communities, a retirement community firm. After only one year, she was promoted to director of resort marketing with responsibilities for sales, advertising, and promotion of the division.

Joining the Clinton Team

In 1979, approached by Clinton's transition team after his successful bid for governor, Haley was intrigued with the governor's economic development plans to bring the state into the global marketplace. Again facing a totally new career, she made a leap of faith into the complexities of international marketing as a trade specialist. However, her first prospective deal at the Arkansas Industrial Development Commission was less than confidence-inspiring. After approaching and receiving a refusal from the owner of a small Arkansas tent manufacturing company who told her, "I ain't selling no tents to no foreigners," Haley resisted the urge to fold up her own tent and elected instead to establish a personal approach aimed at developing trust and confidence between her office and the statewide network of companies that could be potential exporters of goods.

During the years from 1979 to 1990, Haley served as International Marketing Consultant and Director of Marketing for the Arkansas Industrial Development Commission (AIDC), a state cabinet agency. She advised Governor Clinton on foreign relations, trade and investment activities; took charge of the state's national and international marketing, export development, and foreign programs; supervised the establishment and expansion of the state's overseas offices in Brussels, Tokyo, and Taipei; and coordinated all of the governor's international business missions. Under her leadership, the agency tripled the number of Arkansas manufacturers exporting goods from the state. In the process, these 752 companies employed over 139,000 Arkansans. In 1991, she became director of communications for AIDC, managing media relations, advertising, and promotions.

When Clinton decided to run for president in 1991, Haley was one of the first of his gubernatorial staff to volunteer for his campaign. At the Democratic Convention, she served as a floor whip and surrogate speaker for Asian Pacific events. During the two months prior to the election, she traveled across the country campaigning on Clinton's behalf in Asian American communities.

After his election in November 1992, she was named deputy director of personnel in the transition team. Once again, Haley took a completely new job which required her to move on twenty-four hours notice, leaving her home of twenty-two years, her friends, and family. "In all my professional life, I can say that I took advantage of opportunities," Haley explained in an article in the *Philippine Review* in May of 1993, "but having done that, I worked very hard to establish and maintain my credibility in whatever area I worked on. My way of achieving is to seize the opportunity that comes your way and to take advantage of it, but once you're there, you work very, very hard to stay, and even do better."

In 1993, Haley was named special assistant to the president and associate director of presidential personnel for economics, commerce and trade. Working from sixty-five to seventy hours a week, she oversees and assists in the appointment process of sub-cabinet, senior, and mid-level positions in the Clinton administration. "Being involved in everything you do" is an essential quality of success, said Haley in the *Philippine Review.* "You may be a very brilliant person, with high academic credentials, but to do well...even if it is working as a housekeeper in a hotel, it's the attitude in how you do your work that counts."

Haley values charity toward others and believes strongly that it is through giving that one receives. Cofounder of the Filipino Youth Scholarship Foundation, which assists youths with college financial aid, she has also served in a variety of community and civic organizations including the Rotary Club of Little Rock, Sales and Marketing Executives Association in Manila and Little Rock, and the Professional Women's Advisory Board of Worthen Bank and Trust.

A future goal of Haley's is to return to school to complete her college degree. Although divorced for the past four years, she maintains active relationships with her three grown stepchildren and their families who live in Arkansas and Texas. In her free time she enjoys listening to music, reading, walking, and makes an effort to stick to a weekly regimen of aerobics and weight lifting.

A U.S. citizen since 1979, Haley has said that she thinks of herself as an American with a Philippine heritage. With Filipino Americans the largest Asian ethnic group in the U.S., Haley would like to see more of them in elected positions, "because that's where one can really make a difference," she proclaimed in an article in the *Sunday Inquirer Magazine.*

Like many other Filipinos who today call the United States their home, Haley's feelings about her adopted country do not discount her love for her family and homeland. As she told the *Sunday Inquirer Magazine,* "The

Filipino in me is my past, my heritage, my homeland. But my present and my future is America."

Ross Masao Harano

Sources:

Periodicals

Gerona-Adkins, Rita M. "Maria Mabilangan Haley: A Filipina at the White House." *Philippine Review,* May 1993.

Krebs, Caroline. "U.S. States Promote Exports." *Advertising World,* February–March, 1984.

Lopez, Mena. "Kababayan in the White House." *Sunday Inquirer Magazine,* July, 11, 1993.

"Mabilangan-Haley Leads FAWN Celebration of Asian Pacific American Heritage Month." *CommLink-Philippine News,* June 1–7, 1994.

Other

Haley, Maria Luisa M. Resume, 1994.

———. Speech given at FAWN Celebration of Asian Pacific Heritage Month, June 1994.

—Sketch by Nancy Moore

Ross Masao Harano
(1942–)
Businessman, political activist

Ross Harano remembers the first time he realized that he was Japanese. "It was the day I graduated from grammar school and I went to a movie with my classmates to see *The Court Martial of Billy Mitchell* with Gary Cooper. During the court martial which takes place in the 1920s, Billy Mitchell states that air power will determine future wars and that Pearl Harbor would be vulnerable to air attack. When asked 'Who could bomb Pearl Harbor?' by the prosecution, Billy Mitchell stated 'The Japanese.' At this point all of my classmates turned and looked at me. For the first time I felt different and slightly uncomfortable." It was that realization that later motivated Harano to learn more about his ethnicity and to take an active role in the Japanese American community. As president of the World Trade Center Chicago Association as well as chairperson of the Chicago chapter of the Japanese American Citizens League, Harano is both a business and a community leader.

Ross Masao Harano was born in California on September 17, 1942, at the Fresno Fairgrounds, which was then an assembly center for Japanese Americans interned during World War II. He and his family were relocated to the internment camp in Jerome, Arkansas, and moved to Alton, Illinois when Ross was a year old. They again moved one year later, heading this time to the south side of Chicago where they resided for seventeen years before moving to the north side. The young Harano grew up in a close-knit extended family that included grandparents, aunts, uncles, and cousins.

Young Leader

By junior high school, Harano was already showing his leadership qualities. "I was the master of ceremonies at many of the school assemblies and, as a result, have always enjoyed public speaking. As a youth, my church provided a series of leadership training retreats which assisted me as a young adult," he told Terry Hong in a written interview. Harano feels fortunate to have had strong role models to guide him. He recalled, "In my early teens . . . my pastor . . . had the uncanny ability to almost read my mind and anticipate my thoughts and actions. He was like my guiding conscience." As a young adult, a local community center youth worker "was most influential in steering [Harano's] energies into constructive activities within the Japanese American community."

In 1960, Harano entered the University of Illinois with the intention of studying engineering. He became more interested in business, however, and graduated with a degree in finance in 1965. A year later, he earned a graduate degree in sociology from DePaul University. Harano began his professional career in insurance and moved on to banking, eventually assuming the position of vice president at the Bank of Chicago in 1978 and at the Community Bank of Edgewater in 1980. From banking, he entered the international trading market, serving as the operating partner for two international trading companies, and as the chief financial officer for a third.

Harano leapt to yet another career path in 1988, joining the Office of the Attorney General of Illinois where he served as the equal opportunity officer, the director of advisory councils, and the chief of the crime victims division before leaving in 1993 to assume the presidency of the Illinois World Trade Center.

Despite his successful career, Harano never neglected his community responsibilities. "Being born in a camp during World War II has made me a firm believer in the Bill of Rights, and as a result, I have been active in human rights organizations supporting this important document," he told Hong. Garnering community awards one after the other, Harano has been recognized by the Japanese Americans Citizens League, the Chicago Junior Chamber of Commerce, the Illinois Department of Human Rights and the Chicago Commission on Human Relations, to name a few. He has served as the president of the Illinois Ethnic Coalition and as the chairperson of the Chicago Chapter of the Japanese American Citizens League. In 1992, he became the first Asian American to be appointed as an elector for the Electoral College in Illinois.

The "Taxi Test"

Since becoming the president of Chicago's World Trade Center, Harano has conducted what he calls the "taxi test" almost every day. He tells the story of how he once got into a cab and told the driver, " Take me to the World Trade Center," to which the driver replied, "OK, but it'll cost you about $800." Explained Harano, "He was going to take me to New York. He didn't know that Chicago has a World Trade Center of its own."

The taxi driver is not alone. In spite of its importance in the business community, the center isn't known to many Chicago natives. Chicago's World Trade Center will need to raise its profile considerably, said Harano. Ideally, Harano would like the center to occupy a high-profile Chicago downtown building that can be called the World Trade Center Building.

Meanwhile, Harano continues to conduct his taxi test. "We have to let people know that we're here . . . let them know where we are," he said. "I'll know I'm making progress the first time I'm able to get into a Chicago cab and have the driver take me to the front door of the World Trade Center without starting out for New York."

Sources:

Periodicals

Yates, Ronald E. "Trade Center Has Global Ambitions—in the Midwest." *Chicago Tribune*, April 4, 1993, Business section, pp. 1,12.

Other

Harano, Ross Masao, written interview with Terry Hong, January 1994.

—Sketch by Terry Hong

Sumi Sevilla Haru
(1939–)
Producer, actor, journalist, writer, poet

"**I** always have six million irons in the oven," laughed Sumi Sevilla Haru. Indeed, describing Haru in one phrase is virtually impossible. Haru is a performing arts program coordinator for the City of Los Angeles. She is a newspaper columnist. She is co-president of the County of Los Angeles Media Image Coalition. She is co-founder and president of the Association of Asian Pacific American Artists. She is a member of the national executive board of the Asian Pacific Labor Alliance. She is a radio commentator and show producer for numerous stations. She is an actress. She is a frequent lecturer and keynote speaker. And, she is a teacher. "Most of the activities I'm involved in," Haru told Terry Hong in an interview, "have to do with fighting for affirmative action in media and the arts."

With so many facets to her multidimensional career, Haru's list of achievements and successes is undeniably long. The achievement of which Haru is most proud is her current position as first national vice-president of the Screen Actors Guild (SAG). "I feel it's a very important position. It's good for an Asian American to be in such a visible position," she said.

Hollywood or Bust

Conceived in Manila, Philippines, Sumi Sevilla Haru was born on August 25, 1939 in Orange, New Jersey. When she was three months old, the family left the East Coast. "My father was working for a colonel in the army who got transferred to Fort Leavenworth, Kansas, so we went, too," explained Haru. After World War II, the family settled in Arvada, Colorado, in 1947. "The population of the town then was about three thousand. We were the only Filipinos around. My sister and I were the only Asians in school. There were about five Mexican families and a few Italians, if you could call them minorities. I grew up not knowing that I was that much different from anyone else," recalled Haru. In school, Haru was a superior student, a cheerleader, the first chair in the Colorado Honor Band, a head majorette and, as she remembered, "I managed to practice the piano for six hours a day."

A model child, Haru was "busy out-whiting the whites," she added with a laugh. "I was more capable than my fellow students," she said. "And that kind of frantic life-style of belonging to everything and being good at many things continued into my adulthood. I feel good about that. I consider myself successful."

At the University of Colorado, Haru studied music with a concentration in piano and flute. She married her childhood sweetheart after college and had two daughters. The marriage did not last long, and Haru, once again single, went on vacation to California in 1963. She decided to go out for a drink with a high school friend. "I got picked up at this bar by Ralph Nelson who was making the film *Soldier in the Rain* with Steve McQueen and Jackie Gleason. And that's how I got into show business," she remembered.

In 1964, Haru moved to Los Angeles to pursue an acting career. She began studying acting and was cast in a few films and musical comedies. In 1967, she became involved with East West Players, the first Asian American theatre company in the United States. "I was working on the movie *M*A*S*H* at the time and I met a number of East West members on the set. I started doing productions over there and spent ten years on the board," Haru recalled. "Unlike what other people have said, Mako [East West Players' founder and artistic director] was very encouraging of East West actors to go out and seek work outside of the company productions."

As an actor, Haru experienced first hand the all-too-common racism in Hollywood. In 1970, with similarities to the *Miss Saigon* controversy of the late 1980s (in which Caucasian actor Jonathan Pryce was cast in the male lead of the Amerasian engineer), a European American actor was cast as the male, Asian lead in *Lovely Ladies, Kind Gentlemen,* the musical version of the play *Teahouse of the August Moon.* The actor, Kenneth Nelson, was pictured in a leading newspaper pulling at his eyes sideways, saying "I shall be pleased to play a straight, slant-eyed Oriental." In reaction, Haru helped form the Brotherhood of Artists to protest the racist casting. "It was the beginning of my activism," Haru claimed.

In 1971, Haru came to national attention when she helped found SAG's Ethnic Employment Opportunities Committee which launched the first concerted efforts

Sumi Sevilla Haru

toward establishing affirmative action in the hiring of actors. In 1976, together with actor Bernie Casey, Haru drafted and negotiated the affirmative action clauses of national theatrical and commercial contracts. The now required phrase, "American scene," referred to realistic depictions in film for all aspects of American life, especially in the portrayals of minorities. Through efforts led by Haru, the phrase became a necessary clause required in all SAG and American Federation of Television and Radio Artists (AFTRA) contracts.

"Twenty years later, we're still struggling for realistic representation, especially for minorities," said Haru, somewhat disappointed. "But we've made progress. I would have given up long ago if we hadn't made any progress," she declared.

Championing Minority Voices

"I want to be remembered for having made positive changes in the entertainment industry and the news media," Haru stated simply. To that end, her list of current projects and involvements seem virtually endless. As the performing arts program coordinator for the Performing Arts Division of Los Angeles' Cultural Affairs Department, Haru recently coordinated the Fiesta Del Maiz and Deaf-estival '94. She is also a producer/host of "L.A. Arts Mix," a television magazine program on the arts and culture of Los Angeles.

In addition to her involvement with SAG, Haru has served on AFTRA's local and national boards since 1976. In 1994, she was the local recording secretary and western national chair of the Equal Employment Opportunities Committee. She serves as a legislative advocate at the national level on Federal Communications Commission and civil rights issues, and is a member of the national Legislative Committee and the national Broadcasters Committee.

Haru is co-president of the County of Los Angeles Media Image Coalition, which seeks balanced media images and career opportunities for under-represented groups in the television and film industry. She is co-founder and president of the Association of Asian Pacific Artists which seeks employment opportunities and balanced images of Asian and Pacific Islanders in film and on television. She is a member of the national executive board of the Asian Pacific Labor Alliance, an affiliate of the AFL-CIO, and is the executive vice-president of the Los Angeles chapter of the organization.

As first vice-chair of the National Conference of Christian and Jews Asian Pacific American Focus Program and member of the Media Image Task Force, Haru initiated the publication of *ASIAN PACIFIC AMERICANS: A Handbook on How to Cover and Portray Our Nation's Fastest Growing Minority Group,* published in cooperation with the Asian American Journalists Association and the Association of Asian Pacific American Artists.

Performer and Artist

While Haru expends considerable time and energy toward promoting affirmative action in the media, she is also an artist, broadcaster, writer, and producer. "I keep forgetting that," she laughed. For seventeen years, Haru worked as a producer/moderator for KTLA-TV, making her the only Filipino who has been consistently on the air in Los Angeles. "The Filipino community is very large in the L.A. area, but there is virtually no Filipino representation on the air. When I have time, I try to do commentary on various stations. I think that's really important, to have Asian viewpoints on the air with regularity," she said. Haru's broadcasts include "Gallery," "70s Woman, 80s Woman" and "Weekend Gallery." She has also also produced and hosted specials on the Philippines, Taiwan, the former East Germany, the former U.S.S.R., and Nicaragua.

Haru has also been a programmer and host on the radio. Since 1990, she has been working with KPFK-FM Pacifica Radio where some of her programs include roundtables on multicultural issues, the "lunch breaks" and wrap-ups during the Clarence Thomas Supreme Court confirmation hearings, a special on the commemoration of the atomic bombings of Hiroshima and Nagasaki, election coverage, and a calendar of events.

The credits of Haru's production company, Iron Lotus Productions, include *Women Pioneer* videos for Los Angeles' Telecommunications Department and television programs for Pacific Asian Alcohol Program and Asian Pacific American Legal Center. The production company currently has in development a dramatic series based on Haru's pilot, "Watch This Space," a series which she created, wrote, produced, and in which she plays the lead. Haru also teaches at Columbia College, where she runs a television production workshop that gives junior- and senior-level students experience comparable to the working environment of the entertainment industry.

Acting, which first brought Haru to Los Angeles, is still her first love. "I'd rather be acting than doing anything I'm doing now," she chuckled. Her television and film credits include "The Young and the Restless," "Sweepstakes," "M*A*S*H," "Hill Street Blues" and *Krakatoa, East of Java*. Given the choice, in ten years, Haru would like to spend most of her time acting. "I'd like to be starring in my own television series. I'd like to play a professional woman—a lawyer perhaps. It could be comedy or drama. I can do both," she said.

In addition to acting, writing is also a vital part of Haru's career. "I want to be acknowledged for the things I write," she stated. She is currently a columnist for the newspaper, *Asian Week,* and her articles have appeared in the *Chicago Shimpo, AsiAm, Korea Times, Neworld, Screen Actor,* and *Dialog*. At a recent meeting in Sacramento, Haru realized the effect her writing has had on her readers: "I was walking with [California's] secretary of state, and he said to me, 'you're the Sumi who writes the column.' I realized then that people are really reading what I write, that I have an effect on my readers."

Through all her many projects and talents, Haru strives to make a difference. "I would like to say that I had some very important Asian Pacific American women who were my role models, but I really can't. Isn't it sad that we don't have more Asian role models? There just weren't any Asian Americans in the limelight when I was growing up. That's why I think it's so important today to have as many Asian Americans who are really visible in their fields." Haru is undoubtedly one of them.

Sources:

Haru, Sumi, telephone interview with Terry Hong, June 27, 1994.

City of Los Angeles. "Sumi Sevilla Haru." Professional resume and press releases, June 1994.

—Sketch by Terry Hong

Lon S. Hatamiya
(1959–)
Businessman, attorney, government administrator

Lon S. Hatamiya

Lon Hatamiya has parlayed two of his family's strongest values—hard work and community commitment—into a successful career in both private business as well as public service. His appointment by President Bill Clinton in September 1993 as administrator of the Agricultural Marketing Service (AMS) of the United States Department of Agriculture (USDA) has been the crowning moment in a lifetime of diverse interests and achievements.

Lon Hatamiya was born on January 26, 1959, in Marysville, California, to George and Kashiwa Hatamiya. His grandfather, Sennichi Hatamiya, had come to Marysville from Hiroshima, Japan, in the early 1900s and purchased a farm after working for a number of years as a farmhand and railroad worker. Today the family farm, H.B. Orchards Company, comprises twelve hundred acres of prunes, peaches, walnuts, and almonds. Hatamiya helped on the farm during his childhood, along with his parents, his two sisters (Kim and Jil), and his two uncles and their families. He played a variety of sports from elementary school through graduate school. Boy Scouts was another important activity for Hatamiya; he received the prestigious Eagle Scout award at the age of fourteen.

Hatamiya told Mary Anne Klasen he recalls two pivotal points of his childhood that helped shape his adult goals. The first was the 1968 presidential campaign, even though he was only in third grade at the time. "Nineteen sixty-eight was a year of great civil unrest—from the Vietnam War to the assassinations of Robert Kennedy and Martin Luther King," he said. "Robert Kennedy came to my hometown to campaign for the presidency during the California primary. His presence and eloquence inspired me to public service. My interest and activity [in politics] have continued to bloom."

The second turning point was hearing about his family's experiences during World War II. When Americans of Japanese ancestry were forcibly removed from areas of the West Coast, his father's family was interned first at Tule Lake, California, and then at Amache, Colorado. His mother's family was interned at Topaz, Utah, and then at Crystal City, Texas. During these years of incarceration, the family's farm was taken care of by neighbors. "Learning firsthand from my parents and grandparents about the traumatic experience of being uprooted from their homes during the Second World War to be interned in concentration camps solely because of their Japanese American heritage left a deep impression upon

my personal development," Hatamiya told Klasen. "My family's experience motivated me to become actively involved in community activities and civil rights issues to ensure that such a tragic, discriminatory event would never occur again."

Hatamiya left Marysville for the first time in 1977 to attend Harvard College, where he graduated in 1981 with a bachelor's degree in economics with honors. His first job after college was as a purchasing manager for the Procter and Gamble Company in Cincinnati, Ohio. He returned to California to earn both a master's in business administration in entrepreneurial studies and international business from the Anderson Graduate School of Management at the University of California Los Angeles (UCLA) and his law degree at the UCLA School of Law in 1987. While in graduate school, he worked in Japan as a consultant for the Sony Corporation, where he developed a marketing strategy for broadcast equipment in Western Europe and served as a consultant to the Port of Long Beach, California in 1985 and 1986. After completing his education, Hatamiya practiced public finance, corporate, and political law with the national law firm of Orrick, Herrington and Sutcliffe in Sacramento, California, from 1987 to 1989, when he returned to Marysville and his family's farm.

Farming and politics, never far from Hatamiya's mind, remained a part of his activities after he moved back to California in 1983. He continued to work with the family farm run by his father and two uncles. In 1991 he founded BHP Associates, an economic development, education, and agribusiness consulting firm in Sacramento. Hatamiya's first foray into formal politics came in 1990, when he ran as a Democrat for a seat in the California State Legislature from the third assembly district in northern California. Although he lost to incumbent Chris Chandler, Hatamiya had made his mark: He was the first Japanese American to run for the state assembly in more than a decade, and he again received the Democratic party's nomination in 1992. Today, Hatamiya credits fellow Californians, congressmen Robert Matsui, Norman Mineta, and Vic Fazio, with being important role models in his political endeavors. "Bob, Norm, and Vic strongly encouraged me to utilize my community involvement and run for public office." he told Klasen. "They not only supported me morally, but financially, and continue to provide invaluable personal advice." His election defeats haven't clouded Hatamiya's reputation as a valuable political resource in California.

In 1991, he was selected for the California Agricultural Leadership Program of the California Agricultural Education Foundation, which consists of top state agriculture leaders. The California State Assembly appointed him in 1992 to serve on the Rural Economic Development Infrastructure Panel. He was also a member of the executive committee and co-chairman of the finance committee of the California Democratic party.

Hatamiya's commitment to community service is reflected in his participation in a wide variety of community activities. He served on the boards of directors of Planned Parenthood of the Sacramento Valley and the Marysville Chapter of the Japanese American Citizens League (JACL). As a student at Harvard—where his senior honors thesis, "The Economic Impact of the Second World War Upon the Japanese in California," gained him recognition as a leading authority on the economic impact of Japanese American internment—as research coordinator for the National Committee for Redress of the JACL, and as president of the Sacramento chapter of the JACL, he worked tirelessly to obtain reparations for Japanese Americans like his parents who were interned in camps during World War II. Hatamiya also has worked with the Yuba Sutter Big Brothers and Big Sisters and the California Association of Family Farmers.

Agricultural expertise, community involvement, business and political savvy, and experience combined to make Hatamiya a logical choice for AMS administrator in 1993. His responsibilities there include managing and directing a variety of marketing programs: commodity grading, classing and inspection for quality; commodity procurement; market news and development; commodity research and promotion; and commodity standardization. Hatamiya also oversees the agency's traditional regulatory programs such as marketing agreement and orders, and laws designed to ensure fair trading in the produce and seed industries. Of his move to Washington, Hatamiya said: "The challenge of administering over fifty federal programs is enormous. As the first Asian American administrator in the history of USDA, I am fortunate to be given the opportunity to be at the cutting edge of implementing government policy as it relates to the marketing of everything we eat. My appointment proves that Asian Americans can and should have an influence within every branch of government."

Hatamiya said he, his wife Nancy, and their two sons Jon and George, are proud of their Japanese heritage. "Nancy and I met while we were both presidents of different JACL chapters. Her shared commitment to our community provides the basic foundation of our successful partnership. Without question, our Japanese American heritage has and will always influence my success," he said. "The cultural values instilled in me by my parents and grandparents have provided me with a solid foundation for hard work and commitment to my community."

Sources:

Hatamiya, Lon, telephone interview with Mary Anne Klasen, July 14, 1994.

U.S. Department of Agriculture, Agricultural Marketing Service. "Lon Hatamiya." Press releases and biographical information, 1994.

—Sketch by Mary Anne Klasen

James Hattori

Journalist

James Hattori is one the few Asia American television journalists covering national and international news at the network level. As a correspondent for CBS News, Hattori reported on a wide range of stories for the "CBS Evening News," "Sunday Morning," "48 Hours," "CBS Morning News," and "CBS This Morning." During the 1992 presidential campaign, Hattori covered the beginning of Ross Perot's bid as an independent candidate for the presidency, as well as the Republican National Convention in Houston. In 1990, he reported on the Gulf War for CBS News, serving as a correspondent with air force and army units in Iraq, Kuwait, and Saudi Arabia. He has also covered the U.S. invasion of Panama, the Exxon Valdez oil spill, drug trafficking in Colombia, and NASA space shuttle missions. Since 1992, he has been serving as CBS News correspondent from Tokyo.

The Roots of Hattori's Success

Hattori was born and raised in Los Angeles, the youngest of three children. He lived with his parents and his older brother and sister in the inner-city Crenshaw neighborhood where there was a community of Japanese American families. When Hattori was in junior high school, his family moved to a community near Torrance, a Los Angeles suburb. Hattori remembers taking many trips with his family to national parks like Yosemite and the Grand Canyon. He was also a Boy Scout and went on frequent camping trips. "I loved to travel, still do," he told *Notable Asian Americans*. "I'm fascinated by seeing new places and people. It's one reason why my job is so great."

According to Hattori, his parents had the most profound influence on him as he was growing up. "I didn't realize or fully appreciate it at the time," he said. "They are hardworking, honest people who live modestly. I feel very lucky to have parents who care so much about their children, and who unselfishly dedicated so much of their lives." His older brother and sister have also been very supportive of him, Hattori added. As a young person, Hattori enjoyed reading, starting from the time when his mother would open a book at bedtime. "It exposed me to new worlds and possibilities beyond everyday life," he said, "which I came to realize were not just 'out there,' but really attainable if seriously pursued."

The Journey Begins

After finishing high school in Torrance, Hattori entered the University of Southern California School of Journalism. It was in college, at about the age of twenty, that Hattori decided to pursue a reporting career. He had been studying broadcast management, but changed to journalism when the two programs merged. "I really decided after taking a course from two well-regarded reporters in Los Angeles." Hattori recounted to *Notable Asian Americans*. "They were award-winning, serious journalists whose jobs seemed challenging and meaningful. That's when it struck me that this was a career that was not only interesting, but could also serve the public interest."

Hattori graduated cum laude from the University of Southern California in 1977. His first job as was a weekend assignment editor and writer at KGTV-TV in San Diego. Shortly afterward, he joined KFMB-TV in Spokane, Washington, as a reporter and midday anchor. Hattori spent the following four years at KREM-TV, his longest time at a station to date. In 1982, he joined KING-TV in Seattle as a reporter, legislative correspondent, and weekend anchor. After five years in Seattle, Hattori joined KPRC-TV in Houston as a reporter in the special projects unit. CBS News soon offered him the post of Dallas correspondent.

As a reporter for CBS Hattori covered stories for the newsmagazine "48 Hours." These included diverse topics such as animal rights, abuse of the elderly, Alzheimer's disease, diets, the fight save the rhinoceros, fire fighting, and juveniles on death row. It was after his coverage of the

James Hattori

1992 presidential race that Hattori was named Tokyo correspondent.

The Drive to do Better

As a reporter, Hattori has enjoyed a steady and swift rise in his profession. He moved from station to station to bigger and better posts and is now in a position that uses both his background and skills. "There's no doubt that being of Japanese heritage is a part of the success I've enjoyed," he said. "It's what makes me distinctive–apart from the crowd, at least superficially. But inside it makes a difference too. According to Hattori, "Growing up feeling like something of an outsider striving to be in the mainstream–whether or not that's a mistaken notion–has made me tougher. More resourceful. More independent. It constantly challenges me to assess myself and where I am and where I want to be." Hattori told *Notable Asian Americans,* "Anything can happen if you put your mind to it. No one can do all things or be everything to everyone. We all choose what we want most. If we're inspired and committed, things work out."

Sources:

CBS News, "James Hattori," biographical information and press releases, 1994.

Hattori, James, written interview with Helen Zia, May 1994.

—Sketch by Natasha Rafi

Samuel Ichiye Hayakawa
(1906–1992)
Senator, educator, writer

Although he was probably known to most as the colorful senator from California who made a national name for himself with his eccentric appearance and behavior (at five-foot three he often wore a colorful tam-o-shanter) and his political unpredictability, Samuel Ichiye Hayakawa was also an esteemed scholar, college administrator, and author of *Language in Action,* a seminal semantics textbook now in its fifth edition (as *Language in Thought and Action*), which has been translated into nine languages. He was also a co-founder of the International Society for General Semantics (ISGS) and *ETC.: A Review of General Semantics,* a scholarly journal dedicated to language and its uses. In addition, from 1983 until 1990, he served as Special Adviser to the Secretary of State for East Asian and Pacific Affairs.

Samuel Hayakawa, known to his family and friends as "Don," was born in Vancouver, British Columbia, on July 18, 1906. His parents were Japanese immigrants who ran an import-export business. He earned his bachelor's degree from the University of Manitoba in 1927 and a master's degree from MacGill University in 1928. For his post-graduate work, Hayakawa came to the United States. He earned his Ph.D. in English and American literature from the University of Wisconsin in 1935, where he wrote his thesis on the poetry and prose of Oliver Wendell Holmes.

Academic and Writer

While teaching at the University of Wisconsin, Hayakawa wrote his best known book, *Language in Action,* based on the ideas of Alfred Korzybski, the man considered to be the founder of the field of general semantics, which can be broadly defined as the study of meaning in language. Hayakawa's book was a distillation of Korzybski's theories and was meant to be used by a more general audience than the academic and scholarly readers of Korzybski. He was shunned by a certain element of academe for doing this. As he said to the *Los Angeles Times,* "It's fatal to your scholarly reputation. If you write things everyone can understand, you're a cheap popularizer." It was this fiercely independent mind—disregarding academic convention when it seemed to him meaningless—that would show throughout Hayakawa's career.

By the time *Language in Action* was published in 1941, Hayakawa had left Wisconsin for an assistant professorship at the Illinois Institute of Technology. World War II had just broken out and Japanese Americans on the West

Samuel Ichiye Hayakawa

Coast were being imprisoned in internment camps for fear they would collaborate in the event—however unlikely—of a Japanese invasion of the continental United States. This action, which was clearly unconstitutional and profoundly anti-American, Hayakawa would later defend as within reason considering the bombing of Pearl Harbor, the number of lives lost in that bombing, and the known ferocity of the Japanese soldier as evidenced in their brutal treatment of Koreans in Korea and Manchurians in China. Hayakawa, a Canadian citizen himself, was spared imprisonment.

A Political Conservative

In 1955 Hayakawa left Illinois for a teaching post at San Francisco State College (later renamed San Francisco State University). He moved up through the ranks and was named president of the school in 1968, by then-governor, Ronald Reagan. This was at the height of the anti-Vietnam War protest movement on America's campuses, and like many American universities at the time San Francisco State was periodically wracked by strikes, sit-ins, and boycotts. At one such event, Hayakawa briefly gained national cult hero status among conservatives for pulling the wires out of a sound truck during a particularly raucous student/teacher strike. His outburst was captured by a television crew and broadcast nationally that evening. The symbolic act was cheered by many Americans who felt deeply threatened by the level of chaos in such demonstrations.

Hayakawa was politically conservative in many areas, an aspect of this high-profile Japanese American that many during his life found unpalatable and that many even today have difficulty overlooking. His admirers, on the other hand, point with pride to the fact that he stood up for what he believed in despite the fact that others of his ethnic background considered him to have sold out—as if one's political beliefs were a product of one's race.

Some feel his conservatism is indeed curious, given the prejudice he himself endured in his lifetime. He was barred from becoming an American citizen until the 1950s on the basis of his race, and his marriage to a European American woman was not recognized as legal in many states. Yet, he not only defended the U.S. government's internment order, but he also voted against the reparations payment bill, saying in the *Los Angeles Times* that when "a small but vocal group demand a cash indemnity of $25,000 [per person] for those who went to relocation camps, my flesh crawls with shame and embarrassment."

The Senate

Hayakawa first ran for the U.S. Senate in 1973, but he was disqualified from the race because he had changed political parties—from Democrat to Republican—within the twelve months prior to his candidacy. He ran again in 1976, and this time won. Perhaps not surprisingly, his legislative record is politically conservative. He voted, for instance, to lower the minimum wage and voted against bills meant to provide bilingual education to recent immigrants. Rather than this legislative record, though, what Samuel Hayakawa became most known for as a member of the senate were his eccentricities, his modest stature, and his habit of dozing off during hearings and briefings. What was not widely known was that the senator suffered from narcolepsy.

Hayakawa was not reelected in 1982, and at the end of his term he returned home to Mill Valley, north of San Francisco, where he lived with his wife, Margedant Peters Hayakawa, and where they had raised their three children. He remained active in politics, however, retaining the position of Special Adviser to the Secretary of State for East Asian and Pacific Affairs from 1983 until 1990. He continued also to write books and articles, and in conjunction with the University of California at Berkeley began working on an oral history project about his life. Hayakawa died of a stroke on February 27, 1992.

Sources:

Periodicals

Fox, Roy F. "A Conversation with the Hayakawas." *English Journal*, February 1991.
"Samuel Ichiye Hayakawa." Obituary, *New York Times*, February 28, 1992.

—Sketch by Jim Henry

Dennis Hayashi

(1952–)

Lawyer, civil rights activist, political appointee

Hayashi, a third-generation Japanese American, has spent a lifetime championing the rights of all Japanese Americans. He was born in Los Angeles on May 31, 1952. His parents, along with thousands of other Japanese Americans living on the West Coast of the United States, were interned in camps during World War II because they were deemed threats to national security by the U.S. government. Hayashi graduated from college cum laude with a degree in philosophy in 1974, and he attended Hastings College, where he earned his law degree in 1978. As a law student, Hayashi worked for one year as a law clerk to the honorable Robert Takasugi of the U.S. District Court. After graduating from Hastings College he worked for the Asian Law Caucus from 1979 to 1991.

Activism and the Law

Based in San Francisco, the Asian Law Caucus is a nonprofit law firm that specializes in defending the civil rights of the Asian Pacific Islander community in the United States. Hayashi specialized in employment and racial discrimination cases. He represented Fred Korematsu in his effort to overturn his conviction for resisting the internment of Japanese Americans during World War II. In the original trial, *Korematsu v. United States* (1944), the Supreme Court had ruled that the government did not exceed its bounds when it made the decision to intern Japanese Americans during World War II. The majority decision, written by Supreme Court Justice Black, said: "Citizenship has its responsibilities as well as its privileges, and in time of war the burden is always heavier. Compulsory exclusion of large groups of citizens from their homes, except under circumstances of direst emergency and peril, is inconsistent with our basic governmental institutions, but when under conditions of modern warfare our shores are threatened by hostile forces, the power to protect must be commensurate with the threatened danger."

The Court's decision effectively prevented Japanese-American internees from collecting compensation from the government after the war.

In other cases, Hayashi represented Vietnamese fisherman who suffered discrimination at the hands of the U.S. Coast Guard and minority firefighters of the San Francisco Fire Department. Hayashi also represented the family of Jim Loo, who was killed in a racially motivated attack in 1989.

Dennis Hayashi

Hayashi continued his civil rights activism when in 1991 he was elected national director of the Japanese American Citizens League, the oldest Asian Pacific Islander civil rights organization in the country. As director, he oversaw all legislative and public policy initiatives and administered the seven regional offices and the national headquarters. He is also co-founder of the National Network Against Asian American Violence, which monitors and investigates cases of anti-Asian violence nationally.

When the Clinton administration swept into Washington, Hayashi was selected as a member of the Clinton/Gore civil rights Transition Cluster. On May 5, 1993, Clinton announced Hayashi as his choice for director of the Office for Civil Rights. He was formally appointed to the position by Health and Human Services secretary Donna E. Shalala on June 27, 1993. His new responsibilities include ensuring that the programs and activities of the office that receive funds from Health and Human Services are in compliance with all civil rights laws. He also oversees the activities of the organization's ten regional offices.

Hayashi is active within the Asian American community in the United States. He has served as director for the National Asian Pacific American Association, the board of directors of the San Francisco Coro Corporation, the San Francisco Legal Assistance Foundation, the Coalition of Asian Pacific Americans, and has served on the Asian Pacific American Democratic Council. He has

also published numerous articles in the *Washington Post, Los Angeles Times,* the *Yale Law Review,* and the Kennedy School of Government's *Asian American Policy Review.* Hayashi has taught at the New College of California Law School in San Francisco. He currently resides in the Washington, D.C., area.

Sources:

Periodicals

"Power Brokers." *A Magazine,* December 15, 1993, p. 25–34.

Other

The White House. "Dennis Hayashi." Official resume and press releases, 1993.
Department of Health and Human Services, "Dennis Hayashi: Director of Office for Civil Rights." Official Biography, 1993.

—Sketch by Douglas Wu

Le Ly Hayslip
(1949–)
Author, humanitarian

Le Ly Hayslip is an award-winning author of two memoirs chronicling her extraordinary life in Vietnam and America: *When Heaven and Earth Changed Places* and *Child of War, Woman of Peace.* These books served as the basis for the 1993 Oliver Stone film *Heaven and Earth.* She is also the chair of the East Meets West Foundation, a humanitarian organization that describes its goals as "improv[ing] the general health, welfare, and socioeconomic condition of the people of Vietnam, and . . . provid[ing] a solid base for the self-sufficiency of our programs, as well as the individuals they serve."

Phung Thi Le Ly was born in 1949 to a devout Buddhist family in the small farming village of Ky La (now called Xa Hoa Qui), near Danang in Central Vietnam. She was the youngest of six children, and as an infant was very sickly and not expected to live long. She was born under French colonial rule which was being subverted by a guerrilla war of independence fought by Ho Chi Minh and his soldiers, known as the Viet Cong. The rebels had widespread support among the peasants at the time, and as a child Le Ly worked as a lookout for them. Along with many of her fellow villagers, she collaborated with them in small ways, such as digging their tunnels. The colonial armies of the

French, and later, the Americans, knew of the villagers' collaboration with the Viet Cong, and so persecuted them viciously, often making the children fill in the Viet Cong tunnels. This the Viet Cong perceived as betrayal, and they would often kill the villagers who were simply obeying the orders of the colonial armies.

It was in this nonsensical hell of war-torn Vietnam that Le Ly grew up. By the time she was fifteen, she had been subjected to incredible cruelty by the French and the Americans, she had served as a lookout for the Viet Cong, she had been arrested and tortured by the South Vietnamese police, and then had been sentenced to death by the Viet Cong, who accused her of collaboration. When she was taken into the jungle by two Viet Cong soldiers to be executed, they instead raped the young girl and then set her free.

Life in the City

After her release by the Viet Cong, Le Ly and her mother fled their village, first for Danang and then Saigon, where they found work as domestic help in the house of a wealthy Vietnamese businessman. Here Le Ly found an unbelievably easy existence compared to all that had led up to it. Eventually, though, the still very young girl was seduced by the master of the house and became pregnant with his child. When the mistress of the house found out, Le Ly and her mother were both forced to leave.

Le Ly returned to Danang to have the child. She struggled for several years to survive in both Danang and Saigon, two cities that were essentially occupied by the American army. To earn a living, Le Ly became a souvenir hustler, black market dealer, and even drug courier. She worked for a while as a nurse's assistant in a Saigon hospital and began dating Americans. She had several disastrous, heartbreaking affairs before meeting and marrying an American civilian contractor named Ed Munro in 1969, a man more than twice her age, by whom she had another son. In 1970 she came to America to join her husband. In 1973 he died of emphysema, leaving Le Ly a widow at age thirty-four.

In 1974 Le Ly married Dennis Hayslip. The American war in Vietnam was then beginning to wind down, leading up to the complete American evacuation of Saigon in 1975. Vietnam was left in chaos, with no real government in place. Le Ly worried about the relatives she had left behind, especially her mother and sister. Her sister, Lan, had two Amerasian children, and so would likely be killed by the Viet Cong as a collaborator. In 1975, Dennis left for Vietnam to rescue Le Ly's relatives. Remarkably, he was able to find her sister and her children and bring back to America.

Le Ly's second marriage, however, had never been a happy one. Dennis was a heavy drinker, clinically depressed, and full of rage. The couple had one child, Le

Le Ly Hayslip

Ly's third, and in 1982 during bitter divorce proceedings, Dennis was found dead in a parked van outside a school building. He had established a trust fund, however, that left Le Ly with some money, and he had insurance that paid off the mortgage of the house. With this money, Le Ly began a series of investments in real estate, the stock market, and small businesses that would eventually make her quite well off.

Writer and Humanitarian

Also at this time Le Ly began work on her memoirs of growing up in Vietnam, the book that would become *When Heaven and Earth Changed Places*. She took notes for years, and her son James helped her with typing and her English. In late 1987, the book was sold and Le Ly founded her nonprofit organization, East Meets West. She also resolved to return once again to her home country. As she said in *Child of War, Woman of Peace*. "I wanted desperately to complete some unfinished business: to return to my home village of Ky La—to burn incense at my father's shrine and sleep in the house he had built with his own two hands."

As president of East Meets West, Le Ly has worked tirelessly to improve understanding between the two cultures her life has straddled and to improve the lives of Vietnamese in Vietnam. East Meets West strives to provide quality health care, educational services, vocational training, and rehabilitation to the Vietnamese. In the years since its founding, East Meets West has established several important facilities in Vietnam. The medical center, located on China Beach just outside of Danang, offers primary health care to more than one hundred patients a day. The foundation's mobile medical outreach program brings mobile health units to remote areas of Vietnam where medical services are not readily available. The facial reconstruction project provides facial prosthetic replacements for disabled persons and trains Vietnamese technicians in their construction. The Compassion School offers educational services for poor children, and the Displaced Children's Center provides a home, health care, and education for one hundred orphaned and abandoned children.

When Heaven and Earth Changed Places was published in 1989 to excellent reviews. The *Los Angeles Times* published excerpts in its Sunday magazine, drawing unprecedented reader response. It was also reviewed on the front page of the *New York Times Book Review*. The second installment in her memoirs, *Child of War, Woman of Peace*, was published in 1993. *Publisher's Weekly* declared, "Alternately shocking and inspiring, this . . . is a drama-packed fairy tale cum horror story, filled with cutting observations about American and Vietnamese victims of war."

In the epilogue to *When Heaven and Earth Changed Places*, Le Ly offers her American readers a challenge: "Most of you who read this book have not lived my kind of life. By the grace of destiny or luck or god, you do not know how hard it is to survive; although now you have some idea. . . . Right now, though, there are millions of other poor people around the world—girls, boys, men, and women—who live their lives the way I did in order to survive. Like me, they did not ask for the wars that swallowed them. They ask only for peace—the freedom to love and live a full life—and nothing more. I ask only that you open your heart and mind to them, as you have opened it to me by reading this book, and do not think that our story is over."

Sources:

Books

Hayslip, Le Ly, and Charles Jay Wurts. *When Heaven and Earth Changed Places.* New York: Doubleday, 1989.

Hayslip, Le Ly, and James Hayslip. *Child of War, Woman of Peace,* New York: Doubleday, 1993.

Periodicals

Review of *Child of War, Woman of Peace, Publishers Weekly,* November 23, 1992, p. 48.

—Sketch by Jim Henry

Irene Yasutake Hirano
(1948–)
Public administrator, community activist

Identifying the problem is only a starting point for Irene Yasutake Hirano, executive director and president of the Japanese American National Museum in Los Angeles, and a determined activist in community affairs ranging from women's issues to Asian American concerns. What keeps her going is the search for solutions.

A *sansei*, or third-generation Japanese American, Irene Yasutake Hirano is that rare person who has managed to combine her chosen field, public administration, with her passion, community activism. As executive director and president of the Japanese American National Museum, Hirano is working to end ethnic discrimination against Japanese Americans and ensure the civil liberties of Japanese Americans. As former executive director of T.H.E. Clinic for Women in Los Angeles, she helped to develop medical and educational services for all women in an economically depressed area of the city. Focusing in particular on the needs of Asian American women, she served as associate director of the Asian Women's Center.

Hirano has served in countless state and national leadership positions in professional and community organizations, among which are Leadership Education for Asian Pacific (LEAP), Liberty Hill Foundation, California Commission on the Status of Women and National Network for Asian and Pacific Women. Her dedication has earned her many civic and professional awards, including Outstanding Young Woman in America of 1977; Outstanding Asian/Pacific Islander Award from the National Education Association (NEA) in 1983; Outstanding Service Award of 1984 from the National Institute for Women of Color; and the Lifetime Achievement Award in 1993 from the Asian Pacific Women's Network.

Formative Influence on Civil Rights

Born October 7, 1948, in Los Angeles, Irene Hirano remembers vividly how her father's family was imprisoned in camps even as he was serving in the U.S. Army. This memory remains a motivating force in her today. Speaking passionately about the connections between the Japanese American experience and that of other ethnic groups which have suffered similar denial of basic rights, she warned in a 1994 interview for the *USC Trojan Family*, "The civil liberties that were denied to Japanese Americans . . . one sees it in the discrimination against ethnic groups that come to this country even today."

Women's Issues

Hirano's formal education culminated in a bachelor of science degree in public administration from the University of Southern California (USC) in 1970. One of only three women in USC's public administration program, she earned her master's degree in health administration under a full scholarship at age twenty-four. Her interest in women's issues emerged as a result of this experience and, after serving as an administrative resident at Children's Hospital in Los Angeles in the summer of 1972, she became associate director of the Asian Women's Center, a project serving the needs of Asian American women, funded by the Department of Health, Education and Welfare, Social and Rehabilitation Services. From 1974 through 1975, she joined several national research projects funded by the Department of Health, Education and Welfare in Washington, D.C., serving as program specialist, project coordinator, and consultant. "The projects focused on the needs of low-income individuals," she explained to Cynthia Takano of *Rice,* "and again, the needs of women continued to come to the surface."

In 1975, Hirano began a thirteen-year career as executive director of T.H.E. Clinic for Women in Los Angeles, which grew from a fledgling nonprofit community clinic providing medical help, counseling, and educational services to poor women, to a facility with a staff of thirty-five health-care professionals serving more than 10,000 patients annually. While working to improve healthcare for minority women, she told Takano, "I had a strong sense of the need for people to understand that there were differences in the needs of men and women and for black, Hispanic and Asian American women—that there were not only cultural barriers, but also barriers related to their gender."

In 1976, selected by the governor to be chair of the California Commission on the Status of Women, Hirano traveled throughout the state, meeting with women's groups, working on legislation and developing statewide programs to meet the needs of women. "Asian American women were invisible," she said, referring to their absence in existing organizations and programs. "Yet, because of my ethnicity, I started to meet Asian American women who were interested in talking to other Asian American women, and who were doing good work and were really involved in the local communities." Need and opportunity coincided, and, in 1980, Hirano helped organize the Asian Women's Network in Los Angeles, becoming its first president. "We went on to form a statewide network and then a national network. Many of those groups are still active, still addressing the needs of Asian American women as they continue to change," Hirano told Takano.

Leadership Development

"If you look at who's in leadership and decision-making positions, you still see an absence of Asian Americans," Hirano commented to Takano. "Even though Japanese

Irene Yasutake Hirano

Americans and Chinese Americans have been in this country longer than other Asian ethnic groups, and although we find many who have been successful as a group and as a community, I think we still have a long way to go." In 1983, to develop leadership training programs to correct this problem, Hirano co-founded LEAP, a nonprofit group that conducts workshops and encourages Asian Americans to assume decision-making positions. These choices naturally involve risk-taking, a skill which she feels needs to be developed by Asian Americans. "Because of our culture and background, we're encouraged to be successful, and the way to be successful, in many respects, is to find the safe way to do things. When you take risks, there's the potential that you're not going to do well. Yet, in order to make things happen, we have to take risks," she declared to Takano.

The Japanese American National Museum

Since 1988, Hirano has been director and president of the Japanese American National Museum, which, under her leadership, exceeded its goal of raising $10.2 million to renovate its historic headquarters in Los Angeles' Little Tokyo and to mount its first major exhibition on the Issei pioneers, the first generation of Japanese Americans. As a resource for research, exhibition, and education, the museum relates the saga of the Japanese American experience. Linking the art and business communities, its more than 150 programs include classes in such diverse subjects as art, culture, storytelling, and cookery. Promoting the museum's work in a larger context, Hirano travels throughout the country and Japan, developing joint programs with other institutions. The future of her work will involve leadership in the second phase of the museum campaign to construct a 65,000-square foot pavilion adjacent to its present site, to create its second major exhibition on the Nisei, second-generation Japanese Americans, and to build an endowment fund.

Sources:

Periodicals

"A Sense of Self." *USC Trojan Family,* Spring 1994.
Takano, Cynthia. "Irene Hirano." *Rice,* November 1988.

Other

Japanese American National Museum. "Irene Y. Hirano, Executive Director and President." Biographical sketch and press releases, 1994.
Hirano, Irene Yasutake. Resume, provided by Hirano, June 1994.

—Sketch by Nancy Moore

Alex Kitman Ho
(1950–)
Film producer

Alex Kitman Ho is an Academy Award-winning producer of feature films. He has long been associated with the filmmaker Oliver Stone, having produced such highly regarded films as *Platoon, Wall Street,* and *JFK*—as well as all of Stone's other directorial projects. Ho's collaboration with Stone began in 1984, when both were working on *Year of the Dragon,* for which Stone had written the screenplay. He has also worked on a variety of other film projects with others, from *One-Trick Pony* to *My Favorite Year* to *Fame.*

Early Life

Alex Kitman Ho was born in Hong Kong on January 15, 1950. His family moved to the United States when Ho was four years old. He was educated at Goddard College in Plainfield, Vermont, where he earned a bachelor's degree in cinema studies in 1972. Following his graduation he enrolled in the Tisch School of the Arts at New York University, where he earned a master's degree in fine arts in 1974.

Throughout his career in film, Ho has been involved in a variety of areas in production. His first major assignment was as a unit manager for *To Kill a Cop* in 1978. Also in that year he supervised production on *King of the Gypsies.* In the next two years he worked on singer and songwriter Paul Simon's film *One-Trick Pony,* as well as other films, including *Heartland, Fame,* and *First Deadly Sin.* In 1981 he supervised domestic production for Warren Beatty's epic *Reds.*

Ho Meets Stone

Ho's work in the eighties continued to be of high quality, and he soon established himself as a producer who could assemble a quality cast in well-written productions. In 1982 he produced the critically acclaimed *My Favorite Year,* and in 1983 he worked on *The Loveless.* The following year, while working on the production of *Year of the Dragon,* Ho met Oliver Stone, who was then struggling to make it as a mainstream director after having made critically successful but commercially overlooked films such as *Salvador. Year of the Dragon* did not do well commercially and caused some controversy in the Asian American community for what its critics charged was a simpleminded and stereotypical portrayal of New York's Chinatown. Nevertheless, Ho and Stone combined their talents in 1986 to produce *Platoon,* which drew critical praise and big box office receipts. The film solidified Stone's reputation as a significant American filmmaker and earned several Academy Award nominations.

In 1987 Ho and Stone released *Wall Street,* a cynical portrayal of greed in America's financial markets. This was followed by a film adaptation of a play by the off-Broadway playwright Eric Bogosian called *Talk Radio,* released in 1988. One year later Ho and Stone released the film that would earn Ho his first Academy Award: *Born on the Fourth of July,* the story of disabled Vietnam veteran who returns to the United States and becomes a national spokesman for the growing antiwar movement. (Oliver Stone also won an Oscar for best director.) Two years later Ho and Stone released *JFK,* a highly controversial, speculative look at the possibility that President John F. Kennedy was killed by a secret group within the government of the United States. The film stirred much debate when it was released; it went on to earn Ho his second Oscar.

Miracle is Born

Ho and Stone have talked about putting their collaboration on hold so that they could each pursue independent projects, and in 1993 Ho produced the directorial debut of the action adventure star Steven Seagal. Entitled *On Deadly Ground,* the film pitted the martial artist Seagal against a gang of toxic polluters. And in 1994, Alex Kitman Ho formed his own production company, called Miracle.

Sources:

"Power Brokers." *A. Magazine,* December 15, 1993, p. 25–34.

—Sketch by Jim Henry

David D. Ho

(1952–)

Medical doctor, AIDS researcher

Before the disease even had a name, Dr. David Ho was already treating AIDS patients in 1981 as the chief resident at Cedars-Sinai Medical Center at the University of California at Los Angeles (UCLA) School of Medicine. In 1984, Ho and his coworkers at Massachusetts General Hospital reported the first isolation of HIV from semen. The same report also documented for the first time the "healthy carrier state" of HIV infection which identified otherwise healthy individuals who tested positive for the virus but did not show any physical signs of the disease. One year later, Ho's studies on the saliva of infected patients established the infrequency of HIV in this bodily fluid and helped assure the public that AIDS cannot be casually transmitted. In the same year, Ho's observations that HIV can invade the nervous system and induce brain dysfunction introduced new investigation on AIDS-related dementia. Ho's work on AIDS dementia led him to conclusively demonstrate that normal monocytes are susceptible to HIV infection and monocytes from AIDS patients harbor the virus. More recently, Ho's quantitative studies on the viral burden showed that HIV infection should not be considered latent but rather an actively persistent process. Moreover, these quantitative techniques developed by Ho to measure viral burden have been widely adopted by clinical investigators worldwide.

Having devoted most of his research career to the problems of AIDS and human retroviruses, Ho is recognized as one of the leading pioneers in the field. In 1990, Ho was named the head of New York City's Aaron Diamond AIDS Research Center, one of the largest AIDS research facilities in the world. Under Ho's leadership the center has earned an international reputation for excellence, attracting top scientists from around the world and serving as a central resource for the latest updates and discoveries that will someday control one of the most devastating epidemics in history.

The New Kid on the Block

Born in Taiwan on November 3, 1952, David Ho immigrated with his family to Los Angeles when he was twelve years old. "I spoke no English at the time, so it was rough at the beginning," Ho told Terry Hong in an interview. "But kids learn fast and after a three-month period, I was communicating reasonably well. After a year, it was no problem and I was managing fine. That was a real dramatic change and I would hate to have to go through that adjustment now."

David D. Ho

After completing junior high school and high school in Los Angeles, Ho pursued a bachelor of science degree at California Institute of Technology. He transferred to the Massachusetts Institute of Technology for one year of study because he thought it would be good to have that variation. He graduated in 1974 from Cal Tech, *summa cum laude,* and went on to Harvard Medical School where he was one of four Asian Americans in a class of 140. "It was a typical medical school experience," said Ho. "There was a lot of work the first year and then the third year was spent with patients. There was an overwhelming amount of information one had to learn, and dealing with patients was a great challenge." It was at Harvard that Ho's inclination toward medical science and research over private practice was solidified. "Harvard is very research-oriented. The faculty really emphasizes medical research. That's what nailed it down for me."

Ho said that he "needed a change of scenery" from Harvard and returned to Los Angeles where he completed his internship and residency in the UCLA hospital systems. During the last of his three years there, Ho came into contact with two of the first five patients ever reported with what would eventually be identified as AIDS. "It was an experience I will never forget," recalled Ho. "Two young gay men with fulminant pneumonia came in. We knew they were dying, their immune systems were depleted. We didn't know the cause but the cases looked similar. We couldn't find any literature on anything like it. It was something new, something that wiped out the immune system. Even though the cases were isolated, it was exciting because it was something new. My interest in the disease was formed from that stage on."

Unfortunately, such isolated occurrences of the disease were short-lived. "In the beginning, one person would come in every few weeks but within a few months, people were coming weekly and then there were multiple cases per week," Ho remembered. By mid-1981, Ho and his colleagues quickly realized that the disease was growing rapidly and that cases were doubling every few months. "It was *dramatic*," Ho shook his head.

Mystery Disease Gets a Name

By mid-1982, AIDS was officially named. At the same time, Ho returned to Harvard and Massachusetts General Hospital prepared to focus on virus research. He began to look at AIDS specifically in search of a virus that caused the disease. From that point on, more than ninety percent of Ho's career has been centered on HIV research. He spent four years in Boston until he returned to UCLA in 1987 to teach at the School of Medicine.

By 1990, the Aaron Diamond AIDS Research Center was being formed in New York City, and they were recruiting for a founding director. Ho was chosen to pioneer a scientific program for the fledgling center. With $13 million from the Aaron Diamond Foundation, the city of New York, and New York University, Ho was hired to create a world-class laboratory and fill it with the best scientists from around the world. To date, only two facilities exist that are directed specifically at AIDS research. Besides the Diamond Center, there is the Gladstone Institute, part of the University of California at the San Francisco School of Medicine.

By combining his patient-based clinical experience with his scientific prowess, Ho has led the center in the areas of HIV pathogenesis—how a patient acquires AIDS and the associated destruction of the immune system; transmission *in vivo*—what the viral and immunological factors are that govern transmission from an infected mother to her infant and from an infected person to a sexual partner; and vaccine development—what the critical viral components are to include in a candidate vaccine.

Together with a team of some forty scientists, Ho is making ground-breaking progress. "But it's like putting together a building. Little by little you see a form, you can see something coming together. Most people expect one fortuitous discovery that will be the answer; that's possible, but not likely in the near future. We're seeing slow, steady progress. There are many drugs that curb the disease and maybe someday AIDS will be more of a chronic disease like hypertension or diabetes."

A Realistic Outlook

Ho is convinced that the development of an AIDS vaccine is about five to ten years away. A cure, however, is "highly unlikely in the short term," he said. "We will find many drugs that will suppress the disease, and in combination those drugs might be a sort of cure, but a true cure is not likely. This is a realistic outlook," he emphasized.

In addition to his work at the Diamond Center, Ho is currently on President Bill Clinton's Task Force on AIDS and a member of the national HIV Vaccine Working Group. He likened his work to "running a marathon." He explained, "If you look at the whole picture, the task is daunting. You've got to approach it one step at a time—pick a topic and do one experiment at a time. There's constant feedback and not every experiment works but each experiment elicits a reaction. That kind of feedback provides the motivation to keep going and carry on. When we find something no one else has previously shown, that's very exciting for those of us in science."

In spite of Ho's preeminent position in the medical world for his AIDS research, it was as Magic Johnson's doctor that he recently earned celebrity status. Since making the athlete's initial HIV-positive diagnosis, Ho says that treating the basketball star "is just part of something I do, but a very, very small part of my professional life that takes maybe .5 percent of my time." Ho recalled with some annoyance a talk that he recently gave in Japan at an AIDS conference: "I was introduced as Johnson's doctor, instead of anything about my scientific accomplishments." He reiterated, "Treating Johnson is just something I do; it's not necessarily something I'm proud of." His humor restored, Ho added, "But I'm convinced that I could keep up with Johnson in a game of free-throw."

Ho lives in Chappaqua, New York, with his wife Susan whom he married while in medical school. The couple has two daughters and one son.

Sources:

Periodicals

Yang, Jeff and Betty Wong. "Dr. David Ho" in "Power Brokers: The Twenty-Five Most Influential People in Asian America," *A Magazine*, vol. 2, no. 3, 1994, p. 30.

Woodard, Catherine. "Unraveling AIDS: City Lab and Its Director Work at the Cutting Edge," *New York Newsday*, September 7, 1993.

Other

Ho, David D., interview with Terry Hong, March 10, 1994.

—Sketch by Terry Hong

Reginald C. S. Ho
(1932–)
Physician

Shortly after Reginald C. S. Ho, a widely respected oncologist, became the first Hawaiian to head the American Cancer Society, his photo appeared on the cover of a Honolulu weekly newsmagazine. It showed him in a sky-blue physician's jacket, staring intently ahead, one hand clenched into a fist with fingers wrapped around several crushed cigarettes. An appropriate picture given that smoking is the most notorious culprit in the fight against cancer. The picture, however, doesn't tell the complete story, because Ho was out to battle more than cigarette smoking. After his appointment in 1992 as president of the American Cancer Society, he worked to raise national awareness about prostate cancer, a disease that is the second-leading cause of cancer deaths in men and one that has touched Ho personally.

Six years earlier, Ho and a friend, Dick Wheeler, were in Boston to attend the American Cancer Society's national board meeting. While en route to a restaurant, Wheeler felt an incredible pain that increased in intensity each time the cab in which they were riding hit a bump. He was diagnosed soon afterward with prostate cancer; he died three years later. Ho believes that early detection could improve a patient's prognosis and as head of the American Cancer Society he worked to institute a public-education program that promotes early screening.

In Honolulu, Ho is a highly-respected fighter of cancer. He has headed the Department of Oncology and Hematology at Straub Clinic and Hospital since 1978, and has published a number of articles on the subject in medical journals. However, his early roots hardly prepared him for a distinguished career in medicine.

He was born March 30, 1932, in Hong Kong. His great-grandfather had emigrated from China to Hawaii in 1876, but the family followed a tradition of sending each generation's eldest son to school in China. The sons usually returned after completing their studies; Ho's father, who went to Hong Kong to study, got married and stayed. Ho's parents had five children—four sons and one daughter—but when the Japanese invasion of China appeared as though it would head for Hong Kong, the family returned to Honolulu. Ho's father managed a bakery; the children, including Reginald, grew up learning the basics of customer service.

Early Career

Ho studied philosophy at St. Louis University in Missouri, and entered the university's medical school in 1956.

Reginald C. S. Ho

He completed his residency in internal medicine at the University of Cincinnati Hospitals, then picked up a fellowship in hematology and oncology at Barnes Hospital in St. Louis. He joined Straub Clinic and Hospital in 1973 as an attending physician.

How did Ho develop his interest in medicine, particularly a field as specialized as hematology and oncology? He traces this choice to a Boy Scout scoutmaster and the Marianist Brothers, who taught him at St. Louis High School in Honolulu. From the scoutmaster, Ho learned early on about the importance of caring for people and volunteerism. The Marianist Brothers, who devote their lives to teaching, drove the message home. Ho also connects his desire to enter medicine to an interest in serving people, drawn from his experience working in his father's bakery. "A lot of my motivation was in interaction with people, rather than interaction with the science itself," he said in a 1992 interview with *Midweek*, a Hawaiian newsweekly.

Medical Family

After completing his residency, Ho decided to choose a specialty. He went through his options, trying to decide what area he knew about the least. He came up with cancer and blood disorders, and decided to take specialty training in hematology and oncology at Washington University's Barnes Hospital. Ho met his wife, Sharilyn, a former nurse, at Straub Clinic and Hospital, and they were married November 14, 1964. His four children—Timothy, Reginald (Reggie), Mark, and Gianna—all are alumni of Notre Dame, largely because Ho's brother and a close friend, both gifted with powers of persuasion, were Notre Dame graduates and convinced the children it was the school to attend. Two of his sons studied medicine; his daughter, Gianna, studied veterinary medicine.

Medicine is, in many ways, a mix of science and human compassion. The scientific side of Ho believes fervently in research, calling it the key to discovering the genetic makeup of cancer cells and the ultimate cure to disease. But, on the human side, perhaps the more important side, Ho cherishes an all-American, home-grown image of what a physician should be: the family doctor who treats patients with care and compassion. He learned this art from a doctor with whom he trained at Barnes Hospital, and when he returned to Honolulu, he placed a painting, titled "The Country Doctor" on his wall. The image remains his ideal of what the medical profession should be.

Sources:

Periodicals

Midweek, November 18, 1992.

Other

Ho, Reginald C. S. Biographical material. Honolulu, Hawaii, February 1994.
Telephone interview with Himanee Gupta, February 1994.

—Sketch by Himanee Gupta

Florence Makita Hongo
(1928–)
Educator, publisher, community activist

In 1969, when few Japanese Americans were willing to discuss their World War II internment camp experience, Florence Hongo brought a dozen Japanese American educators together to discuss how to teach it in the public schools. Twenty-five years later, Hongo has transformed that group into the nation's largest nonprofit clearinghouse for Asian American books and educational materials—the Japanese American Curriculum Project (JACP). And she served all those years as a full-time volunteer, working to build the image of Asian Americans through her teaching, lecturing, curriculum development, and as

a consultant to writers and publishers. Today, Hongo continues to serve as the general manager of JACP, which operates a storefront at 234 Main Street in San Mateo, California.

"Florence put a lot of her own money and time into the organization," said Shizue Yoshina, one of the participants at that first meeting in Hongo's living room and vice-president of the JACP board of directors. "She was committed. She was a great leader for us to follow."

Childhood and Internment

Hongo was born Florence Makita on November 21, 1928. She grew up in Cressey, California, a small rural town located in north Merced County, along the Sante Fe Railroad line. She was the fifth of seven children of immigrant parents who were brought together through an arranged marriage. Her father, Haruzo, was a ranch foreman. When he wasn't overseeing the ranch workers, Hongo's father was helping out others in the community. Hongo's mother, Shizu, also had "a charitable spirit," recalled Hongo. "We were basically a community of immigrants."

As a child, Hongo was a voracious reader and keen on learning to play the piano, but she remembers being bored with school. Hongo said she never experienced discrimination in Cressey, until World War II began. "People who never called us names before started calling us names," she told Steven Chin in an interview. "We began to get into physical fights with other kids all of a sudden." She remembered crying when her family was forced, under the internment order, into a Merced assembly center and later sent to Amache Detention Center in Colorado.

Hongo said that as a teenager, she felt she actually benefited by attending high school in the camp, because it allowed her to "mature in a very supportive environment. We didn't have to deal with racism," she told Chin. "There were no concerns about height or blond hair." But while in camp, her father became tuberculant and was placed in a sanitarium. Her three eldest brothers either served in the army or went to work. "It was very traumatic for my mother," recalled Hongo. "She never had this kind of responsibility. I remember many, many times seeing her just in tears." When the family finally returned to Cressey in 1946, vines had overtaken the house and the family's belonging had vanished. "I'll never understand why that happened," said Hongo. "That first year back, I lived in constant fear of being harmed by those racists who hated us."

In 1950, Hongo married Andrew Yoshiwara (they divorced in 1971). She spent the next two decades raising three girls and two boys, and living the life of a "well-to-do suburban matron," which revolved around church, the San Mateo Dental Auxiliary, the PTA, Boy Scouts, and Girl Scouts. She conceded that most of her life she "didn't understand the need to be involved in social causes."

Florence Makita Hongo

Birth of an Activist

It was many years later when Hongo began to realize the deep psychological effects the camp experience had had on her and her family, as well as on the Japanese American community. "The realization of what happened brought me to a commitment to share that experience with school children and others," she told Chin. In 1969, the San Mateo School District brought Hongo in as a community specialist to help the district adjust to its newly integrated classes. Hongo recalled mentioning the internment camps to her black and Chicano colleagues. "They almost fell out of their chairs," she said. "They had no idea."

Soon after, Hongo picked up *America's Concentration Camps* by Alan Bosworth. It changed her life. "A big light went on," she said. "I became so emotional. I couldn't understand what was going on inside me. I sat down and forced myself to read this book. It revolutionized me." For the first time, Hongo understood why her family, along with 120,000 other Americans of Japanese descent, had been forced to live behind barbed wire for three-and-a-half years. "I was so angry," she said. "At that moment, I decided I was going to teach this experience and make sure people knew about it so it wouldn't happen again."

The group of teachers meeting in Hongo's living room in 1969 soon doubled in size. Because no Japanese American history books existed in English, the group started out by translating Japanese language sources. The group

quickly found itself embroiled in controversy. Prior to 1970, few Japanese would talk to their children about the camp experience, let alone discuss it in public. "Our group was considered a bit radical," recalled Hongo.

In 1970, the group produced *Japanese Americans, the Untold Story,* for Holt Reinhart publishing company, but the book was "immediately condemned by many established segments of the Japanese American community," Hongo told Chin. "The reaction approached hysteria," she said. "The Buddhist church called it anti-Buddhist and launched a campaign to block distribution. It was as if the community feared being exposed by bringing up the camp experience in public. . . . For many, it was very comfortable being invisible."

Although the book was submitted to the state for adoption as a supplemental textbook, strong community outcry led to its rejection. The event proved pivotal, however, cementing JACP teachers as a united group. "There was a commitment to getting this story out that was part of U.S. history," said Yoshina, a retired school teacher and a member of JACP. Hongo showed her "stamina," she added. "The group could have gone to pieces over that book. Instead Florence helped us get closer." The group moved on to create several internment camp filmstrips, including "The Inside Look" for elementary schools and "Prejudice in America" for high schools and colleges. In the mid-1970s, JACP broadened its scope to include all Asian American materials and books and become a mail-order operation, initially shipping from Hongo's garage.

In the early 1970s, Hongo earned her Community College Teaching Credential and Secondary Teaching Credential at San Francisco State University. She went on to earn a master's degree in U.S. and Asian history from San Francisco State University, and from 1978 to 1992, was an instructor at the College of San Mateo. In 1981, Hongo married Masanori Hongo. In addition to her role as activist and entrepreneur at JACP, Hongo spends her leisure time gardening, fishing, sewing, cooking, and following her favorite baseball team, the San Francisco Giants.

Honors and Awards

In May 1994, during Asian Pacific American Heritage Month commemorations in San Francisco, Hongo was honored by the Public Broadcasting affiliate, KQED-TV. The citation read "In recognition of your outstanding service to the Bay Area Asian Community [by] providing schools and the community with resources that enhance understanding of the Asian American experience." In 1993, Hongo had received a Special Service Award for a "lifetime of work in advancing Asian American Studies" from the Association of Asian American Studies. Also in 1993, JACP was ranked as one of the top ten companies in "Honoring Excellence in the Bay Area Workplace" awards by the Community Career Education Center in San Mateo. Hongo was also honored for "outstanding service in the field of education" by San Francisco Nikkei in Education in 1989.

Hongo has written for numerous publications, including the history chapter in *Strength and Diversity: A Study Guide for Elementary Schools on Japanese American Women* (1990) and "Shattering Myths: Japanese American Educational Issues" in *The Education of Asian and Pacific Americans,* published in 1982. She was general editor of *Japanese American Journey: The Story of a People,* published by JACP in 1985.

JACP, which changed its name to Asian American Curriculum Project or AACP in 1994, continues to be the vehicle through which Hongo teaches. "I can always call Florence when I need a resource or a book," said Carol Hayashino, associate director of the Japanese American Citizens League. "If we are to appreciate ethnic and cultural diversity in America, we need people like Florence. She and her organization will ensure that the American public understands the history of Asian Pacific Americans."

Sources:

Hongo, Florence, telephone interview with Steven Chin, May 1994.
Japanese American Curriculum Project. "Florence Hongo." Biographical materials and press releases.

—*Sketch by Steven A. Chin.*

Jeanne Wakatsuki Houston
(1934–)
Writer

One day in 1971, Jeanne Wakatsuki Houston's nephew came to visit. He was taking a sociology course at the University of California at Berkeley and wanted to know more about the concentration camps that had incarcerated approximately 120,000 Americans of Japanese descent during World War II. The nephew, who had been born in one of the camps, Manzanar, asked to know more about the family's experiences. "Whenever my family got together and we happened to talk about camp, we would joke about the lousy food, the dust storms or the communal showers, or we talked lightheartedly about recreational activities. I reiterated the same stories to my nephew in the same superficial way," Houston recalled in an autobiographical essay she wrote in 1992 for *Contemporary Authors Autobiographical Series.* The nephew wanted more answers. "'Aunty, you're telling me all these bizarre things. I mean, how did you feel about being locked up like that?'" he

prodded. Houston was stunned. "He asked me a question no one had ever asked before, a question I had never dared ask myself. Feel? How did I feel? For the first time I dropped the protective cover of humor and nonchalance. I allowed myself to 'feel.' I began to cry. I couldn't stop crying," Houston wrote in her essay.

Houston realized that the camp experiences were too difficult and too painful for her to talk about. "[P]erhaps I could write a memoir, a history—just for the family," Houston considered. That history became Farewell to Manzanar, a haunting recollection of the Wakatsuki family's memories of three-and a half years of unjustified imprisonment. Co-written with her husband, James D. Houston, who is also a writer, *Farewell to Manzanar* was a breakthrough accomplishment. For the first time since the actual event, the Houstons' book gave voice not only to the Wakatsuki family, but to the thousands of Japanese Americans who had silently endured similar experiences. In the more than two decades since its publishing, *Farewell to Manzanar* remains an invaluable contribution to the annals of American history.

An All-American Family

Born on September 26, 1934, in Inglewood, California, Houston was the last of ten children born to Ko and Riku Wakatsuki. At the time, Ko was a farmer on the outskirts of Los Angeles. When Houston was two years old, he turned to commercial fishing and moved the family to Ocean Park, a predominantly Caucasian, small coastal community whose main attraction was an amusement pier. Houston fondly recalled in her essay, "The pier was my nursery school, the amusement attendants my sitter. The neighborhood kids and I spent most of our days there."

On December 7, 1941, when Japanese planes bombed Pearl Harbor, Houston was just seven years old. That night, her father burned the flag he had brought from Hiroshima, Japan, thirty-five years earlier. He burned papers and documents and anything else that might suggest a connection with Japan. His precautions proved to be in vain. Two weeks later, he was picked up by the FBI and arrested under false charges that he had delivered oil to Japanese submarines offshore. He was taken into custody and shipped to an unknown location. The family would not see him again for almost a year.

With the family's patriarch gone, Riku Wakatsuki moved the family out of the racially isolated Ocean Park to Terminal Island, a nearby island fishing community filled with Japanese Americans. "[T]he island was a country as foreign as India or Arabia would have been," Houston wrote in *Farewell to Manzanar.* "It was the first time I had lived among other Japanese, or gone to school with them, and I was terrified all the time." In February of 1942, the U.S. Navy decided that having so many Japanese, even those who were American-born, living so close to the Long Beach Naval Station was dangerous and the island was cleared completely. Forced to move again, the

Jeanne Wakatsuki Houston

family went briefly to Boyle Heights, another minority ghetto in downtown Los Angeles. They did not stay long.

On February 19, 1942, President Franklin Roosevelt signed Executive Order 9066, which called for the incarceration of 110,000 Americans of Japanese descent to some thirty concentration camps throughout the West. By April, the family was again forced to move. After selling or abandoning their possessions, the Wakatsukis were piled into a bus heading east. Their new "home" for three and a half years was Manzanar, a barbed-wire, fenced-in, barracks-filled compound in a scorching, fiercely dusty desert somewhere between Los Angeles and Reno, Nevada. Approximately 10,000 Japanese Americans were imprisoned there during World War II.

Houston's first experience with books occurred in the beginning months at Manzanar. In an open area between barracks was a two-story high mountain of books that had been donated by charities for a camp library that had yet to be built. At first the children used the mountainous pile as their playground, sliding and scrambling over the scattered books. Walking by the pile one day, Houston passed an opened book whose pages were fluttering in the wind. The story of long-haired Rapunzel came to life in gilded illustrations, enchanting and entrancing the young Houston. That afternoon, she read every story in Hans Christian Andersen's *Fairy Tales*. She returned to the mountain again and again, always in search of a new literary adventure. "Books became my major form of recreation, my channel to worlds outside the confined and monotonous routine of camp life," Houston wrote in her autobiographical essay.

A New Life

At the end of the war, the family was relocated to the housing project Cabrillo Homes in Long Beach, just a few miles from Terminal Island. "What a different world!" recalled Houston in her essay. "From a racially homogenous one-mile square community, I entered a multi-racial and cultural matrix, a ghetto where our only common denominator was poverty. It was my first experience living among African Americans and Latinos."

In seventh grade, Houston first considered the idea of becoming a writer. She won a place in the school's new journalism project on the strength of an essay she wrote about one of her happiest memories from before the war—hunting grunion fish with her family on full-moon nights and the beach barbecue that followed. Houston soon became the editor-in-chief of the school newspaper. "[T]his experience in junior high school was one of the crucial events in my life. That I could write was clearly programmed in my mind by a wise teacher who knew about validating youngsters, about directing them to higher goals—even when circumstances did not seem to support it. In the late '40s, with the Second World War barely over, who would encourage a young Japanese American girl living in a ghetto to work toward becoming a writer? Only an idealistic, fair-minded person. I was lucky enough to have met such a person in junior high school, my English teacher," recalled Houston in her essay.

Throughout high school, Houston continued to write for the newspaper. During the summer before her senior year, in 1952, the Wakatsuki family moved again, this time to San Jose where Ko tried one last time to make a living at farming. From high school, Houston entered San Jose State University, where she majored in journalism during her first two years, and dreamed of being an Asian Brenda Starr, a comic strip character who was a glamourous newspaper reporter. Discouraged by the department adviser from completing her degree in journalism due to the lack of opportunities for women journalists—especially the near impossibility of an Asian American woman entering the field—Houston changed her major to sociology and social welfare. After graduating from college, Houston took a job at Hillcrest Juvenile Hall, a detention hall in Northern California where she worked as a group counselor, supervising teenage girls brought in for violating probation, running away from home, and sometimes more serious crimes.

On Valentine's Day 1957, the year after graduation, Houston received a card from fellow journalism student, James D. Houston, whom she had dated through college. Inscribed in the card was a marriage proposal. Within a month, the two were married on the beach during a particularly spectacular sunset in Hawaii where Jim was working at the time.

Almost immediately after the honeymoon, the new couple moved to England, where Jim was stationed with the U.S. Air Force in fulfillment of his ROTC responsibilities. While living amidst the East Anglian fog, Houston developed an especially close relationship with a photographer, Bertl Gaye, who had fled Austria in the 1930s and whose family had been killed in Hitler's death camps. A staunch believer in peace, Gaye proved to be a beacon of tolerance from whom Houston drew great knowledge and learning. Houston wrote years later in her autobiographical essay: "I now see my time with Bertl taught me to be an activist of another kind. I, too, believe in peace and abhor nuclear weaponry. But Bertl's greatest lesson for me was about forgiveness."

After three years in England and nine months in Paris, France, the Houstons returned to California in 1961. They lived in Palo Alto while Jim attended graduate school at Stanford University and moved to Santa Cruz soon thereafter, where they continue to live today.

A Writer at Last

With three children, being a wife and mother became a full-time job for Houston. It wasn't until years later that she would remember her initial life goal, to become a writer. Being asked by her nephew how she *felt* about the years of her family's incarceration was the impetus to finally bring her back on the path to becoming a writer. "I had not written for years. I tried to begin. But I found myself in tears, unable to concentrate. Was I having a nervous breakdown? It was apparent my nephew's innocent question, a question he had a right to ask, had opened a wound I had long denied ever existed," Houston recalled in her essay. She turned to her writer husband for help and guidance. In her essay, Houston wrote, "Through tears I told him what I could. I was emotionally honest for the first time. I remembered the feelings—of loss, of shame and humiliation, of rage, of sorrow. [Jim] sat quietly listening. Then he said, 'I have known you for almost 20 years, married to you for 14 . . . and I never had any idea you carried all this around. This is not something to write just for your family. It's a story everyone in America should read.'"

What began as a personal memoir proved to be one of the most important postwar historical texts, still taught in classrooms throughout the country. The Houstons spent a year working on *Farewell to Manzanar,* interviewing family and other internees and researching in libraries. When the book was published in 1973, Houston's life changed dramatically. She recalled in her essay, "I reclaimed pride in my heritage. I rediscovered my ability to write. I realized I could no longer hide 'in the country of my husband's shadow.' With Jim's encouragement and support, I left the comfortable safety zone of domesticity and ventured out into the open field. I began to write again." Houston commented to Terry Hong: "It was not until I wrote about the camps that I realized my own self-image as a woman, and as an Asian American woman. That was all jumbled up with the internment crisis within and I had to unscramble all that so I could start writing again."

More than two decades later, Houston has continued to fulfill her seventh grade dream. She is the co-author of three books and a contributor to more than ten others. She is also a writer of at least three screenplays and countless essays, articles, and reviews for such diverse publications as *California, Der Spiegel, Mother Jones,* and *Reader's Digest.*

In 1994, Houston was at work on a novel, tentatively titled *Fire Horse Woman.* "Women born in the Chinese year of the Horse were considered very dangerous. They were women who always outlived their husbands. What that all meant was that she was a very strong woman," Houston explained to Hong. The book, which she began many years ago, opens in 1906 with a Japanese picture bride coming to the United States for the first time. To portray an accurate account of a turn-of-the-century Japanese woman, Houston spent a rewarding six months alone in Japan in 1992, conducting in-depth research through a grant from the U.S.–Japan Friendship Commission and the National Endowment for the Arts.

Houston explained to Hong that she had ended an earlier draft of the book "just before World War II. I couldn't write any fictionalized accounts of the war, specifically about the camps. In the past, I could only write from my own memories, from the family's history. But more recently, I've written three short stories about fictionalized accounts of camp. So in the second draft of my novel, I plan to go beyond the war, to include the war and the camps."

When Houston is not writing, she said she especially enjoys reading about spirituality. "I've been studying Buddhism for about twenty years. I'm very interested in healing," she explained to Hong. "There seems to be two different paths to my life—half of me is the healer and the other half, the more male part of me, is the writer. Perhaps the healer part of me will help me finally finish this year the novel the writer part of me began," she laughed.

Sources:

Books

Houston, Jeanne Wakatsuki. Autobiographical profile in *Contemporary Authors Autobiography Series,* edited by Joyce Nakamura. vol. 16. Detroit: Gale Research, 1992.

Houston, Jeanne Wakatsuki, and James D. Houston. *Farewell to Manzanar.* New York: Bantam Books, 1973.

Other

Houston, Jeanne Wakatsuki, telephone interview with Terry Hong, August 4, 1994.

—Sketch by Terry Hong

James Wong Howe
(1899–1976)
Cinematographer

James Wong Howe was one of the finest cinematographers of Hollywood's golden age. In 1933 he was the highest paid cinematographer in the world, a position he had arrived at with no formal education in the art of cinematography, and as a high school dropout whose first job in the movies was as a janitor. In a career that spanned more than fifty years, Howe photographed 125 films and earned ten Academy Award nominations, winning two. Notable films he photographed include *Peter Pan* (1924), *The Thin Man* (1934), *The Rose Tattoo* (1953), *The Old Man and the Sea* (1957), *Hud* (1963), and *The Heart is a Lonely Hunter* (1965).

Howe was born Wong Tung Jim on August 28, 1899, in Kwantung, China. His father, Wong How, left for the United States soon after his son's birth, leaving the child with his stepmother until Wong Howe could afford to have his family join him in the States. That opportunity came in 1904, when Jim was five years old. Wong How set up a general store in a small town called Pasco, Oregon, where the family were the only Chinese. It was here that Wong Tung Jim became James Wong Howe, when a well-meaning teacher anglicized the young boy's name.

Howe's father died in 1914, and his stepmother, with whom Howe had never gotten along, began pressuring him to take over his father's business, as would be customary for a first son to do in a Chinese family. But Howe wanted more from life and he moved out on his own, staying with a friend of his father's. He then began three years of aimless wandering up and down the West Coast, working variously as a professional boxer, a delivery boy, a darkroom assistant, and a bell boy. In 1917 he landed a job as a janitor as Lasky Studios (now Paramount) in Los Angeles. He was eighteen years old.

Janitor to Filmmaker

Howe soon proved himself a dedicated worker, and through luck and determination he eventually began intermittent work as an assistant cameraman in some of the early productions Hollywood film mogul Cecil B. DeMille. His first job as chief cameraman came in 1922 when he filmed *Drums of Fate,* starring the popular actress Mary Miles Minter. He continued working for Lasky studios through most of the twenties and then, in 1927, he was let go. He did some free-lance work and returned briefly to China, where he shot some film for a movie he hoped to make some day, and saw his natural mother for the first time since leaving China at age five. When he returned to Hollywood in 1930, he had difficulty finding work.

In his critical biography, *James Wong Howe, Cinematographer,* Todd Rainsberger describes these early years as a time of learning for Howe. According to Rainsberger, Howe's work from this period is uneven, with scenes alternating between brilliant and poor: "Howe had formulated his own ideas from five years of observation on studio sets and from his own work with a still camera, but these concepts were largely theoretical and not developed into a coherent approach. The first years were a matter of testing his own ideas against ideas gleaned from others and refining the two into a workable and individual style. The results of this process were technically uneven and lacked any kind of comprehensive visual concept. In the course of his experimentation, Howe would produce occasional scenes which demonstrated striking skill and imagination in films, which, overall, were visually undistinguished."

In 1930, Howe was once again hired by a major studio. He worked for three years at what was then called the William Fox Studio, where he established an excellent reputation for professionalism and artistry in the newly emerging "talkies." Howe's work was consistently above reproach, but the films he was working on were low-budget and not very memorable. In 1933 he left Fox for MGM, where he was the director of photography for *The Thin Man* and *Manhattan Melodrama*. In 1936, Howe left MGM to work in England, where he was regarded as an artist and became a celebrity. He returned to the United States to work for David O. Selznick, and in 1938 he received his first Academy Award nomination for his work on *Algiers*. Later that year he was signed by Warner Brothers to a seven-year contract. From 1938 to 1947, Howe shot twenty-six films for Warner Brothers and four others for different studios.

When Howe's contract with Warner Brothers ended he decided against renewing it. He enjoyed working freelance and also had a project in mind that would require filming in China. He had bought the film rights to a novel called *Rickshaw Boy* which he planned to produce and direct. He returned to his homeland in 1948 to film and spent nearly a year working on the project when he was forced to leave when the Communist forces of Mao Zedong defeated the Nationalists in that country's long civil war.

Upon returning to the States, Howe had difficulty finding work. He had over the years gained a reputation as a perfectionist with a quick temper, and studio heads were reluctant to hire him. His patriotism was also called into question by members of the House Un-American Activities Committee, which was then on a paranoid witch hunt for Communists in the film industry. Howe was "graylisted" by the committee, meaning his name was put on a list of undesirables the committee would prefer not be hired. He made his living during the next several years working on low-budget independently produced films.

Shift in Artistic Approach

Howe's artistry was changing in this period of his career. In his early years he had relied on intricate schemes of lighting, but he began to regard such work as overly stylized, lending the film an unnatural air. In the late forties, he became a more naturalistic cinematographer. Howe spoke of the change in his camerawork for *American Cinematographer* magazine in 1963: "I used to light a lot of things with lights that I shouldn't have been doing. You believe at the time it is the thing to do and it shows what a fine cameraman you are. You want to demonstrate what you can do with all those tricky lights, but the tendency sometimes is to get carried away with lighting, to overdramatize."

Films Howe worked on in the late forties and early fifties include *Body and Soul; Come Back, Little Sheba;* and *The Brave Bulls*. He also directed briefly for television, and he directed his first American feature film, a documentary about the founder of the Harlem Globetrotters entitled *Go, Man, Go*. Howe also produced, directed and edited a documentary about the life and work of the artist Dong Kingman. In 1953 Howe won an Academy Award for his cinematography on *The Rose Tattoo*, which helped revive his career with the major studios. Later in the fifties he would shoot *Picnic* and *The Old Man and the Sea*.

In the late fifties and early sixties, Howe worked briefly directing television commercials and documentaries and as a teacher at the University of California at Los Angeles. In 1963 he received his second Academy Award for his work on *Hud*. After this, Howe became ill and did not complete a film again until 1974, when he took over the financially troubled *Funny Lady*. Howe worked furiously on the film, despite his illness, and he was rewarded with an Academy Award nomination. Not long after, Howe again became quite ill, and on July 12, 1976, he died.

Sources:

Books

Rainsberger, Todd. *James Wong Howe, Cinematographer,* La Jolla, California: A.S. Barnes & Co., 1981.

Periodicals

Lightman, Herb A. "The Photography of *Hud*," American Cinematographer, July 1963, p. 416.

—Sketch by Jim Henry

David Henry Hwang
(1957–)
Playwright, screenwriter

As a senior at Stanford University, in the second week of an introductory play writing tutorial, David Henry Hwang turned in a play called *FOB*. The term, FOB, referred to a new immigrant, someone who was "fresh off the boat." It was first performed in the spring of 1979 by students in Hwang's dormitory under his direction. Then, only weeks before Hwang's graduation, the Eugene O'Neill Theater Center in Waterford, Connecticut—one of the country's most prestigious launching sites for new plays—called to say they wanted *FOB* for their National Playwright's Conference. "Of all the moments in my career so far," says Hwang, "just on a visceral level, that's probably been the most exciting." Less than a year later, the producer Joseph Papp mounted *FOB* in New York at the Public Theater. In the spring of 1981, barely two years since Hwang graduated from college, *FOB* won an Obie for Best New Play.

Seven years later, Hwang's 1988 Tony Award-winning play, *M. Butterfly,* became one of the most successful non-musical works in Broadway history. The show was eventually produced in three dozen countries all over the world, making Hwang an international phenomenon at age thirty-two. In 1989, *Time* magazine referred to Hwang as "potential[ly] . . . the first important dramatist of American public life since Arthur Miller, and maybe the best of them all."

Born on August 11, 1957, David Henry Hwang was the only son of a Shanghai-born banker who founded the first Asian American-owned national bank in the United States and of a Chinese pianist raised in the Philippines. Growing up in San Gabriel, California, Hwang describes himself as a "Chinese-Filipino-American, born-again-Christian kid from suburban Los Angeles" who had always thought of his Chinese heritage as an interesting detail, "like having red hair."

Meshing East and West

Hwang attributes his "rather nice sense of self" to his parents. His father, Henry, was determined that his children be assimilated into Western culture, while his mother, Dorothy, brought to the family a tradition of Protestant fundamentalism. Although the Hwang family seemed Westernized, the ancient Chinese culture with its myths and fables was "subliminally" transmitted into Hwang's psyche. His maternal grandmother told him stories about an ancestor sold into slavery and other tales from the old country. When he was ten, the young Hwang wrote a ninety-page "novel" based on his grandmother's memories.

Hwang attended the Harvard School, a private institution for children of the Los Angeles elite. (There he was on the debating team with Joe Hunt of the Billionaire Boy's Club who was later convicted of murder.) At Stanford University, Hwang first tried journalism and instrumental music before he attempted playwriting. More and more, he was exploring what it meant to be Chinese American. He lived in an Asian American dormitory and played in an all-Asian American rock band, Bamboo.

Hwang's first play was about a musician. When he showed it to a professor, Hwang was told that he obviously knew nothing about writing plays. He found a teacher who was willing to work with him and wrote *FOB*. Based on a night out Hwang had with a Chinese American cousin who was dating a boy from Hong Kong, *FOB* tells the story of the cultural clash between the new immigrant and the Westernized Asian American. From a first production in a dormitory to an Obie Award-winning staging at New York's Public Theater, Hwang's first play propelled him toward certain stardom at an age when most young adults have not even decided on a career.

Hwang's second play, *Dance and the Railroad*, was inspired by the experiences of Chinese railroad workers in the United States in 1867 and was nominated for a Drama Desk Award in 1982. He then wrote *Family Devotions*, a semi-autobiographical play in which Hwang questions the Christian tradition that had obstructed his journey into his cultural past. In 1983, the Public Theater produced a pair of his one-act plays, *The House of Sleeping Beauties*, inspired by a short story of the same name by Japanese novelist Yasunari Kawabata, and *The Sound of a Voice*, about a samurai who intends to kill an old witch but instead falls in love with her as she rejuvenates into a beautiful woman.

Crisis at Twenty-Six

For the next two years, Hwang found himself unable to write. "I lost belief in my subject matter—I dismissed it as 'Orientalia for the intelligentsia'—and virtually stopped writing for two years. I thought seriously about going to law school."

When he finally started writing again, he created his first non-Asian play. "*Rich Relations* was another attempt to write a spiritual farce," explained Hwang, "and it was about my family—except they're not Asians." The play was his first flop, and he said it was the most liberating thing that happened to him since the phenomenal success of *FOB*. "I realized, it's okay. I'm still alive. It's not the end of the world."

Shortly after the closing of *Rich Relations*, Hwang heard the story of a French diplomat who was involved in a twenty-year affair with a male Chinese spy whom he

David Henry Hwang

believed to be a woman. The diplomat even claimed to have fathered a child by his mistress. Even after he is confronted in court with undeniable evidence as to his lover's true gender, the diplomat refuses to believe it. "What interested me the most," Hwang recalled, "was the idea of the perfect woman. A real woman can only be herself, but a man, because he is presenting an idealization, can aspire to the idea of the perfect woman. I never had the least doubt that a man could play a woman convincingly on the stage."

M. Butterfly debuted on Broadway in March 1988, and eventually was produced in three dozen countries around the world. It grossed more than $35 million. In addition to the Tony Award, the play also garnered the Drama Desk, Outer Critics Circle, and John Gassner awards in 1988, followed by a 1991 L.A. Drama Critics Circle Award.

New Paths, New Plans

The worldwide success of *M. Butterfly* brought Hwang new opportunities and venues for creative expression. A few months after the opening of M. Butterfly, Hwang and avant-garde composer Philip Glass produced *1000 Airplanes on the Roof*, a multi-media extravaganza about a close encounter with aliens. Hwang would later write the libretto for Glass's opera *The Voyage*.

In 1992, Hwang premiered another one-act play *Bondage*, at the Humana Theater Festival at the Actors Theater of Louisville. The play, which starred his wife, Kathryn

Layng (the beautiful nurse in the television series *Doogie Howser, M.D.*) boldly confronts the inherent racism and sexism rampant in today's society. Hwang explores similar themes in *Face Value*, a farce inspired by the controversy over the casting of a white man in the lead role of the Eurasian pimp in the blockbuster *Miss Saigon*. His second play to open on Broadway, it closed after less than a week of troubled performances.

Hwang turned to screenwriting and completed a script for the screen version of *M. Butterfly* which was directed by David Cronenberg and released in late 1993. Another of his screenplays, *Golden Gate*, a mystical tale about an FBI agent who falls in love with the daughter of a Chinese American laundryman he sent to jail on false charges of Communist involvement, was released in early 1994.

For the time being, Hwang is spending his time on "non-Asian projects." He has just finished the fourth draft of a screenplay based on British author A.S. Byatt's Booker Prize-winning novel, *Possession*. "Now they have to finally decide whether to really make the movie or not," he chuckles. He is also adapting Isaac Asimov's Foundation trilogy for the screen and is working on a screenplay for an as-yet unpublished novel, *The Alienist*, by Caleb Carr.

"I want to be done by the spring," he says. I really want to be doing my own work. I'm hoping to do a play and an original screenplay by the end of the year." By 1995, Hwang will assume a new role as a director. "I prefer writing for the theatre because of the practical issue of control. A play can't be changed without the playwright's involvement, but with movies, it's very common that changes get made in the filming or editing process that the writer just isn't aware of. Even though I relish working in the theatre, at the same time there are some stories that come to mind that I think will make better movies than plays, and the only way to do that is to become a director."

A Community Spokesperson

Hwang has already been a director of sorts ever since the phenomenal success of his early plays thrust him into the role of spokesperson for the Asian American community, directing the public's perception of Asian Americans through his writings. "Being a spokesperson has been somewhat of a mixed bag," he muses. "I appreciate having a platform, having visibility, especially in regard to issues I really care about. On the other hand, it creates an additional job for an artist. Sometimes, I look with envy at artists that can write whatever they want to write about and not have any political implications attached to their work. I could only do that by not writing plays with any Asian American content, but since that's what I continue to write about, there must be something there I'm interested in."

In the last few years, Hwang has begun to "become very comfortable with the fact that there are many more Asian American writers out there than when I started." He is no longer the lone voice. "I don't feel I have to express *the* Asian American aesthetic anymore. One person can't represent a whole community. That there are so *many* voices now is the hopeful direction of the future. . . . 'I don't like *M. Butterfly*, but I like Chin's works or Gotanda's.' That people can say that is real progress."

Sources:

Periodicals

Gerard, Jeremy. "David Henry Hwang: Riding on the Hyphen." *New York Times Magazine,* March 13, 1988, pp. 44—45 and 88–89.

Henry, William A., III. "When East and West Collide." *Time,* August 14, 1989, pp. 62, 64.

Smith, Dinitia. "Face Values: The Sexual and Racial Obsessions of Playwright David Henry Hwang." *New York Magazine,* January 11, 1993, pp. 42—45.

Other

Hwang, David Henry, telephone interview with Terry Hong, February 9, 1994.

—Sketch by Terry Hong

I

Paul M. Igasaki

(1955–)

Attorney, activist

Paul Igasaki is the executive director of the Asian Law Caucus (ALC), a San Francisco-based civil rights and legal advocacy organization that has represented the Asian American community for twenty-one years. Prior to his position with the ALC Igasaki served as the Washington, D.C., representative for the Japanese American Citizen's League, a lobbying group concerned with promoting the interests of Japanese American citizens. He worked briefly as a fund-raiser for Representative Robert Matsui in his abortive bid for the U. S. Senate, and he has recently been nominated for a chairmanship of the Equal Employment Opportunity Commission.

Paul Igasaki was born in Chicago, Illinois, on July 25, 1955. His father was a corporate officer in accountancy and his mother was a homemaker. He was educated in the public school system and graduated from Niles West High School in 1973. From there he went to Northwestern University in Evanston, Illinois, where he studied political science. While an undergraduate Igasaki worked as a reporter for the *Daily Northwestern,* the campus newspaper. He also served as a congressional intern to then-congressman Abner J. Mikva (Democrat of Illinois). He graduated from Northwestern in 1976.

After graduation Igasaki moved to the West Coast to enroll in the Martin Luther King, Jr. School of Law at the University of California at Davis. While a student Igasaki worked as a law clerk for Asian Legal Services Outreach, a legal rights advocacy organization headquartered in Sacramento. Later in his schooling he worked as an intern for the California Agricultural Labor Relations Board, joining its full-time staff after earning his law degree in 1979.

Legal Activist

After passing the California bar exam in 1980, Igasaki went to work for Legal Services of Northern California, where he was a Reginald Heber Smith Fellow. In this position Igasaki worked as legal representative for impover-

ished clients in a variety of civil matters. At this time legal services to the poor around the country were being cut back due to the budgetary conservatism of the administration of president Ronald Reagan. The American Bar Association set up a program to defend against such budget cuts, and Igasaki was made director of the program, which was called the Private Bar Involvement Project. This organization, headquartered in Chicago, worked to increase resources available to legal service offices around the country through the provision of grants, on-site technical assistance, conferences, and information delivery systems.

In 1985 Igasaki left this position to serve Harold Washington, the mayor of Chicago, as the liaison to the city's Asian American community. In this capacity, he provided legal and management counsel to the Commission on Human Relations, the city's civil rights agency, and worked with all city departments in an attempt to make government more responsive to the Asian and immigrant population in Chicago. He served on the mayor's affirmative action council and as the first director of the Commission on Asian American Affairs.

Following Washington's death, Igasaki stayed on with the city of Chicago for two more years before moving to the nation's capital to become the Washington, D.C. representative for the Japanese American Citizens League, where he worked on such issues as the Civil Rights Acts of 1989 and 1991, immigration reform, access to higher education, confronting and eliminating media stereotypes, and funding for the Japanese American redress program. In this capacity Igasaki had the opportunity to work with legislators from around the country and in 1991 he joined Representative Robert Matsui's campaign for the U. S. Senate. He served as the Asian funding director of the campaign, which was aborted when Matsui withdrew for family reasons.

Asian Law Caucus

After Matsui abandoned his campaign, Igasaki was named executive director of the Asian Law Caucus (ALC), headquartered in San Francisco, California. The ALC provides legal services to the poor in the areas of civil rights, discrimination, immigration, housing, and worker's rights. He has served as executive director for three years. In the summer of 1994, Igasaki was nominated by President Bill Clinton to serve as a chairman of the Equal Employment Opportunity Commission, the nation's chief enforcer of employment discrimination laws. As of July 1994, Igasaki was awaiting Senate confirmation of this important posting.

Igasaki currently serves on several civic and legal affairs organizations. He is a co-chair of the civil rights committee of the American Bar Association, serves on the executive committee of the State Bar of California Legal Services Section. (He was a founder and vice president of the Asian American Bar Association of Chicago.) Igasaki is the co-chair of the legislative committee for the National Asian Pacific American Bar Association.

Sources:

Asian Law Caucus. "Paul Igasaki." Biography and press release, San Francisco, California, 1994.

Igasaki, Paul, telephone interview with Jim Henry, August 2, 1994.

—*Sketch by Jim Henry*

Daniel K. Inouye
(1924–)
Politician, war hero

United States Senator Daniel K. Inouye was the first American of Japanese descent to serve in the Congress. A highly decorated war hero, he has served as a representative of the state of Hawaii since it entered the union in 1959, first in the House of Representatives and then in the Senate, where he has served continuously since 1962. He first came to national attention at the 1968 Democratic National Convention in Chicago, where he made a poignant appeal in his keynote address for racial understanding. In 1973 and 1974 he once again drew national attention as a member of the Senate Watergate Committee, which investigated alleged wrongdoing by Republicans during Richard Nixon's 1972 reelection campaign. Aside from these high profile achievements, Inouye has had a distinguished legislative career and is currently one of the senior members of Congress.

Daniel Ken Inouye was born in Honolulu, Hawaii, on September 7, 1924, the oldest of four children of Hyataro and Kame (Imanaga) Inouye, first-generation Japanese immigrants. The elder Inouye worked as a file clerk to support his family. As a child, Daniel went to a special Japanese language school, as well the Honolulu public schools. As soon as he was old enough, he began working part-time jobs, including parking cars at the Honolulu Stadium and giving hair cuts to his friends. He spent most of his money from these jobs on his youthful hobbies of stamp collecting, chemistry, electronics, and keeping homing pigeons. In 1942 he graduated from McKinley High School and enrolled in the pre-med program at the University of Hawaii. He dropped out of college within a year, however, to enroll in the U.S. Army.

The 442nd Regimental Combat Team

After the bombing of Pearl Harbor in 1941, Japanese Americans had been petitioning the government to allow them to serve in the armed forces as a way of proving their loyalty to their country. In response the army established the 442nd Regimental Combat Team. Inouye enlisted in the army in 1943 and was assigned to this all-volunteer, all-Japanese unit. Inouye and the 442nd fought for nearly three months in the bloody Rome-Arno campaign, and then went on to France where they rescued an American Battalion surrounded by Germans. The Battle of the Lost Battalion is listed in the annals of U.S. military history as one of the most significant military battles of the twentieth century.

Back in Italy in the closing months of the war, Inouye fought in a battle and was hit in the abdomen by a bullet that came out his back, barely missing his spine. Despite his injury, he continued leading his platoon and advanced alone against an enemy machine gun nest that had his men pinned down. He tossed two grenades into the nest, crippling the machine-gunners before his right arm was shattered by a rifle grenade fired at close range. Inouye threw his last grenade with his left arm and was finally knocked down the hill by a bullet to the leg. For this remarkable display of bravery and selflessness, Inouye was made a captain and awarded a Distinguished Service Cross (the second highest award for military valor), a Bronze Star, a Purple Heart with cluster, and twelve other medals and citations.

Civilian Life

After being discharged from the army, Inouye reenrolled in the University of Hawaii on the GI bill, this time to study government and economics. He earned a bachelor's degree in 1950 and went on to law school at the prestigious George Washington University Law School in Washington, D.C. While in law school Inouye was elected to the professional law fraternity of Phi Delta Phi, served as editor of *George Washington Law Review*, and volunteered for the Democratic National Committee. He received his law degree in 1952.

Back in Hawaii, the young Inouye immediately became involved in politics. He befriended many important civic and Democratic party leaders and was appointed deputy public prosecutor for the city of Honolulu. In 1954 he ran for the territorial house of representatives. He won that election and was eventually made majority leader of the

Daniel K. Inouye

house. In 1958 he decided to run for election to the territorial senate; he won that race too. Inouye had become a very popular figure in Hawaiian politics, and when the territory was admitted into the United States as the fiftieth state he was elected to its first seat in the House of Representatives in an election that garnered him the largest number of votes ever cast for a candidate in a Hawaiian election.

In his first term Inouye served on the Banking and Currency Committee, but made a name for himself as an outspoken supporter of civil rights legislation. He also made important friends, including then-speaker Sam Rayburn. In 1960 he was reelected and moved to the Agriculture Committee where he was an advocate for sugar and pineapple growers and exporters, a major segment of the Hawaiian economy. In 1962 Hawaii's first senator, Oren E. Long, retired and endorsed Inouye as his successor. Inouye easily won the primary election and then defeated his Republican opponent in the general election by a two-to-one margin.

During his first term in the Senate, he supported the programs of Democratic presidents John F. Kennedy and then Lyndon B. Johnson. Bills of special concern to the senator were those directed at redressing racial discrimination—which he himself had routinely suffered—including Johnson's ground-breaking Civil Rights Act of 1964.

He was also a strong proponent of the liberal agenda of the time, topped by the Johnson administration's social welfare policies known as the Great Society. He also backed his president's policy of continued involvement in Vietnam.

Inouye was appointed to several posts within the Democratic party during his first term, including assistant majority whip and vice-chairman of the Democratic Senatorial Campaign Committee. His name was repeatedly mentioned as a possible vice president on a future Democratic ticket, and in 1968 he was chosen to deliver the keynote address at the party's convention. In that same year he was reelected to the Senate seat with 83 percent of the vote, an incredible margin.

Inouye's second term was marked by a reversal of his support for American involvement in Vietnam. He supported the Cooper-Church and McGovern-Hatfield amendments to end the war and co-sponsored the historic War Powers Act of 1973, which was intended to limit a president's power to commit American military forces to overseas conflict without congressional approval, a bill that has been largely ignored since its passage.

In 1973 Inouye was named by Senate Majority Leader Michael Mansfield to sit on the Senate Select Committee on Presidential Campaign Activities, known commonly as the Senate Watergate Committee. The committee had been set up to look into allegations that the Nixon administration had engaged in, or conspired to cover up for others who had engaged in, illegal activities on behalf of Nixon's 1972 reelection campaign. The committee's hearings were nationally televised and widely watched, and Inouye distinguished himself as a sincerely concerned finder of fact. At the conclusion of the hearing a Gallup poll gave the young senator favorable ratings of 84 percent.

Other nationally prominent committees Inouye has served on or chaired include his chairmanship of the 1976 Senate Select Committee on Intelligence, which was set up to formulate regulations for covert operations abroad and internal operations against American citizens by the intelligence community. Until that time, U.S. intelligence organizations had operated with seeming impunity around the world and at home, engaging in practices that horrified most Americans when they were exposed in the mid-seventies.

In 1987 he was again appointed chairman of a committee looking into executive abuse of power, the Senate Select Committee on Secret Military Assistance to Iran and the Nicaraguan Opposition, known popularly as the Iran-Contra Committee. This committee was set up to look into reports that members of President Ronald Reagan's National Security Staff had sold arms to Iran—a violation of international law and official American policy—and then sent the profits to a band of resistance fighters seeking to oust the Sandinista government of Nicaragua in violation of a congressional ban on such aid. The hearings of this committee were televised nationally.

Inouye's Legislative Record

Since his election to the Congress in 1958, Inouye has voted in the liberal tradition on most social issues and moderately on economic and defense issues. He is a strong supporter of abortion rights, desegregation of public institutions, and tough gun control. He champions consumer rights and has voted in favor of public works programs to put the unemployed to work. In matters of defense his voting has been less partisan. He voted in favor of many cold war military systems, including funding for the development of the neutron bomb, a nuclear device designed to kill populations while leaving structures intact. He opposed many Reagan-era defense programs, however, most notably the Strategic Defense Initiative, an elaborate, expensive (and many thought scientifically dubious) scheme meant to protect the United States from nuclear attack with a system of space-based laser beams and nuclear devices.

Today the senior senator from Hawaii chairs the Committee on Indian Affairs, the Appropriations Subcommittee on Defense, and the Commerce, Science, and Transportation Subcommittee on Communications, where he is having a major impact on the formation of national information delivery systems. His recent bill to allow cable and telephone companies to directly compete in the information delivery market has had an important effect on the growth of this vital industry.

Inouye married Margaret Shinobu (Awamura) in 1949. They live in Bethesda, Maryland, and Honolulu, Hawaii. They have one son, Daniel Ken, Jr.

Sources:

Books

"Daniel K. Inouye." *Who's Who in American Politics*, New York: R.R. Bowker, 1993.

Periodicals

Yang, Jeff. "Power Brokers." *A. Magazine*, vol. 2, no. 3, December 15, 1993, pp. 25–34.

Other

Inouye, Daniel. "Biography, Daniel K. Inouye, United States Senator." Washington, D.C., May 1994.

—*Sketch by Jim Henry*

Paul Isaki
(1944–)
Business executive

Since 1993, Paul Isaki has been vice-president for business development for the Seattle Mariners major league baseball team—the all-American dream job. But his birth in Topaz, Utah, where his family was imprisoned with other West Coast Japanese Americans, was anything but an all-American beginning.

Paul Isaki was born June 6, 1944—D-Day (the day on which allied forces landed at Normandy Beach to begin the invasion of France during World War II)—at Topaz, Utah, an internment camp. When the internment order was lifted in 1945, the Isaki family returned to Oakland, California. Shigeyoshi Isaki, Paul's father, who had been born in Oakland, started a small trucking company. Remembering the attitudes in the San Francisco Bay area toward Japanese Americans immediately following World War II, Isaki told Susan Gall, "My father would comment that it was often necessary to fight his way onto and off the docks on the San Francisco waterfront to pick up shipments to be able to earn a living. Anti-Japanese sentiment did not disappear when the camps closed." Isaki's mother, Haru Michida was born in San Francisco and worked as a clerical worker for the same trading company that had employed Isaki's father's trucking company before the war.

Isaki grew up in Oakland and attended public schools which, in his neighborhood, served primarily African American children. His childhood environment had a powerful effect on Isaki. "I think my strong social and economic justice motivations go back to my childhood in west Oakland, a predominantly African American community. Many of my attitudes were shaped by those early friendships, where I could observe firsthand what it meant to be black and poor. In my early life, this was a much fuller experience [than the internment, or Japanese American experience], and shaped my attitudes before I could fully appreciate the experience of my parents' generation. I am better able to feel, sense, and articulate the effects of social and economic injustice because I saw it firsthand," he said. "My urban experience was not all that different from my other Sansei [third generation Japanese American] friends in San Francisco or Los Angeles. We grew up with and went to school with a lot of minority children. It was not at all uncommon for Japanese Americans and African Americans to be friends."

Public Service Beginnings

After graduating from high school, Isaki entered the University of California, Berkeley, with the plan, directed

Paul Isaki

by his parents, to become a dentist. "That changed almost immediately. At the time, the focal point at Berkeley was social justice, including the early seeds of the civil rights movement and the free speech movement. This definitely affected me. I was caught up in the drive toward significant social change," he recalled. "I remember listening to James Farmer [then-head of the Congress for Racial Equality (CORE)] in 1962. He was speaking on a street corner in Berkeley. This was before the Voting Rights Act of 1964. But that was how things were in Berkeley then."

Isaki graduated from Berkeley in 1965 and became involved in the "War on Poverty," a government-sponsored program to help the economically disadvantaged. Isaki worked in various community agencies in rural central California, serving primarily migrant workers, and in the urban San Francisco Bay area, working with African Americans. In 1971, he moved to Seattle to take a position with the Seattle Opportunities Industrialization Center, a skills training center for federally funded job training programs. In 1973, he left to take a position with the city of Seattle, where he was instrumental in setting up a two-county, seven-city regional job training and placement program as a federally funded demonstration. As he progressed in his career, Isaki's skills for development were honed. In Seattle, he was responsbile for developing a new $3.1 million job training center in the inner city. "Among the last things I was doing in California had less to do with social services and more to do with physical development. I was tackling capital development projects,

bringing public and private interests together," Isaki recalled.

He moved next to become assistant director of a four-county, public/private economic development project, where he stayed until 1979. It was then that Isaki decided to capitalize on his aptitude and skill for real estate development, forming a company with a partner to provide consulting in urban development for public and private interests. "Our clients were municipalities looking to attract private investment, and private developers seeking local government partners. We were interpreters—my partner and I had an interesting mix of commercial and public development experience, and we helped others make the transition," he related. One of their clients was a large hotel management company based in Denver, which bought out Isaki and his partner in 1981, and they became part of the national company. "They made us the proverbial offer we couldn't refuse," Isaki said. "We were responsible for hotel deals...ranging from a $4 million restoration and redevelopment project in Chattanooga, Tennessee to the development of a $20 million hotel in San Diego. I marvel today that they actually paid us to do that work. My partner and I were taken under the wing of the company's CEO, and we learned a tremendous amount."

In 1984, Isaki left the management company with the intention of doing real estate development on his own. "While I was putting that together, I was approached by a friend who was directing the transition for Booth Gardner, who had just been elected governor of the state of Washington. Gardner had based his campaign on a theme of economic development, and they invited me to join his team," Isaki said. "I was furiously trying to do my own venture, but the governor-elect did not take 'no' for an answer. I served in the Governor's administration for eight years, ultimately heading up the department of trade and economic development."

In Washington State, trade development is one of the most important aspects of the state's operation. "From the standpoint of jobs and business sales, Washington is the most trade-dependent state in the United States. [In] my role in the governors' office. . . . I was charged with finding ways to help Washington companies become more trade-competetive." Isaki said. As an illustration, Isaki described a project that the Washington government and industry took on, in partnership with the Hyogo prefecture [provincial] government in Japan. This project, a symbolic experiment with strong economic repercussions, involved building a western style subdivision, designed by a Washington architect working with a Japanese architect. The concept was for Japanese builders to construct 170 houses, using materials from Washington state. The homes, 100 of which had been built and sold by late summer 1994, are very expensive and very popular. Isaki related that this project, which he spearheaded from 1986 to 1992, "came to symbolize a partnership, with Japan as consumer and the United States as producer. The results have been incredible, in terms of stimulating the wood products manufacturing sector in Washington to recognize Japan as source of new business." And Isaki is not alone in viewing the project as successful. In 1991, the Washington Village Project, as it is known, was recognized as one of twenty-five national finalists by the Innovations in State and Local Government program. This juried program, sponsored by Harvard University's Kennedy School of Government, annually assesses worthy undertakings by state and local governments. This may have been one of Isaki's first forays into a business relationships with Japan, but it was just a taste of things to come.

It was in 1985 that major league baseball and Isaki first crossed paths. Isaki was on the governor's staff in charge of business and economic issues when a dispute over renegotiation of the Mariners' Kingdome lease heated up over a period of months, with the owners threatening to move the Mariners out of Seattle if the lease terms with King County were not satisfactorily settled. Isaki recalled, "[The governor and his staff, including Isaki] had business in Japan during that period, and our Japanese contacts displayed more than a casual interest in the plight of the Mariners. They wanted to know what the governor was doing about it, and expressed their strong feeling that it would be a shame if Seattle lost its major league baseball team." Gardner realized that major league baseball was a high-profile international issue, and Washington's most important trading partner, Japan, was concerned about it. Isaki continued, "He then assigned me to work on a resolution of the [Kingdome lease] issue full time." Isaki's role in resolving the impasse in the lease negotiations, clearing the way for Seattle to keep the Mariners, is universally recognized.

Drafted by the Majors

In 1992, John Ellis, board chairnan and chief executive officer of the Mariners, approached Isaki about joining the new Mariners' organization in a job specially created for him, vice-president of business development. His assignment is to develop Mariners' business interests both in the Pacific Northwest and in Japan. "I'll be involved with building an advertising base regionally to support a strong broadcast program…and evaluating Japan to see what opportunities there are for the Mariners," he told *Washington CEO.* The Mariners' objective to increase exposure in Japan is viewed as positive by both major league and the players. The Mariners' link with Japan drew national attention in 1992, when a majority interest in the team was purchased by Hiroshi Yamauchi, president of Nintendo, the entertainment game conglomerate whose U.S. headquarters are in Redmond, Washington.

Although the players' strike in the summer of 1994 will delay it, Isaki is putting together the terms for the Mariners to play a regular season game against another American League team in Japan, along with possible exhibition games against Japanese teams. Isaki hopes this will be a reality in the 1996 season. "Baseball fans in Japan acknowledge that major league baseball in the United States is the pinnacle," Isaki told Gall. "Playing in Japan would increase our visibility to Japanese businesses with whom we hope to develop expanded relationships," he explained to Susumu Awanohara of the *Far Eastern Economic Review.* If the terms can be worked out, much of the revenue derived from game tickets, merchandise, advertising, and broadcast rights sold there would go to the league's twenty-eight teams, but Isaki still feels the benefits would be great for the Mariners.

The theme of economic development being a public/private venture is a strong one in Isaki's career. The expansion into an international arena is an added dimension in his role with the Mariners. "I enjoy the international aspect of this business," he told Gall. And, as an enthusiastic baseball fan since childhood, the nature of his business is something he enjoys as well.

Isaki lives in Seattle with his wife, Lucy, who is a partner in the law firm of Bogle & Gates. Isaki told Gall that after growing up in west Oakland, he feels "fortunate to have options and opportunities, and to be able to achieve some measure of success." Given the nature of his assignment with the Mariners, the skills he has developed along his career path seem to have prepared him well. "They [the Mariners' management] didn't set out to hire a Japanese American. I was recruited directly by the president and CEO specifically because they felt I was uniquely qualified to do the things they wanted to get done from a business standpoint. . . . The fact that I'm Japanese American was a bonus." he told Mike Habata of *Rafu Shimpo.* He added, "If the work I do here serves that purpose [as a role model for minorities who want to work in professional sports], I am really pleased."

Sources:

Periodicals

Awanohara, Susumu. "Marketing: Major-League Gambit." *Far Eastern Economic Review,* December 23, 1993, p. 50.

Boardman, Paul. "The State's Japanese Partnerships & Relationships: The Beat Goes On." *Team Washington News,* vol. 4, no. 2, fall 1991, pp. 1+.

Day, Connie. "Former State Trade Chief Steps to Mariners' Plate." *Washington CEO,* nd, p. 52.

"Editorial: Step 1 for Regional M's: Hiring New Business Veep." *The Seattle Times,* December 4, 1992, p. A16.

Habata, Mike. "Swinging for the Fences." *The Rafu Shimpo,* February 4, 1993, pp. 1+.

Lim, Gerard. "Paul Isaki Lands Front Office Job with Mariners." *Asian Week,* January 22, 1994, p. 4.

Mochizuki, Ken. "Paul Isaki: Seattle Mariners VP Hustles for Major League Support," *Northwest Nikkei,* vol. 5, no. 4, April 1993, pp. 1+.

Other

Isaki, Paul, telephone interviews with Susan Gall, August 2 and 18, 1994.

Seattle Mariners. "Paul Isaki." Professional bio and press releases, 1994.

—Sketch by Susan Gall

Eiko Ishioka

Eiko Ishioka

Graphic designer, art director

Having won prestigious awards for her design work in both Japan and the United States, Eiko Ishioka is one of the most gifted costume, set, and graphic designers working on the international scene. Her work ranges from award-winning advertising to Academy Award-winning costume design. No matter what her medium, Ishioka's designs are powerfully thought-provoking.

Eiko Ishioka was born July 12 the oldest daughter of Tomio and Mitsuko Ishioka. Her father was a well-regarded graphic designer in Japan. In 1957, Ishioka entered the Tokyo National University of Fine Arts and Music, where she studied industrial design until her final year when she switched to graphic design. After graduation in 1961, she joined an advertising division of Japan's oldest cosmetics company, Shiseido. Within two years, the young designer was winning awards, including the Tokyo Art Directors Club Gold Medal. In 1965, she was the first woman to be given the Japanese advertising industry's most coveted award, the JAAC Prize (Japan Advertising Artists Club) for a series of nine posters entitled *Symposium: Discovery Today*. During the mid-1960s, Eiko (as she prefers to be called) began to expand her horizons beyond Japan. She traveled first to Hawaii for advertising photo sessions, and then spent several months in Europe and North America, seeking ideas and insights from the international design industry.

International Career Is Launched

In 1968, Eiko created *Power Now*, a poster which was included in a Gallery Nippon exhibit in Tokyo, and in the "Graphics I: New Dimensions" exhibit at the Museum of Modern Art (MOMA) in New York. MOMA acquired the poster for their permanent collection, and it went on to win the bronze medal in the Politics and Society section of the Fourth International Poster Biennale in Warsaw. In late 1968 Eiko left Shiseido and accepted art direction assignments for magazine advertisements and record covers for the then-new CBS/Sony recording company.

She was also intrigued by the design challenge of books, creating a noteworthy design for a multivolume anthology of critical essays.

In 1970, Eico Design, Eiko's own design studio, was born. Her first projects were both a continuation of her previous work as an in-house designer doing posters and advertising, and an exploration of new fields with such assignments as art director for Susumu Hani's film, *Slave of Love (Aido)*. Eiko also began exploring new applications for design, doing fabric designs for the fashion designer Issey Miyake, and corporate logotypes. She achieved another first for women in the design profession when, in 1971, she became the first woman to be elected a member of the Tokyo Art Directors Club.

In 1975, Eiko created a sensation with her advertising campaign for Parco, a chain of Japanese shopping complexes. The posters she designed had nothing to do with shopping, but rather were dramatic artistic statements. For example, one featured a nude black model bent forward with her hands on the floor, eyes wide, grinning into the camera, with the verse "A nightingale flatters no one and sings for herself." In another, the American actress Faye Dunaway, dressed in traditional Japanese clothing, is wrapping two Japanese children into the folds of her cloak, with the accompanying text: "Can the West assimilate the East?" Throughout the seventies, Eiko pursued the thought-provoking approach to advertising, winning attention and acclaim from her colleagues, clients, and the general public.

Eiko continued to design posters, two for the Japanese release of Francis Ford Coppola's *Apocalypse Now.* In 1979, the Japanese distributor for the film, Nippon Herald Films, sent Eiko to New York to view the film and to interpret Coppola's message for the Japanese audience. She returned to Japan with ideas for two large posters which eventually came into Coppola's hands without his knowing who the designer was. Eiko wrote in *Coppola and Eiko on Bram Stoker's Dracula,* "I remember that, years later, I was greatly surprised and delighted to see my posters of the helicopters and surfer motif framed and displayed side by side on the wall of Francis's dining room in his New York apartment." Eiko also designed the Japanese edition of Eleanor Coppola's book, *Notes,* about the making of *Apocalypse Now.*

In 1980, Eiko closed her Tokyo studio and went to New York for an extended vacation that lasted until February 1982, and that included one semester of study at New York University. It was during this New York stay that she first met Eleanor Coppola. Of that meeting, Eiko wrote: "At our first meeting, Eleanor told me she liked my book design [for the Japanese edition of *Notes*] very much, and immediately we became good friends."

When Eiko's father died in 1982, Eiko returned to Japan. In 1983, Eiko designed *Eiko by Eiko,* a 240-page collection of two thousand illustrations accompanied by tributes to her work, published simultaneously by Callaway in New York and Kyuryudo in Tokyo. She sent a copy to Eleanor Coppola, who promptly installed it on the coffee table in the Coppola home.

The Next Design Phase—Feature Films

Although Eiko was familiar with the visual presentation of a film's concept for advertising and promotional purposes, it wasn't until 1984 that she became involved in the actual design of film sets. Paul Schrader and Francis Ford Coppola came to Japan as director and executive producer respectively to begin shooting a film titled *Mishima* about the life and death of the novelist Yukio Mishima. Tom Luddy introduced Eiko to Coppola during this time, and she met Schrader shortly thereafter. Shrader invited her to become production designer for *Mishima,* and she accepted. The film, which had its world premiere at the Cannes Film Festival in 1985, won a special jury prize for artistic achievement citing cinematography by John Bailey, the musical score by Philip Glass, and art direction by Eiko.

Both Coppola and Eiko are fascinated by the conflicts and contrasts of Eastern and Western culture. In April 1988, Coppola attended a preview of *M. Butterfly,* a theatre production that was truly international—the producer, Stuart Ostrow, was American; the director, John Dexter, was English; the playwright, David Henry Hwang, was Chinese American; and the scenic and costume designer, Eiko Ishioka, was Japanese. Writing in *Bram Stoker's Dracula,* Eiko said, "I think we must call this sort of creative expression 'Global Style.'"

In the spring of 1991, Francis Ford Coppola invited Eiko to join the team working on *Bram Stoker's Dracula* as costume designer. In describing his vision of the costumes, Coppola said "In this film the costumes will be the set, and the set will be the lighting." Eiko was intrigued enough to travel from New York to California to the Coppola home for further discussions, and she enthusiastically accepted the assignment.

Eiko's designs for the film are startlingly fresh and unique. In describing her design process, she noted during the preproduction phase of *Bram Stoker's Dracula:* "I never use a design element straight from the source. I get ideas from different materials, and then I keep them filed in the drawers of my mind until they are needed. My sources ranged from armadillos and frilled lizards to Buddhist figurines." The resulting costumes won the 1993 Academy Award for best costume design.

In a May 1992 interview with Francis Ford Coppola published in *Eiko and Coppola on Bram Stoker's Dracula,* Coppola said: "My strategy in hiring someone like her [Eiko]—an independent, a weirdo outsider with no roots in the business—it worked in the end. Because I could look at the screen and say, well, these costumes are truly irrational and artistic and absolutely unique." The "absolutely unique" designs are predictably deserving of awards and accolades, no matter what venue she is working in.

Sources:

Dworkin, Susan, ed. *Coppola and Eiko on Bram Stoker's Dracula.* San Francisco: Collins, 1992.
Ishioka, Eiko. *Eiko on Eiko.* New York: Callaway Editions, 1983.

—Sketch by Susan Gall

Lance A. Ito
(1950–)
Judge

Los Angeles County superior court judge Lance A. Ito is a highly regarded jurist in the state of California. He served for ten years as a county prosecutor, serving on both the hard-core gang and organized crime units of the office. He served as a municipal court judge for two years prior to his elevation to the superior court, and in 1992 the Los Angeles County Bar Association named him trial judge of the year.

Lance Ito was born on August 2, 1950, in Los Angeles, California. Both of his parents were schoolteachers. Ito was educated in the Los Angeles public school system and graduated from John Marshall High School in 1968. In the fall of that year he enrolled in the University of California at Los Angeles. He studied political science and graduated *cum laude* in 1972. From there he enrolled in the Boalt Hall School of Law at the University of California at Berkeley, from which he graduated in 1975. Ito was admitted to the California Bar on December 8, 1975.

A Career in Law

Ito's first job after law school was in the office of the firm of Irsfield, Irsfield, and Younger, where he practiced for two years. In 1977 he left private practice to work for the district attorney's office as a prosecutor. He stayed in this position for ten years and prosecuted cases involving street gangs and organized crime. From 1984 until 1987 he served on the board of directors of the Los Angeles County Association of Deputy District Attorney's. He also served as vice-chair of California State's Task Force on Youth Gang Violence in 1986 and 1989. Additionally, he served on California State's Task Force on Victim's Rights in 1988.

In December 1987 California governor George Dukmejian appointed Ito to fill the newly created position of municipal court judge of the Los Angeles Judicial District of Los Angeles County. In 1989 Ito was appointed, again by Dukmejian, to the Los Angeles County Superior Court to replace retiring Judge Franciscus. In 1990 Ito ran unopposed in an election to retain his appointed seat. As of summer 1994 Ito's position was as assistant presiding judge of the Los Angeles Superior Court.

Ito is a very highly regarded judge of the superior court. In 1992 he was recognized for his outstanding service by the Los Angeles County Bar Association when it named him trial judge of the year. Since 1987 he has been a member of the California Judges Association, and in 1990 he was named to its board of directors.

High Profile Cases

In 1991 Ito presided over a nationally prominent case as the judge assigned to the securities fraud prosecution of Charles Keating, the former owner of the infamous Lincoln Savings and Loan Association, one of the hundreds of failed Savings and Loans that plagued the nation in the late eighties and early nineties. Keating was accused of cheating investors out of their savings to support his own lavish life-style. Ito caused a national controversy while presiding over this case when he dismissed about half of the government's charges. When the trial was over and Keating had been convicted, Ito sentenced him to the maximum allowable prison term.

Lance A. Ito

In 1994 Ito was assigned to another high-profile case when it was decided that he would hear the case against Hall of Fame runningback O. J. Simpson, who in mid-1994 was accused of murdering his ex-wife and a friend of hers. This case, which dominated the attention of the national media in an unprecedented and at times unseemly manner, made Ito one of the most discussed judges in the nation. In the *New York Times* several prominent attorneys, those associated with the Simpson case and others who were not, were given an opportunity to discuss the judge's record and credentials.

Commenting to the *New York Times,* Blair Bernholz, a Los Angeles defense attorney, said: "He [Ito] is very sensitive to the needs of trial lawyers and allows them to do their work. But there's never any question who is in control of the courtroom. He keeps a firm hand." Janet Kerr, a law professor at Pepperdine University in Malibu, California: "I believe him to be a brilliant judge who's willing to listen to many different sides of an issue and who makes very well-reasoned decisions. He does have a dry sense of humor. I think he adds a lot of personality in the courtroom." Robert Shapiro, who represented Simpson said that Ito was "an excellent choice because he is one of the finest judges in the state of California."

Ito is married to Margaret Ann York, a former homicide detective and currently a captain in the Los Angeles Police Department. They have been married since 1981.

Sources:

Periodicals

Mydans, Seth. "Judge in Simpson Case Goes by the Rules." *New York Times,* July 23, 1994, p. 9.

Other

Los Angele Superior Court. "Lance Ito." Press release and publicity. Los Angeles, California, 1994.

—Sketch by Jim Henry

Pico Iyer
(1957–)
Writer

Pico Iyer is a contributing writer to *Time* and *Conde Naste* magazines. He is also the author of three books, *Video Nights in Katmandu,* an account of his travels in Southeast Asia, *The Lady and the Monk,* about a year he spent living in Japan, and *Falling off the Map,* a collection of his travel essays written for various publications. In 1995 he will publish his first novel.

Pico Iyer was born on February 11, 1957, in Oxford, England, to Asian Indian parents, both of whom were teaching at Oxford University. When Iyer was seven his parents moved to Santa Barbara, California, and Iyer, who had already started school at the Dragon School, stayed behind as a boarder. After finishing junior high school, Iyer won a King's Scholarship to attend Eton, one of the most prestigious private preparatory schools in England. While there, Iyer was the editor of the student newspaper, the *Eton College Chronicle.* Iyer was an excellent student and after graduating from Eton in 1974 was awarded a scholarship to Oxford University.

Before starting college Iyer took a year off, a tradition among English private school graduates. During this time he traveled to the United States and worked for a time as a busboy in a Mexican restaurant, disguising himself as a Mexican. He then went with a friend on a long overland journey from California through Central America to Bolivia. Iyer remembers the journey fondly and as a transforming experience in his life. In an interview with Jim Henry he said, "It's a great thing to take a journey like that when you're seventeen or eighteen because you're relatively reckless and you don't really know what the dangers are. And then once you've done it, anything seems possible thereafter."

Following his travels Iyer returned to England to attend Oxford. He studied English literature at Magdalen College and worked as the arts editor for *Isis,* the main university magazine. He also began writing professionally at this time, sending book reviews and travel articles to small journals and magazines. His main source was *London Magazine,* a relatively small but modestly prestigious magazine known for its sponsorship of young, unknown writers. Iyer graduated from Oxford in 1978 with a bachelor's degree in English, and with the distinction of a "congratulatory double first," meaning that he scored in the highest categories in two final year examinations.

After finishing at Oxford Iyer went to graduate school at Harvard, where he began studying for his master's degree in English and American language and literature, which he earned in 1980. Afterward he spent two more years at Harvard, teaching expository writing and working toward his Ph.D., for which he has completed all the requirements but writing a dissertation. Also during this time Iyer worked as a writer for the travel books published by St. Martin's Press called the *Let's Go* books; the standard student and budget travel guides to the countries of the world. Iyer wrote parts of seven books, including *Let's Go Britain, Let's Go France,* and *Let's Go Europe.* This work was especially helpful later in Iyer's career as a travel essayist. He also wrote freelance pieces, mainly book reviews, for magazines such as *Saturday Review* and *The Nation.*

Writing for *Time*

In 1982 Iyer left Harvard with his master's degree to take his chances doing freelance writing rather than pursuing an academic career, and he was hired by *Time* magazine as a staff writer for the world affairs section. He also continued writing literary and performance reviews for other magazines, such as the *Village Voice.*

During his first year on the staff of *Time,* Iyer took a vacation to Southeast Asia and was enthralled by the area. He took a couple of other extended vacations there in the preceding years and then in 1985 he took a six month leave-of-absence from *Time* to write a book about his experiences is Southeast Asia. He spent the first three months of his leave traveling through ten countries and spent the next three months writing what would become his first book, *Video Nights in Katmandu,* published by Knopf in 1988.

When Iyer returned to New York in 1986 he resigned his position with *Time,* thinking that he couldn't stand the thought of writing in a cubicle in New York after having spent so much time traveling. *Time* offered to keep him on in a new capacity, however, one that would allow him a degree of freedom and still keep him writing for the magazine. Iyer accepted the offer and became a contributing editor in 1986.

The following year, having fully completed the manuscript of his first book, Iyer traveled to Japan, a place that

Pico Iyer

had always fascinated him. He spent a year living in the city of Kyoto. He wrote about this year abroad in his second book, *The Lady and the Monk*, which received generally good reviews when it was published in 1991. Writing in *Time* magazine, Stefan Kanfer said, "Iyer combines an acute sense of place with a mordant irony. The revealing detail is his specialty."

In 1989 Iyer returned to the United States, staying at his parents' home in Santa Barbara, California, living both there and in Japan since then. He continues to write for

Time magazine and has since become a contributing editor to *Conde Naste Traveller.* In 1993 Knopf published a collection of his travel essays called *Falling off the Map.* In the summer of the 1994, Iyer had just completed his first novel, tentatively titled *Cuba and the Night,* which will be published by Knopf in early 1995.

Reflections on Life in America

Iyer describes America as the perfect country to be a foreigner in. He sees himself as a perennial outsider, having spent his childhood and early adulthood as an Indian growing up in England and then living as an English-educated Indian in America, and then finally as an Indian from England and American living in Japan. Of all of the cultures he has been exposed to, Iyer finds the American most accommodating to his otherness. He goes so far as to say that being an Asian Indian in America is an advantage in that Americans' preconceived ideas about Asian Indians are rather positive in general.

Speaking about the success he has achieved, Iyer suggests that the most obvious advice he could give a young writer would be to write as much as you can; rather than just thinking of yourself as a writer, actually do the writing. The second piece of advice would be that if you have the courage of your convictions, the rest will take care of itself.

Sources:

Periodicals

Kanfer, Stefan. "Review of *The Lady and the Monk,*" *Time,* September 23, 1991. p. 70.

Other

Iyer, Pico, telephone interview with Jim Henry, July 7, 1994.

—Sketch by Jim Henry

J

Philip Jaisohn
(1864–1951)
Physician, civil servant, newspaper publisher

Philip Jaisohn

Philip Jaisohn was a man of many firsts. In his native Korea in 1881, he was a member of the first group of Korean students to be sent abroad to study. He was a leader in the first reformist uprising in Korea's history, a failed coup d'etat in December of 1884 during which he and his fellow reformers held power for just three days. In April of 1885, Jaisohn arrived in San Francisco, California, as a young exile and three years later, he became the first Korean to become an American citizen. In 1892, he became the first Korean American to receive an American medical degree. Four years later, Jaisohn returned to Korea where he founded the first Korean newspaper, *The Independent (Toknip)*, which was published in the vernacular *onmun* (the Korean language character set) rather than the less accessible Chinese characters known only by scholars and the upper classes. Throughout his life, he would be remain loyal to both his motherland and his adopted homeland, serving both to the best of his abilities.

Childhood

Philip Jaisohn was born Suh Jae-pil in Kanaeri, Tong-Bok District in the South Cholla Province of Korea. Although the exact year of his birth is uncertain, it is believed he was born on November 28, 1864. He adopted the name Philip Jaisohn upon his arrival in the United States, using an Anglicized version of his Korean name in reverse order: Philip for Pil, Jai for Jae, and Sohn for Suh.

In the late 19th century when Jaisohn was born, Korea was known as the Hermit Kingdom, named so for its fierce isolationism. Korea was very much a feudal nation, ruled by an absolute monarchy to which it had been subjected for thousands of years. By the 1860s, the Korean government not only rejected contact with foreign nations, it absolutely forbade contact between Koreans and foreigners. Moreover, the nation was segregated by an extremely rigid social stratification, known as the *yangban* system. *Yangban* was not originally a social class but rather the word referred to a group consisting of high government officials. During the Yi Dynasty (1392–1910), Korea's last dynasty, the class system changed and the *yangban* came to refer to the highest of the hierarchical social class system.

Born into this rigid, yet greatly privileged *yangban* class., Jaisohn was the second son of the magistrate of the Tong-Bok District in South Cholla Province. His parents had come from two of the most illustrious and wealthy families in Korea. He was described as a happy and energetic child with a beautiful singing voice and a precocious nature. He enjoyed a carefree childhood until he was sent, at age seven, to live as the adoptive son of one of his family's clansmen, who was without a male heir. His relationship with his adoptive parents was not one of mutual affection. In his new home, he was sternly told that playing with the children of poor peasants was a frivolity unacceptable to the son of a yangban. Jaisohn was made to realize, much younger than most children, that he was not born to enjoy life but to fill a role assigned to him for the maintenance of a social system.

As the male heir of his adoptive father, Jaisohn was expected to bring fame and fortune to the new family. To that end, he needed only to pass the *kwago* (government service examination) to begin the expected government career. Since the advanced education necessary to pass this examination could not be found outside of Seoul, Jaisohn was sent off to the capital city to live with a wealthy, powerful uncle and his family.

For six years, he attended the private school established by his uncle for his own son, Jaisohn, and half a dozen sons of his friends. With his photographic memory and high intelligence, Jaisohn was the best student. At age 13, the youngest in a group of nineteen candidates, he not only passed the *kwago*, but he was declared the winner of the highest award. He had a promising government career before him.

Bringing Down the Government

As Jaisohn entered young adulthood, he came into contact with other young men of the yangban class who were unhappy with Korea's isolationist, socially stratified absolute monarchic rule. A political movement for governmental and social reform was just forming, led by a young liberal named Kim Ok-kiun. A core group of reformers began to emerge, with Jaisohn the youngest among them. With the help of a Buddhist monk who had traveled to Japan and a Japanese book in the monk's possession, *The History of the Occidental World*, the group began to learn about the world outside of isolated Korea. Convinced that Korea could enter the modern age by studying Japan's military and scientific advances of the last twenty years, Kim Ok-kiun convinced the Korean king and queen to send a group of young men for such training to Japan in order to revitalize Korea.

In December 1882, Jaisohn and fourteen fellow students—screened and selected by Jaisohn himself—left Korea for Tokyo. After spending six months studying Japanese, the young men enrolled at the Toyama Military Institute, completing their studies in May of 1884. They immediately returned to their homeland ready to renovate Korea's tiny defense force. However, instead of being welcomed home, they were met by angry relatives and friends who considered the young men traitors for going to a country considered an historic enemy of Korea. Moreover, instead of putting their newly acquired military skills to beneficial use, the young men were ordered to report for duty at the royal palace as palace guards.

By this time, the ruling Korean royalty had come under heavy Chinese influence. Antagonism was growing between the multiplying Chinese troops in Korea and the Korean people. The Chinese were usurping more and more power away from the Korean people and the royalty did nothing to stop the abuses. In order to free the country from the Chinese, as well as the virtually ineffectual monarchy, Kim Ok-kiun began to regather his group of Korean independence supporters, including Jaisohn and

the rest of the original fifteen students who had traveled to Japan. With Japanese military support behind them, the group of young reformers led a surprise attack on the royal palace on December 4, 1884, capturing the king and queen. The following morning, Kim Ok-kiun and his colleagues announced the formation of a new government, the first reform regime in Korean history. Jaisohn, who at age twenty was the youngest of the leaders, was given operational command of all forces. The fledgling reform did not last long, however, and on December 6 fell to powerful Chinese troops who overtook the palace. Jaisohn and his fellow reformers escaped Seoul and soon thereafter left Korea.

A New Life in a New Country

Jaisohn fled to Tokyo, where he remained for five months, living with and giving Korean language lessons to an American missionary and his wife who were waiting to enter Korea. From them, Jaisohn learned firsthand about life in America. He also had plenty of time to ruminate over the failed coup. He realized that to best serve his beloved Korea, he must find a way to educate first himself and then the Korean people. To that end, he decided to pursue an education in the United States.

In April 1885, Jaisohn landed in San Francisco. He found a job that paid him two dollars a day for distributing advertising circulars for a furniture store. He took English lessons at the local YMCA, and attended Bible classes, worship services, and prayer meetings at Mason Street Presbyterian Church. A church elder took a deep interest in Jaisohn and introduced Jaisohn to William Hollenbeck, a wealthy coal magnate from Pennsylvania. Hollenbeck proposed that Jaisohn be sent to school to be trained for the ministry, then sent back to Korea as a missionary. Jaisohn readily agreed, eager to obtain the education for himself for which he had come to America.

Jaisohn attended Harry Hillman Academy in Pennsylvania, completing a four-year course in two and graduating in June 1888 with high honors. Also in 1888 he became the first Korean to be naturalized as an American citizen. He soon realized that he no longer felt called to the ministry, however, and looked for a way to continue his education without Hollenbeck's financial help. He eventually landed a job at the U.S. Army Surgeon General's Library in Washington, D.C., after scoring high marks on a civil service exam. There he catalogued medical books and periodicals from Asia. He became interested in medicine, and while continuing to work at the Library, he enrolled at the Corcoran Scientific School, a division of Columbia College which has since become George Washington University. He finished his medical degree in three years, becoming in 1892 the first U.S.-educated Korean to receive a medical degree.

Upon graduation, Jaisohn began his internship at Garfield Hospital in Washington, while retaining his position as a civil servant. Feeling his opportunities were limited, he resigned from the civil service in 1894 and opened his own medical office, where he specialized in pathology. That same year, he began courting Muriel Armstrong, a socialite of Chicago and Washington. The two were married on June 20, 1894.

An Exile's Return

With the outbreak of the Sino-Japanese War in 1885, Jaisohn decided to return to Korea and do whatever was possible to keep Korea independent. He feared that whichever country proved victorious in the war, Korea would be the loser as it would fall under either Chinese or Japanese rule. He closed up his medical office and in December, he left the U.S. by ship with his very supportive wife.

Arriving New Year's Day 1896, the Jaisohns entered Seoul virtually unnoticed; he was unsure of how he would be received after 12 years of exile. Once the Korean government learned of his return, however, he was appointed to the post of Adviser to the Privy Council. Perhaps intended as an honorary position; the post nevertheless allowed Jaisohn both public visibility and personal access to the government's dealings.

Foremost in Jaisohn's mind was maintaining Korea's faltering independence. To that end, with an initial grant from the government and relying on his salary as Adviser, Jaisohn began to publish *The Independent (Toknip)*, Korea's first-ever newspaper, by late March 1896. Most important was that it was written in the vernacular *onmun*. The four-page nonpartisan, independent paper was comprised of three pages written in Korean and one page in English; by 1897, the paper expanded to eight pages. Jaisohn's goal was two-fold: to reach the Korean masses and spread knowledge of democratic ideals and parliamentary procedures, as well as to accurately inform foreigners about Korea and Koreans.

Simultaneous with the birth and growth of the newspaper was the formation and evolution of the Independence Club, a political group which Jaisohn helped establish whose prime concern was parallel to that of the ideals published in *The Independent*: that Korean independence was the concern of all Korean people. As the group grew in number and influence, so, too, did Jaisohn's detractors. Eventually, the government came to view Jaisohn as a potential threat to the monarchy and in April 1898, Jaisohn was politely dismissed from both his advisory post and Korea. Jaisohn left Korea on May 14, 1898.

Back in the U.S., Jaisohn conducted medical research in pathology at the Wister Institute of Anatomy and Biology at the University of Pennsylvania until 1905, when he and a friend founded a printing and office equipment business. The company proved greatly successful, eventually allowing Jaisohn financial independence. He began to devote more and more time to promoting Korea's liberation from Japan, which had invaded and annexed Korea in 1910. He organized the First Korean Congress, held in Philadelphia in April of 1919, where two hundred Kore-

ans from all over the United States, Hawaii, and Mexico gathered in hopes of involving the U.S. government in the fight for Korean liberation. In spite of considerable Korean appeal, President Wilson decided that Japan's cooperation was more important for the establishment of the League of Nations than Korean independence; U.S. support would not be forthcoming.

While Jaisohn devoted the majority of his time and energy to Korean causes, he neglected his business completely. By 1924, he was forced to declare bankruptcy and suffered a physical breakdown. One year later, he attempted to establish an import and export business which also failed. In 1927, he decided to return to medicine and pathology and took a position in Washington. In order to reestablish his private medical practice, Jaisohn returned to school and entered the Graduate School of Medicine at the University of Pennsylvania. Remarkably, he was more than sixty years old. After working for four years at various hospitals as a pathologist, he established his own office in 1934 and within five years, had a thriving practice. During World War II, Jaisohn volunteered his services as an examining physician to the Draft Board. His beloved wife died in July 1941.

The Final Return

In June 1947, accompanied by his daughter Muriel, Jaisohn again returned to Korea, almost fifty years since he was exiled. This time, he entered as a U.S. appointee in two capacities, chief adviser to the Commanding General of the U.S. Army Forces in Korea and as special counselor on Korean Affairs. Newly liberated from Japan and U.S.-occupied in the south, Korea was on the verge of its first election. Although Jaisohn's original intent was to avoid Korean politics, within eight months he was inevitably drawn in. However, after Syngman Rhee was elected president of South Korea on July 19, 1948, a man with whom Jaisohn had once been very close and was now at ideological odds, Jaisohn decided to return to the United States. Although he wanted to remain in Korea to work for democracy and peaceful reunification of Korea, he did not want to be involved with the Rhee government. On September 11, 1948, Jaisohn left his motherland for the final time. After a visit to Los Angeles and a few months of recuperation, Jaisohn opened a new office in June 1949 in Media, Pennsylvania. He remained deeply involved with Korean developments, constantly voicing his concern and uneasiness over the Rhee regime's growing authoritarianism. In 1950, amidst outbreak of the Korean War, he was diagnosed with bladder cancer. On January 5, 1951, he quietly passed away with both his daughters at his side. On the day of his death, all flags throughout South Korea were flown at half-mast.

During a life devoted to Korean independence, Jaisohn remained true to his given Korean name Jae-pil, "assumer of service." Indeed, throughout his long life, Suh Jae-pil was a man of service in many capacities, both in his homeland and his adopted country.

Sources:

Book

Liem, Channing. *Philip Jaisohn: The First Korean American.* Kyujang Publishing Company, 1984.

Other

The Philip Jaisohn Memorial Foundation. "Philip Jaisohn," biographical information, Elkins Park, 1994.

Sketch by Terry Hong

Gish Jen
(1955–)
Writer

Gish Jen cites her husband, David O'Connor, as "the liberator" who helped her write again. Newly married after completing her master's degree in fine arts, Jen had put her writing aside to become, as she said in an interview with Terry Hong, "a dutiful wife," a role that eventually frustrated and enraged her. The turning point came when she and her husband were preparing to move from San Francisco, California. to the East Coast. "We had this set of fancy glasses that I had just finished packing up to bring to California and now I was going to have to pack them all up again to bring to Massachusetts. And I didn't even like them! But they were a wedding gift, and I felt I had to do it. So my husband just picked up one of the glasses and threw it out the window. It was such a liberating experience. Then we had a huge garage sale and got rid of all these things that were tying me down, and I started to write again," Jen remembered. "I wrote a short story, 'In the American Society,' which later became *Typical American*," Jen's first novel. It was published in 1991 and was a resounding success. It was a finalist for a National Book Critics' Circle Award. *Time* magazine called it an "engaging tale of one immigrant family's pursuit of the American Dream." From the *San Francisco Chronicle* to the *New York Times Book Review* to the *Boston Globe,* Jen was praised and lauded for *Typical American.*

The Dutiful Daughter

Born in Queens, New York, on August 12, 1955, to immigrant parents from Shanghai, China, Lillian Jen was the second of five children. She would later adopt the name "Gish"—as in the actress Lillian Gish—while in high school. "It was part of becoming a writer," she told the *New York Times* in 1991, ". . . not becoming the person I was supposed to be."

From her earliest memories, Jen was the one person in her family with an insatiable interest in books. "My parents were very academically inclined. My mother was a schoolteacher and my father a professor of civil engineering. But we were a very aliterate family. We didn't even get any magazines at home. Although my parents were educated, they were struggling so much as newcomers in this country that there was no room in their lives for leisurely things like reading. I think my book was the first non-technical book that my father ever sat down to read."

Growing up, Jen moved from the predominantly working class neighborhood of Yonkers, New York, to the more affluent town of Scarsdale. She quickly discovered that the Scarsdale school library had far more titles to offer than the limited Catholic school library in Yonkers. She told Hong, "I felt like a kid in a chocolate factory. I must have read every book. I read indiscriminately, whether it was Albert Camus or Walter Farley. They all made me say 'wow.'"

In class, Jen was more interested in math and sciences than in English. "By eighth grade, I had decided to get a Ph.D. in math. But by high school, it was socially unacceptable for girls to be science-and math-types. My parents thought that was great, but my friends considered it nerdy, and I think that social pressure helped me switch over to English," said Jen.

In 1972, Jen entered Harvard University where she majored in literature. As the dutiful daughter, Jen also took the required courses to be designated pre-med. But during her junior year, Jen took her first writing class, a course on prosody taught by famed translator, Robert Fitzgerald. Jen recalled, "It was the first English class at Harvard that engaged me." The first assignment was to write something in Catullan hendecasyllables. "I wrote this piece and Fitzgerald passed it out to the class. Later, he pulled me aside and asked if I had ever thought about writing as a career. 'No, I'm pre-med,' I said to him and he shook his head. Even so, I never really considered being a poet. I loved writing, and told my roommate that if I could write poetry for the rest of my life, I would be happy. But I had never known anyone who became a writer of any sort, and it just seemed like a crazy idea."

In Search of the Writer

After graduating from Harvard in 1977, Jen worked in publishing at Doubleday. "Fitzgerald got me that first job. He picked up the phone and the next thing I knew, I had a job." At Doubleday, Jen was "around people who were writing books all the time." In such literary surroundings, she became more and more interested in writing and took further writing classes paid for by Doubleday. "Working in publishing, however, was in between being a writer and

Gish Jen

being a practical person. I didn't want to be stuck in the middle. Finally I decided that if I couldn't decide, I might as well try being practical first. And so I applied to business school." With three siblings who went to business schools (and a fourth who went to medical school), Jen was in good company.

Although she was accepted at Harvard Business School, Jen said she chose Stanford University's Graduate School of Business "because it had a good writing program." Jen struggled through the first year. "I knew the first day that I was not in the right place. I read more than 100 novels that first year and took as many writing courses as I could. I should have dropped out but I couldn't because I was being the dutiful daughter." On the first day of the second year of the program, Jen overslept and missed her classes. She overslept again on the second, third and fourth days. "By then, it became obvious that I was never going to go to class," she laughed.

When Jen left Stanford, her parents did not speak to her for almost a year. She was cut off financially and suffered an extremely difficult emotional period. "I was on the verge of a nervous breakdown. What I realized was that I had to become a writer. I had no choice. People say that no one becomes a writer who can do anything else, and I think that's true. So I was very lucky, in a way, to find out early that I didn't have any other option—to discover that I had to become a writer or die."

Leaving California, Jen spent a year in China, teaching English to coal-mining engineers slated to study in the United States. "It was a wonderful experience in every way," she recalled. "Not only was it a discovery of my roots, but it was also the first time that I really felt I was contributing to something larger than myself.... Also, it was the first time I asked some serious questions. It was the first time I thought about language. It was the first time that I understood what culture was. . . . I couldn't have written *Typical American* without that trip."

When she returned to the U.S., Jen headed to Iowa for the University of Iowa's Writers' Workshop. After she graduated in 1983, she returned to San Francisco and married David O'Connor, whom she had met during orientation week at Stanford. "My parents' worst fear was that I would become a writer. Their second worst fear was that I would marry a writer. At least I didn't do that," she laughed.

Author, Author

Married life for Jen was initially trying. "I was married to a very successful businessman and I didn't know what it meant to be a wife. I made the beds every morning and prepared candlelight dinners at night." When she finally freed herself with her husband's supportive encouragement from all her self-inflicted expectations of 'being a dutiful wife,' Jen was finally able to return to writing. "Every day, I prided myself on not making the beds," she chuckled.

The move to the East Coast landed Jen in a "fixer-upper" home in Cambridge, Massachusetts. She referred to the home renovation as her "next great temptation." "I spent so much of my time fixing up this fixer-upper that I lost my way again. Luckily, I had enough sense to sign myself up to go to MacDowell (a writers' colony in New Hampshire), where I wrote 'The Water Faucet Vision.' It's no surprise, looking back, that the story involves a man who throws his wife out the window. That's the level of frustration I felt."

Back in Cambridge, Jen was still uncertain about her future. "I was writing, but nothing particularly was happening for me as a writer. I thought maybe I should go back to publishing." Jen even went so far as to take a typing test as part of a job application at Harvard University Press. She flawlessly typed ninety words per minute and was told by the university employment office that a job would certainly become available to her. "My heart leapt up. I was so ecstatic at the prospect of a job . . . but in the end, there was no job. I waited and waited, and nobody called."

In 1986, Jen finally succeeded. Awarded a year-long fellowship from the prestigious Radcliffe Bunting Institute, Jen now had both the motivation and the means to write full time, without distraction. "The fellowship seemed to happen out of nowhere. I had never given serious thought to applying, much less actually getting it." At the Bunting Institute, Jen found herself surrounded by ambitious women. "I came in expecting to do a collection of short stories. But after a week of being around that kind of ambition, I thought—no, I'm going to write a novel."

As a prelude to the completion of her first novel, *Typical American,* Jen began to publish her short stories with regularity. Her works appeared in *Atlantic Monthly,* the *New Yorker,* the *Southern Review,* the *Yale Review* and the *Iowa Review,* among others. Her stories have also been widely anthologized in such collections as *Norton's Worlds of Literature, The Heath Anthology of American Literature* and *Best American Short Stories 1988.*

"Beyond My Wildest Expectations"

Typical American is the often comic, at times tragic story of the immigrant Chang family. Ralph comes to the United States in search of an American Ph.D. in engineering and finds his American dream in a fried-chicken palace. His wife, Helen, lives out her dreams through glamour magazines, blindly entrenched in suburban life, while his sister, Theresa, the strait-laced doctor, finds solace with a married man. The three strangers in their new land are initially bound together, struggling to make sense of the American culture they do not understand. As they slowly adjust to America, Ralph, Helen, and Theresa are each transformed by changes that eventually drive the Changs apart. Each of the characters must learn enough about his or her own self in order to come back together as a family.

"Since I wrote *Typical American,* honors have fallen out of the sky," Jen marvelled. "It's all so far beyond my wildest expectations." Having achieved success, Jen is often asked by aspiring writers "what to do to crack the market, as if it's some big conspiracy," she said with a laugh. Her answers are simple: "Develop your own voice. Publishers are always looking for something fresh. If you can develop your own voice, your own vision, the vaulted doors will open of their own accord. As for how to develop your own voice: don't be too nice. I don't mean that you should be rude to people. I mean that you should seek to understand conventions of behavior and of writing, and that you should seek not to be unconventional, but to free your voice of those fetters. A teacher in graduate school once told me, 'There's no such thing as a nice writer, and there's no one so nice as the daughter of an immigrant.' That's something I've always bore in mind as a writer."

Currently, Jen is working on a new novel, tentatively titled *Mona Changowitz.* At the center of the work is Mona, the oldest daughter of Ralph and Helen. Jen believes the novel will be the second volume in a Chang family trilogy. "I hope to finish it by the end of 1994 which means it would be out in late 1995 or early 1996," Jen predicted. Reflecting on her career as a writer, Jen mused, "I think perhaps there are many different things I *could* be doing. But being a writer, I'm grateful that I ended up doing something so interesting."

Sources:

Periodicals

Mojtabai, A.G. "'The Complete Other Side of the World,'" *New York Times Book Review,* 31 March 1991, p. 9–10.
Simpson, Janice C. "Fresh Voices Above the Noisy Din," *Time,* 3 June 1991, v. 137, no. 22, 66–67.

Other

Jen, Gish, telephone interview with Terry Hong, June 15, 1994.

—Sketch by Terry Hong

K

Cynthia Kadohata
(1956–)
Writer

Cynthia Kadohata is an award-winning novelist and short story writer. Her short fiction has appeared in the *New Yorker, Grand Street*, and *Pennsylvania Review*, and her two novels, *The Floating World* and *In the Heart of the Valley of Love*, have been generally well received. She has received grants from the National Endowment for the Arts and a prestigious Whiting Award.

Cynthia Kadohata was born in Chicago, Illinois, in 1956, and spent much of her early life moving with her family. She lived in Chicago, Arkansas, Georgia, Michigan, and then at the age of fifteen in Los Angeles, where the family settled down. Kadohata was a shy young woman. She told Lisa See in *Publishers Weekly*, "It got to the point that going to the grocery store and talking to the cashier really made me nervous." After finishing high school she held various part-time jobs before enrolling in Los Angeles City College. From there she transferred to the University of Southern California where she earned a degree in journalism in 1977.

Beginning to Write

In 1977 Kadohata moved to Boston after being severely injured in a freak car accident in Los Angeles. In Boston she supported herself with temporary office jobs while working on her writing. Kadohata had not read much fiction until this time in her life, only just discovering it when she began going to bookstores in Boston. She told See, "I started looking at short stories. I had always thought that nonfiction represented the 'truth.' Fiction seemed like something that people had done a long time ago and [like something that] wasn't very profound. But in these short stories I saw that people were writing *now*, and that the work was very alive. I realized you could say things with fiction that you couldn't say any other way."

In 1986 Kadohata sold her first short story to the *New Yorker*, after having received twenty-five rejections from the magazine. Thereafter she had more success publishing in

Cynthia Kadohata

literary journals. She enrolled briefly in the graduate fiction writing program at the University of Pittsburgh later that year, and then decided to transfer to the writing program at Columbia University in New York, thinking it would be a good way to get to New York. In 1988 Kadohata was contacted by an agent who had read one of her stories in the *New Yorker* and wanted to see more of her work. She eventually signed with the agent and began working on converting her short stories into a novel. In the spring of 1988, her agent sold her novel *The Floating World*, to Viking. It is in many ways an autobiographical work, telling the story of a Japanese American family traveling across the country in the 1950s.

Reviewing the book in the *New York Times Book Review*, Diana O'Hehir described it as being "about families, coming of age, guilt, memory and, especially the magic [of being on the road]." She described Kadohata's narrative as "straightforward and direct . . . Her aim and the book's seem to be one: to present the world affectionately and without embroidery. To notice what's there. To see it as clearly as one can."

The success brought Kadohata a certain amount of fame, and she was lauded by segments of the Asian American community as a new, artistic voice, a position she has ambivalent feelings about. "For the first time in my life, I saw that there could be expectations of me not only as an Asian American writer," she told See. "On the one hand, I felt like, 'leave me alone.' On the other hand I thought, 'This is a way I can assert my Asianness.' I wrote the book and I'm Asian, and I'm the only person that could've written it."

Asian Americans—Many Voices

Kadohata finds the current climate in the Asian American arts community a difficult one in which to maneuver, when groundless accusations of pandering to whites are tossed around with impunity. "My grandparents were already married when they came to this country," she told See. "Well, I've been told my book isn't historically correct because most Japanese weren't married when they came here. One Japanese interviewer accused me of being socially irresponsible. He asked me if in *The Floating World* I was saying that all Japanese grandmothers were abusive and in conflict with themselves. Of course not! . . . He said that Amy Tan and Maxine Hong Kingston were catering to white people, but I think they and other Asian American writers are just writing from their hearts. Why should their work or my work stand for all Asians? That's impossible."

Kadohata's second novel, *In the Heart of the Valley of Love,* is a realistic story set in the Los Angeles of the near future, in the year 2052. Society has degenerated into a state of near eternal class warfare. This effort was not as well received as her first. A reviewer in the *New York Times Book Review* found the novel "haphazardly constructed out of [the main character's] deadpan stream of consciousness observations, which read like a bad translation of Camus. The result is like listening to someone describe a long and pointless dream."

Kadohata is a frequent traveler who believes her experiences on the road in America enrich her fiction. She told See, "I feel if I don't go out there and do wacky things, like traveling, it will make my writing dry. Besides, you can't help admiring people who never went to school, travel around, and are incredible writers. There's something romantic about that."

Sources:

O'Hehir, Diana. "On the Road with Grandmother's Magic." *New York Times Book Review,* July 23, 1989, p. 15.

Quick, Barabara. Review of *In the Heart of the Valley of Love. New York Times Book Review,* August 30, 1992, p. 14.

See, Lisa. "Cynthia Kadohata." *Publishers Weekly,* August 3, 1992, pp. 48–49.

—Sketch by Jim Henry

Duke Kahanamoku
(1890–1968)
Olympic athlete, surfer, actor

Shortly before the Olympic trials in August of 1911, the first Amateur Athletic Union (AAU) swim meet was held in Hawaii. When young Duke Kahanamoku broke the world record for the 100-yard freestyle event by an astonishing 4.6 seconds and tied the 50-yard freestyle world record, mainland officials refused to believe the times were accurate. They first asked if the Hawaiian timekeepers had been using alarm clocks for stopwatches and then claimed that the ocean currents had aided the swimmer.

Eager to prove that Kahanamoku's performance was not a fluke, Hawaiian locals raised the funds to send the swimmer to the mainland. In Chicago, Kahanamoku swam for the first time in a pool, dominating the 50-yard and 100-yard freestyle events. At the Olympic qualifying trials in Philadelphia, Kahanamoku won the 100-meter freestyle and was the top qualifier for the 4 x 200-meter relay team. The young swimmer not only went to the 1912 Olympics, but he would go on to compete in four Games, altogether winning three gold and two silver medals.

Royal Roots

A full-blooded Hawaiian, Duke Paoa Kahinu Mokoe Hulikohola Kahanamoku was born on August 24, 1890, in the palace of Princess Ruth in Honolulu. A descendent of the early nineteenth century King Kamehameha, Kahanamoku could trace his name to the Duke of Edinburgh, whose 1869 visit to the Hawaiian islands coincided with the birth of Kahanamoku's father, Duke Sr., who passed the name on to his first-born son. Young Duke grew up near the Pacific Ocean in a section of Waikiki now occupied by the Hilton Hawaiian Village resort. Duke always loved the ocean, and he left school after the eleventh grade to pursue a life in the water by concentrating on his swimming.

Even before his sensational debut at the 1912 Olympic Games in Stockholm, America had already begun to take notice of this swimming sensation. The *New York Times* wrote glowingly of Kahanamoku, describing him "as a wonder at 100 yards...a giant, ebony-skinned native about twenty years old standing over six feet in stockings, weighing about 190 pounds, and a magnificent specimen of manhood, straight, well-muscled and perfectly formed. He...goes through the water with shoulders high above the surface, moving at fast speed."

In Stockholm, Kahanamoku tied the world record in a qualifying heat for the 100-meter freestyle. At the time of

Duke Kahanamoku

the final, however, he was nowhere to be found. The story is a favorite of Sergeant Kahanamoku, Duke's younger brother: "Brother Duke slept 99 percent of the time. He could sleep while he was sitting there talking to you. And I always thought that was what made him a great swimmer. He was clear in the head. So at the Olympic finals, they found him asleep under a bridge, snoring. He got up, said sorry, got in the water to loosen up, and then won the race. His mind was clear." So clearly did Kahanamoku swim that at the halfway mark he took the time to look back and survey the pool. Realizing he had a comfortable lead, he allowed himself a more leisurely pace, and still won by two yards.

The Stockholm Games made Kahanamoku an international sensation. Although the 1916 Games were canceled because of World War I, he spent the following eight years traveling extensively, defending his titles at AAU meets and demonstrating the powerful "Kahanamoku kick." It was also during that time that Kahanamoku began to teach the world to surf. His 1915 visit to Australia is remembered by today's Aussie surfers as nothing less than the appearance of a prophet. During a 1916 Red Cross fund-raising tour through the East Coast, Kahanamoku stopped for surfing exhibitions in Atlantic City and Coney Island. In New York, officials even named a Brighton Beach thoroughfare after him. At the 1920 Olympics in Antwerp, Belgium, Kahanamoku broke his own world record for the 100-meter free style just in time for his thirtieth birthday. He was also the anchor for the world-record setting 800-meter relay team.

Hello Hollywood

During the 1920s, Kahanamoku split his time between Honolulu and Los Angeles as he began a movie career that would span twenty-eight years and dozens of films in which he usually appeared as a bare-chested Hawaiian king. The highlight of his career was perhaps a role as a Polynesian chief in the 1948 adventure film *Wake of the Red Witch* with John Wayne.

At the same time, Kahanamoku was unofficially designated as Hawaii's greeter. He welcomed almost every well-known person who came to visit the islands. Photos collected through the years show Kahanamoku in a boat with Babe Ruth, on the beach with Shirley Temple, holding Groucho Marx on his shoulders, chatting with John F. Kennedy, and giving an impromptu hula lesson to Britain's Queen Mother Elizabeth.

Olympic Defeat

Kahanamoku's first defeat was in 1924 at the Paris Games where he was beaten in the 100-meter event by 19-year-old Johnny Weissmuller, who later played Tarzan in several Hollywood movies. During the final, Weissmuller swam between Kahanamoku on one side and Kahanamoku's 19-year-old brother Sam on the other. The young Weissmuller remembered Kahanamoku's encouraging words: "Johnny, good luck. The most important thing in this race is to get the American flag up there three times. Let's do it." When the race was over, Weissmuller had won, leaving Kahanamoku with a silver, Sam with the bronze (Sam reportedly had slowed down in deference to his older brother.) Years later Kahanamoku would joke, "It took Tarzan to finally beat me."

A Hero for Life

Despite his defeat at the Olympics, Kahanamoku will always be remembered as a true hero. In 1925, he and a group of friends saw a boat capsize during a fierce storm off the coast of southern California. Without hesitation, Kahanamoku grabbed his surfboard and, making three trips through violent waves, personally saved eight people in a disaster that claimed seventeen out of twenty-nine lives. The local chief of police was later quoted in newspapers, "Kahanamoku's performance was the most superhuman rescue act and the finest display of surfboard riding that has ever been seen in the world."

Kahanamoku did not compete in the 1928 Games in Amsterdam due to illness. In 1932, at the age of forty-two, he missed qualifying for the Los Angeles Games although his trial times were faster than the world records he had set twenty-one years earlier. He did earn a spot as an alternate on the bronze-winning water polo team, though he did not play.

From Los Angeles, Kahanamoku returned to Hawaii to settle down. He first operated two gas stations (a derisive song at the time was called "Duke Kahanamoku, Former Olympic Champion, Now Pumping Gas"). Soon after, he began his twenty-six-year career as Honolulu's sheriff. However, the spirit of competition remained with him well into his fifties—under his guidance, Hawaii's Outrigger Canoe Club won seven straight championships.

Although Kahanamoku passed away at age seventy-seven, Hawaii commemorated the 100th anniversary of his birth by dedicating a nine-foot bronze statue on Waikiki Beach. Standing with his back to the ocean, a twelve-foot surfboard at his side, the "Bronze Duke of Waikiki" continues to greet all visitors to his island, his arms outstretched in grand welcome.

Sources:

Books

Wallechinsky, David. "Swimming, Men." In *The Complete Book of the Olympics*. New York: Little, Brown, 1991, p. 475.

Periodicals

Gullo, Jim, "The Beloved Duke of Waikiki." *Sports Illustrated*, September 17, 1990, p. 97.

—*Sketch by Terry Hong*

Ken Kashiwahara
(1940–)
Broadcast journalist

Ken Kashiwahara is a correspondent for ABC News and one of the first Asian American journalists to work in network television. He has been a correspondent for ABC News since 1974, and has served as San Francisco bureau chief since 1978.

Ken Kashiwahara was born on July 18, 1940, in Waimea, Hawaii, on the island of Kaui. The son of schoolteachers, he was an average student in high school. After graduation in 1958, he enrolled in Washington and Jefferson College, in Washington, Pennsylvania. Here he was confronted with racism when he tried to join a fraternity. As he told *A. Magazine*: "My first two years of college were in Pennsylvania and there was a lot of prejudice then. I couldn't join a frat in college because of all-white clauses; it was very traumatic, and I went through a period when I was ashamed of being Asian. I didn't want to speak Japanese or eat Japanese food. It was that bad."

His experiences of racism at Washington and Jefferson prompted him finally to leave, and he returned to Hawaii, where he enrolled in the pre-med program at the University of Hawaii. He stayed at the university for one year, and then decided that he didn't want to be a doctor. He'd become very interested in broadcasting and decided to transfer to San Francisco State College, where he earned a bachelor's degree in broadcasting in 1963.

At that time, there was a military draft and, rather than be drafted into the army, Kashiwahara enlisted in the air force and became an information officer. In this capacity he was stationed in both Europe and Vietnam, and wrote and published several articles in both the civilian and military press.

Beginning of His Career

After serving in the military for five years, Kashiwahara returned to civilian life in Hawaii, where he began pursuing a career in television news. Describing his decision to *A. Magazine*, Kashiwahara said: "I saw the makeup of the [Hawaiian] population: mostly Asian. And I saw the people on television: all white. And I thought, well, for a guy with absolutely no experience, this might be a way to get in." He was hired as a political reporter for KGMB-TV in Honolulu where he became a popular and well-liked personality. In 1971 he became an anchorman.

In 1972 Kashiwahara moved to KABC in Los Angeles where he served as a reporter and the co-anchor of weekend

Ken Kashiwahara

news broadcasts. In 1974 he became a network correspondent with ABC. In this capacity he covered several stories in Southeast Asia, where America was then losing its war against the Communist forces of North Vietnam, while its handpicked government in Cambodia was falling as well. Kashiwahara covered these events and was one of the last American journalists to be airlifted from Saigon in 1975 as the city fell to the North.

In 1975 Kashiwahara was named the ABC News bureau chief in Hong Kong. He served at this post for three years and covered many regional stories, as well as the civil war in Beirut, Lebanon, in 1977.

During the eighties Kashiwahara covered a wide range of stories for ABC News, including Ronald Reagan's presidential campaign from the earliest primaries through the Republican National Convention in Detroit and on to the general election. He also covered the eruption of Mount Saint Helen's, the Washington volcano. In 1986, Kashiwahara won a National Emmy Award for his story "In the Fire's Path," which was broadcast on ABC's newsmagazine show "20/20." The report told the story of the 1985 brush fires that devastated Ojai, California, and surrounding areas. In 1988, he won a second Emmy as a correspondent for the documentary "Burning Question—The Poisoning of America."

In 1988 and 1989, Kashiwahara accompanied American veterans of the Vietnam War on a return trip to Vietnam.

The trip resulted in a special report on the network evening news broadcast about three veterans' reunions with children they'd fathered while in Vietnam. He also contributed to a one-hour "Nightline" special focusing on eight veterans with post-traumatic stress disorder who were coming to terms with their wartime experiences. Also in 1989, Kashiwahara covered the aftermath of the Tiananmen Square massacre in Beijing, in which hundreds—perhaps as many as thousands—of unarmed prodemocracy demonstrators were killed by government troops.

A Pioneer in Network Broadcasting

Kashiwahara was awarded a Lifetime Achievement Award in 1993 from the Asian American Journalists Association. When he began his career in 1974, he and Connie Chung were the only two Asian Americans on the air in network news. In an interview with *A. Magazine*, Kashiwahara recalled, "It stayed that way for a long time, until three years ago or so—when CBS hired correspondents James Hattori and Linda Taira. Coincidentally, around that time NBC hired two Asian American reporters. But before that, I kept saying it was only the two of us."

During his career, Kashiwahara has been an outspoken critic of discrimination against Asians in the media. Such discrimination, he asserts, often takes the form of media blindness or indifference to Asians. One incident Lilian Huang notes in *A. Magazine* was when the *New York Times* observed that "the Senate was 100 percent white. The glib ignorance of this statement shocked [Kashiwahara]: 'Well, excuse me, but what about Senator [Daniel] Inouye and Senator [Spark] Matsunaga?' Kashiwahara asks. 'I don't think they're white.'" Another example of media blindness, according to Kashiwahara, is the fact that the first Asian American astronaut made almost no news, while the first African American astronaut and the first female astronaut were headline stories. This, Kashiwahara maintains, is the kind of blindness the media shows to Asians in America, and the kind he seeks to remedy. One solution Kashiwahara proposes is using Asian journalists to cover all stories, regardless of their specific concern to the Asian community. As he told *A. Magazine*: "I think the media has to realize that Asian Americans are part of America—we are Americans. Asian Americans ought to be used in stories that have to do with general things in the country, whether it be the economy or politics, or how Americans feel about the Middle East."

Further, he believes that the Asian American community should launch a concerted grass roots effort to demand wider political representation. Kashiwahara told *A. Magazine*, "In California, where Asian Americans are the fastest growing minority group, we do not have a single Asian American state legislator. . . . The generation before wanted to remain very low key, and not go out front, but it is the next generation, and it is time for us to assume the responsibility and take our place in society."

Sources:

Periodicals

Chin, Curtis, Lilian Huang, and James Wang. "Correspondent Force." *A. Magazine,* vol. 1, no. 1, Fall 1992, p. 16.

Huang, Lilian. "A Newsroom of Our Own." *A. Magazine,* vol. 1, no. 1, Fall 1992.

Other

Kashiwahara, Ken, telephone interview with Jim Henry, April 20, 1994.

—Sketch by Jim Henry

Joyce Kennard
(1941–)
Judge

Described as a hard-working, independent, and thorough judge with a keen intellect, Joyce Luther Kennard is well respected by her friends and colleagues. Throughout her life she overcame seemingly insurmountable difficulties and remained steadfast in pursuit of her goals. Her efforts were rewarded when in 1989 she became only the second woman to be appointed to the state of California's highest bench.

Joyce Luther Kennard was born on May 6, 1941, in Bandung, West Java, Indonesia (formerly known as Dutch East Indies). Wilhelmine, her mother, was Chinese Indonesian, with a sprinkling of Dutch and Belgian. Her father, Johan, was a mixture of Dutch, Indonesian, and German. Her eclectic heritage made her feel that she did not belong to any particular group; it also tended to draw discrimination from all sides.

Kennard was a "war baby." During World War II, her father died in a Japanese prison camp. The Indonesians considered people of mixed heritage to be Dutch. Kennard and her mother, fearing the rising Indonesian terrorism, moved to a protective camp for women and children on Java, where they waited for the war to end. Kennard's mother had to endure a lot of pain and abuse to take care of her child, of whom she was fiercely protective. Kennard led a very subdued and bare-bone life, without any toys or dolls. A playmate once showed her a Sears catalogue, and Kennard recollected in an interview with Visi R. Tilak, "It was the most beautiful book I had ever seen."

When Java became independent in 1949, and Kennard's mother was forced to become an Indonesian citizen, the family decided to move to Dutch New Guinea (now Irian Jaya) when Kennard was ten years old. As Indonesians in a town dominated by a Dutch oil company, they had to live in the natives' section, which had inferior housing, stores, and education. Kennard's mother worked as a typist for the oil company to make ends meet. An oil drum as a bath tub, a cement ditch at the edge of the jungle as the toilet, sharing a small hut with four families—nothing stood in the way of Kennard's quest to learn.

Determination to Learn and Excel

She would borrow the fattest book from the library because it would last the longest, she learned English from a little missionary school, listened to pop songs on Radio Australia, and practiced business correspondence by writing fictitious orders to bicycle companies in England. When she was fourteen years old Kennard and her mother moved to Holland, where she finally was exposed to telephones, television, and the ways of modern life. With her mother's help, Kennard was admitted to a lyceum, where she was coached in college prep courses. She was soon on her way to the university.

Just before her sixteenth birthday, a tumor appeared on her right leg, and having been diagnosed as a life-threatening condition, her leg had to be amputated. With a $20,000 prosthesis, Kennard's disability goes largely unnoticed today, except for the slight hitch in her fairly slow walk. At the time, Kennard handled her physical and emotional trauma with grace and courage. She was hurt most by the fact that she would no longer be able to be on the university track team.

Kennard enrolled in a business school to study secretarial skills and Dutch/English interpreting. "I never expect much, and then things just happen," she said in an interview while talking about the unexpected path her career took. When the United States announced that it would accept a large immigrant quota of Dutch nationals, Wilhelmine persuaded Kennard to go, insisting that she herself would stay to ensure that her daughter had a home to come back to.

In 1961, Kennard immigrated alone to the United States "with no illusions of grandeur," as she told Tilak. With her shorthand skills she landed a $280-a-month secretarial position with Occidental Life Insurance. She was twenty years old. Her mother visited her only once when she was in South Pasadena, California. In 1968, Kennard returned to Holland to tend to her mother, who was dying of lung cancer. She stayed two months and flew back to California. A few days later her mother died, leaving behind a bequest of $5,000 for her daughter. "That legacy was the key to my education," Kennard recalled.

Joyce Kennard

Her mother's bequest, scholarships, and a part-time job helped Kennard through Pasadena City College and then the University of Southern California (USC) in just three years. She received a bachelor's degree in German from USC, but her boss, for whom she was working as a legal secretary, encouraged her to try law school. Hoping that a law degree would open doors she enrolled in USC's Gould School of Law and graduated in 1974. Only 15 percent of the students in Kennard's law school class were women, and they were more or less classified as second-class citizens in the legal world. Her friends from school described her as hardworking, and ambitious about public service, though not about personal fortune.

After earning degrees in law and public administration within another three quick years, she applied for a job in the civil division of California's state attorney general's office. When she was told that it was just a secretarial position, Bob Kennard, the tall, handsome Kentuckian whom she had met at a car repair shop and had been dating, told her not to take it. She took his advice and did not take the job, though she did marry Bob Kennard in 1976. They have no children.

Life in the Courts

Kennard instead applied to the criminal division of the attorney general's office and was hired in 1975. Soon after she went on to California's court of appeals in 1979 and

spent seven years there as a research attorney. She was deputy attorney general from 1975 until 1979, when she moved up to senior attorney at the court of appeals.

Even though her first application for judgeship to Governor Jerry Brown was unsuccessful, once Governor George Deukmejian discovered her, there was no looking back. The Republican prosecutor was on a "bullet train" to success. Multicultural diversity was the in-thing at the time, and her ethnicity combined with her excellent reputation made her politically irresistible. In 1986 she was named to the municipal court in San Fernando, she became the superior court judge in 1987, and a year later she was made associate justice to the Second District Court of Appeals. In 1989 Deukmejian appointed her to the California Supreme Court as an associate justice. Kennard's 70-year-old aunt came from Holland to celebrate. The only sad thing about her rise in her was the obvious absence of her mother. "She sacrificed so much," Kennard said in an interview, tears welling up in her eyes.

Kennard has a number of awards to her credit. In 1993 she received the Margaret Brent Women Lawyers Achievement Award 1993, which is given to honor outstanding women lawyers throughout the country who have achieved professional excellence within their area of specialty and have actively paved the way to success for other women lawyers. Among her other awards are Women of the Nineties Award; First Annual Netherlands-American Heritage Award; Chinese-American Pioneers from South California in the Judiciary Award (1992); Justice of the Year Award (1991), Honorary Degree of Doctor of Laws from Southwestern University School of Law (1991).

Today, Kennard is one of the most respected professionals in the legal world. An editorial in the *San Francisco Chronicle* refers to her as one of the two most respected justices on the court. She is also well known for speaking her mind. The *Los Angeles Times Magazine* reported: "Fairly unpredictable on the lackluster California Supreme Court, Justice Joyce Kennard stands out. What really surprised court watchers were Kennard's numerous and trenchant dissents."

Kennard has carved a niche for herself. From a journey that began in Java to where she is today, Kennard has traveled a long path, but steadily and with confidence. She respects people and their rights and she rigorously holds herself to the same principles of equality and justice that she endorses on the court. At a retirement dinner Kennard sat at a table with her staff rather than at the table shared by other justices. When court staff members were asked to take unpaid four day furloughs to ease the budget crunch, she gave up four day's pay. Kennard modestly told Vislak, "I try to do what Helen Keller said—I long to accomplish a great and noble task, but it is my chief duty to accomplish small tasks as if they were great and noble."

Sources:

Periodicals

Los Angeles Times Magazine, February 7, 1993.
"The Wrong Dose" *San Francisco Chronicle* editorial, November 24, 1993.

Other

Kennard, Joyce. Biographical information provided by Kennard, June 1994.

—*Sketch by Visi R. Tilak*

Le Xuan Khoa
(1931–)
Educator, community leader

Le Xuan Khoa is the current president and executive director of the South East Asia Resource Action Center (SEARAC), a Washington-based national advocacy organization. SEARAC's mission is to assist Southeast Asians in the United States make their transition from dependent refugees to productive U.S. citizens.

In an interview with Visi R. Tilak, Khoa explained the impetus behind his involvement with SEARAC: "When I came to America in 1975 as a refugee there were two things that came to my mind. First, I knew I couldn't pursue my teaching profession because of language barriers and area of expertise. Second, I thought of the increasing number of my fellow compatriots coming to the country. Seeing ourselves as an emerging minority in America, I saw the need to establish ourselves to help our people adjust and become productive and contributing members of the American society."

Born in Hanoi, Vietnam, to a family of well-educated people, Le Xuan Khoa is the eldest of six children. His father was a scholar and helped him set his goals in life. "My father deeply influenced my life. He taught me all about Asian traditions and helped me set my motto," he told Tilak. He describes his mother as being a loving and compassionate woman who supported her children in all their endeavors. "She was very dedicated to her family and I am grateful to her for her care and support," he said.

Teaching and Travel

After graduating from the University of Hanoi, Khoa moved to the south of Vietnam in 1953. He began his career as a high school teacher and later taught at the college level. In 1958 he went to the Sorbonne in France to submit his doctoral dissertation on oriental philosophy.

Khoa traveled extensively in Thailand and India doing research. One of the highlights of his travels was his visit to Darjeeling, India, in 1959, to visit the Dalai Lama, the head of the dominant order of Tibetan Buddhists. He was also a former deputy minister for culture and education in Vietnam and the vice-president of the University of Saigon, where he also taught oriental philosophy for fifteen years before he came to the United States as a refugee in 1975.

Since his arrival in the United States, Khoa has been active in refugee affairs. He spent the first three years as a researcher with a consulting firm in Washington, D.C., where he conducted a series of surveys on refugee settlements across the nation. In 1978, he became the associate director of the Indochinese mental health program at the Eastern Pennsylvania Psychiatric Institute in Philadelphia, Pennsylvania. When this program ended in 1980, Khoa worked at the Center for Applied Linguistics for a year before joining the Indochina Refugee Action Center as the deputy director. A year later he became chief executive of the organization which later changed its name to Southeast Asia Refugee Action Center (SEARAC). Since its inception in 1979, SEARAC has served as a voice and a resource to all Southeast Asian ethnic groups in the United States. SEARAC functions as a leading advocate for refugee protection and human rights. In addition, SEARAC serves as a national clearinghouse for information on Cambodia, Laos, and Vietnam, and as a technical assistance center for the empowerment of the Southeast Asian American community.

Khoa often speaks and writes on issues dealing with refugee protection and assistance. He is editor-in-chief of *The Bridge*, SEARAC's quarterly publication reporting on refugee issues, and he has testified before the U.S. Congress on refugee policies and programs.

Respected Leader

Khoa is a frequent and influential attendee at international meetings on refugee protection, human rights, and durable solutions to the Southeast Asian refugee problem. His work has earned him a number of prestigious awards. He was chosen in 1984 by the Citizens' Committee for Immigration Reform to be honored as one of a select group of nationally prominent refugees and immigrants who have made significant contributions to the United States. In 1988 the Asian and Pacific American Civil Rights Alliance honored him with its Civil Rights Award.

Khoa serves on the boards of the American Council for Voluntary International Action, National Immigration

Forum, Federation of American Cultural and Language Communities, National Asian Pacific Center on Aging, National Institute Against Prejudice and Violence, and Refugee Voices.

Khoa is married to Tuyet Truong Le, a retired registered nurse. They have five children who are all professionals working in business, banking, and state and federal government. Buddhist by tradition but not by practice, Khoa has been deeply influenced by Buddhism, Taoism, and Confucianism. "I have read a lot about Horatio Alger, a self-made man who was very successful. I see him as a role model for my community," he told Tilak.

Khoa said his own guiding motto for success is: "Accepting life as it comes while still striving for your goal, not to be discouraged by failure and not to become over-confident with success." This principle, he said, is grounded in the essence of Asian philosophy and is the key to him achieving his goals. He added, "My Asian American heritage has also helped me be successful. I have been able to use my life experiences as an Asian American to help other Southeast Asian refugees."

The willingness of refugees to help one another, Khoa believes, is integral to the success of organizations like SEARAC and the people they serve: "People who come to America as refugees and not as immigrants are unprepared to face life here. They have language, career, and cultural problems, among others. So I see a vital need to create programs and form self-help groups to aid these people. The best way to help these people is for those who came earlier as refugees to share their experiences with the newcomers."

Khoa finds his work both challenging and frustrating. The trend of the American government to reduce the number of refugees and immigrants entering the country is challenging to those providing services to refugees. It makes is difficult for advocacy groups like SEARAC to get funding and to attract and retain effective personnel.

Nevertheless, Khoa vows to maintain his commitment and to avoid becoming discouraged—the refugees who are following in his path are depending on it.

Sources:

Khoa, Le Xuan, telephone interview with Visi R. Tilak, May 3, 1994.

—Sketch by Visi R. Tilak

Har Gobind Khorana
(1922–)
Biochemist

The 1968 Nobel Prize for Physiology or Medicine was presented to Har Gobind Khorana, Robert W. Holley, and Marshall W. Nirenberg for deciphering the genetic code and its role in the control of protein synthesis. Two years after receiving the Nobel Prize, Khorana and his colleagues were also the first researchers to synthesize a gene of yeast, the first eucaryotic (an organism of one or more cells with a distinct nucleus) species from which a gene had been synthesized. Later he also was the first to synthesize a gene of the intestinal bacterium *Escherichia coli,* a procaryotic (an organism that does not have a distinct nucleus) species. Among the numerous awards and honors received by the Alfred P. Sloan Professor of Biology and Chemistry at the Massachusetts Institute of Technology are the Merck Award of the Chemical Institute of Canada (1958), the Louisa Gross Horwitz Prize of Columbia University (1968), the Albert Lasker Basic Medical Research Award (1968), and the Willard Gibbs Medal of the American Chemical Society (1974).

Born on January 9, 1922, in Raipur, India, a village in Punjab which today belongs to Pakistan, Har Gobind Khorana was the fifth child of Ganpat Rai Khorana, a tax clerk for the British colonial government, and Krishna Devi Khorana. His parents were both Hindus and his family, although poor, was one of the few who were literate in Raipur. Khorana received his early education in the village school. He attended D.A.V. High School in Multan, Punjab, and in 1943, earned a bachelor of science degree, with honors, in chemistry from Punjab University in Lahore. Two years later he completed his master's degree, again with honors. In 1945, he entered the University of Liverpool on a government of India fellowship to study organic chemistry, receiving a Ph.D. in 1948 for his dissertation on the chemical pigment violacein, a coloring agent for certain bacterial cells. After spending a year with Vladimir Prelog at the Federal Institute of Technology in Zurich studying the chemical structure of certain alkaloids, Khorana returned to England as a Nuffield fellow at Cambridge University working with Alexander Todd. This was where he first became interested in the biochemistry of nucleic acids, large molecules found in the cell nucleus.

In 1952, Khorana was appointed director of the Section of Organic Chemistry of the British Columbia Research Council at the University of British Columbia in Vancouver, Canada, where he began his study of the chemical structure of acetyl coenzyme A.

Har Gobind Khorana

Discovered in 1945 by Fritz Lipmann, acetyl coenzyme A is a complex molecule essential to the cellular biochemistry of carbohydrates, fats, and proteins. In 1959, Khorana earned international recognition for developing a new, simpler, and less expensive method for isolating acetyl coenzyme A from yeast, which made it accessible for research on cellular processes like the breakdown of sugar molecules to release energy.

Deciphering the Genetic Code

In the early 1960s, Khorana set a goal to decipher the genetic code. In 1960, he moved to Madison, Wisconsin, to become codirector of the Institute for Enzyme Research at the University of Wisconsin, where he published *Some Recent Developments in the Chemistry of Phosphate Esters of Biological Interest.* After being named editor of the

Journal of the American Chemical Society in 1963, he was appointed Conrad A. Elvelijem Professor of the Life Sciences at the University of Wisconsin, where he directed his research in the biochemistry of nucleic acids, the biosynthesis of cellular proteins, and the nature of the gene.

At the University of Wisconsin, Khorana used Marshall Nirenberg's system for the synthesis of protein molecules to perform a series of experiments that enabled him to determine the DNA base sequences in the triplet codes for all twenty amino acids. Khorana's discovery led to the realization that some amino acids were represented by more than one base triplet. This was important because it revealed that every change in the gene would not necessarily result in a corresponding change in the protein that the gene coded for, which meant in turn that the organism could remain unchanged from an evolutionary point of view. Khorana and his researchers also studied the secondary chemical structure of transfer RNA, which reads the genetic code and links the amino acids in their appropriate sequence.

Nobel Prize

In recognition of his work, Khorana shared the 1968 Nobel Prize for Physiology or Medicine. At the award ceremony, Peter Reichard from the Karolinska Institute equated Khorana's achievement to deciphering the genetic dictionary, comparing nucleic acid and proteins to language, and their building blocks to the letters of the alphabet. "It is the chemical structure of the nucleic acid which determines the chemical structure of the protein. The alphabet of nucleic acids dictates the alphabet of proteins. The genetic code is the dictionary which gives us the translation of one alphabet into the other," he was quoted as saying in *Nobel Prize Winners*.

Har Gobind Khorana and his wife, Esther Elizabeth Sibler, a native of Switzerland, have been married since 1952. They have a son and two daughters. Khorana became a U.S. citizen in 1966. Although devoted to his research, he also enjoys listening to music and hiking, which doubles for him as an outlet for creative thinking and problem solving.

Sources:

Books

Wasson, Tyler, ed. *Nobel Prize Winners: An H.W. Wilson Biographical Dictionary*. Princeton, New Jersey: Visual Education Corporation, 1987.

—Sketch by Nancy Moore

Andrew Byongsoo Kim

Andrew Byongsoo Kim
(1936–)
Businessman

Andrew Kim is the president of Sit/Kim International Investment Associates, a joint venture with Sit Investment Associates and the Fremont Group, formerly known as Bechtel Investment. In addition to his distinguished work in the financial world, Kim actively participates in many civic, cultural, and industry associations and organizations.

Andrew Byongsoo Kim was born on September 12, 1936, in Seoul, Korea, which was then occupied by the Japanese, who ruled the peninsula brutally. When the Japanese were defeated in World War II, Korea was liberated, but remained in turmoil through much of Kim's childhood. As a child, Kim worked as a radio actor for the Korean Broadcast Service as a regular character in a dramatic series. He also did some theatre work.

In 1950, when he was fourteen, the North Korean army invaded the South and for the next three years the country was engulfed in a war involving not just the North and the South, but the two superpowers—the United States and Soviet Union—as well. The war was over in 1953 and in 1955 Kim graduated from high school.

Coming to America

After high school Andrew attended Seoul National University's College of Commerce, but soon left the country for the United States to study at Adelphi University where he earned a bachelor of arts degree in 1960. He continued his education at Columbia, remaining for one year before transferring to the Johnson Graduate School of Management at Cornell University where he earned a master's of business administration in 1963.

After graduation Kim began a distinguished career in investment research, financial analysis, and fund management. In 1963 he was hired as a financial analyst for the brokerage firm of Francis I. duPont, then the second largest such firm in the country. In 1965 he was hired as a research analyst for the asset management, investment banking, and institutional brokerage firm of F. Eberstadt and Company. As a researcher he dealt primarily in the air transportation and aerospace industries. In recognition of this work he was named by *Institutional Investor* magazine as a member of the All America Team for investment research twelve years in a row. In 1977 he was named director of research, and then executive vice president, a post he held until 1985. From 1985 until 1989, Kim served in a variety of positions on Wall Street.

In 1989 Kim formed his own company, Sit/Kim International Investment. The firm was established as a joint venture with Sit Investment Associates of Minneapolis—an Asian-owned firm—and Bechtel, one of the world's largest privately held corporations. Sit/Kim is a pension fund management firm that includes Bechtel and three of the regional Bell system companies on its client list. Sit/Kim manages exclusively the overseas investments of these huge pension funds.

A Pioneer on Wall Street

When Kim began his career on Wall Street there were almost no other Asians working in the investment community. In an interview with Jim Henry, Kim attributed this to the fact that there was at the time no tradition of securities trading in Asian countries. In addition, those Asians who did study business and management in the United States usually took their education back to their native countries.

Kim could recall only one instance of bigotry in his early career. It was during recruitment prior to graduation when a representative of Chase Manhattan Bank asked Kim how he felt he would be able to "fit in" with the Chase image. Kim was not discouraged by this humiliating question, and in fact, many years later related the story to Chase Manhattan head David Rockefeller himself, who was very apologetic.

Kim theorizes that in the sixties and seventies it was easier than it is today for Asians to succeed on Wall Street because at the time he and the very few other Asians in the financial community were seen as anomalies. Today, however, he believes that minorities of all kinds are seen as threats by the establishment. The traders in large firms like Goldman Sachs or Merryl Lynch are about 10 percent Asian, and Kim feels it will be difficult to go beyond that kind of representation.

Kim is involved in several cultural and political organizations. He is the donor of the Gene Y. Kim Gallery at the Dartmouth College Museum of Art, named in honor of his son, an alumni of the college. He also serves on the Council on Foreign Relations, a quasi-public, quasi-private organization of current and former political and financial leaders from Europe, America, and Asia. The council holds off-the-record meetings at which leaders are free to express themselves on a wide range of concerns without fearing political repercussions. Kim finds this feature of the council very conducive to international cooperation.

In 1992 Kim was named a trustee to the Asia Society, a New York-based organization dedicated to promoting an understanding of all Asian cultures, both in the United States and internationally. Speaking about the society in the organization's newsletter, Kim said, "In my view, the Asia Society has a unique opportunity to speak to second and third generation Asian Americans who, like most other Americans, know very little about contemporary Asian cultures. I would like to see more programs that educate audiences about the contributions of Asia today and about the difference that Asian Americans can make to the future of the United States."

Kim is married to Wan Kyun Kim, a painter and collector of Asian art, and the couple has two sons. He has an older brother who is the Archbishop of the Anglican Church in Korea, and an older sister who is a professor and social worker.

Sources:

Periodicals

"Profile: Andrew Kim." *Asia: The Newsletter of The Asia Society,* vol. 10 no. 2, Winter 1993–94, p. 4.

Other

Kim, Andrew Byongsoo, telephone interview with Jim Henry, April 14, 1994.
Sit-Kim International. "Andrew Kim." Selected press releases and internal documents. New York, April 1994.

—*Sketch by Jim Henry*

Elaine Kim

(1942–)

Academic, author, activist

Elaine H. Kim is a professor of Asian American studies at the University of California at Berkeley, perhaps the foremost university in the country in the promotion of ethnic studies. She is a leading national activist and a prolific writer in mainstream, ethnic, and academic newspapers, magazines, and journals. Kim also produces educational videos and in 1992 made a documentary called *Sa-I-Gu: From Korean Women's Perspective.* Shot three months after the Los Angeles riots which devastated the city's Koreatown, the film details the destruction from the

Elaine Kim

point of view of Korean women whose businesses and homes were destroyed in the riot.

Elaine H. Kim was born in New York on February 26, 1942, and grew up in Tacoma Park and Silver Spring, Maryland. Her mother had immigrated to Hawaii in 1903 as an infant and spent her childhood working on the tenant farms and plantations of California and Hawaii. Kim's father had come to America as a student in 1926. Kim was subjected to a lot of racism in school, where she was the only minority student. Recalling her grade school days in a speech she delivered at the University of Maryland in 1994, she said, "When I was in the second grade, we read an illustrated book that pictured a globe with a blonde-haired white child standing upright on top of the world, and an upside down Asian child on the bottom, complete with buck teeth, slitted eyes, a long upside down pigtail, and orange skin. Later on the school bus going home, the girl sitting in front of me turned around, put her arm against mine and said, "You're *yellow*.""

Elaine graduated from high school in 1959. She earned a bachelor's degree in English and American literature from the University of Pennsylvania in 1963. From there she went to New York City to study at Columbia University, where she earned a master's degree in English and comparative literature in 1965. One year later, she left the United States for Korea. She described her thoughts behind this decision in her 1992 keynote speech to the Women's Organization Reaching Koreans: "When I was

twenty-three years old, I went to work in Seoul [South Korea] for a year, armed with an Ivy League education and buoyed by a burning desire to 'become Korean.' I returned feeling neither 'Korean' nor 'American.'…[M]y encounters in Korea convinced me that I was clumsy, ugly, and hopelessly inadequate as a woman besides." She stayed in Seoul until 1967, working as a lecturer in the English department of Ewha University.

In 1968 she moved back to the states and enrolled in the University of California at Berkeley as a Ph.D. student in English. Again she was confronted with, if not outright racism of the type from her childhood, a cultural bias that discouraged her interest in studying the literature of non-Western cultures. Frustrated, she transferred to the education department, which she found to be more open to cultural diversity.

Third World Strikes on Campus

In 1969, the Berkeley campus of the University of California was racked by student strikes initiated by students of color who felt underrepresented numerically and culturally. The striking students, whom Kim joined, wanted greater representation on the faculty and student bodies and the establishment of ethnic studies programs. These activities strengthened Kim's interest in Asian American studies and her dissertation, published in 1982 by Temple University Press, was a reflection of this interest. Entitled *Asian American Literature: An Introduction to the Writings and Their Social Context,* it was the first scholarly study of Asian American literature.

Beginning in the early seventies, Kim worked to establish Berkeley's Asian American studies program within the newly formed Ethnic Studies Department. She was instrumental in the development of remedial English equivalency programs. These courses, which teach critical reading and writing skills, use literature from African American, native American, Asian American, and Chicano writers, a practice that is widespread today but in 1970 was groundbreaking.

Community Activist

Kim was granted tenure in 1981, and she began devoting her time to community activities in support of San Francisco-area Korean Americans. From 1981 until 1982 she served as project director of Asian Women United of California Project on Asian Women's Education and Employment for the U.S. Department of Education. Under her direction the project produced four books and four thirty-minute television programs designed to increase awareness of job options among Asian American girls and young women.

Kim also has worked for many years and in various capacities for the Korean Community Center of the East Bay (KCCEB). She is currently that organization's president. In her tenure with the KCCEB she has helped to raise more than $650,000 for a variety of programs servicing the community. The KCCEB recently bought a small shopping center in Oakland, California, which it operates as a for-profit business, using the money it makes to help fund its social projects. The project is a first for the Korean community anywhere in America and a model combination between community service organization and entrepreneurship.

Other community organizations Kim has served on include the Center for Women Policy Studies, on whose national advisory council she served; the project on equal education rights for the NOW (National Organization for Women) Legal Defense Fund; the Northern California Korean Coalition; the U.S.-Korea Foundation; the Japan Pacific Resource Network; and many others.

Kim has written extensively on issues of concern to Asian Americans. Her first published article, "The Myth of Asian American Success," appeared in 1975 in *Asian American Review*. Her dissertation was published in 1982, and in 1983 she published *With Silk Wings: Asian American Women At Work*. Other articles by Kim have been published in magazines and newspapers such as the *Philadelphia Inquirer, Newsweek*, the *San Francisco Bay Guardian, A. Magazine*, and *Korean Journal*. She served as editor for several anthologies, including the highly regarded *Making Waves: Writings By and About Asian American Women*. As of spring 1994, Kim was at work on two publications, *Korean American Life Stories: Portrait of a Los Angeles Community*, and *Fierce Dreams: Lives and Work of Asian American Visual Artists*. Kim is also a much sought-after speaker and academic panelist.

The Third Space

Kim has spoken and written often of what she sees as a "third space"—a place in the American community that exists between blacks and whites as a kind of buffer. As she wrote in the *San Francisco Bay Guardian* in an essay to accompany the San Francisco opening of her film *Sa-I-Gu*: "I am optimistic that if Asian Americans understand our situation clearly, we will refuse roles as apologists for the status quo, as decorative gatekeepers, and petty functionaries.... Instead, I hope that we will create a space for ourselves, that we will shake things up, working tirelessly to transform society with our eyes on a time when racial inequality and injustice will be remembered as part of a distant past."

Sources:

Periodicals

Kim, Elaine H. "Creating a Third Space." *San Francisco Bay Guardian*, March 10, 1993.
———. "They Armed in Self-Defense." *Newsweek*, May 18, 1992, p. 10.
———. "Women's Organization Reaching Koreans Keynote Speech."A speech delivered to the Women's Organization Reaching Koreans, November 13, 1992. Published in *KoreAm Journal*, December 1992, p. 32.

Other

Kim, Elaine H. "Asian Americans and Higher Education." An Address for the University of Maryland Conference on Education Equity, March 2–28, 1994.

—Sketch by Jim Henry

Jay C. Kim
(1939–)
Politician, civil engineer

As the nation's first Korean American congressman, Jay C. Kim hopes to be a model for all Asian Americans: "They can look at me and say, 'He made it as an immigrant with a strong accent. Why can't I?'" In a surprise landslide victory, Kim, a Republican, was elected to Congress in November 1992 as the representative for the newly created 41st District of California, a racially mixed, solidly Republican district that comprises parts of San Bernardino, Orange, and Los Angeles counties. Following the election, Kim was selected by his colleagues to serve on the Public Works and Transportation Committee and the Small Business Committee. This representative is anything but a typical politician on Capitol Hill. For example, those members of Congress who seek selection to the Public Works and Transportation Committee often have particular projects they want to see financed. Not in Kim's case. Convinced that there is far too much waste and unnecessary spending by the government, Kim joined Public Works determined to trim budgets and drastically curtail spending.

Born in Seoul, South Korea on March 27, 1939, Kim arrived in California in 1961 at the age of twenty-two, just out of the South Korean army. After a series of menial jobs, Kim attended the University of Southern California where he earned both bachelor's and master's degrees in civil engineering. Having earned his degrees, Kim officially marked his adoption of the United States as his home by legally changing his given name from Chang Joon to Jay.

In 1976, Kim founded Jaykim Engineers, a highly successful engineering design firm. Under Kim's leadership, the firm specialized in building roads and water reclamation projects. It was one of five minority-owned companies hired to demolish buildings damaged during the 1992 Los Angeles riots. Following his election to Congress, however, Kim sold his firm to avoid any appearance of conflict of interest.

Jay Kim

An Alternative to Professional Politicians

Kim's political career began in 1990 with his election to the city council of the town of Diamond Bar in eastern Los Angeles County. He then served as the mayor of Diamond Bar from 1991 to 1993. Kim decided to run for Congress in January of 1992 when, as he faced having to lay off more than twenty Jaykim employees, Congress was voting a 40 percent pay raise for itself. "Talk about being out of touch," he said.

In a campaign that touted Kim as an alternative to the polished professional politician, Kim's heavy accent—despite his more than thirty years of living in the United States—combined with his tendency for blunt honesty undoubtedly served to his advantage. In addition, Kim's entrepreneurial success appealed to the voter of California's new 41st district—a predominantly white-collar, conservative, and affluent district. One of the most noticeable ways Kim distinguished himself among his five fellow competitors was in his departure from the national Republican party's stance on abortion. Unlike the flock of anti-abortion Republicans on the ballot, Kim generally supports abortion rights. Consistent with his hands-off economic views, Kim argues that decisions such as abortion are none of the government's business.

With his no-nonsense conservative platform that favored less taxes and fewer regulations on businesses, Kim surprised both political observers and his opponents by surpassing the two presumed front-runners for a 899-vote victory in the Republican primary. He then easily defeated his Democratic opponent, winning almost double the number of votes and gathering 60 percent of the votes overall.

The 103rd Congress with Jay Kim

As a member of the 103rd Congress, Kim is recognized as a staunch opponent of deficit spending, higher taxes and government mandates. He is critical of President Bill Clinton's economic plan and is especially wary of the proposed increases in government infrastructure spending as well as an increase in the national debt limit. Kim is also determined to personally track every proposal which involves spending money on construction projects, especially if the result would be a tax increase or larger deficit.

Appearing before the Republican National Convention in 1992, Kim said, "Like most immigrants, I did not come to America looking for more government." In his first year in Congress Kim remained true to his words. In 1993's key votes Kim voted against the "motor voter" registration bill, against the president's budget proposal, and against the economic stimulus plan which would have increased the deficit.

Today, the civil engineer from Diamond Bar represents almost 600,000 people in the nation's House of Representatives.

Sources:

Booth, Cathy, Wendy Cole and Sylvester Monroe, "California/Jay Kim," *Time*, November 2, 1992, 46.
"Jay C. Kim," *Congressional Quarterly.* January 16, 1993, 58.

—Sketch by Terry Hong

Ki Ho Kim
(1929–)
Doctor of Pain Management

Ki Ho Kim is one of the country's most renowned specialists in the fields of physical medicine and rehabilitation and in the treatment and management of chronic pain. He is the founder of the Kim Institute of Rehabilitation Medicine in East Orange, New Jersey, which treats the physically disabled and those suffering disorders of the central nervous system from spinal cord injuries and brain damage, and of the Kim Rehabilitation Institute/Central Nervous System and Pain Management Institute, also in

West Orange, New Jersey. Kim is a diplomate of the American Academy of Physical Medicine and Rehabilitation, American Academy of Pain Management and a council member of the International College of Acupuncture and Electro-Therapeutics.

Early Life

Ki Ho Kim was born in Mu-ju, Korea, on April 9, 1929, the oldest of four children, into a family of wealthy landowners and textile factory operators. In 1946 he enrolled in the pre-medical program at Severance Medical College in Seoul, from which he graduated two years later. He then went to medical school. In 1950 the North Korean army invaded South Korea and occupied Seoul, where Kim was studying medicine. The entire college had to be evacuated to Pusan, at the southern tip of the Korean peninsula. In 1952, Kim graduated from Kwang Ju Medical College of Chon Nam University in Kwang Ju City.

In 1952 Kim volunteered for the air force where he served a rotating internship at the Air Hospital of the Republic of Korea. When his internship was completed he became the chief of preventive medicine with the 217th Medical Squadron of the Korean Air Force. During this time Kim saw a great deal of suffering in the servicemen he treated. It occurred to him that many of the soldiers' illnesses were rooted in emotional distress, most likely homesickness. Kim believed that these illnesses could be treated by sending the soldiers home for weekends, but the military hierarchy was not easily persuaded, and resisted his efforts. Eventually, though, Kim was able to convince them that traditional medical treatment would have no affect on psychologically induced illnesses and the only solution was to institute a furlough program for homesickness. It was in this way that Kim began his career-long work in holistically treating illness.

In 1955, after his tour of duty in the air force, Kim was named by presidential appointment to the post of medical director of the Korean National Rehabilitation Center, where he served until 1957. That year he left his country for what was intended to be a short stay in the United States, serving a residency in physical medicine and rehabilitation at the Bellevue Medical Center of New York University. Here he studied under Dr. Howard A. Rusk, who Kim described in an interview with Jim Henry as "one of the great fathers of rehabilitation medicine in the world." Another pioneer in the field was Dr. Henry H. Kessler, founder of the Kessler Institute for Rehabilitation in West Orange, New Jersey. Kim and Kessler found that they were compatible in their ideas and that they worked together well, and in 1959 Kim joined Kessler's institute, becoming the clinical director in 1967.

Kim stayed at the Kessler Institute for several years, making his stay in America much longer than he had intended. Around the time he started thinking about

Ki Ho Kim

returning to his country, South Korea was undergoing serious political turmoil and he was advised not to return. Kessler helped Kim to stay in the United States, which Kim was happy to do. Although he missed Korea, he felt lucky to be doing the work he had always wanted to do. He became a U.S. citizen in 1967.

Kim Institute of Rehabilitation Medicine

In 1969 Kim left the Kessler Institute to found the Kim Institute of Rehabilitation Medicine, a 162-bed facility that specialized in in-patient pain management and rehabilitation of the severely disabled. Kim founded his institute because he was dissatisfied with quality and level of rehabilitation in the area of spinal cord- and brain-injured patients. He wanted to introduce new ideas into treatment of such patients that would go beyond traditional approaches and modalities. In spite of a great deal of resistence, he introduced accupuncture treatment to brain-injured persons in comas and to those suffering severe pain and paralysis from spinal cord injuries, strokes, or muscular-skeletal injuries. He not only used accupuncture, he inisted on treating patients like healthy people. Consequently, there was no hospital clothing at the institute; all the patients dressed as they normally would. Kim also built an apartment in the hospital for the husband or wife of a patient to stay in prior to the patient's release so the couple could practice living together again: often an extremely difficult process in cases of severe paralysis. Kim would counsel the couple in everything from the manner in which their sexual relations would change, to how to get around a kitchen in a wheel chair.

Kim also taught at the New Jersey College of Medicine and Dentistry in Newark, New Jersey. He continued to serve as director of the Kim Institute until 1976 when he became director of the Central Nervous System and Pain Management Institute, a separate entity with close medical connections to the institute.

In 1982 Kim opened the Kim Rehabilitation Institute in West Orange, New Jersey. His new institute replaced the old, offering only out-patient treatment, although he was still practicing in the same field: brain and spinal cord injuries and pain management. A widely respected expert in his field, Kim served as a consultant to the insurance industry and to the legal community, evaluating the severity of catastrophically caused spinal cord and brain injuries, and establishing the prognosis and the degree to which patients can expect to recover. He also serves as a member of the Accupuncture Examining Board of New Jersey and the vice-president of the faculty of the International College of Accupuncture and Electro-Therapeutics.

Inventor

In addition to this work, Kim has written and lectured widely in his field and has patented an invention, the Kim self stander. Developed in 1952, this device allows paralyzed patients to simulate standing to help bones and muscles continue to develop in the absence of motion. He is currently working on a second invention, an electronic, patient-operated pain controller. It is in the clinical trial process and in need of funding, which Kim is confident he will be able to secure.

Kim believes that the values instilled in him by his parents have been of great value to him. They taught him—as he taught his three children—not to make life or career decisions based on earning potential. He believes that in pursuing goals, one should strive for personal and spiritual satisfaction and to do work to the best of one's ability. With that, Kim believes, happiness will come.

Sources:

Kim, Ki Ho. "Curriculum Vitae" supplied by Kim, 1994.

——, telephone interview with Jim Henry, July 22, 1994.

—Sketch by Jim Henry

Wendell Kealohapauloe Kim
(1950–)
Baseball manager, coach

"**N**ever be satisfied" is the credo of Wendell Kealohapauloe Kim, the first and only Korean American to wear a major league baseball uniform. Born in Hawaii in poverty, abused by his prizefighter father who died when he was seven, and reared in a tough Los Angeles neighborhood rife with violence and crime, Wendell Kim is a man who has triumphed over many obstacles, rising from pro-ball infielder and minor league manager to become one of the top coaches in baseball—the third base coach of the San Francisco Giants.

Kim was born on March 9, 1950, in Honolulu, Hawaii, to Doris Kim, a woman of Irish and Hawaiian descent, and Philip "Wildcat" Kim, a renowned professional welterweight boxer of Korean descent. "My father didn't have much of an education. When he was young his mother didn't want him. He lived in a crate box behind a market," Kim told the *Contra Costa Times* in 1992.

Challenging Childhood

While Kim was still young, the family moved from Hawaii to a rough Los Angeles neighborhood between Watts and Compton where his home life became as tough as the streets. When he was six, Kim's father gave him a pair of boxing gloves and asked him to hit him. When Kim refused, his father punched him, nearly breaking his nose. The whole family was totally dominated by Philip, who forced his three children to be in their pajamas every day by 3 p.m., made them eat every bite of food on their plates, and punished them for making too much noise by standing them in a corner where they often fell asleep on their feet. Once after beating their mother who then fled the house for a week, Philip, in a fit of depression, contemplated killing himself and his children. A short time later, he was murdered in a gangland-style assassination, probably in connection with a comeback he was making and a refusal to throw a fight. Kim was eight years old.

Bequeathed with a jungle mentality, the diminutive Kim grew up on the streets using his own "anything-goes" book of tricks to fight and survive. "I was a tough, rough kid. Someone would get mad and I'd punch him. You didn't fight fair. You had to win," Kim related to the *Contra Costa Times*. Kim fought his way out of that environment not only with his fists but also with his brain. Although he graduated from Banning High School tenth in his class with a 3.4 (B+) grade point average, his friends never caught him with a book. "I would stay out with the tough guys at my school until midnight on school nights and

Wendell Kealohapauloe Kim

then stay up for two hours doing my homework," said Kim in a 1993 article in the *Modesto Bee*. He did this by keeping one set of books at home and another in school.

On the Diamond

Kim joined the Coast Guard after high school and went on to play four years of varsity baseball at California State Polytechnic University in Pomona as an infielder while studying to be a teacher. While there, Kim set the Bronco single-season record for runs scored (93), walks (91), and games played (124), and he was twice named to the All-California Collegiate Athletic Association team. In spite of his stellar college record, the five-foot-five-inch, 160-pound second baseman was passed over by every major league team in the 1972 draft.

Undeterred, Kim drove to the Giants camp in Casa Grande, Arizona, slept in his car for two nights, and showed up for tryouts. Jack Schwarz, San Francisco's director of minor league development, looked at him, shocked. "There must be a mistake. Son, if I let you on the field, you'll embarrass me, yourself, and the San Francisco Giants," Schwarz told him, joking that they would need to find a bat boy's uniform for Kim, according to a 1993 article in the *Vacaville Reporter*. In the tryouts, he played twenty-four of twenty-seven innings of a double-header, went four for six with two triples, five stolen bases, and five runs scored, and also helped turn nine double plays. The Giants signed him three weeks later.

Kim spent seven seasons in the minors. He batted .306 in 1974 and was an honorable mention California League all-star for Fresno. In 1976, Kim led the Texas League in hits (164) and at–bats (537). He ended his playing career in 1979 after two seasons in Phoenix hitting a career high of .313.

Known throughout the Giants organization for his hustle, enthusiasm, and knowledge of the game, Kim was offered a job managing in the Giants' minor league system in 1980 where he worked for eight years with Phoenix, Shreveport, Fresno, and Clinton. He was named California League Manager of the Year after leading Fresno to the California League title in 1983. He was voted Texas League Manager of the Year in 1986 after leading Shreveport to an 80–56 mark. Kim led the 1987 Phoenix Firebirds to a 77–67 mark, coming within one game of the Pacific Coast League play-offs, and also piloted them to a 67–76 mark in 1988, breaking a personal string of five straight above–.500 finishes.

In his early years with Fresno, Will Clark remembers playing for Kim, his first professional manager. "When I first went to Fresno, the first game I had a couple of home runs. That's what everybody talked about," said Clark, quoted in the *Oakland Tribune* in 1992. "They forgot to mention that after that I pulled something like an 0–for–25. Wendell got me in the cage for three or four days straight. We talked, we worked on things and everything after that went well."

Major League Talent

Rising quickly through the Giants' organization, Kim served three years (1989–91) as their first base coach. Hard to miss because of his seemingly perpetual motion, Kim flies about the dugout, perching momentarily on the edge of a bench stretching, then suddenly appearing at the opposite end, legs spread and arms akimbo, his eyes on the field. Whether galloping to the pitcher's mound, first base or third, which he has coached since 1992, Kim's hustle, zeal, and energy are applied to almost every task at hand from coaching to preparing lineup cards, setting up defensive alignments, leading calisthenics, and even pitching batting practices.

But in addition to being the "everything coach," according to Giants' manager Dusty Baker, Kim is also respected for his confidence and intelligence. "Kim brings with him a lot of baseball experience. In his twenty-one years, he's seen a lot of different players and a lot of different baseball. He wouldn't be on third base if he couldn't do the job. Players trust him," said right fielder Willie McGee in 1993 in the *Modesto Bee*.

Kim wants to take the step someday to managing a major league team, though for now he'll continue in his capacity as coach for the Giants. Kim lives in Mesa, Arizona, with his third wife, Natasha, and their three children. In his spare time he pursues his only hobby, magic tricks, and is contemplating writing a book about his life. He even has a title in mind: *The Hard Way Up.*

"I'm proud that I never gave up," Kim told the *Modesto Bee.* "I'm still doing something that I love. I was in the minors sixteen years before getting up here. A lot of people never get up here. I kept working hard—the main thing I've done is survive."

There never has been an Asian American manager in the majors, but considering the odds that Kim has beaten so far in his career, breaking that barrier would seem to be a fair bet.

Sources:

Periodicals

Jackson, Ron. "Diminutive Coach Performs Big Job." *Vacaville Reporter,* August 18, 1993.
Newhouse, Dave. "Kim Escaped From a Rough Childhood." *Contra Costa Times,* July 11, 1992.
Rocha, Elisa. "Mr. Excitement." *Modesto Bee,* August 13, 1993.
Schulman, Henry. "The Life and Times of Wendell Kim—That's Adversity." *Oakland Tribune,* August 23, 1992.

—Sketch by Nancy Moore

Willa Kim

Costume designer

With a career in costume design that spans well over thirty years, Willa Kim must be one of the most decorated artists working in theatre. Since her first Broadway show in 1966—Edward Albee's *Malcolm* at the Schubert Theatre—Kim has been designing costumes for the theatre and dance to rave reviews. She won Tony awards for Duke Ellington's *Sophisticated Ladies* (1981) and Tommy Tune's *The Will Rogers Follies* (1991). She received Tony nominations for Peter Allen's *Legs Diamond* (1988), Andrew Lloyd Webber's *Song and Dance* (1985), Bob Fosse's *Dancin'* (1978), and Joel Grey's *Goodtime Charley* (1975). She won an Emmy for the San Francisco Ballet's production of *The Tempest* (1981); Drama Desk awards for Maria Irene Fornes's *Promenade* (1969), Sam Shepherd's *Operation Sidewinder* (1988), and Jean Genet's *The Screens* (1971); and an Obie for Robert Lowell's *The Old Glory* (1976).

While Kim admits to a preference for musical theatre, to say that she single-handedly revolutionized the look of the dance world early in her career would not be an exaggeration. She pioneered the use of stretch fabric long before the Capezio name became synonymous with the leotard. Thick, woolly nylon had been the dancer's choice material before Kim began working with thin stretch fabric. No longer encumbered with a heavy layer, the new fabric celebrated the lines of a dancer's body, accentuating the elongated torso. The sheer, sleek body delineations became a hallmark of late twentieth century ballet and modern dance. In addition, with her fine arts background in illustration, Kim was the also first to try fabric painting, convincing a Brooklyn factory to lend her dyes and teach her how to color nylons. Her experimental methods quickly became the industry standard.

An Artist, not a Designer

A second-generation Korean American, Willa Kim grew up in Los Angeles. Although as a child Kim spent many hours drawing and making paper dolls, she was convinced that she would become a painter. "I was trained as an artist, not a designer, and my work reflects that," Kim told *TheatreWeek* in 1991. After receiving a scholarship, she studied fashion illustration at the Chouinard Institute of Art in Los Angeles. She happened onto costume design straight out of art school: "One of my art instructors insisted that I take my portfolio around to art studios and department stores. I was so delighted when Western Costume asked me to leave it. It was as big as I was and it was so heavy to carry around. The next thing I knew, I was working in the studios," she told Lynn Pecktal in *Costume Design: Techniques of Modern Masters.*

In the late 1950s, Kim moved from Los Angeles to New York City. Her first New York production was Arnold Weinstein's 1961 off-Broadway play, *Red Eye of Love.* "I had to create fifty costumes with a budget of $250. I used to fall asleep on the floor in the theatre and get up and sew at the strangest hours," Kim told the *New York Times* in 1981. In spite of the sparse, difficult beginning, the experience proved to be a great training ground and Kim was hooked. Just five years later, she was designing on Broadway for Edward Albee's *Malcolm.*

In the same way she fell into costume design, Kim waltzed into the dance world. In 1962, a young choreographer at the time, Greg Tetley, approached Kim to design a ballet he was choreographing. Called *Birds of Sorrow,* the production was well-received and proved very successful. "[A] lot of choreographers saw that evening of dance and started calling me. Once again, it was something I hadn't thought about doing any more than I had thought about designing," Kim told Pecktal. "It seems events kind of occurred and the next thing I knew I was a ballet designer." Since her dance debut, Kim has worked regularly with the Joffrey Ballet, the American Ballet Theatre, the San Francisco Ballet, the Alvin Ailey Company, and the Feld Ballets/New York with whom Kim has maintained a two-decade-plus collaborative relationship.

The Tonys

After being nominated twice before, Kim won her first Tony Award in 1981 for Duke Ellington's *Sophisticated Ladies.* Plagued by changing directors (there were three of them), revolving choreographers (there were also three of them), and countless numbers constantly being cut and added with each directorial change before the show even made it to Broadway, it was not surprising that Kim referred to the show as "a pain in the neck" in the *New York Times* shortly after winning the award. In spite of the frustration of creative battles, Kim proved tenacious and justly triumphed with theatre's highest award.

Kim's second Tony Award was not nearly as frustrating. Working with choreographer Tommy Tune with whom she has collaborated on numerous shows, Kim created the glamorous costumes for *The Will Rogers Follies* from rough sketches supplied by Tune. In spite of a nearly impossible timeline, Kim told *TheaterWeek,* "It was an easy show to do, compared to a lot of them." The 1991 Broadway spectacular was a far cry from Kim's first New York show with its $250 costume budget. This time her budget had escalated to $1 million with costumes each costing in the thousands. Because designers were not allowed to make acceptance speeches, when she was awarded her Tony, Kim stood up in the audience and held up a fan inscribed with thanks to Tune and the costume shop of Parson Meares.

The Kim Process

When she is designing for the theatre, Kim begins by reading the script, researching the period, and then meeting the performers. "It's ideal to wait until the show is cast before beginning the design," she said in a 1989 interview in *TheaterCraft.* In the same way, when she is designing a ballet, Kim insists on seeing the dancers rehearse the finished choreography. "I can reflect and help to emphasize what the choreographer is doing in the way of movement," she explained. "I try to take advantage of the best points of the performer."

Kim claims that her favorite part of her designing process is watching things being made in the costume shops. She stays involved from conception to the final stitch, careful to examine the smallest of details. Kim is also known for lengthy and frequent fittings, often because part of the invention of the design takes place on the body, noted a frequent collaborator.

While she continues to design for the ballet and opera, Kim has often voiced a preference for musical theatre. "The challenge is much more exciting," she explained in *TheaterCraft.* "There's more to contend with. Not only the number of people but the complexity of the problem. You have to delineate a character within a time and a period and show a progression of ideas. You also have to flatter the performers."

Kim's career shows no signs of slowing down and she remains one of the busiest women working in theatre. If it's musicals Kim wants, it's musicals Kim gets. She designed costumes for the revival of *Grease* which opened on Broadway in late spring of 1994. Her upcoming projects, also musicals, are Blake Edward's stage version of *Victor/Victoria* starring Julie Andrews and *Busker,* the latest from Tommy Tune.

Sources:

Books

Pecktal, Lynn. "A Conversation with Willa Kim." *Costume Design: Techniques of Modern Masters.* New York: Backstage Books, 1993.

Periodicals

Duka, John. "She Made 'Ladies' Look Sophisticated." *The New York Times,* September 20, 1981, p. D3.
Dunning, Jennifer. "Backstage Partners: Ballet's Kim and Feld." *The New York Times,* August 9, 1991.
Howard, Beth. "Designers on Designing: Willa Kim." *TheaterCraft,* March 1989, pp. 29–33+.
Pais, Arthur J. "Willa Kim's Fashion 'Follies'." *USAir Magazine,* October 1993, pp. 64–67+.
Wong, Wayman. "Willa-Mania!" *TheaterWeek,* July 8-14, 1991, pp. 24–27.

Other

Kim, Willa, telephone interview with Terry Hong, March 14, 1994.

—Sketch by Terry Hong

Lillian Chiyeko Kimura
(1929–)
Community leader

In 1993, the government of Japan held a special ceremony to honor three Japanese Americans who were recognized as leaders in promoting relations between the United States and Japan. Among the three was Lillian Kimura who received the prestigious Order of the Precious Crown, Wisteria. During the ceremony, the Consul General of Japan referred to Kimura as a "person who personifies the spirit of the words 'public service' . . . someone who cares very much about people and the society in which they live.'"

Lillian Chiyeko Kimura

Trained as a social worker, Kimura has spent the majority of her life in service to others. When she retired in 1992, she left behind a legacy of commitment and dedication at the Young Women's Christian Association (YWCA) where she served as the associate national executive director for five years. Also in 1992, Kimura became the national president of the Japanese American Citizens League (JACL), the first woman president in JACL's six-decade history.

Lillian Chiyeko Kimura was born in Glendale, California, on April 7, 1929. She was the second of three daughters born to Hisaichi Homer and Hisa Muraki Kimura, both originally from Japan. The family remained in Glendale until 1942 when they were evacuated to Manzanar in Lone Pine, California, one of the ten relocation camps for Japanese Americans during World War II. When the war was over, the family moved to Chicago. After completing high school in Chicago, Kimura received her bachelor's in psychology and a master's in social work from the University of Illinois.

A Career in Service

Following graduation, Kimura joined Chicago's Olivet Community Center as a group work supervisor. Olivet was a neighborhood center that provided after-school and summer recreational and social activities for young people, a nursery school, a seniors' club, as well as extensive community development programs to improve the

neighborhood's housing and living standards. During her sixteen years at Olivet, Kimura supervised the center's many community activities. In addition, she led local public schools and other community agencies in efforts to prevent gang activities from growing. By the time Kimura left Olivet in 1971, she was the center's director.

In the same year, Kimura joined the YWCA as a program consultant in the Chicago field office. She provided technical assistance and consultative help to YWCAs throughout the midwest. She also trained YWCA staff in program planning and development. When the YWCA reorganized in 1978, the Chicago office was closed and Kimura was transferred to St. Louis, Missouri, where she was appointed director of the mid-states office. There she supervised a staff of six women who provided services to 175 YWCAs throughout the mid-states.

Two years later, Kimura was promoted to executive of the field services unit. She moved again, this time to New York. Together with her staff of twelve people, located in three regional field offices, Kimura was responsible for providing technical assistance and management training for staff and board members of 400 YWCAs throughout the country.

In 1983, Kimura became the assistant national executive director and then in 1987 was promoted to associate national executive director. As such, she supervised the agency's work with all member YWCAs, including training, consulting, evaluating, organizing new YWCAs, providing model program ideas and monitoring the quality of service provided by the individual YWCAs. Working closely with the national director and the national president, Kimura also interfaced with other national youth services and women's groups.

First Woman President ... Twice

In addition to working at YWCA, Kimura remained actively involved with the Japanese American community. In 1973 Kimura became the first woman to serve as president of the Japanese American Service Committee (JASC). The group was organized in 1946 to assist Japanese Americans in their adjustment period from leaving the relocation camps to rebuilding a new life in mainstream American society. During Kimura's six-year tenure, JASC experienced a period of expansion, especially in aiding older first-generation Japanese Americans by providing meals, day care, and housekeeping services.

In 1992, Kimura decided to retire from the YWCA in order to devote more time to her involvement with the Japanese American Citizens League. In the same year, Kimura became the first woman to be named national president of JACL, a 25,000-member, 113-chapter organization with more than a six-decade history. Founded in 1929, JACL was organized by second-generation Japanese Americans who sought to overcome social and economic discrimination based on race. At the time of JACL's founding, laws prevented first-generation Japanese Americans from owning property and becoming U.S. citizens.

Kimura's involvement with JACL is more than two decades old. From board member to chairperson of the Long Range Planning Committee to past New York chapter president, Kimura's list of accomplishments is indeed long. She instituted the concept of "Program for Action" to help the organization better prioritize upcoming issues of concern and she saved the *Pacific Citizen,* JACL's national weekly newspaper. She led JACL's public relations efforts to offset any anti-Japanese sentiment resulting from the commemoration of the 50th anniversary of the bombing of Pearl Harbor. Perhaps most importantly, Kimura played a primary role in the success of the redress issue in which the U.S. government admitted to the unconstitutionality of the World War II relocation camps and offered monetary compensation for camp survivors and their descendants.

As JACL president, Kimura has just a few goals on her agenda: to increase JACL membership to 30,000; to recruit and train third- and fourth-generation leaders; and to position JACL to become a major player in national civil and human rights issues as well as in the broader issues of the economy, heath care, and education. Given Kimura's past track record, she will undoubtedly succeed.

Sources:

Kimura, Lillian Chiyeko. Biographical materials and press release. December 1993.

—Sketch by Terry Hong

Dong Kingman
(1911–)
Artist

One of America's foremost watercolorists, Dong Kingman is recognized around the world as a major artist of the century. His paintings are in collections at some of the most prominent museums in the United States, including the Museum of Modern Art, the Metropolitan Museum of Art, and the Art Institute of Chicago. He has taught painting at Columbia University, Hunter College, and at the Famous Artists School in Westport, Connecticut. He has also illustrated several books, magazine articles and covers, and movie posters.

Dong Kingman was born in Oakland, California, in 1911, the second of eight children born to first-generation Chinese immigrants from Hong Kong. When Kingman was still quite young his family left the United States. His father feared that his older children might be somehow dragged into World War I, then being fought in Europe. He sold his dry goods store and returned his family to Hong Kong where he ran a successful department store. The young Kingman showed artistic ability from an early age, and he was encouraged in his paintings and drawings by his mother, who had painted for years. As a teenager, Kingman was sent to Lingnan Branch School in Hong Kong, where he studied painting with Szetsu Wei, a highly regarded Chinese painter. Here he studied both traditional Chinese approaches to art and the Western masters as well, especially the French Impressionists.

In 1929, at the age of eighteen, Kingman left Lingnan for the United States, where his father thought he would be better able to pursue a career in art. He arrived in San Francisco and worked at a variety of jobs—from a laborer in an overall factory owned by his brother to proprietor of a failed restaurant—to support himself and his art. He began to show some of his paintings in group shows, and then in 1936 he was hired as an artist by the federal government through the auspices of the Works Progress Administration, a Depression-era program of the New Deal. Kingman had his first solo show that year. Held at the San Francisco Art Center, it received generally good reviews.

Watercolor painting was enjoying wide popularity on the West Coast at this time, and Kingman had the further good fortune to have the patronage of a prominent collector who donated several of his Kingmans to museums. Then, in 1940, the Metropolitan Museum of Art in New York bought its first Kingman watercolor. This purchase was the first acquisition made by that museum of work by an Asian American artist. In 1941 Kingman's stature as an artist of importance was further enhanced when he received a two-year Guggenheim Fellowship that funded an extended tour of the United States during which the artist would produce paintings reflecting the vast array of American landscapes.

Cityscapes

Of all of America that Kingman saw during this tour, New York City most fascinated him. In 1942 he had a one man show at the Midtown Gallery. Again, he was accorded wide acclaim in several prominent publications including *Time, Newsweek,* and the *New Yorker.* In 1943, the artist was drafted into the military where he served in Washington, D.C., working as an illustrator for the Office of Strategic Services (OSS), the forerunner of today's CIA. While serving in Washington, Kingman produced a series of paintings of the nation's capital that would later serve as the basis of his first postwar show in New York.

In 1945, after being discharged from the military, Kingman decided to move to New York, the city that had captured his interest. In *The Watercolors of Dong Kingman and How the Artist Works*, Allan D. Gruskin quotes the artist as writing about New York: "What did I see [in New York]? Man-made monumental structures; dynamic streets and avenues; locomotives, buses; BMT, IRT, and IND—the fast and quick ways of transportation; the birds, pigeons, and ducks; the animals, lions, monkeys, dogs, cats, people—some happy, some sad; the atmosphere, noise, dirt and odors. Summer is hot, winter is snow; subjects dirty or clean. I enjoy sketching in the asphalt jungle—the big city."

Throughout the remainder of the forties and the early fifties, Kingman continued showing and selling his paintings. He taught painting at Columbia University and then, in 1948, became a full-time instructor at Hunter College. In 1951, the Midtown Gallery had a retrospective of the artist's work, marking the tenth anniversary of his first show with the gallery. In 1953, Kingman was invited to tour Asia as a part of the U.S. State Department's educational exchange program. The tour was very successful, with large audiences attending lectures wherever Kingman went, including Hong Kong, Singapore, Malaya, Bangkok, New Delhi, and Istanbul. He returned to the United States via Europe, stopping in Vienna, Copenhagen, Oslo, London, and Reykjavik, Iceland. His paintings of this trip were sent on a State Department-sponsored touring show of the cities that he had visited.

Artist as Teacher

Beginning in 1957, Kingman began teaching annual painting workshops in different countries around the world. He has taught in Europe, Asia and Latin America. He continues to paint and show as well, with his favorite topics being urban landscape and his favorite urban landscape being that of New York, his home for more than fifty years.

Reflecting on his career as a painter in *Dong Kingman's Watercolors*, he said: "Over the years, I've had some difficult times. But whenever I felt discouraged, I would stop and think of how something had always come along which enabled me to continue learning. I would tell myself to have faith and that with time and perseverance I could overcome anything. And I did."

Sources:

Gruskin, Allan D. *The Watercolors of Dong Kingman and How the Artist Works*. New York: The Studio Publications, Inc., 1958.

Kingman, Dong and Helena Kuo Kingman. *Dong Kingman's Watercolors*. New York: Watson Guptil Publications, 1980.

—*Sketch by Jim Henry*

Maxine Hong Kingston
(1940–)
Writer

"**Y**ou must not tell anyone what I am about to tell you." So begins Maxine Hong Kingston's first book, a 1976 memoir called *The Woman Warrior: Memoirs of a Girlhood Among Ghosts*, which won the National Book Critic's Circle Award and catapulted her into national literary prominence. Kingston has since written two other critically acclaimed books. *China Men*, a sequel to *The Woman Warrior*, appeared in 1980 and also received the National Book Critic's Circle Award. Kingston published her first novel, *Tripmaster Monkey: His Fake Book*, in 1989.

Kingston's work explores the Chinese American experience and the roots of that experience. Drawing on historical fact and her artistic imagination, she depicts the lives of Chinese men and women who immigrated to this country in the nineteenth and twentieth centuries. She also tells of their American-born descendants and examines how their Chinese heritage has affected their adjustment to American society.

"The one thing about which I am absolutely sure is that I am a Chinese American woman. That feeling affects my writing in a particular way. I know that what I have to say is what a Chinese American person is thinking. I don't have to go out and make a survey," she told Timothy Pfaff.

"When I wrote *The Woman Warrior* and *China Men* . . . I was trying to find an American language that would translate the speech of the people who are living their lives with the Chinese language. They carry on their adventures and their emotional life . . . in Chinese. I had to find a way to translate all that into a graceful American language. Which is my language."

Maxine Hong Kingston grew up in Stockton, California. Her father, Tom Hong, came from Sun Woi, China, to New York City in 1924, where he started a laundry with three friends. For fifteen years, Hong lived the freewheeling life of an unattached young man. In 1939 Hong sent for his wife, Chew Ying Lan, who at his urging had earned a medical degree and launched a flourishing practice in Sun Woi. Chew Ying Lan's arrival put an end to the men's fun. Whereas Hong and his friends had eaten take-out from restaurants on tablecloths of newspapers with little regard for manners, Chew Ying Lan cooked elaborate meals which the men ate with due formality. Angered by the loss of their freedom, Hong's friends swindled him out of his share of the laundry, and he and his wife moved to Stockton penniless.

Work and Education

In Stockton, the couple ran a gambling house for a few years (naming their first child, Maxine, after a blonde gambler who always won) and then opened a laundry. Maxine and her five brothers and sisters joined their parents in working long, arduous hours at the laundry.

With the help of eleven scholarships, Kingston attended the University of California at Berkeley. She intended to study engineering, but changed her major to English literature. "When I went from engineering to English, I felt I had abdicated all my responsibilities! I was just living life for the fun of it. I guess it was the way I was raised, but everything had to be hard. But English was easy for me. . . . [I thought] there was something wrong with me if I did something that was easy and fun," she told Marilyn Chin.

Kingston graduated with a bachelor of arts degree in 1962. In November of that year, she married Earl Kingston, who had been one of her classmates in an English course. The two were both involved in the antiwar movement of the sixties and shared an interest in theatre.

Kingston obtained a teaching certificate from Berkeley in 1965 and taught for a year with her husband at Sunset High School in Hayward, California. In 1967, they moved to Hawaii. Earl worked with a theatre company that toured high schools, and Kingston financed her writing by teaching at various institutions, including Kahuka High School, Kahaluu Drop-In School, Honolulu Business College, and Kailua High School. From 1970 to 1977, she held a teaching position at a private school, Mid-Pacific Institute. The success of *The Woman Warrior* in 1976 eventually enabled her to write full time.

The Woman Warrior

In *The Woman Warrior*, Kingston portrays the conflicting messages sent to her from both cultures of which she is a part. In *The Woman Warrior*, she writes that Chinese legends tell girls "that we failed if we grew up to be but wives or slaves. We could be heroines, swordwomen." The same culture, however, propagated folk sayings that proclaimed the worthlessness of women, such as "When fishing for treasures in the flood, be careful not to pull in girls." Kingston tells of her lifelong struggle to fashion an identity on her own terms and to draw sustenance from her Chinese culture while rejecting its sexist values.

In her attempts to claim her identity as an American while growing up, Kingston experienced further alienation and confusion. Pressured by her Euro-American teachers and classmates to speak in class, Kingston nevertheless felt silenced by her sense of herself as a foreigner. "When I went to kindergarten and had to speak English for the first time, I became silent. . . . I spoke to no one at school, did not ask before going to the lavatory, and flunked kindergarten. . . .The other Chinese girls did not talk either, so I knew the silence had to do with being a Chinese girl," she wrote in *The Woman Warrior*.

China Men resembles *The Woman Warrior* in that it explores the Chinese American experience through the lives of Kingston's parents and kin. Indeed, Kingston thinks of the two as one book, having written them "more or less simultaneously," she explained to Timoth Pfaff. Yet whereas the narrators in *The Woman Warrior* are all women, and include Kingston herself, the voices in *China Men* are exclusively male—those of Kingston's grandfathers, father, and brothers. Kingston weaves a tapestry of images from these men: a grandfather clearing forests on Hawaii "so thick they shut out sunlight" for sugar cane farms; another grandfather dynamiting mountains for the Central Pacific Railroad Company; a brother who enlisted in the Navy during the Vietnam War teaching remedial English to his fellow recruits.

"What I am doing in this book [*China Men*] is claiming America," Kingston told Pfaff. "That seems to be the common strain that runs through all the characters. In story after story Chinese American people are claiming America, which goes all the way from one character saying that a Chinese explorer found this place before Leif Ericsson (sic) did to another one buying a house here. Buying that house is a way of saying that America—and not China—is his country."

A New Literary Hero

Kingston's third book, *Tripmaster Monkey: His Fake Book*, takes place in San Francisco in the 1960s. The second half of the title, Kingston says, is a reference to its fictional content. The book's protagonist is Wittman Ah Sing, a manic, playful, highly verbal young man who is a year out of the University of California at Berkeley. Wittman was named for Walt Whitman, and like that poet, seeks to claim America for himself through his writing. Fired by a toy company for setting up a pornographic encounter between a Barbie doll and a battery-operated monkey, Wittman turns his enormous energies to writing a contemporary epic play based on an old Chinese novel.

Some maintain that the way Kingston has draw Wittman—his energy and self-absorption and anger at a flawed world that misunderstands him—makes him a sixties version of such heroes of American literature as Holden Caulfield and Huck Finn. Yet he also recalls Chinese literary figures, wrote John Leonard in the *Nation*: "[Wittman is] the incarnation of the Monkey King in Wu Ch'eng-en's sixteenth-century *Journey to the West*, a kind of *Pilgrim's Progress*. He's the rebel/mischief-maker who helped bring back Buddha's Sutras from India; the shape-changer (falcon, koi fish, cormorant) who annoyed Lao-tse by eating the peaches of the Immortals, even though he hadn't been invited to their party."

In an interview with Marilyn Chin in 1990, Kingston speculated on the direction her work would take in the future: "I'm beginning to have an idea that Wittman ought to grow up. . . . American literature is made up of great novels about young men. It has to do with our being a young country. . . . If I can write a novel in which Wittman grows up to be a socially responsible, and effective, good man—forming a community around him, bringing joy to people . . . then it means I will have made Holden Caulfield grow up; I would have made Huck Finn and Tom Sawyer grow up. . . . Then I would have helped us all grow up."

Sources:

Books

Kingston, Maxine Hong. *China Men.* New York: Knopf, 1980.
———. *Tripmaster Monkey.* New York: Knopf, 1989.
———. *The Woman Warrior.* New York: Knopf, 1976.
Lim, Shirley Geok-Lin, ed. *Approaches to Teaching Kingston's The Woman Warrior.* New York: The Modern Language Association of America, 1991.

Periodicals

Chin, Marilyn. "A MELUS Interview: Maxine Hong Kingston." *MELUS,* vol. 16, Winter 1989/90, pp. 57–74.
Pfaff, Timothy. "Talk with Mrs. Kingston." *New York Times Book Review,* June 15, 1980, pp. 1+.

—*Sketch by Anne P. Standley*

Harry Kitano

(1927–)

Academician, author

Harry Kitano, professor of Social Welfare and Sociology at UCLA, has crystallized for many Americans the identity crisis and trauma suffered by Japanese Americans as a result of their internment in U.S. camps during World War II. His book, *Japanese Americans,* provided the first coherent account of the experiences of Japanese Americans after the war. published in 1969 and translated into Japanese, the book was a success and led to Kitano lecturing throughout the United States as well as in Japan, where he enjoyed near celebrity status.

"I hope that through my own search and self-discovery I can help others benefit from the experience," Kitano told *Notable Asian Americans.*

The Ethnic Experience

Following the release of *Japanese Americans,* Kitano wrote dozens of other articles and books on Asian Americans and race relations, including *Asian Americans: A Success Story?; Generations and Identity: The Japanese American;* and *Applied Research on Health and Ethnicity: Asian and Asian American Elderly.* Kitano said his keen interest in studying and writing about his own ethnic group was almost therapeutic and helped him to deal with his insecurity and low self-esteem caused by the internment. "My writing became increasingly more autobiographical and it allowed me to put forth my own ideas," Kitano told *Notable Asian Americans.* "Even though I've learned that ethnic identification is central and that I would never be fully accepted on all levels. I've reached a point where I feel I don't have to prove to my American colleagues that I am just as good as they are."

The youngest of seven children, Kitano grew up in San Francisco's Chinatown. His questions about identity and his Japanese American heritage began early in childhood, coming as a result of barbs and taunts from other children who called him "Jap." Kitano recalls several incidents of prejudice and discrimination, but those experiences with racism were minor until the Japanese attack on Pearl Harbor in 1941. Then a high school freshman, Kitano recalled feeling confused and even guilty that Japan had attacked the United States, but he thought that it wouldn't drastically affect his life. He was wrong. Soon afterward the FBI came to his home and removed his father as a prisoner of war.

Internment Camps

Thus began the nightmare for Kitano and thousands of other Japanese Americans incarcerated during World War II. Considered potential traitors and dangerous to the war effort, they were ordered by the U.S. government to close their businesses and homes, sell their belongings and property, and assemble at designated sites. There they were herded into railroad cars and transported to temporary camps. Kitano and his family, along with 20,000 other Japanese Americans, were detained in Santa Anita, California, until more permanent inland camps were developed. The experience intensified Kitano's silent struggle for an identity. He felt like an American. "I belonged to the ROTC band at Galileo, and played 'The Stars and Stripes Forever,' marched behind the flag, and had little identification with Japan," he wrote in *A History of Race Relations Research.* Yet he was treated like an outcast by the very people he identified with.

Kitano later moved to Topaz, a permanent camp set up in the middle of the desert in Utah where he lived from 1942 to 1945. Unlike the camp in Santa Anita, where he could see cars driving by and detainees could even wave to acquaintances on the street, this camp was guarded by armed soldiers and its perimeters sealed with barbed-wire fences. All detainees had to answer a questionnaire that was used to determine whether inmates were loyal to Japan or to the United States. Responses of "yes, yes" were interpreted to mean that one identified with the United States, and "no, no" responses were generally interpreted to mean a strong identification with Japan. "I answered

Harry Kitano

'yes, yes' on the questionnaire because I knew nothing about Japan, and I felt that my future was in America, no matter what the cost," Kitano wrote in *A History of Race Relations Research.*

After his release from Topaz, Kitano traveled to Milwaukee and worked briefly as a farm hand. Although the war was over, lingering racial hostility toward Japanese Americans worried Kitano, so he changed his name to Harry Lee. He played trombone with several bands in Minnesota, where he had the opportunity to work with black musicians. It was an eye-opening experience for Kitano, for here was an ethnic group that suffered even more hostility and discrimination than his own.

In 1946 Kitano returned to California to attend the University of California at Berkeley where he earned a bachelor's degree in 1948, a master's in social work in 1951, and in 1958 a doctorate. It was at Berkley that Kitano met Davis McEntire, a labor economist who strongly influenced Kitano and gave him his first professional job in the field of social research. Working for McEntire, Kitano developed a survey of Japanese Americans and their housing needs that eventually was published in a volume entitled *Studies in Housing and Minority Groups.*

Work Experience

Kitano credits two other jobs for helping to shape his career. As a caseworker at the International Institute of San Francisco from 1953 to 1961, Kitano's major task was to work with new Asian immigrants as they adapted to American society. Kitano found it particularly interesting to study the children of these immigrants, whose problems were not unlike those he had experienced in his own childhood.

While working as a therapist for minority children in the Child Guidance Clinic of the San Francisco Schools from 1954 to 1958, Kitano was introduced to the principles of psychoanalysis. He was excited by the intricacies of psychoanalysis, the use of dreams, and the rich variety of symbolic interpretations that could be applied to the behavior he was studying.

Kitano has spent the better part of his career trying to make sense out of what happened to Japanese Americans and to determine whether such action could take place again in a democratic society. He believes that the lessons learned from such studies can help other minority groups who feel despair, frustration, and alienation much like the Japanese Americans once did.

Kitano now makes his home in Bel Air, California, where he lives with his wife Lynn and his daughter Christine.

Sources:

Books

Stanfield II, John H., ed. *A History of Race Relations Research.* Newbury Park: Sage Publications, 1993.

Other

Kitano, Harry, written interview with Grace Wong, November 1993.

—Sketch by Grace Wong

Harold Hongju Koh
(1954–)
Attorney, law professor

It's almost as if Harold Hongju Koh's life as a Yale Law School professor, author, and frequent commentator on international law issues of the day had been pre-ordained. His father was a scholar and a U.S. diplomat, and his mother was a Ph.D. in sociology who taught at the college level. Together, his parents were the first Asian Americans to teach at Yale University. And today, one of Koh's younger sisters is a colleague of his at Yale.

Harold Hongju Koh

Harold Hongju Koh was born December 8, 1954, in Cambridge, Massachusetts, one of six children. Koh's mother had immigrated to the United States from Korea in 1948. One year later Koh's father, Kwang Lim Koh, a graduate of Seoul National University, came to the United States to study at Harvard Law School. The couple met in their newly adopted country and married in 1950.

Impressive Legacy

In 1960, Koh's family moved to Washington, D.C., when his father accepted an assignment as acting ambassador of South Korea. In the late 1950s and 1960s, Kwang Lim Koh also led South Korean missions to the United States and the United Nations. After the elder Koh's stint as a diplomat ended, the family left Washington for New Haven, Connecticut, where Koh's parents both landed teaching positions at Yale Law School, becoming the first Asian Americans to teach at the university.

Koh's father went on to teach for twenty-three years at Central Connecticut State University. He wrote fifteen books in Korean and two in English. He lectured at Boston University Law School and earned five postgraduate degrees, including a master's and doctorate at Harvard Law School and a doctorate at Boston College Law School. Kwang Lim Koh also helped found the first Korean studies program at Harvard.

Koh said he grew up very much in the mainstream of American life with very few Asian American counterparts

as friends or classmates. By virtue of their professions, his parents immersed themselves in American culture but managed also to incorporate some Korean American or Asian American philosophy in the upbringing of their children. "I learned about the tremendous importance of family, a reverence for tradition and respect for the elderly, as well as the value of a harmonious society," Koh said in an interview with Felicia Paik.

After graduating summa cum laude in 1975 as a government major, Koh told Paik: "My father initially encouraged me to become a physicist. I think he was concerned I might not succeed as a lawyer, that as an Asian there might be discrimination, and because back then there were very few Koreans who were lawyers. He was secretly very pleased with my decision."

Law Career Begins

Koh graduated from Harvard Law School in 1980 after receiving a bachelor of arts degree in philosophy, politics, and economics from Magdalen College at Oxford University. Koh worked as a law clerk to U.S. Supreme Court Justice Harry Blackmun and then joined the law firm of Covington and Burling as an associate for one year before returning to public service. From 1983 to 1985 Koh was an attorney-adviser in the office of Legal Counsel in the U.S. Department of Justice. During this period, he also lectured in the evenings at the George Washington University National Law Center where he met his wife, Mary-Christy Fisher, who was a law professor there. The couple has two children.

In 1985 Koh joined the Yale Law School as an associate professor and received tenure five years later. He specializes in international law and is the director of the Orville H. Schell Center for Human Rights. From his post as a Yale Law School professor, Koh has become a well-known pundit on cases of international law. In recent years he has weighed in with his opinions on the Iran-Contra affair and whether John Demjanjuk, an accused Nazi war criminal, should be allowed to return to his home in the United States after being cleared of his crimes in Israel.

Awards, Honors

In 1990 Yale University Press published Koh's book, *The National Security: Sharing Power After the Iran-Contra Affair.* The book won the Richard E. Neustadt Award from the Presidency Research Section of the American Political Science Association as the best book in 1990 that contributed most to the research and scholarship on the American presidency.

However, to date, Koh has received the most media attention as the attorney who argued in front of the U.S. Supreme Court on behalf of the Haitians' right to seek asylum hearings. In June 1993 the Supreme Court ruled that refugees fleeing Haiti for the United States may be stopped at sea and returned home without asylum hearings. The eight-to-one opinion, with Justice Blackmun dissenting, dealt a blow to thousands willing to take a risky ocean passage in search of freedom and upheld a policy developed by the Bush administration and adopted by President Bill Clinton.

For his work on behalf of Haitians and in other areas of international law, Koh has received several accolades, including the 1993 Justice in Action Award from the Asian American Legal Defense and Education Fund. In 1992 he was a corecipient of the Human Rights Award from the American Immigration Lawyers' Association, Asian Law Caucus. He is active in a variety of associations including the Connecticut Civil Liberties Union and the American Bar Association. He also serves as secretary of East Rock Institute, a New Haven nonprofit research educational and cultural organization studying Korean and American cultures, which his parents founded in 1956.

Considering his young age and the prominence he has achieved as a champion of human rights, some people say Koh is poised to one day lead Yale Law School or even ascend to the U.S. Supreme Court.

Sources:

Koh, Harold Hongju, telephone interview with Felicia Paik, April 1, 1994.
———. "Harold Hongju Koh." Resume. New Haven, Connecticut, March 1994

—Sketch by Felicia Paik

Tomia "Tommy" T. Kono
(1930–)
Weightlifter, Olympic medalist

Tommy Kono is one of the great Olympic athletes in American history. As a weightlifter, Kono won three Olympic medals—two of them gold—in three Olympic games and in three weight classes. During his lifting career Kono won eight consecutive World Championships and broke twenty-six Olympic records, seven world records, and eight Pan American Games records. In 1982 *World Weightlifting,* the official magazine of the International Weightlifting Federation, named Kono as the greatest lifter in history, and in 1990 he was inducted into the United States Olympic Hall of Fame. Kono and diver Sammy Lee were the first Asian American inductees.

Tomia "Tommy" T. Kono

Introduction to Weightlifting at Tule Lake

Tomia Kono was born in Sacramento on June 27, 1930. At the age of twelve his family was imprisoned with other Japanese Americans due to the anti-Japanese war hysteria brought about by the Japanese bombing of Pearl Harbor. He was sent, along with his family, to the Tule Lake Detention Camp in northern California for three and a half years. In an interview with Bill Kwon in the *Honolulu Star Bulletin,* Kono said, "Of course I remember it. How can you forget it when you spend three and a half years? But it was rough on my dad and my older brother." After the war the family was released and they returned to Sacramento. Kono was sixteen.

During his imprisonment Kono met a couple of friends who introduced him to weight training. Kono was asthmatic and had trouble sustaining his strength. He found the training helped him physically as well as psychologically, as he endured being a prisoner in his own country. He continued training after his release and in 1948 he placed second in his first weightlifting competition.

Kono was inducted into the army in 1952 and was sent to Camp Stillman in California to prepare for combat in the war then being fought on the Korean peninsula. It was originally intended that Kono be shipped to the conflict, but some people who knew of his skill as a weightlifter intervened, thinking he was quite possibly an Olympic candidate. Kono was transferred to Fort Mason in San Francisco so he could be near Oakland, then the center of American weightlifting. The army funded Kono's training and paid for him to attend the Olympic trials in New York. The Olympics that year were held in Helsinki, Finland, and Kono competed as a lightweight, winning his first gold medal.

Following his Olympic victory, Kono began an unprecedented string of victories in international competitions. In 1953 he won the world middleweight championship in Stockholm, Sweden; in 1954 he won the world light-heavyweight championship in Vienna, Austria; and in 1955 he won the world light-heavyweight championship in Munich, West Germany. In 1956 Kono again qualified for the Olympics, held that year in Melbourne, Australia, and he put in a stellar performance. He set two Olympic and two world records, bringing home his second gold medal.

In 1957 his international domination continued when he won the world middleweight championship in Teheran, Iran; in 1958 he repeated at that weight in the championships held that year in Stockholm, Sweden; and in 1959 he won his third consecutive middleweight championship in Warsaw, Poland. In 1960 Kono went to his third Olympic Games, where he won a silver medal and set an Olympic record.

Mr. Universe in Triplicate

Kono also competed in bodybuilding. He won the Mr. World competition in 1954 and went on to capture three Mr. Universe titles in 1955, 1957, and 1961. Kono told Kwon that movie star and former bodybuilder Arnold Schwarzenegger, at age fourteen, saw Kono compete in one such competition. Following his amateur weightlifting career, Kono worked as a coach. He coached the Mexico national team in the 1968 Olympics held in Mexico City, and then served as coach for the West German team for their home stand at the 1972 Munich Olympics. In 1976 he coached the U. S. team at the Montreal Games, and from 1987 until 1989 he served as coach of the U.S.A. Women's World Team. Kono also serves on the board of the U. S. Weightlifting Federation.

Today Kono lives in Hawaii, where he moved in 1955 when he married Florence Rodrigues, a native of the island of Kauai.

Sources:

Kwon, Bill. "Kono in U.S. Olympic Hall of Fame," *Honolulu Star Bulletin,* July 5, 1990, p. D5.
United States Weightlifting Federation. "Tommy T. Kono: Titles and Achievements." Press release, 1990.

—*Sketch by Jim Henry*

Fred T. Korematsu
(1919–)
Internment Order resister, draftsman

One day in 1967, a young Karen Korematsu ran home from school brimming with excitement. In a presentation on the internment of 112,000 Americans of Japanese descent, she learned of a U.S. Supreme Court case called *Korematsu* v. *United States,* in which a young man challenged the government's orders to lock up an entire group of people simply on the basis of race. The young man turned out to be her father, Fred T. Korematsu.

The Internment Order

In 1942, Korematsu defied government orders that all Japanese Americans, like himself, turn themselves in. Instead of reporting to the assembly centers as he was directed, he continued living his normal life until he was finally picked up and jailed. Korematsu took his case to the U.S. Supreme Court and lost. He lived with this decision, a convicted criminal, for forty years. Then in November 1984, forty years after the Supreme Court ruled that the internment program was justified by wartime exigencies, his conviction was overturned by a judge in the Federal District Court in San Francisco.

"Fred Korematsu represents every Japanese American's desire for the trial they never had, to the extent that the internees felt victimized or treated unjustly," said Donald K. Tamaki, a partner at Minami, Lew and Tamaki in San Francisco, and one of the dozen or so attorneys on Korematsu's appeal. "Fred's a regular guy," Tamaki said. "To me, he's the epitome of the ordinary man who, under extraordinary circumstances, became heroic."

Besides Korematsu, the convictions of Gordon Hirabayashi and Min Yasui were also overturned in 1984. All three lent their names to cases that in some way challenged the government's wartime internment program. And they are familiar citations in law books describing the low points in the history of the Supreme Court's civil liberties rulings.

Private and Lonely Hero

But in the Korematsu household, the case was not discussed with the children, Karen and Kenneth. For all Japanese American internees, the internment camp was a bitter memory. Korematsu, had not only fought internment and the U.S. government and its justice system, he had also found himself ostracized by the Japanese

American community, which viewed him as a trouble-maker for even challenging the civil and military orders. It was a chapter in his life he would have preferred to forget. His decision to defy the evacuation orders was based on the simple notion that he had a right to live his life as all other Americans had.

A Childhood of Japanese and Football

Korematsu was born Toyosaburo Korematsu, in Oakland, California, in 1919. He was the third of four sons born to Japanese immigrants. His parents ran a flower nursery on twenty-five acres and spoke Japanese in the home. Korematsu remembers observing Japanese festivals, but spending much of his time playing sports—tennis, basketball, and football—with his classmates.

Soon after the Japanese bombing of Pearl Harbor on December 7, 1941, the U.S. government, wary of spies and saboteurs, began cracking down on the Japanese American population of the West Coast. Curfews were imposed and it became illegal to travel beyond a twenty-five-mile radius of a residence. Many Japanese Americans were interrogated by the FBI. Then on February 19, 1942, President Franklin D. Roosevelt signed an executive order that formalized the anti-Japanese sentiment. It called for the forced evacuation of Japanese Americans and resident aliens from the West Coast to internment camps inland.

Evacuees were first confined to temporary assembly centers. Korematsu's family was sent to the Tanforan center, a former racetrack. But twenty-three-year-old Korematsu did not go with his family. Instead, he changed his name to Clyde Sarah and had his eyelids surgically altered to make himself appear more Caucasian. He worked several welding jobs and lived in a boarding house. He planned to move East with his fiancee, an Italian American. "I felt just like before, as any American felt at that time, busy doing their own thing, working," recalled Korematsu in an interview with Steven Chin.

But on May 30, 1942, police picked up Korematsu as he waited outside a San Leandro, California, pharmacy. They took him to San Francisco County Jail. A short time later, he was approached by Ernest Besig, director of the American Civil Liberties Union in northern California, with a proposal to test the legality of the internment. Korematsu agreed to become a plaintiff in a test case to challenge the relocation program in court.

Internment and Legal Battles

Korematsu, free on bail, was sent to Tanforan where he joined his family. They were then sent to the Topaz internment camp in south-central Utah. Meanwhile, Korematsu lost his trial and was sentenced to five years probation. With attorney Wayne Collins, he appealed his conviction

to the Ninth Circuit Court of Appeals and lost. The final step was the U.S. Supreme Court. In December, 1944, shortly after the Wartime Relocation Administration had decided to close the camps, the Supreme Court handed down its decision.

"All legal restrictions which curtail the civil rights of a single racial group are immediately suspect," Justice Hugo L. Black wrote. But Korematsu "was not excluded from the Military Area because of hostility to him or his race," the justice continued. "He was excluded because we are at war with the Japanese Empire, because the properly constituted military authorities feared an invasion of the West Coast." Dissenting Justice Frank Murphy, one of three justices filing dissents, wrote that the exclusion order "goes over the very brink of constitutional power and falls into the ugly abyss of racism."

When the internees were permitted to leave the camps, Korematsu headed to Detroit, where he lived from 1944 to 1949 and worked as a draftsman. It was here that he married his fiancee, Kathryn, on October 12, 1946.

Korematsu's case resurfaced unexpectedly in 1982. Peter Irons, a historian and lawyer teaching political science at the University of California at San Diego, found new evidence while researching the internment cases. Irons discovered that government prosecutors possessed, but did not disclose, intelligence reports that Japanese Americans were, as a whole, loyal, and that the original final report by General John DeWitt, commander of the Western Defense Command, had been altered.

There was also evidence that the Office of Naval Intelligence had concluded that the Japanese American population was of no danger. Irons proceeded to contact Korematsu, Hirabayashi, and Yasui, and then contacted Dale Minami, a Japanese American attorney who had researched the cases, to ask if he would form a legal team.

Minami assembled the San Francisco Bay Area attorneys. In all, some two dozen attorneys from the Bay Area, Seattle, and Portland joined forces to retry the three cases, working on a pro bono basis. In San Francisco, key lawyers included Minami, Donald K. Tamaki, Dennis W. Hayashi, Karen N. Kai, Robert L. Rusky, Lorraine K. Bannai, Eric Yamamoto, and Leigh-Ann K. Miyasato.

On January 19, 1983, the attorneys filed a writ of *coram nobis* in federal court in San Francisco in *Korematsu v. United States*, arguing that the conviction should be reversed based on the evidence uncovered by Irons showing government agencies falsified, suppressed, and withheld evidence from the high court. The evidence, the petition said, concluded that there was no "military necessity" to forcibly detain Japanese Americans.

The hearing, which was held on October 4, 1983, was packed with three hundred Japanese Americans. Korematsu was permitted to make a statement on his own behalf. "Your Honor, I still remember forty years ago when I was handcuffed and arrested as a criminal here in San Francisco," he said, going on to describe the horrible camp experience. "As long as my record stands in federal court, any American citizen can be held in prison or concentration camps without a trial or a hearing. I would like to see the government admit that they were wrong and do something about it so this will never happen again to any American citizen of any race, creed, or color." Judge Marilyn Hall Patel granted the writ of *coram nobis*, vacating Korematsu's conviction.

Since the issuance of the verdict in her father's case, Karen Korematsu has established a civil rights fund in her father's honor. Additionally Korematsu, along with Yasui and Hirabayashi, are the subjects of a documentary by Steven Okazaki, entitled *Unfinished Business: Three Men who Fought the Japanese American Internment.* Korematsu has since moved back to the Bay Area and has become a celebrated elder spokesman for the Japanese American community.

Sources:

Books

Chin, Steven A. *When Justice Failed: The Fred Korematsu Story.* Austin, Texas: Raintree Steck-Vaugn, 1993.

Irons, Peter. *Justice At War: The Story of the Japanese American Internment Cases.* Oxford: Oxford University Press, 1983.

____. *Justice Delayed: The Record of the Japanese American Internment Cases.* Middletown, Connecticut: Wesleyan University Press, 1989.

Periodicals

Kawamoto, Jon J. "The Korematsu Legacy." *Daily Journal,* February 19, 1992.

Margolick, David. "Nisei Carves a Niche in Legal Lore." *New York Times,* November 24, 1984.

Other

Korematsu, Fred, interviews with Steven A. Chin, 1991-1993.

Korematsu, Karen, interviews with Steven A. Chin, 1991-1993.

Korematsu, Kathryn, interviews with Steven A. Chin, 1991-1993.

Irons, Peter, interviews by Steven A. Chin, 1992.

Minami, Dale, interviews by Steven A. Chin, 1992.

Tamaki, Donald K., interviews by Steven A. Chin, 1992.

—Sketch by Steven A. Chin

K.V. Kumar
(1945–)
Businessperson, political activist

K.V. Kumar is the president and chief executive officer of American Systems International, a Maryland-based software development and professional services company. He is also the founder and a former president of the National Indian American Chamber of Commerce and a powerful Republican party activist who has volunteered his time in numerous congressional elections. Kumar served in a variety of posts in the Bush/Quayle 1988 and 1992 election campaigns and served on the president's transition team following George Bush's election in 1988. He serves on a voluntary basis in a number of social service organizations, most notably the National Head Injury Foundation, the services of which he himself has needed since he suffered multiple head injuries in two separate accidents in 1992.

K.V. Kumar was born in Bangalore, India, on April 14, 1945. His father was a successful businessman, working as a management consultant. Kumar was an average student in school. He had trouble concentrating on his studies, he told Jim Henry in an interview, because, although he saw the value of academic training, he was more interested in "the practicality of life, and helping others" than in the abstract teachings of school. He attended private schools in India (what in America would be called public schools), graduating from high school in 1962.

Kumar went to college at the Bangalore Polytechnic, earning a diploma in industrial and production engineering in 1967. He came to the United States in 1968 as a student first to New York City, and later to Washington, D.C. To support himself while a student, Kumar was a messenger for embassies and international organizations. He also served as a priest at the Vittala Hindu temple, the first Hindu temple in the Washington area. Kumar also went to school part time at the University of the District of Columbia, and then finished his graduate studies at Southeast Asia Interdisciplinary Institute (SAIDI) in Manila, Philippines. He also began working at the World Bank, where he eventually became an operations analyst.

Banking in the United States

In 1987 Kumar left the World Bank to seek other opportunities. He was one of the founders of the First Liberty National Bank in Washington, D.C. He began work as a management consultant, working for a variety of concerns, mostly small businesses. As he became more successful as an entrepreneur, Kumar began getting more involved in American politics. In 1988 he worked as a strategic planner for the Bush/Quayle presidential campaign where he focused on getting the campaign's message out to minority voters. After Bush was elected Kumar worked as a deputy chief to the director of systems management in the telecommunications center at the Presidential Transition office.

After leaving this position, Kumar worked primarily as a management consultant, serving a variety of entrepreneurs, private/public sector and nonprofit organizations, and others in his fields of expertise—organization and management strategies, policy planning, business and organizational development, and negotiating strategies. In 1991, Kumar founded the National Indian American Chamber of Commerce. Writing in *India Globe,* Geeta Toteja noted: "One finds in the U.S. today, there are about 100,000 businesses owned and/or operated by Indians. Furthermore, there are manifold entrepreneurs, professionals, and corporate executives. Bearing this in mind, a group of dedicated and determined individuals recognized the need for a national organization to represent its interests before the public and private sector."

Charity Interests

In addition to his business success and his political activism, Kumar is a strong advocate of charitable works. He is especially interested in helping those in American society that are largely ignored, such as the elderly and the homeless and impoverished. He worked as a volunteer leader for the Washington, D.C.-based group Help the Senior Citizens, and became friendly with an elderly couple he assisted in a medical emergency some fourteen years ago. Kumar told Henry that he used to spend a lot of time with his grandparents in India, and that he had gained a lot from being in their company.

In addition to his charitable work, Kumar is a founding member of and management consultant to the Cauvery Medical International (CMI) in Anaheim, California, an organization made up of Indian American physicians and other professionals interested in establishing technologically advanced medical centers in developing countries. CMI is currently involved in a project that is building a 500-bed hospital in Kumar's hometown of Bangalore, India, expected to open in January 1995.

He has become involved with the National Head Injury Foundation (NHIF), working as a volunteer beginning in June 1994. The NHIF works to assist medical research in the field of head injuries and in providing social services to those who have suffered head injuries. Kumar works in family counseling with family members of patients, many of whom never completely recover. He became involved in this organization after suffering his own head injuries in 1992 following two separate falls that left him seriously impaired. This life-altering experience has had a profound

K.V. Kumar

impact on Kumar, changing forever his perspective on the meaning of status and accomplishment.

Kumar's recovery from his head injury has been long and difficult, and he told Henry that it would have been impossible without the support of his wife and the expertise of several doctors whose names he specifically asked be mentioned: Drs. George and Shobha Matthews; Dr. Robert S. Wilkenson; Dr. Sambhu Banik, a friend and political guru, and the man who helped Kumar regain his memory after six months of amnesia following his injury; and Dr. Nomita Sonty of the National Rehabilitation Hospital in Washington, where he now works as a volunteer.

Sources:

Periodicals

Toteja, Geeta. "NIACC Convention-A Grand Success," *India Globe,* June 1, 1993 p. 35.

Other

Kumar, K.V., telephone interview with Jim Henry, June 27, 1994

—Sketch by Jim Henry

Paul Kuroda
(1954–)
Photojournalist

Paul Kuroda

"**I** choose subjects that do not have a voice, that have been trapped in a dark corner of society," Paul Kuroda explained to Terry Hong in an interview. "I want to bring light to subjects that have been overlooked, that have gone unnoticed, that seem invisible. . . . I want to tell stories through my pictures, especially stories that will help rid our world of racism." Through his haunting pictures of the silent, the forgotten, and the downtrodden, Kuroda has gained distinguished recognition as one of the most effective photojournalists working today.

In 1991, Kuroda was named Newspaper Photographer of the Year by the National Press Photographers Association and the University of Missouri School of Journalism. The competition, for which 1,750 entrants submitted 35,000 photographs in thirty-five categories, is considered among the most prestigious in the world. The title is the most coveted recognition in newspaper photojournalism. The bulk of Kuroda's portfolio was comprised of two subjects: desperate Mexicans attempting to illegally cross the border into California, driven by the promise of earning wages to send back to waiting families; and young, lost Vietnamese gang members trying to survive day-to-day in Orange Country, California, caught between an unaccepting new country and the unbending cultural expectations of the faraway motherland. Kuroda was lauded for his ability to get close to his subjects, to develop a certain rapport that translated onto his vivid, startling images. In 1992, those same images of the illegal immigrants made Kuroda a Pulitzer Prize finalist in photojournalism.

Resolving the Anger

Born on February 13, 1954, in Fresno, California, Paul Kuroda was one of three children of a Japanese mother and a second-generation Japanese American. Kuroda grew up on the family farm, a twenty-acre plot at the edge of Fresno. "We lived on the farm," Kuroda told Hong, "in a very dilapidated home. It was falling apart when I was growing up, but it's still standing today—just barely."

Kuroda's father had been interned, along with thousands of loyal Japanese Americans, during World War II and, as a result, had lost a successful trucking business. Farm life was extremely difficult for the family and Kuroda spent his childhood in poverty. "Because of the internment, I think I also lost a lot of cultural things that might have tied me to Japan, like swords and other samurai things. These things were destroyed or given away because my father didn't want to appear Japanese in any way. He wanted to prove that he was an American," Kuroda remembered. "My father never talked about being interned. Instead, he was extremely proud of having served in the U.S. Air Force during World War II. His one wish at his death was to have a U.S. flag draped over his coffin. . . . And he got his wish.

"I spent so many years carrying around great anger over what happened to my father. That anger finally resolved a few years ago when I spent an entire day at Arlington Cemetery in Washington, D.C. I read the gravestones of the fallen Japanese Americans from World War II who were buried there. I visited the graves of John and Robert Kennedy. The inscription on R.F.K's grave was something to the effect that all the different people in this country have learned to work together, that we're more united than divided. That really hit home for me. That's when I finally came to terms with the unconscious animosity I felt toward our country."

Little Boy Lost

Growing up in Fresno was not easy for the young Kuroda. "Fresno is very small town. It doesn't have the diversity of San Francisco or Los Angeles. It was very difficult to find role models, especially Asian male role modes and that lead to a lot of problems in my life. I felt like a little boy who never belonged in this world. I spent a great deal of time pondering over why I was here," said Kuroda. An extremely shy child, Kuroda took to the camera early.

He bought himself a miniature camera from the local drug store and attempted to shoot pictures of a rare P-51 Mustang at the local airport. "I wanted to preserve the excitement, to capture the moment of having seen a P-51. Then I remember developing the film in water, hoping a picture would come out of it, and of course, failing," he recalled in an interview with *Photographer's Forum* in 1992.

Kuroda's interest in photography continued into college. He enrolled at California State University at Fresno in 1972 because, as he said, "it was close and it was cheap." Although he spent four years there, he never graduated. "I got a lot out of the four years there, I just didn't get that one piece of paper." Kuroda began his journalism career as a freshman when he was a reporter for the student newspaper. He also did photo-related work at the school's audio-visual center. To support himself, Kuroda worked in the library, bussed tables at Denny's restaurant, sold photo equipment at a mall camera store, clerked at Woolworth's, and delivered Chinese food.

At school, Kuroda took as many diverse courses as possible. "I was pretty much a rebel at the time and didn't believe in the system. I took ethnic study courses, such as Asian American studies, plus journalism courses . . . radio and TV writing, ethics in journalism," he told *Photographer's Forum*. He actually flunked the Introduction to Photojournalism course, but later became friends with the instructor with whom he "couldn't get along" at the time. The highlight of Kuroda's academic career was the creation of two 16mm films which began his career-long dedication to helping the disadvantaged. One of the films depicted the plight of elderly immigrant Filipino men living in what was San Francisco's International Hotel, which served as a form of low-income housing. Kuroda had hoped that a documentary might forestall the hotel's demolition, but the site eventually became a parking lot. Kuroda's next film captured the relationship between Japanese farmers' organizations and the United Farm Workers Union, exploring the possible racism of the Japanese American farmers toward their predominantly Mexican labor forces. "But I couldn't find anyone to air [these films]. So I decided that still photography was it."

In 1976, Kuroda joined the staff of the *Clovis Independent and Tribune*, a small community newspaper, where he worked for two years. "It was my first job. I didn't really understand the concept of a *job* then. I had a mission, instead. My mission was something simple that I determined when I was young—to make a change in the world before I die," Kuroda said. At the *Independent*, Kuroda was the only photographer. "I . . . was responsible for doing everything . . . making and shooting assignments, helping in layout. It was up to me to deal with the community, to make connections, to find the stories. But I was shooting real hokey things, for instance, kids making faces. It was very shallow photography at its worst," Kuroda told *Photographer's Forum* in 1992.

Acclaim, Acclaim

Kuroda quickly moved from the *Independent* to the *Fresno Bee*. "I really enjoyed the people there. It had a family-type atmosphere. Unlike other places I've worked, the *Bee* was a very loving place in many subtle ways." That family atmosphere nurtured Kuroda to national acclaim when, in 1984, the *Fresno Bee* was a finalist for a Pulitzer Prize for its coverage of the Coalinga, California earthquake. At the forefront of the coverage were images Kuroda captured so soon after the first shake that even the police had not yet begun to cordon off potentially dangerous streets.

After some eleven years, Kuroda joined the *Orange County Register*. "It was very good for me to work for a larger paper," he recalled. "My career really leap-frogged there. My boss was great. He let me run, while removing the hurdles I encountered in the *Register* building. He allowed me to crack through the shooting style of the *Register* which was known for its lighting. I don't artificially light my pictures. You end up putting yourself in the picture by using a strobe. You end up falsifying the subject. If it's dark, let it be dark, because that's the true representation." After six years, Kuroda left behind a solid legacy: "I changed the shooting style there. I proved that the paper can actually run dark pictures. I developed a documentary style of photo essays that the *Register* adopted."

Two projects brought Kuroda considerable acclaim—one on Vietnamese gang violence in southern California's Little Saigon and the other documenting illegal aliens crossing the Mexican border into southern California. Kuroda caught the young Vietnamese gang members between their two worlds—the strict Vietnamese and the more permissive American culture. Over three months, Kuroda became part of the dark gang world, often shooting at 2:00 or 3:00 in the morning. "It helped that I am of Asian descent. It would have be been very difficult for a photographer of non-Asian descent to do this essay. I tried not to stand out," he told *Photographer's Forum*. Little by little, he gained the members' trust, slowly understanding their involvement in gang life. "These kids—some of them as young as twelve—are frustrated and rebelling, and it can get ugly with guns. People do get killed. I wanted to show the tragedy of this . . . that these are in fact good kids, smart kids. But they just don't have the right support groups."

Kuroda spent six months working on the illegal immigrant photo essay. Shooting again at night, Kuroda once more developed strong bonds with his subjects. He himself made the border crossing several times, starting from the Mexican side. In order to protect the individuals and the position of their crossing, Kuroda shot the photos on black-and-white infrared film. The dark, haunting images show no distinguishable faces, yet capture the desperation of the night travelers.

Both essays helped Kuroda win the coveted award Newspaper Photographer of the Year in 1991. The competition is considered among the most prestigious in the world. Then in 1992, Kuroda became a finalist for the Pulitzer Prize for his images of the fleeing illegal immigrants. "When I take pictures, I try to dissolve any walls within myself that might inhibit me from opening up to the subject. I open up to the point that I become a part of the subject. When I was shooting the gang members, I became Vietnamese. When I was shooting the immigrants, I became Mexican. And that's when I become able to take real pictures."

Shoot for the Stars

After six years, Kuroda left the *Register* in 1993. "They didn't have the heart that I wanted them to have. I needed them to truly want me to do stories that were not just for greater profits or to boost the circulation, but because they really wanted these stories," he explained. "It all came back to my mission—to be an agent of change. I'm still reaching for it, still reaching high. I always say, 'Reach for the stars and if you fail, you'll land on the moon; aim for the sidewalk and fail, then you land in the gutter.' People should always have something unreachable, something to always keep you reaching high."

Convinced he could not achieve his personal mission at the *Register,* Kuroda moved to the *Daily Breeze* in Torrance, California, where he became the director of photography. He remained a mere six months. "I was the only minority in the newsroom. I was the director of a staff of only white males. There was not even a single female on the staff. I tried gently to apply my vision, which meant we went into the predominantly black population in Inglewood and the predominantly Hispanic population in Lenox. But the staff didn't really connect with these subjects, although

they tried. So I finally decided to head to San Francisco, a city that I had always wanted to live in."

Early in 1994, Kuroda became a photo editor for Associated Press. He is currently responsible for a staff of photographers based from Sacramento to San Francisco, covering the area from Fresno to northern Nevada. "AP's reputation in the past has been that their work is boring, superficial, but there are many who have been trying to change that. I saw that as a great opportunity for me," he commented.

In addition to enjoying his new job, Kuroda is enthralled with San Francisco. "I can actually feel the humanity around me. Even though I have a car, I enjoy taking mass transit all over the city. I enjoy seeing the diversity of the people. There are so many different people all around me, and they aren't isolated in their cars as they were in L.A. . . . Anyone can live here without being looked at funny. . . . There's just so much here. I want to stay here for a very long time. It makes me sing inside," he exclaimed.

Sources:

Periodicals

Hofland, Alison. "Paul Kuroda." *Photographer's Forum,* September 1992, pp. 46–52.

Other

Kuroda, Paul, telephone interview with Terry Hong, July 6, 1994.

—Sketch by Terry Hong

L

Cheryl Lau
(1944–)
Politician

Even as a student at Hilo High in Hawaii, Cheryl Lau was fascinated with politics. A voracious reader, just like her father, she read about politicians, their issues, and their personalities. She liked probing the organizational aspects of the political structure and the issues that politicians encountered. But the woman who is Nevada's secretary of state, the state's first Asian American to hold elected office at the executive level, and the woman who is strongly considering a bid to become the first Asian American woman to be elected a state governor, never dreamed of making politics a career. "In the 1960s, when I graduated from high school, women were encouraged to go into nursing, teaching, professions like those. I wanted to follow my mother's footsteps and teach music. So, I never considered politics."

Lau did go on to study music, obtaining a bachelor's degree from Indiana University, a master's degree from Smith College, and her doctorate from the University of Oregon. But her interest in politics never disappeared. In 1990, at age forty-five, a few years after obtaining a law degree from the University of San Francisco, Lau—an underdog and a political novice—entered the race for Nevada's secretary of state as a Republican and won.

Independent Thinker

Lau's affiliation with the Republican party often produces lively debate when she gets together with her father, mother, and two sisters. Hawaiians, after all, tend to vote Democratic, and Lau's younger sister, who campaigned for President Bill Clinton, served on Clinton's transition team. But the political differences encourage only debate, no barriers. "That's the kind of background I grew up with," she said. "My mother and father encouraged us to think our own thoughts, to always be willing to hear from both sides."

Lau draws much of her inspiration and inner strength from her family. She was born December 7, 1944. Although

Cheryl Lau

her father, Ralph K.Y. Lau, has only a high school education, he taught his daughters the importance of balancing a good education with a strong work ethic and respect for other people. Her father owns a dry goods store, which has been in her family for generations. He had to leave school to help his father run the store after it fell into bankruptcy. Over the years, Lau said, her father worked hard, read as much as he possibly could, and used his almost innate desire to show respect for others to make the business a financial success. He still runs the store in Hilo today. Lau, who worked at the store as a teenager, believes that experience shaped many of her political views. "I learned early on about the economies of running a business," she said. This shaped her belief in free enterprise, which she feels fits well with basic Republican party philosophy.

From her mother, Beatrice, Lau learned the importance of community service. Her mother has worked as a teacher, administrator, band teacher, and dental hygienist. She also remained active in community affairs. Lau also counts her grandmother, who spoke very little English and received no formal schooling, as one of her role models. "She had an innate philosophy of life that I see disseminated time after time in scholarly theses now," Lau said. "I have a great deal of respect for her."

Music and Politics

Lau studied piano and flute and entered Indiana University's highly-reputed School of Music intending to go into performance. She gave her final recital, however, shortly before receiving her bachelor's degree and began to focus on the teaching and research side of music. After earning master's and doctorate degrees, she became a professor of music at California State University in Sacramento. She eventually became director of the graduate division of the university's music department.

Lau got into politics almost by accident. While on a tenure track to become a full professor of music, she took some time off to attend law school at the University of San Francisco. Unsure whether she wanted to pursue law or continue her teaching and research, she took the bar in 1986. Shortly after, she was offered a position as a deputy attorney general in Nevada. "I thought of that job as a legal position, not politics," she said. "The thing that stimulated me about it wasn't politics at all. It was the opportunity to understand contract policies more. That was something I enjoyed while studying law."

She decided to make a bid to be secretary of state in a roundabout way. Shortly before the 1990 election, the attorney general, her supervisor, decided not to run for re-election. Instead, the secretary of state decided to make a bid for the attorney general post, which left the secretary of state position open.

Lau approached the Republican party to ask for support. Party leaders were encouraging but naturally hesitant. Newspaper editorial boards, too, tended to wave her off as inexperienced and endorsed her opponents. Nevertheless, Lau won both her primary and general election race handily. Her victory was even more unusual, considering that the eventual winners of the gubernatorial, attorney general, and majority of general assembly seats were Democrats. "I'm still trying to determine what made me win, and win (the general election) by 30,000 votes, a large margin at that. I felt I had the background and knowledge to do the job, but because I had not been very involved in politics, the Republican party didn't know me. Perhaps Nevadans were looking for a new face."

The Next Step

During her election, Lau talked about streamlining the secretary of state's office and bringing it into the computer age. During the last four years, she said she has cleaned up corporation codes, which makes it easier for businesses to obtain licenses in Nevada. She also has eased

antiquated problems in elections, regulations, which often had made it difficult for people to vote, and tightened the state's securities laws. After considering her options and the record she has built on such issues, Lau decided to try to climb the next step on the political ladder: On April 28, 1994, she announced she will run for governor.

Her personal secretary calls her a vibrant and exciting leader, who "ought to be president." Lau acknowledges laughingly that some people have asked her to consider running for a national office. Though she hasn't ruled out the possibility, she is not considering it currently.

As she spends her spare evenings and weekends campaigning, Lau occasionally reflects on her first career, music. "My father, he calls me up from time to time and says, 'Now, Cheryl. We spent all this money on you so you could play piano. Tell me, are you practicing?'" She isn't. But she hopes to get back to playing piano for enjoyment someday. For her, it's a wonderful way to relax.

Sources:

Lau, Cheryl, telephone interview with Himanee Gupta, March 16, 1994.

—Sketch by Himanee Gupta

Fred H. Lau
(1949–)
Law enforcement officer

Fred H. Lau is chief of inspectors for the San Francisco police department. He is one of the highest ranking police officers of Asian American descent in the United States.

Fred Lau was born on June 26, 1949 at San Francisco's Chinese Hospital, where his father, Harry, and most of his paternal relatives had also been born. The Lau family came to San Francisco in the early 1920s, when Lau's grandfather, Lau Cheuck Tong, immigrated from what was then the Territory of Hawaii. He operated Wing Duck, a store specializing in importing and selling Hawaiian food products, until his death at over 100 years of age. Lau's parents met when Harry traveled to Hong Kong. There he met his future wife, Carol. They were married and returned to San Francisco in 1948. Lau related to Susan Gall his early childhood memories of his mother studying English and American history for her citizenship exam at the same time he was learning to speak Chinese.

"It was a very proud day for me, the day my mother became a U. S. citizen."

Lau also has memories of his parents working very hard. "My dad was absent, but what I didn't realize at the time was that he was working two and three jobs to provide for us [Lau has a brother, Gregory]. Today, I appreciate so much all that he did."

Early Experience with Conflict Resolution

Lau received his education, from elementary school through college, in San Francisco. He attended Garfield Elementary School and graduated in 1967 from Galileo High School. While in high school, Lau had an experience that he describes as very significant is shaping his commitment to community service. "It was around 1967. There was a teenage dance in Chinatown's Victory Hall. A big gang fight broke out between two rivals groups, and I was struck in the head with a chair and knocked to the ground. A social worker, who eventually became one of my mentors, got me out of there safely. He began to tell me how important it was to stay out of such situations, to get an education. This incident led me in the direction of doing community work."

Lau became involved with Youth for Service, an agency which worked to convert African American gang leaders into "street workers," paraprofessional social workers. Lau became one of the first Asian Americans to volunteer, first while he was still in high school and then continuing through his junior college years. He told Gall, "I gained a tremendous amount of experience working within the city system. While helping to keep the community peaceful, I was trying to help myself also, trying to understand my own goals. My social worker mentor kept telling me, 'You can't represent your people until you represent yourself.'"

As adjunct professor at San Francisco State University, Lau shares with students his views on the importance of community service. "I'm a guest lecturer, trying to motivate people to do community work, to work within the city system. I convey my own commitment to community service—that it's important to substantiate your own personal identity, to return it to younger people." Lau has observed that as the Asian American community has grown up, many have dispersed to suburban communities, and no longer live in a strong ethnic community. For this reason, understanding and preserving his Chinese American heritage and sharing its importance with young people is vital to Lau.

Police Recruit, Give or Take an Inch

The seeds of Lau's interest in law enforcement were planted at that dance at Victory Hall in 1967. A lot of the problems in the urban neighborhoods where Lau was volunteering involved confrontations between young people on the street and the police. "There were very few recre-

Fred H. Lau

ational facilities. The streets became the meeting places. The alleys became the playing fields. Large groups of people hanging around led to misunderstandings and confrontations with the police." Lau and the other volunteers were trying to keep the young people out of the criminal justice system, and he became acquainted with the only two Chinese Americans on San Francisco's police force at that time. "They encouraged me to get involved with the force. They basically told me, 'You're always talking about how to keep the young people out of trouble. Why don't you join the force?'"

In 1971, as a police recruit in the San Francisco police department, Lau was only the 5th Chinese American to join the force in its entire history. (Preceding him were Herbert Lee, Donald Tong, Adrian Lim, and Alan Lim.) But his first attempt to join the force ended in disappointment—he was three-quarters of an inch shy of the minimum height (5 feet 8 inches) to join the police force. "I didn't quite meet the requirement, but I felt it was unfair. Many Asian Americans are a little smaller in height that other recruits, but we're as strong, as caring, as capable, as willing. I competed successfully on the physical agility test against other recruits who were six feet tall." The Asian American community joined Lau in challenging the height requirement, and he was able to get the requirement lowered by one inch so that he qualified. (Today there is no height requirement for police recruits in San Francisco). Lau views this experience, where he succeeded because of the support of his community, as another building block in his own commitment to community.

Lau has continuously advanced through the ranks in the police force. In November 1980, when he attained the rank of sergeant/inspector, he was only the second Chinese American to earn that position. And in each of his next advancements—to lieutenant (1984), captain (1986), commander (1988), deputy chief (1990), and chief of inspectors (1992)—Lau was the first Chinese American to have reached that rank. While with the police department, Lau has served in the patrol force, in community relations, in the gang task force, in the tactical company, in field operations and the administrative bureau, and has taught criminal law at the Police Academy. In his current position as chief of inspectors, Lau oversees criminal investigations.

Public Service, Lau Style

In his career with the police department, many would say that Fred Lau is already devoting his life to public service. But Lau goes beyond the challenges of public service in law enforcement to involvement with other spheres of the San Francisco Bay area community. Frequently invited to speak before groups of young people, Lau relishes the opportunity to share his philosophy with others. "It's a matter of self-esteem. Other ethnic communities have highly visible role models, whereas Asian Americans have been much less visible. I want kids to have someone they can look up to, to say, 'Hey that's somebody I want to be like.'"

Lau states his basic philosophy in terms of what he describes as his three families: his law enforcement family, his community family, and, most of all, his own family: "I have a tremendous responsibility to my three families. . . . Their expectations are high, but not nearly as high as my own. My families are my foundation. I will never forget them. I will make them proud." He tirelessly seeks ways to strengthen his three families, while at the same time achieving his own personal and career growth.

Although he is years away from retirement, Lau has more than twenty years with the San Francisco police department. During those years, he has received numerous awards for bravery and outstanding criminal investigations. Among these are the Bronze Medal of Valor, three Meritorious Conduct awards, two Police Commission Commendations, numerous Captain's Complimentaries, and, in 1990, the City College of San Francisco Government Award. In reflecting on his success, Lau points to his greatest role models, his parents, because "of everything they went through, so quietly. They are so caring and loving, first with us, and now with my brother's two sons."

Lau lives in San Francisco with his wife Barbara, who is from Hawaii. They expect their first child, a son, in December of 1994. His greatest hope is that he will be for his son the kind of role model his parents have been for him. The message he wants to share is : "Be proud of who you are. And be confident that your past generations were building blocks to your present life, and that your life will be a building block for your children."

Sources:

Lau, Fred. "Short Biography of Fred Lau." May 1994.
Lau, Fred, telephone interview with Susan Gall, August 18, 1994.
San Francisco Police Department. "Fred H. Lau, Chief of Inspection." Professional resume, August 1994.

—Sketch by Susan Gall

Ang Lee
(1954–)
Filmmaker

Ang Lee is an award-winning filmmaker, whose two films, *Pushing Hands* and *The Wedding Banquet,* have enjoyed considerable critical and commercial success in America, his native Taiwan, and in Europe. *Pushing Hands* won nine Chinese Academy Award nominations, and *The Wedding Banquet* took prizes at the Berlin and Seattle Film Festivals.

Ang Lee was born in Taiwan on October 23, 1954. His father was the principal of Lee's high school, so he was expected to do well academically. But when it came time to take the annual college entrance examinations, he failed them. As he told Jeff Yang in the *Village Voice,* "For my generation, that's like death."

Emigration to America

Unable to attend college in Taiwan, Lee came to America to study and enrolled in the theatre arts program at the University of Illinois. After graduation he enrolled in the prestigious New York University film school, where he was a classmate of Spike Lee, the noted African American film director. While in school, Lee worked on his student film and took odd jobs as cameraman on other student projects. He also won best student film award for his thesis, *Fine Line,* a comedy about an Italian trying to escape the Mafia and a Chinese woman hiding from the Immigration and Naturalization Service. While student films are rarely seen by people other than students, *Fine Line* did attract the attention of an agent with the giant William Morris agency. He put the young filmmaker in contact with the principals of Good Machine productions, Jim

Ang Lee

Schamus and Ted Hope, who had earned a reputation for making quality, critically respected low-budget films.

After he graduated in 1984 Lee entered what film insiders refer to as "development hell." He spent six years trying to sell Hollywood on making his films. He was continually encouraged and strung along in meeting after meeting, but nothing came of any of it. Finally in 1990 he entered his two screenplays in the Taiwanese government's annual screenplay competition. Remarkably, he won both first and second prize, with *Pushing Hands* taking first. The prize consisted of funding of the film. Lee received $500,000 to complete his first feature.

With funding he was able to work with Good Machine productions, who found the half million dollar budget more than ample. The film tells the story of an old tai chi master who moves in with his son and his son's white wife. Although the film was made in the United States, it was never released here. It was seen, however, at the Berlin film festival and in Taiwan, where it made so much money that Central Motion Picture, Taiwan's largest studio, signed him to make another picture. That picture would be *The Wedding Banquet.*

The Wedding Banquet

The Wedding Banquet tells the story of a gay Chinese American landlord who marries a female tenant of his to appease his parents, so afraid is he to face letting them

know the truth about his sexuality. The woman he marries goes along with the ruse to get a green card, the documentation immigrants need to stay in America. The film was well received in Asia, America, and Europe. Writing in the *New York Times* Stephen Holden said, "Considering that it cost only $750,000 [it] is a remarkably polished looking film. But its biggest strengths have little to do with production values. It is the unusual film comedy in which humor springs as much from character as from situation." In Taiwan it earned $4 million, which made it the highest grossing film in that country's history.

In 1994, Lee began work on the film *Eat Drink Man Woman,* which concerns a widower with daughters who are trying to find him a wife. It is to be filmed in Taiwan and will be distributed in America by the Samuel Goldwyn Company, the distributors of *The Wedding Banquet.* After that, Lee plans on "going Hollywood." As he told the *Village Voice,* "If all the variables are right, sure. Twenty-five million dollar budgets—that's a dream. But I want to do something I'm comfortable with. I don't want a Sony executive looking over my shoulder."

Lee is married to the former Jane Lin, a microbiologist whom he met while a student at the University of Illinois. They have two children and live outside of New York City. Lee considers spending time with his family to be of utmost importance, and as soon as the hectic pace of the last several years slows down, he plans on doing as much of that as possible.

Sources:

Holden, Stephen. "Inconvenient Marriage of Convenience." *New York Times,* August 4, 1993.
Hornaday, Ann. "A Director's Trip from Salad Days to a 'Banquet'." *New York Times,* August 1, 1993, sec. 2, p. 25.
Yang, Jeff. "Wedding Dues." *Village Voice,* August 24, 1993.

—Sketch by Jim Henry

Brandon Lee
(1965 - 1993)
Actor

Young Brandon Lee did not want to be known only as Bruce Lee's son. "When you have a built-in comma after your name, it makes you sensitive," he told *People* magazine shortly before his death. In life, the comparisons between father and son were unavoidable; ironically, in death, the two will remain even further intertwined.

Brandon Lee

Brandon Lee was suddenly killed while making his sixth film, his fourth feature; he was only twenty-eight. Bruce Lee was making his fifth film when he died mysteriously from brain swelling in 1973 at the age of thirty-two. Both achieved fame in action films; on celluloid, both were known for their martial arts performances. Years after the older Lee's death, a schlock kung fu movie called *Game of Death* was put together from all of the disjointed footage ever recorded of Bruce Lee; in the film, Lee portrayed an actor who is shot after mobsters substitute a live round for a fake bullet on a movie set. Fourteen years after that film was released, the young Brandon Lee died from a wound inflicted by a "live" shell that had somehow mistakenly been lodged into a prop gun on the set of his last film. Even more eerie, the film, *The Crow*, is about a rock musician who returns from the grave to avenge his and his girlfriend's murders; it was released one year and one month after the young Lee's death. In the posthumous film, the first image of Lee the audience sees is the actor in his grave, kicking vigorously, trying to break free.

Coming to Terms with Death

Born in 1965 in California to a Chinese American father and a Caucasian American mother, Brandon Lee was whisked away as an infant to Hong Kong. There in his native land, the not-yet legendary Bruce Lee hoped to build a more substantial film career than he was able to in the United States. By the age of two, Brandon Lee began training with his father in the martial art of Jeet Kune Do.

Living in Hong Kong as part of an American family, Lee grew up fluent in both English and Cantonese.

When Bruce Lee died mysteriously in 1973, the autopsy reported that the death was a result of brain swelling due to an allergic reaction to a painkiller. The sudden death left young Brandon fatherless at age eight. The young Brandon and his sister Shannon, three years old at the time of her father's death, moved to Seattle with their mother soon after the funeral. The family eventually settled in posh Rolling Hills, California. Being the son of a legendary film idol proved difficult for Lee. "When I was growing up, we moved around a lot, and whenever I'd get to a new school, there'd be somebody there trying to kick my ass," Lee said in 1992. When his mother took him for martial arts lessons at age nine, Lee noticed a poster of Bruce Lee on the wall of the studio, began to cry, and fled the room. Coming to terms with his mythologized father was a challenge Lee faced through most of his short life.

As a student, Lee was a rebel. He dropped out of high school twice and was expelled for misbehavior just months before graduation from the private Chadwick School in Palos Verdes, California. He finally received his diploma at another nearby high school.

Lee, who had wanted to be an actor since he was a young boy, began to take his training seriously. Unlike his father, who had no formal dramatic training, the young Lee studied drama at Boston's arts-oriented Emerson College and took acting lessons in New York City. He headed to Hollywood at age twenty, but finding roles proved difficult. Immediately, Lee was pigeonholed as Bruce Lee's son. He finally gave in to the inevitable in 1985 and made *Kung Fu: The Movie*, a television film with David Carradine. Like his father, Lee had to travel to Hong Kong to get on the big screen. There he made his first martial arts feature, *Legacy of Rage*, in 1987 entirely in Cantonese. Then came *Laser Mission* in 1989 and *Showdown in Little Tokyo* with Dolph Lundgren.

A longtime Lee family friend told *Premiere* magazine in 1993, "Brandon said to me, 'You know, for years I was in my father's shadow, and I resented it. I wanted to be an actor, not do marital arts films. But it finally dawned on me—I am who I am, and I might as well accept it. Once I realized that, doors started to open for me. I'll go in and do what they ask of me, and I'll use it to get to the kind of movies that I want to make.'" Although *Little Tokyo* was not exactly a blockbuster, it did begin to establish the young Lee as an actor to watch. After years of struggle, he spent his first paycheck from the film lavishly, buying an $80,000 Acura NSX sports car.

Lee's first starring role came with another action film, *Rapid Fire*, which was released in August 1992. He signed a three-picture contract with Twentieth Century-Fox, then embarked on a worldwide publicity tour to promote the film. "He was living for this," a friend told *Premiere*. For the young Lee, the contract, the tour, the potential fame was, in essence, a coming out from beyond the long shadows of his father's fame.

The Crow

The leading role of Eric Draven, a comic book hero from a series created by James O'Barr, in the film, *The Crow,* was to be Lee's career turning point. A strange, cartoonish horror film that defied categorization, *The Crow* little resembled the shoot-'em-up kung fu films that Lee was usually offered. Although not without its violent, bloody scenes, the story was one that intrigued Lee.

Ed Pressmen, one of the most respected independent producers in Hollywood, initially wanted Christian Slater for the role of Draven, a rock musician who returns from the dead to avenge his murder. Slater passed and Pressman signed on Lee who had lobbied heavily for the part since he had first read the script in the summer of 1992. Lee came relatively cheap, or rather he was considerably less expensive than Slater; Lee was promised $750,000 plus a small percentage of the gross. So enthusiastic was Lee about *The Crow,* he had already agreed to two sequels.

The first feature film directed by Alex Proyas, a young Australian filmmaker, *The Crow* was ominously plagued with problems from the first day of shooting—February 1, 1993. Filmed in Wilmington, North Carolina, where production costs were far less than in New York or Los Angeles, the crew worked under a constant cloud of fatigue, usually putting in twelve- and fourteen-hour days. "They wanted to make a $30 million movie but they only wanted to spend $12 million on it," one crew member who quit a few weeks into filming told *Premiere.*

A carpenter was almost electrocuted on day one. A storm destroyed sets. They were shooting at night in the worst of winter, often with forced rain, so it was always dark, wet, and cold. A crew member jammed a screwdriver through his hand. A stuntman fell from a roof and broke a couple of ribs. And director Proyas steadily became harder and harder to satisfy.

Fifty days into the shoot on March 30, Lee appeared on the set shortly after midnight. The planned shot was to be a flashback to the night of Draven and his girlfriend's murder in their apartment. Lee was to open the door and enter the apartment, bag of groceries in hand, to find his girlfriend on the verge of being raped by a group of thugs. One of the thugs pulls out a pistol and shoots him, the groceries scatter everywhere and Draven slumps to his death.

The death of Draven's character, however, would lead to Lee's own some twelve hours later. The .44 Magnum revolver was supposed to have been loaded only with dummy bullets (bullets without gunpowder) for Lee's final scene. It had been used in prior scenes and after

each use, it should have been properly examined and cleaned; however, with mishandling and lax precautions, a "live" bullet had dislodged itself deep into the barrel of the gun and had not been detected between uses. That bullet pierced a hole the size of a quarter through Lee's abdomen, ripped through his body with great force, and lodged next to his spine. Half an hour after the accident, Lee arrived at the New Hanover Regional Medical Center, but at the end of a five-hour operation, the blood could not be stopped and Lee's condition worsened. At 1:04 p.m. on March 31, Lee passed away, with his fiancée, Eliza Hutton, by his side. Hutton had rushed to North Carolina from Los Angeles and arrived an hour before Lee's death. His mother, unfortunately, did not arrive in time from Boise, Idaho, where she currently lives.

"The Lee Family Curse"

On April 17, 1993, just after *The Crow* was to have finished shooting, Lee and Hutton had planned to fly to Ensenada, Mexico, where they were to be married on the beach at sunset. Tragically instead, on April 3, Lee was buried at Lake View Cemetery in Seattle, next to his father. The next day, some three hundred mourners gathered at the Los Angeles home of actress Polly Bergen, a longtime family friend with whom Lee used to play backgammon.

Lee's sudden death brought back rumors of the legend of the "Lee family curse." Fans of the elder Lee referred to his posthumous, pieced-together film, *Game of Death,* as a foreshadowing of young Brandon's death. According to the legend, when Bruce Lee bought a house shortly before his death in a Hong Kong suburb called Kowloon tong ("Pond of the Nine Dragons"), he incurred the jealous wrath of the neighborhood's resident demons. The curse, it is said, lasts three generations.

Ironically both Lee actors have become almost mythic screen figures due to their early deaths. *The Crow,* its fate uncertain for many months following the tragedy, was finally finished on June 18, 1993. It lost its original distributor, Paramount, and was picked up by Miramax. The film opened in New York and Los Angeles on May 11, 1994, and was released on one thousand screens two days later in the company's widest release ever. The film opened to mixed reviews, amidst an air of great eeriness. Critics and audiences alike found it hard to separate the character Draven and the actor Lee.

The last interview Lee gave was less than two weeks before his death. Published posthumously in *Entertainment Weekly* just before the release of *The Crow,* Lee's words about his character leave behind a haunting, prescient quality: "You tend to take a great deal for granted, because you feel like you're going to live forever. It's only if you lose a friend, or maybe have a near-death experience [that] many events and people in your life suddenly attain real significance. When you take into account the fact that that could have been the last time I would ever see this person [or] do something so mundane as go out to dinner. . . . This is [where] this character is coming from. [He realizes] just how precious each moment of his life is."

Sources:

Periodicals

Ascher-Walsh, Rebecca. "How The Crow Flew," *Entertainment Weekly,* May 1 1994, pp. 18–21.
"Brandon Lee's Last Interview," *Entertainment Weekly,* May 13, 1994, pp. 22–24.
"Dying Young." *People Weekly,* April 12,1993, p. 63.
Goodell, Jeffrey. "Chronicle of a Death Foretold." *Premiere,* July 1993, pp. 70–78.
Lipton, Michael. "Lethal Weapon." *People Weekly,* April 19, 1993, pp. 80–86.
———. "Son of Bruce Breaks Loose." *People Weekly,* September 7, 1992, pp. 111–113.

—Sketch by Terry Hong

Bruce Lee
(1940-1973)
Actor, martial arts master

Before Hollywood discovered Bruce Lee the actor, he was already gaining fame as Bruce Lee the martial arts master. Blending elements of ancient kung fu with philosophy, Lee created a new technique called *jeet kune do,* literally meaning "the art of intercepting the first," the principles of which were published in his book, *The Tao of Jeet Kune Do.* The technique, which was far more psychological and spiritual than physical, was a fast and direct approach to martial arts which stripped away everything except the bare essentials. Lee's credo, as quoted by the *New York Times* in April of 1993, was the following: "The martial arts are ultimately self-knowledge. A punch or kick is not to knock the hell out of the guy in front, but to knock the hell out of your ego, your fear, or your hangups."

Lee's innovations with jeet kune do aroused tremendous outrage and skepticism in traditional martial arts circles, but eventually, its following packed martial arts competitions around the world. Hollywood came calling in the 1960s and 1970s to train such celebrities as Steve McQueen, Kareem Abdul-Jabbar, and James Coburn. Eventually, Lee the actor emerged in small television roles until his major break in 1966 when he co-starred in the television series, "The Green Hornet," as Kato, the hero's masked sidekick. In spite of Lee's success, he was convinced that his Asian features would not get him far in Hollywood and eventually, he relocated to Hong Kong where starring roles were readily forthcoming.

By 1973, Lee was well on his way to stardom with only four feature films completed. Already his films were the top-grossing ventures throughout Asia. His just-finished fourth film, *Enter the Dragon,* which was to catapult him to international stardom, was a mere three weeks away from its premier. He was already working on his next feature, ironically titled *Game of Death.* He had just finished shooting a death scene for the partially finished film when he died mysteriously on July 20, 1973. He was thirty-two years old.

The Star is Born

In 1939, Lee Hoi Chuen, a well-known Chinese opera star from Hong Kong, brought his wife and three children to San Francisco, California, while he performed there in a Chinese play. On November 27, 1940, in the Chinese year of the Dragon, another son was born to the Lee family. Because in Chinese tradition a new child is not named until the naming ceremony a short time after the birth, a name had not yet been selected for the infant. At the time of the birth, the father was performing in New York and the mother had not planned on an American name. However, in order to fill out the birth certificate, a name had to be chosen. At the suggestion of the physician, the infant was named Bruce, which means "Strong One" in Gaelic. His Chinese name was Jun Fan, which, according to *The Legendary Bruce Lee,* means "ever or always San Francisco."

The infant Lee made his film debut at age three months when he appeared as a stand-in for a baby in the American film, *Golden Gate Girl.* Shortly afterward, the Lee family returned to Hong Kong. According to Chinese superstition, jealous demons were said to carry away male children to the netherworld. Since Chinese culture long stipulated that female children were not as valued as their male counterparts, the Lee family dressed the young Bruce in female clothing, told strangers he was a girl, and called him the Little Phoenix (the legendary bird of Egyptian origin which was reborn out of its own ashes, and which represents the female side of the dragon). For most of his young childhood, Lee was even sent to an all-girl school.

With his father in the entertainment industry, Lee often visited movie sets. At four years old, he had his first walk-on, together with his two older sisters. Two year later, he had his first real part: "When Bruce was six years old, the director of his father's latest film saw him on the set and was so impressed that he offered him a part. His creative instincts instantly told him that there was something very 'special' about Bruce. At first both Bruce and his father thought he was joking, but he assured them he was

Bruce Lee

serious. Bruce, wide-eyed, open-mouthed, and deliriously happy, immediately accepted," recalled Lee's mother in the book, *Bruce Lee: The Untold Story.*

As a child, Lee was both mischievous and good natured. The same boy who would engineer elaborate practical jokes and clever pranks would also be helpful at the most unexpected times: "One day, I . . . saw him intently looking out the window down into the street. Suddenly he started running toward the door. I asked him where he was going in such a hurry but he didn't answer and just raced out. I walked over to the window to see what he had been looking at and saw him helping a blind man across the busy street. He later told me that everyone else was just walking past the poor man and he looked so sad and frustrated that he felt he had to do something," recalled Lee's mother in *The Untold Story.*

Enter the Little Dragon

As the young Lee grew out of childhood, he became more and more involved with street gangs. A strong, hot-tempered youth, Lee was constantly getting into trouble. On the streets, he became known as the Little Dragon. Lee was always an enigma—while he was turning into a street-wise ruffian, he was also cultivating himself as a dancer. With natural grace and agility, Lee proved to be an extremely talented dancer. His favorite was the cha-cha and eventually, he was crowned the Hong Kong Cha Cha Champion.

At the same time, Lee's darker side made him afraid that one day, he might not be able to defend himself. In order to develop himself into an invincible fighter, Lee decided to study the traditional martial art of kung fu. "Kids [in Hong Kong] have nothing to look forward to," he was quoted in the biography *Bruce Lee: Fists of Fury.* "The white kids [British] have all the best jobs and the rest of us had to work for them. That's why most of the kids became punks. Life in Hong Kong is so bad. Kids in slums can never get out. *I* always fought with my gang behind me. . . . I only took kung fu when I began to feel insecure. I kept wondering what would happen to me if my gang was not around when I met a rival gang."

In order to become a better fighter, Lee began studying at the Wing Chun School, which offered a sophisticated Chinese martial arts system that stressed economy of movement and springing energy. Reportedly founded more than 400 years ago by a woman, Yim Wing Chun, the style was based on the techniques of a Shaolin nun, Ng Mui. Yim felt that Ng Mui's style was too complex with too much emphasis on power techniques. Yim took the basics and created a simpler and more efficient method of defense which eventually came to be known as *wing chun.*

Under the tutelage of wing chun master, Yip Man, it became clear that Lee was especially adept in martial arts. After quickly learning the techniques, Lee began to add his own adaptations and variations to the traditional moves. Frowned upon by the established wing chun community, Lee was asked to leave the school. Years later when Lee became famous, the wing chun group attempted to reclaim Lee.

In spite of the street fights and gang activity, Lee continued to appear consistently in films, completing some twenty films before the age of eighteen. Not surprisingly, he was often cast as a rebel or juvenile delinquent. He was popular for his good looks and dramatic facial expressions. His pout and his scowl became trademarks of his performance.

Not yet out of high school, Lee was offered a film contract with Run Run Shaw, a powerful producer at the time. Lee announced to his mother that he would quit school and accept the offer. Although his mother was certain that Lee would someday be successful, she was also concerned that he at least earn his high school diploma. When Lee was picked up by the police for street fighting, his mother forbade him to accept Shaw's offer, and sent him to the United States to live with family friends and to finish high school.

An American Returns

Upon arrival, Lee settled in Seattle, Washington, and finished high school at Edison. He earned money giving dance lessons and waiting tables. After graduating, he entered the University of Washington, where he majored in philosophy. To support his education, Lee worked at Ruby Chow's, a popular Seattle restaurant, living in the restaurant attic and working at night as a busboy and waiter. In spite of financial hardship, he never asked his parents for money. After a few months of restaurant life, Lee quit and began teaching kung fu to his fellow students. One of those students was Linda Emery, whom Lee married in 1964.

Shortly after, the couple moved to California where Lee devoted all his time to teaching his new technique called Jeet kune do. He chose his students intuitively—if there was anything about a prospective student he did not like, he would not accept him or her. Eventually, Lee operated three schools for jeet kune do, in Seattle, Oakland, and Los Angeles' Chinatown. He called these establishments the Jun Fan Kung Fu Institute, bearing his Chinese name. Lee would later be approached by European investors to open a commercial nationwide chain of "Kato's Kung Fu School," but he refused, feeling that was not the correct way to promote his art.

As Lee became more and more successful as a martial arts pioneer, he struggled to become an American actor. Offers were small and slow in coming. After a few minor television roles, Lee finally had his first big break in 1966 with ""The Green Hornet" television series. The series which lasted only one season would later become a pop culture phenomenon and be remembered not for the man for whom the show was named, but for Lee's performance as Kato, the Hornet's sidekick. For the role, Lee literally created a fighting alter ego with fancy wide stances, flowing hands, cat calls, leaps, and high kicks. While it was in complete opposition to Lee's real-life fighting style as a martial arts master, that dramatic, overzealous style would come to epitomize Lee the screen actor.

After "The Green Hornet," Lee made guest appearances on such television series as Raymond Burr's "Ironsides" and "Here Comes the Bride." He had a small part in the film *Marlowe* starring James Garner. His performance in a few episodes of the series "Longstreet" with James Franciscus was critically well received. However, Lee's acting career on the whole was not progressing. Roles for Asian Americans were either stereotypical and demeaning, or small and forgettable, or a combination of both.

In an effort to change that, Lee helped develop the idea for the television series ""Kung Fu" about a martial arts expert who wanders through the Wild West, fighting villains with his wits and the ancient techniques of kung fu. When the starring role was given to David Carridine, a Caucasian American actor, Lee believed that he would not find the stardom he sought in Hollywood. Convinced his Asian face would only prove to be a hindrance in the United States, Lee packed up his wife and two young children—Brandon, born in 1965, and Shannon, born in 1967—and returned to Hong Kong.

In Hong Kong, offers poured in. Lee signed a two-film contract with producer Raymond Chow and Golden Harvest. His first feature film, *The Big Boss* (retitled *Fists of Fury* in the United States), was released in October 1971. Nervous about his first starring role, Lee would often slip into a movie theatre unnoticed and watch the reactions of the audience. Lee need not have worried, as the film quickly became the highest-grossing film in Hong Kong. The film also marked an important departure in the martial-arts film genre: "Most Chinese movies followed the Japanese," Lee said in *Bruce Lee: Fists of Fury,* "and there were too many weapons—especially swords. So we used a minimum of weapons and made it a better film. I mean people like films that are more than just one long, armed hassle. With any luck, I hope to make multilevel films here [in Hong Kong]—the kind of movie where you can just watch the surface story, if you like, or can look deeper into it. Most of the Chinese films to date have been very superficial and one dimensional. I tried to change that in *The Big Boss.*"

Lee's second film, *The Chinese Connection* (confusingly titled *Fists of Fury* for Asian audiences), which appeared a short year later, broke the records set by his first film. With his contract fulfilled, Lee launched his own production company, Concord Pictures. He now had full creative control not only to star in and choreograph his films, but he directed and co-produced his project well. The first film from Concord Pictures was *Way of the Dragon* [retitled *Return of the Dragon* in the United States], co-starring a very young Chuck Norris, and was not released until after the posthumous release of Lee's fourth film, *Enter the Dragon.*

The Lee Legacy—Promise Unfulfilled

For a vibrant man in such superb physical condition, Lee was obsessed with death. He talked often of dying young. That he died a thousand deaths on the screen only added to emphasize his mortality. When he did die suddenly on July 20, 1973, while in the midst of filming his fifth film, *Game of Death*, rumors of foul play circulated endlessly. The official version, according to the *New York Times,* was that he had died in the apartment of his mistress in Hong Kong, of a cerebral edema, or brain swelling, after an adverse reaction to aspirin which he had been taking for a back injury. Other reports stated the Lee's long and rigorous training schedule had literally exhausted him to death. Another theory suggested he had been given an untraceable oriental poison. Still more outrageous variations said that Lee had been given what was known in martial arts legends as the "death touch" by a rival master. Other rumors circulated that Lee had been murdered by the Chinese Mafia or greedy film producers with whom he had refused to work.

Whatever the cause of his death, the result was the same. Lee was three weeks away from achieving international stardom. *Enter the Dragon*, U.S.-produced by Fred

Weintraub and Paul Heller for Warner Brothers, was the film that would finally re-introduce Lee to American audiences as a bona fide action superstar. Two decades since its release, *Enter the Dragon* has grossed $100 million. Lee's final film, the unfinished *Game of Death*, was poorly pieced together and eventually released in 1979 by Columbia Pictures. Although intended by the studios to be a tribute to the late Lee, the film proved both an artistic and commercial disappointment.

With the mystery still shrouding his death, Lee remains a mythical legend, leaving behind an inarguable legacy that changed the course of martial arts films throughout the world. Tragically, his son, Brandon, would also die a mysterious death at twenty-eight while in the midst of filming *The Crow*, the film that was predicted to finally propel the young Lee out of the action genre, out of his father's shadow, and establish him as a film star of his own right.

Both father and son struggled to achieve their lifelong dream on the elusive silver screen. Both died just on the verge of certain success. Ironically, with their premature deaths, father and son are assured immortality—not so much for what they accomplished, but for promise unfulfilled.

Sources:

Books

Bruce Lee: *The Untold Story, Bruce Lee's Life Story as Told by his Mother, Family, and Friends.* Hollywood, California: Unique Publications, 1980.

Gross, Edward. *Bruce Lee: Fists of Fury.* Las Vegas: Pioneer Books, 1990.

Uyehara, M. "Bruce Lee: The Man, the Fighter, the Superstar." in *The Legendary Bruce Lee* by the editors of *Black Belt Magazine.* Burbank, California: Ohara Publications, Inc., 1986.

Periodicals

Phantom of the Movies. "The Lee Legacy." *Daily News,* {April-Jun 1993, deduced from contents of article], pp. 16-17.

Sharkey, Betsy. "Fate's Children: Bruce and Brandon." *New York Times,* May 2, 1993, pp. 1 and 22.

Sinclair, Abiola. "Bruce Lee: His Life and Times." *New York Amsterdam News,* May 22, 1993, pp. 28 and 53.

———. "Bruce Lee: His Life and Times (Part III)." *New York Amsterdam News,* May 29, 1993, pp. 30 and 56.

———. "Return of the Bruce Lee Story." *New York Amsterdam News,* July 24, 1993, p. 26.

Weinraub, Bernard. "Bruce Lee's Brief Life Being Brought to Screen." *New York Times,* April 15, 1993, pp. C15-16.

—*Sketch by Terry Hong*

Carol F. Lee
(1955–)
Lawyer

Carol F. Lee, one of Washington, D.C.'s most respected international corporate lawyers and general counsel of the Export-Import Bank of the United States, plays a key role in determining how the bank handles its more than $15 billion in annual loans, guarantees, and export credit insurance to support U.S. overseas sales. "She is creative and open-minded and smart enough to understand the intricacies of international finance. She has the ability to understand the changing dynamics of the world, and the fact that internationalization is a force to be reckoned with. And what the bank is doing is absolutely key to linking the global network that so many American companies need to and want to achieve," Claudette Christian, a lawyer in Washington, D.C., was quoted as saying in *Appointments with Power.*

As a member of the agency's senior management team, Lee provides advice on policy and program issues to the chairman and members of the board of directors. Lee and her staff of twenty lawyers negotiate and document all the bank's loans and guarantee transactions with governmental entities, commercial banks, corporations, and joint ventures around the world. Because of the Clinton administration's high priority on environmental protection, Lee has recently worked with administration officials to develop an environmental export program that safeguards both the environment and U.S. jobs by exporting pollution control equipment and other environmentally-friendly technologies. With the rapid growth of market economies in countries with which the Ex-Im Bank deals, Lee's department has also developed innovative structures for transactions with private sector borrowers in such big-ticket sectors as telecommunications, power generation, and oil and gas.

Carol Lee was born on September 17, 1955, to parents of Chinese ancestry. The Lee family lived in an English-speaking suburb of Montreal, Canada, until Carol was eleven, when they moved to southern California.. Lee demonstrated her brilliant intellect early in her life. In 1976, she not only earned a bachelor of arts degree *summa cum laude* with distinction in history from Yale University, but also won the Warren Memorial Prize for the graduating Yale senior majoring in humanities with the highest scholastic rank and the Fellows' Prize from Jonathan Edwards College. In addition, she distinguished herself by election to Phi Beta Kappa in her junior year and as a Yale National Scholar. Lee attended Oxford University in England as a Marshall Scholar. In 1978, she earned a bachelor of arts degree in philosophy, politics, and

Carol F. Lee

economics (PPE) with First Class Honors and the Highest Marks. She was also named an honorary college scholar at Wadham College. In 1981, she earned her J.D. from Yale Law School, where she was article and book review editor of the *Yale Law Journal* and teaching assistant to Professor Owen Fiss. In the 1980 Jessup International Law Moot Court Competition for the New England Region, Lee captured Best Individual Oralist, and her team won Best Team and Best Memorial.

After graduation from law school, Lee clerked for one year each for U.S. Court of Appeals judge J. Skelly Wright and for Supreme Court justice John Paul Stevens. As an associate at the D.C. law firm of Wilmer, Cutler & Pickering from 1983 to 1988, and as a partner from 1988 to 1993, she focused primarily on international corporate law and the regulation of international aviation in the United States and Europe. Lee also handled appellate and Supreme Court litigation and worked on federal election campaign finance law.

"She is that rare combination of a brilliant intellect and sound judgment. You sometimes get one without the other," remarked John Pickering of Wilmer, Cutler & Pickering, Washington, D.C. in *Appointments with Power.* "She also has the incredible capacity for hard work, the ability to organize, and to concentrate on what's important. She worked for me here . . . on some complex, difficult accounting issues in royalty matters involving leases on

Indian lands. It was a subject she had known absolutely nothing about, and she mastered it. She went on to carve out an important area of work in our international field."

In addition to writing many articles, Lee has been a lecturer in law at Harvard Law School and a visiting lecturer at Yale Law School. From 1985 to 1993, she served as a moot court panelist for the National Association of Attorneys General (NAAG), preparing state advocates for U.S. Supreme Court arguments, and won NAAG's Volunteer Recognition Award for Sustained Assistance in January, 1992. From 1988 through 1992, she was a member of the board of directors of the Association of Marshall Scholars. Lee also served as Vice-Chair of the Election Law Committee of the American Bar Association from 1991 to 1993 and is currently a member of the ABA Section of International Law, Section of Administrative Law and Regulatory Practice, and Section of Individual Rights and Responsibilities. In addition to joining the executive committee of the Yale Law School Association in 1990 and becoming a vice-president in 1993, Lee has served since 1988 on the selection committee for the J. Skelly Wright Fellowship at Yale Law School.

Lee's professional contributions also include a significant commitment to community service. For nearly ten years, she provided pro bono advice on campaign finance regulation to Common Cause. In addition, she gave legal assistance and wrote Supreme Court briefs for refugees seeking asylum in the United States and did constitutional research for the National Council for La Raza and the Lawyers' Committee for Civil Rights Under Law.

As a highly skilled lawyer who knows the international corporate world well, Lee told *Appointments with Power* that her future goals as general counsel for the Export-Import Bank of the United States include helping to "lead the bank to improved levels of service to U.S. exporters and their customers." As the bank is faced with the need "to do more with less" in response to significant budgetary pressures, Lee wants to help rethink procedures and programs to adapt them to the increasing demand from the private sector for Ex-Im support.

Sources:

Books

Rushford, Greg. "Carol Lee." In *Appointments with Power: An Insider's Guide to the Clinton Administration's Top Business Policy-Makers.* Washington, D.C., Legal Times Books, 1993.

Other

Lee, Carol, written interview with Helen Zia, July 21, 1994.

—Sketch by Nancy Moore

Christopher Lee
(1956–)
Entertainment executive

Christopher Lee

$\mathbf{T}$he fact that Tom Hanks won the 1994 Best Actor Oscar for his portrayal of a young homosexual lawyer with AIDS in the film *Philadelphia* was yet further proof that Christopher Lee, senior vice president of motion picture production for TriStar Pictures, is one Hollywood's top executives. "It's a project I championed with the studio. I believed the film could be both educational and entertaining. It would open people's eyes and teach them something as well as be a success, which it proved to be," Lee told Terry Hong in an interview. He considers the film, for which he was supervising production executive, to be his greatest professional achievement. "It was a great opportunity, an honor, really, to work with such incredibly talented people like Jonathan Demme, Tom Hanks, and Denzel Washington. I was just an advocate actually," he added modestly.

Born on October 30, 1956, in New Haven, Connecticut, to a Chinese American father and Scottish American mother, Christopher Lee is fifth-generation Asian American, with ancestors who first arrived in the United States to work on the transcontinental railroad. When he was very young, the family moved to Hawaii, which he considers home. He explained, "The main reason my parents moved us was because of the chance to live in a multicultural society. I feel very fortunate to have grown up among so many other Asian Americans."

Lee returned to New Haven where he attended Yale University, following in the footsteps of his father. He graduated in 1980 with a degree in political science. Considering his career in entertainment, he said with a chuckle, "I might have been better off with a philosophy or English background." He admitted, however, "Politics and entertainment are intimately codependent. There really is no formal training for going into entertainment. I do have creative instincts but I also have some political instincts. The political instincts are very important in this business."

Going to the Movies

Lee left New Haven and headed south to New York City where he began his entertainment career in television. Working on ABC's *Good Morning America*, Lee was an entertainment segment producer which meant he "did a lot of movie reviews, award show coverage, and things like that." For three years he learned about the small screen world until he left New York in 1983 to join Wayne Wang (possibly Asian America's preeminent director) on the set of Wang's second feature film, *Dim Sum.* Lee worked as first assistant director and assistant editor on the film. "It was a low-budget project so everyone had to do a bit of everything. It was like going to film school without paying any money for it but hardly getting paid, and in the end we had a good little product," he recalled. Most importantly, working on the film taught Lee that he "did not want do production or post-production, which left only one choice—project development as a studio executive."

Toward that goal, in 1985, Lee walked into the offices of TriStar Pictures as a free-lance script analyst. The job, however, lasted all of two weeks before he was hired as assistant story editor. "I got lucky," he chuckled. His goal to become a studio executive was clear. "There are only three ways to become a studio exec," he explained. "You have to either be someone's assistant first, be a reader or be a Beverly Hills High School graduate." He laughed, then added, "Seventy percent of my colleagues are related to or grew up knowing someone in the business. I didn't. And I also didn't have the right last name." But he did quickly gain experience reading scripts.

Regardless of his name or his diploma, Lee moved up quickly through the TriStar ranks. He remained an assistant story editor for a couple of years, then director of creative affairs for about a year, then moved on to vice-president of production for less than two years. Then in 1989, Lee took his current position as senior vice-president of motion picture production.

Lee's fast-track career is crowded with credits. He has recruited new and innovative filmmakers to TriStar, including Gus Van Sant (*Drugstore Cowboy*), John Woo (*The Killer*) and Cameron Crowe (*Singles*), while developing successful new projects with established talents, such as Paul Verhoeven (*Basic Instinct*) and Jean Jacques Annaud (*The Lover*). Lee's latest projects include a new Anthony Hopkins film, *Legends of the Fall*, also starring Brad Pitt and Aidan Quinn, due out in fall of 1994; Norman Jewison's romantic comedy, *Only You*, with Marisa Tomei and Robert Downey, Jr.; Paul Verhoeven's new sci-fi flick, *Starship Troopers*; and an American remake of the all-time lizard legend, *Godzilla*, which, Lee promises, is "going to be great." But, says Lee, who is always working on twenty or thirty projects at a time, "It's always easier to talk about what *did* get made rather than speculate on what *might* be made."

Not Your Typical Exec

A typical working day for Lee begins at 8:00 a.m. and usually goes until 11 p.m., although later-than-midnight evenings are far from rare. "There are a lot of meetings, phone calls, reading, social engagements, always a lunch and dinner." He cited as a recent example that after a full schedule in his office, he "went to a panel discussion, a fund-raiser, a film premiere, then had three scripts waiting for [him] when he got home." As reading scripts is one of his more important tasks, Lee averages two every night and ten on weekends. "I probably read all the way through half of them and read thirty to forty pages of the others," he remarked.

While Lee has earned one of the top seats in Hollywood, he has also established himself in the Asian American community as an invaluable resource. He is a member of the Board of Governors of the Los Angeles Festival and a founding member of the Coalition of Asian Pacifics in Entertainment. In 1991, he served as executive producer of the 1991 Association of Asian Pacific American Artists Media Awards. In 1992, he was cited as Asian Business Person of the Year by the Asian Business League of Southern California.

Informally, Lee continues to give back to the Asian American community by helping Asian Americans find jobs and by hiring Asian American writers. In addition, he has "worked very hard to connect Asian executives together, to facilitate the executives getting to know one another better." Most importantly, he has made himself readily available to the Asian American community. "I think I'm an accessible person," he commented, and many would agree.

Regardless of the countless demands of his professional schedule, Lee is a frequent speaker on minority empowerment for schools and multicultural groups. He admitted that he prefers speaking in front of students: "I'm always looking for that new generation of writers, directors, and producers. I already know a lot of actors but if they have

no roles to play, no movies to be in, then there's only frustration all around." To the young Asian American who is interested in a career in entertainment, Lee advised, "Decide what aspect of the entertainment business you want to be involved with. I wanted to be an executive and was really focused toward that goal. If you want to be in production, then be a production assistant. If you want to be a writer, write. If you want to be a director, go to directing school or go work on a film if you can't go to school."

What the Future Holds

Lee is the first to admit that the bastion that is Hollywood is finally changing. "In the past, Hollywood has flirted with Orientalia. What was different was that none of the older movies were produced, written, or directed by Asian Americans; Asians starred in the films, although a lot of times, not even that." Lee is convinced that the recent influx of Asian and Asian American films which have brought such successes as Chen Kaige's *Farewell My Concubine*, Ang Lee's *Wedding Banquet* and Wayne Wang's *Joy Luck Club* to the mainstream screen will continue. "What people don't realize is that these films were made by people who have been making films for a long time. We've known each other for ten or fifteen years; we've been struggling together. It just happens that the timing is all coming together now. Of course, they will continue to make films. These people are not suddenly going to become accountants or dentists or anything—they're going to keep on making films," he emphasized.

Regarding his own future, Lee offered, "Hopefully I'll continue with the studio making films. Eventually, I hope to become a producer. That's what happens to everyone."

Sources:

Lee, Christopher, telephone interview with Terry Hong, April 27, 1994.

—Sketch by Terry Hong

C.Y. Lee
(1917–)
Author

Chin-Yang Lee is a pioneering Asian American writer, most notably of the best-selling 1957 novel—his first—*Flower Drum Song*, which was turned into a Rodgers and Hammerstein musical on Broadway and a movie. He is often cited as a source of inspiration by the many young Asian American writers of today.

Chin-Yang Lee was born on December 23, 1917, in the Hunan province of China. His father was a landlord of moderate means and the head of a family of eight brothers and two sisters. China was in the midst of many years of civil war and unrest during Lee's childhood, and by the time he went to college the family could not afford to send him anywhere but the Southwest Associated University in Kumming, a school for refugees and the poor. Lee earned his bachelor's degree in 1942 and then decided to sell his personal possessions in order to come to the United States.

In the United States

Lee arrived in the United States in 1942 and enrolled in the graduate comparative literature program at Columbia University in New York City. He transferred to Yale's graduate writing program after a friend suggested he could make a living writing screenplays for China's then-forming film industry. Ann Elmo, a New York literary agent, saw one of his plays performed at Yale and signed Lee on as a client.

After his graduation from Yale in 1947, Lee set out to return to China. While in Los Angeles, though, he got word from his family that things were not going well in the ongoing civil war and that it looked like the Communists would come to power. He remained in the United States and found a job as a daily columnist for *Chinese World*, a Chinese-English newspaper published in San Francisco's Chinatown. His column was called "So I Say" and was very popular. In 1949 Lee won $750 in a contest sponsored by *Writer's Digest* for his short story "Forbidden Dollar," which was anthologized in *Best Original Short Stories* that same year. Also in 1949 he became an American citizen.

Flower Drum Song

Lee began working in earnest on his novel after he became a full citizen. He delivered it to Elmo in mid-1955 and she began sending it out. Like many first novels it was rejected by nearly every major publishing house in New York. The story of how the book was finally picked up by Farrar, Strauss, and Culhady, an eminent literary publisher, is one Lee relishes. In an essay entitled "The Short-short That Changed My Fate," Lee recounted, "According to John Farrar . . . the manuscript had at first landed on the sick bed of an 80-year-old reader. The elderly gentleman, having finished the book, didn't have enough energy to write a detailed critique. With his last bit of strength he scribbled on the dog-eared cover, 'Read this' and died."

Flower Drum Song exceeded everyone's expectations, including the publisher's. The book became something of a sensation, making it on to the *New York Times* best-seller list and creating a bidding war among Hollywood studios for the film rights. Lee had become a celebrity overnight and met such Hollywood notables as Gene Kelly, Groucho Marx, Marlon Brando, Steve Allen, and Shirley MacLaine. In 1959 the mayor of San Francisco presented Lee with a key to the city, and the governor sent him a letter of congratulations at his success.

The fame also earned Lee a job as a screenwriter and story editor at 20th Century Fox. He went from editing the San Francisco newspaper *Young China* where he was paid $175 a month to making $1250 a week at Fox. His career in Hollywood was short-lived, however. The first project he was to work on for Fox, a film about Buddha, was scrapped when a production company in Japan began work on a similar project. Lee lost his job at Fox and then devoted himself to his fiction. In 1958 he published *Lover's Point*; in 1959 *The Sabwa and His Secretary: My Burmese Reminiscences*; in 1960 *Madame Goldenflower*; in 1961 *Cripple Mah and the New Order*; in 1964 *The Virgin Market*; and in 1967 *The Land of the Golden Mountain*. This marked the end of an incredibly prolific period in Lee's life—five novels and two memoirs in a decade.

Lee did not publish again until the 1987 historical novel *China Saga*, which follows four generations of a family through a century of Chinese history, from the Boxer Rebellion through the cultural revolution. In 1990 he published *The Second Son of Heaven*, another historical work, this one about the Taiping Rebellion. Lee was deeply affected by the pro-democracy movement in his homeland in late 1989 and by the massacre at Beijing's Tiananmen Square in which government tanks moved to disperse peacefully demonstrating students. In response to this horrific event, Lee wrote a novel called *Gate of Rage: A Novel of One Family Trapped by the Events of Tiananmen*, published in 1991.

Lee has remained considerably involved and interested in the events of his native land since coming to America. Much of his fiction details life in China rather than the experience of the immigrant in America. Considering the scope of historic upheaval China has endured in the space of Lee's lifetime, his choice of subject matter is not surprising. He discussed his position as a Chinese writer living as an American citizen in a *Publishers Weekly* interview published in 1987 to coincide with the release of *China Saga*: "I am an American citizen and my loyalties are here in this country, but I have always hoped that China would become prosperous and raise its standard of living. Though the people are still poor, they're not dying in the streets anymore. But in order to catch up with Western countries, the government will have to continue to encourage free enterprise and personal freedom."

Sources:

Lee, C.Y. "The Short-short That Changed My Fate."
See, Lisa. "C.Y. Lee Interview." *Publisher's Weekly*, August 14, 1987, pp. 84–85.

—Sketch by Jim Henry

Gus Lee

(1946–)

Writer

Gus Lee, one-time attorney, now full-time writer, began his first book in 1989 as a private memoir. "My daughter asked me to write a family journal and it turned out to be *China Boy*," he explained in an interview with Terry Hong. Not only was the work Lee's first novel, but it was also the first time he had ever attempted fiction writing. "I just wrote this book. For me, it was a miracle," he recalled. Using a favorite analogy, Lee compared his literary success to baseball: "Say you always wanted to bat .300, but had never played a game before. You're at the ballpark and they let you hit. Everything they pitch, you hit, and you didn't even know you could hit before. That's the way I feel about writing. I never had any literary training, did any workshops. *China Boy* just happened."

The semi-autobiographical *China Boy* introduced audiences to Kai Ting, the American-born son of transplanted Chinese parents, who grows up in the predominantly African American Panhandle neighborhood of San Francisco, California. The book was widely heralded: the *New York Times Book Review* compared the novel to Amy Tan's *The Joy Luck Club* and Gunter Grass' *The Tin Drum; Publishers Weekly* referred to it as "the Chinese American experience as Dickens might have described it"; the *Washington Post Book World* praised it as "marvelous"; and *Time* magazine called it "delightful." *China Boy* proved to be a six-month best seller, a Literary Guild selection, a Random House Audio-Book and one of the *New York Times* Best 100 for 1991.

In 1994, Lee produced the second installment in the life and times of young Kai Ting, following him through his training at West Point where Lee himself was educated. *Honor and Duty* also received glowing praise from the *New York Times Book Review, Publishers Weekly, The Chicago Tribune, The Los Angeles Times* and numerous other major publications. It, too, has proved to be a best seller, and was chosen as a Book of the Month Club selection and a Random House AudioBook.

Growing up Asian American

Born August 8, 1946, in San Francisco, Gus Lee was the only child born in the United States to parents Tsung-Chi and Da-Tsien (née Tsu) Lee. Lee's four older sisters (including one who died in infancy) were all born in China. "My family was very lucky to get out," said Lee. The once wealthy and aristocratic Lee family fled China during the Japanese invasion and arrived in the United States in 1945 to settle in the poor and mostly African American Panhandle district of San Francisco.

Gus Lee

"I lived in the Panhandle through junior high school," Lee recalled. "At times it was very tough, but eventually it just became my world. My objective was to become a successful black youth," he added with a laugh. "I never completely mastered it, but it was an honorable objective. Just not one for which I was naturally suited." From the age of nine, Lee worked part time at the local YMCA at various odd jobs. "I was the only kid hired back then. I actually handled the cash register, which was especially rare for a Chinese kid," he recalled.

In high school, the Lee family moved to the Sunset district where Lee graduated from Lincoln High School. He entered West Point at the urging of his father, who had been an officer in China. "It was unusual and different being Chinese at West Point, but it was very hard being a cadet for everyone," Lee remembered of his experiences. "I was supposed to be there for four years and we got rice maybe once a week," he laughed.

During Lee's third year, he took an engineering class from H. Norman Schwarzkopf, who would later become famous as the American field commander in the Persian Gulf War. He did well in the class, but not so well in other engineering classes. "The humanities department thought I was a pretty good student, but the engineering department thought I had been dropped on my head. I really was a bad engineering student," he confirmed. "I just didn't do my homework. I read lots of Chinese history, military history, studied the Vietnam War avidly. I was studying, just not the curriculum."

With one failed electrical engineering class, West Point discharged Lee and he left to assume his assigned post as a drill sergeant. "It was a painful separation, one that affects me to this day," he said. Although Lee was eligible to be sent to Vietnam, he was not. He returned to California and applied to the University of California at Davis which initially denied him admission because, as he recalled, "I had flunked out of a major college back east." It took a letter from then Major Schwarzkopf for Lee to finally be admitted and, in three quarters, he earned his undergraduate degree.

The Education Continues

Lee remained at the University of California to begin a Ph.D. program in Chinese history which evolved into a nine-year commitment. "I loved the subject, but I didn't have the will to go on that long so I went to law school instead," Lee said. While a graduate student at Davis, Lee was an assistant dean in the Educational Opportunity Program, serving low-income and minority students. He helped found the school's Asian American studies department and the Third World Council, and he coordinated the national Asian American Studies Conference.

After graduating in 1976 from law school, Lee returned to the army and was sent to Korea where he served as a criminal defense lawyer. He returned to California in late 1978 when he was reassigned to the Presidio in San Francisco. "Then I met my wife Diane. We had a whirlwind romance and got married after knowing each other for six months. Pretty amazing for a die-hard bachelor like me," Lee recalled.

At his wife's urging, Lee finally left the army in 1979. "But I really hated leaving," Lee said. "I was not comfortable being a Chinese man in the real world. In the army, everyone is green. In the real world, you're the color that's on your face." As a civilian, Lee said he quickly realized that "the politics of discrimination are always with you, whether you're pro-active or not." He added, "So if it was always going to be there, I decided I might was as well do something to make it better."

With that goal in mind, Lee took the position in 1980 of deputy district attorney in Sacramento. Three years later, he was a senior deputy district attorney, trial team leader, and police and attorney trainer for Sacramento County. In 1985, Lee was named deputy director for the California District Attorneys Association, where he created and directed skills-based trial advocacy training programs for California's prosecutors with an emphasis on child sexual assault and domestic violence. Four years later, as a senior executive for the State Bar of California, Lee designed and implemented mandatory continuing legal education for California's 130,000 attorneys.

During his legal career, Lee conducted over two hundred criminal trials and received awards for trial advocacy, legal education, community work, and military service, including the University of California at Davis Alumni's 1991 Citation for Excellence, Outstanding Instructor Awards from the California District Attorneys Association and West Point, the army's Meritorious Service Medal with first oak leaf cluster, and the Order of the Silk Purse.

The Writer Emerges—Fully Formed

In 1993, Lee left law to become a full-time novelist. With the 1991 success of *China Boy*, his first novel, in addition to fulfilling the duties of his legal career, he was constantly in demand to give lectures and presentations throughout the United States. Unable to spend the time he desired with his wife and two children, he finally chose one career.

No longer professionally tied to California, Lee moved the family to Colorado the same year. "In California, I was under a great deal of stress between my work, my volunteer activities, my writing. I was gone all the time and was a very inadequate father. The irony was that on the outside, I might have looked like a good father, because I was giving talks all the time about being a good father since I had learned all those lessons of accountability from writing my book . . . but at that time, I really wasn't doing what I was preaching. So I literally asked the kids if they would be willing to move and leave California in order to get their dad back. I had a genuine fear that they might just say, 'No, thanks, nice of you to ask but no,' etc. But they said yes and so we headed for Colorado."

Writing came naturally to Lee. "It's easy for me to write stories with a moral core," Lee stated. "It's not because of anything in me, but because of experiences that have unfolded in my life and because it's a gift. I would love to tell you it's been an arduous process, that I've struck out at bat in fields all over the country and it finally culminated in my hitting the ball. Writing is just something I can suddenly do now. I find myself regarding the gift as a religious experience. I have a rational mind, but I have no way to explain this. I just recognize it as something that is as amazing as the sun coming up every morning."

After writing *China Boy*, getting the novel to the public proved virtually effortless, which Lee credits to his agent, Jane Dystel. "I had no problems finding a publisher. It was preposterously easy. But that wasn't my job, it was Jane's. She was the one who made it so easy. Yes, I've been lucky with publishers and editors, but it all starts with your agent," he insisted modestly.

Following the success of *China Boy*, it was Dystel who suggested to Lee that he submit a proposal for a second book. "She told me 'You don't have to write the whole book, just get me a proposal.' So I did and lo and behold, the proposal went to auction and it got sold. So I wrote the book." *Honor and Duty* shows every indication that it will be as successful as his first book. Published by Knopf, the novel is slotted for paperback publication in 1995.

Lee is currently at work on a third book, *To Pull the Tiger's Tail.* "It's the capstone to the trilogy about Kai Ting. He gets to have an excellent adventure and then he'll get a vacation after a very happy ending. In the first two books, he was still growing up and going through his tutelage. He was a boy becoming a page, then a page struggling to be a knight . . . without all the armor. Now he's finally a knight, no longer in training, someone who must deliver and serve." He paused, then added with a laugh, "Sounds like he's a waiter . . . which isn't a bad job, either."

A Bit of Advice

Although Lee cannot explain his writing gift, he offered a few words about taking a project to completion. "I think you need to have a certain amount of relaxed persistence about writing. It's like kung fu or baseball. You can't force it and be successful, but at the same time, you can't not practice and expect to be successful. I paid my dues by having a miserable childhood. So I had angst early on and then had an easy time writing. Although I think it's probably better to have a good childhood and then a lousy time writing.

"The other thing is you really have to have time. If you can't create adequate time for writing, then you'll have to lower your expectations for what you're going to accomplish." Lee paused with a last warning, "I have to go back to baseball. . . . So if you're in mid-swing, and you stopped to say, 'oh, I have to answer the phone,' or 'I have to go to that meeting,' what kind of contact can you possibly make with the ball? So time is very, very important.

"Also, I think it's crucial not to focus on what the writing will do for your economics or for your profession. It's very important to focus on what the writing can do for your own learning and your teaching of others. If you say you're going to write the great American novel, there are too many ways of failing. Whereas, if you say you're going to write about something you know, something where you can see a moral core to the message, and you're truly interested in telling the story, then how can you go wrong?"

Sources:

Lee, Gus, telephone interview with Terry Hong, June 6, 1994.

—Sketch by Terry Hong

Harry Lee
(1932–)
Sheriff

Harry Lee, known by many as the "Chinese Cowboy" of Louisiana, is one the first Asian American sheriffs in the United States. He has served as sheriff of the parish of Jefferson, a suburb of New Orleans, since 1980. The parish, one of the state's largest counties with about 470,000 residents, consists mostly of white, upper-class neighborhoods. Seen as a tough crime fighter, Lee is responsible for operating the sheriff's department's $60 million budget and supervising about fourteen hundred employees as of 1994.

The son of Chinese immigrants, Lee was born in New Orleans, Louisiana, on August 27, 1932. The third of six children, he grew up working in his father's restaurant. He was elected class president and student body president in grade school. Lee received a bachelor's degree in geology from Louisiana State University, where he was named an outstanding ROTC cadet. After graduating, he served in the U.S. Air Force for nearly three years, during which he was rated in the top two percent of junior officers.

After his stint in the air force, Lee returned home to help open and manage his family's new restaurant, the House of Lee Restaurant, in the Jefferson Parish community of Metarnie for eight years. During that time, Lee was elected president of the New Orleans chapter of the Louisiana Restaurant Association in 1964. He was credited for helping lead the peaceful integration of New Orleans' restaurants after the enactment of the 1964 Civil Rights Act.

While working seventy-two hours a week at the family restaurant, Lee took law classes at Loyola University in New Orleans. He also served as an unpaid aide to the late Louisiana congressman Hale Boggs, a high-ranking Democrat in the House of Representatives and one of the few Southern congressmen who supported civil rights legislation.

Career in the Legal System

After Lee received a law degree in 1967 and had a few years of law practice under his belt, he was appointed a U.S. magistrate for the Eastern District of Louisiana with the help of Boggs. And in 1973, he was elected president of the National Council of United States Magistrates. Lee resigned from the federal office after four years of service as a U.S. magistrate, and later accepted an appointment as parish attorney for the parish of Jefferson, an office he held for another four years until he resigned to run for the sheriff's office.

He is serving his fourth term as sheriff of the parish of Jefferson, an office he has held since April 1980. During Lee's reign as one of the state's top law enforcement officials, the outspoken and blunt sheriff sparked controversy for a comment deemed racist by some. In response to a crime spree in which robbers followed shoppers home and mugged them in their driveways in 1986, Lee issued a statement saying that if there were young blacks found driving a car late at night in a predominantly white area, they would be stopped.

Civil rights organizations, including the American Civil Liberties Union and the National Association for the Advancement of Colored People, protested his announcement. Lee apologized, but said that he was misinterpreted in addressing a way to stop a particular type of crime in a specific area. Despite the furor, he was re-elected to office when many constituents rallied behind him.

Lee has been actively involved with numerous civic groups, including the Lions Club, American Legion, and Organization of Chinese Americans. He also is a member of several law enforcement organizations.

Sources:

Office of the Sheriff. "Harry Lee." Professional resume. Jefferson Parish, Louisiana, 1994.

—Sketch by Kim Moy

K.W. Lee
(1928–)
Journalist

K.W. Lee is considered by many to be the dean of Asian American journalism. In a career that spans more than three decades, he distinguished himself as an investigative reporter, founded the first Korean American English-language newspaper, *Koreatown,* and worked as an editor of the Los Angeles-based weekly, the *Korea Times.*

Lee is perhaps best known as the reporter who dug into the case of Chol Soo Lee, who was convicted of the 1973 murder of a Chinese gang leader in San Francisco. After Lee's stories in the *Sacramento Union* revealed weaknesses in the case, ethnic newspapers across the country carried the reports, galvanizing support among Asian Americans for a retrial. Chol Soo Lee (no relation of K. W. Lee) was eventually acquitted and released from prison, where he had been on death row.

K.W. Lee

Lee saw the case as a dramatic example of ignorance and insensitivity in law enforcement. After covering the case, which later formed the basis for the Hollywood film *True Believer,* Lee said he felt a calling to leave the *Sacramento Union* to join the ethnic press. He founded *Koreatown,* a twenty-four-page weekly that became the first Korean American newspaper in English. For two years, he took turns with two staff members driving copy from their Los Angeles base to Sacramento printing presses each week, an 800-mile round trip.

Lee had spent $5,000 of his own money to jump-start the paper, which grew to a circulation of 3,000 before folding. The newspaper was the predecessor to the ethnic weekly newspaper, the *Korea Times.* As English section editor of the *Korea Times,* Lee edited stories and wrote editorials for about two years serving as a bridge between mainstream society and Korean Americans, until an illness forced him to retire. "Immigrants are very much isolated from mainstream society. [I] always wanted to provide the American perspective," Lee said in an interview with Kim Moy.

A Career in Journalism

Born Kyun Won Lee in Kaeson, Korea, on June 1, 1928, Lee immigrated to the United States at the age of twenty-one, following a childhood spent largely in Japan and a stint in the Japanese Air Force after that country occupied Korea. Lee studied journalism at West Virginia University and the University of Illinois. After college, he moved to California, where he taught at the Military Defense Language Institute for the U.S. military and worked for local papers in the area.

Lee's next career stop was in Kingsport, Tennessee, where he worked at a daily newspaper from 1956 to 1957. He then moved to Charleston, West Virginia, where he covered segregationist practices in the South from 1958 to 1970 as the daily paper's civil rights reporter. He also did stories on the plight of Appalachian coal miners as well as exposes on vote-buying in West Virginia. In Sacramento he did investigative reports on perks for state legislators in Sacramento, and corruption in the Sacramento Housing Authority.

Lee's Korean name, Kyung Won, means "source of good news," and articles appearing with his byline have helped to initiate change, including state legislation and resignations of city officials. Lee, who is fluent in Korean and Japanese and can read and write in Chinese, has inspired dozens of Asian American students across the country to enter journalism, law, and politics.

Among his two dozen awards are citations from various journalism organizations for investigative reporting and outstanding public service. The Asian American Journalists Association awarded him the organization's first Award of Excellence for print media in 1987.

Sources:

Lee, K.W., personal interview with Kim Moy, May 1994.
————, telephone interview with Kim Moy, June 1994.

—Sketch by Kim Moy

Ming Cho Lee
(1930–)
Set designer, professor

If you've seen pipes and scaffolding, if you've noticed collage on the theatre stage, you've seen Ming Cho Lee. With literally hundreds of plays, operas, and dance credits to his name, he's been called the dean of American set design and is considered the most influential figure in the history of set design. For that matter, any reference to Lee is usually peppered with countless *mosts* and *bests*, with a few other superlatives thrown in. After almost thirty years of teaching, more than half of the set designers working today either have been trained by Lee or have been his assistants. The others wouldn't hesitate to admit that they've been influenced by his style and method in some way.

Born in Shanghai, China, on October 3, 1930, Ming Cho Lee "came from a family engaged in business." He told Terry Hong in an interview that he "grew up in a very Westernized family." When Lee was six years old, his parents were granted one of the first divorces in China. His father was awarded custody because, "at the time, women usually did not have any rights to the children," Lee explained. During the week Lee lived with his father, a Yale University-educated international insurance representative, and spent weekends with his mother. "I treasured the time with my mother," Lee told Hong, "It was with my mother that I went to theatres, films, operas, and art galleries. It was through my mother that I started studying Chinese landscape painting. . . . If it had not been for my mother, I would not have entered a career in the arts."

"An American Liberal Arts Education"

With the Communist takeover in 1949 of China, Lee fled with his family to Hong Kong. Following his father's advice, Lee came to the United States on a student visa and enrolled at Occidental College in California. In spite of a strong Yale connection (Lee's father, stepfather, and maternal uncle were all Yale graduates), Lee's father believed that a smaller college would be a better environment. Today, Lee readily agrees. "The best thing that could have ever happened to me was to get an American liberal arts education at a small college. It made me look at everything about myself, about education, about society. . . . My father made a great choice."

At Occidental, not yet comfortable with the English language—"I was in serious trouble with my English," Lee admitted—Lee took as many studio art courses as he could, including watercolor, figure drawing, and basic drawing. "At least I managed to get good grades in art courses," he laughed.

Lee recalled, "At the time—the late forties and early fifties—abstract expressionism controlled the art world, so much so that any kind of representational painting was not considered serious art. Even though I understood abstract painting very well, I had trouble doing it myself." From the art department, Lee switched to speech, which housed the theatre major. "Since I had seen quite a lot of theatre and opera in Shanghai, I thought it was a good idea that I should at least try theatre. . . . In the theatre department, I was very appreciated because I could draw and paint. And that was the beginning."

After receiving his degree in 1953, Lee spent one year doing graduate work in theatre arts at the University of California at Los Angeles. "But I quickly realized that I was just sick of school," he said. He moved to New York with an introduction to Jo Mielziner who was then Broadway's premier set designer. In 1954, Lee became Mielziner's apprentice, then his assistant. They worked together on and off for six years.

Ming Cho Lee

Stage Debuts

In 1955, within weeks of passing the examination for membership in the theatrical designers union, United Scenic Artists, Lee designed his first professional show, a revival of the musical comedy *Guys and Dolls* for the Grist Mill Playhouse in Andover, New Jersey. Three years later, on February 3, 1958, Lee made his New York debut at the Phoenix Theatre as set designer for *The Infernal Machine,* Jean Cocteau's adaptation of the Oedipus legend. While the play received mediocre reviews, Lee attracted the attention of several important critics for his striking design.

In the late 1950s, Lee began working for set designer Boris Aronson. "He was a great influence on my work," Lee told Hong. "Jo and Boris were very different designers. Jo had a French impressionistic style; he sketched superbly, did incredible watercolors, created a poetic realism. Boris had a different background. He was from Russia and when he was young, he was very involved with the avant-garde movement in Russia—especially the Cubists.

He trained as a painter and sculptor so his approach to plays tended to go way beyond realism; in fact, his approach was always a metaphoric approach. He was always trying to get at the core of the play and make a total visual statement rather than an illustrative form. All my early work was very influenced by Boris."

In its initial stages, Lee's solo career seemed focused on opera. He designed numerous productions for the Peabody Institute of Music in Baltimore, the Baltimore Opera Company, and the Opera Company of Boston. In 1961, Lee moved his family to California where he became designer-in-residence of the San Francisco Opera. He stayed for one season, returning to New York in 1962. "I came back to do my first Broadway show, which was given to me through Jo [Mielziner]," Lee said. He also began a collaboration that would last for eleven years with Joseph Papp, the legendary of the New York Shakespeare Festival and longtime artistic director of the Public Theatre. Lee assumed the post of principal designer for the Shakespeare Festival's annual summer presentations at the outdoor Delacorte Theatre in Central Park. Because of the Festival's constant budget limitations, Lee created adaptable sets, usually constructed of pipe scaffolding and raw wood planks. This minimalist look, which became Lee's signature, gave rise to a sculptural style in American set design in the 1960s and 1970s.

In addition to the Festival's outdoor productions, Lee designed the sets for many of the company's productions in the Shakespeare Festival's downtown theatre, including the controversial musical *Hair.* Beyond the sets, Lee created an Elizabethan-style, multilevel mobile stage, which because of its ease in setting up, allowed the company to take its open-air productions to parks and playgrounds throughout the five boroughs of New York City. He redesigned the Delacorte Theatre itself, changing its shape from a fan to a horseshoe to bring the audience closer in to the stage, improving the sound quality and allowing more fluid staging. Other theatre-designs credited to Lee include the Florence Sutro Anspacher and Estelle R. Newman theatres in New York Shakespeare Festival's Public Theater complex and the Garage Theatre at the Harlem School of the Arts. Lee was also involved with the designs of the Performing Arts Center at the State University of New York at Purchase, the acoustical shell and proscenium arch at the Cincinnati Music Hall, and the Patricia Corbett Pavilion at the University of Cincinnati's School of Music.

While designing for the New York Shakespeare Festival, Lee simultaneously began working as principal designer for the Juilliard Opera Theatre, later called The American Opera Center of the Juilliard School of Music. In 1966, Lee also began creating sets for the New York City Opera, an affiliation that lasted for seven years. In 1974, Lee made his Metropolitan Opera debut with his design for Boris Gudonov and went on to do three more shows.

In addition to theatre and opera, Lee has built a substantial career in designing sets for dance. In 1962, he was tapped by the well-known modern ballet choreographer Martha Graham to create the set for *A Look at Lightning.* His affiliation with her company lasted into the mid-1980s. In 1963, Lee began designing for Gerald Arpino of the Joffrey Ballet, eventually creating the sets for eight ballets.

Other dance credits include designs for the choreography of Alvin Ailey, Lew Christenson, and Eliot Feld.

Moving away from Broadway

In spite of Lee's indisputable success in opera and dance, he readily admitted to a "terrible Broadway career." He added, almost jovially, "I've had more Broadway flops than anyone in the history of theatre." Bluntly honest, he stated very matter-of-factly, "It's very difficult to work on a theatre project where the ultimate goal is everyone's greed." He repeated the words of Aronson: "In every show, there must be a victim. The trick is not to be that victim," and continued, "How can you do real work in an environment like that?" Another Broadway hazard Lee pointed out is that "whole lives' works are based on one reviewer. You always have to be guessing whether or not Frank Rich—now David Richards—[the former *New York Times Theatre* critic and his replacement] will like something or not. It's like Russian roulette." He added in all seriousness, "I didn't go into theatre to gamble."

While Lee may not be comfortable on Broadway, it was at a Broadway theatre, the Brooks Atkinson, that Lee realized what is perhaps his greatest success—the 1983 staging of *K2*, a drama by Patrick Meyers about two mountain climbers, one of them injured, trapped on an icy ledge near the summit of the world's second highest mountain. With its behemoth structure soaring beyond the audience's view, the set won for Lee the Tony Award, the Outer Critics Circle Award, the Drama Desk Award and his third Joseph Maharam Award.

Nevertheless, Lee limits his Broadway stagings. The few times he does agree to a show, he said he must "make sure not to get emotionally involved, to always step back so [he] doesn't find [himself] devastated from the work if something goes wrong." But that kind of objectivity, he maintains, presents other problems. "I don't want to work in that detached way all the time. If you do it all the time, ultimately, it will affect your attitude and your ethics toward the work you're doing. One thing about art is that you must involve your whole heart and soul."

It is in regional and experimental theatres such as the Arena Stage in Washington D.C., the Mark Taper Forum in Los Angeles, and the Guthrie Theatre in Minneapolis, that Lee prefers to involve his "whole heart and soul." Away from the demands for profit that drive larger theatres, the smaller venues are more likely to stage new or controversial works. These are the commissions that continue to take Lee all over the country and throughout the world.

"I Love Teaching"

Beyond the stage, Lee has also been teaching for almost thirty years. In 1967, he began at New York University then moved to Yale University in 1969. Now in his twenty-fifth year at Yale, he currently chairs the design department at the drama school, commuting three or four days a week between New York and New Haven. "I love teaching," he stated simply.

Lee commented that he has had very few Asian American students who have graduated in design. "It's very frustrating that after more than twenty-five years of teaching, I've only had one set designer, Wing Lee," he cites as an example. "I think a career in the arts is not really totally acceptable to Asian families, especially for male offspring. In a way, there seems to be a distrust of the arts. Earning a living at it is very difficult. Asian Americans, especially first-generation Asian Americans, tend to be pragmatic people and it's very hard for them to imagine a life of insecurity for their children. The arts and theatre somehow don't always have tangible results. A career in the arts can be enormously meaningful and have nothing to do with success."

Referring to his own decision to enter set design, Lee remembered, "It was a crisis in my family." But after countless awards and fellowships (including Guggenheim and National Endowment for the Arts) and at least two honorary doctorates, the only crisis Lee might have to deal with is where he will find the time to finish all his endless projects.

Sources:

Books

Lee, Ming Cho. "Designing Opera." In *Contemporary Stage Design U.S.A.* Edited by Elizabeth B. Burdick, Peggy Hansen and Brenda Zanger. Middletown, Connecticut: Wesleyan University Press, 1975.

———. Introduction to *American Set Design 2*, edited by Ron Smith. New York: Theatre Communications Group, 1991.

Periodicals

Huang, Yu-mei. "The Twists, turns, trials and triumphs of a Theatrical Life," *Free China Review*, January 1984, 63–75.

MacKay, Patricia. "Designers on Designing: Ming Cho Lee," *Theater Craft*, February 1984, 15–21+.

Other

Lee, Ming Cho, telephone interview with Terry Hong, February 6, 1994; telephone interview with Hong, March 6, 1994.

—Sketch by Terry Hong

Ronald D. Lee

(1959–)

Attorney

In 1994 Ronald D. Lee was named the general counsel of the National Security Agency (NSA), the highly secretive government intelligence-gathering agency linked with the Department of Defense. As general counsel, Lee is the chief legal officer of the NSA and supervises the work of the attorneys and other personnel in the office of the general counsel. Prior to this posting, Lee was a partner at the Washington-based law firm of Arnold and Porter where he specialized in the areas of product liability litigation and food and drug regulatory proceedings.

Ronald Derek Lee was born in Seattle, Washington, where his father, an avionics engineer, was working on a temporary assignment for Boeing Aircraft. The family was originally from Montreal, Quebec, and they returned there when Lee was one year old. When Lee was seven, his family moved to southern California. Lee recalled for *Notable Asian Americans,* "Our trip across the United States was a great adventure for me (less so for my parents), with a new motel, new rest stops, and fresh scenery every day." Lee loved southern California and said of his family's move there, "I viewed the climate and the elimination of snow clothing as one of the region's primary advantages; I later understood that my parents had moved to the Los Angeles area in order to give their family a better life and a broader array of opportunities. Like my grandparents, who emigrated to Canada from rural villages in southern China, my parents were determined to enhance their children's futures."

Table Tennis and Travel

Lee was an excellent student and was active in athletics. While in high school he attended a summer table tennis camp where he was put through a rigorous schedule of training and calisthenics. He told *Notable Asian Americans,* "I ended the summer with a much stronger sense of determination, discipline, and inner reserves." Two summers later, Lee had another pivotal experience when he accompanied his older sister, then a senior at Yale, on an extended trip through Europe. He was exhilarated by the trip and told *Notable Asian Americans* that he "was also learning German that summer and found the complete immersion in foreign cultures and in two millenia of history fascinating." He added, "I realized my aptitudes were verbal rather than mathematical and that I enjoyed learning about peoples and their pasts."

In 1976 Lee enrolled in Princeton University in Princeton, New Jersey, where he began studying history. Again,

Ronald D. Lee

he excelled at his studies and earned several distinguished honors. In 1978 and 1980 he was awarded Book Prizes by the consulates of West Germany and Austria in recognition of his excellent performance in German language courses. In 1979 he was awarded the William Koren, Jr., Memorial Prize in history for having the highest departmental standing as a junior, and in 1980 he was awarded the Laurence Hutton Memorial Prize in history for having the highest departmental standing as a senior. Upon his graduation in 1980, Lee was elected to the Princeton chapter of Phi Beta Kappa, won the M. Taylor Pyne Prize for excellence in scholarship and effective support of the interests of Princeton University, the highest general award available to graduating seniors, and was awarded a Rhodes Scholarship for graduate study at Oxford University in Oxford, England.

Legal Career

Lee earned a master's degree at Oxford in international relations in 1982, and then returned to the United States where he attended Yale Law School. While at Yale, Lee was a summer associate at Covington and Burling in 1984, and at Lord, Day and Lord in 1985. He also served as article and book review editor at *Yale Law Journal.* After graduation from Yale in 1985, he served as a law clerk to Judge Abner L. Mikva of the U. S. Court of Appeals for the D.C. Circuit. In 1986 he went to the Supreme Court where he clerked for Justice John Paul Stevens.

In 1988 Lee joined the international law firm of Arnold and Porter where he specialized in product liability and food and drug regulatory proceedings. He also represented domestic clients in antitrust, breach of professional duty, and other types of litigation and government investigations and has counseled foreign clients on the legal aspects of international joint ventures and transnational litigation as they apply to U.S. law.

Lee has also served on the firm's hiring committee, its summer associate committee, and its pro bono committee. In 1992 he became involved in the management and administration of Arnold and Porter's Los Angeles office. Lee has published several papers in prestigious law reviews and in 1993 he served the new administration of President Bill Clinton by writing a briefing paper outlining selected judicial opinions of potential Supreme Court nominee Ruth Bader Ginsburg.

Sources:

Arnold and Porter. "Ronald Lee." Professional resume, June 1994.
Lee, Ronald, written interview with Helen Zia, July 1994.

—Sketch by Jim Henry

Rose Hum Lee

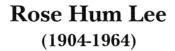

Rose Hum Lee
(1904-1964)
Sociologist

Rose Hum Lee fought the traditional values of both society and her family to become a renowned expert on Chinese American life. She is best known for her study *The Chinese in the United States of America*, which examines the social structure and assimilation patterns of Chinese Americans in the United States. Published in 1960, the book combines autobiographical information and sociological research to depict a Chinese American society in conflict between "sojourners"—Chinese Americans who resist efforts to become Americanized—and "American Chinese," who want to join the mainstream. When she was appointed chairman of the sociology department at Roosevelt University in Chicago in 1956, Lee became the first woman of Chinese ancestry to reach such a position at an American university.

Rose Hum was born on August 20, 1904, in Butte, Montana. Her father, Hum Wah-Lung, worked as a ranch hand, miner, and laundry worker in Montana after immigrating from Kwangtung province, China. In 1900, he married Lin Fong, a mail-order bride from Kwangtung.

Lin Fong would prove to be a major influence on both Rose and her six siblings. Illiterate herself, Lin Fong resisted family pressures to lead her children into traditional roles as family breadwinners. Rather, she encouraged education, independence, and love of learning.

A Decade in China

Many details of Lee's life are not known, but it is documented that she graduated from Butte High School in 1921. She was working as a secretary sometime thereafter when she met and fell in love with Ku Young Lee, a Chinese student from Philadelphia. Despite her mother's objections, they married and left the United States to live in China in the late 1920s. During her decade in China, Lee worked in a variety of jobs, sometimes simultaneously, using what she had learned in high school business classes. She worked for the Kwangtung Raw Silk Testing Bureau from 1931 to 1936; the National City Bank of New York in Canton and Kwangtung from 1936 to 1938; the Sun Life Assurance Company in Canton from 1936 to 1938; and the Kwangtung Municipal Telephone Exchange from 1937 to 1938. Each of the jobs enriched her understanding of Chinese business practices and everyday life.

When the Sino-Japanese War broke out in 1937, she assisted the Chinese government by working in the Canton Red Cross Women's War Relief Association, the Overseas Relief Unit, and the Kwangtung Emergency Committee for the Relief of Refugees. When the Japanese invaded Canton, initiating an eighteen-month siege, Lee worked as a radio operator and translator of Japanese transmissions. She also worked in hospitals and helped care for and settle war orphans, one of whom she adopted as her daughter and brought back with her to the United States in 1938. Lee's husband is not mentioned in biographical material after her return to the United States. It is unclear if he returned with her or remained in China.

Fulfilling a Dream

Again with her mother's encouragement, Lee returned to school hoping to become a writer and teacher. She received a bachelor's degree in social work from the Carnegie Institute of Technology in 1942, a master's from the University of Chicago in 1943, and, four years later, a Ph.D. While her studies and her daughter, Elaine, kept her busy, Lee found time to write two children's plays. One, *Little Lee Bo-Bo: Detective for Chinatown*, was produced in 1945 at Chicago's Goodman Theatre. Also in 1945, Lee made a move that would affect the rest of her career: She joined the sociology department at Roosevelt University, a new college in Chicago that, even amid the ethnic and racial tensions immediately following World War II, encouraged diversity among its students and faculty.

Lee's graduate dissertation studied the growth and decline of Chinese American communities in the Rocky Mountain region. In 1949, with a grant from the Social Science Research Council, she expanded her research to new Chinese immigrant families in San Francisco. *The Chinese in the United States of America* developed out of this research and proved controversial. Lee was ostracized by some in the Chinese community for her belief that parochial attitudes on the part of many Chinese people prevented them from fully participating in American society. Nevertheless, Lee's study proved to be a valuable foundation for future studies. The hostility did not derail Lee's other efforts. During the 1950s and 1960s, she studied a wide variety of racial and urban problems. Another major work, *The City: Urbanism and Urbanization in Major World Regions*, was published in 1955.

Meanwhile, Lee's career at Roosevelt University progressed impressively. Eleven years after joining the faculty, she became department chairperson. Three years later, in 1959, she was promoted to full professor. Lee discussed her leadership position in the *Chicago Sun-Times:* "I was a woman, I was in a man's field, and I was Chinese. That meant three strikes against me," she said. "The fact that I was able to overcome these barriers is a tremendous encouragement to others, particularly women who belong to minority groups."

In 1951, Lee married Glenn Ginn, a Chinese American lawyer from Phoenix, Arizona. She took a leave of absence from Roosevelt in 1961 to teach at Phoenix College, where she stayed through 1963. There, she continued to teach her belief that racial hatred and separatism must be overcome for true democratic equality.

Sources:

Books

"College's First Lady: Dr. Lee Blazes Trail at Roosevelt," *Chicago Sun-Times*, April 10, 1950.

Other

Roosevelt University. "Rose Hum Lee." Biographical material. Chicago, 1994.

—Sketch by Mary Anne Klasen

Sammy Lee
(1920–)
Olympic diver, physician

When Dr. Sammy Lee, Olympic gold medalist and ear specialist, was in junior high school, he attended a party given by a classmate. When the hostess' parents realized that Lee, then student body president, was not white, he was asked to leave. Returning home in tears, Lee asked his father why he was not born white. "My father wisely told me how lucky I was to be an American and that if I did not act and perform by showing the fine qualities of my Korean heritage, I would never become a good American," Lee recalled in an interview with Terry Hong.

Some ten years later, Lee proved to the world that he was an exemplary citizen of the United States. Even after graduating medical school with a specialization in diseases of the ear, Lee became in 1948 the first American-born Asian to win an Olympic gold medal in platform diving. Four years later, he became the first male diver to win consecutive gold medals. Lee's talents and accomplishments are many—during his illustrious life, he has been and continues to be student, teacher, leader, champion, doctor, lecturer, American representative to the world, husband, father, and more recently, tennis and golf player. While he is full of sparkling humor and bursting with charismatic energy, underneath Lee's playful exterior radiates a deeply rooted pride in his Korean ancestry. He has always strongly believed that "immigrants are the lifeblood of America." He emphasized, "We need fresh blood to make the American dream a reality."

The American Dream come True

Born on August 1, 1920 in Fresno, California, to immigrant parents, Lee was raised on the ideal that in America—the land of freedom and choice for all, regardless of

Sammy Lee

race, color or creed—he could be anything he wanted. Lee explained, "My parents used acts of discrimination to their advantage. They told me that prejudiced people were like the pupil of an eye. The more light you try to shine in them, the more it contracts. Born in America, you have all the rights and privileges. It's in the law. And if you allow these pickpockets, these bigots, to pick from your pocket full of dreams, then you won't have any dreams. Life without dreams is like a bird without wings. You can't fly. And so it was. We [Lee and his two sisters] all fulfilled our dreams."

In 1932, Lee was twelve years old when the Olympic games were held in Los Angeles, where the Lee family had settled. When the young boy learned for the first time what the Olympic games were, he precociously announced to his father that he would someday be an Olympic champion. When his father asked in which sport, Lee answered, "I don't know yet, but I'll find one."

That summer, Lee recalled, "I noticed that I was doing things off the diving board that my honky brothers couldn't do." Under the tutelage of Hart Crum, a well-respected local black athlete and "one of [Lee's] heroes," Lee took to the board. "Hart double-bounced me and I did my first forward one-and-a-half somersault. I was so excited that I ran all the way home and breathlessly told my dad that I'd found the sport I was going to be an Olympic champion in." Still in high school, Lee's diving career had begun.

However, the local Brookside pool where Lee practiced was only open to non-whites on Mondays, referred to as International Days. By declaration of the health department, the pool was then drained, cleaned, and disinfected for white swimmers by Tuesday morning. Forty years after Lee swam there, Brookside pool's ex-director approached Lee after a speaking engagement. He revealed to Lee that Brookside pool was too large to be drained in one night, and that the water level was lowered just enough to convince passersby that, indeed, the water was being changed. Later, in the darkness, the pool was refilled to its capacity level. Lee chuckled, "We were swimming in the same water after all."

With Crum's patient teaching, Lee earned the attention of ex-Olympic coach Jim Ryan. Day after day, month after month, year after year, Lee listened to Ryan's curses and demands and met his grueling expectations. Surviving Ryan's relentless practices, Lee was ready to face any challenge. "Don't let people ever tell you anything is impossible," Lee told Hong. "Only you know the limit to your abilities."

A Credit to His Profession

Amidst his training, Lee graduated high school as valedictorian of his class and student body president. Already gaining national recognition in diving, he entered Occidental College with plans to pursue a medical career. However, by his junior year, Lee's grades had fallen so low that he almost was not recommended to medical school by his academic adviser. "My adviser thought I would probably be the first Occidental graduate to flunk out of medical school, but out of respect for my father who was also an Occidental graduate, he gave me a recommendation."

In 1942, Lee enrolled at Southern California Medical School. He remembered, "It was so traumatic to meet all those brains with photographic memories, guys who could make 4.0s without even trying. It was one of the most traumatic things in my life, to realize that I couldn't be the best in everything. I had to really evaluate myself and I realized that I could still be on the medical team if I passed. I may not be Phi Beta Kappa, I thought, but I'm going to stay in and be one of the most compassionate doctors and a credit to my profession."

In spite of personal hardship, Lee finished his medical degree by the time he traveled to London in 1948 as a member of the U.S. Olympic Diving Team. There he became the first American of Korean descent to win a gold medal. He was also the first non-white to win a gold medal in diving. Lightheartedly, he recalled with laughter in his eyes, "If 12,000 people hadn't been looking at me, I would have pee-ed in my pants." He continued, "The 'Star Spangled Banner' never sounded so good. I was proud of two things. I was wearing the flag of my country on my chest and I was wearing the flag of my Asian ancestors on my face." He added with humor, "For the first time, American sports weren't in black and white. I added a little yellow."

Four years later, America was involved in the Korean War. Lee had entered the U.S. Army's specialized training program in 1942 to help finance medical school. After graduation, he had received his post as a lieutenant in the Army Medical Corps and was serving his residency. When asked by the U.S. Olympic coach to compete in the 1952 Olympics, Lee anxiously asked his commanding officer, "Is it morally right that I should ask to compete in the Olympics again when my country is at war in my ancestral land of Korea?" He received his answer: "There's only one doctor who can win the gold medal for the U.S. and we have thousands of doctors who can repair the wounded. If you do not make a comeback, the U.S. will lose the gold medal to Mexico." With that approval, Lee repeated his winning performance in Helsinki, setting new diving records with his second Olympic gold medal. It was August 1, 1952—his thirty-second birthday. "You know what great philosophical thought was running through my mind as I hit that pool? Happy Birthday, you SOB. You did it again," he chuckled.

In 1953, Lee was presented with the James E. Sullivan Award, the most prestigious award given to America's outstanding amateur athlete. The State Department sent him on a goodwill exhibition tour through ten different Southeast Asian countries. He toured the world, expounding on the freedom and opportunities available in America. After each exhibition, he addressed his audiences: "If the majority of the American people did not practice what they preach, how I could I be here as a two-time Olympic gold medal winner, a doctor of medicine and the winner of the James E. Sullivan Award? In America, we have a commitment to excellence. And we have every opportunity."

Ironically, back home in California, Lee could not purchase a home. He wrote to CBS news correspondent, Robert Pierpoint, a personal friend and later godfather to Lee's daughter: "Things have really improved in California. They no longer slam the door in our faces like they did to my father saying, 'no Chinks' or 'no Japs,' but I can't buy a home in Orange County." Pierpoint contacted Edward R. Murrow and together they orchestrated a widespread media blitz—"Sammy Lee cannot buy a home in Orange County." The response was overwhelming. Personal telephone calls and telegrams came from such people as then-vice-president Richard Nixon, television show host Ed Sullivan, Korean president Syngman Rhee, army generals, famous athletes, and entertainers. "Nothing I had ever accomplished in my life touched me as much as this response did," Lee recalled. His ideals of America and American freedom were once again renewed.

Serving His Country Well

During his extraordinary career, Lee has served numerous U.S. presidents. He was President Dwight D. Eisenhower's personal representative to the 1956 Olympics in Melbourne, Australia. He was a member of the Presidential Council on Physical Fitness and Sports between 1970 and 1975 under President Richard Nixon. He served as Nixon's personal representative to the 1972 Olympics in Munich, Germany, and as President Ronald Reagan's representative to the 1988 Olympics in Seoul.

In addition, Lee has coached both U.S. and international diving teams. In 1979, he was the first foreign coach invited to China to evaluate their diving program. He has also been instrumental in the career of individual divers, coaching Bob Webster. to gold during the 1960 Games and the legendary Greg Louganis, whom Lee described as "another son," to his first Olympics in 1976 where he captured silver. As if to bring Lee's Olympic legacy full-circle, Lee was a proud Olympic torch runner and flag bearer when the Games returned more than half a century later to Los Angeles in 1984. Today, Lee is retired from being a physican and surgeon and is an avid tennis player. In the last year, "I got shamed into playing golf," he said with a laugh. "Tennis has made me bilingual in both English and profanity. And golf has made English a second language," he claimed.

In describing his philosophy of life, Lee explained, "I believe that success in life is like the steps of a ladder, with each step being necessary in order to get to the top of our life's ambition. Too many of us ask to be boosted up three and four steps at a time, totally ignoring the time spent by our victorious competitors. That's what I used to do. I used to pray every night that someday I would be an Olympic champion. But I remember my dad saying that when I lost a diving contest, 'Never use an excuse of your racial background. Just work harder. If you're not proud of the color of your skin and your ancestral heritage, you'll never be accepted as an American." Lee took his father's words to heart.

Indeed, Lee is an American who has achieved his ambitions. He has left his indelible mark on American history. As he told Hong, "You can't have youth forever, but if you have courage and endurance, your character can live forever.

Sources:

Books

Wampler, Molly Frick. *Not Without Honor: The Story of Sammy Lee.* Santa Barbara, California: The Fithian Press, 1987.

Other

Lee, Sammy, interview with Terry Hong, June 1988.
Lee, Sammy, phone interview with Terry Hong, May 14, 1994.

—Sketch by Terry Hong

Tsung-Dao Lee
(1926–)
Scientist, Nobel Prize winner

Tsung-Dao Lee is a theoretical physicist who was awarded the Nobel Prize in 1957 in recognition of his theoretical and experimental work in contradicting the long-held scientific belief in the conservation of parity, a tenet of nuclear physics having to do with the interactions of colliding subatomic particles that had gone unchallenged since the 1920s. He shared the prize with Chen Ning Yang, and together their discovery owes much to the experimental work of Chien Shiung Wu of Columbia University, all Chinese American immigrants.

Tsung-Dao Lee was born in Shanghai, China, on November 25, 1926. His father, Tsing-Kong Lee, was a businessman and his mother, the former Ming-Chang Chang. Lee graduated from high school in 1943 and enrolled in college at the National Chekiang University in Kweichow, from which he earned a bachelor's degree in physics in 1946. China at that time was fighting a long war against an invading Japanese army, and Lee's education was at one point disrupted when Chekiang University was forced to flee south, consolidating itself with other colleges and universities which also had relocated because of the war.

After earning his bachelor's degree Lee came to America on a government scholarship to study physics at the University of Chicago. While at Chicago, Lee studied under Enrico Fermi, one of the world's most prominent nuclear physicists. He earned his Ph.D. in 1950, writing his dissertation on white dwarf stars. Later in 1950, Lee worked as a research associate in Lake Geneva, Wisconsin, at the Yerkes Astronomical Observatory. In 1951 he left Yerkes to work as a research associate at the University of California at Berkeley. Later that year he transferred once again, this time to the Institute for Advanced Study at Princeton, where he was reunited with a fellow student from his undergraduate days in China, Chen Ning Yang. In 1953, Lee moved to Columbia University in New York City where he served as an assistant professor, and then in 1956, at the age of twenty-nine, he became a full professor at Columbia, the youngest person ever to attain such a title in Columbia's history. Lee worked at Princeton again from 1960 until 1963, when he returned to Columbia as the Enrico Fermi Professor of Physics.

The Nobel Work

In the mid-fifties Lee and Yang, who was then at Princeton, began to study a curious phenomena in particle physics. Physicists had for years been bombarding subatomic

Tsung-Dao Lee

particles in high speed accelerators to observe the nature of their structures. In the course of these experiments, two new particles, called K-mesons, were discovered. Upon further experimentation, it was observed that these K-mesons behaved in a way contrary to the laws of conservation of parity in that one K-meson would decay into two pi-mesons, while the other would decay into three. Established physical law does not allow for such differences in behavior; the natural world is expected to behave in symmetrical ways.

Lee and Yang began further experimentation. The question they sought to resolve was whether the two types of K-mesons were in fact the same particle (which would mean the fall of the concept of parity conservation), or whether they were different in a way science had not yet been able to observe. The decisive experiment Lee and Yang conducted was in 1956 and 1957, and involved observing the subatomic decay of radioactive cobalt in a controlled environment. The pattern of the decay they observed proved that the law of conservation of parity was invalid, a conclusion that surprised the young scientists.

In 1957 the Royal Swedish Academy of Sciences awarded Lee and Yang the Nobel Prize in physics. H.W. Wilson's *Biographical Dictionary* quotes O.B. Klein of the academy as presenting Lee and Yang the award with these words: "Through your consistent and unprejudiced thinking, you have been able to break a most puzzling deadlock in the field of elementary particle physics where now experimental and theoretical work is pouring forth as a result of your brilliant achievement."

Lee has received other honors for his work as well. In 1957 he was awarded the Albert Einstein Commemorative Award of Yeshive University, and in 1958 Princeton University awarded him an honorary degree. Lee is also a longtime member of the National Academy of Sciences and is a fellow of the American Physical Society. He has been a citizen of the United States since 1963, and has been married since 1950. Lee has done substantial theoretical work in areas other than particle physics, including statistical mechanics, astrophysics, hydrodynamics, and turbulence.

Sources:

Wasson, Tyler, ed. *Nobel Prize Winners.* Princeton, New Jersey: Visual Education Corporation, 1987.

—*Sketch by Jim Henry*

Yuan T. Lee

Yuan T. Lee

(1936–)

Chemist, Nobel Prize winner

Yuan Tseh Lee and Dudley R. Herschbach shared the Nobel Prize for chemistry in 1986 for their ground-breaking research into the nature of chemical reactions. Adding to the work Herschbach had initiated as assistant dean and chemistry professor at Harvard University, Lee successfully designed a mass-spectrometer, a technologically advanced detector used in analyzing chemical reactions. Lee is also noted for his work in physics and physical chemistry and has several awards for his accomplishments.

Yuan T. Lee was born in the city of Hsinchu, Taiwan, on November 29, 1936. His mother was an elementary school teacher and his father was an artist and an art teacher. Lee was an outstanding student, and when he graduated from high school in 1955, he was able to enter the elite Taiwan University without taking the normally required entrance exam.

In college he discovered a love of science and of chemistry in particular. He later recalled that he was impressed by the biography of Marie Curie, winner of the Nobel Prize in chemistry in 1911. As part of his college work he conducted research on the separation of the elements of strontium and barium in the presence of an electric field.

Upon graduating from Taiwan University in 1959 he entered graduate school at Tsignua University. He earned a master's degree in chemistry in 1961 and came to the United States to attend the University of California at Berkeley. In 1965 he received his Ph.D. from Berkeley and spent a year and a half doing his postdoctoral work before moving on to Harvard University.

Study of Molecules Begins

At Harvard, Lee joined Herschbach's research team in 1967. When he was at the University of California at Berkeley in the late 1950s, Herschbach had proposed that chemical reactions could be studied as soon as the molecules combined using a crossed molecular beam technique.

In 1963 Herschbach had returned to Harvard and continued his research in reaction dynamics. He performed several successful experiments involving alkali atoms. Essentially, Herschbach's technique used a crossed molecular beams of fast-moving particles so that the molecules of the reaction being studied can combine under controlled conditions. The beams consist of molecules that are flung together at very high speeds. When the molecules collide in the crossed beams, new molecules are formed.

Advanced chemical detectors could then trace where the molecules had ended up, what new molecules had been created, and whether energy had been created or absorbed. At the time the method used a surface ionization detector to analyze the results, so only systems involving alkali atoms could be studied.

When he joined Herschbach's lab, Lee immediately began designing a better detector so that a wider range of molecules could be studied. The detector was state-of-the-art for the late 1960s. It was a mass-spectrometer which applied magnetic and electric fields to deflect different ions along different paths to separate and identify them. The technical challenges were difficult, but within ten months the detector was producing significant results. The first study was a halogen exchange between chlorine and bromine.

Lee, who left Harvard in 1968 to become an assistant professor of chemistry at the University of Chicago, continued his research into chemical reactions. He left the University of Chicago in 1974 to become a professor of chemistry and principal investigator at the University of California at Berkeley's Lawrence Livermore Laboratory. While at Berkeley, Lee's laboratory became known for its work in physics and physical chemistry. He studied reactions between oxygen and small and large hydrocarbon molecules.

Nobel Prize

In 1986 Lee and Herschbach shared the Nobel Prize in chemistry with John Polanyi, a University of Toronto chemist, who studied the same problem as Lee and Herschbach, but took a different approach. He studied the faint infrared light emitted when molecules react to form new substances.

Lee's other awards in chemistry include the Peter Debye Award in physical chemistry awarded by the American Chemical Society (1986) and the National Medal of Science from the National Science Foundation (1986). He also holds an honorary degree for the University of Waterloo, Canada.

Lee is married to Bernice Chinli Wu, whom he has known since elementary school. They have two sons and a daughter. Lee has been a U.S. citizen since 1974.

Sources:

Books

"Lee, Yuan T." In *Current Biography*. New York: H. W. Wilson, 1987, p. 167.

Periodicals

"Chemistry: Nobel Prize for 'Detailed Understanding of How Chemical Reactions Take Place.'" *Scientific American*, December 1986, p. 86.

Gwynne, Peter. "Nobel Prizes Focus on Science of the Ultra Small." *Research and Development*, December 1986, p. 37.

Peterson, Ivars. "Chemistry: Probing Reaction Dynamics." *Science News*, October 25, 1986, p. 262.

Zoglin, Richard, Joe Levine, Michael D. Lemonick, Paul Gray, and Barbara Rudolph. "Nobel Prize Winners." *Time*, October 27, 1986.

—Sketch by Douglas Wu

Russell C. Leong
(1950–)
Poet, editor of *Amerasia Journal*

Russell C. Leong is a widely published poet and short story writer. He is the co-founder of the national interdisciplinary *Amerasia Journal* where he has served since 1977 as editor. He also works as an editor at the Asian American Studies Center at the University of California in Los Angeles.

Born in 1950 to Charles, a journalist, and Mollie Joe, a businesswoman, Russell Leong was raised in a fourth floor Chinatown flat on Stockton and Washington Streets in San Francisco. His father was a fairly prominent newsman who worked for a number of publications, including *Young China*, the *Chinese Press*, the *San Francisco Examiner*, and the *San Francisco Chronicle*. In an interview with Stephen Chin, Leong said he grew up in a home where "there were always a lot of broken pencils and paper."

As a teenager, Leong's first interest was in painting. At age fifteen, with assistance from his father, he produced *My Chinatown, A to Z*, a Chinatown guide that sold for one dollar at Grant Avenue gift shops. Around the same time, Leong met local artist and filmmaker Loni Ding, North Beach artist Bernice Bing, and Chinese art historian Bill Wu. "Besides my parents, it was living in Chinatown, the atmosphere, that encouraged me," Leong told Chin. "The community was being revitalized by new immigrants from Hong Kong and the third generation who were growing up."

After graduating from Lowell High School in 1968, he attended San Francisco State College, as it was then known. If Leong's later writing often took on a decidedly political edge, it was a reflection of his experiences growing up in the Bay Area in the 1960s—a time when his own Chinatown community witnessed tremendous growth as a result of the liberalization of U.S. immigration quotas for Chinese in 1965. America's college campuses, especially

San Francisco State College and the University of California at Berkeley, were undergoing social and political turmoil at this time as well. Leong was drawn to the turbulence and became active in Chinese for Social Action, one of the many student groups that emerged during the Third World ethnic studies strikes then being waged on several California campuses. "During the strike, we tried to connect ourselves to the Third World," Leong told Chin. "It was important for all our identities. It was the first time meeting native Americans, Chicanos, and blacks. It influenced our thinking, what we read—Mao Zedong, Che Guevara, Regis Debray. Whether we read it well or not was beside the point—we were open to it."

While in college, Leong joined the Kearny Street Writers Workshop, which spawned a number of well-known Asian American writers, poets, and filmmakers. Working out of the basement of the International Hotel, the writers tied their works to the political issues of the day—fair housing, the creation of ethnic studies, the plight of native Americans, and international liberation movements in the Americas and Asia. In 1972, they published a book of their writings *We Won't Move,* in support of the elderly tenants threatened with eviction from the International Hotel.

After graduation Leong spent a year in Taipei at Taiwan National University studying comparative literature. These studies, in Sung poetry and early Chinese literature, combined with his undergraduate work in such topics as Mexican philosophy and Asian American literature, broadened Leong's perspective. Topping Leong's reading list, however, were Mao Zedong's writings on literature and art, discussing their role in serving the people. "[Being exposed to Mao's works] was a positive thing," Leong told Chin, "because we did not want to side with the Chinese Six Companies [a fraternal group of Chinese Americans], and the feudal ideas that we found in the community—so we looked to China."

In 1977 Russel Leong co-founded *Amerasia Journal* with the noted Asian American social scientist Don Nakanishi. The journal has become over the years one of the foremost voices of Asian American literature and scholarship in the country, and is published today by the University of California at Los Angeles.

The Poetry of Russell Leong

Notwithstanding his academic career and varied political activities, Leong considers himself first and foremost a poet. His works tend toward the longer narrative, as in "Unfolding Flowers, Matchless Flames," a seven-part poem about Buddhism and the Los Angeles riots, published in *Tricycle: The Buddhist Review,* a literary and philosophical journal. The poem attempts to draw links between the Vietnam War, the Persian Gulf War, and the Los Angeles riots, set against a landscape of personal life, loss, and Buddhist beliefs.

In other works, Leong incorporates the theme of Chinese migration and broadens the scope to include the other peoples of Asia. In "Aerogrammes," a poem included in his 1993 collection *The Country of Dreams and Dust,* for instance, the younger Leong, following a 1984 visit to his ancestral village in Sunwei, China, sees himself as a bridge between the culture of his ancestors and that of his home country, the United States.

Discussing the themes of his work, Leong noted that, "In my poetry, through juxtaposition, I try to show the contradictions in people's lives. I try to break certain colonized patterns of thought, assumptions, which we all have." One example is the title poem of his collection *The Country of Dreams and Dust.* Following his father's death in 1984, Leong was cleaning out his father's office when he discovered a small English and Chinese reader, published in 1882 by a Reverend I.M. Condit. It had been used to teach Chinese immigrants to speak English and to convert them to Christianity. "The missionary book ditties struck me as both innocuous and insidious," recalled Leong.

To highlight the cultural insensitivity of the nineteenth century Americans who would use such a book, Leong wove phrases from the reader into his poem, which is about Chinese immigration, religion and sexuality. "The second generation [of Asian immigrants] never acknowledged things like institutional racism or colonization, that type of thing. They usually blamed [their second-class status] on themselves," said Leong. "So maybe my father, by leaving me some of his books, was giving me the opportunity to tell it like it was for his generation." The narrative of *The Country of Dreams and Dust* begins in the Canton Delta of China and ends in the drained swimming pool of a Los Angeles tract house in the Little Saigon section of Los Angeles.

Leong's Fiction

Leong is also an author of short stories. In 1973, he wrote "Rough Notes for Natos," under the pen name Wallace Lin, published in the 1974 landmark collection of Asian American writing, *Aiiieeeee!* edited by Frank Chin. In contrast to his long narrative poems, brevity characterizes Leong's stories. His most recently anthologized short story, "Geography One," is included in *Charlie Chan is Dead: An Anthology of Contemporary Asian American Fiction* edited by Jessica Hagedorn.

In an essay on Asian American fiction in the *Los Angeles Times Magazine,* Nina Easton commented on Leong's story: "Southern California is . . . a place where writer Russell Leong can realistically transform a tract house off the Garden Grove Freeway into a Buddhist temple, a haven for his Vietnamese character, a man of water 'born in the Delta plains between the Red and Black Rivers,' but transported to this desert of 'jerry-built towns of plastic pipe and drywall. . . . 'Geography One' represent[s] the diversity of stories that ring true in 1990s L.A.".

In 1993, Leong won the PEN Oakland Josephine Literature Award. As of the middle of 1994 he was working on an experimental novel based on the themes of his poetry.

Sources:

Books

Chin, Frank, et al., ed. *Aiiieeee!* Washington, D.C.: Howard University Press, 1974.

Hagedorn, Jessica, ed. *Charlie Chan is Dead: An Anthology of Contemporary Asian American Fiction.* New York: Penguin, 1993.

Leong, Russell. *The Country of Dreams and Dust.* Albuquerque, New Mexico: West End Press, 1993.

Periodicals

Easton, Nina J., *Los Angeles Times Magazine* September 5, 1993.

Other

Leong, Russell, interview with Steven Chin, 1993.
———. Vitae provided by Leong.

—*Sketch by Steven A. Chin*

Channing Liem
(1909–)
Diplomat, scholar, minister

Channing Liem is a longtime Korean expatriate living in the United States. A fervent, lifelong supporter of Korean democracy and independence, he served briefly as the Republic of Korea's ambassador to the United Nations and emissary to several southwest African states. During this time he was a strong supporter of the establishment of a nonaligned South Korea, and the eventual establishment of a unified Korean state free from superpower geopolitical manipulation. Liem is also the president of Han Min Yun, the United Democratic Movement of Overseas Koreans, a multinational organization working toward peace and unification of Korea.

Early Life

Channing Liem was born on October 30, 1909, in Ul Yul, a rural village just north of the thirty-eighth parallel, the line that since World War II has divided the historically unified Korean peninsula. At the time of Liem's birth, Korea was occupied by the Japanese. He was educated at a school established by American missionaries in conjunction with Korean patriots who didn't want their children educated in the Japanese-imposed system. In 1930 he graduated from Sung Sill College in Pyongyang, in modern-day North Korea. With the help of the president of the school, Liem immigrated to the United States where he enrolled in Lafayette College in Easton, Pennsylvania. There he earned his first American degree, a bachelor's of science, in 1934.

After graduation, Liem was offered a fellowship to Bucknell College, where he taught part time and studied sociology. He had intended to earn his master's degree at Bucknell but left after a year, primarily because the professors he was looking forward to studying with left. In 1936 Liem moved to New York where he entered the New York Theological Seminary, an institution affiliated with New York University. Here Liem studied sociology and religion, becoming a pastor and clergyman at the Korean Church and Institute, at the time the only Korean church in the United States. He worked in the church for six years, primarily performing social services for the immigrant Korean community in New York which was made up mostly of single men living in or near poverty.

Liem had been hoping to save enough money to return to school, but his work with the church did not pay well and kept him too busy. In 1942 he decided that he would return to school whether he could afford it or not. He applied to both Princeton and Yale, explaining to them his situation and his history, in the hopes of getting a scholarship—something which he had always thought he was unqualified for because of unexceptional grades. To his great surprise, both schools offered him full scholarships with stipends, and he decided on Princeton.

During the World War II, Liem was recruited by the U.S. government to work in the Office of Censorship, where he helped to translate sensitive documents seized from the Japanese consulates and embassy in the United States. The government paid him well for this important work, and along with the stipend he was receiving from Princeton, Liem was able to finish his graduate studies. He had decided to pursue a degree in constitutional government at Princeton, and while there he studied under Edward S. Corwin, whom Liem described in an interview with Jim Henry as an internationally renowned scholar on the U.S. Constitution. Liem earned his master's degree in 1943 and Ph.D. in 1945. He then earned a postdoctoral fellowship, which he retained for two years.

During the 1950s, Liem taught government and political theory at various colleges, including Chatham College and the State University of New York at New Paltz. Meanwhile, in Korea, the government established by Syngman Rhee after the defeat of the Japanese in World War II was deposed in 1959, and Rhee's vice-president, John Myung Chang, was elevated to the presidency. Chang and Liem had met in the United States while Chang served as the

Channing Liem

Korean ambassador shortly after Korean independence in 1945, and the two had become friends. When Chang became president he asked Liem to return to Seoul to help form the new South Korean delegation to the United Nations.

Delegate to the United Nations

Liem met many challenges in this position. The government of South Korea was still quite fragile and fractured and was at the center of superpower geopolitics which, in Liem's view, had no real concern for the interests of the Korean people. He found himself immersed in a political culture that for several years had fostered a heavy dependence on anti-communism as a foreign policy, a tenet Liem found simpleminded and irrelevant. Early in his term as ambassador to the UN, Liem toured several newly independent southwest African countries. The governments of these countries, like Liem, believed in neutrality in the Cold War realizing that the superpowers had no intention of fighting their skirmishes on their own soil. He returned to Korea and used these countries as examples of what Korea should strive for. He told Henry, "I was determined gradually to help wean away the ideological dependence of the Korean government on the United States, and, you might say, its rabid anti-communism."

Liem was moderately successful in pushing his neutralist agenda, and had even persuaded a skeptical Korean assembly that his views were in the best interests of Korea. Then in 1961 there was a coup in Korea led by Park Chung

Hee, a virulent anti-communist who was seen by many as a puppet for the United States' interests on the Korean peninsula. Liem refused to work for Park, and he resigned his post with the government after only ten months.

International Activism

After leaving the government of Korea, Liem became an international activist in support of democracy, independence, and neutrality in his homeland. Since 1976 he has made four trips to North Korea to promote peace and reconciliation on the peninsula, and in 1977 he founded Han Min Yun, the United Democratic Movement of Overseas Koreans, whose goal is also to pursue peace in Korea.

Liem retired from teaching in 1975, but continues to speak around the country. He expressed hope that the problem of the reunification of Korea can someday be stripped of the ideological constraints forty years of Cold War rhetoric has imposed on it, and the people of North and South Korea can be left to determine their own future.

Sources:

Liem, Channing, telephone interview with Jim Henry, July 27, 1994.

Liem, Ramsey, written interview with Susan Gall, July 20, 1994.

—Sketch by Jim Henry

Maya Lin
(1959–)
Architect, sculptor

At the remarkably young age of twenty-one Maya Lin gained widespread attention as the winner of a national competition to design a monument commemorating—in what the sponsors of the competition specified be an apolitical way—America's longest and most politically controversial war. Her design for the Vietnam Veterans Memorial in Washington D.C. features a black granite wall inscribed with the names of the nearly eighty-thousand American servicemen and women who died in the Vietnam War. The monument has become one of the most visited sights in Washington and has earned a reputation as being a place of great emotion and healing. Other significant works by Lin include the Civil Rights Memorial (1989) in Montgomery, Alabama; the new lower Manhattan home of the Museum for African Art; and *The Women's Table* at Yale University in New Haven, Connecticut.

Maya Lin

Maya Lin was born in Athens, Ohio, on October 5, 1959, into an academic and artistic family. Her father, Henry Huan Lin, came from a distinguished family of anti-Communist politicians and intellectuals in Beijing, China, and was a well-known ceramist and the former dean of fine arts at Ohio University. Her mother, Julia Chang Lin, is a professor of Asian literature at Ohio University. Maya was a reclusive child and spent much of her free time in solitary pastimes, such as hiking and reading. She also experimented with many artistic media, such as silversmithing and bronze casting. She was a good student and was co-valedictorian in her high school. After graduation she applied to and was accepted by Yale University in New Haven, Connecticut.

The Vietnam Veterans Memorial

As her senior thesis project at Yale in 1981, Lin submitted a design to a national competition then underway for a Vietnam Veterans Memorial. The site planned for the memorial was on The Mall in Washington, D.C., between the Lincoln Memorial and the Capitol. Artistic considerations aside, the memorial would be difficult to design for other reasons. There was a great moral ambivalence about America's long military involvement in Southeast Asia, which ended in 1973, with those that favored it and those that opposed feeling equally as passionate. There was also the matter of the veterans of the war who had been, in many places, treated like criminals upon their return. Politically, morally, and culturally, America's war

in Vietnam had caused, or significantly contributed to, many rifts in society. The memorial was envisioned as a first step in healing those rifts.

The memorial Lin designed reflected her artistic bias toward simplicity. It called for two highly polished walls of black granite, set in a "V" to be inscribed with the names of the almost 58,000 dead or missing veterans of the Vietnam War. In a statement she composed to accompany her design, Lin describes the effect the monument is to have in terms of movement—that people are to experience the losses of the war as they "Move into and out of it." Lin's design was chosen as the best from 1420 entries.

Advanced Study in Architecture

The selection of Lin's design proved to be controversial. Some veterans and their families felt its simplicity and starkness recalled the domestic controversy engendered by the war rather than the heroics of those who served in it. Protesters petitioned for another design—a bronze sculpture of three servicemen with an American flag submitted by sculptor Frederick Hart—to take its place. Eventually a compromise was reached. Hart's sculpture would stand 120 feet away from Lin's wall near the entrance to the memorial.

During the time of this controversy, Lin had graduated cum laude from Yale University in 1981. In 1982, she coordinated the construction of the memorial, which was completed and dedicated in 1982. At the dedication ceremony Lin's name was never mentioned, and the program distributed during the ceremony had a picture on its cover not of Lin's memorial, but of Hart's. The controversy that had swept through the country concerning Lin and her memorial had taken its toll on the still quite young woman, and she left graduate school at Harvard for most of 1983 to work for an architectural firm in Boston. In the fall of that year she resumed her studies, this time in Yale's graduate architecture program, from which she received a master of architecture degree in 1985. In 1986, Yale conferred upon her an honorary doctorate of fine arts, and in 1987 Lin moved to New York City where she set up a studio practice, working continuously in sculpture and architecture.

The Civil Rights Memorial

In 1988 the opportunity to work on another large outdoor memorial presented itself when the Southern Poverty Law Center in Montgomery, Alabama, asked Lin to design a memorial to those who had given their lives in the struggle for civil rights. She told Richard Howard of *Smithsonian* magazine that she was surprised by the call: "I thought surely one had already been done. But there had only been specific monuments to specific people; no memorial existed that encompassed the movement itself and caught what that whole era was about." She began studying the history of the civil rights movement: "I was horrified to realize that many of the these murders had taken place during my lifetime," she added.

The design Lin came up with was inspired in part by a phrase from the Book of Amos used by civil rights leader Martin Luther King, Jr., on two occasions: "We will not be satisfied until justice rolls down like waters and righteousness like a mighty stream." That phrase is engraved in the monument, along with important dates in the history of civil rights and the names of forty men, women, and children who lost their lives in the movement. The memorial is constructed of a polished black granite wall and conical table over which a thin pool of water flows.

In recent years Lin has created three other pieces of public artwork. In 1991 the Charlotte Coliseum in Charlotte, North Carolina, installed *TOPO,* an environmental landscape sculpture. In 1993 *The Women's Table* was installed at Yale University. The granite sculpture and water table, dedicated to women, past and present, at Yale, consists of a granite table with a series of numbers spiraling out from its center representing the number of women students at Yale for each year of its existence. With the preponderance of the numbers being zeros, Lin graphically represents women's historical exclusion from Yale. And, as an artist in residence at the Wexner Center for the Arts in Columbus, Ohio, Lin was given the first permanent sculpture commission to that newly-created, well respected arts facility. Her landscape installation *Groundswell* is made of 43 tons of recycled tempered glass and is installed in multiple locations throughout the center, highlighting, for instance, a corner near the floor, the sill of a window. Lin continues to devote time to public art and is currently working on two new projects scheduled for completion in 1994. Another project is *Eclipsed Time,* a sixteen-by-thirty-foot glass and steel clock that has been installed in the ceiling of the Long Island Railroad/Pennsylvania Station terminal in Manhattan.

Lin also produces highly regarded studio sculpture in such media as beeswax, lead, steel, and broken glass. These have been shown in group shows in New York, Los Angeles, and San Francisco and were exhibited at the Wexner Center for the Arts in 1993 in her first one-woman show.

Lin also works in architecture, and has recently designed two houses: one in Williamstown, Massachusetts, and one overlooking the Pacific Ocean in Santa Monica, California. The Williamstown house is a one-story home constructed around a courtyard, reminiscent of traditional Japanese design. And, indeed, much of Lin's work is regarded as Asian in sensibility rather than Western, an observation with which she readily concurs. Of the difference in the two artistic traditions, she wrote in *Art in America,* "Much of the Western architectural training has left me cold. But when I walk into a Japanese garden, I respond immediately. I find its simplicity lets me think and come to my own conclusions; I find it more sympathetic than the didactic, assertive stance of most Western architecture."

Lin is very interested in environmental concerns and serves on the boards of the Energy Foundation and the Presidio Council, two nationally active conservation organizations. She is also a board member of the Smithsonian Institution's Commission on the Future, a public policy think tank comprised of eminent persons from many disciplines and fields.

About her ethnicity Lin wrote in *Art in America,* "If you ask, I would identify myself as Chinese American. If I had to choose one thing over the other, I would choose American. I was not born in China, I was not raised there, and the China my parents knew no longer exists . . . I don't have an allegiance to any country but this one, it is my home."

Sources:

Periodicals

Gandee, Charles. "Life After Vietnam." *Vogue,* February, 1993.
Howard, Richard. *Smithsonian,* September, 1991, pp. 33–35, 42.
Lin, Maya. "Maya Lin." *Art in America,* September, 1991.

—Sketch by Jim Henry

Jahja Ling
(1951–)
Conductor/Pianist

Jahja Ling is recognized as one of the most talented young conductors in the music world today. He has earned a reputation for insightful and highly expressive interpretations as both conductor and pianist, and has already amassed an impressive list of guest conducting engagements with some of the most renowned orchestras in the world. Currently he holds two posts: resident conductor of The Cleveland Orchestra and music director of the Florida Orchestra.

Jahja Ling was born in Jakarta, Indonesia, to a family of Chinese descent. His father, who had been Dutch educated, enjoyed many aspects of Western culture, especially classical music. His grandmother had once been a violinist and provided the Ling household with the piano that young Jahja first began to play when he was four years old. At that young age, Jahja was able to reproduce pieces on

Jahja Ling

1977 Artur Rubinstein International Piano Master Competition in Israel and a certificate of honor at the 1978 Tchaikovsky International Piano Competition in Moscow.

In 1979, Ling was accepted as a scholarship student into the noted conducting program at the Berkshire Music Festival at Tanglewood. As Ling recalled in an interview with Marilyn Eppich: "1979 was a critical year. I came to Tanglewood as an unknown and was given a lot of encouragement. Bernstein even told me that I would be a big conductor one day." Not wanting to disappoint the man he later regarded as his mentor, Ling proved his worth and the following summer was awarded a Leonard Bernstein Conducting Fellowship. There he studied with some of the world's most accomplished conductors–Bernstein, Colin Davis, Gustav Meier, Seiji Ozawa, Andre Previn, and Gunther Schuller. This opportunity also provided Ling with the recognition that would quickly propel him into the professional ranks.

A Leader of Youth

In 1981, Ling joined the conducting staff of the San Francisco Symphony through the Exxon/Arts Endowment program, where he served as assistant conductor and then associate conductor until 1984. During his tenure, Ling founded the San Francisco Symphony Youth Orchestra and in a short time created a top-quality ensemble.

In 1984, Christoph von Dohnanyi, music director of The Cleveland Orchestra, offered Ling a job as associate conductor. Ling's performance led to his appointment the following season as The Cleveland Orchestra's resident conductor, becoming only the fourth person (joining the ranks of Louis Lane, Matthias Bamert, and Yoel Levi) to hold the title. "This orchestra needs people with very strong integrity and that integrity he's got," said Dohnanyi about Ling. "He's modest, and maybe in some ways, too modest, but he's a terrific musician and a wonderful colleague."

Ling has a commitment to developing the talent of young musicians and believes, as he told Marilyn Eppich in an interview, "Young people need to be exposed early to classical music. It has to be passed on to the next generation, and that's why working with young people gives me tremendous joy." In 1986, Ling founded The Cleveland Orchestra Youth Orchestra and was regarded as a benevolent leader by the young musicians with whom he worked. In 1993, due to his increasingly busy schedule, he had to step down as music director of the ensemble.

The year 1988 provided Ling with two distinctive honors. He was one of three conductors to receive the Seaver/National Endowment for the Arts Conductor's Award, a career development grant made to American conductors judged to be of extraordinary promise. That same year, Ling was appointed music director of the Florida Orchestra, which serves the Tampa Bay area. Since

the piano that he heard the kindergarten teacher play for the group of children that assembled daily in his family's home. At age six, he began formal piano instruction and by age twelve had taught himself Tchaikovsky's *Piano Concerto No. 1*. At age seventeen, he won the first of two Jakarta Piano competitions, and when he graduated from the Jakarta Music School, his sights were set on becoming a soloist. He then left for the United States as the recipient of a Rockefeller grant to study at the Juilliard School of Music under the tutelage of famed teacher Mieczyslaw Munz.

Early Experience on the Podium

While a Juilliard student in New York, Ling got his first taste of conducting as the director of his church choir. He became interested enough to sign up for a conducting course at Juilliard where his teacher, John Nelson, recognized his talent and encouraged him to pursue conducting seriously.

After graduating from Juilliard in 1975 with a master's degree in music, Ling was accepted into the highly competitive conducting program at the Yale University School of Music. As a student of Otto-Werner Mueller, Ling's career as a conductor began and he eventually earned a doctor of musical arts degree in 1985.

While training as a conductor at Yale, Ling also wanted to maintain his position as a pianist. He entered several piano competitions, winning the bronze medal at the becoming music director in Florida, he has been credited with bringing a degree of confidence and a high level of expectation to an organization that was losing ground. The doubling of subscriptions since his arrival as music director has been attributed to his dynamic leadership and commitment to the community.

One of Ling's most notable appearances with the Florida Orchestra was at Super Bowl XXV in January 1991. Ling led the orchestra in the performance of "The Star Spangled Banner" with Whitney Houston before a worldwide audience of 750 million. Subsequently, the recording of the performance on Arista Records earned a gold record with sales of more than 860,000 copies.

Other recordings on Ling's discography include an album of classical trumpet works with Rolf Smedvig and the Scottish Chamber Orchestra, which earned a Grammy nomination in 1990, and the Dupre Organ Symphony and Rheinberger Organ Concerto with soloist Michael Murray and the Royal Philharmonic Orchestra.

Jahja Ling has earned critical acclaim as a guest conductor for many of the world's leading orchestras. Along with the "Big Five" orchestras (Boston, Chicago, Cleveland, New York, and Philadelphia) he has led the North American ensembles of Cincinnati, Detroit, Houston, Los Angeles, Minnesota, Montreal, and San Francisco, among others. In 1988, he made his European debut with the Leipzig Gewandhaus Orchestra as the first conductor of Chinese descent to lead the ensemble and he was asked to return to the podium in October 1994. Other engagements abroad have included the Hong Kong Philharmonic, Netherlands Radio Philharmonic, Royal Philharmonic, National Symphony Orchestra of Taipei, and Tokyo's Yomiuri Nippon Symphony.

One of the highlights of Ling's career was his New York Philharmonic debut in 1993. Substituting for the ailing Kurt Masur, Ling conducted the world premier of Ellen Taafe Zwillich's *Symphony No. 3*. Ling recalled the significance of the event: "Because of the world premiere, there were thirteen critics in the audience. Having so many critics there was added pressure, but receiving good reviews from all of them was very satisfying."

In addition to his conducting duties, Ling continues to perform at the keyboard. He has appeared as soloist and conductor/soloist with the Cleveland, Florida, and St. Paul Chamber orchestras. He sees these performances as an opportunity to enhance his ability to communicate as a conductor, explaining, "When you play with the orchestra as part of the team, it makes a feeling of being a colleague. It makes the music flow better and they know what you mean musically."

In the summer of 1994 Ling stepped in to conduct the Los Angeles Philharmonic in a performance to Tchaikovsky's *Symphony No. 2*. The *Los Angeles Times* music critic Martin Bernheimer began his review, "His name is Jahja Ling. Remember it. . . . Ling capitalized on expressive restraint, crisp articulation, dynamic variety, and rhythmic propulsion. It was lovely.'"

Classical Music Ambassador

Ling is also committed to expanding the classical music audience. Since 1990, he has led free concerts of The Cleveland Orchestra in several of the city's downtown locations for Fourth of July celebrations, drawing as many as 100,000 listeners. "It gives me great joy when I can see so many people at concerts they wouldn't normally come to," he says. "There's a danger that classical music is thought only to belong to the elite, and we need to change that. When you can touch people with music, you have made an important connection."

Jahja Ling has relied on his strong Christian beliefs to guide him along the way. When faced with choices, he uses the power of prayers to guide him to a decision. He also feels this guidance during music-making, because "when you have an orchestra of over 100 musicians, from all different backgrounds, the focus that brings everyone together to convey a singular idea has to be from a greater power."

To keep his life's goals in perspective, Ling holds this philosophy: "Stay focused. . . . Don't underestimate or overestimate the talents you have been given. . . . Aim for your own target." Ultimately, he would like to take the reigns of a major orchestra and continue with guest conducting engagements. Paramount to his plan is finding a post that will not only provide him with quality conducting opportunities but also time to spend with his wife Jane, and sons, Gabriel and Daniel. "He'll always be busy and always working," ventured Michael Steinberg, part-time annotator for the San Francisco Symphony, and long-time colleague of Ling's. "He has a sort of magical personality. He'll bring people joy for years to come."

Sources:

Periodicals

Fleming, John. "From Red, White and Blue to Gold," *St. Petersburg Times*, November 22, 1991.

Rosenberg, Donald. "Jahja Ling: a Consummate Wielder of Orchestra Baton" *The Plain Dealer*, April 3, 1994.

"They Loved Ling in L.A." *Cleveland Plain Dealer*, August 6, 1994, p. B4.

Thomas, Michael. "A man of many movements." *City Reports*. October 15, 1992.

Other

Ling, Jahja, personal interview with Marilyn Eppich, July 8, 1994.

—Sketch by Marilyn Eppich

Gary Locke
(1950–)
Politician

As the first Chinese American to head a county government in North America, Gary Locke must be all things to all people: a visionary, a manager, and a leader. In his eleven years as a state legislator in Washington State, Locke earned a reputation for brilliance in budget-writing, for working sixteen-hour days, and for his obsession with detail. King County, encompassing the greater Seattle, Washington area, is an area where newer, affluent communities contrast with older urban neighborhoods and rural areas. As executive of this complex region, Locke is grappling with the same issues facing many regional governments in the mid-1990s: managing growth, providing services to a burgeoning population, balancing the concerns of city and rural residents, of developers and environmentalists, and planning for the future. King County faces enormous change, and, as its leader, Gary Locke mirrors that change.

Being a legislator was easy, he said in an interview with Himanee Gupta. "All you had to do was know every line of the state's budget, work frantically for four months to get your bills passed, and go home." As county executive, however, Locke must set the government's vision, identify goals, and choose how to go about carrying them out. "I am impatient sometimes," he admitted. "I have to learn that change doesn't happen overnight."

A Crucial Test

Locke's leadership skills passed a crucial test in late May 1994, when he was put in the position of bringing environmentalist and pro-growth forces together on the Seattle area's regional growth-management plan. After pondering the issue for months, Locke brokered a compromise that allowed some growth to expand into rural areas if developers also created a buffer of park land between urban areas and rural parts of eastern King County. The compromise, announced moments before elected officials from King County, Seattle, and the area's suburban areas were to start voting on new twenty-year growth-planning policies, stunned—and pleased—many observers. "You really have to give him credit for coming in and taking on an issue a lot of us have mulled over for years," longtime King County councilwoman Cynthia Sullivan told Gupta. "He brings a new perspective."

Seattle Childhood

Gary Locke was born January 21, 1950, in one of Seattle's poorest neighborhoods, the son of a Chinese immigrant mother and a World War II army combat officer. His

Gary Locke

father, James, owned a restaurant in the Pike Place Market and later a grocery. Locke grew up speaking Chinese at home, learning English only after starting kindergarten.

A straight-A student and a Boy Scout, Locke went to Yale in the late 1960s to study political science. Though smart, he often felt out of place among his wealthier, blue-blooded classmates, and he found himself missing Seattle. Nevertheless, he graduated in 1972 and earned a law degree from Boston University in 1975.

After earning his law degree, Locke returned to Seattle and took a job as a King County deputy prosecutor, which eventually led him into politics. He started out campaigning door-to-door for politicians such as future Seattle mayor Norm Rice, Seattle city councilwoman Dolores Sibonga and future congressman Jim McDermott. He found he liked the work, and after a 1981 staff job with the state senate's higher education committee, he was hooked. He ran for the state house of representatives in 1982, and came into office calling for reform in Seattle schools to improve education for poor and minority students.

His colleagues recall that in his first years in the state legislature, Locke played the role of angry agitator, who often made enemies. Over time, he became known more as a consensus builder, who would fight for his bills aggressively and eventually pull all sides together to broker an agreement. Eventually, he rose to chair the powerful house appropriations committee, where he acquired a reputation for brilliance in budget-writing. He was widely seen as a rising star, possibly a future U.S Senate candidate or Washington State governor.

Locke made his run for King County executive at a time when the county was gaining new clout and power. Before 1994, King County controlled a vast 2,200 square miles of territory but always seemed politically inept. A nine-member council set policy, tone, and agency. For eight years, Republican Tim Hill, Locke's predecessor, for eight years had entrusted the running of government to department heads. The region's real power base lay at Seattle City Hall.

A vote to merge King County with Metro—which provides the area's bus and sewer services—changed that. The day Locke was sworn into office, county government grew from 7,000 to 11,000 people. The county council grew to thirteen members, giving suburban representatives a majority and clout for the first time. Locke was assigned the role of regional leader, a job second in power only to governor.

Locke threw himself into office, becoming the region's leading decisionmaker. Yet, his critics chastised him at first for making decisions too slowly. Locke defends his pace, saying that his advisers suggested that he take things slowly, hire the right people, and get them working together. "Reshaping government takes time," he told Gupta.

The Politics of Inclusion

At the core of Locke's philosophy is a need to reach out to people that government has traditionally ignored. During his first six months in office he visited rural areas such as Duvall, a small community in the county's dairy lands, where local officials briefed him about road and bridge improvements, and the North Bend Senior Center where he promoted the idea of setting up offices in rural locations to make the county more responsive to all of its residents, who range from the rural, and largely conservative to the generally liberal population of the city of Seattle.

Locke frequently talks about a Nordstrom-style government, referring to the department store chain famous for its exceptional customer service. Locke's way of adapting the Nordstrom philosophy to government is to treat people with respect and to make government more accessible to ordinary people.

It seems Locke's philosophy is working. In 1994, he successfully led the King County Council and area developers into a compromise which brought together pro-growth and environmental forces. In the agreement Locke and the other parties forged, developers would build on 325 acres of a 2,025-acre area, preserving the rest to open space. All sides were ecstatic with the decision.

The compromise symbolized unity. County councilwoman Sullivan said at a press conference that she'd "rarely been prouder of an elected official than I am today of the County Executive." County councilman Larry Phillips, with whom Locke had had serious disagreements in the past, also was pleased, saying he was happy to see "a new way of doing business in King County."

Sources:

Periodicals

Gupta, Himanee. "Opposing Sides Praise County's Agreement on Grand Ridge." *Seattle Times,* May 19, 1994.
———. "Locke Faces Big Tests with Growth-Plan Vote—County Executive Learning Nuances of Job." *Seattle Times,* May 23, 1994.
Kno, Fidelius. "Man of the Year: Gary Locke's Star Rises in the Northwest." *Asian Weekly,* December 4, 1993.
Lim, Gerard. "Gary Locke's for Honest, No-Frills Legislation in King County, Washington." *Asian Week,* March 1994.
Moody, Fred. "The Man Who Mistook His Life for the Legislature." *Seattle Weekly,* February 27, 1991.
Schaefer, David. "Two Very Private Candidates—If You Find Locke off Duty, He's Likely to Have a Wrench in Hand." *Seattle Times,* October 31, 1993.

Other

Locke, Gary, interviews with Himanee Gupta, February–May 1994.
King County, Seattle, and suburban city officials and community activists, interviews with Himanee Gupta, February–May 1994.

—*Sketch by Himanee Gupta*

John Lone
(1952?–)
Actor, director, choreographer, composer

After almost a decade of classical training with the Beijing Opera, John Lone left his home in Hong Kong to move to Los Angeles where he spent three years in night school learning English well enough to take acting lessons. He struggled in Hollywood, discovering East West Players, the first Asian American theatre company in the United States, where he came to the attention of its founder and then-director, Mako, who cast him in a play written by a young, virtually unknown playwright, David Henry Hwang. Both the play and Lone won Obie Awards

John Lone

in 1981. Lone and Hwang worked together on additional projects, including Hwang's *The Dance and the Railroad,* for which Lone won his second Obie, and *M. Butterfly,* the 1993 film adaptation of Hwang's Broadway blockbuster. With a growing list of theatre and film acting credits to his name, Lone is fast distinguishing himself as one of Hollywood's most versatile actors.

"Not Chinese Enough"

John Lone's actual date of birth, although set in 1952, remains unknown. As an orphan, proper records weren't available on the details of his birth. As he grew older and needed travel documents, a birth date and name were chosen for him. At the age of about ten, Lone was taken by his guardian from his impoverished home in Hong Kong to join the Beijing Opera, a company that had fled China during the Revolution, which took in and trained children who did not have money but had the promise of talent. Lone remained in the company's near-monastic regimen, learning classical Chinese theatre techniques. The strenuous training included poetry, acting, dance, mime, singing, acrobatics, and martial arts.

Lone was trained in a style of opera that was so specialized that he was separated from his fellow students who were not even allowed to watch him rehearse. The only time any of the students were allowed to venture beyond the Beijing Opera walls was for performances. Isolated from any outside influences, academically and socially,

Lone began to grow more and more curious about the outside world. While in his teens, with the help of his guardian and the contrived story of an ill grandmother, Lone escaped. Two years short of his contract with the opera company, he spent months in fearful, guilty hiding. During this time he began to frequent movie houses, sometimes seeing two or three films a day, and discovered that he preferred American and European films over those that were Hong Kong-made.

Eventually, Lone began performing again. His acting and athletic abilities did not go unnoticed by the public. It was not long before he was offered a ten-year film contract to star in kung fu action movies for a major Hong Kong studio. At the same time, he was invited to join the Maurice Béjart dance company from Brussels. He declined both offers, choosing instead to immigrate to the United States.

Lone first settled in Los Angeles, and attended Santa Ana Junior College, where he earned his associate of arts degree. As he prepared to return to the world of performance, he became more and more fascinated with the possibilities of Western acting. He explained to the *New York Times* in 1983, "I grew up in this old world, this secret world, this religion of perfection. [Beijing] Opera is a total theater form with no psychological reason behind it. They teach singing, acting, tumbling, acrobatics, form, symbolism, everything except psychological understanding. . . . When I started studying Method, Western acting, I loved it. Now I understand there's a reason for a character's behavior. The approach is much more immediate, knowing the thoughts behind the character, the history. I was so excited."

Although his life in the small town of Santa Ana had been protected and free of racism, Hollywood proved to be less tolerant and virtually unsupportive. As he struggled to establish himself as an actor, Lone was told again and again by producers and directors that he was not Chinese enough for the Asian roles and too foreign for the leading roles.

David Henry Hwang's Interpreter

"There was really nothing for an Asian actor to do here," Lone told the *New York Times* in 1981. "The men we must portray are basically cooks or gangsters, and the women are prostitutes. My agent was sending me out whenever a movie or a television show needed an Asian actor for atmosphere or to introduce the plot. I did a couple of things—I hope they are forgotten—and used the money to pay for acting classes and unemployment time. I found myself very frustrated and going nowhere."

Then came Mako and the East West Players. Having read the script of David Henry Hwang's first play, *FOB,* Mako was convinced that the part of the fresh-off-the-boat immigrant cousin from Hong Kong unfamiliar with the ways of the West would be the perfect role for Lone. Lone went on to meet Hwang, land the title role, and appear in the production at the Joseph Papp/New York Public Theater. *FOB* won the Obie in 1981 for Best New Play and Lone won for Best Actor. The collaboration between Lone and Hwang was cemented. Don Shewey of the *New York Times* referred to Lone as "the key ingredient in Mr. Hwang's plays." Lone quickly gained a wide reputation as *the* interpreter of Hwang's plays.

Later in 1981, Hwang wrote a play specifically for Lone. In *Dance and the Railroad,* the two characters named Lone and Ma (for the actor Tzi Ma) are two Chinese men working on the transcontinental railroad, one of them a disciplined performer training for the Beijing Opera and the other a happy-go-lucky hedonist. Lone not only starred as the opera performer, but he directed, choreographed, and composed the music for the play, as well. He also picked up his second Obie. Hwang told the *New York Times* in 1983, "In *FOB* and *Railroad* I was consciously trying to blend Chinese theater techniques with a Western-style play. . . . What John has made possible is for me to physicalize a relationship between the two cultures."

In 1983, Lone directed and played the lead in Hwang's next production, a set of one-act plays, *The Sound of a Voice* and *The House of Beauties,* collectively known as *Sound and Beauty.*

In 1984, Lone made his film debut in the feature film, *Iceman,* about a prehistoric man found frozen in the Arctic ice and brought back to life by an anthropologist played by Timothy Hutton. Lone won the title role after the director, Fred Schepisi, saw him in *The Dance and the Railroad* at the Public Theater. In spite of working seventeen-hour days in heavy makeup and enduring five months of arctic winter, Lone found the challenge exhilarating. He recalled that during filming he had injured his knee and had to be flown by helicopter to the nearest health center. Arriving in full makeup and wardrobe as the prehistoric man, he startled more than one nurse.

Following the *Iceman,* Lone portrayed the leader of the Chinese Mafia in Michael Cimino's *(The Deer Hunter)* controversial *Year of the Dragon.* In spite of angry protests from the Asian American community that the film negatively portrays Chinese Americans and Chinatowns, Lone remained enthusiastic about his part in the film and did not waver in his support of Cimino.

Lone's subsequent roles were not nearly as controversial. In 1987, he spent six months in China filming the title role in Bernardo Bertolucci's *Last Emperor* which won the Oscar for Best Picture. Almost immediately following his return, he appeared in Alan Rudolph's *The Moderns* as an enigmatic businessman/art collector living among the expatriates in Paris of the 1920s. He then portrayed a Hong Kong businessman in a political thriller, *Shadow of China,* and an underworld crime lord in a gangster epic, *Shanghai 1920.* Both were Asian-produced and Asian-directed English-language films with an international cast.

In 1993 Lone returned to the world of David Henry Hwang, starring in David Cronenberg's film adaptation of Hwang's Broadway hit, *M. Butterfly.* Lone drew on his past with the Beijing Opera for the title role as the captivating opera star who carries on a long affair with a French diplomat. In 1994, Lone appeared opposite Alec Baldwin in the film *The Shadow* as Shiwan Khan, the last warrior descendant of thirteenth-century Mongol conqueror Genghis Khan. As determined as Lone's character is to take over the world, the Shadow is equally stalwart in stopping him. In 1995, Universal Pictures will release *The Hunter* starring Christopher Lambert and John Lone with director Jonathan Lawton.

From immigrant to prehistoric man to potential world ruler, Lone's roles have been as diverse as his many talents. He chooses each role carefully, allowing the audience to rediscover him with every new project. In a 1994 press release, Lone said: "Ideally, acting, even directing, is about revelation and sharing. I've been lucky to have the opportunity, the good fortune, to have a life and career which lets me experience that so often."

Sources:

Periodicals

Barnes, Clive. "A Workin' Railroad." *New York Post,* July 17, 1981.

Broeske, Pat. "Shanghai Surprise." *Calendar,* December 2, 1990, p. 26.

Harmetz, Aljean. "Japanese Make a U.S.-style Movie, in English, Aiming for Global Appeal." *New York Times,* October 14, 1989, p. 11.

Hilton, Pat. "The Sudden Success of John Lone." *Drama-Logue,* October 10-16, 1985, pp. 14–15.

"John Lone." *New York Times,* July 31, 1981, p. C2.

Shewey, Don. "His Art Blends the Best of Two Cultures on Stage." *New York Times,* October 30, 1983.

Watson, Steven. "The Primitive Innocence of a Lone Iceman." *Newsday,* April 22, 1984.

Other

Block-Korenbrot Public Relations. "John Lone." Press release, 1994.

Universal News. "John Lone, 'Iceman'." Press release, March 9, 1984.

—*Sketch by Terry Hong*

Bette Bao Lord

(1938–)

Author

Bette Bao Lord is a best-selling author of novels and works of nonfiction that have been translated into more than fifteen languages. She is also a civic activist who serves on many boards and is currently the chair of Freedom House, an organization established in 1941 by Wendell Willkie and Eleanor Roosevelt to monitor violations of political and civil rights and to promote the growth of democratic institutions around the world. She is a frequent lecturer on the topic of foreign affairs, and, specifically, on her native country, China.

Bette Bao was born on November 3, 1938, in Shanghai, China, to Dora and Sandys Bao. Sandys, her father, had been educated in England and China as an electrical engineer. When the Japanese invaded China he was commissioned in the army as a colonel. He spent much of the war building a power plant in Hunan Province, in China's interior. When the war was over Sandys was sent to the United States by the Nationalist government to buy heavy equipment to rebuild China. It was initially intended that he serve this time in America alone, but he was finally able to persuade the authorities to allow his wife and two of three daughters to join him. A third, the youngest girl, Sansan, was left behind with relatives because her parents thought the long boat journey across the Pacific would be too much for the infant.

Within a couple of years China's Nationalist government would become embroiled in a civil war with the communist forces of Mao Zedong. When the government fell in 1949, the Baos knew they could never go back, and further, that getting Sansan out would be nearly impossible.

The Baos settled in Brooklyn, New York, where Bette went to grammar school. Soon, though, the family moved to New Jersey, and Bette went to high school in Teaneck where she was a very popular, excellent student. She was elected secretary of the student council and was a member of the debating team. Upon graduation she enrolled in Tufts University in suburban Boston.

Bette's parents wanted her to study chemistry, and for her first year she did, until discovering that it wasn't right for her. Instead she earned a bachelor's degree in history and political science in 1959. From there she went on to earn a master's degree at Tufts's Fletcher School of Law and Diplomacy the next year.

Beginnings of Her Career

Bao's first job after graduate school was as assistant to the director of the University of Hawaii's East-West Cultural Center. The center grew considerably while she was there, due mainly to a large increase in federal funding, and by the time Bao left the job in 1961, she was in charge of a department of thirty-five people. From there she accepted a job in Washington as adviser to the director of the Fulbright Exchange program. In Washington she was reunited with Winston Lord, a man she'd met in college. In 1962 they were married. Also in that year, Bao's mother, feigning a serious illness, convinced authorities to allow her youngest daughter, Sansan, to visit her in Hong Kong. After making it to Hong Kong, Sansan escaped to America with her mother.

Bao Lord's First Book

Bao Lord continued in her job with the Fulbright Foundation while her husband pursued his career in diplomacy. In 1963 she was encouraged by some friends who had heard the story of Sansan and her separation from the family to write a book about her sister's life. The idea seemed very intriguing to her and she quit her job and devoted herself to the project full time. She interviewed Sansan extensively and in 1964 Harper published *Eighth Moon: The True Story of a Young Girl's Life in Communist China*. The book did remarkably well both critically and commercially. It was issued as a *Reader's Digest* condensed book and continues to be taught in high schools. Bao Lord also gave birth to a daughter that year, Elizabeth Pillsbury Lord.

In 1965 Bao Lord's husband was sent to Geneva as a member of the United States negotiating team at the Kennedy round of international tariff discussions. While in Switzerland, Bao Lord taught modern dance, something she'd been involved in since college. Upon returning to Washington two years later she had her second child, a son, Winston Bao Lord.

Winston Lord's political prospects brightened considerably when Richard Nixon was elected president in 1968. Nixon's chief foreign policy adviser was Henry Kissinger, and Lord was one of Kissinger's top assistants. When Kissinger was named secretary of state, Lord left his post with the national security council to follow him to the state department. As a top Kissinger aide, Lord accompanied him on five meetings with Mao Zedong in preparation for American recognition of Communist China. Bao Lord was not allowed to go with her husband on any of these missions, but in November 1973 she was allowed to return with her husband to the country of her birth.

Photographs she took during this trip were published in the *Washington Post* when she returned—they went on to win the National Graphic Arts Contest—and she signed a

Bette Bao Lord

contract with Harper and Row to write an account of her return to China.

In 1976 the Republicans were voted out of the presidency and the Lords decided to leave Washington for a while. They moved to Colorado where Bao Lord began work on her book. Her original intention was to write a nonfiction account of her return to China, but she was concerned that she might jeopardize the lives of some of the family members she had met with while there. China was at the time in the grips of the vehemently anti-Western Cultural Revolution, and people were routinely imprisoned or killed for having contact with what were considered "anti-revolutionary" Westerners. So she decided to write a novel instead. It was called *Spring Moon* and was published in 1981 to glowing reviews. It was nominated for a National Book Award, was on the *New York Times* bestseller list for thirty weeks, and earned an award from the Literary Guild.

In 1984 Bao Lord published her first children's book. Intended for fifth and sixth graders, *In the Year of the Boar and Jackie Robinson* is a fictionalized account of her first year in America, which she spent as a grade-schooler in Brooklyn, New York.

Ambassador's Wife

In 1985 Lord was appointed the American ambassador to China, and she returned with him to her native country.

While stationed in Beijing, Bao Lord immersed herself in the local arts community, and in 1988 she co-produced the play *The Caine Mutiny* at The People's Art Theater. The production was directed by the American film star Charlton Heston and the premiere was attended by Herman Wouk, the play's author. The play received excellent reviews—including Wouk's, who said it was the best production he had seen of his play since its world premiere.

Although Bao Lord had no official title in the diplomatic corps, she was an invaluable assistant to her husband during this period, which was an especially difficult one for the rulers of China. By the end of Lord's stay in Beijing, the city was in the midst of the student-led pro-democracy movement. Lord's ambassadorship ended in April of 1989, but Bao Lord stayed behind to help interpret events for CBS News. She had left, however, by the weekend of June 3rd, when government troops massacred hundreds, perhaps thousands, of unarmed students in Tiananmen Square.

In 1990 Bao Lord published her second work of nonfiction, *Legacies, A Chinese Mosaic*, which tells the story of her return to China as the wife of the American ambassador. The book became a *New York Times* bestseller, a Book of the Month Club selection, has been translated into ten languages, and was named one of the top ten books of nonfiction for 1990 by *Time* magazine.

Bao Lord holds honorary doctorates from Notre Dame, Tufts, Skidmore College, Marymount College, Bryant College, and Dominican College. She is a New York Public Library Literary Lion, is in the International Women's Hall of Fame, and has won the Exceptional Achievement Award from the Women's Project and Production.

Since the spring of 1993 she has been the chair of the Freedom House, a New York-based organization that seeks to foster democracy around the world. It issues yearly reports on the state of freedom in the world, listing countries that hold free and fair elections and those that don't. Another of the guiding premises of Freedom House is that it is in the best interests of the United States to remain engaged in the international community, resisting isolationist impulses at home.

Writing in *Newsweek* in 1992, Bao Lord addressed recent national concerns over ethnicity and the barriers that members of racial minorities experience in their attempts to succeed. In this climate, she observed, there is a tendency for groups to splinter from the mainstream, to cut themselves off into an enclave. She warned that this is a dangerous impulse, but she predicted that the need for it will be overcome "when we engage our diversity to yield a nation greater than the sum of its parts; we can be as different as brothers and sisters are, and belong to the same family; and we bless, not shame, America, our home."

Sources:

Books

Fox, Mary Virginia. *Bette Bao Lord: Novelist and Chinese Voice for Change.* People of Distinction series. Chicago: Children's Press, 1993.

Periodicals

Lord, Bette Bao. "Practice of Liberty Begins at Home." *USA Today,* December 20, 1993, p. 13A.
———. "Walking in Lucky Shoes." *Newsweek,* July 6, 1992, p. 10.

Other

Lord, Bette Bao, telephone interview with Jim Henry, April 18, 1994.

—Sketch by Jim Henry

Greg Louganis

(1960–)

Olympic diver, actor

As Greg Louganis mentally prepared for his last dive at the 1984 Olympic Games in Los Angeles, he quietly sang "Believe in Yourself" from the musical *The Wiz.* As he stood on the platform ready to launch into a reverse 3 1/2 somersault tuck—a dive so difficult that it had killed a man a year earlier—Louganis thought, "No matter what happens, my mother still loves me." When he emerged from the water, the scoreboard showed five 9s, one 9.5, and a 10. His final score for the competition was 710.91, an unheard-of feat. Not only had Louganis won the gold medal with a 67.41-point lead over the silver medalist, but he became the first diver in history—man or woman—to break the 700-point mark. He also became the first man in fifty-six years to win Olympic springboard and platform diving titles at the same Olympics. All this for someone who believes diving is an art, rarely a competition.

Four years later at the Seoul Olympics, Louganis at age twenty-eight was already considered an old man. With graying temples, he was exactly twice the age of his main competitor, a tiny sprite from China. But with the same grace and elegance that had always defined his unprecedented style, Louganis repeated his near-perfect reverse-3 1/2-somersault-tuck-of-a-final-dive to win gold and become the first man ever to take home two diving gold medals in successive Olympics. The day after his victory,

he left for Los Angeles where he was to serve as the host of a cable-TV show taped at a well-known local comedy club. "I picked up some *fabulous* jewelry over there," he teased the audience as he flashed his twin gold medals.

Born in 1960 of Samoan and Northern European ancestry, Gregory Efthimios Louganis was adopted shortly after his birth by Peter and Frances Louganis. Raised in El Cajon, a suburb of San Diego, Louganis was just eighteen months old when he began taking dancing lessons with his older sister, Despina. During these lessons, Louganis learned the concept of visualization which would prove crucial to his later championship diving technique. To help students memorize new dance combinations, the teacher would dim the lights, turn up the volume of the music, and ask the children to visualize the routine from beginning to end. "I didn't leave the room until I could do the routine flawlessly in my head," remembers Louganis.

From the age of three, Louganis performed in recitals and local talent competitions. He gained a self-confidence on the stage that he did not have when he was off it. In a school full of blond and blue-eyed children, the brown-skinned Louganis hardly fit in. "Nigger!" the children taunted him. Already uncomfortable among his unaccepting peers, Louganis's childhood was made more difficult due to a stutter so serious that it could only be overcome with speech therapy, and dyslexia which was mistakenly interpreted by teachers as mental impairment.

To compensate for the ridiculing he endured at school, Louganis concentrated his energies on dancing as well as gymnastics which he took up on the advice of a doctor who believed that the vigorous exercise might help cure Louganis's asthma. He began practicing his acrobatic routines off the diving board into the family's backyard pool. It was then that his mother Frances decided to enroll her son in a local diving class.

The Greatest Talent Ever Seen

Two years later, Louganis scored a perfect ten in the diving competition at the 1971 Amateur Athletic Union (AAU) Junior Olympics. Among the spectators was Dr. Sammy Lee, a physician and gold medalist in the ten-meter platform diving event at the 1948 and 1952 Olympic Games. "When I first watched him, I said to myself, 'My God, that's the greatest talent I've ever seen!'" Lee recalled. Four years later, Peter Louganis enlisted Lee's help in coaching his son to prepare for the 1976 Olympics in Montreal. During the six months before the Games, Louganis lived at Lee's home and practiced. He qualified easily for the team, but the actual Games proved to be a trial. First Lee had difficulties gaining entry to poolside to guide Louganis because Lee was not an official coach. Louganis, unable to concentrate on the day of the springboard final, finished sixth. The platform proved to be a better event. Louganis, just sixteen years old at his first

Greg Louganis

Olympics, earned second place, a mere 23.52 points behind the winner, Klaus Dibiasi, who took his third successive gold medal. "Next Olympics, I watch you," Dibiasi said to Louganis.

The eighteen months following the Olympics were dismal for Louganis. "When I came back from Montreal, a lot of my friends at high school wouldn't talk to me because they thought I had changed. It was very hard on me at the time," he said. Illness and injuries added to his pain and frustration.

By 1978, Louganis had a new coach, Ron O'Brien, who would not only take him through the 1988 Olympics, but more importantly, would become a close friend. That year, Louganis garnered four national diving titles, a world championship (where he succeeded Dibiasi as the gold medalist), and a scholarship to the University of Miami in Florida. In freshman English class, he was given "dyslexia" as a vocabulary word. When he checked the dictionary, he was elated. "For the first time, I knew I *wasn't* retarded." Louganis spent two years in Miami before he transferred to the University of California at Irvine where he could be closer to O'Brien who was now coaching at the world-famous Mission Viejo Club near San Diego. Two years later, Louganis graduated with a degree in theatre and dance.

Due to the Carter Administration's boycott of the 1980 Olympics in protest of the Soviet invasion of Afghanistan,

Louganis, who had been heavily favored to win gold, had to wait another four years. O'Brien made sure that he continued to learn more difficult dives. The first time Louganis attempted the inward 3 1/2 somersault tuck, he stood on the platform for thirty minutes, only to climb back down. O'Brien called him back saying, "If you have to eat dinner off the platform tomorrow you're going to stay until you learn that dive." For Louganis, it was an important choice: do the dive or quit the sport. The next day, he nailed it on the first try.

'I want to be just like Greg Louganis'

In spite of his extraordinary diving, Louganis's personal life was falling apart. He was sneaking a cigarette every chance he got and drinking more and more. The turning point finally came one day at a meet when he noticed a very young diver puffing a cigarette. "Why are you doing that?" asked Louganis. "I want to be just like Greg Louganis," replied the child. Louganis was finally cured.

At the 1984 Olympics, Louganis went into the first event, the springboard competition, under great pressure. As the reigning champion in both the platform and springboard, he felt that the judges expected greater feats from him: "[The judges] have seen probably the best dives that I've ever done in my entire life. Now they want to see something better. They don't want to see the same dives because their expectations are higher." Still, Louganis easily won the springboard competition with a 92.10 lead over the silver medalist. Two days later, he won the platform with his signature reverse 3 1/2 somersault tuck. His total score was an unprecedented 710.91. His performance could hardly have been more perfect—if he had scored a 10 from every judge on every dive, his total would have been only 79 points higher. "I doubt this performance will ever be equaled," Lee told a reporter. "It won't happen in my lifetime—or yours."

The next year, Louganis received the prestigious Sullivan Award, given to the nation's outstanding amateur athlete. More than the perfect athlete, he was quickly becoming a role model for thousands of teenagers. Finally breaking out of his binding shyness, Louganis spoke of his own difficulties as a youth. By sharing his experiences, he was able to release his own demons and fears while empowering struggling young people. They had choices to make, he told them, both positive and negative. Smoking, drinking, and drugs were negative. Sports and the arts were positive. "Feel good about yourself," he told them.

By the time Louganis appeared in Seoul for the 1988 Olympics, he had garnered forty-seven national diving titles, six Pan-American gold medals, five world championships, and the two Olympic golds. Victory in Seoul, however, proved to be a greater challenge. Louganis arrived with an injured wrist and a low-grade fever. Then he picked up the same sore throat that made its round to most of the participants. On top of that, there was the famous three-inch head gash injury he sustained during a preliminary round. In spite of everything, Louganis won the gold for the springboard event by just over twenty points. But the pressure only got worse. "I was the defending world and Olympic champion," he recalled, "and if I came back without two medals, I would have been considered a failure because everyone expected that I would get both. After I hit my head, I suddenly became an underdog. So that made each dive more important. I also knew but no one else knew at the time that these were going to be my last competitive dives. I didn't even tell Ron O'Brien and that added even more pressure to do well."

In spite of the obstacles, Louganis won gold again for the platform event. In the final dive of the day, he needed a hefty 85.57 points to take the lead from his fourteen-year-old rival. The last dive of his Olympic career brought him 86.70 points. He became the only athlete in the world to win two diving medals in successive Olympics. To add to his glory, Louganis was awarded the Olympic Spirit Award at the closing ceremony—in layman's terms, that made him the most inspiring athlete among the 9,600 assembled in Seoul. As Preston Levi, director of research services at the International Swimming Hall of Fame, told *Notable Asian Americans*, "Greg Louganis is the diver of the century."

The World's a Stage

Life after the Olympics has kept Louganis in the limelight, making use of his theatre and dance degree. On the theatre stage, Louganis has danced with the show Dance Kaleidoscope, starred in *Cinderella* at the Los Angeles Civic Light Opera, performed in *The Boyfriend* at the Sacramento Music Circus, sung and danced with the Cincinnati Pops Orchestra, and most recently appeared Off-Broadway in the comedy, *Jeffrey*, as Darius, a dancer in the chorus of the musical *Cats* who succumbs to AIDS. "It was a great experience for me to be in *Jeffrey*," commented Louganis. "It's a play that deals with AIDS and HIV, and I think that the two biggest problems facing the world today are with the environment and AIDS."

Besides the theatre, Louganis also has numerous movie and television credits, including guest commentating spots for national, international, and Olympic diving events. In addition, he has appeared in television commercials and in movies such as *The Mighty Ducks*. "I really enjoy film or television work more. I do enjoy the theatre, but making a living at it is impossible unless you're on Broadway," Louganis says realistically.

Not only does Louganis have an acting career, but so do his Harlequin Great Danes, which Louganis raises and trains. "My dogs got work before I did this year," he laughs. Two of his Great Danes were featured in the canine hit, *Beethoven II.*

In addition to his acting, Louganis is writing his autobiography, due out in 1995 from Random House. A few years ago, Random House released an unauthorized biography by Joyce Milton titled *Greg Louganis: Diving for Gold,* which Louganis describes as "a children's book, real cute,

but not completely accurate." The new book, he hopes, "will set the record straight."

Sources:

Books

"Louganis, Greg," *1984 Current Biography Yearbook,* New York: H.W. Wilson, pp. 239–242.

Periodicals

Anderson, Dave. "The State of the Art," *The New York Times,* August 8, 1984.
Hirshey, Gerri. "Arc of a Diver," *Rolling Stone,* September 22, 1988, pp. 87–91.
Janofsky, Michael. "Louganis Wins Historic Springboard Gold Medal," *The New York Times,* September 20, 1988.
Leerhsen, Charles. "True to the Olympic Ideal," *Newsweek,* October 10, 1988, pp. 63–64.
Michelmore, Peter. "Greg Louganis: High Diver with Heart," *Reader's Digest,* June 1988, pp. 163–170.
Neff, Craig. "It's a Bird, It's a Plane, It's Supergreg!" *Sports Illustrated,* August 20, 1984, pp. 80–83.
Skow, John. "A Soaring, Majestic Slowness," *Time,* August 20, 1984, pp. 62–63.
Stathoplos, Demmie. "No One Does it Better." *Sports Illustrated,* July 18, 1984, pp. 480–93.

Other

Louganis, Greg, telephone interview with Terry Hong, February 10, 1994.

—Sketch by Terry Hong

David Wong Louie
(1954–)
Writer

David Wong Louie is the author of the critically acclaimed short story collection *Pangs of Love, and Other Stories.* Published in 1991, *Pangs of Love* was reviewed in the *New York Times,* the *Voice Literary Supplement,* and the *Los Angeles Times,* among others—a considerable amount of attention for a first collection of short fiction. Louie holds a master's degree in fine arts from the University of Iowa, home of one of the country's finest graduate writing programs, and a bachelor's degree from Vassar. He has taught English since the early 1980s and today is an associate professor of English at the University of California at Los Angeles.

David Wong Louie was born in the suburban community of Rockville Center, New York, in 1954. His parents were first-generation Chinese immigrants who worked as laundry owners. Louie was a good student, attending the public school system in various cities on Long Island, New York. Invariably, there were very few Asians in the schools he attended and he grew up being constantly aware of feeling different. In high school, Louie took his first writing course and worked on a small literary journal, producing what he described for *Notable Asian Americans* as "bad high school poetry." Still, he claims he never really considered a career as a writer; he was more interested in geology. Louie graduated from East Meadow High School in East Meadow, New York, in 1973, near the top of his class.

As graduation approached, Louie met with his high school's guidance counselor to discuss where he should go to college. His parents had never gone, and he was not clear about what sorts of choices he had. A friend of his older brother's had gone to Vassar, and so he had a vague sense he might like to go there. The counselor tried to dissuade him and suggested that he instead go to the local community college, a move that was surely beneath someone of his academic standing. Looking back on this today, Louie attributes her condescending attitude to a racist belief that a Chinese American had no business at one of the country's premier private colleges.

Vassar College

In the fall of 1973, Louie began studies at Vassar College in Poughkeepsie, New York. At Vassar, he felt much as he had growing up on Long Island. He was once again in an area nearly without Asian Americans, feeling like an outcast and wondering how he fit in. This, however, may have had more to do with class than race, Louie told Jim Henry in an interview. In his first year he took a course in geology and found it utterly tedious and decided he would look for another major. He took some liberal arts classes, notably in Asian American studies, including some Chinese language courses. He also took some English courses, including a couple of advanced writing courses that piqued his interest in writing and diverted him, finally, from the "bad poetry" of his high school years to the writing of short fiction.

After graduating from Vassar in 1977, Louie moved to New York and took a job at a small advertising firm, Zolinko and Zolinko, which worked mainly in trade magazines. Louie hated the job and he wanted to get out of New York so he applied to graduate school at the University of Iowa, where many of his writing friends at Vassar had talked about going. He hadn't been doing any creative writing and still wasn't seriously considering a career as a writer, but he thought a master's degree would be helpful.

Louie describes his experience at Iowa as very helpful. He found it stimulating being around people who were

David Wong Louie

passionate about what they were studying, and he caught their passion in his second year when he really began to apply himself to his writing. Many of the stories collected in *Pangs of Love* were first written during this time. He graduated from the University of Iowa in 1981, and in 1982 he married and moved with his wife to the Los Angeles area, where he taught composition part time, devoting the rest of his time to writing and rewriting. He taught at various schools in southern California, including Cal State and San Bernadino.

During this time Louie's short stories were being published by some of the most prominent literary journals in the country, including the *Chicago Review, Fiction International,* the *Iowa Review,* and *Ploughshares.* In 1989 his story "Displacement" was included in *Best American Short Stories, 1989,* published by Houghton Mifflin.

After a few years, Louie had collected enough stories to publish them in book form and he began sending them around to various literary contests. He made the finals a few times, but he never won. Then he decided to do what all writers are warned not to even try doing, so seldom does it work: he sent it out to publishers, unsolicited, hoping to get an editor at one of the major houses to read it. To his astonishment, it worked, and an editor at Crown made him an offer. With an offer from a major publisher, Louie was able to find an agent, and the agent negotiated him a better deal with Knopf; in 1991 his collection was published.

Pangs of Love, and Other Stories was widely reviewed by the press when it was published. Sybil Steinberg writing in *Publishers Weekly* called it a "notable debut collection [in which] Louie paces off the perimeters of alienation as he portrays a series of characters emotionally imprisoned and isolated. . . . Louie transmits rage and bitterness into an impressive matrix of plot and character conveyed in biting prose." Richard Eder wrote in the *Los Angeles Times,* "It must be said right off that Louie is the furthest thing from a genre ethnic writer. He is elegant, funny, a touch spooky, and has as fine a hair-trigger control of alienation and absurdity as any of the best of his generation."

Gary Krist said in the *New York Times,* "The characters in *Pangs of Love . . .* are a remarkably varied group, but most of them have one thing in common—a distinctly unstable sense of identity." And the *Voice Literary Supplement* remarked that Louie differs from the current flock of Asian American writers in saying "In making sense of America, some Asian American writers have focused on historical epic or ancient myth. Although it's not a wrong, or even undesirable, way to go about it, this approach tends to overlook the subtler psychological and emotional contours of being there. In this sense, David Wong Louie breaks new ground: his stories are more impressionistic than expressionistic, his characters more quirky than emblematic."

Louie currently lives in Los Angeles with his wife and their child, a son named Julian. He told Henry that he is currently working on a novel and is spending time rewriting his short stories, a habit in which he says he indulges to excess.

Sources:

Periodicals

Eder, Richard. "Meeting the Twain," *Los Angeles Times Book Review,* June 16, 1991, p. 3.

Krist, Gary. "The Ratchety Process of Change." *New York Times Book Review,* July 14, 1991, pp. 13–14.

Steinberg, Sybil. Review of *Pangs of Love Publishers Weekly..* vol. 238, no. 21, May 10, 1991, p. 270.

Voice Literary Supplement. Review of *Pangs of Love,* vol. 101, December, 1991, pp. 13–14.

Other

Louie, David Wong, telephone interview with Jim Henry, May 6, 1994.

—Sketch by Jim Henry

Elwood Lui
(1941–)
Judge, attorney

Although Elwood Lui's fast-track career is marked by such achievements as becoming the first Chinese American appellate court judge and the fourth Chinese American judge appointed in California, that does not mean that getting through law school was easy. "It seemed impossible at the time," he remembered. Working full time as a Certified Public Accountant (CPA) with a family of four to support, Lui also had U.S. Army Reserve duty during the Vietnam War years—all this in addition to attending law school at the University of California at Los Angeles (UCLA). "I don't remember sleeping very much at that particular time of my life," said Lui with a chuckle.

Born on February 4, 1941, in Los Angeles, Lui was the youngest of seven children. His parents had immigrated in the 1920s from Canton, China, and settled in the Los Angeles area. "They came over for the usual economic reasons, to start a new life and to raise a family," explained Lui. As a child of immigrant parents, Lui faced racial tensions and witnessed the resulting difficulties his parents endured. Although securing housing and buying property were made difficult for his parents, Lui's father prospered nonetheless in the wholesale produce business, helping farmers deliver their merchandise to businesses and retailers. "Immigrants often had to be their own boss because they couldn't get jobs anywhere else," said Lui. " My father was one of the early businesspeople who was able to give jobs to people—Chinese, Hispanic, any kind of worker."

High School Success

Education was always the first priority in Lui's home. "My parents really stressed education," explained Lui. "Actually, the correct word was *pressure.* They pressured me toward a good education." Fortunately, in high school, Lui "hung around with a lot of people who wanted to go to college and become professionals and do well in life." He also kept his life well-rounded, balancing academics with sports as a member of both the track and basketball teams. Lui recalled that "high school was one of the best experiences of [his] life." Los Angeles High School was ethnically, racially, and economically balanced. "It was a real blessing to have grown up in an area that was a true melting pot," commented Lui.

When Lui entered UCLA as an undergraduate, he was at first unsure as to what career he would pursue. "My parents left me alone to choose," he said. He began in engineering, moved to history, and finally settled on accounting. "I thought accounting looked like a good way to learn business and get a good job," he commented. Upon graduation in 1962, Lui volunteered for the Army Reserve as a way to avoid interrupting his schooling. He didn't want to get drafted, preferring instead to fulfill his military duties on his own schedule.

Lui Takes to the Bench

After six months in the army at Fort Ord near Monterey, California, Lui returned to UCLA, this time for his master's in business administration. Graduating in 1964, he embarked on a career as a CPA. One year in the field made him realize that a career in law would be more appealing and provide greater opportunities for a varied career. He began taking night classes in law at Loyola University, then transferred to the full-time program at UCLA. Graduating in 1969, Lui was the only Asian American in his law class that year. He spent two years as a deputy state attorney general, concentrating on anti-trust and consumer protection cases. From the public sector, he then moved into private practice with Mori and Katayama, a predominantly Asian firm with a base of major Japanese clients.

In 1975, barely six years after Lui had been admitted to the bar, then-California governor Jerry Brown appointed Lui a municipal court judge. Lui spent a few weeks in the traffic court, six months at the arraignment court, a year on preliminary hearings, and another year on a misdemeanor master calendar before getting a trial assignment. In 1980, Lui was elevated to the superior court and was given a juvenile court assignment. Just over a year later, he was again elevated, this time to associate justice of the California Court of Appeal, Second Appellate District. He enjoyed his six-year tenure there more than the other judicial posts because it gave him the opportunity to have a significant impact on the law.

Lui took early retirement in 1987 and joined the second largest law firm in the world—Jones, Day, Reavis and Pogue. Among the more than 1000 lawyers in the firm, Lui was the first Asian American partner. His decision to leave the bench was partly economic. Like his parents, he "wanted [his] children to have the best education possible." He added with a laugh, "It's hard to pay for a Yale education on a judge's salary," referring to his elder son who graduated from Yale University and is also a lawyer.

His prior experience as a judge makes Lui well-suited for his current specialization in appellate and litigation work. Focusing predominantly on business matters, Lui also counsels clients on tax and government law matters. "The legal world is very different now," he said. "Twenty years ago, Asians never had the opportunity to represent major companies like GM, Toyota, and Isuzu. With more and more Pacific Rim businesses entering the U.S., doors that were previously locked are now open to Asian Americans."

As Delbert Wong, the nation's first Chinese American judge, had inspired Lui to his own great achievements,

Elwood Lui

Lui today serves as a role model for aspiring Asian Americans entering the legal arena. Hopeful candidates seek out Lui for advice and guidance. "I tell them that it's a great career, but if they want to be a judge, they have to be motivated by something other than economics. If they have the right attitude, they can really do a lot for society," he advised.

In spite of his successful legal career, Lui is "most interested in public service." He asserts that his most rewarding experience was as the Interim Director for the Los Angeles County Department of Children's Services in 1990. In charge of the abuse and neglect department, Lui was responsible for some 50,000 children in foster care. "As a lawyer, my job is to advise and serve clients. That role doesn't often offer you an opportunity to make an impact on social issues. Being involved with the Department [of Children's Services] gave me a renewed sense of what a person in the public sector can do to impact society."

Something besides Engineering

According to Lui, he plans to stay with Jones, Day, Reavis and Pogue for the foreseeable future. After that, he may seek a position in the public sector, including returning to the bench: "It depends on who the president or governor is and the political situation at the time."

"Being a lawyer is a great experience, a great opportunity for Asian Americans to do something that a few years ago just didn't seem possible," said Lui. He added with a laugh, "Besides, non-Asians will start to see that Asians can do something outside the area of science."

Sources:

Periodicals

DeBenedictis, Don. "Profile," *The Los Angeles Daily Journal,* October 5, 1982, pp. 1 and 17.

Distad, Carl. "Profile," *The Los Angeles Daily Journal,* August 11, 1980, pp. 1 and 23.

Other

Lui, Elwood, telephone interview with Terry Hong, January 24, 1994.

—Sketch by Terry Hong

M

Yo-Yo Ma
(1955–)
Cellist

Under his father's tutelage, Yo-Yo Ma began playing a child-sized version of the cello at age four. Remarkably, he started with a Bach suite. So pronounced was his exceptional talent that he gave his first public recital at age five at the University of Paris, playing both the cello and the piano. At nine, Ma began studying with the legendary cellist Leonard Rose at the Juilliard School in New York City, an arrangement orchestrated by the noted violinist Isaac Stern. By fifteen, Ma had graduated high school and by nineteen, he was being compared to such famed cellists as Mstislav Rostropovich and Pablo Casals. As he entered his twenties, he was acclaimed as one of the world's greatest instrumentalists. Ma was hailed unequivocally not only for his technical superiority, but for his astoundingly mature powers of interpretation. Today, he is indisputably the most extraordinary cellist alive.

Yo-Yo Ma

A Method to His Madness

Yo-Yo Ma was one of two children born to musical expatriates living in Paris, France. Ma's father, Hiao-Tsiun Ma, a violinist and former professor from Nanjing University in mainland China, had arrived in 1936 to further his musical studies. Ma's mother, Marina, gifted with a beautiful voice, was Hiao-Tsiun's former student at Nanjing and moved to Paris in 1949. The two were soon married and in 1951, had a daughter, Yeou-Cheng. Four years later on October 7, 1955, Yo-Yo was born.

Hiao-Tsiun Ma taught music to his children at an early age. Yeou-Cheng began the violin at age two-and-a-half while Yo-Yo began studying the cello and piano at age four. "My father was a born pedagogue," Ma told the *New Yorker* in 1989. "He wanted not only to advance himself through learning but to share that learning. He wanted to teach everybody; it was his way of life." The older Ma tutored his precocious children in French history, Chinese history, mythology, and calligraphy. For music, he developed a method of teaching young children how to concentrate intensively. The premise of his method was to break down musical works into small, fully comprehensible pieces. "I would learn only two measures a day which is no strain at all," recalled Ma in a 1981 article in the *Saturday Review*. After just a year of study, Ma had learned, two-by-two, all the measures of three Bach cello suites. "Everyone would say to my father, 'Ma, you're driving your kids crazy!' But it wasn't hard work. My father didn't believe in long hours of practicing; he really believed in very concentrated work. It was mentally hard work. I used to practice only five to 10 minutes a day, but whatever I did had to be with tremendous concentration. And you know, I hated those 10 minutes."

Later, Ma explained further to the *New Yorker,* "I found this method ideal, because I didn't like to work hard. When problems in cello techniques arose, my father would apply the principle, '*Coupez la difficulté en quatre.*' [Cut the difficulty in quarters.] This helped me avoid the kind of strain young cellists often experience. When a problem is complex, you become tense, but when you break it down into basic components you can approach each element without stress. Then, when you put it all together, you do something that seems externally complex, but you don't feel it that way. You know it from several different angles."

Hiao-Tsiun's pedagogical techniques were the foundation for what became Ma's unparalleled technical superiority. Again and again, Ma would return to that foundation whether learning a new piece or reinventing an already mastered composition.

A New Life

So quickly did the precocious Ma learn compositions, he gave his first public concert at age five at the University of Paris, playing both the cello and the piano. One year after that first performance, in 1962, the Ma family moved to New York City. Originally, Hiao-Tsiun had planned a visit for the sole purpose of convincing his discouraged brother who had recently immigrated to the United States not to return to China. The six-month visit grew to sixteen years.

In New York, Ma began lessons with Janos Scholz, the distinguished cellist. Scholz told the *New Yorker* in 1989 that Ma was "the most natural and eager boy you could imagine." He continued, "We went through a mountain of repertoire in two years. He learned with lightning speed. He was everything one could wish for in a student, and the last I ever took."

Already the child Ma was gaining notice, performing regularly since his debut, playing with orchestras and symphonies throughout the world. Isaac Stern was one of many who quickly recognized Ma's prodigious talent. "I first heard Yo-Yo play in Paris when he was five or six years old," Stern told the *New Yorker*. "The cello was literally larger than he was. I could sense then, as has now been confirmed, that he was one of the most extraordinary talents of this generation. I was so taken by him that when he was nine, I arranged for him to study with Leonard Rose. Lenny told me that, unlike any other student he could remember, Yo-Yo would come to every lesson perfectly prepared. It's not just that he had practiced. He played every piece from memory and had obviously worked constantly on everything he had been assigned. He bloomed under Lenny." For seven years, he studied with Rose. Ma began as a timid child who literally tried to hide behind the cello. "I was afraid to speak to Mr. Rose above a whisper. . . . He tried to get me to overcome my timidity by constantly urging me to sing out on the instrument," Ma told the *New Yorker*.

While he developed and matured as a musician with Rose's paternal nourishment, Ma had difficulty adjusting to puberty and his teenage years. "As soon as we moved to America I had to deal with two contradictory worlds. At home, I was to submerge my identity. You can't talk back to your parents—period. At school, I was expected to answer back, to reveal my individuality. At home, we spoke only Chinese; we were taken to Chinese movies to remind us of our traditional values. But I was also American, growing up with American values. . . . My home life was totally structured. Because I couldn't rebel there, I did so at school. In the fifth grade, I began to cut classes, and I continued to so do through high school. I spent a lot of time wandering through the streets, mainly because I just wanted to be alone," Ma told the *New Yorker*. Eventually, in 1968, Ma enrolled in the Professional Children's School, where the teachers, convinced that Ma was skipping classes out of boredom, placed him in an accelerated program. By age fifteen, he graduated high school.

First Freedom

At Rose's suggestion, Ma spent the summer after high school graduation at Meadowmount, a music camp in the Adirondacks run by the late Ivan Galamian whose students included such notables as Itzhak Perlman and Pinchas Zukerman. That summer was Ma's first experience away from home, completely on his own. Suddenly he was free. Ma recalled to the *Saturday Review:* "I just went wild: Never showed up at rehearsals, left my cello out in the rain, beer bottles all over the room, midnight escapades to go swimming, and just about everything." In spite of his undisciplined behavior, Ma told the *New Yorker*, for the first time he had discovered "uninhibited freedom—just letting go, in a way that had never happened before" in his playing. Ma suddenly leapt into a new dimension—his virtuoso playing now commanded a newly unleashed imagination and creativity.

Ma's unbridled behavior continued when he returned from Meadowmount. He shocked Rose by appearing for his first lesson that fall wearing a leather jacket and uttering a string of obscenities. "I'm embarrassed when I think of the language I used," Ma told the *New Yorker*. "But Mr. Rose took it in his stride and saw me through this phase. At some level, he must have been very happy to find me opening up in that way. And, for some reason, he kept his faith."

After high school, while continuing his lessons with Rose, Ma entered Columbia University. Still living at home, Ma quickly realized that taking college classes was little different from going to high school. Without telling his parents, he eventually dropped out and began hanging around Juilliard. Trying to act older than his age, he got himself a fake I.D. and began drinking. "One day," he told the *New Yorker*, "I passed out in a practice room, having thrown up all over the place. They thought I had O.D.'d on drugs. So they carted me off by ambulance to Roosevelt Hospital, where they recognized that I was suffering from the effects of alcohol. As I was a minor, my parents were sent for. A moment of deep shame in the Ma household. . . . The news of my drinking spread to friends in France. All I was trying to do was to be accepted as one of the guys, and not be considered a freak. But for the next five years everywhere I went people would look at me and think, 'This guy is trouble.'"

Into the Ivory Tower

At the age of seventeen, following the advice of Isaac Stern among others, Ma entered Harvard University. His older sister had studied at Radcliffe, eventually going to Harvard Medical School and becoming a pediatrician, in addition to remaining a superb musician.

In four years, Ma finished a full course of study while continuing to keep up with his cello career, continuing to give regular performances. He took whatever classes interested him; in addition to music, he took courses in the rise and fall of civilization, Chinese and Japanese history, anthropology, French civilization, fine arts, modern Chinese literature, German literature, Dostoyevski, astronomy, math, sociology, and natural sciences. With characteristic modesty, he explained to the *New Yorker* how he was able to juggle both a full academic load and an active performing schedule: "I was able to manage because I was unbelievably lazy in everything. I had very low standards—I didn't feel compelled to get high grades, or to practice many hours every day. I worked in spurts. If I could no longer put off writing a paper, I studied into the night. And when I had a concert to give and didn't want to make an absolute fool of myself I'd put in a few more hours of practice. . . . my generally undisciplined approach to life offers me the possibility of doing many things."

For Ma, college was a period of maturation and growth, both personally and professionally. "I wanted to try and tie together the various threads of my life—my Chinese upbringing, the atmosphere of Paris, my totally different experience in America. Studying history was a way of putting these diverse cultures in perspective." At the same time, his musical knowledge grew vastly. "While I was at Harvard, I gained a new vocabulary for understanding music: linear polyphony, harmonic rhythm, hidden scale relationships." As Stern observed to the *New Yorker*, "[Ma] learned musical analysis and a good deal about life in general. But above all, he learned how to learn. . . . He learned how to apply himself in the best possible way to everything he needed for his artistic development."

Ma made his London debut during his years at Harvard. As concert requests began to come more frequently, Ma realized it would be possible for him to support himself as a musician. At the same time, so crowded was his calendar with concert dates that his academic work suffered to the point that he considered dropping out. At his father's insistence, he remained and limited his performances to one a month. "In retrospect, I'm happy I followed [my father's] advice," he admitted to the *New Yorker.*

Not only did Ma survive college, but his long-term, long-distance relationship with Jill Horner, whom he had met

at age sixteen, blossomed through intense correspondence and astronomical telephone bills. The two were married in 1977. Although Ma's father initially disapproved of the marriage—he feared that Ma's marriage to a Westerner would threaten the continuation of family traditions—he eventually came to accept Jill as his daughter-in-law and when the two grandchildren were born, he gave them each Chinese names.

A Musical Career

After graduation, the Mas spent three more years at Harvard with Yo-Yo as artist-in-residence at Leverett House and Jill teaching German. They eventually settled in Cambridge, Massachusetts, and figured out ways to survive Ma's demanding concert schedule. "When we married, we never imagined how busy my career would become," Ma told the *New Yorker.* "We had visions of an equal relationship, where we would share the cooking, share taking out the garbage—share everything. To make matters worse, I've proved horrible at all domestic chores. During my first years of performing, all the traveling and concertizing seemed terribly exciting. . . . [I ended] up with as many as a 150 concerts a season. I was always flirting with getting burned out from exhaustion."

Two major events finally convinced Ma to reevaluate what was most important in his life. In 1980, Ma had an operation for scoliosis, a curvature of the spine. He was faced with the very real possibility that he might never play the cello again. "Long before the operation, I was prepared for the possibility that it might not turn out successfully," Ma said to the *New Yorker.* "I had decided that there's more to life than the cello. There are so many things that I find enormously exciting. . . . perhaps I'd do social work, or become a teacher." Fortunately, the operation proved a total success and even after six months in a body cast, Ma's cello playing was unimpaired. Gladly, he re-embraced and accepted his chosen musical career.

The second event that dramatically changed Ma's life was the birth of his first child, Nicholas, in 1983. "When you have your first child, everything changes. You realize that life is finite, that you absolutely have a limit to your energy. You give, you love, you care, and it's all different," Ma recalled in the *New Yorker."* So I finally sat down and wrote out a list of the things I care most about. First of all, I promised myself that if I ever felt really burned out and lost enthusiasm for giving concerts I'd be responsible enough to quit. After all, if I lose interest in what I'm doing how can anyone else be interested? Second, I decided that every concert I played—no matter if the city was big or small—was going to be special. Third, I accepted the fact that only one person is responsible for what's going on, and that person is me. . . . So if someone suggests adding just one more concert at the end of a tour—it's always just one more—you just have to say no. Itzhak Perlman, who is dedicated to his family, showed me how to take a good, hard look at a schedule and protect time for my family." With his family as first priority, Ma has learned well how to balance both the professional and personal aspects of his fast-paced, ever-changing life.

Yo-Yo Ma, the Performing Musician

While the rest of the world can only speak of Ma in the most intense superlatives, Ma described himself to the *New Yorker* as "just a performing musician." He gives all credit to the music's composers: "I feel that when a composer writes a piece of music he's translating a human experience into sound." Ma's intention, as a musician, is to bring that experience, whether it was written 100, 200 years ago, or just 100 days ago, to the audience through an imagination based on empathy. "One must go out of oneself, finding empathy for another's experiences, forming another world."

This is the kind of interpretation, the formidable power of imagination that has earned Ma deserving acclaim. "I know my greatest joy as a musician when I am playing a concert dedicated exclusively to Bach," he explained to the *New Yorker*. "Then for a whole evening I'm living in one man's mind— and a great man's mind. That's how I can justify being a performer. One is involved in a process that is larger than oneself."

While he is lauded for his interpretations of Bach, as well as Mozart and Beethoven, Ma constantly challenges his own abilities by determinedly expanding his repertoire. Ma plays a considerable amount of twentieth century music, including Samuel Barber, Benjamin Britten, William Walton, Penderecki, Lutoslawski, Kirchner, Carter, Henze, Dutilleux, as well as new American works. Ma has taken on new projects that push the boundaries of traditional music. In 1992, he performed with jazz vocal artist Bobby McFerrin to create *Hush,* a collection of duets that paired Ma's cello and McFerrin's chameleon voice. The same year, he gave a series of concerts at Tanglewood in Massachusetts in collaboration with the technology gurus from Massachusetts Institute of Technology's Media Lab who created a series of computer "hyperinstruments" with which Ma performed the world premier of a work by Tod Machover, *Begin Again Again.*

With over fifty recordings and eight Grammy awards, Ma's genius has already proven itself both sustaining and prolific. Whether in collaborative efforts with such diverse performers as his long-standing colleague, pianist Emanual Ax, to the jazz pianist Claude Bolling, or playing solo, Ma's future will undoubtedly include a few surprises.

For his performances, Ma told the New Yorker he has one simple goal: "I hope that people will want to come to concerts, and that those who already do will continue to be excited by the music they hear." Always and foremost, for Ma, it is the music that should draw audiences and nothing more. He added, "The listener should develop a personal relationship to the music."

Sources:

Periodicals

Blum, David. "Profiles: A Process Larger Than Oneself." *New Yorker.* May 1, 1989, p. 41+.
"The Courage to Go Forth: Yo-Yo Ma in Conversation." *Economist,* vol. 322, no. 7746, February 15, 1992, p. 107+.
Eisler, Edith. "Yo-Yo Ma: Music from the Soul." *Strings,* May/June 1992. pp. 58–62.
Kupferberg, Herbert. "Yo-Yo Ma." *Stereo Review.* vol. 55, no. 4, April 1990, p. 70+.
Thorne, Richard. "The Magic of Yo-Yo Ma." *Saturday Review.* July 1981, pp. 55–58.

Other

ICM Artists. "Yo-Yo Ma." Promotional material. New York, New York, August 1993.

—*Sketch by Terry Hong*

Mako
(1933–)
Actor, director

When veteran actor, Mako, returned from New York to Los Angeles in 1960, he spent five years doing what he described to Terry Hong as "small features and next-to-nothing-parts." During those years, he got to know many Asian American actors with whom he would meet informally. "All we talked about," remembered Mako in an interview with Hong, "was . . . the lack of decent roles for Asian Americans. Even actors who were more established than I was were talking about the same thing. So one thing led to another and eventually it came down to a group of seven of us who were totally committed to forming an organization."

In 1965, the young group of Asian Americans, under Mako's leadership, founded East West Players, the first Asian American theatre in the United States. For the first time in theatre history, Asian Americans had a venue in which to perform rewarding roles in realistic settings. During Mako's more than two-decade reign, he "discovered" such playwrights as Wakako Yamauchi and Philip Kan Gotanda. Under his artistic direction, the fledgling company matured into a premiere showcase of Asian American talents.

While he devoted much of his energies to developing and growing East West Players, Mako continued his career as an actor outside the realm of Asian America. In 1966, he earned an Oscar nomination as Best Supporting Actor in *The Sand Pebbles*, starring Steve McQueen. He also won a Golden Globe Award for the same performance. In 1975, he received a Tony nomination for Best Actor in the Broadway musical, *Pacific Overtures.*

An East/West Beginning

Makoto Iwamatsu, later shortened to just Mako, was born on December 10, 1933, in Kobe, Japan. "For political reasons," Mako spent the majority of his childhood in Japan with his grandparents although the rest of his immediate family was already living in the United States. The family was reunited after World War II when Mako arrived in New York in 1949. "It was a big adjustment coming from Kobe to New York," he recalled to Hong. "I came from post-war Japan where people had nothing to speak of, where they were just beginning to reconstruct Japan. When I arrived in New York, the first thing that came to mind was how fat, how obese the people were. In post-war Japan, there were very few fat people. In the US there were so many."

Mako lived with his parents on the Lower East Side of Manhattan. "There were so many derelicts and winos on the sidewalks," he remembered. "I thought this was a very strange country that had come up victorious in World War II."

Quickly accepting his surroundings "for what they were," Mako eventually enrolled at the Pratt Institute in New York to study architecture. He was asked one day by a classmate to help in designing and building a theatre set. Mako was quickly drawn into the theatre world: "It seemed more interesting than remaining in school . . . and I became more involved in theatre, artistically and emotionally," he told Hong. He missed so many of his own classes that he soon lost his draft deferment and for two years, he served in the U.S. Army in Korea and Japan. "I was confused about my future, so while I was in the service, I had two years to think about what that future should be."

In the meantime, Mako's parents had moved to Los Angeles and upon his discharge, he joined them there and began studying at the Pasadena Playhouse on his G.I. Bill. "Acting was the farthest thing from my mind at the beginning . . . but I thought I was young enough to attempt learning something about theatre and then I could decide if I should pursue acting," he said to Hong. At the Playhouse, Mako at first felt overwhelmed. "My initial impression of my classmates was that it seemed they had done so many things in theatre, with acting, before having come to Pasadena. They seemed so seasoned, even though they were only in their late teens and early twenties. I felt I had nothing and in essence, I was in awe of these people." The Playhouse's system of weeding students out each quarter proved to Mako that he had the talent to continue in acting.

Mako

Following graduation, he returned to New York. "I wanted to study more. The Method was the rage at the time. Paul Newman, Marlon Brando were using it. They were my idols so I wanted to study where they had come from, The Actors Studio.... I auditioned two years in succession and didn't make it, but I decided to follow someone who was teaching the Method ... and studied for the next two years," he told Hong.

Making His Own Roles

Mako returned to Los Angeles and was confronted with the difficulties of being an Asian American actor at a time when film giants such as Marlon Brando and Alec Guinness were playing the few leading Asian roles, complete with prosthetic make-up and a pidgin accent, while Asian American actors could only get negligible roles as houseboys, gangsters, and No. 1 sons. Mako found small roles in television, including "McHale's Navy," "Ironside," and "M.A.S.H.," and a few movies.

In an effort to establish a venue that would give Asian American actors a chance to perform substantial roles, Mako—together with James Hong, June Kim, Guy Lee, Pat Li, Yet Lock, and Beulah Quo—founded East West Players in 1965. The fledgling company's inaugural production was staged in a small church basement in 1966. *Rashomon*, a play based on the short story by Japanese writer Akutagawa Ryunosuke, was well received. Mako urged director Robert Wise who was then casting the film,

The Sand Pebbles, to come see the show which eventually led to the role that earned for Mako an Oscar nomination and a Golden Globe Award in 1966. "It was a very, very good experience," Mako recalled to Hong.

By 1968, East West Players found a permanent home on Santa Monica Boulevard in Los Angeles's Silverlake area. Under the artistic direction of Mako, East West Players initially focused on play adaptations by Asian novelists such as Yukio Mishima. At the same time, the group staged Western classics by such writers as Lorca and Goldoni, providing Asian American actors with the opportunity to try roles that had been previously inaccessible to them due to their skin color. Soon after, the company began to concentrate on plays written by Asian Americans, premiering at least one original work almost every season. During Mako's more than two-decade reign, he not only directed and performed in plays, he even wrote an original production, *There's No Place for a Tired Ghost,* about Japanese Americans who died in internment camps during World War II. Since 1977 when East West Players won three Los Angeles Drama Critics awards for the debut production of Wakako Yamauchi's *And the Soul Shall Dance,* the citations and awards have continued almost every year, including numerous Drama-Logue and L.A. Weekly Theatre awards.

In 1989, Mako resigned from East West Players after disagreements with the Board of Directors could not be reconciled. He told Hong that in retrospect, two elements were outstanding regarding his experience: "One—being able to teach acting, to share my experiences with aspiring actors, which meant sharing an understanding of the craft of theatre as well as exposing them to the racist-oriented conditions of the theatre; and two—being able to develop a short story writer or novelist into a playwright and making them aware of the collaboration that goes on in theatre." Although he is no longer involved with the group he helped found, Mako remains a seminal figure in Asian American theatre, producing plays on his own—"the right pieces for which [he] personally sees potential."

A Star, a Star

In February 1994, thirty Hollywood Walk of Fame stars were dedicated, including one marked for Mako. *Asian-Week* columnist Sumi Haru reported that the cheering by Mako's fans topped those of Sophia Loren's. "We were proud, happy that one of our own was finally being recognized as an honest-to-God Hollywood star. This means big time; but, of course, that doesn't mean he'll be offered better parts or more money," wrote Haru. Mako was equally realistic as he explained, "In a way, it was anti-climactic, as opposed to getting an Oscar or a nomination which opens more doors. The Stars event was sponsored by the Hollywood Chamber of Commerce as opposed to the industry and so it has little impact on one's career."

Mako's career, however, remains active. After appearances in more than three hundred television shows and thirty plays, after directing more than one hundred performances

and starring in dozens of films, Mako has built a reputation as a performer, in addition to building his most important legacy in East West Players. As an actor, Mako talks about the struggle between taking the less than perfect roles in order to work and maintaining the idealism of searching for more meaningful roles. Realistically, Mako himself uses the word "compromise" in describing his own approach to roles. "Compromise happens with almost every role, in any job," he told Hong. "One learns to compromise one's ideals, though not sacrifice them. A give-and-take situation happens every time."

Today, Mako is looking forward to a future of producing and directing his own projects. "Movies or theatre, it doesn't really matter," he said. "But it will have to relate to Asian American history in this country. About Asian American contributions to this country."

Sources:

Periodicals

Fields, Sidney. "Only Human." *New York Daily News,* January 9, 1976. p. 81.

Haru, Sumi. "Mako." *AsianWeek,* February 18, 1994.

Pacheco, Patrick. "When Worlds Collide." *Los Angeles Times,* Calendar section, April 19, 1992. pp. 3+.

Other

Mako, telephone interview with Terry Hong, March 7, 1994.

—Sketch by Terry Hong

Beckie Masaki

(1957–)

Social worker, women's advocate

Beckie Masaki is a co-founder and executive director of San Francisco's Asian Women's Shelter. Founded in 1988 by a small group of Asian activists in the Bay Area, the shelter provides safe shelter and a wide array of social, economic, and legal services to women from the Asian community who are suffering abuse in their relationships. The shelter is capable of housing up to six or seven families at a time, provides a twenty-four hour telephone hotline, and performs valuable community outreach services, educating the Asian community about domestic violence and offering victims a badly needed alternative to enduring it.

Beckie Masaki was born on December 9, 1957, in Sacramento, California, to second-generation Japanese American parents. Her father owned a small fish store in Sacramento at the time of Masaki's birth, which he built up after he lost everything during World War II when the Masakis, along with 120,000 other Japanese Americans, were imprisoned as threats to national security. In an interview with Jim Henry, Masaki described her knowledge of this event as being pivotal in the formation of her sense of injustice in this society. She said it taught her "that anything can be taken away, even your home, through no fault of your own."

Fine Arts and Psychology

Masaki was educated in the public school system of Sacramento. She was a good student and was especially interested in art. After graduating from high school in 1976 she enrolled in the University of California at Berkeley, where she began studying fine arts. This choice caused a stir with her parents, who believed it was a foolish course of study. She was, after all, a member of the first generation of the family to have the resources to go to college. Masaki partially acquiesced and took up psychology in addition to art and graduated with a double major in 1980.

While at school, Masaki had become interested in the various forms of political activism on Berkeley's campus, though she didn't quite know how she could fit in. She saw that the third world movement and the ethnic studies programs were dominated by men and the women's organizations were dominated by whites; she felt marginalized in both these areas.

After graduation Masaki took a job with the Educational Guidance Center, which sponsored a program in which Masaki travelled to inner city schools and counseled students interested in higher education. She later worked for a program called Upward Bound, a federally funded project that brings students from inner city schools to college campuses to interest them in college. She worked in these two programs for a year and then decided to return to school to work toward a master's degree in social work.

In 1981 Masaki returned to Berkeley where in a class of two hundred there were eight Asians, six of whom were women. Masaki told Henry that this was her first contact with socially active women of Asian descent. Masaki and these colleagues formed a group called the Asian Caucus of the Social Welfare Program, which met primarily to address support issues of its members. Also during this time, Masaki met other women of color from other backgrounds who shared her interests in social activism.

Shelters for Battered Women

In 1983 Masaki graduated from Berkeley with a master's degree in social work and went to work for a women's shelter in San Francisco called La Casa de las Madres. This

Beckie Masaki

was her first experience working with battered women and Masaki found the politics of the battered women movement disheartening. When she asked about why there were no Asian women being served by the shelter she was told by a director that there was very little domestic abuse in the Asian community, and what little there was was generally handled within the family in accordance with Asian custom. Masaki was shocked to hear such an ignorant statement coming from a women's activist, especially one at a shelter serving women of color. She told Henry that it was less indicative of a mindset at La Casa than it was of society and the battered women's movement in general, both of which were just beginning to understand the need for ethnic pluralism.

Masaki quit her position at La Casa in protest over such ignorance and stereotyping. She took a half-time job with California State University at Hayward counseling students at an inner-city community college in Oakland. With her remaining time Masaki began working on starting a shelter for Asian women, a goal she and a core of like-minded activists had been working toward since about 1983. They spent the next three years making their idea a reality. In 1988 they opened the shelter in a rented four bedroom house in San Francisco. At the insistence of her colleagues, Masaki became executive director, a position she still holds.

The shelter's commitment to the Asian community goes beyond providing a safe space for abused women. Masaki told Henry that she was especially proud of the work they do in breaking cultural ties that feed Asian women's beliefs that they must preserve the family above all—even above their own health and safety. The shelter teaches the women that there is an alternative, and that the deep Asian commitment to family stops applying when the family becomes abusive. Masaki said that it was especially gratifying seeing how this message frees so many women.

The shelter also provides economic assistance, job training, legal advice, and translation services for the more than forty languages spoken by the immigrant Asian community in San Francisco. For legal services, the shelter refers women to community law groups, but then continues to work with and support them throughout any legal battles.

At its first home, the Asian Women's Shelter was turning away 75 percent of the women who came to it for lack of space. In 1994, however, they bought a building in San Francisco that allowed them to double their capacity. They have also initiated a broader outreach program in which they attempt to reach disabled and lesbian Asians.

Masaki told Henry that she felt that the "notable" thing about the work she has done is not that she did it, but that it was done. She said that there were many people who played just as significant a part in the founding of the shelter as she did, and mentioned specifically the shelter's women's advocate Mayseng Saetern, and two of its original founders, Debbie Lee and Deeana Jang. Masaki has continued to work on her art—she works in mixed media and printmaking—and has had several shows at local community cultural centers in the Bay Area.

Sources:

Masaki, Beckie, telephone interview with Jim Henry, August 4, 1994.

—Sketch by Jim Henry

Donald Masuda

(1961–)

Gay rights advocate

Donald Masuda is a health care professional and longtime community activist who in 1987 co-founded Gay Asian Pacific Alliance (GAPA), a non-profit support group and social service provider headquartered in San Francisco, California. In addition to this work, Masuda also co-founded GCHP, the GAPA Community HIV Project.

Donald Masuda was born in San Francisco on January 17, 1961. His father is a retired army officer and a retired guard at San Quentin Federal Pententiary and his mother is a retired seamstress. Masuda was educated in the San Francisco public school system, where he was a high achiever in academics. He was also a member of the Boy Scouts, an experience, he told Jim Henry in an interview, that helped shape his lifelong commitment to serving society. He attended Lowell High School, an academic high school with high admission criteria and high expectations of its graduates. The administration of Lowell High also influenced Masuda, who said that graduates of Lowell are "expected to go out and change the world." He further said that he's "always felt that . . . you need to be a good citizen and contribute to society and community, because you only get out what you put in."

Start in Health Care

Masuda graduated from high school in 1978 and enrolled in a local community college, working part time and saving money with the hope of eventually transferring to the University of California at Berkeley. After two years at the community college, Masuda transferred and majored in physiology, expecting to use his degree to get into medical school. While in school, Masuda helped organize the Asian Health Students Alliance of UC Berkeley, which provided students with information about career alternatives in the health field, such as nursing, health education, health administration, and public health. The Alliance also encouraged students to become involved in volunteer work at hospitals. Masuda was also active in the Alpha Phi Omega service fraternity, which performs service projects for groups such as day-care centers and the Special Olympics.

After graduating from Berkeley in 1983 with a bachelor's degree in physiology, Masuda was hired by the emergency room at the University of California at San Francisco Medical Center, where he had been volunteering. Today he serves as the unit coordinator of the emergency room.

Political Activism

Also after graduation Masuda got involved in politics and was elected to the board of the Alice B. Toklas Democratic Club, a gay political organization in San Francisco. He was very interested in learning about the political process of effecting change, but eventually found himself discouraged by forces within the various movements he participated in that expected him to, as he told Henry, "choose . . . that either you're gay or you're Asian when it came to issues: you're either for us or against us." This mindset prompted Masuda to form GAPA to provide a forum where gay Asians would not be forced to take sides on issues. He founded the organization in October of 1987, serving as co-chair until January of 1990.

Also in 1990, GAPA started its own HIV education and social services agency called GCHP, the GAPA Community

HIV Project, which as of 1994 had twenty-three full-time employees. GCHP offers services to the Asian community in education, outreach, medical support, translating, case management, living well groups, alternative medicine services, and special support services for surviving friends and family of AIDS victims. Masuda currently serves on the boards of both organizations and is the special liaison between the two boards. He is also the international affairs chairperson of GAPA and as such is in contact with gay advocacy groups in Japan, Hong Kong, Singapore, the Philippines, and Korea, where gay men face a variety of stigmas and government discrimination and harassment.

Masuda serves the gay and Asian communities in several other capacities as well. He has worked for the Asian AIDS Task Force, a precursor of GCHP, and he was co-chair of the Asian Pacific AIDS Coalition. He is the current chair of the opening night committee of the Asian American Film Festival, a fund-raising event for the HIV-Asian community. He also served on the board of the San Francisco AIDS Walkathon from 1989 until 1992.

Among the many awards Masuda has received for his work are the Harvey Milk Democratic Club Award in 1991, the GAPA Man of the Year Award in 1989, the University of California at San Francisco's Service Excellence Award (1991), and UCSF's Edison Uno Award for Public Service. Masuda works as a retreat facilitator for various ethnic gay organizations and was recently funded by the Centers for Disease Control to serve as a consultant to GCHP to work nationally on helping other Asian gay organizations get to the point where they can open an HIV project.

Sources:

Masuda, Donald, telephone interview with Jim Henry, August 4, 1994.

—*Sketch by Jim Henry*

Tom Matano
(1947–)
Automotive designer

Tom Matano is the executive vice president of the design division of Mazda Research and Development of North America. Since becoming vice president his studio has produced the designs for such popular cars and trucks as the Navajo, MX-3, 929, MX-6, 626 and the B Series trucks introduced in 1994. He was also a contributor to the design of the Miata, one of the most successful and sought-after new cars when it was introduced in February 1989.

Tom Matano was born on October 7, 1947, in Nagasaki, Japan. When the United States dropped nuclear bombs on Hiroshima and Nagasaki in 1945 in a successful effort to end World War II, Matano's family lived on the other side of a mountain from "ground zero" and thus survived the destruction. Matano's father was a salesman with the industrial giant Mitsubishi Heavy Industry, working in the shipbuilding division. His mother was a traditional housewife. The family moved from Nagasaki to Tokyo when Matano was still an infant, and for the remainder of his childhood they lived in and around Tokyo. Throughout his life, though, he would spend his summer and winter vacations with his grandparents in Nagasaki.

Early Exposure to Automobiles

As a young boy Tom was exposed to automobiles. He had an uncle, a former kamikaze pilot with Japan's Royal Air Force, who had built a car from spare parts and took the family on frequent trips. His father had a very wealthy uncle, as well, who owned a 1951 Cadillac, which he later traded in for a 1957 model, the elaborate design of which fascinated the young boy. This much exposure to automobiles was rare in Japan, where the personal automobile did not become a commonplace item until the 1970s.

In high school, Matano was an above-average student. The Japanese education system does not offer classes in automobile shop or design, so Matano would on occasion skip school to hang out in race shops. After graduation from high school he entered Seiki University in Tokyo, where he studied analysis engineering. He had wanted to study design, but he would have been required to take an additional two years of classes before even being allowed to apply for admittance to the program. While attending Seiki, Matano worked part-time for a large Tokyo advertising agency, which hired him to drive cars—often in the middle of the night—to remote sites for photographic shoots. Soon he was working on the production team scouting the sites used for the shoots.

In 1969, Matano visited America for the first time. He arrived, via cargo ship, in Everett, Washington, and took a bus to Los Angeles. From there he traveled to New York and then back again. As he told *Notable Asian Americans*, "I had seen the States, and this trip gave me a taste of long-distance driving." By this time Matano knew he wanted to work in the design field, and he had been told by friends and business connections that he had the talent, all he needed was the degree. He went to the U.S. embassy in Tokyo to research American schools of design, and in 1971 he began classes at the Art Center College of Design in Los Angeles.

While in school, Matano observed that most of the Japanese students kept to themselves. He didn't want to isolate himself, however, so he spent his lunch hours sitting with the Americans, listening to how they spoke, trying to learn the language more completely. For doing this, he said in

Tom Matano

an interview with Jim Henry, he was shunned by the Japanese students. In 1974 he earned a bachelor of science degree in transportation design.

An International Career in the Auto Industry

After graduation Matano was hired by General Motors to work on the design staff in Warren, Michigan. After eighteen months, however, he was unable to renew his visa to remain in America. In 1976 he left this country for Australia to work for General Motors' Holden design team there. He stayed in Australia for six and a half years. He then accepted a job with BMW AG in Munich, Germany. He liked the working environment at BMW, but couldn't adjust himself to the cold Bavarian climate and so he left to join the Mazda design team in California where he works today.

He joined Mazda in the winter of 1983. Two of his first jobs were the MPV, Mazda's entry in the lucrative minivan market, and the Miata, a classic roadster. A sporty two-seater with a ragtop, the Miata became so popular Mazda had tremendous difficulty keeping up on orders for it. Matano told Henry that when he worked on the design for the Miata, he relied on his belief that one can literally "plan" to make history. With the correct attitude, Matano explained, one can, from the outset of an endeavor, plan to make it succeed in a history-making way. With the Miata, this has certainly worked.

Matano was made vice president of the California design team in 1991. As such, he is responsible for distilling the work of several designers into a finished, final design, which is then sent to Japan to be reviewed. Along with the designers' drawings and computer images of the final product, a full-scale handcrafted clay model is sent along. Even as vice president of design, Matano still works on these clay models, trying to instill in them his philosophy of design, which he described for *Metropolitan Home* magazine: "Think of a raindrop when it falls on a curve. As long as the raindrop doesn't have to think twice about where it's going to go next, then the design is good. So, in my imagination, I become a raindrop and I go all over the surface to find the stoppages. Then I go back and smooth them all out." This remarkably poetic philosophy of design may explain the success Mazda has had in recent years, and the singularity of the design of its cars in an industry increasingly dominated by what some consider to be formless, unimaginative design.

Personal Beliefs

Matano thinks of himself as having the temperament and belief system of an American. He loves southern California and intends to apply for citizenship in the future. He says he has never encountered any racism or stereotyping in America and believes that the success stories collected in *Notable Asian Americans* should serve as inspiration to all Americans, and not just Asian Americans. He added that it would be a shame if *Notable Asian Americans* was only read by that segment of this vast and diverse country.

Matano told *Notable Asian Americans* that his motto is: "Don't be afraid of mistakes, and never repeat the same mistake twice. . . . When I was growing up, I read many success stories, and one of the common threads was that every one of them had made huge mistakes . . . so I thought if I could organize my mistakes and my many unique and interesting experiences, then one day I may get to tell a story or two."

Sources:

Periodicals

"Thinkers." *Metropolitan Home,* vol. 26, no. 2, March/April 1994, p. 52.

Other

Matano, Tom, telephone interview with Jim Henry, April 13, 1994.
Matano, Tom, written interview with Jim Henry, March 28, 1994.
Mazda Corporation, Department of Research and Development. "Tom Matano." Press releases and internal documents. April, 1994.

—Sketch by Jim Henry

Prema Mathai-Davis
(1950–)
Organization executive

Prema Mathai-Davis

For many an adventurous woman traveling alone, the sight of the familiar Young Woman's Christian Association (YWCA) sign means safe lodging and a welcoming smile. Established in 1858, YWCA's success as an international association has been phenomenal. It is the oldest and largest women's organization in the U.S., boasting a membership of nearly two million girls and women. On February 1, 1994, the YWCA of the United States took an unprecedented step. It selected Dr. Prema Mathai-Davis as its national executive director. An American of Asian Indian descent, Dr. Mathai-Davis became the first foreign-born woman to lead the group.

Actually, the appointment is a homecoming for Dr. Mathai-Davis, whose family has a long tradition of involvement with the YWCA. Her great-grandmother helped start two YWCAs in India at the turn of the century, and her maternal grandmother, several aunts, and mother have been YWCA leaders in India and Pakistan.

Born in the state of Kerala, India on October 28, 1950, Prema Mathai was brought up in a Syrian Christian family. She shone brightly as a student and attended Delhi University's prestigious Lady Irwin College, where she received her bachelor of science degree in 1970 and then went on to earn a master's degree in child development in 1972. After graduation she decided to travel to Massachusetts to continue her education. In 1979, she completed her doctorate in human development at Harvard University. While at Harvard she met Wallace Davis, whom she married in 1978. The couple lives in New York with their three children, a son and twin daughters, as well as Mathai-Davis's parents, who came from India to live with them in the U.S. Starting their own tradition by joining both their last names, Mathai-Davis, Prema and Wallace have created their own intergenerational household in this country.

A Public Service Tradition

Interest in public service was instilled in Prema Mathai from early childhood. She grew up in a multigenerational household resplendent with love and achievements. Her father, Stephen, established the largest relief effort in India, Christian Agency for Social Action, which delivered needed services to refugees from Tibet and Bangladesh at critical times in recent history. He retired as an advisor to the United Nations World Food Program for the Pacific region. Her mother, Susy, was also an ardent volunteer for several public service efforts. "My parents were my role models," recalled Mathai-Davis in an interview with Shamita Das Dasgupta. "They taught me the value of public service. I knew I wanted to leave a mark in this world."

Mathai-Davis started her career in academia, instructing in universities and colleges in India and Western Samoa. However, academia did not hold her attention for long. Soon she moved into the public service arena and took on leadership positions in the field of institutional health care. Her first such position was as director of New York's Mount Sinai School of Medicine-Hunter College Long Term Care Gerontology Center, where she worked from 1979 until 1981. She left that position to serve as director of Social Service Programs with the Community Service Society of New York, where she worked until 1985. She then became president and chief executive officer of the Community Agency for Senior Citizens, Inc., of Staten Island, New York, a position she held until 1990. In all her work, Mathai-Davis showed consistent dedication to the welfare of the elderly.

Mathai-Davis became nationally recognized as an advocate for the aged when in 1990, Mayor David Dinkins appointed her as New York City's Commissioner in the Department for the Aging. There she managed and oversaw the delivery of comprehensive services to 1.3 million older adults, working with a budget of $150 million and a staff of 400. She is the first person of Asian Indian descent to hold cabinet rank in the city of New York. In 1991, New York governor Mario Cuomo appointed her to the board of directors of the Metropolitan Transportation Authority of the State of New York. She is the first Asian to be appointed to the board of the country's largest transportation network. Her reputation as a visionary leader preceded Mathai-Davis and ultimately led to her appointment in 1994 as the national executive director of YWCA.

Although Mathai-Davis took the helm of the YWCA at a time when the organization is experiencing downsizing and budget retrenchment, she has great plans for it. Mathai-Davis wants to make the 126-year-old organization into a significant national presence. Her goal is to break YWCA's image as only a service provider. Mathai-Davis told Dasgupta, "We are about the empowerment of women and children, and the elimination of racism. I think we are on the cutting edge of the future."

Mathai-Davis believes that her cross-cultural background and international professional experience are assets in working with the diverse population of the United States. "My being an American of Indian roots and the experience of living in a variety of countries give me a multicultural and multiracial perspective," she observed. Mathai-Davis asserts that this special perspective will provide YWCA with its new directions.

Breaking Tradition

The path to success has not been easy for Mathai-Davis. Being an Asian Indian woman in the U.S. workforce has meant dealing with stereotypes and preconceived notions. "People tried to put me into prelabeled baskets that did not fit me. I would not allow them to do it. I broke all barriers by excelling in everything I did," Mathai-Davis stated. Nevertheless, such treatment has helped her become sensitive to differences in others. "I became careful about prejudging anyone. One must be treated as an individual at all times and not be boxed in from the start." She brings this philosophy to all her activities. For instance, while working for the elderly, Mathai-Davis focused on destroying all stereotypes that exist between the generations, and has encouraged intergenerational interactions to dispel myths about the elderly. In the same vein, she has established a unique program for minority communities, a program that addresses the needs of Latino, African American, and Asian elderly in New York City.

Mathai-Davis's accomplishments are impressive. By 1994, she had developed a national Aging Agenda by creating a partnership with 675 area agencies and the National Council of Leadership Organizations. This agenda was presented to key House and Senate members and was incorporated into the Republican and Democratic party 1992 platforms. In addition, she organized a forum with Japan's Ministry of Health and Welfare to discuss Japan's ten-year strategy for addressing older citizen's needs. She was involved in coordinating the United Nation's international conference on population aging, and also convened the first national conference on intergenerational programming for at-risk children and youth.

Mathai-Davis has received several awards and recognition for her exemplary career achievements, among them New York's Spirit of the City Award in 1994.

As a working mother Mathai-Davis shares issues and problems with all women with similar life-styles. "It is a life of juggling everything—being a wife, mother, daughter, daughter-in-law, everything," said Mathai-Davis. However, she declared women can overcome all this with "a sense of self, a passion for the goal, and a stubbornness to move forward." She believes that no obstacle can ever deter one from the desired goal. Mathai-Davis's career is a living testimony to her belief.

Mathai-Davis's Asian Indian roots have given her some enduring values: a strong sense of family responsibility and a dedication to public service. She deeply believes that all of us must give something back to our society. Her advice to all new immigrants, especially Asian Indians in the United States, reflects her strong convictions about social responsibility. "If we are to be considered in equal terms with the rest of Americans, we must become fully participating members of this society. We must give something back to our land of choice, America."

Sources:

Periodicals

McNatt, Robert. "Y Chief Preaches Revival Message." New Executive Profiles, *Crain's New York Business*, March 7, 1994, pp. 31.
Melwani, Lavina. "YWCA's National Director: An Advocate for Women of All Ages." *India West*, February 11, 1994, pp. 41, 44.

Other

Mathai-Davis, Prema, telephone interview with Shamita Das Dasgupta, June 14, 1994.

—*Sketch by Shamita Das Dasgupta, Ph.D.*

Robert Matsui

(1941–)

Politician, attorney

Congressman Robert Matsui has represented California's fifth district, the Sacramento area, in the House of Representatives since 1978. In time he has become a senior member of the House Ways and Means Committee, perhaps the most powerful committee in Washington, and has taken the lead on many public policy issues dealing with tax policy, social issues, health care, and welfare reform. In late 1993, he was entrusted by the Clinton administration with marshaling congressional support for the North American Free Trade Agreement (NAFTA), a hotly debated free trade agreement among the United States, Canada, and Mexico. The treaty at times seemed to be floundering and in grave danger of being rejected by Congress, which would have been a major defeat for the new president who had staked his political reputation on its passage. Matsui's leadership on the issue put him in the national spotlight, and the treaty's ultimate approval—considered a remarkable political achievement for the young administration—was due in no small part to Matsui's efforts.

Robert Takeo Matsui was born in Sacramento, California, in 1941, to second-generation Japanese-American parents. This was a dark time in American history for civil rights of Japanese Americans. With tremendous loss of life, Pearl Harbor had been attacked by the Japanese, and the country had been whipped into an anti-Japanese hysteria that led to the now infamous Executive Order 9066 mandating the imprisonment of Japanese Americans on the West Coast. In April 1942, Matsui—then less than a year old—and his family were sent to an internment camp where the young boy spent the next three years of his life. Recalling his imprisonment for *A. Magazine* the congressman said, "I have no memory of it, just flashbacks; we were released when I was about four. My parents rarely talked about it, since it was an issue of shame that our loyalty was put into question. They were citizens, born in this country. Yet because we were at war with a country our ancestors happened to come from, we were considered a security risk."

An Early Interest in Public Service

After their release at the end of the war, the Matsuis returned to Sacramento and attempted to rebuild their lives. A pivotal event in Matsui's younger years was reading the autobiography of Clarence Darrow, the famous trial lawyer. Darrow, he told *A. Magazine*, "said the basis of law is to protect the underdog, and that appealed to me—the need to protect those in need, who are not part of the system." This sense of protecting the interests and rights of the underrepresented would stay with Matsui all his life and serves today as the drive behind his legislative agenda.

After high school, Matsui enrolled in the University of California at Berkeley, where as a sophomore he recalls being inspired by President John F. Kennedy's now famous call to public service. After graduation, he enrolled in Hastings College of Law where he earned his J.D. in 1966. In 1967 the young lawyer returned to his hometown of Sacramento with his new wife, Doris (Okada), to begin a private practice. The early years of his law practice were difficult, and the young couple had to struggle to get by. Within a few years, however, Matsui had become an established member of the community, joining

Robert Matsui

such civic and cultural organizations as the Japanese American Citizens League, the Barrister's Club, and the 20-30 Club, all of which he later served as president.

In 1971 Matsui saw his opportunity to run for public office when Sacramento's city council districts were redrawn, leaving the incumbent Republican in his district vulnerable. Matsui ran an inexpensive campaign, utilizing community support earned in his years of networking. According to Matsui in *A. Magazine*, his first political race "was really an interesting campaign, and it shows how an Asian American can run for public office. A lot of my parents' friends helped, the Asian American community helped, and, at the same time, a lot of the friends we'd made . . . helped. It really was a shoestring operation—we ran it for about $8600—but we all pitched in." Matsui won the race and served on the Sacramento City Council until 1978 when he ran for the U.S. Congress.

The idea to run came when the incumbent congressman from Matsui's district told Matsui that he would retire after his next term. Three contenders immediately jumped into the race, with Matsui far behind the others in initial polling. But as was the case in his council races, Matsui ran a grass roots campaign, relying on volunteers and calling upon his extensive connections throughout the local community. In *A. Magazine*, Matsui recalled that "hundreds of people . . . were showing up at the headquarters, willing to walk the wards. The Asian American community, and all the different organizations we were involved in, really mobilized behind us." He won the race, and in 1992 was reelected to serve his seventh straight term as representative.

In Congress

In his first year in Congress, Matsui expressed interest in sitting on the House Judiciary Committee, believing his law practice and the work he had done as a businessman would be useful to the committee's work. Here he encountered racial stereotyping, something he has fought against all his career. He was told by the Democratic leadership that they had imagined he would be more interested in serving on the immigration committee. "Here I was," he said of that moment in *A. Magazine*, "thirty-seven years old, I had just won a very competitive primary and a tough general election, and I had reached a position which only 435 people in a country of 260 million people are able to achieve, and *still* I was immediately stereotyped as an Asian." Instead of being defeated by such incidents, Matsui says he learns from them and overcomes them. He sees himself not only as an example for other Asians, but for the population at large. He hopes they will see what he has achieved and recognize those abilities in other Asians. "I'm a politician who happens to be Asian American," he told *A. Magazine*. "I take my experience with me; I don't deny my past, and I *shouldn't* deny my past."

In his second year in office Matsui realized his ambition and was granted a seat on the Ways and Means Committee, generally considered the most powerful committee in either house of Congress. Today the congressman is the ranking Democrat on the Ways and Means subcommittees on trade and human resources, and is the eighth ranking member overall. As leader of the forces supporting NAFTA in 1993 in Congress, Matsui worked with a bi-partisan team that included academics, business leaders, environmentalists, and former cabinet secretaries, and he was a frequent guest on television news and talk shows. Other legislation Matsui has worked on includes the Enterprise Capital Formation Act, an economic growth initiative, various child welfare reforms, mass transit subsidies that encourage employers to contribute to the commuting expenses of employees who use public transportation, and a tax credit for the production of renewable energy sources.

Honors and Awards

Matsui has received many honors for his years of public service. In 1993 the Children's Defense Fund honored him for his work on behalf of children. He was named as one of California's outstanding legislators by Claremont College in 1990 and 1992. Also in 1992 he received the Excellence in Public Service Award from the American Academy of Pediatrics, was recognized by the American Wind Energy Association for his work on renewable energy, and was cited by the American Public Transit Association for his success in promoting public transportation. He has also been honored with a Lifetime Achievement Award from the Anti-Defamation League and has received

from Yale University the Chubb Fellowship, the highest honor that institution confers upon visiting lecturers.

Matsui has served as treasurer of the Democratic National Committee since 1991. He lives with his wife, Doris, a deputy assistant to the president in Washington, D.C. They have one son, Brian, a student at Stanford University.

Sources:

Books

"Matsui, Robert." *Who's Who in American Politics*. New York: R.R. Bowker, 1993.

Periodicals

Yang, Jeff. "The Power of Two: An Interview with Bob and Doris Matsui." *A. Magazine*, vol. 2, no. 3, December 15, 1993.
———. "Power Brokers." *A. Magazine*, vol. 2, no. 3, December 15, 1993.

Other

The office of Congressman Robert Matsui, Sacramento, California, 1994.

—Sketch by Jim Henry

"Spark" Masayuki Matsunaga
(1916–1990)
Politician, attorney

Spark Masayuki Matsunaga, a decorated veteran of World War II and a leader in the 1988 Senate campaign to bring war reparation to Japanese Americans imprisoned in internment camps during the Second World War, served fourteen years each in the United States House of Representatives and Senate. A longtime champion of environmental causes, the liberal Democratic senator from Hawaii, ill with cancer, cast his final votes from a wheelchair on the floor of the Senate in 1990 in support of an extension of the Clean Air Act. Matsunaga was also well-known for his efforts toward peaceful resolution of international disputes and Soviet-American cooperation in space exploration. A member of the 100th Infantry Battalion, one of the most highly decorated in U.S. history, Matsunaga was awarded the Bronze Star Medal with Valor, Purple Heart with the Oak Leaf Cluster, Army Commendation Medal, and five Battle Stars.

Born on October 8, 1916, on the island of Kauai to a poor Japanese immigrant family, Spark Matsunaga and his three brothers and two sisters embraced the immigrant ethic which connects hard work and success. Through high school, he had many jobs including stevedore, warehouseman, bookkeeper, and sales clerk. At the University of Hawaii, he earned his bachelor of education degree in 1941 along with many honors, including election to Phi Beta Kappa.

Military Service

Matsunaga was commissioned as a second lieutenant in the U.S. Army in 1941. However, after the Japanese invasion of Pearl Harbor on December 7, and the extreme devastation and loss of life that followed, he and other Japanese Americans, their loyalties in question, became victims of wartime anti-Japanese hysteria. With the issuance of the now infamous Executive Order 9066 mandating the imprisonment of Japanese Americans, Matsunaga was consigned to a Wisconsin internment camp. After petitioning President Franklin D. Roosevelt, he and other internees were released and permitted to form the 100th Infantry Battalion which became one of the most highly decorated military units in history. Twice wounded in Italy during the war, he was released as a captain in 1946 with a long record of honors and commendations. He married Helene Hatsumi Tokunaga in 1948.

Under the G.I. Benefits Bill, Matsunaga earned his law degree from Harvard University in 1951. From 1952 through 1954, he was a Honolulu prosecutor, executive board member of the Democratic Party of Hawaii, and a delegate to the County and State Democratic Convention. Elected to the Hawaii territorial House of Representatives in 1953, Matsunaga served as a member and majority leader. In 1962, he was elected U.S. representative from Hawaii and went on to serve seven consecutive terms in the House in Washington, D.C. Elected to the U.S. Senate in 1976, he served until his death in April of 1990. Surviving him were his wife, three daughters, two sons, and three grandsons.

Tributes

In a statement issued after Matsunaga's death, Governor John D. Waihee III of Hawaii hailed him as a humanitarian. "He will be remembered most for his vision of peace and his faith in the human spirit," said Waihee, as quoted in the *New York Times* on April 16, 1990. Indeed, "Sparkie," as the diminutive, good-natured senator was known to his friends, never stopped trying to make the world a more peaceful place. For twenty-two years, he worked tirelessly, ultimately persuading Congress to create a peace academy program in 1984 to award graduate degrees to those who help settle disputes within and among nations. Neither did he ever cease his efforts to fight intolerance and bigotry. Once Matsunaga attacked vice-presidential candidate Spiro T. Agnew for a racial slur

"Spark" Masayuki Matsunaga

leveled in supposed jest at a Japanese American reporter on the campaign trail. The result was an apology by Agnew.

Ironically but not surprisingly, Matsunaga's greatest humanitarian accomplishment was inspired by his own bitter experience as a Japanese internee during the war years. Never yielding the quest for justice for his fellow Japanese Americans interned during the Second World War, Matsunaga was the main Senate leader who lobbied for passage in 1988 of the $1.25 billion bill which offered a formal apology and $20,000 in reparations to each Japanese American interned in the United States.

Sources:

Books

Who's Who in American Politics 1987–88, 11th Edition. New York: R.R. Bowker Co., 1987.

Periodicals

Flint, Peter B. "Spark Matsunaga Dies at 73: Senator Led Fight for Reparations." *New York Times Biographical Service*, April 1990.
"Milestones." *Time*, April 30, 1990.
"Transition." *Newsweek*, April 30, 1990.

—Sketch by Nancy Moore

Nobu McCarthy
(1934–)
Actress

Nobu McCarthy was "discovered" by a Hollywood film agent four decades ago while eating dinner in a Los Angeles restaurant. Newly arrived in the United States, she had left Japan just six months earlier where she had been the country's leading high fashion model. She had briefly tried film acting in Japan, but had not enjoyed the experience. Understandably, she was reluctant about the agent's offer, but hesitantly agreed to at least visit Paramount's studios.

McCarthy met with funny man Jerry Lewis who was casting his latest film, *Geisha Boy,* which is about a magician and his rabbit who are lured by a luminous beauty away from the United States to the theatres of Japan. McCarthy was dressed in a Japanese kimono at the first meeting and Lewis turned her down. They met again, and this time, McCarthy was attired in chic Western clothes. Lewis immediately cast her in her first starring role.

McCarthy's acting career was quickly established. Both film and television offers were abundant. "There were times when I would finish at the Twentieth-Century Fox lot in the morning and work at Paramount in the afternoon," she recalled in an interview with Terry Hong. Before long, she was keeping company with some of the industry's best. "I had the chance to meet and be friends with many of the giant stars—Gary Cooper, Cary Grant, Fred Astaire, Sammy Davis, Jr., Marlon Brando, Anthony Quinn, and others."

In spite of her fairy-tale-like "discovery" and the many subsequent offers, McCarthy quickly realized that roles for Asian Americans were limited: "I was really working so much," she told Hong, "but almost always in the frame of stereotypical roles." The turning point in McCarthy's career came at the age of thirty-seven when she played the fifty-three-year-old mother in the film, *Farewell to Manzanar.* Ironically, she began to be typecast predominantly in, as she put it, "old mother, granny roles," although she continued to be described as "exquisite-looking" and "glamorous" by *the New York Daily News* and other publications. The typecasting, however, worked to McCarthy's advantage as she was from then offered more honest, human roles, contrasted to ingenue type roles.

To be a Success in Anything I Tried

Nobu McCarthy was born Nobu Atsumi on November 13, 1934, in Ottawa, Canada, where her father was serving as a diplomatic attaché to Prince Tokugawa. When she

Nobu McCarthy

was a few months old, the family returned to Japan and settled in Tokyo.

"At the age of four . . . my mother took me to see *A Midsummer Night's Dream* and from that time on, I wanted to be on the stage," McCarthy told Hong. By the age of six, she was already studying the piano, modern dance, and voice. A precocious performer, she was contracted to King Records in Japan and became a child singer on stage and on radio. At age eleven, McCarthy enrolled in the Pavlova School of Ballet in Tokyo where she studied dance seriously for the next seven years.

Growing up in Japan proved difficult at times for McCarthy. "Because my father spoke English and I was born outside of the country, the children were very cruel." McCarthy told Hong. "I remember as a child being ashamed because I wasn't born in Japan. At school, my classmates often teased me and called me 'Mary,' a name reserved for those who were pro-Western in their thinking and behavior. . . . [That] negative response from my peers . . . only served to motivate me. In fact, if there was one single thing that I had to point out as the catalyst that moved me forward, it would be that. I vowed I would show everyone that I could be a success in anything I tried to do. Luckily, my father was my strongest supporter, and my mother was never far behind. They counseled me to finish whatever I started, and to do it with zest!"

That dedication to succeed catapulted McCarthy to the highest ranks of professional modeling in Japan. Her father, who had resigned from his diplomatic career to pursue a career in fashion design, created all of McCarthy's clothes. She recalled for Hong, "A friend who was close to the editor of a teen fashion magazine suggested to the editor that he do a feature story about a teen-aged ballerina who wore beautiful clothes designed by her father. The photos and the article so impressed the editor that he hired me to be his personal model for the magazine and my career began." Within a year, McCarthy was one of Japan's leading models. "Things were tough in early postwar Japan, but with the money I made as a model, I was able to put my four brothers through school."

Star of Film, Television, and Stage

In 1955, McCarthy married a young GI named David McCarthy and amidst woeful objections from Japan's fashion industry, she arrived in the United States and settled in Los Angeles. Six months and a starring role later, McCarthy was back before the cameras, steadily appearing in films and on television. Although she divorced David McCarthy in 1970 and later married William J. Cuthbert, an attorney, in 1976, she has remained Nobu McCarthy in her career. "Sometimes people get confused because of my name, but in real life, I'm Mrs. Cuthbert," she patiently explained.

McCarthy's film credits include *Five Gates to Hell, Wake Me When It's Over* (with Ernie Kovacs), *Two Loves* (with Shirley MacLaine), *Walk Like a Dragon* (with Jack Lord), *Karate Kid II* (with Pat Morita and Ralph Macchio), and *Pacific Heights* (with Michael Keaton). She has made more than one hundred television appearances, including guest appearances on episodes of *Playhouse 90, The Man from U.N.C.L.E., Batman, Quincy, Happy Days, T.J. Hooker, Hawaii Five-O, Magnum, P.I.,* and *China Beach*. McCarthy also played the starring role in the award-winning television film, *Farewell to Manzanar,* based on Jeanne Wakatsuki Houston's ground-breaking memoir of the same title, about her family's internment during World War II.

In the late 1960s and 1970s, McCarthy decided to try stage acting. "In those days, what was called 'Oriental' was no longer in vogue. Instead, the black movement was very big. I had been such a busy actress and then suddenly, there seemed to be very few jobs in film. I wanted to continue to learn acting, so I decided I would continue learning in the theater. Learning was my hunger. So I agreed to do Momoko Iko's *The Gold Watch* at the Inner City Cultural Center in L.A." In 1971, McCarthy played opposite the venerable actor, Mako, the founder of East West Players, which was the first Asian American theater company in the U.S. "Since then, it was set that Mako was one of my stage husbands," she laughed, referring to future roles that would pair the two actors together. McCarthy eventually became actively involved with East West Players, honing her acting skills and discovering her directing talents.

During the 1970s and 1980s, McCarthy's stage credits grew steadily. Among her numerous performances, McCarthy originated the leading role in David Henry Hwang's *As the Crow Flies* for which she won, among other honors, the Los Angeles Drama-logue Award. She also created the leading role of Masi in Philip Kan Gotanda's *The Wash,* making her New York debut at the Manhattan Theatre Club and later reprising the role at the Mark Taper Forum in Los Angeles and other regional theatres. She won another L.A. Drama-logue and the San Francisco "Bernie" for her performances.

From 1982 to 1987, McCarthy taught acting at California State University, Los Angeles, and was the director of the Asian American Theatre Project. Since 1991, she has also taught acting at various other universities, including the University of California at Los Angeles. In 1989, she added a new element to her career when she assumed the artistic directorship of East West Players, six months after Mako had resigned. "When the Board first asked me, I said 'no,' but eventually I had to agree. My thought at the time was that I could feed my passion for helping Asian American actors. I would do the job for three years, put my life into it and then search for a successor," McCarthy told Hong. Those three years grew into five during which she set forth a mission to upgrade Asian American acting talents. To do so, she expanded East West Players from being predominantly a theatre group to a formal artist training facility, developing and directing the theatre's Professional Actors' Training Program and founding the David Henry Hwang Writers' Institute. In the meantime, McCarthy trained fellow East West member Timothy Dang to be her successor. "We worked together closely for two years, and in my mind I was always clear that he would be the next artistic director," she said.

"Never Give Up"

Freed from administrative duties, McCarthy returned to acting full-time. "I thought that once I left, I would go back to the theatre all the time, to check on how things were going and to see how the members were getting on. But I haven't gone back since. I've been too busy." Just recently, McCarthy appeared once again as Masi in Philip Kan Gotanda's *The Wash* at the Studio Theater in Washington D.C. Earning rave reviews, McCarthy proved that she was still a leading actress. In a recent review, *The Washington Post* called the play "graceful, subtle and moving . . . much more powerful than an evening of Strindbergian fireworks" and referred to McCarthy's performance as "truly remarkable."

"I've been very lucky in that I don't have to take roles to eat," McCarthy told Hong. "But acting is really a blade with two sides. If you really do pick and choose your roles, then you end up never acting." In spite of the undeniable lack of accurate, honest roles for Asian Americans, McCarthy is encouraging of young actors. "Yes, it's a very tough road, but you cannot give up your desires," she asserted. "You have to keep that fire burning in your heart. You just have to do it. It's quite a bit of suffering, but you can't count just the suffering. There's so much joy, too. Just never, ever give up. That's the key to success."

Although McCarthy is not currently taking any new roles, she is determined to continue acting. "At my age," she told Hong, "family is the most important thing in my life—my very supportive husband and two children. But acting is what makes my soul soar, so I'll have to keep doing it." For now, McCarthy is looking forward to "taking it easy for awhile, enjoying just being Mrs. Cuthbert." She added with a hint of mischief in her voice, "Now I finally have the luxury of just sitting back and thinking about what I want to be when I grow up."

Sources:

Periodicals

Gardella, Kay. "'Star of 'Manzanar' Film Gives Japanese View of US," *New York Daily News,* March 5, 1976, p. 98.
Rose, Lloyd. "'The Wash': Delicate Cycle," *Washington Post,* March 17, 1994, pp. D1, D5.

Other

McCarthy, Nobu, telephone interview with Terry Hong, May 28, 1994.

—Sketch by Terry Hong

Ruthanne Lum McCunn

(1946–)

Writer, teacher

During the early years of her life, Ruthanne Lum McCunn was known as Roxey Drysdale. Born to a Scottish American father and a Chinese mother, McCunn's features are not recognizably Asian. But growing up in Hong Kong surrounded by her mother's extended family and living the majority of her adult life in California, McCunn's identity today is completely Asian American. That synthesized identity is reflected in her name: Lum is her mother's maiden name—"When I started to write, I felt it was important to have the Lum in there. Everything I write comes from that source"—while McCunn is her married name. "It's really because of both my mother and my husband that I am able to do the work that I do," she told Terry Hong in an interview. "I'm able to write about Chinese America because of my mother, and I'm also able to write because it was my husband who encouraged me to go for it."

McCunn wrote her first book, *An Illustrated History of the Chinese in America,* for her students in a junior high school in San Francisco where she was working as a bilingual teacher. She had discovered that virtually no books existed about Chinese Americans, much less Chinese American history.

By the time *An Illustrated History* was published in 1979, McCunn had left her decade-long career as librarian and teacher to become a full-time writer. Her work since then has steadily added to the growing library of Asian American literature. She has written three novels, a children's tale, a book of proverbs, and a compilation of personal histories of Chinese Americans. Her books have won awards, including the American Book Award from the Before Columbus Foundation and the Outstanding Academic Book from *Choice* magazine. She is also a recipient of the Distinguished Achievement Award from the National Women's Political Caucus.

Chinese Beginnings

Ruthanne Lum McCunn was born February 21, 1946, in San Francisco's Chinatown. Her father was a merchant marine of Scottish American descent, and her Chinese mother was from Hong Kong. While visiting the United States as a tourist, McCunn's mother married the merchant marine. In 1947 when the infant McCunn was a year old, the family relocated to Hong Kong. Though McCunn's father was at sea for much of her childhood, she grew up in the midst of her mother's extended family that included her mother, an aunt, uncle, cousins, and a great aunt.

McCunn's first and only language until she was five was Cantonese. She lived in a Chinese neighborhood where she attended Chinese school. Although she was very blonde as a child, McCunn recalled, "It was no big deal looking different as long as I was going to the Chinese school." However, when McCunn was six years old, her father returned from sea and, concerned that his child could not speak English, placed her in a British school. "Once I started going to English school, I was no longer part of the Chinese neighborhood. To the Chinese neighborhood children, I was the white devil foreigner and at the English school, I was the 'Ching Chong Chinaman,'" she told Hong., In an attempt to express the confusion and isolation she felt being trapped between two worlds, McCunn started writing at the age of seven in a diary that her father had given her.

At age sixteen, one year after her father's death, McCunn returned to the United States. A college education in Hong Kong would have been very expensive, if even possible, and in America, McCunn had heard that college was much more accessible and that one could work to support her education. She was also eager to see more of the world than Hong Kong's at times claustrophobic 240 square miles.

Encouraged by her mother, McCunn first arrived in Boise, Idaho, where her sister had already settled with their father's relatives. "Because I left when I was only a

Ruthanne Lum McCunn

year old, coming back was like coming to America for the first time. I had very much an immigrant mentality. And I spoke English with a British accent," she told Hong. Unhappy in an area with only one Chinese family, McCunn left Idaho for the San Francisco Bay area where she lived with a friend of her mother's in Walnut Creek. For two years, she attended Diablo Valley Junior College, working odd jobs from janitor to short-order cook. She then transferred to the University of California at Berkeley, marrying Donald McCunn at the end of her junior year. The couple moved briefly to Austin, Texas, where McCunn finished her undergraduate degree in English at the University of Texas at Austin in 1968. McCunn earned her teaching credentials from the University of California at San Francisco when the couple returned to San Francisco the following year.

Career Changes

McCunn first worked as a librarian and then as a teacher in a Santa Barbara elementary school before the couple settled for good in San Francisco in 1974 where McCunn was an English and bilingual teacher in the public school system. For four years, she continued to teach until she made the decision to write full–time. With the exception of a few terms of teaching creative writing and Asian

American literature at the University of California at Santa Cruz and the Cornell University, McCunn has remained a full-time writer. "I loved teaching. I loved it at

every level, from elementary to graduate school. But even though I enjoy it, I've found that I can't write and teach at the same time. To be a good teacher is a very creative endeavor and that saps all my creativity. At this time, at this place, I prefer writing," she told Hong.

Since McCunn's first book, *An Illustrated History of the Chinese in America*, was published in 1979, it has been used as a college text. She finds it very alarming that so many of her readers are older students since the book was written for schoolchildren at a fifth-grade reading level.

Her second book, *Thousand Pieces of Gold* was published in 1981. McCunn believes it is the first biographical novel of a Chinese American pioneer woman. The story concerns Lalu Nathoy, who was shipped to the United States as a slave and became Polly Bemis, a well-loved pioneer woman of Warrens, Idaho. The novel, McCunn's best-selling work to date, was the basis a 1991 film made by independent filmmakers Nancy Kelly and Kenji Yamamoto. McCunn was unhappy with the celluloid translation. She told Hong, "It was very different. The character names and the title were the same, but everything else was different."

The next book McCunn wrote was a children's story, *Pie-Biter*, published in 1983, about a young boy named Hoi whose legend is somewhat akin to that of Paul Bunyan or John Henry. "I came across the story while I was doing research for *Thousand Pieces*. It seemed so astonishing that there were no Chinese American folktales in print. There were Chinese tales, but none that were truly Chinese American. It was way past time that we had a Chinese American tale," she said. *Pie-Biter* won the American Book Award from the Before Columbus Foundation in 1984.

McCunn followed the tale with another biographical novel, *Sole Survivor*, in 1985. The novel was based on the true story of Poon Lim, a Chinese sailor who miraculously survived 133 days adrift in the Atlantic Ocean after his ship was sunk during World War II. The book won Best Book in the Nonfiction Adventure category from the Southwest Booksellers Association.

In 1988, McCunn published *Chinese American Portraits: Personal Histories 1828-1988*. "I had, over the years, come across a number of interesting stories while doing research and I wondered what I should do with all this material," she recalled. "When I wrote *Thousand Pieces*, I wanted to dispel stereotypes of the passive Asian woman. When I wrote *Survivor*, I wanted to dispel the misconception that Asians do not value life. So with *Portraits*, I wanted to bring together many stories like that, to show that stories like Polly's and Poon's were not just an exception here and there. I wanted to show the many Chinese Americans in history who have not been acknowledged and I wanted to show the great diversity of Chinese America." In 1990, the book received the Outstanding Academic Book award from *Choice* magazine.

In 1991, McCunn published a collection entitled *Chinese Proverbs*. "These proverbs were something that I have been collecting over the years out of a personal interest, so when a publisher approached me to put a collection together, I thought 'Aha! This is why I've been collecting all these years.'" She told Hong, "It was just a fun thing to do."

Something New

Wooden Fish Songs is McCunn's latest book, due out in 1995 from Dutton. "My husband is printing out the final revision at this moment," she told Hong gleefully. *Wooden Fish Songs* was the novel McCunn was researching years ago when she got side-tracked by *Portraits*. The title of the work comes from stories told in the Canton delta region of China, stories told from women's points of view about husbands and lovers in Gum San, the Chinese name for the gold mountains of far-away America. McCunn's novel is the story of one Chinese American man, told by three different women: his mother in China, his European-American mentor in Massachusetts, and the mentor's cook in Florida. The Chinese American man in question is based on a true figure who was one of McCunn's subjects in *Portraits*. In order to research the novel, McCunn traveled to Toisan, China, where the man was originally from, then to North Adams, Massachesetts. and DeLand, Florida.

McCunn's latest project has returned her to the mid-1800s. She is currently researching Chinese Americans who served during the Civil War. "I have about twelve of them identified. More of them were on the Union side," she told Hong. "It's been very difficult to research because all except two or three of the soldiers have Western surnames although they were ethnically Chinese. . . . Several of them came over as children on ships and they took the names of the ships' captains. I think the name-changing was just happenstance, not deliberate."

For the foreseeable future, McCunn plans to continue writing. "My writing grew out of a desire to teach and share, to do so not in a dogmatic, teacherly way, but to do it in a fun way. Through my writing, I've found that story-telling is really a way to pass on information."

Sources:

Periodicals

Seto, May. "An Interview With Author Ruthanne Lum McCunn," *Sampan,* January 1982.
Stein, Ruthe. "Inside Look at Growing Up As an Outsider," *San Francisco Chronicle,* 21 September 1983, p. 39.
Stix, Harriet. "Author Leads, Writes About a Double Life," Los Angeles Times, 25 September 1983, Part VIII.

Other

McCunn, Ruthanne Lum, telephone interview with Terry Hong, April 25, 1994.

—Sketch by Terry Hong

Ajai Singh "Sonny" Mehta
(1942–)
Book publisher

Indian-born Sonny Mehta spends his days wrestling with pushy agents, desperate writers, and oversized egos, but he takes it all in stride. He is the president and editor-in-chief of Alfred A. Knopf, a division of Random House. He is also the president of the Knopf Publishing Group, which includes Knopf, Pantheon Books, Schocken Books, Vintage Books, and Random House Large Print Publishing. Random House is the largest general trade book publisher in the United States and the English-speaking world.

Mehta became head of Alfred A. Knopf in 1987. His division publishes the works of John Updike, John Hersey, Andre Gide, and Albert Camus, among others. In recent years Knopf has published the works of Toni Morrison, V.S. Naipaul, John le Carre, Gabriel Garcia Marquez, Michael Crichton, and Cormac McCarthy. Alfred A. Knopf writers have won more Nobel Prizes than those of any other publisher. Its writers have also won Pulitzer Prizes and other literary awards.

Ajai Singh Mehta was born in India in 1942, the son of a diplomat. He was educated at the Lawrence School in Sanwar, India, and Cambridge University. He began his publishing career in London at Rupert Hart-Davis. After founding Paladin Books, he became editorial director of Granada Paperbacks, where he oversaw the operations of the Panther, Mayflower, and Paladin book line. In 1972 he became publishing director of Pan Books and launched the highly successful Picador trade paperback line.

When Mehta joined Alfred A. Knopf in 1987, he headed the publishing house in a new direction. Knopf was known for publishing critically acclaimed books that sold well, but not great, in book stores. Mehta decided to look for more commercially viable projects.

His first hits as publisher were *American Psycho* by Bret Easton Ellis and *Damage* by Josephine Hart. Both novels were panned by critics but were commercial hits. Mehta used his marketing genius to propel the books to the top of the *New York Times* best-seller list shortly after the books were released. With the success of *Damage* especially, he proved to the skeptical publishing world that he could take a book from nowhere and put it on the best-seller list.

On a typical day Mehta gets up and reads manuscripts. He breaks only to change CDs—his musical tastes range from Beethoven and Mozart to Biber—and watch cricket

Ajai Singh "Sonny" Mehta

matches on cable TV. At 4:00 p.m. in the afternoon he generally stops reading and returns phone calls until it is time for dinner.

Mehta is married to Gita Mehta, a writer who splits her time between New York, London, and India. The couple has one son who lives in London and manages an art gallery.

Sources:

Periodicals

Conant, Janet. "The Very Furry Feet of Sonny Mehta." *Esquire.* April 1993, pp. 106–109.

"Power Brokers." *A Magazine,* December 15, 1993, pp. 25–34.

Streitfeld, David. "Life at Random: Reading Between the Lines at America's Hottest Publishing House." *New York.* August 5, 1991. pp. 30–44.

Other

Alfred A. Knopf. "Ajai Singh Mehta." Official biography, January 1, 1994.

—Sketch by Douglas Wu

Gita Mehta

(1944–)

Writer

Gita Mehta is a writer in every sense of the word though she doesn't consider herself a professional writer. She is a journalist, documentary filmmaker, promoter of the Indian experience, and writer. She writes nonfiction books and novels because she has something to say about her varied experiences.

Gita Mehta was born in southern India in 1944. Her father was an industrialist, flying ace, and politician. Mehta witnessed India's transition from a jewel in Britain's crown to a member of the Commonwealth of Nations. Mehta's childhood was far from typical. She was born barely three weeks before her father, Biju Patnaik, was carted off to jail by the British during India's struggle for independence. One of her father's cousins, a nineteen-year old poet, had been shot dead on the steps of the Chittagong armory in a bold bid inspired by the Easter uprising in Dublin, Ireland. Another cousin, aged fourteen, was taken in chains to the Andaman Islands and imprisoned for seventeen years. When Mehta was barely three, she was packed off to a boarding school in the Kashmir run by nuns (although Mehta has said that she doesn't think it remarkable to have been separated from her family when she was so tiny). Her mother, even though sheltered by her family, was now linked to the revolutionary movement, and was busy trying to get her father out of jail. It was into this unique family setting that Mehta was born, at a juncture in India's evolution which energized people with the dream of what India could be. Mehta's father, who had been a leading industrialist in India, abandoned his business interests to devote himself to politics. In 1994, he was chief minister of Orissa, an eastern state in India with a population of thirty-two million.

Risk-Taker

It is said by people who know her that Mehta is a witty, opinionated person who is always open to new ideas and experiences. At age forty, she did a parachute jump with a British military squadron. But she did not challenge herself with physically taxing adventures in pursuit of eternal youth, she assured Christa Worthington of *Harper's Bazaar* in 1989: "I am an Asian woman. . . . Possibly because one is Indian, it's not terrifying to grow up. As we grow older, we're given more authority and respect."

She traveled to Britain to study at Cambridge University, and immediately felt at home with the intellectual atmosphere there. It was while at Cambridge that Mehta met her husband, Sonny Mehta, who in 1987 was made president and editor in chief of the publishing house Alfred A. Knopf. Richard Eyre, a friend from Cambridge commented about the Mehtas as a couple in 1993 in *Vanity Fair*: "They were preternaturally well-read, politically, culturally, musically literate in the widest sense; in a perfectly obvious way they were made for each other."

The Mehtas were living in London in a basement flat in Belgravia when their son, Aditya, was born. In 1993, at the age of 26, Aditya was working in London and living in that same flat. Gita Mehta divides her time between London, India, and New York, although she spends at least three months every winter in India.

During the Bangladesh war in 1971, Mehta was the only Indian woman to go out with an American film crew. When asked about her reasons for undertaking such a risky venture, she told Joan Juliet Buck of *Vanity Fair*: "When you see things that are terribly unjust, you realize something has to be done. It's not an act of courage; it's an act of anger."

Evolution of a Writer

Mehta wrote her novel, *Karma Cola*, published in 1979, in three weeks on a whim. The book is a mixture of polemic and travel literature. In the book, she trampled on India's phony Eastern mysticism, and on Americans who adopted the philosophies in defiance of Western materialism. Mehta said in an interview with Christa Worthington for *Harper's Bazaar*, that in the 1960s and 1970s, "Both [societies] were looking for instant gratification. We [Indians] wanted gratification of toys of America, which promised eternal adolescence. The West wanted gratification of tranquility of India, which is another kind of lobotomy."

Mehta's first novel, *Raj*, published in 1989, documents the Hindu, Muslim, and Sikh princes' torn loyalty between the British Raj and loyalty to their own history and traditions. Royal India was a collection of 565 princely states ruled by an assortment of scholar kings and sportsmen, tribal chieftains, Oxford graduates, reformers, and despots. The novel depicts their struggle through the eyes of a prince's daughter destined to become a leader in free India. *Raj* includes Queen Victoria's Diamond Jubilee in 1897 and India's partition and independence in 1947. The epic tale ends with Indira Gandhi's parliamentary bill of 1970 discontinuing privy purses and abolishing the concept of rulership.

Mehta believes India's road to independence was difficult because India does not have a homogenous society. According to Motihar, Mehta explains that fragmentation in India occurred because a 19th century European idea of nationalism was imposed by the British, and therefore, India was never a nation. It was a civilization that had been there for five millennia, carried on by great, enduring principles of government. As an illustration, Mehta cites the fact that British government is based on majority rule; whereas royal Indian government was based on political consensus. India was historically a great, open, welcoming

presence for other cultures. Mehta feels that in many ways it still is.

In 1993, Mehta published *A River Sutra*, a collection of mystic tales about the many forms of love. In it, she takes a decidedly Indian approach to explain India to the Western world. Rahul Jacob of the *Los Angeles Times* wrote: "The tales are explorations in the power of desire, of love, or religious longing and of covetousness. Every yarn begins the lazy circle again, another variation on the novel's central themes. Each story ends with a beguiling tung into the next one. The simplicity of Mehta's writing nicely complements the novel's profound concerns. Nor does the wheel stop, when you finish the book."

Writer Michael Herr was quoted in *Vanity Fair* about Mehta's strengthening reputation as a writer: "As long as I've known [Mehta], she's refused to allow me to call her a writer. When I read *A River Sutra*, I said, 'You've really lost your amateur status on this one. . . . This is a wonderful piece of work.'"

Sources:

Periodicals

Buck, Joan Juliet. "A Mehta of Style." *Vanity Fair*, May 1993, pp. 16+.
Worthington, Christa. "Gita Mehta." *Harper's Bazaar*, 1989, p. 73.

Other

Motihar, Kamla. "Gita Mehta." unpublished essay, 1994.

Sketch by Douglas Wu

Ved Mehta
(1934–)
Author

Since his entry into the world of American letters in 1957 with the publication of his critically and commercially successful autobiographical work *Face to Face*, Ved Mehta has become one of the most widely read and respected writers in the English language. His novels, books of nonfiction, screenplays, and autobiographical studies reflect his sense of himself as an Indian expatriate living in the West and how the two vastly disparate worlds in which he has lived formed him. As Bernard Nossiter noted in the *Chicago Tribune*, Mehta's work expresses "a rare synthesis, an attitude that draws strength from both his heritage and the insights of his adopted culture."

Ved Prakash Mehta was born in British colonial India on March 21, 1934, in the town of Lahore, in present-day Pakistan. He was the fifth of seven children born to Dr. Amolek Ram Mehta and Shanti (Mehra) Mehta. The Mehta family had become fairly anglicized during years of British colonial rule. Mehta's paternal grandfather, Bhola Ram Mehta, had encouraged his six sons to take advantage of the educational opportunities afforded by British rule. His eldest son, Amolek, did so, obtaining scholarships to study medicine and public health in Great Britain and the United States. When Amolek returned to his home country he became a public health officer who worked tirelessly to fight epidemic diseases that wracked India following World War II. As head of the anti-tuberculosis campaign, he toured the British provinces with the Red Cross Society, and after Indian independence in 1947 he was named deputy director general of the health services in the newly formed Indian government.

An Early Illness Leads to Blindness

At the age of three Mehta was struck with spinal meningitis, which left him completely blind. Throughout most of his early life, he was sent to various boarding schools, hospitals, and institutions for the blind. Mehta's 1982 book *Vedi* chronicles four years in the Dadar School for the Blind in Bombay, India. According to critic Janet Malcolm of the *New York Review*, the school was "a mosquito-ridden industrial slum, where [Mehta] was to contract typhoid within three months (and suffer repeated bouts of it), and where he lived for four years under the harshest physical conditions and received the most pitifully rudimentary of educations." After twelve years of being sent to different schools in India, the young Mehta was accepted into the Arkansas State School for the Blind in Little Rock. The school was underfunded, underequipped, and understaffed, yet it gave Mehta something he had heretofore lacked: confidence in his ability to move through the world without sight.

After graduation Mehta enrolled in Pomona College in Pomona, California. During summers he attended sessions at Harvard and the University of California at Berkeley. He was elected to the Phi Beta Kappa Society in his junior year and earned his bachelor of arts degree in 1956. From there he went to England to study modern history at Oxford, which granted him another bachelor of arts degree in 1959. When he returned to the United States he received a fellowship to attend Harvard and after a year and a half he earned his master of arts degree.

A Career in Writing

For years it had been Mehta's intention to pursue an academic career. Yet his success as a writer along with the encouragement of others—most notably, the legendary former editor of the *New Yorker*, William Shawn—convinced him to write full–time. In 1960 he published *Walking the Indian Streets*, a first-hand, journalistic account of a trip he made to India and Nepal with a friend. In it, he recorded his impressions of his home country and the

Ved Mehta

conversations he had with the people he met there. One such person was Prime Minister Nehru, whom Mehta had previously criticized for opposing Hindu nationalism and seeking to strengthen India's ties to the Western world.

In 1961 Shawn invited Mehta to join the staff of the *New Yorker* magazine. In addition to writing for the *New Yorker*, he continued his autobiographical, critical, and fictional writing, gaining increasing recognition and respect for both efforts. After *Walking the Indian Streets* he published *Fly and the Fly-Bottle: Encounters with British Intellectuals* in 1963, a collection of interviews with leading British philosophers and historians. Three years later he did another collection of interviews, this time with religious scholars, entitled *The New Theologian* .

In 1967 Mehta published the novel *Delinquent Chacha*, which in 1980 was made into a British film for which Mehta wrote the script. It was followed by *Portrait of India* (1970), *John is Easy to Please* (1971), *Daddyji* (1972), *Mahatma Ghandi and His Apostles* (1977), *New India* (1978), *Mammaji* (1979), *The Photographs of Chachaji* (1980), *A Family Affair: India under Three Prime Ministers* (1982), *Vedi* (1982), *The Ledge Between the Streams* (1984), *Sound-Shadows of the New World* (1986), *Three Stories of the Raj* (1987), *The Stolen Light* (1989), and *Up at Oxford* (1993).

The Themes of His Work

Though the majority of Mehta's work revolves around India, he says that he is not ultimately concerned with interpreting his native culture to the West. As he told *Publishers Weekly,* "I think I can leave that to sociologists, anthropologists and political scientists." He added "These books in the autobiographical series are really to be read more like a novel than a tract of any kind."

In an interview with Jim Henry, Mehta credited his success in America to his high profile as a staff writer with the *New Yorker,* a magazine he speaks of with discernible reverence. "The *New Yorker* has done more for writers than any other institution in the world," he told Henry. He described the magazine as a "free association of writers [that] unless you've been a part of . . . it's hard to imagine." He also cited another institution, the John D. and Catherine T. McArthur Foundation, for its invaluable help. In 1982, the McArthur Foundation gave him a genius award, an anonymously nominated cash grant given outright to people who do outstanding work in a variety of fields. Mehta said the $236,000 grant has given him financial security, something he believes has been very helpful to his work as a writer.

Of all of Mehta's writings, his autobiographical series are most popular and have drawn the most positive critical attention. The first series, *Daddyji, Mammaji,* and *Vedi,* chronicles his early life in India and focuses, in turn, on his father, his mother, and the years he spent at the Dadar School in Bombay. His subsequent series, comprised of *The Ledge Between the Streams, Sound-Shadows of the New World,* and *Up at Oxford,* chronicles his life as an expatriate in America and Britain.

Legendary for the long hours he puts in at his office at the *New Yorker,* Mehta is also currently working on the finishing touches to his new book, *Rajiv Ghandi and Rhama's Kingdom,* to be published by Yale University Press. He lives in New York with his wife Linn and daughters Alexandra Sage and Natasha. Looking back at his life's work, Mehta told Henry that he's not "trying to interpret India or blindness or any of that. All I'm trying to do is to tell a story of not one life, but many lives—and through those stories, to try to say something that's universal."

Sources:

Periodicals

Dong, Stella. "Interview with Ved Mehta." *Publishers Weekly,* January 3, 1985. pp. 57–58.

Malcolm, Janet. "School of the Blind." *New York Review of Books,* October 7, 1982.

Nossier, Bernard D. "Whatever Can Be Said of India, the Opposite Also Is True." *Chicago Tribune,* May 10, 1970.

Other

Mehta, Ved, telephone interview with Jim Henry, February 1994.

—Sketch by Jim Henry

Zubin Mehta
(1936–)
Conductor, music director

"**B**orn to the baton" aptly describes the extraordinary career of Zubin Mehta. Maestro Mehta has served as music director of the New York Philharmonic, the Los Angeles Philharmonic, the Montreal Symphony, and the Israel Philharmonic, to name a few.

Born April 29, 1936 in Bombay, India, Zubin Mehta grew up in a home filled with music. His father was a co-founder of the Bombay Symphony, and the young Mehta heard chamber music and Beethoven quartets before he heard a symphony. He learned to sing what he heard before he could read music. At the age of sixteen, Mehta began conducting concerto accompaniments, leading the orchestra when his father was away on concert tours. At eighteen, Mehta abandoned his medical studies to pursue a career in music at the Academy of Music in Vienna. "I always had the intention of becoming a conductor, not just because I wanted to wave a stick, but because orchestral music appeals to me most," he said.

By the time he was twenty-five, Mehta had conducted both the Vienna and the Berlin Philharmonics and was the music director of the Montreal Symphony. In 1962, at age twenty-six, he became the youngest conductor of a major American orchestra when the Los Angeles Philharmonic appointed him music director. In 1978, he accepted the music directorship of the New York Philharmonic. Mehta's powerful stage presence translates into a strong, provocative management style. "In Los Angeles [as compared to New York] I'm the absolute boss. It's my orchestra," he said.

During Mehta's thirteen-year tenure with the New York Philharmonic, he conducted more that one thousand concerts, and he held the post of music director longer than anyone else in the orchestra's modern history. However, his relationship with the orchestra was a stormy one. "An American should lead the Philharmonic," concluded Mehta. "He should be able to deal with both the orchestra—they step over conductors—and New York."

An intriguing question is the role that being Indian has played in the success of his career. "Mehta's career in this internationally minded age has possibly profited from the exotic value attached to being the only India-born conductor to attain prominence," speculated Albert Goldberg, music critic of the *Los Angeles Times.* "But [Mehta] does not trade on such externals. . . . His musical abilities alone have been sufficient," concluded Goldberg. "Zubin has one of the best techniques around," agreed Los Angeles Philharmonic tympanist William Kraft. "Even the way he holds the baton makes it easier for the orchestra to follow him." In addition to his unquestioned talent, audiences respond to Mehta's impassioned, almost spiritual, performances and to his personal magnetism. Mehta, whose name means "powerful sword," understands the importance of showmanship on stage.

Mehta retains strong ties to his native country and still retains his Indian citizenship. He has taken the New York Philharmonic to Bombay, and when the Festival of India came to the United States, its gala opening on September 11, 1985, was led by Mehta conducting the New York Philharmonic. Mehta's religious roots are also quite deep. He belongs to the Zoroastrian religion, a group commonly known in India as "Parsis" because they emigrated from Persia in the sixth through eighth centuries. There are currently about ninety thousand Zoroastrians in India, twenty-five thousand in Iran, and fifteen thousand in Pakistan. Mehta has participated in a feature-length docudrama entitled *A Quest for Zarathustra* on the life of Zoroaster and his religion. "It is based on my quest for knowledge of my religion," explained Mehta to John Rockwell of the *New York Times.*

His religious background and his membership in a minority community contribute to Mehta's strong identification with the state of Israel. "We are the Jews of India, the Persians who didn't mix," explained Mehta to Rockwell. "We enjoy the same minority complexes as the Israelis except we were not persecuted." In 1969 the Israel Philharmonic Orchestra appointed Mehta its music adviser, in 1977 its music director, and in 1981 its music director for life. Altogether he has conducted more than fifteen hundred concerts with the Israel Philharmonic.

Mehta had a mentor in his father, and he clearly has an extraordinary talent, but he also credits his success to taking opportunities when they were offered. "I made half my career by jumping in for others at the last moment. I sometimes think my success was due almost entirely to the misfortunes of my elderly colleagues," he told Goldberg.

Numerous honors have been bestowed on Mehta, including the Nikisch Ring, the Vienna Philharmonic Ring of Honor, and the Hans von Bulow medal bestowed by the Berlin Philharmonic Orchestra. Mehta has been awarded the Padma Bhushan (Order of the Lotus) by the Republic of India, has received the Defender of Jerusalem Award, and is an honorary citizen of the city of Tel Aviv. He is also the only non-Israeli ever to receive the Israel Prize.

Mehta looks forward to continuing his participation on the international music scene. On June 20, 1994, from the burned out shell of the National Library in Sarajevo, Mehta conducted Sarajevo's orchestra and chorus in a

Zubin Mehta

benefit that was broadcast around the globe. In August 1994, he conducted a concert at Dodger Stadium in Los Angeles at the close of the World Cup Soccer Tournament, a concert that brought together a trio of popular tenors—Jose Carreras, Placido Domingo, and Luciano Pavarotti. He is a leader in the classical music world, staging events to bring performance of great musical works to the largest possible audience.

Sources:

Periodicals

Bernheimer, Martin. "Don't Call Him Zubi-baby." *New York,* April 5, 1978, p. 67.

Henahan, Donal. "Ruffles and Flourishes on an Old Tune." *New York Times,* April 5, 1981.

Rockwell, John. "Zubin Mehta Will Appear in a Film About Zoroaster." *New York Times,* April 10, 1985.

Sudetic, Chuck. "In the Very Ashes of War, a Requiem for 10,000," *New York Times,* June 20, 1994.

Stereo Review, September, 1978.

Other

Goldberg, Arthur, "Zubin Mehta." In *Commentary on the Music Center and Zubin Mehta,* Los Angeles, California, n.d.

—*Sketch by Shazia Rafi*

Ismail Merchant

(1936–)

Film producer

A world-renowned filmmaker, an accomplished chef, and a charmingly persuasive financier, Ismail Merchant is the business brain behind Merchant Ivory Productions, the world's leading independent film company that has produced a number of award-winning feature films such as *A Room with a View, The Bostonians, Howards End, The Europeans, The Remains of the Day* and *Heat and Dust.* Merchant, along with director James Ivory and writer Ruth Prawer Jhabvala is part of a team that has been successfully working together for almost thirty-two years, producing more than sixteen feature length films. This fact has them listed in the Guinness Book of World Records as having the longest creative partnership in film history. In 1990 Merchant received the Alumnus of the Year Award from New York University, and in 1992 he and Ivory received the Filmmaker of the Year Award from the Motion Picture Bookers Club. In addition, Merchant is the first South Asian to successfully produce movies for an international audience using mixed Indian and American casts.

The Roots of Merchant's Success

Merchant was born Ismail Noor Mohammed Abdul Rehman on December 25, 1936, in Bombay, India. He was the only boy in a family of seven children. His father, Noor Mohammed Haji Abdul Rehman, was a middle-class Muslim trader who was also the president of the Bombay branch of the Muslim League. His mother, Hazra Memon, was a homemaker.

His parents wanted Ismail to be a "professional" so they enrolled him in both Muslim and Jesuit schools to give him the best English schooling in Bombay. However, Merchant's interest in drama was evident from an early age. He began staging variety shows while he was still in secondary school.

The partition of India had a significant impact on the nine-year-old Merchant, particularly since his father was involved in politics. Many of his relatives left for Pakistan leaving only his immediate family in Bombay. In that turbulent period, the young boy delivered a speech at a political rally in front of 10,000 people. Coached by a Muslim preacher, Merchant impressed and stirred the crowd, a moment that he recalls to this day. In Robert Emmet Long's 1992 book *The Films of Merchant Ivory,* Merchant compared the start of his film career to that moment, saying that once he had begun, "there [was] no going back, no stopping."

Through his network of friends and relatives Merchant met his first mentor, the Indian actress Nimmi. Although he was only thirteen years old and she was in her twenties they became good friends and she encouraged him to pursue a career in the film industry. According to Merchant that was when he made up his mind to go to the United States and produce cross-cultural films. Meanwhile, he attended St. Xavier's College in Bombay where he studied political science and English literature.

Even in college his interest in drama continued, and he produced a number of variety shows to raise money for the school. He persuaded the head of the Jesuit college to let him stage shows in the school's quadrangle to attract larger audiences. In 1958 Merchant graduated with enough money from his last show to pay his travel expenses to New York City and his tuition for a master's degree in business administration from New York University (NYU).

The Journey Begins

Merchant excelled academically at NYU, and even though the business courses did not interest him, the knowledge he gained helped him in his career. His real interest lay in the concerts and films he saw in New York. America had opened up a whole new world of art and culture for him. It was in the United States that he discovered the films of Satyajit Ray, the renowned Bengali director. Merchant was also profoundly affected by the European art films that he saw in New York. Seeing the possibilities of film when not hindered by the marketing concerns of Hollywood budgets excited a passion in Merchant. Among the directors and films that most influenced him were Ingmar Bergman, Vittorio De Sica, and Federico Fellini. A special favorite was the Ingmar Bergman film *Smiles of A Summer Night.*

While a student in New York, Merchant worked as a messenger for the Indian delegation to the United Nations and accumulated contacts for his entertainment projects. After several months at the United Nations he got a job as an account executive at the advertising firm McCann-Erikson. It was with the help of contacts that he made at this job that he made his first film in 1960. Produced in one weekend, the fourteen-minute film called *The Creation of Woman* was well-received. Encouraged by his efforts, Merchant left for Hollywood as soon as he received his degree at NYU. Even though he had no money, Merchant was optimistic and cunningly creative. Before leaving for California, he sent a fake press release to all the media outlets in Los Angeles announcing that a famous Indian producer would soon be arriving in Hollywood.

However, the first few months in Hollywood forced "the famous Indian producer" to take a night job in the classified department of the *Los Angeles Times* and a part-time day job at a clothing store. Optimistic as ever, Merchant continued to seek out opportunities.

Ismail Merchant

Through careful investigation he discovered that a film needed to be played three days at a commercial theatre to be eligible for Academy Award consideration. He persuaded the owner of a fine arts cinema in Los Angeles to show *The Creation of Woman* along with Bergman's film *The Devil's Eye*. As a result *The Creation of Woman* received enough exposure to be nominated for an Oscar. Merchant's persistence and optimism had set him on his way. "I never take no for an answer," Merchant said in a *Time* magazine interview. "It simply does not exist as an option."

Merchant Meets Ivory

In 1961 Merchant met James Ivory at the screening of Ivory's documentary, *The Sword and the Flute*. According to Merchant it was Ivory's extraordinary knowledge of India that drew them together. A few months later Merchant and Ivory became partners and set up a production company with a view to make films in India for a Western audience. Later that year they met Ruth Prawer Jhabvala, who would become their screenwriter, and the enduring partnership began.

The Drive to Always be Better

Their first film was based on Jhabvala's novel *The Householder,* and was a black-and-white feature released in 1963. It was this film that gave the company its first break when Columbia Pictures agreed to distribute it in the United States. Although most of the early films that followed were based on India, they were not very popular with Indian audiences, perhaps because they depicted a Western point of view. *Shakespeare Wallah* (1965), received the most critical acclaim. Their next major release, *Savages* (1972), did well in Europe but it opening in the United States was disappointing. It was not until *The Europeans* was released in 1979 that Merchant Ivory managed to capture the imagination of both European and American audiences. *The Europeans* heralded a new era of beautiful period films, produced on a grand scale with a surprisingly low budgets.

To celebrate the twenty-first anniversary of their partnership in 1982, Merchant and Ivory produced a screen adaptation of Jhabvala's prize-winning novel, *Heat and Dust*. This film was the first in a series of successful screen adaptations of famous novels. These included Henry James's *The Bostonians* (1984), which received an Oscar nomination, E.M. Forster's *A Room with a View* (1986), Evan Connell's *Mr. and Mrs. Bridge* (1990), and Forster's *Howards End* (1992).

Although all were successful, *A Room with a View* was a blockbuster. The movie was produced on a budget of $3 million grossed $60 million worldwide, a record for an art film. It received eight Academy Award nominations and won three—best art direction, best screenplay, and costume design.

Before *A Room with a View,* Merchant and Ivory risked all their money on a new film and did not have an extravagant lifestyle. After their phenomenal success they were encouraged by Hollywood executives and Wall Street to go public. However, they decided not to. According to Merchant, the film scripts they were sent by Hollywood studios were "shallow." "This was not how we saw ourselves," he told Long. "None of it had any link to our methods of moviemaking. And we didn't want to become the flavor of the month." Merchant strongly believes that to succeed in life one must do what one does best and continue to perfect it. Perhaps that is why Merchant Ivory films are all very similar; they evoke nostalgia for a seemingly beautiful past and are meant to enchant.

Described by Long as "an emotional man with fast-changing moods and remarkable self-discipline," Merchant has a unique way of conducting business that is rare in the industry. His contracts involve no businessmen or lawyers and conclude in twenty-four hours rather than months. He is a persistent and persuasive fund-raiser. Merchant has always insisted that the money he raises go toward production costs and not inflated salaries, even for himself and his partners. He also manages to get well-known stars to work for less money. Even for props and set designs Merchant is able to beg and borrow whatever is needed, thereby further reducing costs. According to him it is not the money spent on a film, but good dialogue that sets it apart. Noted Long, Merchant "represents the paradox of being intensely and deeply idealistic and intensely and deeply practical."

Merchant has also tried his hand at directing. In 1985, he made the *Courtesans of Bombay,* and most recently *In Custody.* Based on Anita Desai's novel, the film is a tribute to Merchant's Indian heritage and depicts Urdu language and Indian culture. Merchant says he felt so strongly about the topic that he could not let anyone else direct it.

Although he is an international celebrity with homes and offices in three continents, Merchant has strong ties to his South Asian roots. A devout Muslim, he wakes up at the crack of dawn to say his prayers. Although he has lived in the United States more than three decades, he is proud to carry an Indian passport. His loyalty toward his heritage is not confined to nationality—he is particularly fond of Urdu poetry and Indian classical music and collects antique Persian rugs, silver, and porcelain. An overall connoisseur, he likes to surround himself with beauty in clothing, ornaments, food, and entertainment.

Merchant divides his time between Bombay, London, and New York where he has both a Manhattan apartment and a home in upstate New York. The Hudson Valley home is filled with curios collected from film sites all over the world. It is a gathering place for artists, writers, and musicians.

Merchant's creative instincts have also led him to writing. He is the author of *Hullabaloo in Old Jeypore,* a book about making movies in India. He is also the author of four cookbooks, *Ismail Merchant's Indian Cuisine* (1986) and *Ismail Merchant's Vegetarian Cooking* (1992), *Ismail Merchant's Passionate Meals* (1994) and *Ismail Merchant's Florence* (1994). He first learned how to cook in the 1950s out of need as a student. Later, he used his skills to establish a congenial atmosphere for writers and artists when in 1972 he began a still-standing tradition of cooking meals once a week for his entire crew. He prepares a combination of Indian, French, and other ethnic cuisine with the same elegance evident in his films, an exquisite blend of East and West.

Sources:

Periodicals

Blowen, Michael. "There Is Always a Way to Get a Picture Made," *The Boston Globe,* July 27, 1983.

Cagin, Seth. "Tracking." *Soho News,* October 27, 1981.

Cohn, Lawrence. "Merchant Ivory's 'Bostonians' Ready for Bow; 3 Rank Pics Next." *Variety,* July 11, 1984.

Giovannini, Joseph. "Merchant and Ivory's Country Retreat." *New York Times,* April 3, 1986.

Harmetz, Aljean. "Merchant and Ivory Strike Gold." *New York Times,* July 5, 1986.

Insdorf, Annette. "A Retrospective Celebrates 21 Years of Movie Teamwork." *New York Times,* December 4, 1983.

Jacobs, Rita D. "An Unforgettable Evening. Food and Film: Dinner with Ismail Merchant." *United Airlines Vis a Vis,* November 1990.

Kythreotis, Anna. "Ismail Merchant Tries a Different Job: Director." *New York Times,* May 9, 1993.

Maychick, Diana. "Ismail Merchant, Crazy Like a Fox." *New York Post,* March 25, 1986.

———."Merchant of Magic." *New York Post,* January 18, 1989, p. 23.

O'Conner, John J. "Film Group is Shown in a Profile." *New York Times,* April 5, 1985.

Sachs, Lloyd. "A Room with a View is Trio's Latest Triumph." *Chicago Sun-Times,* April 6, 1986.

Weinraub, Bernard. "Bombay: Poor Find Escape in Films." *New York Times,* May 7, 1973.

Other

Ginsberg, Mark. "Ruth Jhabvala, Ismail Merchant, James Ivory," Interview from Theatre Collection. The Research Libraries, New York Public Library, December 1983.

Myrna Post Associates Inc., "Ismail Merchant," New York, 1994.

—Sketch by Natasha Rafi

Midori
(1971–)
Violinist

Even before she celebrated her twentieth birthday, Midori—who uses only her first name—was considered one of the world's most celebrated violinists. A child prodigy, she trained at Juilliard School of Music and performed at Carnegie Music Hall by the age of eighteen. She won the respect of even the most cynical critics at age fourteen, when a series of broken strings forced her to complete a difficult concerto on two borrowed violins. Now in her twenties, she commands performances with world-famous ensembles: the Philadelphia Orchestra under Wolfgang Sawallisch; the Maggio Musicale in Florence, Italy; the NDR Symphony Orchestra in Hamburg, Germany; La Scala Philoharmonic; Orchestre de Paris; and the Frankfurt Radio Symphony, among others.

Midori was born October 25, 1971, in Osaka, Japan. Her father was an engineer; her mother was a professional violinist. From the beginning, her mother was her close friend, her coach, and confidante. About her father,

Midori knew little. Her initial music lessons came from her mother. But, because her mother was working, the young girl often practiced on her own. "When she came home, she was cooking and I would practice in the kitchen," Midori told Robert Schwarz of the *New York Times Magazine* in 1991. Through this process, she memorized works by Bach, Bartok, and Paganini. At age eight, an American colleague of her mother heard Midori perform and made a tape, a homemade version which also included sounds of the family dog barking in the background. Nevertheless, the tape found its way to Dorothy DeLay, a world-renowned music teacher at Juilliard School of Music in New York. DeLay was impressed enough to bring Midori to the 1981 Aspen Music Festival as a scholarship student. Midori made her U.S. debut and, with her mother, settled in New York City.

"A Miracle"

Pinchas Zukerman, a well-known violinist and one of Midori's early idols, heard the girl perform for the first time at Aspen. "She tuned, she bowed to the audience, she bowed to me, she bowed to the pianist—and then she played the Bartok concerto and I went bananas," he told Schwarz in the *New York Times Magazine*. "I sat there and tears started coming down my cheeks." Later, Zukerman turned to the audience and said, "Ladies and gentlemen, I don't know about you, but I've just witnessed a miracle."

In 1982, Midori began studying with DeLay at Juilliard's pre-college division. She rapidly learned vast amounts of repertory, despite going through the shock of adjusting to a new culture and juggling schooling with music lessons, practice, and a slowly growing concert schedule. Added to this pressure came her parent's divorce in 1983. Nevertheless, she seemed to grow into adolescence relatively comfortably. Much of this seemed to come from her own ability—and desire—to lose herself in her music. Playing the violin was always her choice, she likes to say. Her mother never forced her to learn; she taught Midori because Midori wanted to learn. Later, when she began working with an agent, Lee Lamont of ICM Artists, her performance schedule was carefully limited. In the beginning, she gave no more than eight to ten performances a year, and they were carefully chosen to help enhance her learning process. She made a Canadian debut in 1985 with the Toronto Symphony and traveled to Japan later that year to perform with Leonard Bernstein and the European Youth Orchestra in a special concert commemorating the fortieth anniversary of the bombing of Hiroshima.

On a hot and humid night in July of 1986, Midori, then fourteen, made a now-legendary appearance at Massachusetts' Tanglewood Music Festival. While playing Leonard Bernstein's "Serenade," her E string broke. She put her violin down and borrowed the concertmaster's instrument. The E string broke again. She picked up the

Midori

assistant concertmaster's violin and finished her performance without a flaw. The audience went wild.

Most teenagers go through a period of rebellion, Midori was no exception. At age fifteen, she decided to leave Juilliard. Her reasons remain vague, but it appears that Midori wanted to stand up for herself and make a big decision. She continued to work with ICM Artists, who kept a careful control over her schedule and made sure she gave no major recitals until she had developed a proper level of artistic maturity.

In October 1989, she made her New York recital debut at Carnegie Hall before a sold-out audience. Her performance was later released on a Sony Classical laser disk. Midori later confided that she wasn't nervous. "I feel so comfortable onstage; I feel safest," she told Schwarz. "The best part of giving concerts is just being out there and playing, nothing else."

Now, as a full-time professional performer, Midori gives about eighty recitals a year, traveling to thirty cities on both sides of the Atlantic. She records exclusively for Sony Classical, and she has received numerous honors, including the Los Angeles Music Center's Dorothy B. Chandler Performing Arts Award, New York State's Asian-American Heritage Month Award, and Japan's Crystal Award for her contribution to the arts.

Mature Artist

In 1992, she founded the Midori Foundation, which seeks to expose children to the arts. She devotes her time to the foundation by giving special concerts in schools, hospitals, and institutions where children often don't have the opportunity to come into direct contact with the arts.

Barely five feet tall, her face cut with fine, porcelain-like features, Midori often looks fragile and vulnerable on stage. She was perhaps one of the most-watched child prodigies of her time. And as with many such prodigies, many wondered whether her extraordinary childhood talent would mature into a sophisticated level of artistry. Or, would she, like so many other child sensations, stumble?

She didn't stumble. A 1993 recital tour and three separate performances of the Sibelius Violin Concerto drew rave reviews. The *Los Angeles Times* reported that Midori played "with all the passion, authority, ease and penetrating detail one has come to expect of all her performances." And the *Philadelphia Inquirer* remarked "Midori's playing had cast such a spell that the audience's rapt attention continued through the pause between movements."

Noting that "Midori isn't a prodigy anymore," *New York Newsday* pronounced that "the tiny twenty-two-year-old violinist has made the transition from phenom to artist . . . The commitment, maturity and richness of Midori's performance was that of the well-established artist."

As she grows, Midori's challenge will be to continue to let her sense of her music mature with her. Schwarz recalled one image of Midori vividly. After a rehearsal she stood on a stage, playing a difficult solo variation. Nearby, stage equipment was noisily being taken apart. Midori, lost in her music, didn't appear to notice the noise. Swaying, bending into her violin, she played on.

Sources:

Periodicals

Cariaga, Daniel. "More Volume than Finesse at the Bowl." *Los Angeles Times,* Aug. 27, 1993.

Goodman, Peter. "Midori: No Longer Just a Superstar." *New York Newsday,* September 27, 1993.

Schwarz, K. Robert. "Glissando." *New York Times Magazine,* March 24, 1991.

Valdes, Lesley. "Haydn With a Twinkle, Spellbinding Sibelius." *The Philadelphia Inquirer,* Sept. 23, 1993.

—Sketch by Himanee Gupta

Anchee Min
(1957–)
Author

Anchee Min is the author of the critically acclaimed 1994 memoir *Red Azalea,* which detailed her life in China during the Cultural Revolution. The book won wide praise in England when it was published there in 1993, and its American release the following year drew considerable attention and excellent reviews.

Early Life

Anchee Min was born in Shanghai, China, in 1957. Her father taught industrial design at the Shanghai textile Institute and her mother taught at a local middle school. Min wrote in *Red Azalea,* "I was raised on the teachings of Mao and on the operas of Madame Mao, Comrade Jiang Chiang. I became a leader of the Little Red Guards in elementary school. This was during the Great Proletarian Cultural Revolution when red was my color."

The Min family lived in squalid conditions, as did most of the residents of Shanghai at the time, but this did not dampen Min's fervent belief in the rightness of the state. She was educated in the public school system and at the age of seventeen the government sent her to a labor camp in the countryside rather than to pursue a higher education. The camp she was sent to was called Red Fire Farm and was in a rural province on the East China Sea. The soil on the farm was too salty to adequately support the crops they were instructed to grow there, but the administration insisted that they continue to try.

Min stayed on the farm for a year, enduring brutal living conditions. During this time she came to question her devotion to the party slogans that had sustained her in her childhood. The reality of life in the camp, especially the fiercely dogmatic governance of every aspect of the workers' lives, shattered Min's illusions about a caring, thoughtful state. She began an affair with a fellow worker at the camp, a woman named Yan, and together they made life endurable.

Actress

In the spring of 1975 Min was chosen by a group of visiting functionaries to audition for a part in a movie that the government was making about the life of Chairman Mao's wife, Jiang Chiang. She was then transferred to Shanghai, where her family still lived, and began preparation for the film, which was to be called *Red Azalea*. There were four other actresses up for the part of Madame Mao, as she was known, and the competition was fierce. Ultimately Min was

Anchee Min

not chosen for the part and instead worked on the set, performing a variety of duties. Midway through production, however, there was a shake-up and Min was chosen to replace the star. Then on September 9, 1976, Mao Zedong died, and his widow, who had been behind the production of the film, was arrested and China descended into a tumultuous period. The production of *Red Azalea* was halted.

For the next eight years, Min worked in Shanghai and attempted to be granted permission to either be admitted to college or be allowed to leave the country to study. In 1984 the actress Joan Chen intervened in her case and helped her to get permission to come to the United States, ostensibly to study at the School of the Art Institute of Chicago. When she arrived in Chicago, Min spoke no English and decided to immerse herself in American culture, taking jobs as a waitress, messenger, textile painter, and baby-sitter.

Author

In 1988 Min met and married Quigu Jiang, an artist from Shanghai who had been forced to flee China that year. She then began writing about her experiences in China and eventually sent a chapter to *Granta,* a British literary magazine, which published the story. On the basis of this story Min signed with a literary agent who secured a hefty advance for a memoir of her experiences in China. Min finished the manuscript in 1992 and the resulting book, *Red Azalea,* was published in early 1994.

The book received generally good reviews and was highly publicized by its publisher, Pantheon Books, in the hopes that its sales would emulate those of Amy Tan's works, which did not happen. Writing in the *New York Times Book Review* Judith Shapiro called it "an entertaining, provocative . . . and extraordinary story."

Sources:

Books

Min, Anchee. *Red Azalea.* New York: Pantheon Books, 1994.

Periodicals

Shapiro, Judith. "Counterrevolutionary Sex." *New York Times Book Review,* February 27, 1994, p. 11.

—Sketch by Jim Henry

Dale Minami
(1946–)
Attorney, activist

Dale Minami is an attorney in private practice in San Francisco, California, who has for many years worked in organizations that fight for the political rights and civil liberties of the Asian American community. He is founder of the Asian Law Caucus, the Asian American Bar Association, and the Asian Pacific Bar of California; he has served Democratic politicians as co-chair of the Northern California Asian Pacific Americans for Clinton/Gore in 1992 and as a member of Senator Barbara Boxer's judicial screening committee; and he has litigated a number of significant cases defending the Asian community's civil rights.

Dale Minami was born on October 13, 1946, in Los Angeles, California to second-generation Japanese Americans. His father was a gardener and owner of a small sporting goods store, where his mother worked as well. During World War II the Minamis were imprisoned, along with 120,000 other Japanese Americans on the West Coast, as national security risks. Their home and business were taken away and they were sent to live first in a horse stable at the Santa Anita raceway. From there they were sent to their final destination, Rowher, Arkansas, where they stayed for the duration of the war.

Minami was educated in the Los Angeles public school system. After graduating from high school in 1964, he enrolled in the University of Southern California, where

Dale Minami

he received a bachelor's degree in 1968, graduating magna cum laude and as a member of the honor society, Phi Beta Kappa.

He then went on to law school at the University of California at Berkeley's School of Law. He earned his law degree in 1971 and was admitted to the California bar in January of 1972. Minami told Jim Henry in an interview that the highly charged political atmosphere of the Berkeley campus during the late 1960s had a major impact on him. He was especially affected by the antiwar movement and the ethnic studies movements.

Following graduation Minami opened a law practice that specialized in personal injury, entertainment law, and civil litigation. He also began teaching and spent one year as an instructor at Mills College in the department of ethnic studies. He also became a lecturer at the University of California at Berkeley in Asian American studies.

Asian Law Caucus

In the early seventies, Ken Kawaichi (now a superior court judge) and Minami began working toward establishing the Asian Law Caucus (ALC), a legal advocacy organization directed to helping the Asian American community in the areas of civil rights, employment and housing discrimination, and immigration. They co-founded the organization in 1972, and Minami became its first attorney. He handled all the cases and wrote the proposals for funding.

Getting the money to start the ALC was fairly easy, but maintaining its operation proved problematic until it was granted a special tax status that allowed it to charge nominal fees—something nonprofit organizations are generally not allowed to do. Minami served as director of the ALC for three years, during which time he also taught at Berkeley and continued in his private practice.

One of the ALC's first prominent cases was *Chan v. City and County of California,* in which the ALC represented Barry Chan, a photography student at Berkeley. Chan had been in Chinatown one day when he noticed police rounding up, seemingly at random, a group of Asian men, handcuffing them and taking them in to the station to be fingerprinted and photographed. Chan took pictures of the police's actions and an officer noticed him, broke his camera, and handcuffed Chan as well. The ALC was alerted to the case by Chan, and they brought suit against the city, which defended these blatantly unconstitutional sweeps as necessary to fight Asian gang violence. The ALC publicized this practice and a huge public uproar ensued that caused the city to settle the case before trial, with promises to end this practice.

Another prominent ALC case was *Wong v. Younger,* in which the ALC sued the attorney general of California to halt distribution of a pamphlet that depicted Asians as criminals, suggesting, among other things, that Chinese love to gamble and smoke opium. The case was lost on First Amendment grounds, but the publicity generated by it caused the state to discontinue use of the pamphlets.

Private Practice

Minami left the ALC in 1975 to devote more of his time to his private practice. In 1989 he formed the law firm of Minami, Lew, Takami and Lee, headquartered in San Francisco. He continues to specialize in employment discrimination and personal injury law. He also works as an entertainment lawyer, representing clients that include noted Asian Americans Philip Kan Gotanda, Mako, and Kristi Yamaguchi.

In addition to co-founding the Asian Law Caucus, Minami co-founded the Asian American Bar Association of the Greater Bay Area in 1976, the first Asian American Bar Association in the United States. In 1988 he co-founded the Asian Pacific Bar of California, a statewide consortium of Asian Pacific Bar Associations. In 1989 he co-founded the Coalition of Asian Pacific Americans, the first Asian Pacific political action committee, which lobbies locally and nationally for issues of concern to the Asian community. He has lectured and written extensively and has received many awards for his career of service. Among these are the State Bar of California's President's Pro Bono Service Award (1984), the Coro Foundation Achievement Award (1986), the Harry Dow Memorial Fellowship "Justice in Action" Award (1988), and the Organization of Chinese Americans Leadership Award (1989).

Sources:

Minami, Dale, telephone interview with Jim Henry, August 4, 1994.

Minami, Lew, Takami and Lee. "Personal Resume of Dale Minami." August 1994.

—Sketch by Jim Henry

Norman Y. Mineta
(1931–)
U.S. Congressman

Norman Y. Mineta

Norman Yoshio Mineta represents one of the nation's most populous congressional districts—California's fifteenth, which includes the south San Francisco Bay, part of the city of San Jose, and a large chunk of Santa Clara and Santa Cruz counties. As chairman of the House's powerful Committee on Public Works and Transportation, he wields considerable influence, for it is up to this committee to determine how the nation should deal with its four million miles of highways and bridges, and 438 mass-transit systems. And, as *A. Magazine* noted in December 1993, "with the nation's highways and railroads careening toward disaster, Mineta's role in the House is likely to balloon in the years to come."

Yet, none of this is why most people know Norman Mineta. Hundreds of thousands of citizens know him for the role he played in 1987, when in the historic 100th Congress, he and another Japanese American congressman convinced their colleagues to approve a measure offering an official apology from the federal government and a $1.2 billion award to the 120,000 Japanese Americans, who, like themselves, were forced to move from their homes during World War II and into isolated relocation camps.

Born November 12, 1931, in San Jose, Norman Mineta was the son of Japanese immigrants. His father had emigrated from Japan in 1902, and his mother had come in 1912. Neither, however, could become U.S. citizens because of the Oriental Exclusion Law of 1924. Nevertheless, Mineta's father, believing in the American dream like many immigrants, established an insurance agency in 1920. The family's life was relatively stable until Japanese troops bombed Pearl Harbor in 1941, essentially forcing the United States to enter World War II. In early 1942, the federal government, acting under an executive order, began deporting Americans of Japanese ancestry to relocation camps. Families often were given only a few hours to dispose of property and set their affairs in order before troops came. They were then allowed to carry only what possessions they could handle in their arms.

The Internment Begins

Mineta remembers one night in early 1942 when his father called the family together. "He said he did not know what the war would bring to my mother and to him, since they were resident aliens," Mineta said during the House of Representatives debate on the redress issue. "However, he was confident that his beloved country would guarantee and protect the rights of his children, American citizens, all. But his confidence, as it turned out, was misplaced."

On May 29, the Mineta family received word that it would be relocated. Under the scrutiny of armed guards, Mineta's father loaded his family onto a train. Mineta, age ten, was wearing a Cub Scout uniform as the train headed for a relocation camp in Wyoming.

Mineta's father wrote to friends in San Jose what happened as the train pulled out. In his remarks to Congress, Mineta quoted from the letter: "I looked at Santa Clara's streets from the train over the subway. I thought this might be the last look at my beloved home city. My heart almost broke, and suddenly hot tears came pouring out, and the whole family cried out, could not stop, until we were out of our loved county." During the congressional hearings, Mineta wiped tears of his own away as he recalled the story.

For three years Mineta's family remained in the camp. At the end of World War II, he and his family—like thousands of other Japanese Americans—returned to their homes and picked up the pieces of their previous lives.

Mineta went to San Jose High School and later to the University of California, Berkeley, where he earned a bachelor's degree in business in 1953. He joined the army and served as a military intelligence officer during tours of duty in Japan and Korea. Meanwhile, his father reopened his insurance agency, and when Mineta left active service in 1956, he went to work for his father.

Over time, as a business executive who believed in active community involvement, Mineta became involved with the Japanese American Citizens League, the Greater San Jose Chamber of Commerce, the Rotary Club, and other civic groups. Community involvement led to government involvement. In 1962, he became a member of San Jose's Human Relations Commission, then later served on the city's Housing Authority. In 1967, he was appointed to fill a vacancy on the city council and became San Jose's first minority councilman. He was elected to the seat in 1969 and ran for mayor in 1971. When elected, he became the first Japanese American mayor of a major city. He quickly established himself as an aggressive advocate for urban areas. At the time, the San Jose area was growing considerably, and Mineta aligned himself with the political forces that called for limits on growth.

National Politics

Mineta's rising in political ranks continued through the 1970s. He ran for Congress in 1974, drawing broad support from a small but cohesive Japanese American community in San Jose, and as a Democrat, won a seat long held by Republicans. He quickly established himself as part of a new Democratic leadership—as one of seventy-five reform-oriented Democrats elected to Congress that year.

In Congress, his influence grew as his tenure increased. He was deputy whip for the House Democratic Leadership and has served on the Budget Committee, the Policy and Steering Committee, and the Post Office and Civil Service Committee. He also held several chairmanships on subcommittees under the Public Works and Transportation Committee he now heads. He is described as a detail-oriented politician, familiar with the mechanics of transportation policy but not the type to micro-manage. When elected to chair the Public Works and Transportation Committee in 1992, he was considered a full-fledged inside player.

But even as Mineta climbed the ranks politically, a feeling of shame lived within him, as it did many Japanese Americans who had tried for decades to forget World War II, the executive order, and living in the relocation camps. For Mineta, this sense of shame was channeled into a desire to right wrongs. He had wanted to obtain some form of redress for more than a decade. In 1978, he won passage of a bill to grant previously denied retirement benefits to Japanese American civil servants who had been interned. But his fight for full justice continued.

When in 1987 the bill for redress for internment came to the floor of the House of Representatives, Mineta urged members of Congress to right the wrongs of the past: "We lost our homes, we lost our businesses, we lost our farms, but worst of all, we lost our most basic human rights," he said. "Our own government had branded us with the unwarranted stigma of disloyalty which clings to us still to this day."

"Injustice does not dim with time," he added. "We cannot wait it out. We cannot ignore it, and we cannot shrug our shoulders at our past. If we do not refute the shame of the indictment here and now, the specter of this tragedy will resurface just as surely as I am standing here before you, and the injustice will recur. . . . The bill's impact reaches much deeper into the very soul of our democracy. Those of us who support this bill want not just to close the books on the sad events of 1942; we want to make sure that such blatant constitutional violations never occur again."

After Congress passed the legislation, Mineta signed the bill on behalf of the House. But, for him, the chapter on discrimination had not completely closed. He later pushed for legislation authorizing a memorial honoring Japanese Americans who served in the military, and he helped pass the Americans with Disabilities Act, which requires businesses and public buildings to make their facilities more accessible to people with disabilities.

And when the Persian Gulf War began, Mineta urged federal law enforcement officials not to target Arab Americans—he didn't want the same discrimination that occurred during World War II to happen again.

Sources:

Kenworthy, Tom. "House Votes Apology, Reparations for Japanese Americans Held During War." *Washington Post,* February 18, 1991.

Mineta, Norman. "Nation's Transportation Moving into a Crossroads." *Nations Cities Weekly,* February 18, 1991.

"Power Brokers." *A. Magazine,* December 15, 1993, pp. 25–34.

Tumulty, Karen. "House Votes to Pay Japanese WWII Internees." *Los Angeles Times,* September 18, 1987.

—Sketch by Himanee Gupta

Patsy Takemoto Mink

(1927–)

Legislator, lawyer

In her thirty-year career as a legislator at the state and federal levels, Patsy Takemoto Mink has championed legislative reforms in health care, education, women's rights, environmental affairs, cancer research, and employment. Taking often unpopular positions on these and other issues has not been uncommon for Mink; she has always believed that challenging the power structure and contemporary wisdom are not simply acts of moral courage, but are the essential obligations of every citizen. And she has practiced this principal not only as a politician but also as a woman, a native of Hawaii who chose to marry a European American man, and a lawyer who has won many lawsuits of national import.

Such choices have not come without a personal cost. Mink has suffered more than a few defeats in her quest for political office, racial and sexual discrimination as one of the first Japanese American woman attorneys in Hawaii, and political isolation because she challenges party politics and powerful business interests.

Nevertheless, Mink has worked to maintain her independence and integrity during her eight terms as Hawaii's representative in the U.S. House and numerous other terms as a lawmaker at the state and municipal levels. Political insiders still consider her one of the few remaining true liberals in Hawaii's Democratic party.

The Roots of Mink's Success

Born in 1927 on the island of Maui, an island in Hawaii, Patsy Takemoto Mink enjoyed a comfortable life in her family's cottage on two acres of land. Her father's work as a civil engineer afforded the family an upper middle-class lifestyle that was affluent compared to the humble living conditions of most other Hawaiians. Mink's penchant for challenging established traditions was borne out early in her life when she insisted on starting school at age four, a year earlier than the normal practice. She later sought admission to the all-European American Kaunoa English Standard School which rarely admitted students of color. Because of the long travel time to the new school and the unfriendly environment, Mink was drawn to reading books and listening to the radio. Reading about leaders like Mahatma Gandhi led her to dream about being a medical doctor, a career she had entertained since undergoing surgery for appendicitis at the age of four.

Patsy Takemoto Mink

Her experiences at school became more unpleasant when the Japanese attacked Pearl Harbor and Japanese Americans throughout the United States—except for Hawaii—were interned in concentration camps. Despite being spared internment, Mink and other Asians in Hawaii were not spared the indignity of frequently being reminded that they were the enemy of the United States. After later transferring to Maui High School, her career interests began to turn to politics when she was elected student body president.

The end of the war brought the return of Nisei, second-generation Japanese Americans, who had fought in the war and were motivated to work for social change to improve the economic and political status quo in Hawaii. This inspired Mink to become more involved in politics. After graduating from high school as class valedictorian, she enrolled at the University of Hawaii where she was elected president of the Pre-Medical Students Club and chosen as a member of the Varsity Debate Team.

Following her sophomore year, she spent her remaining college years transferring to two different colleges before finally graduating from the University of Nebraska. Her post-graduation year was frustrating and boring: She worked at a clerk-typist job in a small museum in Honolulu while trying to decide what to do with her life after having been rejected by every medical school to which she had applied.

The Journey Begins

Heeding the suggestion of a mentor that she pursue a law career proved to be a major turning point in Mink's life. She was soon admitted to law school at the University of Chicago, where she met John Mink, a graduate student in geophysics. Despite opposition from her parents the two married six months after that first encounter in January 1951, the same year they graduated. Their first and only child, Gwendolyn Rachel, whose nickname was Wendy, was born a year later.

Although John found immediate employment after graduation, Mink was unable to find work. Not only was she a woman, but she was an Asian American woman in an interracial marriage, and no one would hire her. She was forced to return to her student job at the law school. She continued receiving job rejections even after the couple moved back to Hawaii following their daughter's birth—even after she passed the Hawaii Bar Exam. So, with the assistance of her father, she started her own law practice taking divorce, criminal defense, adoption, and other cases shunned by established law firms. She also taught business classes at the University of Hawaii.

In 1954, Mink was elected president of the Young Democrats, a powerful political group that started as a result of Everyman's Organization, an Oahu-based group that Mink founded whose mission was to push for Democratic party participation among young Democrats.

Between 1957 and 1964, Mink held elected positions as a representative and a senator in the legislature of Hawaii, which at the time was a U.S. Territory. There she developed a reputation for supporting the underdog. As a senator she authored the "Equal Pay for Equal Work" law, and while serving as a representative, she sponsored a successful resolution protesting Great Britain's nuclear testing in the South Pacific.

Six-Term Congresswoman

Her reputation as a political maverick and a liberal continued when she took the oath of office in January of 1965 for the first of six consecutive terms as Hawaii's—and the nation's—first Asian American woman elected to Congress. During her tenure as a congresswoman, she supported the regulation of strip mining, sponsored the Women's Educational Equity Act, was outspoken in her opposition to the U.S. role in the Vietnam War when it was considered politically risky to do so, and successfully sued the federal government in a Freedom of Information Act case that was later cited as legal precedent for obtaining the tapes in the Watergate scandal which led to Richard Nixon's forced resignation as president. Her commitment to liberal causes was also demonstrated in her legislating in education and child care issues.

Following an unsuccessful campaign as the first Asian American to run for the presidency in 1972 and a campaign for the U.S. Senate that bore similar results, Mink served for three years in the Carter administration as Assistant Secretary of State for Ocean and International, Environmental and Scientific Affairs until she resigned in 1980 to serve for three straight terms as national president of the Americans for Democratic Action.

More Lawmaking in Hawaii

After successfully bringing a lawsuit for a community group opposing the construction of a nuclear power plant in Honolulu county, she returned to Hawaiian politics. In 1983 she was elected to the Honolulu City Council where she served for four years.

A Return to Congress

Though she was defeated in subsequent races for state governor in 1986 and Honolulu's mayor in 1988, Mink won an election in 1990 to serve the remainder of Representative Daniel Akaka's unexpired term in the U.S. House; Akaka had been appointed to the Senate seat left vacant after the sudden death of Senator Spark Matsunaga that same year. In 1991, she authored legislation that eliminated prior restrictions that prevented many nontraditional college students from receiving federal aid and that excluded the value of a family home in the formula for determining federal student aid, a provision that enabled more families' sons and daughters to qualify for such assistance.

In 1992, she introduced legislation that provided full funding of the Headstart Program, incentive grants to school systems for quality education achievement, and increased federal funding levels for secondary and elementary schools. She also worked diligently in 1993 to get Congress to enact legislation that banned the practice of permanently replacing employees who participated in labor union strikes.

Despite her belief that "women who have a brain and an idea" will encounter hostility in public life, Mink has chosen to counter that hostility with constructive action as a highly successful lawmaker.

Sources:

Mink, Patsy Takemoto. *Resume and press release* provided by Mink, 1994.

—Sketch by Samuel R. Cacas

Janice Mirikitani

(194?–)

Poet, community activist

Janice Mirikitani is a poet, community activist, choreographer, artist, feminist, church administrator, and preacher's wife. Her strong, passionate voice defies categorization. A Sansei (third generation Japanese American) internee, a sixties student radical, an incest survivor, and an advocate for the homeless and downtrodden of San Francisco, Mirikitani writes on all the aspects of her life.

Describing herself in "Who is Singing This Song" she writes:

> I am your own, a child in dark streets,
>   woman seeking safety in a world of shadows,
> I am the present, struggling to be free
>   a crusader in these spiritless prisons,
>   pinnacles to greed and sterility.

Mirikitani's first book of poetry, *Awake in the River,* was published in 1978. In it she writes about her anger at racism and her experiences as a Japanese American. Her second book, *Shedding Silence* appeared in 1987. It is a collection of poetry and prose about an assortment of topics—Hiroshima, Chernobyl, abuse of women, the internment, racism, incest, and sexism.

Internment

Mirikitani was only an infant in 1942 when her family was shipped to Rohwer, Arkansas, one of the ten internment camps that held Japanese Americans during World War II. She and her parents, chicken farmers from Stockton, California, were incarcerated until she was three. After the war they moved to Chicago; her parents divorced a few years later.

Her mother's remarriage brought her back to northern California and closer to other family members. Along with the stability of family came years of sexual abuse, a subject on which Mirikitani courageously and eloquently has been outspoken. She wrote of her abuse by family friends and relatives in *No Hiding Place*, a book by her husband, Reverend Cecil Williams: "For eleven years, almost daily, I was stalked in the darkness of closets, the barn, in muffled bedrooms, I would not tell anyone; I remained silent. My mother would scold me and tell me that I should not allow those 'things' to happen. She gave me, a young child, the responsibility to stop an adult male. I couldn't."

Janice Mirikitani

Through these difficult life experiences, a sensitive yet steely young woman emerged. After graduating from the University of California at Los Angeles (UCLA), she was pursuing her master's studies at San Francisco State University when she heard the call of the civil rights movement and the demands for "Yellow Power." Her voice as an Asian American woman grew stronger. She divorced her first husband, a Caucasian, and for the next decade was a single mother raising her daughter Tianne. At the same time, she collaborated with other writers and poets, joining Third World Communications, an arts and literary collective, and helped found the Kearny Street Writers Workshop.

Editor and Writer

Mirikitani edited and directed numerous anthologies, including *AION* magazine, *Third World Women, Time to Greez! Incantations from the Third World,* and *Making Waves.* Her most recent anthology, *Watch Out! We're Talking,* focuses on issues of incest and abuse. She and her husband have also produced a collection of children's writings, *I Have Something to Say About This Big Trouble: Children of the Tenderloin Speak Out.*

A reflection of the many worlds her life traverses, Mirikitani's writings are only one way she expresses her passion for people and social change. In the sixties she joined San Francisco's famed Glide Memorial United Methodist Church, where she has worked with homeless people, battered women, drug addicts, street kids, gay men and lesbians, poor people, survivors of sexual abuse, and prostitutes. She is president of the Glide Foundation and director of Glide's programs, where she administers some two hundred different services and activities. Mirikitani has received numerous awards and honors for her work.

It was also at Glide that she met her husband, Cecil Williams, the charismatic spiritual leader of Glide. She writes of their marriage in her poem "Soul Food":

> We prepare
>   the meal together.
> I complain,
>   hurt, reduced to fury
>   again by their subtle insults
>   insinuations
>   because I am married to you.
> Impossible autonomy, no mind
>   of my own.
>
> You like your fish
>   crisp, coated with cornmeal,
>   fried deep,
>   sliced mangoes to sweeten
>   the tang of lemons.
>
> My fish is raw,
>   on shredded lettuce,
>   lemon slices thin as skin,
>   wasabe burning like green fire.
>
> You bake the cornbread flat
>   and dip it in
>   the thick soup
>
> I've brewed from
>   turkey carcass, rice gruel,
>   sesame oil and chervil.
>
> We laugh over watermelon
>   and bubbling cobbler.
>
> You say there are few men
>   who can stand to have a woman equal,
>   upright.
> This meal
>   unsurpassed.

Sources:

Books

Williams, Cecil. *No Hiding Place: Empowerment and Recovery for Our Troubled Communities.* San Francisco: Harper, 1992.

Periodicals

Holt, Patricia. "Shattering the Silence." *San Francisco Chronicle,* July 5, 1987.

Nakao, Annie. "The Lifeblood of a Poet." *San Francisco Examiner,* September 20, 1992.

Ohnuma, Keiko. "Breaking through the Wall of Silence." *Tenderloin Times,* June 1991.

Oktenberg, Adrian. "No More Madame Butterfly," *Women's Review of Books,* February 1988.

Tepperman, Jean. "She's a Me." *San Francisco Bay Guardian,* May 4, 1994.

—Sketch by Helen Zia

George Sukeji Morikami
(1886–1976)
Farmer, real estate developer, philanthropist

"**D**o for your life's work whatever you want to do. If you like to be a farmer, do not allow it to bother you that people say you get your hands and knees dirty. Be a farmer."

—George Morikami's self-written epitaph

It is the classic immigrant tale whose ending rejoins its beginning. In 1904, George Morikami came to this country as a penniless nineteen-year-old Japanese immigrant who hired on as an indentured worker in the Yamato Colony, the first settlement of Japanese farmers recruited by land developer Jo Sakai, to clear, plant, and farm a tract of land near the Boca Raton area of Florida at the turn of the century. He died in 1976 at age eighty-nine a millionaire landowner, but, true to his epitaph, a wizened old farmer who lived the simple life in a rickety trailer and took catnaps in the middle of his pineapple fields.

Born on November 5, 1886, in Miyazu, Japan, near the city of Kyoto, George Sukeji Morikami was the eldest of four children—three sons and a daughter—born to Takezo and Soyo Morikami. At the time of his birth, the Morikamis earned their living farming, although his father was of former *samurai* status, being descended from retainers of the Isshiki clan, which held Miyazu and much of the Tango Peninsula in the sixteenth century. At the age of fourteen, Morikami graduated from Yosa-gun Higher Elementary School in Miyazu in 1901, after eight years of schooling. He had a dream to raise fruit trees and ship the produce to markets on the East Asian mainland. However, lacking the financial resources to do so, he signed on with American-educated Japanese expatriate, Jo Sakai, also a native of Miyazu, to join the Yamato Colony in the United State, where he hoped to earn the capital to realize his dream. Sponsored by one of the colony's organizers, Mitsusaburo Oki, a silk merchant from Miyazu, Morikami was provided his passage and room and board (approximately $150). In exchange for three years of work in the pineapple fields, he was to receive a $500 bonus and a small grant of land. According to family history, Morikami made his decision to go to America after his proposal of marriage was refused by the parents of Hatsu Onizawa, whom he was courting.

Yamato Colony

Joining the Yamato Colony in 1906, Morikami and the other settlers, all of whom were male, tackled the mosquito-infested, swampy wilderness of southern Florida clearing the land acre by with grubbing hoes, rakes, and shovels. The seasonal rains that flooded fields and ruined crops, the insects that forced the settlers to wear head-nets before going out during summer months, and the relentless heat forced the less hardy colonists to leave. Shortly after his arrival in Florida, Morikami's sponsor, Oki, died in a typhoid epidemic that swept Yamato. Thus he was left without the possibility of receiving his bonus and return passage to Japan. At the end of three years in America, he had no money and spoke no English. Resolving to change his fate, Morikami tried working as a hired hand for a local family for room and board and $10 a month. Learning no English, but working long hours for little pay, the twenty-four-year-old Morikami decided he had to seek a formal education. Boarding with another Japanese friend, he attended the local elementary school in Brevard County. The one year he spent in elementary school was the full extent of Morikami's formal education. Morikami supported himself by renting a small garden plot, farming it, and selling his produce door-to-door throughout town.

Morikami returned to the Yamato settlement in 1911 and lived with the Sakai family in their big two-story house. A friend let him clear a half-acre of land and keep the proceeds from its harvest. The local storekeeper loaned him the tools, seed, fertilizer, and groceries to live on until he was able to sell his tomato crop. By the end of that season, Morikami had paid all his debts and realized a profit of $1,000 for his labors. With his capital, he bought land in Palm Beach County. Over the following years, he planted larger crops and hired on workers, reinvesting the profits in more land. Ever the astute businessman, he began a mail-order produce business in the 1920s, bypassing the commission men who amassed handsome profits by handling the shipping and marketing of produce for a percentage of earnings. But again, his fortune was short-lived. When the banks failed in 1929 beginning the Great Depression, Morikami lost every cent he had—a quarter of a million dollars.

George Sukeji Morikami

Investment in Land

From that time on, Morikami's earnings bought land. During the Second World War, when more than 120,000 Japanese immigrants and Japanese Americans were being interned and relocated in the interior of the country, Morikami, vouched for by his friends, remained on his farm producing agricultural yield for the war effort. After the war, he continued to add additional parcels of land to his holdings until they numbered 150 acres. As Florida experienced the postwar land boom and development soared throughout the state, Morikami's financial future was secured.

Despite that fact, he continued to live the same simple, frugal existence in his old trailer, working his fields, planting pineapples, and living alone. By 1967, he was growing 20,000 pineapple plants. He had a large lake dug near his trailer which was stocked with fish. He landscaped it with trees and built a boat dock. In the middle of the lake he built a floating feeder for migratory ducks. Fashioning a mound out of the dirt from the excavation of the lake, Morikami dubbed it jokingly, "Little Mount Fuji." He ate and slept according to his own internal time clock, eating when hungry and sleeping even in the middle of the day between rows of pineapple plants. Many days, he worked tirelessly into the night using his tractor headlights to illuminate the fields. He worked alone, even in his eighties devising ways to perform tasks which ordinarily could not be done without help.

In 1967, Morikami realized his long-standing dream to become a U.S. citizen. As a result of the Walter-McCarran Act of 1952 which made it possible for Orientals to become naturalized U.S. citizens, at age eighty-nine, he went to Miami, applied, and was sworn in at the federal courthouse.

Philanthropy

Grateful to the country that had been his home for seventy years, Morikami decided to offer the city of Delray Beach land for a park. However, after the proposal languished at city doorsteps for several years for want of funds, Morikami made a similar offer of land to the county with the same result. Undeterred, Morikami was quoted as saying in *Palm Beach Life*, "I've never done anything for this country. I'm only eighty-two. If I live to be one hundred, that gives me eighteen more years, and you can do a lot in eighteen years." That same year, Morikami was honored by the city council for his contributions and years of good citizenship with a plaque naming him honorary mayor of Delray Beach. It was not until 1973 that his offer of 35 acres of land was accepted by the county. Morikami Park was dedicated the following year. Two additional gifts of land in 1974 and 1975 brought the total parkland to 155 acres.

George Morikami died peacefully in his sleep at age eighty-nine on February 29, 1976. In 1977, the Morikami Park, Museum of Japanese Culture, and Japanese Gardens was opened to the public providing an appropriate memorial to Yamato Colony's last pioneer.

Sources:

Periodicals

Pozzetta, George E., and Harry A. Kersey, Jr. "Yamato Colony: A Japanese Presence in South Florida." *Tequesta: The Journal of the Historical Association of Southern Florida*, 1976.

Snyder, Virginia. "Sole Survivor." *Palm Beach Life*, May 1993.

Other

The Morikami Museum and Japanese Gardens Booklet, Del Ray, Florida: Mirkami Museum, 1991.

Unpublished Morikami Museum exhibit texts, August 1994.

—*Sketch by Nancy Moore*

Noriyuki "Pat" Morita
(1933–)
Actor

Pat Morita is a star of television and film who is probably best known for his role as the karate master in the film *The Karate Kid*, for which he received an Academy Award nomination. He also appeared in the film's two sequels, *The Karate Kid: Part II* and *The Karate Kid III*, and has been a regular in several television shows, including *Sanford and Son* and *Happy Days*.

An Early Illness

Noriyuki Morita was born on June 28, 1933, in Isleton, California. His father was a migrant farmer in the fruit orchards of California. Noriyuki was a very sickly child; he suffered from spinal tuberculosis—at that time a usually fatal disease—and spent nine years, from age two to eleven, in a hospital. (He did not learn to walk until he was eleven years old.) In a 1986 interview for the *New York Daily News*, Morita recalled, "there was this wonderful priest who used to visit me all the time. . . . At one point he wanted to baptize me, and he picked out my name. I was to be Patrick Aloysius Ignatius Xavier Morita. . . . But he'd always call me Pat when he stopped by, and the name kind of stuck."

Right around the time Morita was released from the hospital, the war between the United States and Japan broke out and Americans of Japanese descent, both citizens and resident aliens, in the Western states were being imprisoned in internment camps in clear violation of the Constitution. The Moritas were sent to a camp in Arizona. Morita recalled those times in *People Weekly* in 1986: "They were enormously difficult years for our people. Suicides, people walking into the desert never to be seen again. Or hanging themselves. It was horrible. Horrible."

When the family was released they moved to Fairfield, California, and his father opened a Chinese restaurant in a black neighborhood of the nearby city of Sacramento. Morita attended public schools and tried college briefly before giving it up to work with his father at the family restaurant. He was married around this time and had a daughter who is now thirty-one and whom he rarely sees.

When the family restaurant closed, Morita found a job at Aerojet-General Corporation near Sacramento. He told the *Cable Guide* in 1985, "That job was just laborious for me. I didn't have a degree so I felt like a second-class citizen. And all the time there was this huge machinery talking back at me or people telling me that I've got to make sure the computer goes on at 6:55 in the morning. . . . It drove me nuts." Morita had always wanted to go into show business, but had never made any attempts. He had always been told by friends that he was funny so he began his career as a stand-up comic in San Francisco.

The Hip Nip

Morita was working as the emcee of a Japanese nightclub in San Francisco when he got his first break in 1964. Singer Sam Cooke had been shot and the owner of the famed Copacabana in Los Angeles needed someone to fill the bill. Morita's agent Sally Marr (comedian Lenny Bruce's mother) got Morita the show. He billed himself as the "Hip Nip" and went on that night. He continued performing for many years under that name, which today may sound racist, but at the time set Morita in with a crowd of many minority comedians (like Dick Gregory and Mort Sahl) who drew attention to their ethnic heritage, using at times slanderous nicknames in an attempt to diffuse the power those names had over people.

In the late sixties and early seventies, Morita was a popular opening act for performers such as comedian Redd Foxx and singers Vic Damone and Connie Francis. He also played small parts on several television shows, including *Love American Style* and *Hawaii Five-O*. In 1973, Morita was offered the role of Arnold, the local hamburger shop owner, on the television show *Happy Days*. This was the first role that brought him national recognition. Two years later, he left the show to star in his own series, *Mr. T. and Tina*.

The show didn't survive one season. The next several years were very difficult for Morita, both personally and professionally. His uninsured home in Tarzana, California, was destroyed in a storm, his second wife's mother died, and then his youngest daughter, Tia, was diagnosed as having a kidney disease. In 1980, Morita left his wife and moved to Hawaii, where he stayed for two years. When he returned to Los Angeles in 1982 for a role that never materialized, he and his wife were reunited.

The Karate Kid

In 1984 Morita was hired to play the role of Miyagi, the master in the movie *The Karate Kid*. Simply getting the role was difficult. The producer of the film, Jerry Weintraub, told *People Weekly* in 1986, "I didn't want him. I've known Pat for twenty years and used to book him into the Catskill hotels when I was a kid. But his audition made me cry." The film was made for the modest sum of $10 million and nothing was really expected of it, even by Morita, who told *People Weekly*, "I thought the film would be a summer in-and-outer, like *Porky's* or *Police Academy*." *The Karate Kid* ended up taking in over $100 million, a 1000 percent profit. It also earned for Morita an Academy Award nomination. In 1986, *The Karate Kid: Part II* was released, and in 1989, *The Karate Kid III*.

Noriyuki "Pat" Morita

Morita lives with his second wife, Yuki, a community organizer, in Los Angeles. The couple has two children. Morita has achieved much of what he has through perseverance. He struggled for many years in Hollywood against heavy odds. About his decision at age twenty-nine to go into show business, he said in the *Cable Guide*, "There are some terrifying moments when we decide whether we want to flop or hope for the rest of our lives. But I have everything to be thankful for, even as scary as it's been along the way."

Sources:

Brady, James. "In Step with: Pat Morita." *Parade Magazine*, February 21, 1988, p. 22.

Burden, Martin. "Money-Making Martial Art." *New York Post*, June 26, 1989, p. 23.

Livingston, David. "Close-Up: Pat Morita." *The Cable Guide*, October, 1985 pp. 39–40.

O'Haire, Patricia. "You Mean He Can't Even Do One Little Chop?" *New York Daily News*, June 19, 1986.

Stark, John. "After a Lifetime of Misfortune, *Karate Kid's* Noriyuki 'Pat' Morita Battles His Way to a Happy Ending." *People Weekly*, June 30, 1986, pp. 101–102.

—*Sketch by Jim Henry*

William Mow

(1936–)

Entrepreneur, engineer

As an entrepreneur, William Mow has achieved phenomenal success in two dramatically different industries: electronics and clothing. In some ways, he came into the retail business quite by accident. He didn't grow up doodling designs for clothes or studying the fashions of the day. In fact, he was skilled at math, gravitated toward electrical engineering in college, and later received his Ph.D. in that discipline.

A twist of fate propelled Mow to preside over one of the leading U.S. clothing companies for middle America: Bugle Boy Industries. Mow is the founder, chairman, and chief executive of the private company he launched in 1977. Bugle Boy boasts annual sales of $500 million, providing the clothing collections coveted by families all over the country.

"We never stay on one trend too long," Mow told *Notable Asian Americans*. "We pick the trends from all over the world. And it's not just by shopping - it's by sitting at an outdoor cafe, seeing what's going on with young kids."

The First Notes

Mow was born in Hangchow, China, in 1936. Mow's father was chief of the military committee for Chiang Kai-shek's Nationalistic government at the United Nations in New York when Mao Tse-tung's revolution swept China. With the communists in power, Mow's father remained in the United States and the whole family, including Mow and his four brothers, emigrated to the United States when Mow was thirteen years old.

Mow grew up in Great Neck, New York, and worked his way through Rensselaer Polytechnic Institute in New York where he studied electrical engineering. In 1967, he earned his Ph.D. in electrical engineering from Purdue University. Mow credits much of his later success to the emphasis his family placed on education when he was a child. All but one of his brothers has a Ph.D.

After graduating, Mow took a job at Litton Industries and two years later in 1969 founded a computer-controlled instrumentation firm called Macrodata, which developed new techniques to test large scale integrated computer chips. In five years, Macrodata posted sales of twelve million dollars annually.

Turning Point

In the mid-1970s, Mow sold control of Macrodata to a Milwaukee-based conglomerate, Cutler-Hammer, but stayed on as chairman and chief executive officer. Within the first year under the new management, the conglomerate accused Mow of concealing $2 million in Macrodata losses. He was forced to resign. Lawsuits from other minority shareholders ensued against the conglomerate, and in 1988 Mow was finally exonerated when a California appeals court found Cutler-Hammer executives engineered the accounting fraud.

The loss of his job at Macrodata and the need to drum up cash for his legal fees against Cutler-Hammer pushed Mow into finding a new line of business, which turned out to be wholesale and retail clothing. Mow said this his motivation to develop a new business was to clear his name and right the wrong he'd experienced with the sale of Macrodata..

Mow met his partner Vincent Nesi in 1976 when Nesi was working at A. Smile, a boutique jeans resource. Mow started Buckaroo International Inc. a year later and signed Nesi on as a merchandise manager. In a 1991 interview for *Nation's Business*, Mow recounted the early days at Buckaroo: "I felt that anybody who could invent equipment with millions of wires and hundreds of thousands of components, measuring accuracies to a billionth of a second should be able to make a pair of pants. How wrong I was!" He was determined not to give up. "I got myself a 'school-of-hard-knocks' Ph.D. in understanding every step in composing a garment."

In September of 1980, Mow reorganized Buckaroo, and promoted Nesi president of the company to take charge of sales and merchandising. Nesi accepted the new responsibility, and the partners decided to focus on one product: jeans and casual pants. The company's name was officially changed to Bugle Boy Industries, a name chosen by Mow to reflect his interest in the Civil War era, after the young men who played bugles during battle.

Elements of Success

Bugle Boy Industries has widespread name recognition, thanks in large part to the marketing strategy to establish Bugle Boy as a brand name through television commercials, magazine advertisements, and billboards revolving around a single piece of dialogue: "Excuse me. Are those Bugle Boy jeans you are wearing?"

Based in Simi Valley, California, Bugle Boy sells its line to more than 7,000 department and specialty stores. Mow was able to find a niche in the competitive retail world by adhering to a seemingly simple strategy, to build brand loyalty by delivering a fresh product to the stores virtually every month. Bugle Boy's goal was to provide its target customer, who is aged fifteen to nineteen, with affordable,

William Mow

comfortable pants with Bugle Boy Design jeans without the designer's higher price. Since 1991, Bugle Boy has become the brand for the whole family, carrying basic as well as fashion clothing for all ages and size ranges.

Products are mostly manufactured outside the United States, in thirty-five foreign countries. In the 1980s many of the items were shipped to retail accounts within two days of arriving at Bugle Boy warehouses in the United States. In the 1990s, Bugle Boy had developed electronic data interchange (EDI), for quick response to cope with the high demands of the marketplace.

Bugle Boy clothing is also sold overseas. Its first foreign licensee was signed in Canada in 1988, followed by an agreement for Japan and Eastern Asia and other arrangements for distribution of Bugle Boy clothing in Australia, New Zealand, Mexico, Spain and the Caribbean Basin in 1990.

As of 1994, Mow and Nesi are the sole shareholders of Bugle Boy. Mow is based at Bugle Boy's Simi Valley, California, headquarters, which handles administration, operations, advertising, and the distribution of Bugle Boy products. The company's merchandising, product design, and sales divisions are located in New York.

As for his own family, Mow and his wife have two small children. He also has two grown children from his first marriage.

Sources:

Periodicals

Barrier, Michael. "From Riches to 'Rags'—And Riches." *Nation' Business,* January 1991, p. 32.

Other

Bugle Boy Industries. "Dr. William C.W. Mow." Biographical information, Simi Valley, California, March 1994.
Mow, William, written interview with Helen Zia, June 1994.

—Sketch by Felicia Paik

Dhan Gopal Mukerji
(1890–1936)
Writer

Dhan Gopal Mukerji was a prolific writer of children's literature. His works, including *Gay-Neck: The Story of a Pigeon,* which won the Newberry Medal from the American Library Association, children's literature's highest honor, incorporate animals in presenting Hindu folktales and philosophy. He was also a poet, playwright, novelist, and nonfiction writer, and served for a time as a Hindu priest in his native India.

Dhan Gopal Mukerji was born on July 6, 1890, near Calcutta, India into a very religious family who for generations had managed the Hindu temple in his native village. As a young teenager, Mukerji followed the traditional dictates of a young man from the Brahmin priest caste and entered study for the priesthood. Before he would actually become a priest though, Mukerji decided to travel a bit, and he began a two-year journey around India and Southeast Asia during which he lived as a beggar. The journey had a major impact on the young man, and when he returned to his village he decided the priesthood, which he actually did assume briefly, was not what he wanted. To go against the caste system's dictates in such a brazen way was very difficult in a tradition-bound culture such as turn-of-the-century India, but Mukerji was determined to have the life he desired irrespective of tradition.

Academia

The life he desired was an academic life. He began his higher education in 1908 at the University of Calcutta. From there he went to the University of Tokyo, where he earned his undergraduate degree in 1909. The following year, Mukerji immigrated to the United States where he enrolled in Stanford University, where he studied comparative literature and earned a Ph.D. in 1914. After his graduation, Mukerji remained briefly at Stanford where he was a lecturer in comparative literature.

It was also at this time that Mukerji began his writing career. In 1916 he collaborated on a play with Mary Carolyn Davies. *Chintamini: A Symbolic Play*, which was adapted from another play by Girish C. Ghose, was published in 1914, the year Mukerji finished his studies. Within the following three years he published another play, *Layla-Majnu*, and two volumes of poetry, *Rajani: Songs of the Night* and *Sandhyu: Songs of Twilight*. In 1918 Mukerji married Ethel Ray Dugan, a teacher, the couple would have one child, a son named Dhan Gopal II.

Mukerji's first children's book was published in 1922. Entitled *Kari, the Elephant*, the book established what would become Mukerji trademarks: jungle settings, animal characters, and a spiritual journey. That same year he also published another play, *The Judgment of India*. In 1923 Mukerji published his first work of nonfiction, an autobiography called *Caste and Outcast*. The book detailed the rigidness of India's caste system and the troubles he had as an Asian in early twentieth century America. Also in 1923 Mukerji published his second children's book, *Jungle Beasts and Men*, a collection of stories filled with exciting descriptions of the life in the jungle he had known as a boy, although through the eyes of its wild inhabitants. The book received glowing reviews, and the next year (1924) Mukerji published two more books, as he had in each of the two preceding years: a children's book and a work of nonfiction. The children's book was called *Hari, the Jungle Lad*, and the work of nonfiction was called *My Brother's Face*.

In the 1920s Mukerji established himself as an extremely prolific and gifted writer. In 1926, he published his first novel, *The Secret Listeners of the East*, and in 1928 he published what would become his most highly praised work, the children's book *Gay-Neck, The Story of a Pigeon*. The book tells the story of a young warrior named Ghond and his pigeon, Gay-Neck, and their adventures making their way through the jungle during a fictitious war called the Great War. *Gay Neck, The Story of a Pigeon*, received excellent reviews and, aside from the Newberry Award, was named by the American Institute of Graphic Arts as one of the fifty best books of the year.

In 1928 Mukerji published a sequel to *Gay-Neck* called *Ghond, the Hunter*. Like its predecessor, *Ghond* was very well received and was also named one of the fifty best books of the year by the American Institute of Graphic Arts. Mukerji himself considered *Ghond* to be his finest work. In an introduction to his book *Bunny, Hound, and Clown*, he wrote: "The work I consider the most valuable juvenile book that I have written is *Ghond, the Hunter*. In it, I have sought to render the inmost things of Hindu life into English."

While attaining success and notoriety in children's literature, Mukerji continued to publish works of nonfiction, mainly dealing with the religious traditions of Hinduism, still considered an exotic religion in the West. In 1929 he edited an English translation of Hindu religious works called *Devotional Passages from the Hindu Bible*. In 1931 he was both editor and translator for a publication of *The Song of God: Translation of the Bhagavadgita*, Hindu's holy book. In 1933 he published *Daily Meditation: or, The Practice of Repose*, and in 1934 *The Path of Prayer*. Two years after his death, *Hindu Scriptures: Hymns from the Rigveda, Five Upanishads, the Bhagavadgita*, for which he had served as editor, was published.

He also continued to publish children's books. Later titles include *Hindu Fables for Little Children* (1929); *The Chief of the Herd* (1929); *Rama, the Hero of India: Valmiki's "Ramayana" Done into a Short English Version* (1930); *Bunny, Hound, and Clown* (1931); *The Master Monkey* (1932); and *Fierce-Face: The Story of a Tiger* (1936). Many of these books were well reviewed, and Mukerji's reputation continued to grow. In 1936, however, eight days after his forty-sixth birthday, Dhan Gopal Mukerji committed suicide by hanging himself in his home in New York City.

Sources:

"Dhan Gopal Mukerji." *Contemporary Authors*, volume 136, Detroit: Gale Research, 1992.
Mukerji, Dhan Gopal. *Bunny, Hound, and Clown*. New York: Dutton, 1931.

—Sketch by Jim Henry

Bharati Mukherjee
(1940–)
Novelist/Writer

Bart Anand and Bernard Sudhir, the names of Bharati Mukherjee's two sons, embody the essence of her writings and her experiences. An Indian immigrant married to a Canadian, Mukherjee has captured the chaos of the melting pot in her short stories and novels about the South Asian, particularly the Indian, immigrant experience in America. A professor of English at the University of California at Berkeley, she is the author of more than a dozen novels and several short stories, many of which are drawn from her own experiences as an immigrant. She depicts the clash of cultures and the ensuing dilemmas and successes with unique understanding and startling sensitivity.

Her writings have held a mirror up to the South Asian community in North America.

A cross-cultural writer, Mukherjee has won several grants and awards from the Canadian government, universities, and the Guggenheim Foundation. She received the National Magazine Award in 1981 for her essay "An Invisible Woman." Prior to that she won the first prize from the Periodical Distribution Association for her story, "Isolated Incidents." However, it was in 1988 when she won the National Book Critics Circle Award for best fiction that Mukherjee's work received national attention. The award was for her collection of short stories, *The Middleman and Other Stories,* which many say is her best work to date. Before Berkeley, Mukherjee had taught at Marquette University, University of Wisconsin-Madison, McGill University, Skidmore College, Montclair State College, and Emory University.

The Roots of Mukherjee's Success

Born in Calcutta on July 27, 1940, to upperclass Bengali Brahmin parents, Sudhir Lal and Bina Banerjee, Bharati was the second of three daughters. She grew up in an atmosphere of privilege and wealth in an extended family that included aunts, uncles, and cousins. Even in a crowded household Mukherjee found the time and space to become a voracious reader. According to her, she knew as early as the age of three that she wanted to be a writer. As a child her favorite pastime was to hear Indian folk tales told by her grandmother. By the time she was eight she had already read several works by Leo Tolstoy, Dostoevsky, and Maxim Gorky, along with Bengali classics. In 1948 Mukherjee moved to England with her immediate family and it was there that she first enjoyed privacy and independence. "I discovered myself in new ways," she told Natasha Rafi in an interview. Living apart from various relatives allowed her to concentrate on what was important to her. At the age of nine, she wrote her first "novel" about a child detective. The family returned to Calcutta after three and a half years and Mukherjee received the best English schooling available at Loretto House, a missionary school. She earned her bachelor's degree from the University of Calcutta in 1959 and a master's degree from the University of Baroda in 1961.

The Journey Begins

That same year Mukherjee moved to the United States to study creative writing at the University of Iowa. She considers this event to have been the turning point in her career. "If I had lived in India, I still would have been a writer, but a very different sort," she said. It was in Iowa that the twenty-three-year-old Mukherjee met and married a Canadian student, Clark Blaise, in 1963. After receiving her Ph.D. in 1968 Mukherjee moved to Canada with her husband, where she became a naturalized citizen in 1972.

Bharati Mukherjee

Her first book, *The Tiger's Daughter,* was published in 1972 by Houghton Mifflin. It is about an Indian woman who returns to India after many years in the West and looks at her native country through changed eyes. The poverty, hunger, and dirt in the country now cloud the memory of the upperclass genteel life-style of her childhood and youth. Yet the longing for the security of home and the comfort of her own culture creates a conflict known only to those born in the third world, burdened with the choice of living in the West. "While changing citizenship is easy, swapping culture is not," said Mukherjee. "I want to write about others, who for economic, social, political, or psychological reasons have had to uproot themselves from a life that was predictable to one where you make up your own rules."

Having the Strength to Succeed

A painful part of immigration is encountering racism in the adopted country. In her short story collection, *Darkness,* published in the 1985, Bharati explores Canadian prejudice against South Asians. The racial intolerance she experienced in Canada compelled her to move back to the United States where she is now settled and claims to have found greater acceptance as a South Asian. In an interview with Sybil Steinberg of *Publishers Weekly,* she described her feelings about America: "Mine is a clear-eyed but definite love of America. I'm aware of the brutalities, the violences here, but in the long run my characters are survivors . . . I feel there are people born to be Americans. By American I mean an intensity of spirit and a quality desire. I feel American in a very fundamental way, whether Americans see me that way or not."

Mukherjee's 1993 novel, *The Holder of the World*, attempts to interchange time, space, and cultures through the story of a researcher from Massachusetts who traces the life of her seventeenth century ancestor, Hannah Easton, a woman who had traveled to India with her English husband. Mukherjee skillfully uses her knowledge of Indian history and Western culture to weave an exotic tale of contrasts and comparison.

On a personal front, a dual-career marriage has forced Mukherjee and her husband into a commuting relationship. Although it is not an ideal situation, Mukherjee said it has made her more independent emotionally and physically and has left her with more time for concentrated writing.

According to Mukherjee, her mother was determined that her daughters' lives would not be confined to the home and family as her had been, and that she was the driving force behind the professional success of her daughters. Mukherjee described her as "a most modest heroic woman" who achieved her goals in "quiet and determined ways." All three children realized their mother's dreams—the eldest is a psychologist in Detroit and the youngest heads the English department at the University of Baroda in India.

Throughout her professional and personal life Mukherjee felt her Indian heritage has shaped the way she views the world. Strong family ties and the love of education that was a vital part of her upbringing have stayed with her through the years. Her advice to others is: "Treat every moment with reverence."

Sources:

Periodicals

Brandmark, Wendy. Review of *The Holder of the World. New Statesman & Society,* November 19, 1993.

Ermelino, Louisa. Review of *The Holder of the World. People Weekly,* October 25, 1993.

Hajari, Nisid. Review of *The Holder of the World, Entertainment Weekly,* October 22, 1993.

Steinberg, Sybil. *Review of Darkness, Publishers Weekly,* April 12, 1992, p. 45.

Walter, Colin, Review of *The Holder of the World. Insight on the News,* November 1, 1993.

Other

Motihar, Kamla. "Bharati Mukherjee," unpublished profile, April 1994.

Mukherjee, Bharati, telephone interview with Natasha Rafi, July 1992.

—Sketch by Natasha Rafi

N

Kent Nagano
(1948–)
Orchestra conductor

Since the 1980s, Kent Nagano has been a rising star in the classical music world. Nagano is the music director of the Berkeley Symphony Orchestra, but he has taken his talents abroad as well. He is director of the Opera de Lyon and the Halle Orchestra in Manchester, England, and is the associate principal guest conductor of the London Symphony Orchestra. He has also moved into the international music recording scene, signing in 1993 a contract with Erato Records to deliver fifteen compact discs over a five-year period.

Kent Nagano was born a third-generation Japanese American in 1948. Raised on a farm in Morro Bay, California, Nagano came from a Japanese-speaking household where, he has said, the Japanese influence was strong and undiluted. Still, Nagano had time for cheeseburgers, surfing, and Beethoven symphonies. His mother, an amateur cellist, introduced the family to music. "We did a lot of family entertainment sort of things," said Nagano in a 1986 *Image Magazine* article. "We'd act out plays together or stand around the piano with my mother playing and we'd all sing."

Nagano has said that he did not experience racism while growing up, although he admitted sensing that he was in some ways made to feel different. He understood why after a 1985 trip to Japan with Seiji Ozawa and the Boston Symphony where for the first time in his life he felt what it was like to blend into a crowd.

Nagano studied at Oxford University in England and graduated from the University of California at Santa Cruz with a sociology/pre-law degree. But he said he was drawn to music, which he saw as a more highly developed means of communication.

A multi-talented musician who plays the piano, viola, clarinet, and koto, Nagano ended up studying for his master's degree in music at San Francisco State University, while serving as assistant to conductor Laszlo Varga and

Kent Nagano

also working for the San Francisco Opera. His interest soon turned mainly to conducting. "I'd always been dedicated to every aspect of music, including composition, and at one point I realized I was doing more conducting than anything else," he said during a June 1985 interview with *Ovation*. The conductor, as Nagano said, "has a very simple and direct function. He's supposed to keep an orchestra together, harness their ability into a unified statement."

Contemporary Music Advocate

In 1978, the young maestro took over the then-financially flagging Berkeley Symphony Orchestra. A passionate advocate for the work of living composers, Nagano told *Ovation* that he chose "the route of contemporary music to give the Berkeley Symphony life. With a semiprofessional group like this you have to have a responsibility to the community around you not to repeat or compete with what the other resident groups are playing."

A master of complex contemporary scores, Nagano is credited with transforming the Berkeley Symphony into a group much respected for its performance of twentieth-century music. With a penchant for moving beyond traditional musical boundaries, Nagano has displayed much inventiveness as Berkeley music director. He has programmed a concerto featuring rock guitarist Ronnie Montrose, the acoustical premiere of Wendy Carlos's "Moonscapes" (originally written for synthesizer), and a Vivaldi violin concerto performed by forty Suzuki students playing in unison. He also premiered "Noosphere," an original composition by Grateful Dead bass guitarist Phil Lesh, who studied composition with Luciano Berio.

Aside from leading the Berkeley Symphony, Nagano has conducted orchestras at home and abroad. He has chosen a path of broad experiences, including tackling such unusual projects as recording Frank Zappa's orchestral works with the London Symphony for Zappa's label, Barking Pumpkin Records.

One of Nagano's most ambitious undertakings came in 1983 at the invitation of Olivier Messiaen, who has deeply influenced Nagano's music. Messiaen, patriarch of the modern French composing world, invited Nagano to conduct the final of eight performances of the world premiere of Messiaen's six-hour opera *St. Francis of Assisi,* the first seven of which were to be conducted by Seiji Ozawa.

Career Highlights

Assisting Ozawa in preparing the *St. Francis of Assisi* score proved memorable for Nagano. As a child he had considered Ozawa a role model. His parents also admired him and "were very proud that a Japanese person was having a career in the United States with no apologies," Nagano told *Image Magazine.* "As a Japanese American, I had always looked up to Ozawa and paid a lot of attention to him," Nagano told *Ovation.*

In December 1984, again as Ozawa's backup—this time with the Boston Symphony—Nagano stepped in without a rehearsal and led the orchestra in what critic Richard Dyer of the *Boston Globe* called "intense and noble" performances of Mahler's *Ninth Symphony.*

In November 1989, Nagano led the Orchestre de Paris in the world premiere of Toru Takemitsu's "A String Around Autumn" as part of a huge celebration of the French Revolution's bicentennial.

A long-time champion of Takemitsu, Nagano conducted Takemitsu's fifteen-minute work, which contained Japanese, as well as French, textures. Nagano's exposure to Japanese music from childhood, combined with his feeling for contemporary scores, may have made him a natural for the work's premiere.

"We live in an international world now and, if only through the media, we all have been exposed to those various sounds," Nagano told the *San Francisco Examiner* in a 1990 interview. "Music has always been an international language, and there are no Berlin walls in culture any more."

In 1985, Nagano won a Seaver Conducting Award, a $75,000 prize intended to foster the development of "American conductors on the threshold of major international careers." Nagano currently lives in San Francisco with his wife, renowned pianist Yvonne Loriod.

Sources:

Marum, Lisa. "Kent Nagano, Conductor." *Ovation,* June 1985.

Pfaff, Timothy. "Trans-bay Conductor." *San Francisco Examiner,* January 3, 1990.

Reynolds, Richard. "Remarkable Conduct. *Image Magazine, (San Francisco Examiner),* December 21, 1986.

—Sketch by Steven A. Chin

Mira Nair
(1957–)
Filmmaker

For filmmaker Mira Nair, home is wherever she aims her camera. The 37-year-old award-winning director specializes in crossing borders, both physical and cultural. From *Salaam Bombay!,* her first feature film about children living on India's mean streets, to *Mississippi Masala,* her 1992 film about Indian immigrants struggling to survive in a southern rural town, Nair has cast an unflinching eye on society's outcasts. "I've always been drawn to stories of people who live on the margins of society; people who are on the edge, or outside, learning the language of being in between; dealing with the question, 'What, and where, is home?'" Nair said in a 1992 interview with *Time* magazine.

Unlike the characters who populate her films, Nair has a strong sense of her own roots. Born in 1957, she grew up in relative affluence in Bhubaneswar, a small town in the delta region of eastern India. There Nair played among ancient stone temples and rice fields.

"I remember the emptiness. Playing hide-and-seek in the temples," Nair said in a 1992 *Vogue* magazine interview. "How there was time to dream because nothing ever happened." Nair has vivid memories of seeing the film, *Dr. Zhivago*, on a hot summer day. "When the power broke down, the cinema manager just got on-stage and said, 'All the fans have stopped, ladies and gentlemen. Now think of Russian snow to become cool,'" she said in *Vogue.*

Nair's first passion, however, was not film, but theater. One of her earliest influences was the avant-garde British theater director Peter Brook. After graduating from an Irish Catholic missionary school in Simia, she attended Delhi University for one year where she was an actress with an amateur theater group that performed Shakespeare. In 1976, when Harvard University offered her a full scholarship, Nair grabbed the opportunity to travel to the U.S. It was at Harvard, where she began to lose interest in theater and discovered her love for film, specifically documentaries. "Documentaries really grabbed me," she said in *Time*. "They were a way of entering people's lives—if they should choose to let you enter—and embracing them."

Nair's first documentary, *Jama Masjid Street Journal,* was made as a student thesis at Harvard in 1979. It explored the lives of a traditional Muslim community in Old Delhi and was told from the perspective of an Indian woman— Nair herself—carrying a camera instead of the burkha or veil worn by most women.

Subsequent films tackled equally complex and socially difficult subjects. Nair's 1982 film, *So Far from India,* told the story of an Indian subway newsstand worker in Manhattan who returns to his wife in India only to find that they have grown apart. In *India Cabaret,* made in 1985, Nair created a stark portrait of the harsh lives of women striptease dancers working in a sleazy Bombay nightclub. The film won best documentary prizes at the American Film Festival and the Global Village Film Festival.

Her 1987 film, *Children of a Desired Sex* , caused an uproar by confronting head-on the culture's preference for boys and the pressure faced by pregnant Indian women to abort female babies.

After completing four documentaries, Nair wanted more control over the filmmaking process and decided to branch out to feature films. Her first attempt was *Salaam Bombay!,* a film written with Sooni Taraporevala, a friend from Harvard, about homeless children living on the streets of Bombay. Made on a $900,000 budget, the film was a commercial and critical success., winning the Camera D'Or and the Prix du Publique at the 1988 Cannes film festival—the festival's top awards. *Salaam Bombay!* was also nominated for an Academy Award that year.

Taraporevala and Nair teamed up again several years later to work on Nair's first English-language film, *Mississippi Masala.* The word *masala* refers to the colorful mix of

Mira Nair

spices used in Indian cooking. The 1992 film was a humorous yet thought-provoking look at the lives of Indians who were forced to leave their native land of Uganda when dictator Idi Amin expelled Asians from the country in 1972. Many moved to the U.S., settling in Mississippi and buying motels. Nair got the idea for the movie from a *New Yorker* magazine article about the subject. "I was so fascinated that I got in a car and started driving through Mississippi, staying in those motels," Nair said in *Vogue.* "Sooni and I worked on a script, going back again and again to Mississippi."

Despite the film's humorous overtones, Mississippi Masala boldly takes on the thorny topic of racism between people of color. The story centers on a young Indian woman named Mina who, much to the consternation of her family, falls in love with Demetrius, an African-American man. Demetrius' role is played by Denzel Washington.

"People think of racism as black versus white, but there's a different kind of consciousness of color within minority groups as we equate beauty with fairness and ugliness with darkness," Nair said in a 1992 interview with *Mother Jones.* "There's a slowness in encountering racism within minority groups and racism against groups that come from abroad."

Nair faced an uphill battle financing this film because of its mostly non-white cast. Even her casting of a big star like Washington and her successful track record would not sway financial backers. After reading her script, one Hollywood producer asked, "Can't you make room for a white protagonist?" Nair told him jokingly, "Don't worry. All the waiters will be white." Eventually she cobbled together the $7 million she needed from Cinecom, her previous distributor, and a British television company.

Nair filmed on location in Uganda during the making of *Mississippi Masala*. At the time, she was getting a divorce from her husband, an American photographer whom she had met as a student at Harvard. In Uganda, Nair met and fell in love with Mahmood Mamdani, a political scientist who was born in India but grew up in Uganda and earned his Ph.D. from Harvard. Mamdani moved to Tanzania after Amin's expulsion order, and returned to Uganda in 1979 when the restrictions against Asians were lifted. The couple eventually married and bought the Kampala home Nair used in *Mississippi Masala*. In 1992, Nair gave birth to a son, Zohran.

Nair said the toughest challenge she faces as a filmmaker of color is revealing truths most communities prefer to hide. "You're expected to put the best foot forward, present the noble face," she said in *Mother Jones*. "But I'm not one for being the ambassador of a community. The challenge is in how to present the idea—if it's done well, it's not just 'airing dirty laundry.'"

Nair is truly a person of the world, having lived in India, England, the United States, and now Kampala, Africa. Yet her roots—and her strong identity—remain firmly planted in India. That sense of home inspires her and fuels her creativity. "Knowing where you come from gives one an incredible amount of self-confidence," she said in *Time*.

Sources:

Periodicals

Mehta, Gita. "Vogue Arts." *Vogue*, February 1992, p. 114–18.

Orenstein, Paggy. "Salaam America!" *Mother Jones*, January/February 1992, p. 60–61.

Outlaw, Marpessa. "The Mira Stage." *Village Voice*, February 18, 1992, p. 64.

Simpson, Janice C. "Focusing on the Margins." *Time*, March 2, 1992, p. 67.

Other

"Mira Nair." Professional resume, 1994.

—Sketch by Valerie Chow Bush

Don T. Nakanishi
(1949–)
Academic, author

Don Toshiaki Nakanishi, director of the University of California at Los Angeles' Asian American Studies Center, is one of the country's foremost authorities on American race relations and the politics of diversity. He is a prolific writer and has published widely in academic journals on issues of education and ethnic diversity. He is also the cofounder and editor of *Amerasia Journal,* a highly regarded academic journal dealing with Asian American studies. In addition, Nakanishi is a frequent guest speaker and panelist at symposia all over the country.

Don Nakanishi was born on August 14, 1949, in East Los Angeles, California, into a working class family of Japanese Americans. His father worked as a produce clerk and his mother was a seamstress. Both of them had been born in America but were educated in Japan, returning to the United States after their education was completed. His family spent much of the Second World War in U.S. concentration camps, as did thousands of West Coast Japanese Americans. His grandparents were killed by the atomic bombs dropped by the United States on Japan in the only use of nuclear weapons on a civilian population in human history.

Nakanishi was an excellent student and planned on becoming a doctor. He graduated from Theodore Roosevelt High School in 1967 and enrolled in Yale University in New Haven, Connecticut, on an academic scholarship. Like many universities in the late 1960s, Yale was struggling to redefine its admission policies with regard to minority students. In an interview, Nakanishi recalled seeing the headline of the school paper his first day in New Haven declaring that year's freshman class to be the most diverse in Yale's history. What that meant in terms of numbers at Yale in 1967 was that of one thousand incoming freshman—all of whom were male—there were seven African Americans, seven Hispanic Americans, and seven Asian Americans.

Turning Point

In his freshman year at Yale, Nakanishi told Jim Henry in an interview, he had an experience that changed his perceptions of himself as an Asian in America and, in the process, changed his career goals as well. Nakanishi had had a lifelong dread of the date December 7, the anniversary of the Japanese bombing of the American naval base at Pearl Harbor, Hawaii. Invariably the significance of the date would be brought up in a history or civics class and Nakanishi would feel shame. He thought it would be different at Yale, but the evening of his first December 7 there, a group of students burst into his dorm room and attacked him with water balloons chanting, "Bomb Pearl Harbor, Bomb Pearl Harbor." Then the leader of the group stepped forward and recited from memory President Roosevelt's speech declaring war on Japan.

This incident brought about a change in Nakanishi, bringing him eventually to intellectually question the role of a Japanese in American society. This led him to pursue research into the history of the American internment of Japanese Americans during World War II. His parents had rarely spoken of their experiences in the camps and nothing had been taught about this shameful chapter in American history in the public school system. This research led him to an interest in the role of minorities in society, and in his sophomore year he decided to major in political science, rather than biology. Nakanishi also became involved in organizations seeking to recruit more minorities and in the establishment of an Asian American studies program at Yale. In 1970 he also co–founded *Amerasia Journal*, which has become the leading journal in the field of Asian American studies.

In his senior year he was awarded the Frank M. Patterson Prize in political science for the outstanding senior essay on American government. He graduated *cum laude* in 1971, and was granted the Saybrook College Fellows Prize as the outstanding graduating senior at Yale.

After Yale, Nakanishi won a fellowship for graduate study at Harvard. In 1973 he won a second fellowship that allowed him to continue his education beyond the graduate level and in 1978 he graduated from Harvard's Center for International Affairs with a Ph.D. in political science. That year he was also awarded a research fellowship as a visiting scholar to the Japan Society for the Promotion of Science, in Tokyo, Japan. While working on his doctorate, Nakanishi was involved in several projects involving ethnic studies and the formulation of desegregation policies in several locations. He served on the Asian American Task Force for Social Studies Guideline Evaluations for the California Department of Education in 1973, he was a researcher and co–chair of the Los Angeles Hispanic Urban Center's project on school desegregation and multicultural education in 1974, and he contributed to a Harvard conference on "Social Scientists and the Making of Public Policy" in 1974.

Tenure Challenge

In 1978, Nakanishi was hired by the University of California at Los Angeles (UCLA) as an associate professor in the Asian American studies program. He continued publishing widely in the field of race relations and diversity and in 1982 he was made director of the program. In 1986 Nakanishi was denied tenure by the UCLA tenure review board in what he considered a race-biased decision. Nakanishi felt that the board's decision was wrong and

Don T. Nakanishi

that he was obligated to challenge it. He felt he had the academic credentials as well as more than enough teaching credentials to have been granted tenure, a contractual relationship between a university and a professor granting him or her a guaranteed job for the duration of a productive career. The granting of tenure is done in secret by an academic board and can seem arbitrary at times. Few professors choose to challenge a denial of tenure for a variety of reasons, but Nakanishi decided that he had a good case against the administration and that their decision had been unfairly arrived at.

The fight lasted three years and is described in detail in an article Nakanishi published in *Amerasia Journal* in 1990 entitled "Why I Fought." The fight made Nakanishi something of an academic celebrity and inspired many others to challenge what they perceived as race-biased decisions in academic areas and other areas as well. The case became a focal point on the campus of UCLA and in the Los Angeles community in general for the expression of rage in the minority community. The mayor of Los Angeles and half of the California State Assembly had declared their support for his tenure. He was eventually granted tenure in a rare reversal of the university's decision, three years after bringing suit.

As of mid-1994 Nakanishi was finishing a book on the political history of Asians in America. He told Henry that the basis to success in a career is pursuing something that you find personally meaningful and important rather than what might be most economically secure. He said that the decision of what career to pursue must be personal and must be arrived at because of a conviction that it is what you really want to do. "After all," he said, "it's what you'll be doing for life."

Sources:

Periodicals

Nakanishi, Don T. "Why I Fought." *Amerasia Journal,* vol. 16, no. 1, 1990. pp. 139–58.

Other

Nakanishi, Don T., telephone interview with Jim Henry, June 13, 1994.
University of California at Los Angeles, Asian American Studies Center. "Resume of Don Nakanishi." Los Angeles, California.

—Sketch by Jim Henry

Philip Tajitsu Nash
(1956–)
Activist, lawyer, teacher, writer

As a civil rights activist, lawyer, teacher, and writer, a single theme runs through the many facets of Philip Tajitsu Nash's life: self-empowerment. "I spend my life trying to help people find their own power," stated Nash in an interview with Terry Hong.

Having worked with Asian American groups throughout his career, Nash's involvement and leadership in the Asian American community is prolific. Currently the executive director of the National Asian Pacific American Legal Consortium in Washington, D.C., Nash has been involved with the Asian American Legal Defense and Education Fund (AALDEF) and has served on the board of the Japanese American Citizens League (JACL) in New York as a legal advocate for Japanese American redress. He helped found the Coalition of Asian Pacific American Associations, which has been responsible since 1979 for the annual Asian Pacific American Heritage Week Festival in New York City, and co-founded the Inter-Change Consultants, the AmerAsian League, the National Asian Pacific American Law Students Association (NAPALSA), and the National Asian Pacific American Bar Association. As a national activist, Nash focuses his energies toward education, family law, labor and organizing, anti-Asian violence, and identity issues.

In addition to activism, Nash also has taught Asian American studies at Yale University, law at Georgetown University and City University of New York law schools, urban legal studies at City College of New York, and metropolitan studies at New York University. He has published numerous articles in both periodicals and books, as well prose and poetry in such publications as *Bridge, Gidra,* and Columbia University's *The Asian Journal.*

"Issues bigger than myself . . ."

Born December 3, 1956, in New York City, Philip Tajitsu Nash was the first child born to a Japanese American mother and a European American father. "I'm fourteenth generation on my father's side, Irish English American. And third generation, *sansei,* on my mother's side," he explained to Hong. Nash spent his childhood in the Bronx and Maywood, New Jersey. His parents made certain that he grew up surrounded by members of every age, racial, and religious group. "My parents . . . took me to a local YMCA to swim in a mostly African American crowd. They encouraged my playing soccer in a mostly Latino crowd. Time was spent going to the cemetery each year to pay homage to the deceased in a ceremony the Japanese call *ohakka mairi* [grave-visiting ceremony]. And I was encouraged to read the sacred literature of and visit the houses of worship of Jews, Moslems, Protestants, Catholics, Buddhists, and others," Nash remembered.

Strongly influenced by his forward-thinking parents, Nash's community activism naturally began early: "my dad, H.B. Nash, took me on the March on Washington to see the Reverend D. Martin Luther King, Jr., in 1963. I can't remember every detail of that day, but I do remember that and other times where I was involved in social justice campaigns from an early age. From this work, I got a sense that there were issues bigger than myself, my family, and my immediate community," Nash recalled to Hong.

In 1978, Nash graduated from New York University with a degree in urban studies and economics. He received his J.D. from Rutgers University School of Law, where he won awards for his civil rights activism. Since finishing at Rutgers University Law School, Nash has devoted himself, both professionally and personally, to empowering the Asian American community.

During and after law school, Nash's growing activism was predominantly focused on the Japanese American redress movement. "I played several roles in the redress movement. As an organizer, I conducted community surveys of opinions, organized meetings, and served (for a short time) as Redress Chair of the New York Japanese American Citizens League. As a journalist, I wrote a weekly column and many long articles about redress for the *New York Nichibei* and other community papers around the country. Finally, as a lawyer, I researched, wrote, and presented materials to government agencies, including Congress, and groups such as the New York State Bar Association," he explained to Hong.

Philip Tajitsu Nash

Nash's interest and involvement with the redress movement began a lifelong career in civil rights. He joined the Asian American Legal Defense and Education Fund (AALDEF) in New York in 1984, and served as a staff attorney, eventually becoming a board member before leaving in 1992. At the same time he was with AALDEF, Nash co-founded Inter-Change Consultants, an organization that offers multi-cultural workshops on cross-cultural communication and conflict resolution. Today, Nash is executive director of the National Asian Pacific American Legal Consortium, a not-for-profit, nonpartisan organization which was formed by AALDEF, the Asian Law Caucus, and the Asian Pacific American Legal Center of Southern California. The Consortium's mission is to advance the legal and civil rights of the nation's Asian Pacific Americans through litigation, advocacy, public education, and public policy development.

Into and Out of the Classroom

In 1984, Nash began to take his personal history of activism into the classroom. His academic career has found him at New York University, Yale University, City College of New York, City University of New York Law School, and Georgetown University Law Center. As a strong advocate of Asian American studies, Nash speaks with great hope and enthusiasm about the future of an Asian American curriculum. He wrote in a 1988 article, "Creating Critical Consciousness: Paulo Freire and the Mechanics of Teaching Asian American Studies": "Some

students, predisposed because of family, employment, or other factors, become empowered the moment they enter the class. More gratifying for me have been those who were less vocal in the class, but who later found their own speed and went on to do other things." He cited examples of a student who became the editor of a Korean American student paper and another who spent the summer volunteering to help a Korean American researcher/educator.

Nash's teaching is not limited to the classroom. He travels throughout the country, giving workshops and making presentations on such topics as race relations, identity issues, immigration, anti-Asian violence, and legal issues specific to the Asian American community.

In recent years, Nash has become considerably involved with the plight of Native Americans. He explained, "While working on redress, I visited the sites of the Minidoka Relocation Center in Idaho and Gila River Relocation Center in Arizona, and was struck by the desolation of the areas my family had been sent to during the war," he told Hong. "Unfortunately, the Native Americans were still there on reservations, so I made up my mind to get involved in their struggles as well.

"The biggest issue for Native Americans in the years before the 1992 Columbus Quincentenary was trying to get a new perspective on the genocide and ecocide done by Columbus and his followers. I helped to found Columbus in Context, a grass-roots group in New York, and worked on *Rethinking Columbus,* a ninety-six-page booklet that has sold over 200,000 copies. . . . I also used my contacts formed during the redress movement to do speeches, articles, and radio shows to help publicize a more accurate view of Columbus and the colonialist world view that he represents."

A Writer with a Cause

From countless articles about the redress movement to anti-Asian violence, opinion pieces, description/analyses of community events, and theatre reviews, Nash is a much-published writer. In addition to periodicals, he has also been published by legal presses, including *New Jersey Law Journal* and *Yale Law Journal.* He has also written chapters for various ESL (English as a Second Language) textbooks for Asian Americans as well as Asian American legal history books.

For Nash, writing is also a creative outlet. "I just write about life," he told Hong. Nash has also written short stories, poetry, and two plays. His family's camp experiences have often proven to be a catalyst for his writing, leading to poetry and what he calls "fragments." Although his mother has been reticent about discussing her experiences, Nash has relied on his maternal grandmother for information and inspiration.

Nash explained, "Writing for me comes from being moved by things. When I'm moved, I end up doing one of two things—either activism, such as being a lawyer or organizer, or writing about it. It's hard to say which process kicks in first. I guess sometimes both."

"Writers need to be involved in issues," he stated with conviction. "I think the abstraction involved in fiction writing is always interesting, but there's a definite need to ground it in something that approximates reality. I'm not saying that everything has to be realistic, but at some point in an Asian American's life, he or she must identify with the struggles of his or her collective life, which enriches a writer's writing, while at the same time bringing our culture and individuals to a broader audience."

Whether helping a student toward self-knowledge through teaching an introductory Asian American studies class or aiding a nation toward self-healing through advocating the reclamation of civil rights usurped from Japanese Americans and Native Americans, Nash has empowered countless Asian Americans to strengthen their identities and struggle together for greater equality. "I never forgot an adage that I learned in Boy Scout camp years ago: always leave the campsite in better condition than you found it. By keeping hope and activism alive in a sea of cynicism, I not only enjoy each minute of camping but make sure my children's children can, too," he added.

Sources:

Books

Nash, Philip Tajitsu. "Creating Critical Consciousness: Paulo Freire and the Mechanics of Teaching Asian American Studies." In *Reflections on Shattered Windows: Promises and Prospects for Asian American Studies,* edited by Gary Okihiro, et. al. Pullman: Washington State University Press, 1988.

Other

Nash, Philip Tajitsu, telephone interviews with Terry Hong, April 13, 1992 and April 21, 1994.

—Sketch by Terry Hong

Irene Natividad

(1948–)

Political activist, feminist, educator

When the phone rings in Irene Natividad's Washington office, one thing is certain—the caller is a person with political power and influence. Natividad is simultaneously at the center of activity in many arenas—as chair of the National Commission on Working Women, which works

to improve the economic status of working women in the United States; as director of the Global Forum of Women, a biannual international gathering of women leaders that convenes to explore leadership issues for women worldwide; as executive director of the Philippine American Foundation, which implements programs to foster grassroots rural development to alleviate poverty in the Philippines; and as principal of Natividad and Associates, which provides consulting services for groups wishing to reach specific segments of the voting constituency. Natividad continues to rise to top executive positions in every activity she pursues.

Born in Manila, Philippines, on September 14, 1948, Irene Natividad is the eldest of four children. Her father's work as a chemical engineer took the family from the Philippines to Okinawa, Iran, Greece, and India. Irene's ability to quickly master new languages was the key to adjusting to the ever-changing schools and communities she encountered while growing up. Partly because of her family's frequent moves, Natividad speaks Spanish, French, Italian, Tagalog, Farsi, and Greek fluently, and is adept at working with people from other countries and cultures.

But if Natividad's international upbringing broadened her understanding of other cultures, it also made her aware of the limited options available to women. In a 1985 interview with the *Bergen* (New Jersey) *Record,* Natividad described how her mother's experience during the family's frequent moves helped to shape her own perspective on women's roles: "My father had his job, we kids had our schools, and she had nothing," Natividad said. "In all those countries, a woman was not allowed to work. . . . I think I have a very intelligent, outspoken, articulate mother, and she had no outlet."

Her parents had high expectations for their three daughters and one son. In Greece, Natividad completed her high school education as valedictorian of her class. A few years later, when her mother indicated that she would not attend Natividad's 1971 graduation from Long Island University unless her daughter was valedictorian, Irene made sure her mother was there by earning the number one spot in her class. In 1973, she received a master's in American literature and a M.Phil. in 1976, both from Columbia University in New York; she has only to complete her dissertation to earn her Ph.D. She has been awarded honorary doctorates from Long Island University (1989) and Marymount College (1994).

Natividad's first forays into the working world were during the 1970s, when she held faculty and administrative positions in higher education. She was an adjunct instructor in English at Lehman College of the City University of New York in 1974; an instructor in English at Columbia University from 1974 to 1976; and director of continuing education at both Long Island University and William Paterson College in New Jersey from 1978 until 1985. In

Irene Natividad

continuing education, she relished the opportunity to support and guide women seeking to return to the work-force or to upgrade their skills.

Political Activism

While working as a waitress, Natividad launched her career as an activist by organizing the other waiters and waitresses to demand higher pay. Although she was fired as a result, Natividad thereafter remained a committed activist employing organizational and political means to achieve a goal. In 1980, Natividad served as founder and president of Asian American Professional Women and as founding director of the National Network of Asian-Pacific American Women and the Child Care Action Campaign.

It wasn't long before Natividad turned her formidable leadership talents toward the political arena. Natividad's first taste of politics came in 1968 when she distributed campaign leaflets for Eugene J. McCarthy's presidential bid. Her appetite for organizing and constituency build-ing had been whetted, and she went on to serve as chair of the New York State Asian Pacific Caucus from 1982 to 1984, and as deputy vice-chair of the Asian Pacific Caucus of the Democratic National Committee. By 1984, when Geraldine Ferraro made history by becoming the first woman from a major party to run for vice-president of the United States, Natividad was tapped by the Democratic party organization to serve as Asian American liaison for

Ferraro's campaign. Ferraro joined Walter Mondale on the Democratic ticket, and although the Mondale/Fer-raro team lost the election to Republicans Ronald Reagan and George Bush, Natividad viewed the campaign as a sig-nificant turning point for women in politics. In 1985, Natividad told the *Honolulu Star-Bulletin,* "[Ferraro's] leg-acy is she broke the credibility gap for all women candi-dates, from presidential down to the local level. I don't consider '84 a loss. I consider it a win."

National Women's Political Caucus

By 1985 Natividad's career as a political activist was in full swing. She was elected to chair the National Women's Political Caucus, becoming the first Asian American woman to head a national women's organization. Com-menting about her election to head the caucus, Nativ-idad told *USA Today* in 1985, "A minority group [Asian Americans] perceived as invisible now has a very visible spokeswoman."

The National Women's Political Caucus, headquartered in Washington, D.C., was founded in 1971 by a small group of feminists (including former congresswomen Bella Abzug, Shirley Chisolm, and Patsy Mink) to focus on putting women in public office. The caucus is bipartisan—as a registered Democrat, Natividad succeeded a Republi-can as leader of the group. But as a very pragmatic politi-cal insider, Natividad acknowledged the need to look to both political parties for support. Natividad described the caucus in the *Bergen* (New Jersey) *Record* as including "friends on both sides of the aisle [in the U.S. Congress]. I'd like to think [the National Women's Political Caucus] is party blind."

Throughout her career Natividad has focused on using organizations to achieve her goals. Her election to head the 77,000-member Caucus was a logical step on her mis-sion to help women gain power and influence through the political system. In a 1985 interview with the *New York Times,* Natividad laid out her goals for the caucus: "One of our missions [at the National Women's Political Caucus] is to transfer the political experience we have developed on a national level to the state and local level. We want to train women to run for local offices because if we don't feed that pipeline we won't have state winners. We have to insure that we have more wins at the local level, for that is where it all starts." During her tenure, the caucus trained candidates and their staffs throughout the United States on the basics of campaigning. The workshops covered top-ics key to running a successful campaign, such as polling techniques, fund-raising, grassroots organization, and strategies for dealing with the news media.

Under Natividad's leadership, the caucus gathered hard data to analyze factors influencing women's con-gressional races and compiled an annual Survey of Gover-nors' Appointments of Women to state cabinets. The caucus also established the first-ever Minority Women

Candidates' Training Program and created the Good Guy Award honoring men who further the cause of women's rights. As a result of their activities, the caucus gained real clout. Through the work of the caucus' Coalition for Women's Appointments in 1988, Natividad was invited to meet with President George Bush to promote women candidates for administration posts. An estimated one-third of all women appointed to high-level positions in the Bush administration had been recommended by the coalition led by Natividad.

In 1989, Natividad stepped down as chair of the National Women's Political Caucus to pursue other interests and to make way for fresh leadership. Her interest in and commitment to women's issues has not waned, but has rather taken on an international dimension.

International Focus of the 1990s

Natividad's interests are truly global in scope. She has frequently written and spoken on topics ranging from the struggle for democracy in Czechoslovakia and her native Philippines, to proposals for changes in the workplace culture that will benefit both women and men. Reflecting her commitment to work at the grassroots level, Natividad is editor of a reference book for public and school libraries, the *Asian American Almanac*, to be published in 1995.

In 1992, Natividad served as a director of the Global Forum of Women, a gathering in Dublin, Ireland, of 400 women leaders from fifty-eight countries to develop strategies for addressing issues facing women worldwide. This international summit was followed in 1994 by a Forum in Taiwan (attended by representatives from eighty countries), for which Natividad developed a program that focused on political empowerment. The basic premise of the Taiwan gathering was that no real change can take place regarding women's lives unless women themselves are the policymakers. Natavidad's program featured practical "nuts-and-bolts" techniques of running for public office and skills-building workshops for policymakers. Natividad develops and leads political training workshops at locations around the world, from Barcelona to Bangkok. Natividad will contribute to planning for a conference that will run in conjunction with the 1995 U.N. Fourth World Conference on Women.

Awards

Natividad's accomplishments have been frequently recognized. In 1994, *A. Magazine: The Asian American Quarterly,* named her to their list of "Power Brokers: The Twenty-five Most Influential People in Asian America." In 1993, she was named as one of the "Seventy-four Women Who Are Changing American Politics" by *Campaigns and Elections* magazine. The National Conference for College Women Student Leaders awarded Natividad its Woman of Distinction Award in 1989, the same year in which she received an honorary doctorate in humane letters from

Long Island University. In 1988, *Ladies' Home Journal* included her in their list of "100 Most Powerful Women in America." In 1987, she received the Innovator for Women$hare Award from the Women's Funding Coalition. Americans by Choice presented the 1986 Honored American Award to Natividad, and the Women's Congressional Caucus presented her the Women Making History Award in 1985.

Natividad is married to Andrea Cortese, director of Digital Communications Services for the Communications Satellite Corporation. They have one son, Carlo Natividad-Cortese, whose birth in 1984 coincided with Natividad's becoming leader of the National Women's Political Caucus. She remarked to *Ladies' Home Journal* on the demanding life of a political activist, "It is satisfying knowing that for a brief point in time you made a difference."

Sources:

Periodicals

"America's 100 Most Important Women." *Ladies' Home Journal,* November 1988.
Benedetto, Richard. "Women's Caucus Loses Cornerstone." *USA Today,* August 2, 1989, p. 2A.
Berger, Leslie. "Feminist Showing that Professionals Can Be Moms, Too." *Bergen* (New Jersey) *Record,* July 15, 1985.
Gamarekian, Barbara. "National Women's Political Caucus: Carrying Word of a Women's Agenda." *New York Times.*
Manuel, Susan. "Leading the Fight to Give Women Political Might." *Honolulu Star-Bulletin,* July 9, 1985.
Phillips, Leslie and Sam Meddis. "Asian-American Leads National Group." *USA Today,* July 1, 1985.

Other

Philippine American Foundation. "Irene Natividad Profile." Washington, D.C., June 1993.

—Sketch by Susan Gall

Josie Natori
(1947–)
Entrepreneur, fashion designer

When Josie Natori left her lucrative career as a Wall Street investment banker in the late 1970s, the last thing on her mind was becoming a fashion industry leader. "My intent was to start a business with products from the

Philippines," Natori said in a telephone phone interview with Valerie Chow Bush. "I never thought in a million years of starting a designer business or being called a designer." But her serendipitous journey led her to just that, and by the 1980s Natori was at the vanguard of the lingerie business.

With her signature beaded bustiers, embroidered leggings, and slip dresses, Natori revolutionized intimate apparel. She rejected the traditional notion that relegated lingerie to sleepwear, to be worn only at home or under layers of clothes. Instead, Natori created a line of high fashion outerwear—elegant clothes women could wear to restaurants, the theatre, or casually on the streets.

Natori's soft, body-hugging designs are made of velvet, Lycra, and lace and are distinguished by their embellishment—delicate golden embroidery, silver beads, and brilliant jeweled appliqués for which the Philippine Islands are renowned.

"My collection is based on my taste level," Natori told Bush. "It's more of an attitude of dressing. Whatever I do, whether it's clothes or jewelry, there's always a feeling of luxury, a lot of detail . . . and evidence of craftsmanship." Natori believes that her clothes are designed for the woman who "believes in pampering herself, in feeling good about herself."

Diverse Interests

Josie Natori was born Josefina Cruz on May 9, 1947, in Manila, Philippines. The eldest daughter in a family of six children, she grew up in relative affluence. Her father, Felipe F. Cruz, owned a construction company, and her mother, Angelita A. Cruz, was a pharmacist who worked as his business partner. Natori had a strict Catholic upbringing and was schooled most of her young life by nuns.

Even as a small child, Natori aspired to be both a concert pianist and a stockbroker, exhibiting the dual artistic and business acumen that would later propel her to success. She began studying piano at four and performed as a soloist with a full orchestra at nine. With her family's encouragement, Natori pursued her second goal at seventeen, when she emigrated to New York City to study economics at Manhattanville College. After graduating in 1968, she joined Bache Securities as a stockbroker. In 1971, she was hired by Merrill Lynch, where she switched to investment banking, rising to a vice president in that division. Natori met her husband, Kenneth Natori, an investment banker for a rival firm, on a blind date. They married in 1972. In 1976, Natori gave birth to a son, Kenneth, Jr.

Two months after her son's birth, Natori returned to investment banking, but was deeply dissatisfied with her career and longed for a more creative outlet. "There's no aesthetic sense on Wall Street," she told *Cosmopolitan* magazine in 1991, "We made creative deals, but there was nothing to look at."

Josie Natori

A Family Business

In 1977, Natori left her six-figure job and, with her husband's assistance and support, pursued their shared dream of opening a business. Initially The Natori Company specialized in importing products such as furniture and baskets from the Philippines. But a traditional hand-embroidered blouse launched Natori into the lingerie business. A Bloomingdales' buyer suggested she lengthen the blouse into a nightshirt. Not even sure what a nightshirt was, Natori took the buyer's suggestion and, in less than three months, had sold $150,000 worth of orders.

Natori's husband left his job as managing partner at Shearson Lehman to officially join the company in 1985. In the beginning, the couple funded the company themselves, relying on subcontractors in the Philippines to manufacture the clothes. Despite their relatively easy start in the lingerie field, the fledgling business partners struggled with "normal business pains," Natori told Bush. Maintaining quality control was difficult. Clothes were not cut to the right size or according to a buyer's specifications. Deals fell through, divisions opened and closed, and the Natoris had to ride out the ebb and flow of rough economic times.

The couple persevered, however, learning by trial and error. A turning point was the creation of their own sewing factory in the Philippines, built and operated by Natori's father, in 1989. The factory allowed the Natoris to have total control over every aspect of their company, and to utilize the designs and craftsmanship indigenous to the Philippines. The Natori Company employs 900 local craftsmen. In recognition of her achievement as one of the prime exporters from the Philippines, Natori was honored with the Galleon Award in 1988 by then-president of the Philippines Corazon Aquino.

An Established Fashion Force

In the 1990s, The Natori Company is a thriving $40 million empire spread out over forty countries. Seeking new markets—and new challenges—Natori has moved into the vanguard of fashion merchandising, following in the footsteps of Ralph Lauren and Laura Ashley. In 1991, she launched Josie Natori Couture, a collection of elegant evening wear and dresses. In fall 1993, Natori introduced a fashion jewelry collection under a worldwide licensing agreement. A Natori day and evening shoe collection debuted in department stores in July 1994. Her next venture is a collection of fragrance and bath products marketed by Avon Products, slated for introduction in spring 1995.

Natori credits her family, particularly the women who raised her, for her self-confidence and business savvy. Her maternal grandmother, Josefa M. Almeda, was particularly influential as a role model. A businesswoman and a workaholic, Natori's grandmother was a feminist in her day. "She believed in women running their own lives and not having to depend on anybody," Natori told Bush proudly.

Natori inherited her drive and business knowledge from her father, a "classic entrepreneur." Her artistic side, on the other hand, came from her mother. "The philosophy of The Natori Company is really very much a product of the influence of my mother," Natori added. Her mother was a pianist and, like Natori, loved to surround herself with luxurious clothes, antiques, and art.

Natori, who is known for her couture-clad diminutive figure (she is five feet two and a half and weighs ninety-four pounds) and precision cut black hair, thrives on being seen as unique and different. "I always say you have to draw on your biggest assets and for me, my biggest assets are one, being a woman, and two, being Filipino," Natori said.

Having grown up with strong women role models, Natori said she never "questioned the power of a woman" and always felt being a female was a strength, not a liability, in the competitive world of business. "My business is about women, and I use what I feel as a woman to determine what women want," she explained.

Being Filipino has also worked to her advantage because she has drawn on her cultural heritage for inspiration. "The whole trademark of Natori is based on craftsmanship out of the Philippines," she said. "I took the best of what I am about, and combined it in this business."

Despite her fame as a fashion industry leader, Natori doesn't want to be remembered solely as a designer who changed the face of lingerie. Fiercely proud of her Filipino heritage, she would like to contribute to the development of the Philippines, beyond her contributions to trade and job creation. "I believe in making a difference in people's lives, and *beyond fashion, please!*" she insisted to Bush.

On a personal level, Natori continues to seek out new challenges, which she manages to fit into her frenetic life as a businesswoman, wife, and mother. Recently, for example, she started to play the piano again after a long absence. Her dream, she admitted laughingly, is to perform a recital at Carnegie Hall someday. "It's just a fantasy. My fingers are rusty so I'm wondering if I can still do it."

But Natori, a self-described positive thinker, remains undaunted by taking this risk or any other for that matter. "You must be willing to take risks and make mistakes . . . or you'll stay in the status quo," she said. "If you have confidence, you can do anything."

Sources:

Periodicals

"Josie Natori: Queen of the Night (gown)," *Cosmopolitan*, vol. 211, no. 6, December 1991, p. 74.
Mall, Elyse. "The Power of Women." *Working Women*, vol. 16, no. 11, November 1991, p. 87.

Other

Natori, Josie, telephone interview with Valerie Chow Bush, April 18, 1994.
Loving and Weintraub, Inc., Public Relations. "Josie Natori." New York, March 1994.

—Sketch by Valerie Chow Bush

Haing Ngor
(1947–)
Physician, actor

Haing Ngor is a physician who survived the murderous reign of the Khmer Rouge in his native Cambodia, fleeing to the United States in 1980. He came to national prominence for his portrayal of Cambodian journalist Dith Pran in the 1985 film *The Killing Fields*. Ngor had never acted before, but his work was so powerful he earned an Academy Award. Since winning the award, Ngor has used his high profile to publicize the holocaust perpetrated on his people by the Khmer Rouge, and

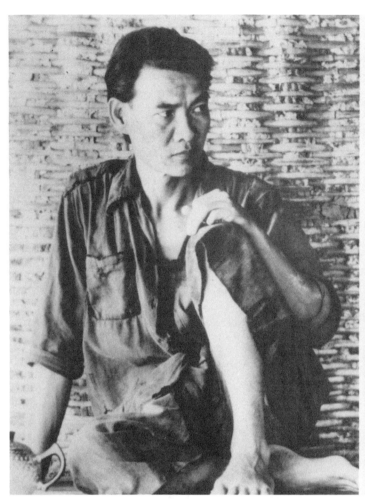 

Haing Ngor

devoted considerable time to organizations serving the refugee population in the United States.

The Early Years

Haing Ngor was born in 1947 in the farming village of Samrong Yong, south of the Cambodian capital of Phnom Penh. The son of a Khmer mother and an ethnic Chinese father, Ngor remembers the Cambodia of his early years as a place of beauty and tranquillity. He recalled in his book *A Cambodian Odyssey*, "Those are my first memories, the rice fields changing with the seasons and the monks coming to our house each morning. And that is how I would like to remember Cambodia, quiet and beautiful and at peace." Unfortunately it would not remain peaceful. By the time Ngor was a small boy, a civil war had already started and his family, like many others, were feeling the repercussions of the strife.

One day when he was very young Ngor had to take his ailing mother to the doctor. The army guards hassled Ngor and his mother, however, and refused to let them go.

This was when Ngor decided on a medical career, much as it was going to be difficult. He had come from a poor family and was expected to work in the fields to contribute to the family's income. Ngor left home to go live in a temple with monks and pursue his dream to become a doctor.

Ngor specialized in gynecology and obstetrics. After medical school, he set up his own clinic in Phnom Penh. He also served as a medical officer in the Cambodian army before the communist forces, the Khmer Rouge, overran the capital in 1975 and began their genocidal regime. The Khmer Rouge was a Maoist guerrilla insurgency led by Pol Pot, who believed that Cambodia had to be freed of all Western influence and the people returned to an agrarian lifestyle, by force if need be. To this end they evacuated cities and towns, sending millions of people into the countryside to do manual labor. Educated people were particularly targeted for "re-education," and Ngor's ability to practice medicine openly was severley curtailed. He could only work in utmost secrecy for fear of losing his life like many other educated people. He was forced to do manual labor to feed himself and his family.

During their reign of terror, the Khmer Rouge exterminated as many as two million people. Along with many other innocent people who had survived under the past regime, Ngor's mother and father and his brothers and their wives were among the early victims of the execution squads. Ngor himself was tortured many times in prison camps.

It was in a forced labor camp that Ngor met and fell in love with Chang My Houy. Ngor recalled in his book, "[She] represented the best of womankind. She never caused pain. She was a healer. She was also much smarter than me. She was not the most beautiful woman in the world, but she was beautiful to me."

Houy and Ngor lived together but were never able to get married. First, it was Ngor's father who denied them permission, and then it was the revolution that prevented them from getting married. In spite of this, they stayed together and decided to have a baby. But due to lack of proper care and nourishment, Houy died before giving birth to their unborn child. Ngor was unable to help her without the proper equipment, medicines, and surgical tools.

Life in America

After Houy's death on June 2, 1978, there were very positive signs that the murderous regime was breaking up. In May 1979, after the Vietnamese overran Cambodia and forced the Khmer Rouge from power, Ngor rescued his niece and escaped to Thailand. He worked as a doctor in refugee camps on the Thai-Cambodian border for eighteen months. He was denied entry into Australia and into America because he did not have close family there. Persistence paid off, however, and finally on October 1, 1980, Dr. Ngor left for Los Angeles.

Life started all over again in America for Ngor. He could not practice medicine since his French medical qualifications were not recognized in the United States. His first job was as a night security guard for a company outside Chinatown. In November 1980 Ngor became a caseworker for the Chinatown Service Center. His job was to help Cambodian refugees find employment. Ngor found the job satisfying because he could do what he wanted to do most—help refugees.

It was in March 1982 that he auditioned for a part in the film *The Killing Fields*. When Ngor's acquaintances first asked him to audition with them, he refused. He was satisfied where he was, helping refugees. However he finally agreed to the audition to satisfy his friends. After six interviews Ngor's attitude about acting in the film changed. He had promised Houy on her deathbed that he would tell the story of Cambodia to people worldwide. He recounted in *A Cambodian Odyssey*, "And it was true. I had changed my mind. If I could be in the film, I decided, in any capacity, I could help tell the story of Cambodia. And that was important because it was a story nobody knew."

Ngor returned to Thailand with members of the film team. He did not know what his role was until he was handed a script and told that he was going to play Dith Pran, a key role in the film. Despite this being his first attempt at acting, Ngor played Pran with such depth and so powerfully that in 1985 it earned him an Oscar for best supporting actor. Ngor says that acting is convincing the others of a new identity that the actor has taken on. That can best be done through the eyes and the heart. The eyes can present everything that an actor wants to portray. Talking about his Oscar-winning performance, Ngor says in *A Cambodian Odyssey*, "My best performances were over before I left Cambodia. And the prize there was much greater."

Other films Ngor has acted in include *The Iron Triangle*, and *Ambition*. He's also appeared on television in the films *In Love and War* and *Last Flight Out* and has had guest star roles on television series such as "Miami Vice," "China Beach," "Highway to Heaven," and "Hotel." Ngor has been the subject of two documentaries, *A Man Without a Country* and *Beyond the Killing Fields*. In 1987 his autobiography, *Haing Ngor: A Cambodian Odyssey*, co-written with journalist Roger Warner, was published to critical acclaim.

Life after the Oscar

Since winning the Oscar and a number of other awards for his role in *The Killing Fields*, Ngor has interspersed occasional acting roles with his life's work, heading six organizations devoted to caring for Southeast Asian refugees and resettling them in the West.

Ngor currently lives alone in Los Angeles, California. Of his three sisters and five brothers, only two brothers are still living, one in the United States and one in Cambodia. He is working on a second book entitled *The Healing Fields*. Ngor is involved with fund-raising efforts to help Cambodian refugees and regularly visits Cambodia armed with medical, school, and other essential supplies.

In his autobiography Ngor remarked, "I have been many things in my life: A trader walking barefoot on paths through jungles. A medical doctor, driving to his clinic in a shiny Mercedes. In the past few years, to the surprise of many people and, above all, myself, I have been a Hollywood actor. But nothing has shaped my life as much as surviving the Pol Pot regime. I am a survivor of the Cambodian Holocaust. That's who I am."

Sources:

Books

Ngor, Haing and Roger Warner. *A Cambodian Odyssey*. New York: Macmillan, 1987.

Other

The Marion Rosenberg Office. "Haing S. Ngor." Biographical information. Los Angeles, California.

Ngor, Haing, telephone interview with Visi R. Tilak, May 6, 1994.

—Sketch by Visi R. Tilak

Sean Nguyen
(1963–)
Entrepreneur

Sean Nguyen

In 1980, Sean Nguyen was a seventeen-year-old youth, tending rice fields in his native town, Rach Gia, Vietnam. Six years later, he started his own business, building and testing computer modems in a makeshift office in a Minneapolis basement. In 1993, with his company's annual sales expected to reach $7 million, Nguyen received a highly sought-after award: the U.S. Small Business Administration's Young Entrepreneur of the Year. He also was named Midwest Manufacturer of the Year by Ernst and Young and *Inc.* magazine. Suddenly, television reporters started calling him, *Fortune* and *Inc.* magazines asked for interviews. A one-time refugee, one of the Vietnamese "boat people" who fled their country by sea for a better opportunity in America, Nguyen had found his pot of gold.

In a 1993 interview with Darlene DePass of the *Minneapolis Star Tribune*, Nguyen seemed almost overcome by his success. "I feel good, proud and happy. I never imagined I would get that far." DePass noted his calm demeanor and his direct and welcoming gaze. But, she said, he seemed uncomfortable wearing a bold, purple tie and suit. He confided that he would have preferred a casual shirt and slacks, but his wife, Terri, the company's general manager, insisted on the formal attire. After all, he had come far.

Flight from Terror

Nguyen was born December 20, 1963, as Nguyen Van Son. He grew up in South Vietnam, tending rice fields, but this peaceful life was shattered in 1980 when the Viet Cong invaded and snatched up his family's lands. One year later, he fled his country on a fragile, wooden boat, along with his father, his brother, and thirty-nine others. Crossing the South China Sea en route to Thailand, his boat was raided seven times in four days by Thai pirates. The pirates raped the women on board and took everything the refugees were carrying: money, clothing, even a worn-out boat engine. The boat drifted for several days, finally scraping the Thai shore. Nguyen wound up in a refugee camp, where he stayed for eight months until a cousin living in Minnesota arranged for him and the family members traveling with him to come to the United States under the sponsorship of the Catholic Church.

In the United States, he lived in his cousin's cramped two-bedroom apartment with eleven other relatives and slept on the floor for several months. He could not speak English, and going to high school to learn the language was not an option. He needed to get a job immediately to support his family in the States, not to mention his mother and sister still living in Vietnam.

Despite the hardship, he felt fortunate to be in America. Everything seemed so big: the people, supermarkets, vegetables sold on produce shelves. "We were lucky," he recalled in his interview with DePass. "It seemed like a land of opportunity."

Through the Catholic relief agency that sponsored his visa, Nguyen found a $4-an-hour job testing personal computer modem boards for a company called Multi-Tech System. On his first day of work, he remembers looking at the inside of a computer with amazement. "Everything looked like a city on the circuit board. It looked like Los Angeles."

Home Work Pays Off

Realizing he needed to improve his technical skills, Nguyen enrolled in an electronics program at Northwestern Electronics Institute in 1987. But $4 an hour wasn't enough to pay for schooling and his family's needs. So he began making extra money by bringing assembly boards home to put together and test. In what *Inc.* magazine called a "stroke of precocious entrepreneurial savvy," he asked to be paid as a separate business entity, rather than as an employee. In 1986, Nguyen Electronics Inc. (NEI) was born. He hired fifteen part-time workers, mostly friends and relatives who like himself spoke little English. In his first year as an independent vendor for Multi-Tech, he earned more than $50,000 in sales. He continued working for the company through 1990, during which time his annual sales at NEI grew to $1 million.

The story of his start-up years might sound familiar to other immigrants who have become successful entrepreneurs. In the first year, he and his family worked every day until 11 p.m. They'd order pizza and keep going until the day's jobs were done. Though Multi-Tech System was a fairly reliable customer, Nguyen knew he couldn't rely on his employer forever. So, in 1989, he poured all of his personal savings into a down payment on a $150,000 automatic assembling machine. Although his monthly profit couldn't cover the $5,000 debt he owed each month, he nevertheless struggled to make payments, never giving up hope that more business would come.

It came, eventually. The automated assembler let him fasten 3,500 electronic components to circuit boards in an hour and gave him the leverage he needed to convince Minnesota companies such as Digi International and Zeos International to sign on as customers. By 1993 he had more than fifteen customers and six automated assembly machines. His annual profit exceeded $1 million, most of which he reinvested in his business.

Diversification

Nguyen diversified his business in 1992 by investing some of his profits in Vid Tech Microsystems, which designs and assembles computer boards. He also has started a second subsidiary, Tertronics, named after his wife, Terri, who also fled from Vietnam by boat as a teenager. Tertronics programs memory chips and floppy disks. Nguyen's goal is to make the best computer boards in the United States.

Nguyen credits his success to a mix of Vietnamese culture and American opportunities. From the Vietnamese side, he gained a strict work ethic, which he sees in himself and in his mostly Asian workforce. From America, he learned that sharing good ideas with other entrepreneurs can lead to much success.

Nguyen seems in many ways like an average American millionaire—he wears ties when his wife insists and his favorite hobby is playing golf. Nevertheless, he still is reminded of his Vietnamese roots whenever he struggles to understand the meaning of certain words. This does, at times, make him uncomfortable. As the boss, he wants to understand everything, but understanding everything sometimes forces him to ask, "What does that mean?"

His company now employs nearly two hundred people, only forty of whom speak English as their first language. For the rest, native tongues are Vietnamese, Chinese, Laotian, and Cambodian. Nguyen says they are hard workers—workers who can't find work elsewhere because their English isn't very good.

The multitude of languages makes communication in the NEI workplace interesting. Team leaders translate conversations that take place in four languages. When no interpreter is around, hand signals are the norm. Nguyen, however, employs three salespeople and a receptionist who speak English fluently, which helps make business transactions go smoothly.

A hard worker himself, Nguyen can hardly be accused of being a lenient manager. When a deadline to finish and deliver a customer's order approaches, he expects his workers to stay on the job day and night. To increase his sales, he began running two shifts, seven days a week. He spends his evenings in the shop, working with engineers to repair equipment, or checking out a part. But while he pushes his workers hard, he tries to reward them well. Salaries for the mostly unskilled jobs start at $5.50 an hour, and he pays both overtime and full health benefits. And he doesn't point fingers when a mistake is made. When a longtime customer received two hundred computer boards with faulty soldering, Nguyen focused not on what caused the problem but on finding a solution. He put two experienced technicians on a quality inspection line and made one supervisor directly responsible for inspections to that company. He also set up regular meetings with the customer to ensure that future quality remained high. Some employers call this "total quality improvement" or "partnering." Nguyen considers it turning problems into challenges. But the end result is the same. Teamwork fosters a sense of cooperation often not found in traditional U.S. companies. Workers help each other, sometimes without asking.

Nguyen recently bought a six-bedroom house in Ham Lake, Minnesota, that overlooks a golf course. He is trying to relax and enjoy life with his young son and daughter. But another goal is driving him. He wants to bring his mother and his sister to the United States. And he also wants to take his business to Vietnam. As trade relations between the United States and Vietnam improve, that goal is getting closer.

Sources:

Caggiano, Christopher. "Entrepreneur of the Year." *Inc.* December 1993.

DePass, Darlene. "From Farmer, to Refugee, to Head of $4 Million Firm." *Minneapolis Star Tribune*, March 22, 1993.

—Sketch by Himanee Gupta

Isamu Noguchi
(1904–1988)
Sculptor, architect

At his death in 1988 at the age of eighty-four, sculptor and architect Isamu Noguchi had achieved worldwide renown few artists of this century have known. His career spanned five decades during which he worked with such seminal twentieth-century figures as George Balanchine, Igor Stravinsky, William Butler Yeats, Ezra Pound, and Martha Graham. His major works include *Red Cube* on the plaza of the Marine Midland Building in New York City, the *Billy Rose Sculpture Garden* in Jerusalem, *2 Peace Bridges* in Hiroshima, and the sculpture garden at the Yale Beinecke Rare Book and Manuscript Library in New Haven, Connecticut. Aside from sculpture and architecture, Noguchi also designed sets and masks for the theater. Most notable among these were his designs for the Balanchine/Stravinsky ballet *Orpheus,* and John Gielgud's *King Lear.*

Isamu Noguchi was born in 1904 in Los Angeles to an American mother and a Japanese father. His father, Yone Noguchi, was a well-known poet and critic who achieved much success in America and Britain as the author of books of verse, a novel, and a wide array of critical works interpreting classical Japanese art and poetry for the Western world. Isamu's relationship with his eminent father was a strained one. The elder Noguchi had left America for his home country shortly before his son was born. He did not see the boy again until two years later, when Isamu and his mother moved to Japan. Although now Isamu and his father were in the same country, they still had almost nothing to do with each other. They did not meet again until the boy was eight and had the measles, and then not again until Isamu was thirteen and was headed back to America to attend boarding school in Indiana. This was in 1918. It would be six years before Noguchi would see his mother again, and thirteen before he would see his father.

The Midwest

In describing his childhood in America Noguchi told the *Journal of Modern Literature* that it "had nothing to do with art, it had to do with the Middle West and the American idealism that flourished in the twenties and thirties." Interlaken, the boarding school in Indiana for which he was bound when he left Japan, had permanently closed by the time he arrived and he found himself stranded and penniless in the Midwest, a thirteen year old of mixed-race parentage. Fortunately, there were two caretakers from the school still in the area and Noguchi was able to stay with them for a year. It was then that the founder of the Interlaken School, Dr. Edward A. Rumley, heard of the young boy's circumstances and found for him lodging in the nearby town of La Porte, Indiana, with a minister and his family. It was in these traditional, middle western surroundings that Noguchi finished high school while supporting himself with a variety of jobs. "So I really grew up in the Midwest," Noguchi emphasized in the *Journal of Modern Literature*, "though I am a mixture of extreme differences in heritage. Please do not forget I am a real product of the Midwest."

After high school Rumley tried to persuade Noguchi to pursue a career in medicine as he himself had, but the young man had already decided he wanted to be a sculptor. The doctor thought Noguchi was foolish to imagine he could support himself as an artist. Nevertheless, Rumley arranged for Noguchi to be apprenticed with the sculptor Gutzon Borglum who at the time was sculpting the presidential monument on Mount Rushmore in South Dakota.

Borglum told Noguchi that he would never make it as a sculptor, and in the mid-twenties Noguchi moved to New York and enrolled as a pre–medical student in Columbia University. Not wanting to give up on his dream, however, Noguchi enrolled in the Leonardo da Vinci Art School on the Lower East Side where he continued to study sculpture. There he met the school's director, who was so impressed with Noguchi's talent he was moved to say that a new Michaelangelo had appeared. Noguchi described his experiences at the da Vinci school as pivotal, and the encouragement he received there prompted him to drop out of Columbia and pursue sculpture full–time.

Noguchi was not ultimately interested in classical sculpture, however, and he immersed himself in the modernist art scene. He spent many days going to galleries, museums, and exhibitions. He was particularly affected by an exhibit at the Brummer Gallery of the works of the famous Romanian-born sculptor Constantin Brancusi, whose pure, simple works were a leading influence on modern sculpture.

Noguchi also exhibited at this time, in a show called the Roman Bronze Exhibit. It was here that Harry Guggenheim saw his work and suggested to the young artist that he apply for one of the newly established Guggenheim Fellowships. Noguchi did so with the help and encouragement of others, including Alfred Stieglitz, the photographer and gallery owner who is credited with helping modern art gain acceptance in the United States. Noguchi won the award and spent the money traveling through Europe, where, in Paris, he spent time under the tutelage of Brancusi.

Noguchi returned to New York in 1929 and earned a living making portrait busts. In 1930 he again went to Paris and then to Asia, via the Trans-Siberian railroad. He studied calligraphy and brush drawing during eight months in Beijing, and then went on to Japan where he lived for six

Isamu Noguchi

months working with clay and studying the classical Japanese garden.

The Beginning of Success

By the beginning of the 1930s Noguchi was attaining limited success. He had exhibited drawings and terra cottas in Europe and America, but he wanted to explore other avenues of expression. Perhaps because of his friendship with the architect and inventor Buckminster Fuller, he became interested in a more elaborate, holistic concept of design that incorporated architecture, sculpture, and landscape. In 1933 he proposed a design for a city park in New York, to be called *Play Mountain,* which incorporated these elements. However, his plan was rejected by the Parks Commission. Noguchi was greatly disillusioned by this rejection and left the United States for Mexico, a country he thought would be more sympathetic to his style of expression. And, indeed, it was in Mexico that Noguchi completed what is considered his first major work, a high relief mural in colored cement called *History Mexico* for the Rodriguez market.

Following the outbreak of World War II, Noguchi founded an organization called the Nisei Writers and Artists for Democracy in an attempt to counter the anti-Japanese hysteria that gripped his homeland following the attack on Pearl Harbor. Noguchi was outraged by the imprisonment of Japanese Americans during the war. Although he was a resident of the East Coast and therefore not subject to the internment laws, as a show of solidarity with other Japanese Americans he voluntarily entered an Arizona internment camp where he was held for seven months. The architect Frank Lloyd Wright was one of many who wrote letters to the War Relocation Authority petitioning for his release.

By the end of the war Noguchi's fame had grown considerably, and his interest in the relationship between sculpture and architecture intensified. He embarked on one of the most prolific periods of his artistic life. It was also at this point that he met and married a movie actress from Japan, Yoshiko Yamaguchi. The marriage was not very happy, produced no children, and after four years ended in divorce in 1955.

In 1956 he was given the commission for the gardens of the UNESCO building in Paris, for which he selected Japanese stones. His other major projects of this period include the *Sunken Gardens* for the Beinecke Rare Book and Manuscript Library at Yale, completed in 1964, and the *Billy Rose Sculpture Garden* for the Israeli Museum in Jerusalem. Completed in 1965, this garden was erected on a hill called Neve Shaanan, meaning place of tranquillity. In 1985 Noguchi wrote that it was his proudest achievement that he was able to retain that quality in his design.

Noguchi was given retrospectives in 1968 at the Whitney Museum in New York and in 1978 at the Walker Art Center in Minneapolis. Writing about the latter in the *New York Times* Hilton Kramer said, "Noguchi is . . . the purest of living sculptors."

In 1982 Noguchi received the prestigious Edward Mac-Dowell Medal for outstanding lifetime contribution to the arts. In 1984 his *Bolt of Lightning*, a 102-foot-tall stainless steel sculpture designed as a memorial to Benjamin Franklin, was installed near the Benjamin Franklin Bridge in Philadelphia, fifty years after Noguchi conceived it. In 1986 he was selected to represent the United States at the Venice Bienale, an international exhibition. In 1987 President Ronald Reagan awarded him the National Medal of Arts and in 1988 the Japanese government gave him the Order of the Sacred Treasure.

Praise for the Artist

Noguchi died on December 30, 1988, from complications of a virus he contracted while working in Italy. In an article in the *New York Times,* several of Noguchi's contemporaries remembered him. Anne d'Harnoncourt, director of the Philadelphia Museum of Art, said of the sculptor: "He never lost his extraordinarily youthful sense of invention and enthusiasm. . . . He was interested in the quality of everything, from the very simple Akari lamps to very elaborate stone sculpture in architectural surroundings. There was a pervasive sense of the individual object as a part of the whole. He was a wonderful free spirit." The sculptor Joel Shapiro said, "His is a broad and inventive body of work. It was very challenging . . . in its range and lack of inhibition." And Martha Graham, the choreographer with whom Noguchi repeatedly worked said, "I feel the world has lost an artist who, like a shaman, has translated myths of all our lives into reality."

Sources:

Books

Noguchi, Isamu. *A Sculptor's World.* New York: Harper and Row, 1968.

Periodicals

Brenson, Michael. "Isamu Noguchi, the Sculptor, Dies at 84." *New York Times,* December 31, 1988, pp. 1, 9.

Hakutani, Yoshinobu. "Father and Son: A Conversation with Isamu Noguchi." *Journal of Modern Literature,* Summer 1990, pp. 13–33.

—Sketch by Jim Henry

O

Gyo Obata
(1923–)
Architect

Architect Gyo Obata's long and remarkable career encompasses projects as diverse as the National Air and Space Museum in Washington, D.C. (the world's most visited museum) to the King Khalid International Airport in Saudi Arabia (the world's largest airport). Yet all of his work, be it large-scale or more modest assignments, has been guided by the same principle: "Never lose sight of the complete picture, of the people who will spend time inside the building, who will be affected by the use of the space," he said in a 1993 *Profiles* magazine story. "I really believe in understanding people's needs, their intuitive and emotional goals as well as their functional needs."

It's a philosophy that has served Obata well over the years. Today, the small St. Louis firm he co–founded nearly three decades ago is one of the largest architecture firms in the world, with offices on four continents. It's a feat made even more amazing by the events that occurred a lifetime ago, when Obata's promising career was nearly derailed before it could start by the outbreak of war and wartime hysteria.

Artistic Roots

Obata was born in San Francisco on February 28, 1923, to Chiura and Haruko Obata. His father, grandfather, and great-grandfather were all painters from Japan, and his mother taught flower arrangement. When he was five years old, the family moved to Sendai, Japan, the family's ancestral home. It was there that Obata attended kindergarten. The family returned to San Francisco the following year, however, and eventually settled in Berkeley, where Obata's father, Chiura Obata, began teaching at the University of California.

As a young boy, Obata was active in baseball and football, sports he credits with teaching him teamwork, a skill essential in his chosen field. It was also during his boyhood that Obata discovered his calling. "I knew I wanted to be an architect by the time I reached the sixth grade,"

Gyo Obata

Obata told *Notable Asian Americans.* "My mother, father, and many other members of my family were artists. I became interested in a combination of science and art, so architecture was a natural choice."

Obata enrolled at the University of California architecture school, quickly distinguishing himself. In his freshman year, his class was assigned to produce five drawings for problems involving historical architectural landmarks. Three of his solutions were awarded first place. But his first semester coincided with the Japanese attack on Pearl Harbor in December 1941, which spawned anti-Japanese hysteria and drew the United States into World War II.

Just months after the attack, those of Japanese descent living on the West Coast were forced to enter internment camps because they were perceived as a national security threat. Because the War Department allowed those accepted to a Midwestern college to leave, Obata's father urged him to continue his education at Washington

University in St. Louis. Obata left for his new school the night before his parents, brother, and sister were bussed to a camp in Utah. "It all happened in about a week, and I didn't really know what would become of them," he told *Profiles.*

In the Midwest, Obata found a more tranquil environment in which to continue his studies. "The comparison between the Bay area and St. Louis was like night and day; no feeling of the war or blackouts," Obata said in a 1992 interview in the *CED News,* a publication of the University of California at Berkeley's College of Environmental Design.

But the relative normalcy he found in the Midwest only heightened the outrage he felt over the treatment of his family and other Japanese. In his *Profiles* interview, he recalled visiting his family in camp at Christmas that year: "There I was studying in St. Louis, not really experiencing any discrimination at all, and my family was being kept there in the desert," Obata said. "Looking back, it was all so absolutely stupid—all prejudice is crazy. But at the time, we all just kept on looking ahead to what we would do later."

After the war his family joined him in St. Louis. Kim Obata, an older brother whom Obata described as a second father figure, later founded Obata Design, a graphic design firm. Now deceased, Kim also established a commercial art studio in Tokyo. Obata's sister, Yuri Kodani, is also an artist and resides in Berkeley.

Career Beginnings

Obata's move to St. Louis had been a turning point in many ways. The experience strengthened his resolve to succeed; he attended school year round and received his undergraduate degree in three years. Just as importantly, exposure to the Midwest broadened his perspective. It was in the Midwest that he met many of the people who would later play important roles in his life, including the man he considers his mentor and greatest architectural influence, Eero Saarinen.

After graduating from Washington University in 1945, Obata received a scholarship to study with Saarinen at Cranbrook Academy, outside Detroit. It was from Saarinen, the famed designer of the Gateway Arch in St. Louis, that Obata learned about urban planning and project design. Saarinen also imparted lessons that have guided Obata throughout his career. "The greatest thing he taught me was this feeling that you could tackle any large-scale problem when you start with the smallest detail," Obata told *Profiles.* "I've never been threatened by the size of a project. I've always known I could take on just about anything."

After a year and a half at Cranbrook, Obata went to Chicago to work for Skidmore, Owings and Merrill. But he was soon drafted, sent to Fort Lewis near Tacoma, Washington, then to the Aleutian Islands with the Corps of Engineers to study arctic warfare. In 1947, he returned to Skidmore. A year later, he worked for architect Minoru Yamasaki in Michigan. He was assigned to the design of a new airport terminal in St. Louis. For several years, he spent most of his time commuting from Detroit to St. Louis.

In 1955, George Hellmuth, who was the resident partner, George Kassabaum, who was running production, and Obata split from the Detroit office after Yamasaki became ill and decided to close the St. Louis office. The move marked the birth of Hellmuth, Obata and Kassabaum, or HOK. Hellmuth ran the marketing programs, Kassabaum took on the management responsibilities, and Obata worked on the designs.

The fledgling company, which began as a twenty-four-person office, benefited from postwar prosperity and the baby boom, which ensured a steady flow of work— mostly elementary and secondary schools and colleges. Today, HOK is one of the largest architecture firms in the world, with eight U.S. offices and four overseas, and more than 900 architects, designers, engineers, and planners on the payroll. HOK's specialties have expanded to include everything from commercial buildings to shopping centers to hospitals. In its Kansas City office, there are 125 people working on sports stadiums and arenas. The firm's credits already include three baseball stadiums: Jacobs Field in Cleveland, Oriole Park at Camden Yards in Baltimore, and the new Comiskey Park Chicago. Its revenues reached $82 million in 1991. Along the way, HOK has established a trendsetting reputation and its designs have won numerous prestigious awards.

Obata, who now serves as co–chairman of HOK, is the only remaining partner; Kassabaum died in 1982 and Hellmuth retired in 1986. Obata still spends the bulk of his time designing. In the *CED News* interview, Obata cited as personal milestones the Priory School and Chapel in St. Louis, the campus of Southern Illinois University, and the Smithsonian Institution's National Air and Space Museum.

Designing the National Air and Space Museum, which attracts some ten million people annually, was a creative and logistical challenge for Obata. "I wanted something that would really involve the average person in the adventure of space travel," he told *CED News.* To do that, Obata brought the skies inside to the visitors by an effect that relies on glass fronted bays; spacious interiors with tall ceilings also permit exhibition of suspended aircraft and space vehicles. The layout of the museum makes it easy for visitors to orient themselves.

HOK has not only altered the visual landscape of architecture, it has also developed its own way of doing business. Early on, the firm adopted a distinct strategy: it maintained a list of projects of different building types in various geographic regions. During recessionary times in the early 1970s, when many large architecture firms foundered, HOK turned to projects in Saudi Arabia. Its $3.5 billion King Khalid International Airport in Riyadh, the world's largest, has a mosque that can accommodate 5,000 worshippers. The firm also worked on a $3 billion national university outside the Saudi capital on a 2,440-acre site.

Major Projects

Other high-profile projects Obata has done include the headquarters for Mobil Oil, the 1980 Winter Olympics facilities at Lake Placid, New York, Taiwan's Taipei World Trade Center, which dominates that city's skyline, and the acclaimed renovation of the St. Louis Union Station. HOK also designed Houston's Galleria, a mini-city that includes hotels, office towers, an Olympic-sized ice skating rink, and a twelve-story mall. It was begun in 1966 and finished eleven years later.

The company's focus continues to be abroad, with a third of the new projects in 1992 originating overseas; there's a new airport in Hong Kong, a resort hotel in Indonesia, and a one million square foot telecom center in Tokyo scheduled for completion in 1995. There are also projects in Moscow, Costa Rica, Warsaw, and Kariuzawa, Japan.

Obata, who is married to Courtney Bean Obata, a ceramist and sculptor, has four children: Kiku (the president of Kiku Obata, a St. Louis graphics firm), Nori (a ceramist), Gen (an architect and painter), and Max (who is in first grade). In recent years Obata has become a strong advocate for environmental issues, pushing his fellow architects to play more of a role in the environmental debate. Obata himself is a member of the Presidio Council, a citizens group established by the Golden Gate National Park Association to formulate the transfer of the San Francisco Presidio from the military to the National Park Service. Obata said he hopes to create a model for sustainable environment by preserving its park, land, and seashores.

"I think architects have to become more vocal—I don't think it's coming from the politicians—or the world is not going to be a very nice place to live," Obata said in the *CED News* interview. "This is an incredible crisis. All this stuff about design and fashion is all secondary. . . . I think that as architects we're supposed to be the humanists, and from that standpoint we need to take a lead in this whole thing and really push on."

Sources:

Periodicals

Biemesderfer, S.C. "From the Ground Up." *Profile*, February 1993.
Montgomery, Roger. "A Conversation with Gyo Obata." *CED News*, University of California, Berkeley, Spring 1992.
Weiss, Julian M. "Forging the Shape of Tomorrow." *COMPASS*, May, 1990.

Other

Obata, Gyo, written interview with Ferdinand M. deLeon, March 18, 1994.

—Sketch by Ferdinand M. deLeon

Angela Eunjin Oh
(1955–)
Attorney, activist

Angela Oh came to national prominence as a spokesperson for Korean Americans in Los Angeles in the aftermath of the 1992 riots, in which more than two thousand Korean businesses were damaged or destroyed. In recognition of her work, Oh was appointed by California State Assembly speaker Willie Brown to co–chair the assembly's special committee on the Los Angeles Crisis. She also serves as chair of Senator Barbara Boxer's judiciary advisory committee, where she is responsible for recommending candidates for judgeships in the central district of California.

Diverse Interests

Angela Eunjin Oh was born in Los Angeles to first-generation Korean immigrants on September 8, 1955. Her mother was a school teacher and her father a laboratory technician. Angela attended public high schools in Los Angeles. She began working at a young age and held various odd jobs while in school. In addition to her studies, Angela played the piano and the guitar and was active in the community as a Mariner Scout. After graduation from high school in 1973, she enrolled in the University of California at Los Angeles (UCLA). After her second year in school, Angela went against her family's wishes and decided not to pursue a career in medicine—a decision that led to her being cut off financially. She then worked to put herself through school, earning a bachelor's degree in 1977 in psychology. While in college she continued working as a community activist, tutoring in the Chicano Youth East Barrio Project, which provided help for public school students in one of Los Angeles' poorer neighborhoods.

After graduating from UCLA, Oh worked in various jobs, mostly in retail. She also became interested in women's issues, especially in the area of health, which led her to community work in public health advocacy. In 1981, in order to increase her effectiveness as an advocate, she enrolled in the doctoral program in public health at UCLA. While in school, Oh took some courses in occupational health. She became preoccupied with labor-related issues and founded LACOSH, the Los Angeles Committee of Occupational Safety and Health. LACOSH was part of a series of loosely affiliated, nationally active worker safety and health advocacy organizations. Oh left the doctoral program early with a master's degree and began working with LACOSH full time. As such she lobbied on the local, state, and national levels for issues related to all aspects of worker health and safety. In 1983, she left LACOSH to become health and safety director of the Federated Firefighters of California, a statewide union representing firemen.

All her work as an advocate brought Oh into contact with legislators and lawyers on a regular basis, and she began to see that she would be better able to advance her political and social beliefs if she were a lawyer. In 1985 she entered law school at the University of California at Davis, and in June of 1986, she earned her J.D. Oh's first job after law school was as a political consultant for an organization called "No On Proposition 63," where she worked to defeat the statewide initiative to make English the official language of the state of California. In an interview with Jim Henry, Oh said that the initiative was driven by a fear of minorities taking over society, and was spearheaded by the often outspoken former senator from California, S. I. Hayakawa. Despite the work of organizations like "No on Proposition 63" the initiative was approved by the voters of the state of California, and English is now, by law, the official language of the most ethnically diverse state in the country.

After the passage of Proposition 63, Oh went to work for the law firm of Levy, Goldman, Greenstone, and Hubel, where she specialized in labor-management relations as a union advocate. In January of 1987, she was offered a position with Silver, Kreisler, Goldwasser and Shaffer. There she continued her work in labor relations but also represented law enforcement officers in official misconduct actions. This work went against her beliefs, however, and she left after only six months, moving to trial law with the firm of Beck, De Corso, Barrera and Oh, where she remains today.

Community Spokesperson

In the wake of the 1992 Los Angeles riots, Oh emerged as a national spokesperson for many of those whose businesses were destroyed in the rampage, especially those business owners in the Koreatown section of the city, the largest Korean community in the world outside of Korea. In the intense media coverage of the riots, Oh frequently was turned to by major media for the Korean perspective on the riots. Often, she was in the position of defending the Korean community, which many people sought to blame at least in part, for the racial tensions in Los Angeles. Writing in *Ms.* magazine, Oh said, "For many Korean Americans, the riots are infused with a sense of community pulling together. This is not an identity crisis for us—it's much more than that. Koreans have been blamed out of frustration with the system. It's not us. We're not the problem."

Oh also made television appearances and wrote several articles for national newspapers such as the *New York Times* and the *Los Angeles Times*. She has become a much sought-after panelist and speaker at academic conferences, where she has tried to draw attention to the plight of the Korean community. In the *New York Times* article, for example, she pointed out that a year after the riot, only one in four Korean businesses destroyed had reopened. At the same time, Oh called for healing the rift between the Korean American and African American communities, which she sees as vital to rebuilding downtown Los Angeles. She told *Open Forum*, a publication of the American Civil Liberties Union (ACLU) of Southern California, "To me [racial harmony] is the critical issue we need to grapple with as a community, as the L.A. community. Because if we don't deal with that, I don't care how many projects you have, I don't care how many buildings you put up, if people don't get along it's not going to work."

In 1992, the California Assembly recognized Oh's work on behalf of the victims of the Los Angeles riots and appointed her special counsel to the Assembly Special Committee on the Los Angeles Crisis. As such she oversaw the state's inquiry into the causes of the riots and helped in the preparation of a report concerning the rebuilding of Los Angeles. In addition, she also produced a video report, which she described to *Open Forum* as "voices from the community, directed to the legislature. It's called *A Share in the Deal*. And basically it talks about what happened—for about thirty seconds. And then it talks about where the hope is for L.A. It's not a glitzy, fashion piece. It's just truthful."

Oh has been involved for years in a variety of civic and community affairs organizations, including the ACLU, where she was a board member; the Korean American Bar Association, where she served as president in 1992; the California Women's Law Center; and the Women's Organization Reaching Koreans, where she served a term as president. In recognition of her expertise in community development issues and the problem of urban conflict, Oh was appointed a fellow of the British America Project, a privately funded annual symposium that brings together academics, artists, politicians, and professionals in several fields to discuss the problems of urban conflict in both Britain and America.

Reflecting on her life, Oh told Henry that almost none of what has happened in terms of her professional choices came about as the result of a plan. Rather, her interests have led her in a variety of directions from health concerns to labor relations to criminal law to community activism. And although she enjoys her current position as a criminal attorney, she expressed a desire to become involved in national policy-making in order to help the United States make the transformation from a country of minorities and majorities into a country of plurality.

Sources:

Periodicals

Oh, Angela. *Ms.*, July/August 1992, p. 43.
Ripston, Ramona. "Ramona Riptson in Conversation with Angela Oh." *Open Forum*, vol. 68 no. 4, Winter 1993, pp. 1–6.

Other

Oh, Angela, telephone interview with Jim Henry, May 10, 1994.

—Sketch by Jim Henry

Yoichi R. Okamoto
(1915–1985)
Photojournalist

Yoichi R. Okamoto was head of the White House photo office and principal presidential photographer from 1964 through 1968 during the presidency of Lyndon Baines Johnson. During the Depression, Okamoto helped pay for his college education working as a nightclub photographer and part-time newspaper photojournalist. These part-time jobs, taken to help pay for his education, led Okamoto to his lifelong interest in photography and set him on a course to becoming a distinguished photojournalist whose famous subjects included J. Edgar Hoover, head of the Federal Bureau of Investigation; Warren Burger, chief justice of the U. S. Supreme Court; and Lyndon Baines Johnson, president of the United States. His work has been featured on the covers of the *Smithsonian* and *Time* magazines. As head of the White House Photo Office, Okamoto made significant contributions to the body of photographic work documenting government in operation.

Okamoto was born on July 3, 1915, the oldest of two boys. His parents, both nisei (first generation Japanese American), divorced when Okamoto was young, and he was raised by his mother up in Yonkers, New York. Like many mothers, Okamoto's stressed the importance of education and hard work. He was a diligent high school student and attended Colgate University in upstate New York. It was while he was a student at Colgate that Okamoto's serious interest in photography developed.

Being Japanese American during World War II

Upon graduation from Colgate University, Okamoto enlisted in the army where he served with the prestigious 442nd, an all-Japanese American infantry regiment in the European theatre from 1942 until 1945. His son, Philip Okamoto, told Margaret Simon in an interview that one major disappointment in Okamoto's life was when he was thrown out of Officer Candidate School because he was Japanese. And, while he was serving in the war, Okamoto's mother and younger brother were sent to an internment camp in Kansas. These events served to make him critically conscious of being Japanese. According to Philip, "My father was always very self-conscious of being Japanese. He was also very proud of his heritage. . . .[and] felt that he had an obligation to show the world that being Japanese was something to be proud of and not to be ashamed of."

Okamoto married and had one son, Philip. Although this marriage ended in divorce, Okamoto received full custody of his son, a most unprecedented decree for the time.

When World War II ended Okamoto transferred to the foreign service and remained in Vienna with the United States Information Agency (USIA) until 1954. While in Vienna, he worked for General Mark Clark as a photographer. In September of 1947, He married Paula Schmuckwachter, an Austrian with a daughter, Karin, from a previous marriage. In about 1950, the U.S. government moved all dependents of personnel working in Vienna out of the city, fearing threat of military activity by the then Soviet Union. The Okamotos were moved to a village outside of Salzburg, Austria, best-known as the setting for the film the "Sound of Music." During these years in Austria, Okamoto fell in love with the city of Vienna and the surrounding countryside.

In 1954, Okamoto was transferred back to the United States to USIA headquarters, where he continued his work as photographer. The Okamoto family settled in Bethesda, Maryland. An auspicious meeting occurred when Lyndon Johnson, then vice president, made a trip to West Germany and requested that the USIA provide a photographer to accompany him on the trip. Okamoto was given the assignment, and the two got along well—so well, in fact, that Johnson requested that Okamoto accompany him on subsequent foreign trips.

Yoichi R. Okamoto

Defining the White House Photo Office

In 1964, Okamoto became head of the White House Photo Office for President Johnson. In addition to managing a team of five photographers, he also served as the primary White House photographer. In that capacity, his main responsibility was to photograph President Johnson's activities on a daily basis. Frank Wolfe, chief of technical services at the LBJ Library in Austin, Texas, and a member of Okamoto's team of White House photographers told Simon: "Yoichi's management style was to let the office run as it did as long as events were covered and the photography was good." Wolfe added that Okamoto was perceived as "a great guy, understanding, easygoing, and always willing to help someone, particularly in photography." Okamoto continued in this capacity until he retired in 1968.

Wolfe shared a story Okamoto often told about his consciousness of being Japanese American. This awareness came at an early age when he and his mother were waiting in line to purchase theatre tickets. Someone pushed ahead of them in line. Yoichi's mother turned to him and said that if that person were Japanese American that is how he would be remembered—as a pushy person. This left an impression on the young Okamoto and he always felt that whatever he did would be a reflection on other Japanese Americans. This experience made him very conscious of the image he conveyed.

Professional Contribution

According to Wolfe, "Okamoto made one of the most significant contributions to government photography, particularly White House photography, of anyone in our time. He set the standards of an up-to-date, in-depth look at the give-and-take of government and politics as it happened. This type of photography never existed before Okamoto." Until that time, most photography consisted of ceremonial setups and other planned photographs. Wolfe continued, using the staff nickname for Okamoto: "Oki's candid look at government through his photographic lens set new standards. Many later presidential photographers modeled their work on [his] style."

In describing a 1991 Austin, Texas, exhibition of primarily Okamoto photos entitled "LBJ: The White House Years," the *Dallas Morning News* wrote: "Granted unprecedented and almost unlimited access to the president, his family and staff, Mr. Okamoto and his team of White House photographers captured President Johnson as he forged civil-rights legislation, sought to create 'The Great Society,' and, in the decade of Vietnam, decided in 1968 not to seek reelection." The article continued to detail Okamoto's dramatic photographs that captured Johnson during moments of triumph and tragedy.

Okamoto listed his role models as Edward Steichen, a U.S. military signal corps photographer, and poet Carl Sandburg—both of whom came to dine with the family on several occasions according to Philip. The photographer Alfred Eisenstaedt was also an influencing force in Okamoto's life. Philip remembered his father as a perfectionist when it came to photography. "He was very critical of his work. He would be thrilled to find one shot in a roll of thirty-six that he liked."

Upon his retirement from the White House in 1968, Okamoto and two others founded a professional photo lab, Image, in Washington, D.C. Okamoto continued his work as a freelance photographer, assembling a long list of photo credits, including all the stage bills for the Kennedy Center of the Performing Arts in Washington, D.C., for a twelve-year period beginning in 1968.

Okamoto also received frequent assignments from such Washington institutions as the Smithsonian and the U.S. Chamber of Commerce. Many Okamoto photographs have been published in the *Smithsonian* magazine, including the first informal photos of Justice Warren Burger of the U. S. Supreme Court. The front and back cover photographs of one issue of the *Smithsonian* magazine were of Burger. Another Okamoto photograph of note was the last formal portrait and photograph of J. Edgar Hoover for the cover of *Time*. Okamoto, on an assignment from Smithsonian, photographed all the judges of the Supreme Court, both at the court and at home.

One hundred twenty of Okamoto's dramatic photographs of Johnson and the White House years are included in a book edited by Harry Middleton, the former Johnson speech writer who directs the LBJ Library and Museum. The book, *LBJ: The White House Years* was published in 1990 to coincide with the silver anniversary of Johnson's inauguration as the thirty-sixth president in 1965. (Johnson was sworn in as president after John F. Kennedy's assassination on November 22, 1963. He was elected to his own term in 1964, and inaugurated in January of the following year.)

For seven years prior to his death in 1985, Okamoto had been working on a book of photographs of Vienna and the surrounding Austrian countryside, making one or two trips to Austria each year and shooting over 500 rolls of film in the process. In 1987, Okamoto's widow, Paula, completed and published *Okamoto Sieht Wien: Die Stadt Seit Den Funfziger Jahren [Okamoto's Vienna]*, (Tafel Spitz Wien, 1987) featuring Okamoto's photographs. (The book was published in two versions, English and German.).

Okamoto's son, Philip, summed up his father's basic philosophy: "Whatever you choose to do, either professionally or as a hobby, learn all you can learn and do it as well as you can. In short, do it right or don't do it at all." Philip described his father as an avid reader, involved and interested in virtually all the arts, especially painting and sculpture. In addition, he had an intense love and appreciation for classical music.

Okamoto felt that he had an obligation to show the world that being Japanese was something to be proud of and not something to be ashamed of. In his business, professional, and personal life, Okamoto felt that he represented much more than himself—he represented the Japanese American. Okamoto's legacy is the wealth of stunning, dramatic photographs that set the standard for White House photography.

Sources:

Periodicals

Feeney, Susan. "Johnson Legacy Saluted." *Dallas Morning News*, April 7, 1990, p. 4A.
"Texas Travels: LBJ Exhibition." *Dallas Morning News*, January 20, 1991, p. 8G.

Other

Okamoto, Philip, telephone interview with Margaret Simon, July 7, 1994.
Wolfe, Frank, telephone interview with Margaret Simon, June 13, 1994.

—Sketch by Margaret Simon

Steven Okazaki
(1952–)
Filmmaker

Winning the Academy Award for Best Documentary Short Subject for his 1991 film, *Days of Waiting*, was a mixed blessing for Steven Okazaki. "What the Oscar means is that a lot of doors open," he told Terry Hong in an interview, "but those doors don't open all that wide if you happen to be Asian American or a documentary maker. There's an aura that goes with winning an Oscar. In some ways, winning has been a real detriment in terms of getting funding. People think that you're no longer the starving filmmaker and that suddenly you have access to a lot of money. So when projects get judged, people tend to say, 'Okazaki doesn't need this grant, let's give it to truly needy people.' So I've been having a hard time getting money."

While funding may not be abundant, Okazaki has remained an independent filmmaker, producing powerful documentaries and what he calls "quirky" features. During the past decade, the body of works from his production company, Farallon Films, has grown steadily. *Survivors*, the first film he made in English, features Hiroshima and Nagasaki survivors telling their stories and was one of the highest rated PBS documentaries of the 1982 season. *Unfinished Business*, which concerns three Japanese Americans who refused to enter U.S. internment camps during World War II, was nominated for an Oscar in 1985. Okazaki then took a break from documentaries to make *Living on Tokyo Time*, a low-budget comedy about a Japanese American nerd with a guitar and a new wife. In 1991 he won an Oscar for *Days of Waiting*, a documentary about artist Estelle Ishigo, a Caucasian woman who chose internment over separation from her Japanese American husband. *Troubled Paradise*, a look at the indigenous Hawaiian population and its native culture, followed in 1992.

Perhaps Okazaki's greatest strength as a filmmaker is his uncanny ability to humanize huge historical events by focusing on selected individual experiences. In his documentaries, Okazaki chooses Asian American subjects such as Asian American history and experiences. "The subject of a work has to be worth devoting two years of my life on," he told Hong. "I want to be able to relate to the subject, so oftentimes, my ethnic background comes into play."

Turning Black during the Summers

Born March 12, 1952, in Venice, California, Steven Okazaki is third-generation Japanese American. As the second oldest of five children and the only boy, Okazaki grew up in a working-class family in which his mother, Rosie, worked as a supermarket clerk and his father, Toll, as a machinist. "My father's name was actually Toru, a common Japanese name, but at the hospital, the name was spelled wrong and somehow it became just Toll."

Living in southern California, Okazaki spent his summers on the beach, he said, "turning black until we had to go back to school." He played in various rock bands in both junior high school and high school, an experience he would later draw on in his feature films. "It was all pretty boring," he joked, "No dark, ugly secrets."

In 1970, Okazaki moved north to studying filmmaking at San Francisco State University. "I wanted to get out of L.A.," he stated simply. In school, behind the camera for the first time, Okazaki created short works he described as "poignant, personal stories and mini-romantic comedies about boys and guitars." He added, "I didn't do any serious work until I got out of school and had to make a living."

Okazaki began his career making cultural and educational children's films for a company in Los Angeles that allowed him to shoot and produce his works in San Francisco. "But the educational market bottomed out in '78 with Proposition 13, which meant that school budgets were cut drastically and the first thing they stopped buying was educational materials." For a few years, Okazaki "floundered with little jobs." He emphasized, "They were really *bad* jobs, doing commercials and some PBS programs. The highlight of that period was when I quit. I was working on a commercial for AM/PM Minimart and I finally decided that I would never do another commercial again."

The Three-Decade Promise

At age twenty-seven, Okazaki made a commitment to himself that before he reached his thirtieth year, he "would make a contribution to the Asian American community by doing something in film." The result was *Survivors*, a documentary about Hiroshima and Nagasaki, which he completed at exactly age thirty. What was unique about *Survivors* was Okazaki's approach. The film was not a direct antinuclear, antiwar statement. It was not a straightforward historical account of the bombings and their aftermath. Instead, Okazaki took the large-scale, immeasurable event and focused on human-scaled details. The resulting film—a thirty-five-minute work which focused on twenty atomic bomb survivors telling their own stories, in their own words—further magnified the more than forty-year-old tragedy, creating a more lasting impact on audiences.

The humanizing of historical events so huge as to be unfathomable became a trademark of Okazaki's filmmaking. In his second film, *Unfinished Business*, he explored the incarceration of Americans of Japanese descent during World War II by focusing on three men who resisted Executive Order 9066, which called for the cattle-like

Steven Okazaki

roundup of Japanese Americans. Rather than tell the story of 110,000 people, Okazaki chose to focus on the lives of Gordon Hirabayashi, Minoru Yasui, and Fred Korematsu, three Americans who deliberately violated government directives and tested the constitutionality of the wartime laws. Deemed "the most powerful and comprehensive film yet on the internment" by the *Los Angeles Times*, *Unfinished Business* was nominated for an Academy Award in 1985.

Two years later, Okazaki made his first feature film, *Living on Tokyo Time*. In creating the low-budget comedy, Okazaki drew on his own guitar-playing experiences. "I took mental notes during my wayward youth," he quipped. Some of those notes were used to create Ken, a third-generation Japanese American whose one source of happiness is playing in a rock band. In spite of the leather jacket he wears, Ken is undeniably a nerd. He finds himself married to a beautiful Japanese woman escaping a bad relationship, who comes to the United States seeking solace and a green card. Ken falls in love with his new wife, but the relationship fails. In the end Ken is alone again with just his guitar.

Although *Tokyo Time* seemed to be only a light, screwball comedy, it challenged the stereotype of the Asian American as a straight-A, successful professional. According to the ever-popular model-minority myth, Asian kids are not supposed to work menial jobs, become punk rockers, and have sex. Okazaki's leading man is indeed a minority, but the hopeless, hapless Ken is far from a model of anything.

Okazaki followed up the feature with his Oscar-winning documentary, *Days of Waiting*, in which he turned again to the subject of Japanese American concentration camps. Although it began as a film about a number of camp internees, *Days of Waiting* finally emerged as a tribute to artist Estelle Ishigo, one of the few Caucasian internees. Rather than be separated from her Japanese American husband, she chose to follow him to the camp in Heart Mountain, Wyoming. Ishigo documented her experiences through hundreds of drawings and paintings, creating a haunting record for future generations.

In 1992, Okazaki produced the acclaimed PBS documentary, *Troubled Paradise*, which offers a view of Hawaii that contrasts sharply with the idealized one presented in commercials and tourism campaigns. While the film is a celebration of the richness of the native Hawaiian culture, it is also an examination of the social and political problems facing the indigenous population, including rampant unemployment, poverty, low life expectancy and high infant mortality rates.

The Latest Projects

Okazaki's most recent works include a short documentary, a drama, and a feature film. He described his half-hour documentary, *Hunting Tigers*, as "a totally *un*serious documentary about pop culture in Tokyo." What began as a serious film about Japanese writer Kenzaburo Oe transformed into a "fun film" as a result of scheduling problems. Okazaki asked the writer—who is a good friend and is in the film—what it was about the current Japanese culture that was troubling him. Oe replied that young people today are too spoiled and too affluent. Okazaki took that statement to "four strange and interesting artists—a pop singer, a performance artist, a dancer, and a collage maker" and recorded their reactions.

Another new work, *American Sons*, which Okazaki described as "a dramatic piece that is based on interviews with real people," is already eliciting strong responses. "I showed it to about four or five people in the editing room and they cried." He made the film because of the increasing incidences of serious violence done to Asian Americans in the United States. "I feel Asian American films have been too polite, too educational in the past, and I've been guilty of this as much as anyone," explained Okazaki. "This film is different. It's very angry, confrontational. It doesn't skirt around the issue of racism; it throws it at you. I'm very anxious to have it out, especially in light of the way the media continues to treat Asians as scapegoats for many problems in this country."

American Sons was, in part, also a reaction to the recent influx of Asian and Asian American films on the big screen. "I have a desire to depict a side of Asian American life that most people don't see or don't want to see." While he admits to enjoying the recent films, including *The Joy Luck Club, Wedding Banquet, Farewell My Concubine,* and *Scent of Green Papaya,* Okazaki said he recognizes "an inherent problem with mainstream, non-Asian audiences." He commented, "In all the recent Asian and Asian American films, there's still the exotic Asian thing going on. Asian women are depicted as mysterious and deep while Asian men are still portrayed as being effeminate and sexless. I don't think that the gay Asian male character was a brave step away from any of the stereotypes. The gay Asian male is exactly what white audiences want. They're more comfortable with him than with an Asian character who is really masculine."

The Continuing Trilogy

Claiming he needed "a creative break" from making documentaries, Okazaki recently made his second feature, *The Lisa Theory.* It is his first film without any leading Asian American characters and, he said, it features "a wonderfully weird cast of promising newcomers" in a story about rock and roll, skateboarding, and getting dumped. "I got a bunch of grunge rockers hanging around the office and together we created a romantic comedy," he told Hong. The film's expected release date is late 1994.

Together with his wife, journalist Peggy Orenstein, Okazaki is currently working on a documentary commemorating the fiftieth anniversary of the Hiroshima bombing. A co-production with PBS and NHK (the Japanese national broadcasting company), the film is both a retelling of the infamous day as well as a look at today's Japan on the verge of reviving its military. The film is scheduled to be broadcast in both the United States and Japan on the actual anniversary, August 6, 1995.

For now, Okazaki's plans for the future include, he said, "a third film about dumb boys and guitars." Together with *Living on Tokyo Time* and *The Lisa Theory,* this film "will complete the trilogy." Afterward, Okazaki said his follow-up film will be "a story about a screwed-up Japanese American family."

If he weren't making films, Okazaki "honestly doesn't know what [he] would be doing." He confessed that there is a part of him that wants "to disappear, have kids, and go surfing for a couple of years." But then there is the responsibility of having won that Oscar. "I take it as encouragement to keep doing what I'm doing, to stay independent and make the films I want to make."

Sources:

Okazaki, Steven, telephone interviews with Terry Hong, February 15, 1994 and May 14, 1994.

—Sketch by Terry Hong

Ayub Khan Ommaya
(1930–)
Neurosurgeon

Ayub Khan Ommaya

Trying to fit Dr. Ayub Khan Ommaya into one professional category is a futile exercise: he has an array of interests and expertise. He is an accomplished authority in all his endeavors—particularly as a neurosurgeon and a scientist. His inspiration, he told Shazia Rafi in an interview, came from his father who "in addition to being a Commissioned Officer in the Viceroy's 12th Bengal Lancers, was a Sufi (religious mystic). . . . As early as eight years old I was fascinated by the interplay of religion and science."

Ayub Khan Ommaya was born April 14, 1930, in Mian Channu, a small rural town in Pakistan, to a French mother and a Pakistani father. He grew up speaking French, English, Urdu, Pashto, and Panjabi. Ommaya told Rafi, "From an early age I was influenced by two streams of culture—an Eastern, Islamic, and especially Sufi one from my father, and a western European one, particularly in the realm of classical music and literature, from my mother."

Early Inspiration

At age fifteen Ommaya read a magazine article about the work of Dr. Wilder Penfield that set the path for his profession. "Dr. Penfield was the pioneer neurosurgeon who made the first clear observations of the brain mechanisms of consciousness; this made me decide to become a neurosurgeon," related Ommaya. He also read about the work of Sir Hugh Cairns, professor of neurosurgery at Oxford University, and was determined to study under his direction after completing his medical training in Pakistan in 1954.

For his academic excellence and versatility, Ommaya was selected as a Rhodes scholar to Oxford where he studied physiology, biochemistry, psychology, and philosophy. His doctorate focused on the mechanisms of traumatic unconsciousness, Ommaya explained, "a subject which has remained my lifelong work because in addition to enabling me to contribute to the field of biomechanics of nervous system injury, it also allowed me to study the reintegration of consciousness after traumatic coma."

Accomplished Career

Ommaya's path from Oxford to the United States was accidental. He had planned to go back and open the first neurosurgery department at King Edward Medical College in Lahore, Pakistan. "K.E. said they were going to advertise the job of the first professor of neurosurgery when I sent in my application," Ommaya told Rafi. "After

three months, some bureaucrat sent me a yellow postcard saying, 'Your qualifications are not adequate'. . . I had had forty papers published by then!"

A fellow Rhodes scholar, Dr. Barry Bloomberg, who later won the Nobel Prize for discovering the hepatitus-B virus, had started working at the National Institutes of Health (NIH) in Maryland. He suggested to Ommaya that he come and work at NIH for awhile. "I had no intention of staying till that yellow card arrived," he told Rafi. NIH arranged for Ommaya's immigration under the exemption that no American scientist could replace his work.

Ommaya eventually became the chief of neurosurgery at NIH. His many appointments in the United States have included Chief of Applied Neuroscience Research, NIH; Chief Medical Adviser, Department of Transportation; Chairman of Committee on Head Injury, North Atlantic Treaty Organization (NATO); Advisory Panels at the U.S. House of Representatives, Bureau of Disease Prevention and Environmental Control. In addition, he continues to serve as consultant and adviser on many international bodies such as the International Red Cross and the International Brain Research Organization, among others. He has published extensively in the United States and abroad.

Ommaya's work at NIH also allowed him to do research and develop new methods of neurosurgery. "I was able to lay the foundations for a novel theory of consciousness based on the evolution of emotions," he explained to Rafi.

"I was also able to contribute some practical methods to neurosurgery and medicine. These included the Cerebrospinal Fluid Reservoire, the first port system enabling diagnostic and therapeutic treatments of the nervous system which can bypass the blood brain barrier. Also, methods of diagnosing vascular malformations of the spinal cord for diagnosis and treatment of leaks of cerebrospinal fluid and for intra-tumural treatment of brain tumors."

Remembering His Roots

Ommaya, while successful in his chosen profession in the United States, remains steeped in his culture and maintains strong ties to Pakistan. He was one of the founding presidents of the Association of Pakistani Physicians of North America. He is a member of the Resident Associate Program at the Smithsonian where he lectures on Reform, Science and Politics in the World of Islam. He is also working to establish a Brain Institute in Pakistan. The government of Pakistan awarded him the Sitari-i-Imtiaz (Star of Achievement) in 1982.

Of his experiences as an Asian American, Ommaya told Rafi, "You have to be not only as good as other Americans but better. . . . Being a first-generation Asian is even more difficult because you don't have connections. In any career you need a mentor; you need guidance through the system. I had trained in England and had no such guide. During my years at NIH I was offered full professorships at UCLA and University of Pennsylvania. I should have taken those offers but there was no one more experienced to take interest in my career development and advise me. I try now to be that person for others like myself."

At age sixty-four, far from thinking about retirement, Ommaya is engaged in new research and is discovering new frontiers in his field. He is currently, among his other appointments, director of the Center for Interdisciplinary Brain Research, where he is testing a new invention, a spinal fluid flow-driven artificial organ for treating type–I diabetes which may also be used to deliver useful substances to the brain in other nervous system disorders such as Parkinson's and Alzheimer's. "I am also continuing my work on head injuries using functional MRI scanning coupled with brain temperature studies. This research will have applications for the early diagnosis and treatment of head injuries as well as testing my theory of consciousness," he told Rafi. In addition to his professional duties, he immerses himself with equal vigor into his hobbies—Italian and French opera singing and, in his words, "good conversation with my family and friends."

Sources:

Center for Interdisciplinary Brain Research. "Ayub Khan Ommaya, M.D." Biographical materials.
Ommaya, Ayub Khan, telephone interview with Shazia Rafi, May 12, 1994.

—Sketch by Shazia Rafi

Ellison Onizuka
(1946–1986)
Astronaut

When Ellison Onizuka was a boy growing up in a small town in Hawaii, he dreamed, like many youngsters, of conquering space and becoming an astronaut. Unlike other boys, whose childhood fantasies soon gave way to other pursuits, Onizuka's interest was unwavering. Over the years, he worked steadily toward his goal and in 1985, as part of the Discovery shuttle crew, he became the first Asian American in space. Later that year he was chosen to be on the crew of another shuttle mission, and the future seemed boundless. But the childhood dreams came to a nightmarish end on January 28, 1986, when, as the nation watched in horror, the Challenger space shuttle exploded seventy-three seconds after liftoff. All seven crew members, including Onizuka, perished.

Early Life in Hawaii

Ellison Shoji Onizuka was born June 24, 1946, in the village of Kealakekua, on the Kona coast of Hawaii. He was the third of four children born to Masimitsu and Mitsue Onizuka. Onizuka's grandparents had emigrated from Japan to work as contract laborers on the island's sugar plantations.

It was, in some ways, an idyllic and ordinary childhood. He explored the island's mountains and caves with friends, picked coffee beans, and played basketball. He also helped out in the small general store run by his mother in Keopu, a coffee-growing community. His mother said he was a good, but not excellent, student, but early on, he displayed a fascination for how things worked. "When he was a young child, we would tease him because he would break things apart and not be able to put them back together," his mother said in a 1986 interview with the *New York Times*.

Space Dreams

Onizuka also showed an early interest in space. He loved to look up at the stars through a telescope at Honolulu's Bishop Museum and constantly daydreamed of imaginary spacecrafts that would take him on distant voyages. Later, as a teenager in the early 1960s, he closely followed the progress of the Mercury space program. His ambition baffled his parents. "He had it inside of him, like a dream," his mother told *the New York Times*. "We didn't understand it, but he knew what he would do."

"Ellison always had it in his mind to become an astronaut but he was too embarrassed to tell anyone," his mother told *Time* magazine after his death. "When he was growing up, there were no Asian astronauts, no black astronauts, just white ones. His dream seemed too big." While in Konawaena High School, Onizuka had other passions that he pursued with intensity. During those years, he became interested in Buddhism and was involved in the 4-H Federation and Boy Scouts, reaching Eagle Scout rank in his senior year.

Onizuka left the islands in 1964 to study aerospace engineering at the University of Colorado in Boulder, as a member of the Air Force Reserve Officer Training Corps. There he excelled in aerodynamics and astronautics. "He felt that discovery was the name of the game in engineering and science," Michael Francis, a fellow student, told the *New York Times*. He received both a bachelor of science degree and a master of science degree in 1969.

That same year he married Loran Leiko Yoshida, a fellow Hawaiian who was also studying in Colorado at a nearby college. The couple later had two daughters, Janelle Mitsue, who was born in 1969, and Darien Lei Sizue, who was born in 1975.

In 1970, Onizuka entered active duty with the U.S. Air Force and became an aerospace flight test engineer with the Air Logistics Center at McClellan Air Force Base near Sacramento. His job was to devise tests to adapt aircraft no new functions and equipment. One of his projects was a system for using heavy helicopters to salvage jets that went down in Vietnam.

He applied for the Air Force Test Pilot School at Edwards Air Force Base and entered in 1974. Fellow students and instructors remembered him for his spirit and for keeping morale up in the demanding program. Onizuka, by then a colonel, stayed at Edwards to become an instructor in the classroom and in the air.

His training as an astronaut began four years later, when he became one of thirty-five people selected by NASA. The family moved near the Johnson Space Center in Houston. His colleagues in the air force and NASA described him as an easygoing professional who could simplify complicated problems. In 1979, he completed a one-year training and evaluation period, making him eligible for assignment as a mission specialist on future space shuttle flight crews. Before his first shuttle crew assignment, Onizuka worked on orbiter test and checkout teams and launch support crews at the Kennedy Space Center. He also helped on numerous other technical assignments.

His turn came in January 1985, as part of the crew of the first space shuttle Department of Defense mission. During the mission, Onizuka was responsible for the primary payload activities. The Discovery completed forty-eight orbits of the Earth before landing at Kennedy Space Center. Despite his training, Onizuka told a friend that the explosive force of the Discovery launching was

Ellison Onizuka

amazing and unnerving, according to the *New York Times* story. "You're really aware that you're on top of a monster, you're totally at the mercy of the vehicle," Onizuka said.

Onizuka became the first Hawaiian, the first Japanese American, and the first Buddhist astronaut, and was the pride of those communities. He spoke at their events, participated in their festivals, and constantly thanked them for helping along his way. Onizuka took pride in his heritage. When he returned from his visits home, he brought back Kona coffee, crates of pineapples, and macadamia nuts for colleagues. Although his dream has come true, he remained unchanged, his family and friends said. "Around us, he was just El," said Claude Onizuka, his older brother, in the 1986 *New York Times* article. "When he'd come home, he'd drink beer and talk story and be just another guy.

In an act of devotion to his faith, Onizuka presented a medallion with a wisteria blossom, the symbol of his Jodo Shinshu faith, to the abbot of Jodo Shinshu Buddhism the year before he died. He had worn the medallion on the Discovery mission.

After the Discovery flight, Onizuka focused on his second space shuttle mission and looked forward to going back in space. But he was also aware of the potential risks. Lorna Onizuka told a Honolulu newspaper that her husband had collected the insurance policies and documents that she would need if he didn't return from the Challenger mission.

"It was so beautiful up there that we didn't want to come back," he reportedly told a neighbor at a welcome-home party for the Discovery crew. On the Challenger, one of his tasks was to film Halley's Comet with a hand-held camera, an assignment he relished. "I'll be looking at Halley's Comet. They tell me I'll have one of the best views around."

It was a view he never lived to see. After Onizuka's death, Bishop Seigen Yamaoka, head of the Buddhist Churches of America, told the *New York Times:* "As a test pilot and an astronaut, he had to deal with life and death. As long as death is seen as the enemy, you fight it, and become more attached to life. In time he came to the realization that death is not an enemy to defeat, but a compassionate friend."

In 1991, the Ellison S. Onizuka Space Center, a two-million-dollar museum built in his memory, was opened at Keahole Airport in Kona, Hawaii, not far from where the young Onizuka first dreamed of the stars.

Sources:

Cohen, Daniel and Susan Cohen. *"Heroes of the Challenger."* New York: Pocket Books, 1986.

Periodicals

Time, February 10, 1986. "Ellison Onizuka: 1946–1986."
Yoshihashi, Pauline. Ellison Onizuka profile in "Three Boys' Dreams of Space, Three Deaths in the Sky." *New York Times*, February 11, 1986.

Other

NASA. Biographical data sheet.

—*Sketch by Ferdinand M. de Leon*

Yoko Ono

(1933–)

Artist, filmmaker, musician

Yoko Ono is an avante-garde artist and filmmaker who became popular in New York's underground art scene in the early 1960s and then became internationally famous in 1968, first as the girlfriend and then as the wife of the late John Lennon, the former Beatle. As a member of the loosely banded group of artists known as Fluxus, Ono made several films, contributed art and sculpture to shows, and worked on many staged productions. With Lennon she orchestrated much of the couple's peace activist performances and the famous "bed-in" of 1969. She and Lennon also formed and recorded with the Plastic Ono Band, and she collaborated on many of his compositions, including "Imagine." In the financially and legally stormy years following the breakup of the Beatles, Ono managed Lennon's finances and parlayed them into one of the largest personal fortunes in the country. Since Lennon's murder in 1980, Ono has recorded two albums, had a retrospective of her art and films at the Whitney Museum in New York, and has written and produced a rock opera for an off-Broadway theatre in New York.

Yoko Ono was born in Tokyo, Japan, on February 18, 1933, into one of Japan's most prominent and wealthy families. Her mother, Isoko, is from the Yasuda family, one of the richest and most powerful families in the country; her father, Eisuke, was descended from a samurai and became the head of the Bank of Japan. As a child, Ono went to the Gakushuin School, which usually enrolls only members of the royal family. When she was seven, her family moved to Long Island, New York, but they returned to Japan just before the outbreak of World War II.

During the war, when the Americans began bombing Tokyo, the Ono children were sent to live in a country house their mother had especially built. Describing it for *Interview* in February of 1989, Ono said, "So instead of going to the [Royal Family's] palace with my school friends . . . my mother thought we should go to the real world. She bought farm land out in the country and had a new house built, all without seeing it. . . . But the farmers [building the house] were not dumb, they just wanted my mother's money. . . . The house didn't have all of its ceiling. There was hardly any food. It was very rough. We were practically starving out there."

Rebelling in America

After the war, Ono briefly attended Gakushuin University in Tokyo before moving with her family to the United States. This time the family settled in Scarsdale, an affluent suburb of New York City. Here, Ono continued her studies at Sarah Lawrence College, where she devoted nearly all her energy to writing poetry and short stories and virtually none to her studies. She remained at Sarah Lawrence for three years and then dropped out without a degree.

In 1957, Ono met and married Toshi Ichiyanagi, a Japanese musician who was in New York to study at the Juilliard School of Music. Describing the marriage for *Interview* magazine, Ono said, "[The marriage was] definitely a rebellion. It was a way to get out of my family situation. He and I were more like roommates." Ichiyanagi was well connected in the New York avante-garde scene at the time, and through him, Ono began to make contacts with luminaries of the avante-garde such as John Cage and Merce Cunningham. In 1958 she began showing her work, mostly events or conceptual art pieces in which the

Yoko Ono

audience or viewer of the art played a significant role in its development.

The High Priestess of Happenings

In 1960 Ono began hosting concerts in her loft at 112 Chambers Street. Performers at these events were from the loosely defined school known as the Fluxus movement. Fluxus art was in part inspired by the composer John Cage's use of everyday noises in his compositions and his introduction of chance into performance. In the catalogue essay that accompanied Ono's 1989 Whitney retrospective, Barbara Haskell described two typical Fluxus pieces from this period: "Allison Knowles' *Proposition*, [in which] performers came out on a stage, made a salad, and exited; [and] La Monte Young's *Composition 1960 #10 to Bob Morris* [which] directed a performer to draw a straight line and follow it."

In 1961, Ono gave her first public concert. It was at the Village Gate in New York and, as Haskell wrote, "consisted of a taped background of mumbled words and wild laughter, musicians playing atonal music, and a performer intoning unemotionally about peeling a grapefruit, squeezing lemons, and counting the hairs on a dead child." Also in 1961 Ono began a series of events at Carnegie Recital Hall that she would stage periodically until 1968. Her first program included *A Piece for Strawberries and Violin* in which a performer repeatedly stood up and sat down in front of a table stacked with dishes for ten minutes. At the end of the piece, Haskell reported, the performer would smash the dishes accompanied by "a rhythmic background of repeated syllables, a tape recording of moans and words spoken backwards, and an aria of high-pitched wails sung by Ms. Ono." In summing up the artistic philosophy of the Fluxus school and Ono's work from this period, Haskell said, "In common with other Fluxus events, Ono's performances jettisoned conventional aesthetics in order to jolt viewers out of self-satisfied assumptions about art."

In 1964 Ono left her marriage to Ichiyanagi and married an underground film producer named Tony Lake. Also in that year she published *Grapefruit*, a collection of surrealist poems and meditations. In 1966, Ono was invited to participate in a multimedia conference/show in London called the "Destruction in Art Symposium." A piece from that symposium that sticks out in the minds of many critics and art historians is a piece called *Cut* in which Ono sat on a stage while audience members cut away her clothes—a white wedding gown—until she was completely naked. She remained in London after the symposium and became such a regular in the London art scene of the time that she became known, according to Haskell's essay, as the High Priestess of the Happening. (Although John Perreault of the *Village Voice* disputes the accuracy of the name, suggesting that "Happenings . . . usually had several things going on at once, [while] the Fluxus event presented single images or occurrences, often, as in Yoko Ono's work, with a Zen-like calm.")

Ono's work of this period was very much based on audience participation. She began exhibiting at London's Indica Gallery such works as *Apple*, which featured an apple on a pedestal that viewers were invited to bite; *Painting to Hammer Nail In*, which was a wood panel with an attached hammer that viewers were encouraged to pound nails into; and *Cleaning Piece*, which consisted of a white cloth, a dark glass box and the instructions "clean it."

From its beginning, the Fluxus movement had been very much involved in filmmaking, and Ono had made several films. In 1966, she made what is perhaps her best-known and most enduring film, *Bottoms*, eighty minutes of nothing but rear-end views of people walking on a treadmill. The film's soundtrack consisted only of what the people were saying as they were being filmed.

Meeting John Lennon

In 1968 Ono met Lennon, who was enthralled by the message of her work, at a show of hers at the Indica Gallery. Both were married at the time to other people, but they began seeing each other and were married a year later, on March 20, 1969, after they had both gotten divorces. By marrying Lennon, Ono instantly became an international celebrity, drawing an amount of attention few could imagine. The couple staged an open honeymoon in Amsterdam, and then, in the spring of 1969, went to Toronto for the now legendary "bed-in," during which Lennon and Ono sat in bed promoting world peace, especially an end to America's war in Southeast Asia, which by that time had spread beyond Vietnam into Cambodia and Laos. The bed-in was attended by many celebrities, including the LSD guru and former Harvard professor Timothy Leary and the comedian/musician Tommy Smothers. Lennon's song "Give Peace A Chance," recorded at the bed-in, became a hit and remains today an anthem of peace activists around the world.

The intensity of international stardom put a strain on Ono's ability to continue doing her work in the way she had prior to her marriage. In 1971 she gave what essentially became her last show of this period. It was at the Everson Museum in Syracuse, New York, and because of her relationship with Lennon, it became a circus of Beatle fans who camped out for days prior to the show's opening to catch a glimpse of the former Beatle. She realized that this atmosphere was counter to her views of art and exhibiting. She began recording and performing with Lennon in his solo work after the breakup of the Beatles. Though Lennon's work was mainly political in nature and decidedly mainstream, Yoko's was still avante-garde. The mix of the two was often less than a commercial success, and for years Ono was blasted by critics for having a negative impact on Lennon's music.

In 1975, Ono and Lennon had their first child, Sean. (Each had one child from previous marriages.) After Sean's birth, Ono began running the vast enterprise of financial holdings Lennon had accumulated through the years, while John took on the day-to-day chores of raising their son. Ono became a notoriously savvy investor in art, real estate, and cattle, and she single-handedly transformed Lennon's large portfolio into one of the country's largest personal fortunes, today estimated variously at between $500 million and $1 billion.

Lennon's Murder

For the remainder of the seventies Lennon and Ono left the public eye. They traveled extensively and spent their time primarily raising their family. Then in 1980, they returned to the recording studio for the first time in five years to work on an album featuring seven compositions by Lennon and seven by Ono. The album was called *Double Fantasy.* Very shortly after its release, the couple was returning home from a recording session when Lennon was brutally murdered—shot six times at close range—right in front of Ono on the sidewalk outside the Dakota, their upper west side apartment building.

In the years following Lennon's murder, Ono has kept a low profile. In 1981 she released an album, *Season of Glass,* which caused some controversy for its cover, which showed the blood-stained broken pair of eyeglasses John was wearing when he was killed, and for a song that consisted of gunshots followed by wailing. In the *New York*

Times of August 5, 1981, Ono defended both decisions saying, "What was I supposed to do, avoid the subject?. . . A lot of people advised me that I shouldn't put that on the cover of the record, but I wanted the whole world to see those glasses with blood on them and to realize that John had been *killed.* It wasn't like he died of old age or drugs or something."

Ono did little in the areas of art or performance throughout most of the eighties. She made videos and some films, and collaborated on several John Lennon memorial concerts and albums. In 1989, the Whitney Museum of American Art in New York staged a retrospective of her work from the sixties, and the Museum of Modern Art showed several of her films, along with those by other Fluxus artists. As of early 1994, she was preparing a rock opera for the WPA Theater in New York City called *New York Rock.*

Ono has been the target of criticism and jokes for more than twenty years. She has been blamed with breaking up the Beatles, something no one with any first-hand knowledge of that band's disintegration finds even remotely possible. As Perreault wrote in the *Village Voice:* "Whether she had anything to do with that or not, they would have broken up anyway. Intelligent little boys often grow up; perhaps their fans do not. Furthermore, isn't it clear that a good part of the hostility to Yoko Ono was racist, sexist, anti-adult and anti-avante-garde?" Ono herself commented on the rage she inspired in people in *Interview:* "Maybe the way John nearly flaunted the fact that he loved me so much was part of the cause. But Paul and Linda [McCartney] have been together for ages now, and he's still a popular person. All in all, though, if John had married a blond upper-crust English lady there would not have been the same sort of reaction. . . . The other side of it was Asian-bashing, it's as simple as that."

Sources:

Periodicals

Palmer, Robert. "Yoko Ono Asks: 'Was I Supposed to Avoid the Subject?,'" *New York Times.* August 5, 1981, p. C17.

Perreault, John. "Yoko Ono at the Whitney: Age of Bronze." *Village Voice,* February 7, 1989, p. 29.

Sessums, Kevin. "Yoko: Life after Lennon." *Interview,* February, 1989, pp. 77–80.

Other

Haskell, Barbara. "Yoko Ono: Objects," Essay published in conjunction with the show "Yoko Ono: Objects, Films." New York: The Whitney Museum of American Art, 1989.

—Sketch by Jim Henry

Alfonso Ossorio
(1916–1990)
Artist

Alfonso Ossorio was an important artist of the New York School, a mid-century group of legendary abstract expressionists that included artists Jackson Pollack, Lee Krasner, and Clyfford Still. Ossorio's work hangs in some of America's premiere museums including the Metropolitan Museum of Art, the Whitney Museum of American Art, the Museum of Modern Art, and the Guggenheim. Later in life, Ossorio dedicated himself to the creation of a large arboretum and sculpture garden, called The Creeks.

Alfonso Ossorio was born on August 2, 1916, in Manila, Philippines, the fourth of six sons, into a wealthy and racially mixed family. His father, a sugar plantation owner and processor, was Spanish and his mother was of Philippine, Spanish, and Chinese descent. At the age of eight, Ossorio was sent abroad to be educated in England. He attended St. Richard's, a Catholic prep school, and at age fourteen he came to the United States to study at the Portsmouth Priory, a school run by Benedictine monks in Rhode Island. By this time he was already very interested in art and showed an extraordinary aptitude for it. During the summers of his junior and senior years of high school, Ossorio studied wood engraving and printing at St. Dominic's Press in England. During the second of these summers, the young Ossorio produced and had hand printed a small book of his poems and wood engravings entitled *Sidrach, Misach, and Abendnego.*

In 1934 Ossorio entered Harvard where he chose to study fine arts. He continued to work mainly in wood engravings and watercolors during his college years. As an undergraduate, he produced an impressive body of work. He made wood engravings for Sheed and Ward, the Catholic publishing house, covers for the quarterly journal *Liturgical Arts*, the cover for an anthology of new writing published by New Directions, and the cover for a translation of poems by Rimbaud, also published by New Directions. He made drawings for the Harvard *Advocate* and designed costumes and programs for two of the college's Poet's Theater productions—the world premiere of T.S. Eliot's *Murder in the Cathedral* and Euripides' *Alcestis*.

Surrealism

Ossorio graduated from Harvard in 1938 and enrolled in the Rhode Island School of Design (RISD), where he studied graphic design. In 1939 he left RISD, took an extended vacation in the West, and then rented a studio in Boston. Early in 1941, Ossorio married Bridget Hubrecht, a woman he had met a year earlier and who was the subject of many of his engravings and drawings. In November of that year, Ossorio had his first one-man show in New York at the Wakefield Gallery. He had one more show at the Wakefield before being inducted into the army in 1943. Stationed in Illinois, he nearly died during a routine surgical procedure and spent most of his time in the Mayo General Hospital where he did medical drawings until his discharge in 1946. Twenty-two of these ink and watercolor drawings were exhibited in 1945 at the Moritimer Brandt Gallery in New York.

B.H. Friedman discussed the exhibit in his critical biography *Alfonso Ossorio*: "One cannot help but wonder how much of his public function in the Medical Corps carried over into these watercolors. They, like much of this exhibition, are grotesque—obsessed with scarred, burned, or diseased flesh; distorted or masked features; anatomical fragments and amputations." Ossorio was gaining a reputation as an American surrealist whose paintings were more absurd and darkly outlandish than Salvador Dali's, then the reigning figure among surrealists. He was also being compared to Bruegel, Bosch, and Goya for his representations of the horrific.

Introduction to Abstract Expressionism

In 1949 Ossorio met the American painter Jackson Pollack and his wife Lee Krasner. They all became good friends. Through the Pollacks he met the French painter Jean Dubuffet and became immersed in what was then becoming the East Hampton, Long Island art scene. Ossorio began collecting the works of some of the eminent abstract expressionists of the time including William deKooning and Pollack.

In 1951 Ossorio began a hectic schedule of exhibiting his own work. His first was in Paris at the Studio Paul Facchetti and consisted of a large series of abstract watercolors he had done while in the Philippines and some new experimental paintings in oil and enamel on canvas mounted on shaped plywood. These three-dimensional works were the precursors of the "assemblages" and "congregations" that would distinguish Ossorio in later years. The show received mixed reviews in the French press but it sold well.

Ossorio had a show in New York six days after the close of the Paris show, which was intended to include some of the large, abstract works from Paris. These, however, were stuck aboard ships due to a dock workers' strike and didn't arrive on time. The show was a disaster. That year, however, did have a bright spot in that Ossorio bought a house on Long Island, a rambling old estate called The Creeks, which he would later turn into an arboretum and sculpture garden.

In the mid-fifties Ossorio began taking his art in a new direction. While the purists of the New York School of abstract expressionism were paring down their paintings, achieving a coolly detached and minimalist effect, Ossorio was experimenting with the old tenets of cubism. As

Friedman wrote, "He was obsessed with breaking through underlying cubist organization and further fragmenting cubist fragmentation." In 1956, Ossorio exhibited some of his new works at the Betty Parsons Gallery in New York.

Assemblages

Beginning in 1960 Ossorio began producing works in three dimensions that were variously referred to as collages or montages, both of which had been done by the cubists, and would later be renamed assemblages by Ossorio himself. In 1963 Ossorio showed his assemblages at Cordier and Ekstrom. It was reviewed in the *New York Herald Tribune* in an unsigned review: "When does the vulgar become the beautiful? Ossorio's constructions are celebrations of the ugly, the terrifying and the screamingly garish. His materials seem like the bizarre treasures of the mad. When combined they blaze in obsessive *horror-vacuui* upon shapes recalling religious altars. But the effect is dazzling—the control never less than arresting and the total statement, one of blood-curdling beauty." Ossorio continued working and showing in this new style and his reputation as a serious artist—although one difficult to pin down with a label—grew. His shows were widely reviewed by the nation's top art critics and his works were being acquired by top museums.

In the 1970s Ossorio worked mainly at The Creeks, his Long Island estate. Through the 1960s he had been collecting exotic trees for the arboretum and by the mid-seventies there were some six hundred varieties present on the eighty-acre grounds. He began adding large outdoor sculptures to the grounds in the mid-seventies, made in classic Ossorio style of found objects inlaid in poured concrete—assemblages, in short. His devotion to The Creeks was evidenced by his willingness to sell works from his impressive collection to finance its building. Describing The Creeks and Ossorio's devotion to it, Friedman wrote, "There [The Creeks] things are freed from the need to be useful or the humiliation of being useless. The collection of objects, the total environmental burgeons, spills out onto the lawn and driveway island and into cleared areas of the woods and down to the pond waterfront. . . . The Creeks is surely Ossorio's single most important *congregation,* as much as an extension of himself as was the Watts Tower for Simon Rodia or the *Palais Ideal* for Ferdinand Cheval. . . . The Creeks is Ossorio's Factory of Dreams."

In the year before his death, there was a highly successful retrospective of Ossorio's work at the Benton Gallery in Southampton, Long Island, where interest in the artist was renewed. Ossorio died in New York City at the New York University Medical Center on December 6, 1990. He was seventy-four years old.

Sources:

Friedman, B.H. *Alfonso Ossorio.* New York: Harry N. Abrams, Inc., 1973.

—Sketch by Jim Henry

George Ow, Jr.
(1943–)
Businessman, arts benefactor

Almost six decades ago, George Ow, Sr., arrived in the United States with two dollars in his pocket. He struggled and triumphed in his adopted country, making land investments that others first laughed at. In 1970, he shifted primary responsibility of the family's many ventures to his son. Today George Ow, Jr., is one of the most powerful, successful businessmen in California. While the family business enterprises are extensive throughout Santa Cruz County and beyond—including large shopping centers, retail outlets, a tennis club, and a book publishing company, to name just a few of the ventures—Ow has also developed a reputation as a reliable, generous supporter of artists and social causes. From bestowing academic scholarships to producing documentaries to commissioning works from struggling artists, Ow is a stalwart supporter of helping others achieve the American dream.

The Ow success story began two generations ago with Lam Pon, Ow's grandfather. Before persistent racism drove him back to China in 1931, Lam Pon helped establish one of the first apple-drying businesses in the United States, founded his own restaurant, and opened the first Chinatown bank in Santa Cruz. In spite of his own frustrations, Lam Pon urged his eldest son to return to the United States and seek his fortune in California. As a teenager, Ow's father returned to Santa Cruz and reconnected with the network of family and friends Lam Pon had left behind. After operating a small grocery store in Monterey, he began building the family empire in 1962 with the purchase of a cow pasture in the small town of Capitola, just south of Santa Cruz, which eventually grew into a major shopping center. The older Ow's theory was to develop the land away from the limited central downtown shopping area in Santa Cruz and establish new business centers in outlying suburbs. "The land downtown was already owned for generations by older families who were unwilling to let go of it. We couldn't break in so we were forced to look elsewhere. I don't think it was a racial thing, but it just happened that the people in power there were white," explained Ow. Following his father's vision, Ow made the family dynasty a reality.

Born Under a Lucky Star

George Ow, Jr., born on January 3, 1943, in Santa Cruz, was the oldest child of George and Emily Ow. "My father always said that Chinese astrologers divined that I was born under a lucky star," recalled Ow in an interview with Terry Hong. "I have always felt that this was true." Although Ow's early years were spent in Santa Cruz's

George Ow, Jr.

Chinatown, Ow was the only Asian in his small elementary school. To avoid being taunted by the other children and feeling unprotected even by the teachers, the young Ow chose to stay in during recess. Instead, he sparked a life-long love of books, eventually reading every book in his classroom library. As Ow told Hong, "One of my greatest motivations for becoming a success was that I didn't want to get stepped on all the time."

As in many Asian families, Ow's parents placed considerable emphasis on education. After high school, Ow graduated *summa cum laude* from Monterey Peninsula College with his associate of arts in 1963, then graduated *cum laude* from San Francisco State in 1965. One year later, he received a master's of business administration from the University of California at Los Angeles. He said with a smile, "I wanted to be just as educated as the next guy."

From 1967 to 1970, Ow served as an officer in the U.S. Army and spent a year in Vietnam with the 101st Airborne Division. After an honorable discharge with the rank of captain, Ow returned home to Santa Cruz. Within a matter of a decade, the Ow family enterprises prospered and grew to encompass King's Plaza Shopping Center in Capitola, King's Village Shopping Center in Scotts Valley, a chain of pizza houses called The Pizza Company, a retro-1950s diner dubbed the Pontiac Grill, the Capitola Book Cafe, where almost every contemporary Asian American literary figure has autographed books, a publishing house called the Capitola Book Company which specializes in

local historical projects, the Imperial Courts Tennis Club in Aptos, as well as innumerable small developments throughout the Santa Cruz County area.

Educate the People

Despite all their success, the Ow family never forgot the community that provided the opportunities to reach their goals. "The Santa Cruz area is our home," Ow proudly said, "and we enjoy returning the money that our businesses and investments generate to it. We feel that the wise placement of our money can contribute to the health and well being of our community."

An old Chinese proverb drives much of the Ow family's philanthropy: "Plan for one year, plant grain. Plan for ten years, plant trees. Plan for 100 years, educate the people." Among the many established scholarships given in the Ow family name are the University of California at Santa Cruz (UCSC) American Dream Scholarships, the Cabrillo College American Dream Scholarships, and the Cabrillo's Women's Reentry Program Scholarships. More importantly, Ow offers personal support where least expected. For example, Ow provided the funds for Maria Gutierrez, the daughter of migrant farm workers with seven younger children to support, to complete her undergraduate studies at UCSC. So phenomenal was her story that a team of local filmmakers documented her life in the award-winning video, *Mi Vida*. Today, Gutierrez is about to finish her Ph.D. in Italian literature from Stanford University and the filmmakers are planning to film a follow-up.

Ow strongly believes that for Asian Americans, education is the means through which success can be achieved. "With education," he stated, "you can get power and money, and the ability to control your own destiny." In addition to supporting formal education, Ow is insistent that the public continue to be educated through books, arts, videos, movies, and other media. He is an important supporter of local artists and musicians, allowing them the opportunities to present their murals and sculptures throughout the Santa Cruz community. He has funded a number of documentaries, including the award-winning *A Dollar a Day, Ten Cents A Dance,* about Filipino farmworkers who came to the United States during the period from 1924 to 1931, and Planned Parenthood's *The Birth Control Film* aimed at teenagers. True to his personal goal of supporting more Asian American producers and directors, Ow has invested in the films of Steven Okazaki (even before he won an Oscar) and Arthur Dong. He is the major supporter of the annual Pacific Rim Film Festival as well as Shakespeare Santa Cruz, a nationally-renowned Shakespeare festival held yearly at UCSC.

Ow's latest projects revolve around his publishing company, which published Santa Cruz historian Sandy Lydon's *Chinese Gold*, a book about the Chinese experience in the Monterey Peninsula area, which later spawned a documentary. Ow is currently working together with Lydon on a new multicultural social history based in Point Lobos, California, and will soon be collaborating on a new manuscript about the Japanese experience in the Monterey area.

Second Chances

Between the business responsibilities and his support of artistic and social causes in his community, Ow lived his life constantly moving in too many directions. It took a heart attack in August 1988 to make him aware of his mortality. Ow's family began to see a substantial change in his priorities. He let go of a number of his ventures, including The Pizza Company, the Pontiac Grill, and the Capitola Book Cafe. He began to pare down his business commitments to land development and management. For the first time, he began the process of passing the leadership onto the next generation. Already, nieces and nephews have begun to take more and more responsibility.

In 1994, Ow's energies are first directed toward his family—his wife Gail Michaelis-Ow and their two sons, as well as an older son from a previous marriage. "I'm spending the time now with my kids that I didn't do early in their lives. I missed out with my first family, but now I'm not missing any Little League games. I'm really glad to have this second chance." And, for the first time, Ow is learning that vacations, which were stressful experiences in the past, now "don't need to have a business tie-in and they can just be enjoyed."

Ow is poised to make the transition into a second career. "I feel very lucky to have been born into a family and country where I could work hard at something, be very successful, and then have the opportunity to switch off and enter a second career in writing and other creative, cultural outlets," he said. His first project as a writer is already well-planned—a children's book about the Victorian home in which he has lived since 1975. When the French-inspired Second Empire Mansard-roofed home was built in 1882—the same year of the Chinese Exclusion Act which severely limited Chinese immigration into the United States—no Asian American would have dreamed of living in it since all Asians were prohibited by law from owning property. "In fact, when we were researching the title on the house, we found out that this house did have a clause specifically saying no Orientals could ever own it. Apparently, it was very common in California until the laws were brought down in the 1960s," Ow explained. His story will begin with a portrayal of his grandfather as a laborer building the house. It will bring the reader into the present with the grandson now living in the home. "It's a good way to tell my kids about the history of both our family and of Asian Americans by relating the story to the history of the house," he added.

The Dream Continues

As a final thought, Ow advises the upcoming generation of Asian Americans: "In spite of the racism and the injustice, the opportunities [for Asian Americans] are greater than ever. It's much better than it was in my father's day or my grandfather's day. Back then, not only would I not have been allowed to buy my house, but I couldn't have legally married my wife in California before 1948 or so. . . . Things will continue to get better, especially as Asian Americans are doing well in terms of education. The success in education will transfer over to economic and business success. I see more and more Asian Americans becoming leaders in business, in different art forms, in science, and I look for Asian Americans winning more and more Nobel prizes, Olympic medals, Hollywood Oscars, to becoming presidents of colleges, high executives. I'm thinking that as that happens more and more, there will be more acceptance throughout the country."

From taunted little boy to powerful community and business leader, Ow has lived the American dream. But more than his own success, Ow is also personally making sure that the American dreams of many others will someday, too, become reality.

Sources:

Periodicals

Scheinin, Richard. "Developing Dreams: The Family Saga of George Ow Jr.." *San Jose Mercury News,* Januray 14, 1990, pp. 1L, 6L.

Other

Ow, George, Jr. interview with Terry Hong, November 1987; telephone interview with Hong, April 8, 1994.

—Sketch by Terry Hong

Seiji Ozawa
(1935–)
Conductor

When Seiji Ozawa was named music director and conductor of the world renowned Boston Symphony Orchestra (BSO) in 1973, he became the first Asian—and the youngest person of any ethnicity—to take the directorship of one of America's major orchestras. Since then he has furthered the Boston Symphony Orchestra's distinguished reputation both at home and abroad with performances in some of America's finest concert halls and on tours of Europe and Asia. He has also continued the BSO's commitment to new music. He commissioned a series of compositions to mark the orchestra's 100th anniversary season in 1981 and a series of works celebrating the fiftieth anniversary of the Tanglewood Music Center, the orchestra's prestigious summer training school for young musicians. Under his direction, the BSO has recorded more than 130 works of fifty different composers on ten separate labels.

Seiji Ozawa was born in Shenyang, in the Manchurian province of China in 1935, the third of four sons. His father was an expatriate Japanese dentist who had gone to China to find work. Ozawa's mother was a Christian and it was through that faith that music first made its way into the Ozawa home. The children were sent to a Sunday school in Beijing where they sang hymns in the choir. As Ozawa recalled in *Opera News*, "Because we didn't have a piano, my older brother started playing the music at home on the accordion and harmonica." Soon, however, the family got an old piano for the boys to play.

When Ozawa was young, Japan invaded Manchuria, and the family moved back to Japan to escape the invading Japanese military force. Although life during the war was uncomfortable, music remained an uplifting force to Ozawa. In 1949 he heard his first live symphonic performance, Beethoven's *Emperor Concerto*. Taken with the breadth and drama of the symphony, Ozawa decided he wanted to conduct. Many people discouraged him from pursuing this dream; it was considered unlikely, at best, that an Asian would ever conduct Western music with a Western orchestra. One person who did encourage him was Hideo Saito, Ozawa's teacher at the Toho Gakuen School of Music in Tokyo and a widely influential source in popularizing Western music in Japan. Under Saito's guidance, Ozawa was soon conducting concerts with the NHK Symphony and the Japan Philharmonic.

At Saito's urging, the twenty-four-year-old Ozawa left Japan for Europe, where he won first prize at the 1959 International Competition of Orchestra Conductors in Besançon, France. The music director of the Boston Symphony Orchestra, Charles Munch, was a judge at the competition and was extremely impressed with the young conductor. He invited him to come to Tanglewood, where Ozawa won the Koussevitzky Prize for outstanding student conductor in 1960. Returning to Europe, Ozawa studied in Berlin with Herbert von Karajan, who emphasized the importance of opera in the development of the conductor.

Ozawa recalled for *Opera News* that Karajan said, "There are two sides to conducting, symphony *and* opera. . . . So I did *Cosi* [*Fan Tutti*, a Mozart opera] for the first time, at Salzburg, with the Vienna Philharmonic." Conducting operatic works has been a passion of Ozawa's ever since. Recalling his early years in opera he modestly attributes much of his success to the singers he had the good fortune to work with. "When I conducted my first *Tosca* at La Scala, you know who my first tenor was? Pavarotti! And when I conducted the same opera in Paris for the first time, my Tosca was Kiri Te Kanewa!"

Seiji Ozawa

Coming to America

During his years under von Karajan, Ozawa came to the attention of Leonard Bernstein, who appointed him assistant conductor of the New York Philharmonic for the 1961-62 season. He made his first professional concert appearance in North America in January 1962, with the San Francisco Symphony. He went on to become music director of the Chicago Symphony Orchestra's Ravinia Festival for five summers beginning in 1964, the Toronto Symphony from 1965 to 1969, and the San Francisco Symphony from 1970 to 1976, followed by a year as that orchestra's music adviser.

Ozawa first conducted the Boston Symphony Orchestra at Tanglewood in 1964, and made his first Symphony Hall appearance in 1968. In 1970 he was made artistic director of Tanglewood and in 1973 he was asked to become the director of the Boston Symphony Orchestra. He remained as music director at San Francisco for the first three years of his tenure in Boston until the traveling became too much for him.

Ozawa's Outstanding Career

Ozawa has led the Boston Symphony Orchestra on seven European tours. They have appeared in Japan on four occasions, most recently in 1989, when they also performed in Hong Kong. The orchestra made its premiere tour of South America under Ozawa in 1992. In addition to his work with the BSO, Ozawa regularly appears with such eminent orchestras as the Berlin Philharmonic, the London Symphony, the Orchestre National de France, the Philharmonia of London, and the Vienna Philharmonic. He made his Metropolitan Opera debut—a longtime dream—in 1992, and appears regularly at La Scala and the Vienna Staatsoper. Ozawa holds honorary doctor of music degrees from the University of Massachusetts, the New England Conservatory of Music, and Wheaton College in Norton, Massachusetts. He won an Emmy Award for the Boston Symphony Orchestra's PBS television series, *Evening at Symphony.* In 1992, in honor of his teacher Hideo Saito, he co-founded the Saito Kinen Festival in Matsumoto, Japan.

Today Ozawa lives primarily in Japan with his wife Vera, who travels with him frequently on his global recording and performance trips.

Sources:

Periodicals

Livingstone, William. "Japan Meets the West," *Stereo Review,* February, 1990.

Scherr, Barrymore Laurence. "Seiji: The Boston Symphony Music Director Attains a Longtime Dream With His Debut This Month in Eugene Onegin." *Opera News,* December 19, 1992.

Other

The office of Maestro Seiji Ozawa. Biographical materials. Boston, February 1994.

—Sketch by Jim Henry

P

I.M. Pei
(1917–)
Architect

When young I. M. Pei embarked on his long ocean journey to the United States, his head was filled with dreams of studying architecture and returning to his home in China to build a career. Although his success as an architect brought him renown worldwide, his dream of returning to China was only partially fulfilled.

Born on April 26, 1917, in the city of Canton (now Guangzhou), Pei was named Ieoh Ming, which means "to inscribe brightly." He was the second child (sister Yuen Hau) and first son born to Tsuyee Pei, a prosperous young executive with the Bank of China, and his wife, Lien Kwun. In 1918, fighting among local warlords in Canton became fierce, making life dangerous in Canton. The Bank of China sent Tsuyee Pei and his family to the safety of Hong Kong, where they lived for nine years, and where Pei's younger sister, Wei, and two brothers, Kwun and Chung, were born. In 1927, Pei's father was made manager of the Bank of China's main office in Shanghai, and the family returned to China.

Pei had deep respect for his father, but he was closer to his mother, Lien Kwun. Although she died when Pei was only thirteen, her influence on him was profound. She took him on two retreats to Buddhist temples, a privilege that only Pei was granted. The deep silence of the Buddhist mountain retreat would remain vivid in his mind. Another image that would provide inspiration to him later in his life was that of the Pei family retreat in Suzhou known as the Garden of the Lion Forest. The skillful design of the Lion Forest gardens impressed the young Pei. He recalled how buildings and nature were harmoniously combined and how the interplay of light and shadow figured prominently in the design. He would return to the Garden of the Lion Forest fifty years later to seek ideas for the design of the Fragrant Hill Hotel in Beijing, China.

Pei was educated at Saint John's Middle School, where he studied under Protestant missionaries who were at the height of their influence in China. Students at Saint

I.M. Pei

John's were granted only a half day a month away for their own amusement. The instruction was given in Chinese, but Pei, along with other top students, read the Bible and Dickens in English.

An Ocean Voyage

Although his father, who had English and Scottish business associates, wanted Pei to study in England, Pei was intrigued by the idyllic image of American university life he had gleaned from American movies and college catalogs. In 1935, at the age of seventeen, Pei embarked on the *S.S. Coolidge* for the ocean voyage to San Francisco. He intended to study architecture at the University of Pennsylvania, but after only two weeks in the program with its heavy emphasis on drawing, Pei realized that he was not likely to excel there. He transferred to the Massachusetts Institute of Technology (MIT) to study engineering.

The faculty at MIT recognized Pei's design talent, and eventually convinced him to return to his original course of study, architecture. He graduated in 1940 with a bachelor of architecture degree, winning the American Institute of Architects Gold Medal, the Alpha Rho Chi (the national professional fraternity of architects) Medal, and the MIT Traveling Fellowship. Yet his intention to return to China could not be fulfilled: during his college years, Japan had invaded China, and Pei's father advised him to stay in the United States.

In the spring of 1942, Pei married Eileen Loo, who had just graduated from Wellesley College. Eileen enrolled in the landscape architecture program at the Harvard Graduate School of Design, and Pei won a fellowship to pursue a master's degree in architecture there also. He enrolled in December 1942, but because World War II was raging, Pei volunteered in January of 1943 to work for the National Defense Research Committee in Princeton, New Jersey, where his assignment was to develop plans for destroying buildings.

In 1944, Pei finished his work with national defense and returned to Harvard's Graduate School of Design. While at Harvard, Pei was strongly influenced by two professors: Walter Gropius, who had created the Bauhaus, a well-known institute of design in Germany which had been closed by the Nazis, and Marcel Breuer, whose interest in light, texture, sun, and shadow was particularly intriguing to Pei. After earning a master's degree in architecture from Harvard in 1946, the Communist takeover of China permanently erased Pei's dream of returning there to pursue his career. He was awarded the Wheelwright Traveling Fellowship by Harvard in 1951, enabling him to travel extensively in England, France, Italy, and Greece. Eileen had suspended her studies in 1945 when the Peis' first son, T'ing Chung, was born.

The Webb & Knapp Years

Although Pei was reluctant to abandon the prospect of returning to China, a meeting in the spring of 1948 with the powerful New York real estate developer, William Zeckendorf, offered him an irresistible opportunity. After seriously evaluating his options, Pei agreed to sign on with Zeckendorf's firm, Webb & Knapp, as director of the architectural division. For the next seven years, Pei would oversee large-scale public housing projects, shopping centers, and similar large-scale urban developments. However, being part of an in-house architectural department had its limitations: because he was considered a "house architect," Pei was excluded from membership in the American Institute of Architects, the profession's governing body.

I.M. Pei & Associates

Pei was joined at Webb & Knapp by former Harvard Graduate School of Design student Henry Cobb and others. Despite the professional disadvantage of being an "in-house" design department, working with Zeckendorf's firm had advantages: Pei and Cobb were working on

projects that would be the envy of many other architects their age. On the other hand, they were not free to pursue, nor were they likely to be considered for, commissions from other important clients.

In 1955 Pei took the first step toward shedding the constraints of Webb & Knapp by establishing I.M. Pei & Associates. In 1959, MIT extended a personal invitation to Pei to design a building for its Earth Sciences Center, which gave the group an opportunity to work outside the commercial development world of Webb & Knapp. By the late 1950s, Zeckendorf's began to suffer. In 1960, I. M. Pei & Associates amicably separated from Webb & Knapp, and Pei and his team faced the daunting task of finding enough commissions to stay afloat while overcoming some powerful negative factors: widespread knowledge of Zeckendorf's financial problems tainted Pei's group by association, and the high-design world regarded the Webb & Knapp experience as inferior preparation for any high-profile commissions.

National Center for Atmospheric Research

One of Pei's first major commissions would establish a pattern for his working relationships: a strong, visionary individual joining with Pei to articulate a building's design and shape its setting. Walter Orr Roberts, the astronomer who headed the National Center for Atmospheric Research (NCAR), presented Pei with the opportunity to create a research complex for NCAR in Colorado. Pei's personal architectural style blossomed, resulting in a complex of buildings that rises over the slopes of the mesa outside Boulder, Colorado. (Few non-astronomers have visited this complex, but many remember them as the setting for the Woody Allen film, *Sleeper.*) Pei would later describe this project, completed between 1961 and 1967, as his breakout building.

In the early 1960s, as commissions came into the offices of I.M. Pei & Associates, Pei assumed a role similar to the one he had played at Zeckendorf: finding clients, envisioning the overall design of the project, and then delegating the execution to others in the firm. In 1966, the firm changed its name to I.M. Pei & Partners to reflect the collaborative nature of Pei's relationship with his associates. In 1989, the evolution of the partnership would be reflected in another name change, to Pei Cobb Freed & Partners. In 1968, the American Institute of Architects recognized the partners with the Architectural Firm Award.

John F. Kennedy Library

In 1964, when Pei was selected over a group of stellar architects to design the high-profile John F. Kennedy Library, it elevated him to the top tier of architects. Although the project would suffer a tortuous course (from concept in 1964 through three designs for three different sites) before its dedication on October 20, 1979, Pei's characteristic capacity to concentrate on the future and to remain true to his course was strengthened by the experience. In addition to the NCAR and the John F. Kennedy Library, Pei has done more than thirty institutional projects including schools, churches, hospitals, and municipal buildings. Nearly a dozen of Pei's commissions have been for museums, where his architectural style and sensitivity to the visitor's experience have created remarkable and award-winning structures.

National Gallery of Art and The Louvre

The reputation of I.M. Pei & Partners grew worldwide with the opening in 1978 of the East Wing of the National Gallery of Art in Washington, D.C. Pei, with benefactor Paul Mellon and then-director of the National Gallery J. Carter Brown, had designed the wing to preserve the stately feel of a monument, while infusing it with energy and allowing for the flow of thousands of visitors.

When planning began for expansion of the most famous art museum in the world, the Louvre in Paris, Pei was invited to take the assignment. Before agreeing, however, he embarked on four months of highly secret research, visiting the Louvre on three occasions to evaluate the prospects. His early plans were also developed in secret, and the French official overseeing the project was enthusiastic about Pei's initial presentation of a crystalline pyramid form to create a new entrance to the Louvre. However, when the presentation was made to an influential French commission, criticisms of the plans were so vehement that the interpreter broke into tears and refused to continue. A counter-attack was mounted, with statements issued by the Louvre curatorial staff supporting the Pei proposal. Finally, French intellectuals and media personalities began to join forces with the Louvre and Pei, but requested that a full-scale model of Pei's pyramid be erected on the sight to give the public an accurate idea of the impact it would have. Pei's designs eventually won approval, and were completed to great acclaim and enjoyment by the public.

Return to China

In 1982, Pei was finally able to realize his long-held intention of returning to China to design buildings when he was invited to design the Bank of China headquarters building in Hong Kong. The resulting Pei design is the tallest building in Asia at seventy-two stories. Equally significant, and reflective of his childhood memories of the Garden of the Lion Forest, is Pei's design for the Fragrant Hill Hotel in Beijing.

Working in China was the realization of a dream for Pei, but political events in China have left the dream only partially fulfilled. In a 1989 editorial published in the *New York Times*, Pei described his feelings about the incident at Tiananmen Square (Chinese government forces attacked protesters, many of whom were students, on Saturday, June 3, 1989. As many as three thousand may have been killed in the massacre, which drew international condemnation.): "More than fifty years ago, my wife and I came to this wonderful country from China. For forty of these years, we dreamed that one day it would be possible to work in our native land. More than anything we wanted to combine our love of the nation that had become our own with our desire to do something for the land of our birth and heritage. . . . In 1978 . . . we were given the chance to work in China. As I worked with a new generation of Chinese, my hopes for the future of China were ever more optimistic. . . . Today, these dreams are dashed by the horrible events of Tiananmen Square. . . . China will not be the same after this terrible tragedy."

Pei remains committed to do what he can to support the growth of China. In 1983, when Pei was chosen the Laureate of the Prizker Architecture Prize, he used the $100,000 award to establish a scholarship fund for Chinese students to study architecture in the United States, with the strict proviso that they return to China to practice their profession.

Awards and Honors

The awards accumulated by Pei during his distinguished international career would fill a large trophy room. Notable among these are the Arnold Brunner Award of the National Institute of Arts and Letters (1963); the Thomas Jefferson Memorial Medal "for distinguished contribution to the field of architecture" (1976); Gold Medal for Architecture from the American Academy of Arts and Letters (1979); Gold Medal of Alpha Rho Chi from the National Professional Fraternity of Architects (1981); The American Institute of Architects Gold Medal, the highest architectural honor in the United States (1979), the Grande Medaille d'Or from the French Academie d'Architecture (1982); and the Medal of Freedom, awarded by President George Bush (1990).

On July 4, 1986, Pei was one of twelve foreign-born Americans (he became a naturalized citizen in 1954) to receive the Medal of Liberty from President Ronald Reagan at the centennial of the Statue of Liberty. Pei stated on that occasion that he had never suffered from racial discrimination in the United States, but that, in the early days, he had sometimes felt like "an outsider." He felt the Medal of Liberty is a symbol that he has been accepted by the American people and rates it above his professional honors in terms of personal importance.

Sources:

Books

Dell, Pamela. *I.M. Pei, Designer of Dreams*. Chicago: Childrens' Press, 1993.

Wiseman, Carter. *I.M. Pei, A Profile in American Architecture*. New York: H. N. Abrams, 1990.

Periodicals

Pei, I. M. "China Won't Ever Be the Same." *New York Times,* June 22, 1989, p. A11.

Other

Pei Cobb Freed & Partners, "I.M. Pei," Resume and biographical information, 1994.

—*Sketch by Susan Gall*

Vincent Perez, Jr.
(1958–)
Investment banker

In 1994 Vincent Perez became the first Asian American partner in the history of Lazard Freres and Company, the New York investment banking firm. Perez's ascent to this level of achievement began with his passionate involvement in an international business and economics students association in the Philippines. In an interview with Felicia Paik, Perez shared his philosophy of success: "Hard work creates luck for you."

Perez, Jr. was born in Quezon City, Philippines, on May 26, 1958, the oldest in a family of five children. His mother, Lucy, was a dietician and his father, Vic, served as a Philippines naval officer and later ran his own shipping services company.

"Safe" Choice of Study

After attending the private Jesuit Xavier School, Perez enrolled as a student at the University of the Philippines, where he graduated in 1979 with a bachelor of science degree in business economics. Perez said he chose his undergraduate studies without too much reflection. "It was really a process of elimination," he told Paik. "I thought it was the safest way to go."

While in college, Perez immersed himself in the activities of AIESEC, an international association of business and economics students which had a chapter on campus. Little did Perez know that this extracurricular activity would end up providing his ticket to the United States and the gateway to his career in the global financial markets.

As national president of AIESEC, representing the Philippines and other Southeast Asian countries, Perez traveled to the United States in 1979 to attend the association's international congress meeting held in Chicago

that year. Also through AIESEC, Perez was awarded an internship at the New Jersey National Bank. After a brief stint there, he decided he needed a master's in business administration to advance his opportunities. In the fall of 1981, Perez was accepted as a student at the University of Pennsylvania's Wharton School of Business. To pay his tuition, Perez did research, studying the labor climate in Southeast Asia, particularly in Malaysia. During the two summers of graduate school, he worked at Citibank M.A. in Manila.

Ladder of Success

In 1983, Perez signed on with Mellon Bank N.A. in Pittsburgh and started climbing the ladder of the credit training program, which landed him a position first as Latin American credit analyst and later as Mexican desk officer. In the mid-1980s Perez put his multi-lingual abilities to use—he speaks Spanish, Filipino, Mandarin Chinese, and English—as one of the early traders of Third World debt. "That was really the stepping stone to my career now," Perez told Paik.

In February 1987, Perez joined Lazard Brothers, the investment banking firm in London, and a little more than a year later was transferred to Lazard Freres in New York. At this post, Perez, specializing in mergers and acquisitions, capital markets and assets management, began the formulation of an emerging markets trading desk, which today boasts a sixteen-member group, up from the two-person office he took over. In January 1994, Perez was named a general partner of Lazard Freres, the first Asian partner at the firm.

To achieve his goals, Perez said he forecasts where he wants to be in his career every five years and then aims to beat the timeline he constructed. "You have to be open to opportunity," he explained. "Some people don't know an opportunity may be sitting right next to them." Perez offered this advice to anyone searching for success: "It's good to be a master of a certain niche and strive to be the best. But you can't rest in your seat. You have to be innovative to stay ahead of the competition."

However, Perez is not so caught up in his ambition that he doesn't find time to enjoy his life. "You have to enjoy the journey and not just the destination," he observed. In 1991, Perez married Leigh Talmage, whom he met while working at Mellon Bank in Pittsburgh. The couple lives in Manhattan. In his spare time, Perez collects sixteenth- and seventeenth-century maps of Southeast Asia. "I love to collect old maps, primarily from the Age of Discovery," he said. "I go to auctions and visit galleries. Right now I have twenty-four in my collection."

Sources:

Perez, Vincent, Jr., telephone interview with Felicia Paik, February 28, 1994.

—*Sketch by Felicia Paik*

Arati Prabhakar
(1959–)
Scientist, government administrator

Arati Prabhakar

In a time when the whole world is taking shape as one unitary marketplace, the National Institute of Standards and Technology (NIST) is apt to play an increasingly vital role in promoting U.S. economic growth. NIST's mandate is to develop and apply technology, measurements, and standards in collaboration with industry to stimulate economic development. In 1994, the appropriated budget for the organization was $600 million, which the Clinton administration plans to increase to $1.4 billion by 1997. The directorship of the agency is indeed a coveted position in the U.S. government. In 1993, President Bill Clinton offered the leadership of NIST to a young India-born engineer-scientist, Arati Prabhakar. With her appointment, Prabhakar became the tenth director of the organization and the first Asian to hold the post.

Arati Prabhakar was born in New Delhi, India, on February 2, 1959. When she was two years old her mother, Raj, immigrated to the United States to pursue an education in the field of social work. Within a year, Arati and her father, Jagdish, followed her. Her father, an electrical engineer, obtained his doctorate in Illinois and then joined the faculty at Texas Tech University in Lubbock.

Science education has been a passion in the family. From an early age, Prabhakar was exposed to the fields of science and technology. These childhood interests later directed her academic and career choices. Her younger brother also has chosen a career in science. Prabakhar pursued her bachelor's and master's degrees in electrical engineering and completed a doctorate in applied physics from the California Institute of Technology (Cal Tech). Although similar to her father in her professional interests, the overwhelming influence in Prabakhar's life has been her mother. "My mother is my primary role model," she told Shamita Das Dasgupta in an interview. "She is the person who first stimulated my curiosity in science. And she told me everything is possible!"

Mother as Role Model

It was Prabhakar's mother who initiated the family's move to the United States, bucking the established trend in which Asian Indian men, not women, lead the migration of the rest of the family. And her decision to come to the United States in 1961 before the post-1965 immigration surge, only confirmed her pioneering spirit. Raj's adventuresome nature and openness to new experiences made an impression on her daughter. Even though Prabhakar grew up in Texas at a time when an Asian Indian community was virtually nonexistent, she feels she did not miss the security of the familiar. Not having a community to fall back on meant an opportunity to interact closely with the local population. "Actually it made me learn more about Americans. I didn't feel isolated at all. I was part of the whole community," she said. She also believes that the rarity of Asian Indians in America then helped her in another significant way. "Since Indians were still an unknown group, we didn't have to deal with any baggage, good or bad." She feels the race biases of the time were focused more on known minority groups.

Prabhakar's mother encouraged and inspired her to be all she could be. "It never entered my mind that there were things that one couldn't do," she said. She chose to do her undergraduate degree in electrical engineering at a time when few women entered the field. Scholastically brilliant, she graduated in three years. Next, she applied to the Bell Laboratories' Graduate Research Program for Women which supported her financially through graduate school.

Despite the harsh academic requirements, Prabhakar persisted at Cal Tech and earned the first Ph.D. in applied physics awarded to a woman at that institution. But a doctorate was not an end for Prabhakar, nor a license to bury herself in further esoteric research. Rather, Prabhakar believed her advanced degree opened doors for further expansion and experimentation. Consulting with her advisers, she decided to set her career goals toward policy-making in the government.

Career in Government

Prabhakar's first job was as a congressional fellow at the U.S. Office of Technology Assessment (OTA). Prabhakar's exemplary work soon brought attention to her and led to the directorship of the Microelectronics Technology Office in the Defense Department's Advanced Research Projects Agency (ARPA). Here she managed a budget of $300 million and contracts and collaborations with hundreds of organizations, firms, and defense contractors. The overall manufacturing programs of the agency was to stimulate and challenge the U.S. semiconductor industry to achieve cost-effective, value-added products. It is from this position that she was selected by the administration in 1993 to take over the helm of NIST. Her appointment broke the longstanding tradition in the agency of selecting directors internally and by seniority. It is a tribute to her expertise and administrative skills that this prestigious position came her way.

Prabhakar is already wooing influential focus on NIST. Her plans for the organization include bringing technology to the center of attention in the government. She is a great believer in the power of technology because it profoundly affects the world around us and challenges all set rules. She said exuberantly: "I always wanted to touch people and change lives. This organization allows me to do that. I love getting up in the morning and coming to work."

Prabhakar credits not only her mother but a few nurturing role models for inspiring her to achieve. Two of her lifelong mentors are her professors, Martin A. Pollock and Robert E. Nahory. In addition to them, Prabhakar speaks with great respect of her graduate school adviser, Tom McGill. All of them have shaped her thinking and directed her career path. "I am extremely fortunate in finding my niche. Most people's careers are a search to match expertise, ability and interest. I have found it,"she declared. "I am proud of my work."

Although totally in tune with her high-powered career, Prabhakar maintains a balanced perspective in everything she does. She acknowledges that her equilibrium comes from her cultural background. "Being an Indian is a permanent part of me. I am extremely fortunate to have been born in it," she said. Her philosophy is to harvest the best from both Indian and American cultures. Her mother, again, was Prabhakar's teacher in the development of this special life-view. "You have to do your work with full focus, yet maintain a distance from it. You have to understand how things measure up from a cosmic perspective. It is only then you can retain your equanimity," she said.

Although Prabhakar has not had a chance to grow up within the thriving Asian Indian community that her counterparts have in the 1990s, she has noticed changes. "When I went to study engineering, it was a novelty. The other day a young Indian high school girl told me that her elder sister was going to college to study electrical engineering, and she didn't even bat an eyelid. It is no longer an exception to the rule." Since her appointment as NIST's director, Prabhakar has unwittingly become a role model for the Asian Indian community. "I have had Indian parents come up to me and say that now they truly believe that their kids can do anything they want," she said. Such adulation from her community has moved her deeply. But, Prabhakar wants to challenge the community and others as well, regarding the notion of role models. "We tend to believe that one's role model has to be of the same sex and ethnicity. However, I believe that choosing a model of a different sex and race may actually have a liberating effect." All of Prabhakar's role models have been white males. She maintains that such a paradigm shift may broaden one's horizons to include characteristics that may normally be out of one's range of experience. "Life is full of possibilities and we must be open to them."

Prabhakar's plans for the future are characteristically open. "I think it is only for one's own entertainment that one plans. I tend to act and interact on a day-to-day basis," she stated. However, she speculated that perhaps in ten years she would be working in manufacturing and product development. No matter what her future activities will be, Prabhakar will surely be touching people's lives.

Sources:

Periodicals

Adam, J. A. "Arati Prabhakar." *IEEE Spectrum*, December, 1993, pp. 48–51.

Other

Prabhakar, Arati, telephone interview with Shamita Das Dasgupta, on June 22, 1994.

—Sketch by Shamita Das Dasgupta, Ph.D.

Dith Pran
(1942–)
Journalist

From 1974 to 1979, Dith Pran, a photojournalist and assistant to *New York Times* correspondent Sydney Schanberg, lived with an almost daily fear of death. He watched his country, Cambodia, turn into a living hell under the murderous regime of the communist Khmer Rouge forces. Many friends disappeared at night, never to return. Others were brutally executed in broad daylight, often clubbed to death with sticks and hoes in order to save bullets. Pran lost more than fifty family members to the Cambodian holocaust: his father died of malnutrition, his mother from the prolonged strain of living in famine and war-torn conditions, and his three brothers, a sister, and their families. One brother, with his wife and five children, was rumored to have been thrown alive to hungry crocodiles.

Pran survived through luck, resourceful planning, and constant prayer. A Buddhist, he felt that if he prayed constantly to Buddha, his life somehow would be spared. When he finally was able to flee Cambodia, enter a refugee camp in Thailand, and move to the United States through the help of his comrade and close friend Schanberg, Pran realized his prayers were answered. Now fifty-two, he lives near New York City with his family. He works as a photographer for the *New York Times*, and often boasts of his four sons who, he said in an interview in the *Los Angeles Times*, have grown tall on a "rich, American diet."

Though he lives in comfort, memories of Cambodia and its holocaust continue to haunt him. Made famous through the 1984 film *The Killing Fields*, Pran has since become one of the world's best-known advocates for justice in Cambodia. He devotes his life to raising awareness of the human-rights abuses in his country. "I'm a one-person crusade," he told *Notable Asian Americans*. "I must speak for those who did not survive and for those who still suffer. I don't consider myself a politician or a hero. I'm a messenger. If Cambodia is to survive, she needs many voices."

Education and Early Career

Pran was born September 27, 1942, in Siem Riep, in the northwestern part of Cambodia near the Angkor Wath temples, once a popular tourist destination. His father, a senior public-works official, supervised road-building in the area. Pran grew up middle class and went to high school, where he learned French in the classroom and English on his own. He finished high school in 1960, and went to work as a Cambodian-language interpreter for a U.S. military assistance group then stationed in Cambodia. Five years later, Cambodia severed its relations with the United States, charging that U.S. troops had launched attacks on Cambodian villages from what was then South Vietnam. After the Americans left, Pran found work as an interpreter for a British film crew and later as a receptionist at a popular tourist hotel near the Angkor temple complex.

In 1970, war broke out between the Khmer Rouge and the Cambodian government, backed by a U.S.-supported puppet, Lon Nol. After an attack occurred in Siem Riep, a group of journalists converged on the township. Pran assisted the journalists as an interpreter and guide. Pained by the human suffering that the war was causing, Pran became infused with a desire to tell the world what his country was going through and decided to move to

Dith Pran

Phnom Penh with his wife and children where he could work as a journalist.

The *New York Times* Connection

Though he had no formal skills, he began assisting several foreign television and newspaper reporters, including Craig Whitney, who was the Saigon bureau chief for the *New York Times*. In 1972, Schanberg, who'd been stationed in Singapore, was drawn to Cambodia and its inadvertent entry into a war it didn't want to go through. Pran began working with Schanberg exclusively, and in 1973, joined the *New York Times* as an official stringer.

Schanberg describes the brotherly relationship that formed between him and Pran during the war years in his book, *The Death and Life of Dith Pran*, on which *The Killing Fields* is based. When Schanberg first landed in Cambodia, Pran was waiting at the airport with a notebook filled with recent events, contact names, and story suggestions. Pran had arranged for a hotel suite and press credentials. Schanberg was ready to go to work. As the two began chasing stories, their friendship grew.

Like close friends, the two cavorted around Phnom Penh and once, Schanberg writes, bayed at a couple of astonished soldiers. They also worked intensely. Schanberg, who eventually won a Pulitzer Prize for his work in Cambodia, was driven, and he drove Pran as well. Others in the press corps labeled Schanberg as Ankalimir, a

Cambodian ogre; Pran, however, saw Schanberg's pace as essential to telling the story of his country. In *Death and Life*, Schanberg writes, "It is difficult to describe how a friendship grows, for it often grows from seemingly contradictory roots—mutual needs, overlapping dependencies, intense shared experiences, and even the inequality of service, one serving the other. Our bond grew in all of these ways."

By 1975, it became clear that the Khmer Rouge eventually would invade Phnom Penh and take over Cambodia. On April 12, the Americans officially decided they would leave. Schanberg, using a connection with a U.S. embassy official, arranged for Pran's family—his wife Ser Moeum and four children—to be evacuated on military planes. Pran, however, wanted to stay. He loaded his family onto a U.S. military truck and watched them leave the country. Early in the morning, six days later, the Khmer Rouge entered the capital city.

In the beginning, Schanberg and Pran hoped—in hindsight, foolishly—that the communist takeover would be peaceful. And, at first, that did seem to be the case. In *Death and Life*, Schanberg recalls the two journalists watching peaceful troops in clean black uniforms marching into the city. But they soon realized that this was not the "real" Khmer Rouge. Later, the actual Khmer Rouge marched into the city and began to ruthlessly drive people to the countryside.

Capture, Hardship

Schanberg and Pran, along with two other journalists, visited a hospital to get some idea of the casualties. As they left, they encountered a group of heavily armed troops who jammed guns to their heads and stomachs and ordered them into an armored truck. Pran, in an effort to save their lives, began talking nonstop in Khmer, the Cambodian language. He wanted the soldiers to know they were journalists and not involved in the war. Schanberg and the other journalist got into the truck, but Pran did not. In *Death and Life*, Schanberg remembers thinking, "For God's sake, Pran, get inside. . . . if you go on arguing, they'll shoot you down in the street." Pran finally climbed inside with the others, and after several hours of captivity inside the vehicle as it drove around the city, the group was allowed to leave. Only later did Shanberg realize that the Khmer Rouge did not want Pran in the van. Pran was trying to stay with the foreign journalists in order to save their lives.

They initially took refuge at the French embassy with other Westerners and their Cambodian friends, but soon the Cambodians—Pran included—were ordered to leave the premises. Though Schanberg and other journalists tried to fake a passport for Pran, the French officials saw through the ploy and told them to give up their efforts. As Pran—armed with food, cigarettes and "bribe" money—walked out of the embassy; Schanberg felt completely helpless.

From the beginning, Pran's supporters believed that his resourcefulness would provide him a way to hide from the Khmer Rouge and flee to Thailand. After returning to the United States, Schanberg distributed photographs of Pran at border camps. He also helped Pran's wife and children settle in and acclimate themselves to American culture.

Pran, meanwhile, began to plan his escape, slowly. He ascertained that the Khmer Rouge intended to brutally return Cambodia to a pre-Colonial, agrarian society, in which people were all of one class, to be treated much like livestock. Realizing his education and middle-class upbringing could work against him, Pran threw away his western clothes and all the bribe money that Schanberg had given him. He donned the clothes of a Cambodian peasant—dirty shirt, short pants, sandals, and a traditional Cambodian neckerchief—made his vocabulary crude and limited, and told people he had been a taxi driver. He found his way to a village east of his hometown, Siem Riep, and was put to work planting and tending rice fields.

For the next two and a half years, he stayed in the village. He nearly died of starvation and of a brutal beating. As famine set in due to the war and disruption of farming, food was reduced to one spoonful of rice per day. Villagers, in a desperate effort to survive, began to eat snails, snakes, insects, rats, and scorpions. Pran heard people were digging up bodies of recently executed victims to eat their flesh. Pran became so weak that he could not stand without a wooden staff. His face became puffy with malnutrition and his teeth began to loosen. He was afraid he would die. One night he crawled into a rice paddy and began stuffing rice kernels into his pocket. Two guards caught him, and a group of a dozen villagers were told to beat him with bamboo-cutting blades. Afterward he was left alone, swollen and bleeding, outside in a rain storm. "I prayed and prayed to Buddha for my life," he says in *Death and Life*. "I said if my mother's milk had value, my life would be saved."

Pran eventually left the village and went to work as a houseboy for a Khmer Rouge commune chief. In 1979, the Vietnamese invaded Cambodia, and he decided to make his way to Siem Riep, where he learned that most of his family had passed away. He also found the "killing fields"—bones and skulls lying in the forests, choking up the wells. He learned to recognize where bodies had been buried; the grass above the graves was always greener.

Escape

Under the Vietnamese, he worked as Siem Riep's administrative chief, but eventually his superiors learned he'd once worked as a journalist. Nervous that he would be killed, he decided to escape. With a group of twelve men, he walked a sixty-mile snakelike path to Thailand, trying to avoid Khmer Rouge guerrillas, Vietnamese patrols, unmarked mines, and other hidden traps. After four days, he reached the border and hid for an additional fourteen days, waiting for an opportune time to slip across into a refugee camp. Once he arrived, he sought out an American relief officer and asked her to contact Schanberg at the *New York Times*.

The Killing Fields ends with an emotional reunion between Pran and Schanberg. In reality, the two men did cry, laugh, and hug a lot when Schanberg arrived at the refugee camp to meet Pran. But Pran's journey isn't over. He spends much of his time traveling to lecture about Cambodia and its human-rights abuses. In recent years, he has returned to the country to provide school materials, blankets, and other supplies to orphaned Cambodian children. He hopes to bring the leaders of the Khmer Rouge to the World Court. He considers Elie Wiesel, who speaks about the Jewish holocaust in Nazi Germany, his hero and a model. Like Wiesel, Pran says, "I try to awaken the world to the holocaust of Cambodia."

He still wakes up at nights in a cold sweat, filled with memories of what the Khmer Rouge did to him. In a 1991 interview with the *Los Angeles Times*, Pran said, "There is no doctor who can heal me. But I know a man like Pol Pot [leader of the Khmer Rouge], he is even sicker than I am. . . . We both have the horror in our heads. In Cambodia, the killer and the victim have the same disease."

Sources:

Books

Schanberg, Sidney. *The Death and Life of Dith Pran.* New York: Viking and Penguin Books, 1980.

Periodicals

Getlin, Josh. "Speaking for the Innocents: As Cambodia Undergoes a Painful Rebirth, Dith Pran Remembers—and Cannot Forgive." *Los Angeles Times,* October 25, 1991.

Grogan, David W. "When Newsman Sydney Schanberg Was Expelled from Cambodia, His Best Friend Was Left Behind in the Killing Fields." *People,* December 10, 1984, p. 65.

Other

Pran, Dith. Personal biography supplied by Pran, March 1994.

———. Written interview with Helen Zia, 1994.

—Sketch by Himanee Gupta

Q

Beulah Quo

Actress

She has acted in films as well known as *Chinatown, Love Is a Many Splendored Thing,* and *Girls, Girls, Girls.* Her television credits include parts in "Starsky and Hutch," "Hawaii Five-O," "Magnum P.I.," and "Trapper John, M.D." On the stage, she was seen in *The World of Suzie Wong* and *Martyrs Can't Go Home.* She was nominated for an Emmy for her role in "Chinese Chess Piece," a feature of the 1990 Los Angeles Film Festival. But unless you have been a long-time member of her "General Hospital" fan club, you probably wouldn't recognize her walking down the street.

For Beulah Quo, this is part of the problem. She believes Asian and Asian American artists don't get the recognition in Hollywood that they deserve and that when a suitable role becomes available, it's often awarded to a Caucasian actor instead. An actress for four decades and now a community activist, Quo has dedicated her life in recent years to trying to change these casting policies—not for herself, but for future generations of Asian American artists to follow. "I would like to get to the point where theater and art know no boundaries," Quo said in a 1991 interview with Sonia Timmerman in the *Port Charles Gazette.* "But first we've got to give people of color a chance to play their own color, and then give them a chance to play roles that were forbidden to them."

From 1985 to 1991, Quo played Olin, a fast-talking, hip housekeeper on the television soap opera, "General Hospital." She was the only Asian American actor whose story line reccurred over several years. This reinforced her belief that more work needs to be done to give Asian American actors a stronger voice on the screen.

"The opportunity for Asian men to play featured and main roles has all but been nil in Hollywood and theater," Quo said in her interview with Timmerman. "This was especially true in the early years of Hollywood. . . . They can always find a female 'dragon lady,' prostitute, or nubile to be had by the white guy, bit it's a stereotypical role usually. However, when it comes to the Asian male, if it's an important role, then the character is invariably

Beulah Quo

played by a white man in yellow face with his eyes taped up." Hard words, perhaps, but Quo says them with a smile. She is, Timmerman notes, a "charming, intelligent, dynamo of a woman" whose "voice wraps you in a cocoon of warmth while her mind takes you on a roller coaster ride through the past and present."

After nearly forty years of working in Hollywood, Quo feels free to speak frankly about the lack of roles for Asian American actors. Now in her seventies, she continues to work in the industry and to derive both professional and personal pleasure from it. The ability to use film and telelvision to touch people and make an influence is what attracted her to acting in the first place.

Early Life

Beulah Quo was born in Stockton, California, a quiet, central California community. Her parents did not have much money, but like many Asian American parents, they wanted their daughter to have a good education. Quo graduated with honors from Stockton High School, graduated Phi Beta Kappa from the University of California at Berkeley, and earned a master's degree from the University of Chicago. She was trained to be a teacher and taught college in both the United States and China.

She and her husband, Edwin, were teaching at Ginling College in Nanjin, China in the 1940s when the Communist Revolution engulfed the country. Quo and her husband fled with a two-month-old baby. Years later, Quo would remember this experience when she acted the "The Children of An Lac," a television drama about the founder of an orphanage in Vietnam who helped save hundred of orphans in Saigon.

Her acting career began by accident. In 1954, she applied for a job as a dialect coach for Jennifer Jones in the movie, *Love is a Many Splendored Thing*. Jones needed to speak with a British-Chinese accent. Quo auditioned for the job, and director Henry King told her that her accent was too "California." But he wondered whether she'd be interested in playing the part of Jones' aunt. One role led to another, and soon Quo was working full time as an actress. Quickly, Quo began to realize that acting was, in many ways, a lot like teaching. Both were vehicles for reaching an audience. She tried to combine careers for awhile, but each eventually proved to be so time-consuming that she needed to make a choice between one or the other. She decided to go with acting. "I felt I could influence people more," she told Timmerman. "I'm a social worker at heart, you see, and I tried to change the general public's concept of a person of color."

Throughout the 1960s and 1970s, Quo acted in films and dozens of popular weekly television dramas. Her film roles included parts in *Flower Drum Song*, *The Sand Pebbles*, and *Chinatown*. One of her favorite roles came in *The Sand Pebbles*, when her petite, five-foot three-inch frame was built up with stuffing so she could play a "fat mama." She also remembers *Girls, Girls, Girls* and working with Elvis Presley. "He was such a gentleman," she recalled to Timmerman. "He always had time to say hello and give a kind word to everyone."

More recently, Quo played the role of empress of Kublai Khan in the NBC production of *Marco Polo*, one of the first major American film projects to be made in China.

Documentaries and Commentaries

Firm in her belief that the media is an important vehicle for reaching out to people, Quo began working in public affairs programming. She ran a talk show for five years, frequently spotlighting Asian Americans and their issues. She also began producing documentaries of well-known Asian Americans, including the Oscar-winning cinematographer James Wong Howe. This documentary, *James Wong Howe:*

The Man and His Movies, aired shortly before Howe died, and won a Hollywood-area Emmy Award.

Always an activist, Quo's list of volunteer activities stretches almost as long as her acting credits. Her volunteer work includes the United Way, El Nido Social Services, China Society, and the Asian Pacific American Friends of the Los Angeles Center Theatre Group. She also has donated volunteer hours to acting as a founder of East West Players (the first Asian American theatre in the United States) and of the Associaton of Asian Pacific Artists, which honored her with its lifetime achievement award in 1990.

Sources:

Periodicals

Timmerman, Sonia. "A Classy Lady, Beulah Quo," *Port Charles Gazette*, January/February 1991.

Other

Quo, Beulah. Biographical materials and press releases provided by Quo.

—Sketch by Himanee Gupta

Safi U. Qureshey
(1951–)
Entrepreneur, engineer

Safi Qureshey and his two friends, Thomas Yuen and Albert Wong, are living proof that the American dream is an achievable reality. They came to the United States as engineering students and established a multi-million dollar manufacturing company. The three Asian immigrants pooled their resources, which amounted to $2,000 in 1980, and started a small electronic design consulting firm which soon expanded into the complete production of personal computers and enhancement products. They used their initials to name the firm AST Research, and drew lots to decide who would be the nominal president of the company. Through the luck of the draw, the job fell to Qureshey.

The trio sometimes called the "three musketeers" could not avoid rising tensions over disagreements, and in 1988 Wong left the company to set up his own business. Yuen followed suit in 1992. Fourteen years from its conception, AST Research, a half-billion dollar manufacturing company is headed by Qureshey, the only remaining founder.

Safi U. Qureshey

AST is based in Irvine, California, and its products are manufactured in Fountain Valley, California, London, Hong Kong, Taiwan, and Ireland, and are sold in eighty-nine countries. The company employs 6,700 people worldwide, ranks 431 on the Fortune 500 list of leading U.S. companies, and is the nation's fourth largest computer maker behind IBM, Apple, and Compaq. In 1991, the company received the "E" award from the U.S. Commerce Department for excellence in exporting. AST is publicly held and is listed on the NASDAQ exchange.

The Roots of Qureshey's Success

"My mother still gets surprised [by my success]," Qureshey told Jim Impoco of *U.S. News & World Report.* "There were no signs earlier on." It is not surprising that Qureshey would not have given an inkling of the success he would achieve in America as a boy growing up thousands of miles away in Karachi, Pakistan. He was born in 1951 in Pakistan, and spent his childhood there. He graduated from the University of Karachi with a bachelor's degree in physics in 1970. He came to the United States shortly thereafter, and received an electrical engineering degree at the University of Texas-Austin in 1975. He became a U.S. citizen in 1984. His work experiences include serving as a project and design engineer at Telefile Computer Products, a minicomputer and mainframe manufacturer. Later he worked as a test engineer for Computer Automation and A.M. International. It was at the former that he met Yuen, who came up with the idea of consulting.

Birth of AST Research

AST was formed as a high tech consulting firm. It was Yuen's idea to develop products to go with IBM's new personal computer. The first deal was not an auspicious beginning. Qureshey was quoted in *Contemporary Entrepreneurs:* "We sold our first board to a customer in Orange County. They sent us a check for $82, and the check bounced. It was not a good feeling." However, by September 1981, the company was shipping "enhancement" products which included a 64K to 256K expansion memory board, a multiprotocol communications board, and an asynchronous communications card. In 1982 banks would not loan AST money to expand so the three partners took out second mortgages on their homes and raised $50,000. In 1984, the company went public.

For the next five years, AST's accessory business was successful. The company continued to come up with innovative products and introduced its first line of personal computers in 1986. The following two years saw further expansion when AST introduced twelve new PC systems and three new enhancement board products. In 1991, the company produced computer number one million, which was presented to President George Bush. AST sales had gone up from $71,000 in 1981 to $688.5 million in 1991.

The Drive to Always be Better

In 1985, IBM started producing its own enhancement products which made a considerable dent in AST's profits. Even the sale of AST's own line of computer products was not enough to keep up. An increasingly competitive market made the company suffer to the point that in 1989 AST reported an $8.9 million loss and laid off 120 employees. It was at this time that Albert Wong left the company over disagreements on how to recover from the setback. Qureshey and Yuen took this opportunity to evaluate past errors and goals. They replaced Wong with a five-member executive committee made up of experts in the field. AST sold its Apple and DEC divisions to pay off debt, and went through a process of restructuring the company to make it both time and cost efficient.

Observers say the key to AST's success has been its long-term strategy combined with a "humane" working environment and an enterprising spirit. Until 1988, AST sponsored pancake breakfasts with employees to discuss company successes and problems. The overall low profile of the company compared to its competitors is a reflection of Qureshey's persona. He is a soft-spoken man, a devout Muslim whose humility is surprising in comparison with other company CEOs. A father of three children, Qureshey believes that it is important to recognize teamwork. "The larger we grow, the more we recognize that each of us could not have accomplished what AST has as individuals," Qureshey told *Contemporary Entrepreneurs.* "The challenge as we become larger and more successful is to suppress the ego."

The Future

In keeping with Qureshey's personal understated style, AST Research's three-building campus is efficient but not lavish. With gray walls and flexible office space, the area is built for expansion. As the company approaches the $1 billion mark, Qureshey is concerned about retaining that image. "Even if we are growing big in terms of people, facilities, and revenue, we have to remain nimble," he told John Longwell of the *Orange County Business Journal.* "We cannot take months and months to make a decision, even though we are reaching a multinational level." The most important task for the future is going to be defining a corporate culture for the organization that retains the energy of a start-up company. Some company employees describe the company work ethic as being "challenging," "fun," and "fast-paced." Others say the challenge lies in long hours and high stress levels. The annual percentage of employee turnover is in the high teens and burnout is frequently cited as the cause. According to one former manager quoted in the *Orange County Business Journal,* workers have to put up with frequent reorganizations and different reporting relationships. Some ex-employees say the management likes really aggressive people with high energy levels.

One theory about the success of the company suggests that the company culture has been shaped by the frugality and hard work of its three Asian immigrant founders. Although AST's bonus program includes everyone, the company is frugal with stock options. Since 1992, Qureshey is the only operating head of the company. However, he believes that that should not be a determining factor for the future of the company. He told Michael Zimmerman of *PC Week,* "I could be hit by a truck tomorrow. AST should go on."

Besides his success as an entrepreneur, Qureshey is also a prominent citizen in southern California. He is a member of the Southern California Technology Executives Network and holds a position on its board of directors. In 1992, he accompanied Congressman Christopher Cox on his visit to see Mexico's President Carlos Salinas de Gortari regarding the North American Free Trade Agreement. Qureshey is a well-known Orange County Republican, who in 1993 welcomed a visit from Vice President Al Gore.

Sources:

Books

"Safi U. Qureshey and Thomas C. K. Yuen," in *Contemporary Entrepreneurs.* Detroit: Omnigraphics, 1992, pp. 402–407.

Periodicals

Armstrong, Larry. "This 12-year-old has come of age" *Business Week,* May 6, 1991, pp. 122–3.

"Award-Winning Exporters: AST Research Inc." *Journal of Commerce,* February 12, 1993, p. 4(A).

Gillin, Paul. "AST bids for the big time as market leaders suffer." *Computerworld,* December 16, 1991. pp. 97–9.

Impoco, Jim. "A smile of recognition: AST finally gets its due as one of America's top computer makers." *U.S. News & World Report,* March 21, 1994, pp. 54–55.

Longwell, John. "Corporate challenge." *Orange County Business Journal,* August 12, 1991, p. 1.

McGuire, Mark. "AST mounts push for big league status." *PC Week,* August 30, 1993, p. 106.

"Safi Qureshey." InfoWorld, April 19, 1993, vol. 15, no. 16, p. 114.

Zimmerman, Michael R. "AST follows its own course—and earns a profit." *PC Week,* November 30, 1992, pp. 161–2.

—Sketch by Natasha Rafi

R

Jhoon Rhee
(1932–)
Martial artist

During a special House committee hearing on aging in 1992, he asked his eighty-eight-year-old mother to perform the "Jhoon Rhee daily dozen" before a group of congressmen. At the same hearing, he himself did one hundred pushups in one minute—though he was sixty years old. He then vowed to repeat the feat in the year 2032, at age one hundred.

Considered the father of American Tae Kwon Do, Jhoon Rhee is credited with adapting and popularizing the Korean martial art form in the United States. He has written books, starred in movies, and hobnobbed with presidents. He creates national teacher appreciation days. He conducts seminars on the importance of being happy. He started his Jhoon Rhee Foundation to teach inner-city elementary school children the "Joy of Discipline," an exercise program he hopes they will continue the rest of their lives. He does this in the name of Tae Kwon Do, health, and happiness. "It takes a year to harvest a crop, ten years to see the full beauty of a tree, and fifty years to make a man," he told the House of Representatives Subcommittee on Aging in 1992. "So let us begin for our young children's education, motivating them to exercise and study."

A small man, Rhee is so flexible that he often is photographed standing on one leg with the other foot flexed toward the ceiling, knee touching his shoulder. His face is a study in intensity, broken only by an unmistakable twinkle in his eyes. He has dedicated his life to spreading happiness, which he believes is enhanced through the practice of Tae Kwon Do. He fervently believes that everyone is born to be happy and that when they have become happy, the world will be a better place. "The purpose of life is to be happy," he told the House in 1992. "And to be happy, we must love and be loved."

Exercise for Life

Jhoon Rhee was born January 7, 1932, in Sanyangri, Asan, Korea. From the beginning, Rhee was taught to respect his

Jhoon Rhee

elders, addressing them as "Sir" or "Ma'am." His grandfather on his father's side was a scholar with a doctorate in Confucian literature, whom Rhee admired greatly as a man of high character and wisdom with a loving personality. His grandfather lived to be ninety-two years old, largely, Rhee believes, because he did thirty minutes of stretching exercises every morning. Today, Rhee's "Jhoon Rhee daily dozen" series of exercises are based in part on his memories of watching his grandfather's morning stretches. From his grandfather Rhee also learned the importance of honesty. While enrolled in a *gul bang*, or a kindergarten, Rhee received from his grandfather a book to study. He left the book at the playground. When he came home, his grandfather asked him to read from the book. Rhee, afraid to admit he'd lost the book, lied and said he'd loaned it to a friend. To his shock, his grandfather then produced the book. After being spanked, Rhee remembers his grandfather telling him that God is watching whatever we do, both good and bad. A simple thought perhaps, but it left an important impression on Rhee that he believes has helped strengthen his character today.

As a child, Rhee was hardly the example of a fit and healthy person. When he was an infant, his sister dropped him on a hard floor by accident, causing his thigh bone to be broken midway between his knee and hip. The same day, his mother's father died of an intestinal problem. Rhee's mother carried the baby to her father's house and used the dead man's hand to massage her baby's wound. Miraculously, the broken bone healed. In school, Rhee always was the slowest runner, the smallest child. In high school, bullies tormented him, often causing him to run home crying and bloody from their assaults. It was this harassment, he realized later, that caused him to seek out Tae Kwon Do. In 1947, at age fifteen, he enrolled in the Chung Do Kwan School of Tae Kwon Do, formed before Korea's liberation from the Japanese.

"Peace Through Strength"

He kept quiet initially about the lessons because his father believed Tae Kwon Do was no different from street fighting. He also kept the practice of the martial art a secret from his school classmates. Then, one day when Rhee was in the eleventh grade, a bully grabbed a pencil from his hand. The time to test himself had come. Rhee told the bully to meet him after school, and in the ensuing fight, punched him in the left eye and kicked him on the throat. By beating up one of the school's biggest bullies, Rhee earned respect and better treatment from his peers. He also gained a sense of what he describes as "peace through strength."

Rhee fell in love with the American dream shortly after World War II when the Korean movie market was suddenly flooded with American movies. He began studying English, with the hope of someday moving to the United States. He planned to attend Dong Kook University in 1950, but the start of the Korean War changed his plans. Then eighteen, Rhee and a nine-year-old brother fled south from their parents' home to their grandfather's house in Asan. But, not knowing where their parents were, Rhee and his brother grew worried. They decided to trek fifty miles north by foot back to their parents' home in Sunan, despite repeated bombings and air attacks. They found their mother unharmed but could not locate their father. Rhee, worried that he might be drafted by the North Korean Communists, hid in a ground cell for two months until word came that General Douglas MacArthur had pushed the Communist forces back. Rhee was so overjoyed by his new freedom that he joined the U.S. Air Force as an interpreter. However, he soon was drafted into the Korean Military in 1951.

After the Service

Rhee came to the United States in June 1956, to work for an aircraft maintenance program at Gary Air Force Base in Texas. Eager to finally be able to pursue the American dream, he attended college in Texas, where he studied engineering. He eventually settled in the United States permanently.

Throughout this time Rhee had kept up his daily practice of Tae Kwon Do, and in the summer of 1962 he moved to Washington, D.C., to teach at a karate school. The school, however, only had six students and no money to pay the teachers. Already energized by the American dream, Rhee decided to open his own school. Within three months, he had one hundred students. Gradually, his teaching of Korean karate styles established him as the father of American Tae Kwon Do. Soon, he was opening schools throughout the United States.

Famous Students

Rhee's style, now known as the "Jhoon Rhee fighting method," differs from traditional Tae Kwon Do in that it stresses learning a series of combinations of moves, rather than relying simply on balance. As an engineering student in Texas, Rhee had applied theories of static, mechanics, speed, and power to his karate moves. Not surprisingly, these ideas have drawn their share of criticism from traditional masters of Tae Kwan Do. Rhee, however, defends his ideas, citing the words of his longtime friend, martial arts master and film star Bruce Lee, who had always said that when you're tied by tradition, there is no improvement.

In a nation wedded to baseball and other all-American sports, promoting a martial art proved to be a tough sell, but Rhee kept his art alive by teaching it to famous people. Boxer Muhammad Ali, for instance, credits Rhee with teaching him a special "accupunch" that helped him win the famous "Thriller in Manila." And in 1975, Rhee brought the concept of Tae Kwon Do to the halls of government by sponsoring a "Capital Hill Grudge Bout" featuring U.S. congressmen. Democrats fought Republicans in a semi-contact karate match. There appears to be no record of who won the match, but it has since inspired dozens of congressmen, including House Speaker Tom Foley, to study Tae Kwon Do under Rhee's tutelage.

Now, in his early 60s, Rhee vows to live to age 136. He promotes a philosophy of life that mixes American utilitarianism with classic Confucianism. He believes that through the practice of Tae Kwon Do, one can strengthen the mind, the body, and the spirit..

Sources:

Periodicals

Segerdal, Alasair. "Jhoon Rhee." *Combat,* February 1978.
Simpkins, Alex and Annellen. "Jhoon Rhee: Born to be Happy," *Tae Kwon Do Times,* January, 1994.

Other

Testimony of Jhoon Rhee, presented before the U.S. House of Representatives' Select Committee on Aging, February 25, 1992.

—Sketch by Himanee Gupta

Syngman Rhee
(1875–1965)
Political activist

Syngman Rhee was the founder and the first president of the Republic of Korea, the first democratic government to rule on the Korean peninsula in four thousand years. The government was formed in exile during the Japanese occupation and ruled from Hawaii, where Rhee lived for many years, both before and after heading the government in Seoul.

Syngman Rhee was born in Whanghai Province, Korea, on March 26, 1875. He was the only son of Lee Kyung Sun and Lee Kim Hai and was a descendant of the rulers of the Yi Dynasty, which ruled Korea from 1392 until the Japanese invasion and occupation of 1910. Rhee was educated by Methodist missionaries in Korea, and as a young man joined the Independence Club, which demanded democratic reform of the monarchy and an end to Japanese influence within the country. In 1895 when the leader of the group fled the country, Rhee became its leader. Also in that year, he founded Korea's first daily newspaper, *Independence*. As he continued pushing for reform he became a nuisance to the monarchy and was jailed and subjected to seven months of torture. While in prison—he was eventually sentenced to life—he was converted to Christianity and became a missionary of sorts within the jail.

Education in the United States

In 1904 the monarchy issued a general amnesty, and Rhee was released. He left Korea for the United States, where he earned a bachelor's degree from George Washington University, a master's degree from Harvard, and a doctorate in international law from Princeton. At Princeton, he was greatly influenced by the teachings of Woodrow Wilson. In 1911 he returned briefly to Korea, which in his absence had been annexed by Japan. Again he was forced to flee, going this time to Hawaii, where he founded the Korean Methodist Church and the Korean Christian Institute. In 1919 in a secret meeting in Seoul, Rhee was elected president of the Korean Provisional Government in Exile. In this post he helped to organize the guerrilla fighters within Korea who fought for the next twenty-five years to destabilize the Japanese colonial government, a notoriously brutal regime.

Independence proved difficult, however, and did not come until the Japanese were defeated by the United States in World War II. In elections held in 1948, after three years of vicious political infighting and superpower posturing over the division of the Korean peninsula—the Soviet Union occupied the North—Rhee was elected to a

Syngman Rhee

four-year term as president. Political turbulence continued during his tenure as president with the military of the Soviet-backed North assuming an increasingly threatening posture. On June 25, 1950, the North invaded the South, beginning three years of warfare between the North and their backers in Moscow, and the South and their backers in Washington. The war was finally resolved with an armistice that resulted in the permanent partition of the peninsula along the heavily fortified 38th parallel.

Exile in Hawaii

Rhee won reelection as president of the Republic of Korea in 1952, 1956, and 1960. The 1960 elections, however, were widely regarded as highly fraudulent and a student protest movement swept the country resulting in Rhee's resignation and exile to the United States. He settled in Hawaii at the oceanside home of a wealthy Korean nurseryman with his wife, Francesca [Donner], the daughter of a Viennese merchant, whom he had met and married in Geneva in 1932.

In 1963 the government of Korea announced that Rhee, until then unwelcome in his country, would be allowed to return. His health, however, was such that the trip was impossible. He died from complications of a stroke at the age of ninety on July 19, 1965, in Honolulu, Hawaii.

Sources:

"Syngman Rhee Dies an Exile From Land He Fought to Free." *New York Times,* July 20, 1965.

—Sketch by Jim Henry

Ninotchka Rosca

(1954(?)–)

Writer

Writing is Ninotchka Rosca's weapon of choice when it comes to fighting the evils of dictatorship and oppression in her homeland, the Philippines. "Mostly I write about how perilous it is to be human in a weak and poor country dominated by Westerners," Rosca told *Contemporary Authors*. Rosca's major works include two short story collections about the Philippines, *Bitter Country and Other Stories* and *Monsoon Collection*. Her novel *State of War,* published in 1988, tells a story of intrigue and betrayal through three fictional characters. When *State of War* was published in paperback edition, it was the first book by a Filipino writer to be published in both hardcover and paperback in more than forty years. In tracing the genealogy of these characters, Rosca in effect relates the history of the Philippines from the days of Spanish occupation through modern times. Summing up much of her writing, Rosca told *Publishers Weekly* in May 1988, "I just wanted to tell the story of my people. I think I'm a populist in my orientation in the sense that I admire Filipinos very deeply. They've struggled so hard, they've fought so hard, and they ask for so little."

Rosca's personal life reflects some of the same conflict she writes about. Born in 1954(?) to a professional gambler father and a botanist mother, she and her two brothers and two sisters experienced the economic ups and downs inherent in their father's career. Rosca credits her mother with shaping her strong feelings about feminism and political activism. "My mother was a beautiful woman, and most people interacted with her on that basis," she told *Publishers Weekly.* "She was also intelligent. But when I was born, I didn't look anything like my mother, and people would say, 'Oh, is that your daughter?' . . . It's tragic for a woman to be beautiful and tragic for her not to be beautiful. It's very difficult being an intelligent female in a country like the Philippines. Being an intelligent male is bad enough."

Activism

Rosca attended both public and Catholic schools in Manila and received her bachelor's degree in comparative literature at the University of the Philippines in 1975. Like many of her contemporaries, Rosca protested against the Vietnam War and the Philippines' role in it as a supporter of U.S. involvement. Her college years were stormy, filled with picket lines and passionate protests. Meanwhile, as the conflict in southeast Asia continued, so did the influence of soon-to-be-dictator Ferdinand Marcos in the Philippines.

Rosca worked for *The Graphic* magazine after graduation and became its managing editor two years later. The job didn't last long because Rosca herself helped to organize a union for staff members, which fired members of management—including Rosca—soon after its formation. She continued to write for various weekly publications in the Philippines and was a scriptwriter for Manila television. She soon became recognized as one of the top writers in the country. Marcos' declaration of martial law in 1972 led to a six-month stay in a detention center for Rosca and other accused dissidents. After her release, she continued to resist the Marcos regime, helping friends escape from Manila while trying to maintain a semblance of normality by attending graduate school. Rosca's experiences during these years later provided material for the stories in *The Monsoon Collection,* published in 1982, and *State of War.*

When Rosca learned in 1976 that she was about to be arrested again, she accepted a fellowship at the International Writers Program at the University of Iowa. The move to the United States proved to be a major turning point; intending to return to the Philippines in 1977 after completing the Iowa program, Rosca was warned by her mother that it wasn't safe. The next seven years proved to be quite dramatic for Rosca, as she struggled to carve out a life in the United States. The Immigration and Naturalization Service (INS) declined to take action on her application for political asylum, and the Philippine government, then under Marcos, twice refused to renew her passport. Forced to exist under these tenuous circumstances, Rosca explained her choices to *Notable Asian Americans:* "I could be very, very quiet and hope the INS won't notice me; or I could be very, very noisy and hope that people will support me if the INS did anything." She elected the high-profile option, and eventually was granted asylum.

During this time, Rosca spent three years teaching Tagalog, the most prominent of the 150 Philippine dialects, at the University of Hawaii. She moved to New York in 1981 with few contacts but high hopes. She wrote free-lance articles for various periodicals, including *Ms.*, the *Nation*, and the *Village Voice*, and worked as an editorial assistant. After hearing about her from a friend, editor Edward Breslin of Franklin Watts hired Rosca to write a book about the tumultuous political activities in the Philippines. *Endgame* was the result, chronicling the rise to power of Corazon Aquino and the inside story of prominent players both within and outside of the Aquino regime. Rosca told *Publishers Weekly* that her return to the

Philippines to research the book generated conflicting emotions. "You could see that people expected so much and that they weren't going to get it," she said. "I looked into the possibility of staying there, but it was impossible. Things were going to turn out so different than what we fought for."

Rosca's writing career has continued to flourish. In 1986 she received a grant for fiction writing from the New York Foundation for the Arts. In that same year, her short story "Epidemic," first published in the *Missouri Review,* was selected for inclusion on the "1986 Raymond Carver's List of Best 100 Stories Published in the US." She won a magazine writing award from the Women's Political Caucus in 1987 for her story "Between the Gun and the Crucifix." Her novel *State of War* was finally published in 1988 after eight publishing houses had rejected it. Rosca's two major commitments, writing and her homeland, have endured throughout years of struggle. In 1993, her novel *Twice Blessed* (published by Norton in 1992) won the American Book Award from the Before Columbus Foundation.

But writing, she told *Publishers Weekly,* is the true cornerstone of her life. "For us to effect social change, to make authority realize it's not doing well, no writing can do it. I say that because in the Philippines we have a tendency to be overdramatic about the writer's role in society. . . . When I went back in '86 and '87, I thought, 'Boy, oh boy, all I want to do is write a good book.' I don't think there is any self-respecting writer in the world who thinks about audiences when she sits down to write. The first thing she thinks about is the story."

Sources:

Books

Trotsky, Susan M., ed. "Ninotchka Rosca." *Contemporary Authors,* vol. 127. Detroit: Gale Research, Inc., 1989.

Periodicals

Mestrovic, Marta. "PW Interviews Ninotchka Rosca." *Publishers Weekly,* May 6, 1988, p. 90–91.

Other

Rosca, Ninotchka, written interview with Susan Gall, July 19, 1994.

—Sketch by Mary Anne Klasen

S

Patricia Saiki

(1930–)

Politician

Patricia Saiki has lived a life of public service. She was the first Republican to represent Hawaii, from 1987-1991, in the U.S. House of Representatives since it attained statehood in 1959. She was appointed in 1991 by President George Bush to head the U.S. Small Business Administration, an agency with 4,000 employees and a budget of $382 million, taught at the Kennedy School of Government at Harvard University, and is a candidate for governor of Hawaii in 1994.

Patricia Saiki was born May 28, 1930, in Hilo, Hawaii, the oldest of three girls born to Kazuo and Shizue (Inoue) Fukuda. Saiki's father's family had come to Hawaii from Japan and labored in the sugar cane fields, earning a dollar a day to support their five sons. Saiki's father worked as a clerk and her mother worked at home as a seamstress. There was no money for extras, not even a car, but the family made a pact to work together and to save every dollar to insure that all three girls would go to college. Pat was the first to go and she lived in a cooperative dormitory where everyone shared chores. She sold stockings and babysat and graduated with a double major in education and history from the University of Hawaii in 1952. All three Fukuda girls graduated and became teachers thanks to their pact and their strong sense of family support.

In an interview with Cobey Black, Saiki recounted: "Dad was the first feminist. But what Dad did that is more important is inspire in me the confidence of my own worth. To believe in myself—that was a wonderful gift." Saiki managed to save enough money from her first teaching job to buy her father a used car and she taught him to drive it. Saiki was helping complete the circle of family support.

In June 19, 1954, Saiki married Stanley Mitsuo Saiki, a doctor twelve years her senior. Shortly after their marriage, Stanley enrolled at the University of Pennsylvania to specialize in the area of obstetrics and gynecology. The

Patricia Saiki

couple left Hawaii when Saiki was pregnant with their first child, Stanley, Jr. The growing family then moved to Toledo, Ohio, for Stanley's residency and the birth of two more Saiki children, Sandra and Margaret. With three young children and her husband's meager pay as a resident, Saiki decided to return to teaching. "Grading papers between three loads of laundry was a nightly ritual," she told Black. Fortunately for the young family, Stanley's mother moved in to help.

Political Beginning

The Saikis returned to Hawaii in the late 1950s, just in time for statehood in 1959. There they welcomed their fourth and fifth children, Stuart and Laura. Saiki entered the political arena as a precinct officer in St. Louis Heights. Angered as she watched the "old war-horses" push their candidates through without opposition, Saiki recounted to Black about how she had begun to speak up. "It didn't seem right, even to a busy homemaker, so I helped work up a slate and the next thing I knew, they'd made me a precinct officer—just to keep me quiet," she quipped.

In the 1960s, while teaching at Kaimuki Intermediate School, Saiki helped to organize a teachers' union. At that time the teachers had no say in educational decisions and worked long hours under poor conditions. Saiki questioned the issue of tracking children and wondered if it only served to demotivate children tracked in the lower levels. She also felt that teachers should help set educational goals and design challenging curriculum. She spoke up and the head of the Hawaii Government Employees Association (HGEA) listened. Saiki helped to organize and teachers joined the Teacher's Chapter of HGEA.

Saiki became increasingly active in politics, serving in a number of different capacities for the Republican party in Hawaii. "I've always been the kind of person who, when faced with something wrong, has to correct it," said Saiki. In 1968, at the urging of her fellow teachers, Saiki ran for public office and was elected a delegate to the Hawaii State Constitutional Convention.

The following year President Richard Nixon appointed Saiki to the Presidential Advisory Council on the Status of Women. She served on the committee for eight years and was reappointed by Nixon's successor President Gerald Ford. During that time, Saiki oversaw the funding of the Hawaii State Commission on the Status of Women and served as a watchdog for women's rights. She was elected to the Hawaii House of Representatives where she served from 1968 to 1974, and the Hawaii State Senate where she served from 1974 to 1982. She authored twenty-five bills dealing with equal rights for women, including the Equal Rights Amendment. In 1987, she was elected to the U.S. Congress and had the opportunity to work on a national level to address her concerns about women's and children's issues.

After a successful term as congresswoman, Saiki decided to run for the U.S. Senate. When she lost her election bid, she was so disappointed she told her family she didn't want to accept any calls. However, she did accept one call—from President George Bush. He consoled her on her loss and asked her to come back to Washington as part of the Small Business Administration.

Two weeks after being sworn in as the administrator of the SBA, Saiki's husband died. They had been successful partners in marriage for thirty-seven years and, together, had watched as their children grew up. Stanley and Sandra became doctors, Margaret a veterinarian, Stuart a computer engineer, and Laura a businesswoman. "I've been blessed with two marvelous, encouraging men in my life, my father and my husband," commented Saiki.

Home to Hawaii

She continued in her capacity at the SBA until November 1992, when she decided to return to Hawaii to be near family. She wasn't home long, however, before she was called by the Kennedy School of Government at Harvard University. The teacher had come full circle and Saiki returned to the classroom, only this time at Harvard University for the spring 1993 term.

During spring break Saiki received another enticing telephone call. An exploratory committee in Hawaii called to ask her to run for governor in 1994. "I really felt that with a lifetime that's been gifted with a devoted family, a great husband, good health, and a political career which has fulfilled the faith of my supporters, I could do a good job as governor." As of fall 1994, Saiki is involved in her political campaign for governor of Hawaii.

The lifelong encouragement and support Saiki has received from family has served to make her an energetic supporter of issues concerning children and families. In a statement issued during her campaign for governor, Saiki said: "If elected, I want to bring new vision and vitality to our plans for the future. I want the people of Hawaii to enjoy the finest quality of life and provide our children a secure future."

Sources:

Books

"Patricia Saiki," *Who's Who of American Women, Chicago: Marquis Who's Who, Inc., 1993/94.*

Periodicals

"Hawaii Business." *In Focus,* September 1991.

Saiki, Patricia. "The Advantages of Making Loans with the SBA (Small Business Administration)." *Journal of Commercial Lending,* November 1992.

"Women Who Won: Seasoned Politicians with Solid Campaign Financing Make Their Mark," *Ms.,* January 1987.

Other

Black, Cobey. "Hilo Girl." Campaign literature, Saiki for Governor '94: A Committee, 1994.

"A Fresh Start: Patricia Saiki '94 Governor." Campaign literature, Saiki for Governor '94: A Committee, 1994.

—Sketch by Margaret Simon

Jo Kamosu Sakai
(1874–1923)
Land Developer

Jo Kamosu Sakai

The shores of Japan are a long way from the coast of Florida. But, in 1904, the dream of Jo Kamosu Sakai, an American-educated Japanese expatriate, brought the two countries closer when he founded a settlement colony of Japanese farmers in southern Florida. It was named Yamato after an ancient name for the country of Japan. The story of Sakai and his colony is the saga of the immigrant dream of opportunity, hard work, and success.

Born Kamosu Sakai on October 10, 1874, in the castle town of Miyazu, Japan, near the present-day city of Kyoto, Sakai was the fourth of seven children born to Takamasu and Masu Sakai. His father, a former *samurai*, had served the last *daimyo* or feudal lord of the Honjo clan, which had occupied the castle since 1758. After receiving his early education in the public schools of Miyazu, Sakai attended the equivalent of private high school at Doshisha, a Christian-based institution of higher learning in the city of Kyoto. Because his family was unable to afford the tuition, his education was financed by his sister's husband, Mitsusburo Oki, an affluent broker of raw silk in Miyazu's local textile industry. The liberal ideas to which Sakai was exposed at Doshisha reflected the philosphy of its founder, Jo Niijima, who became a lifelong role model for Sakai even to the extent that he adopted his first name.

Education in the United States

After completing a six-year curriculum at Doshisha, Sakai left for the United States in 1895 to continue his education at a Western university. According to his family, he wanted to study electrical engineering under Thomas Edison, a well-known figure in Kyoto, respected for his development of the incandescent light bulb whose filament material was made from carbonized bamboo from the grounds of a Kyoto shrine. Sakai did not succeed in joining Edison's organization, however. Although no actual records exist, newspaper reports indicate that he studied briefly at Yale University and then received his bachelor's degree in 1903 from New York University's School of Commerce, Accounting and Finance.

It was with letters of introduction from the dean of NYU's School of Commerce that he presented himself to the Jacksonville (Florida) Board of Trade, explaining his development scheme: He planned to import fifty or sixty Japanese families and establish them in individual farming colonies, ten families per colony. His purpose was to conduct agricultural experiments in the cultivation of silk, tea, tobacco, pineapples, and rice. Welcomed by Floridians and officially endorsed by Governor William Jennings, the U.S. Commissioner of Immigration, and the U.S. Secretary of Agriculture, Sakai capitalized on the American stereotype of the Japanese as ingenious agricultural specialists who could revitalize agriculture in the region. He ultimately signed an agreement with the Model Land Company, a subsidiary of the Florida East Coast Railway, to locate a proposed colony of Japanese farmers in the Boca Raton area. Returning to his native village of Miyazu in 1904 to recruit settlers and arrange for their passage, he succeeded in bringing five Japanese men to the colony he named Yamato.

Yamato Colony is Launched

The first settlers had to clear and plant the land, and it was rare that one settler could clear more than an acre a season. They planted heavily in pineapples and to a lesser extent in other crops such as silk and tea. The need to endure hardships brought on by the tropical climate with its rains, floods, heat, and insects did not deter the small but steady flow of immigrants attracted by the promise of future economic prosperity in Florida. By 1907, the Florida East Coast Railway had established a station at Yamato which provided access to outside markets. That same year, Sakai petitioned the state government to incorporate the settlement under the name Yamato Colony Association and established a governing system for it with constitution, rules, and elected officials. However, the initial promise of economic success was not to be. A blight that struck the pineapple fields in 1908 crippled the crop, and competition from Cuban plantation growers dealt the death blow to that cash crop. Those Japanese settlers who could afford to leave Yamato did. Those who could not remained behind looking for other ways to support themselves. In addition to the economic problems, by 1912 a decisive strain of anti-Japanese sentiment among native Floridians produced discussion of discriminatory laws aimed at preventing Japanese ownership of land in the state. Although this proposed legislation was never passed, new arrivals of settlers virtually ceased. Perhaps the final blow to Sakai's Yamato Colony came in 1919, when the U.S. Post Office Department closed the Yamato post office.

Throughout his relatively short lifetime, Sakai never stopped his tireless efforts to promote the colony. He died of tuberculosis on August 21, 1923, at the age of forty-nine in Asheville, North Carolina, where he had gone to convalesce.

Land Confiscated

By the 1930s only about thirty settlers from the Yamato Colony remained in the area. When World War II broke out, few Japanese were left. The Yamato farmers, unlike their countrymen on the West Coast, were not relocated in internment camps in the country's interior, probably due to the fact that their agricultural production was needed to support the war effort. In May 1942, however, the remaining farmland in the Yamato area which was still owned by Japanese was confiscated by the U.S. government and used to complete a U.S. Army Air Force installation. The last pioneer of the Yamato Colony, George Morikami, died without heirs in 1975.

The Morikami Museum and Japanese Gardens located in Delray Beach in Palm Beach County, Florida, have permanent exhibits depicting the history of the Yamato Colony, its founder, Jo Sakai, and its last pioneer, George Morikami.

Sources:

Periodicals

Pozzetta, George E. and Harry A. Kersey, Jr. "Yamato Colony: A Japanese Presence in South Florida." *Tequesta: The Journal of the Historical Association of Southern Florida,* 1976.
"Sakai Funeral." *Delray News,* August 31, 1923.

Other

"A Guy Named Jo." Text from a forthcoming publication on the Yamato Colony.
The Morikami Museum and Japanese Gardens Booklet. Unpublished exhibit texts, Morikami Museum, 1993.

—*Sketch by Nancy Moore*

Richard Sakakida
(1920–)
Counterintelligence agent

Retired Lieutenant Colonel Richard M. Sakakida of the United States Air Force is a career military officer and a decorated undercover agent who worked as a counterintelligence agent in the Philippines from April 22, 1941, to September 20, 1945. During this time Sakakida was held as a prisoner by the Japanese, who repeatedly tortured him to find out his position with the U.S. military. He was eventually released by the Japanese, but continued to work among them, and used an underground network of Filipino guerrilla fighters to transmit intelligence to General Douglas MacArthur's command in Australia.

Richard M. Sakakida was born November 19, 1920, in Maui, Hawaii. His parents, both of Japanese descent, raised their three children—two sons and one daughter—in Honolulu. His father was a boilermaker and his mother was a housewife who stayed at home to raise Sakakida and his two siblings.

Intelligence Work in the Philippines

Sakakida was involved in military training at Honolulu's McKinley High School where he had achieved the rank of cadet colonel in his senior year. Sakakida's instructor at McKinley, Major Jack Gilbert, would later recruit Sakakida into the Corps of Intelligence Police (CIP), the counterintelligence agency of the U.S. Army. Sakakida graduated from McKinley in 1939, two years before the American involvement in the World War II. In 1941, nine months before the Japanese bombing of Pearl Harbor, Sakakida was sworn in as a sergeant in the CIP.

Sakakida was sent along with another Japanese American, Arthur Komori, to the Philippines on April 7, 1941. Although the United States had still not officially entered the war, the government was clearly concerned with Imperial Japan's military expansionism throughout Asia and the Pacific area. The United States had a variety of colonial and quasi-territorial interests in the area, and was deeply committed to keeping them out of the hands of the Japanese. The Philippines was such a territory. The United States had a clear historical, colonial interest there and Sakakida's mission was to pose as a deserter from the American military, and to keep tabs on Japanese nationals living in the Philippines.

Sakakida moved into the Nishikawa Hotel in downtown Manila, where he posed as a representative of the Marsman Trading Company, Sears and Roebuck's outlet in the Philippines. Sakakida blended well into Manila and he began his work. One of his opportunities came on July 25, 1941, when the United States froze all Japanese assets, including those in the Philippines, in protest of Japan's military aggression throughout Asia. Sakakida volunteered his services to assist Japanese nationals in complying with U.S. financial disclosure requirements. During interviews with Japanese Filipinos, Sakakida would ask questions that were not actually required, such as about their military training, if any. He would then pass this information on to his superiors.

On December 8, 1941, a day that will live in infamy in the Philippines, the Japanese air force bombed Manila, beginning their invasion of the islands. In the aftermath of the bombing, Japanese nationals were rounded up for detention by the American officials. Sakakida, whose mission was secret even to American officials in Manila, was arrested on suspicion of being a spy for Japan. He spent a few days in prison with his fellow agent Komori before being released by his superiors. After his release, he was taken out of cover and began working in uniform translating military prison interrogations and intercepted enemy signals.

Early in 1942 the Japanese began making significant advances in fighting to control the Philippines. General Douglas MacArthur ordered the linguists who remained on the islands to evacuate, and arrangements were made to send Sakakida and Komori to headquarters in Australia. Sakakida, however, felt he would be better able to help in the Philippines and persuaded his superiors to let another man take his seat on the evacuation plane. On May 6, 1942, the U.S. forces in the Philippines surrendered to Japan. Sakakida was arrested and spent six months in jail being interrogated by the Japanese who doubted his cover story of being an American deserter. They considered him a traitor and tortured him cruelly throughout his imprisonment, burning him with cigarettes and purposely dislocating his shoulders, all the while trying to pierce the credibility of his cover story while his defenses were down. Sakakida kept his wits about him, however, and was never tripped up by their tactics.

Finally the Japanese gave up on Sakakida, released him from prison, and sent him to work in the office of Colonel Nishiharu, the chief judge advocate of the Fourteenth Army Headquarters. His duties would be to assist in the office in any way he could and then to serve as the colonel's houseboy when not at the office, even living at the colonel's residence. After Sakakida was caught pilfering American cigarettes from the colonel's personal stash, he was sent to live elsewhere, but continued his work with the colonel. His work at Nishiharu's office allowed him privileged access to regulated documents and he began issuing visitor's passes to the families of Filipino guerrillas being held by the Japanese. These contacts then put him in touch with the guerrillas themselves and Sakakida arranged a daring prison break to free the fighters. This was a remarkable and brave endeavor, and it led to the

Richard Sakakida

freedom of nearly five hundred guerrilla fighters, many of whom rejoined the resistance in the hills.

Sakakida was now in contact with active members of the resistance, who were in turn in contact with American headquarters in Australia, and on at least one occasion he was able to transmit crucial military information through this chain that helped the military prepare for a Japanese offensive.

Jungle Escape

In December of 1944 the United States launched its invasion of the Philippines. Sakakida joined up with a band of guerrillas in the jungles. During a fight with a Japanese unit, Sakakida was wounded and separated from the guerrillas. He wandered through the jungle until he came upon an American unit. The Americans were of course suspicious of Sakakida's story, but the major in charge checked it out and within hours a jeep from the counterintelligence corps was sent for him.

Sakakida continued to work for the U.S. military, first, from 1946 to 1948 in helping the intelligence community round up persons suspected of committing war crimes. He would later return to testify as a key witness in the war crimes trials after the war. Sakakida was awarded the Bronze Star Medal for his distinguished, selfless, and crucial service to the American military.

Lea Salonga

From 1948 to 1975, Sakakida served the air force in its Office of Special Investigations (AFOSI) until his retirement on April 1, 1975. At the time of his retirement, he was commander of AFOSI in Japan.

In 1994, Sakakida was honored by the government of the Philippines with the Legion of Honor (Degree of Legionnaire) presidential award in recognition of his exceptionally meritorious service to the Filipino-American Freedom Fighters and as a U.S. Army undercover agent.

Sources:

Books

Bray, Ann. "Undercover Nisei," in *Military Intelligence: Its Heroes and Legends,* U.S. Army Intelligence and Security Command, Arlington Hall Station, Virginia.

Periodicals

"WWII Nisei MIS Vet Receives Legion of Honor Award," *Nichi Bei Times,* May 5, 1994.

Other

Sakakida, Richard, written interview with Jim Henry, July 18, 1994.

—Sketch by Jim Henry

Lea Salonga
(1971–)
Actress, singer

"**T**he last time Americans were treated to the singing of a Filipino woman, they got Imelda Marcos, shoeless in Hawaiian exile, warbling 'Don't Fence Me In' on *60 Minutes.* But on opening night of *Miss Saigon*'s long awaited run on Broadway, Lea Salonga showed the pipes and pathos that had made her a star in her native Manila, and raised her above the 1,200 other aspiring Saigon auditioners," declared an exuberant reviewer in *People Weekly.*

In 1988, British producer Cameron Mackintosh went to Manila in search of a female lead for his stage production of the musical *Miss Saigon.* At the time, seventeen-year-old Lea Salonga, born in February of 1971 and described as an ethereal beauty, was a pre-med student at the Jesuit university, Ateneo de Manila. She also had eleven years of stage experience and TV roles to her credit. Salonga decided to put aside her surgical instruments and audition for the part of the Vietnamese lover in *Miss Saigon.*

Miss Saigon

Salonga's mother was skeptical that the audition would be legitimate, fearing the casting directors had come to the Philippines to take advantage of young girls. Salonga had to overcome her mother's objections before she captivated everyone with her pure, sweet, soprano voice at the audition. By all accounts, Salonga gave a stunning audition, and then went on to give remarkable performances. A review of the play in *Time* noted: "*Miss Saigon* is not a documentary, not journalism. But it remains stunningly relevant by the standards of Broadway, and triumphantly Broadway in meeting the standards of relevance."

Salonga's performance in the play was lauded by one and all. In 1991 she received the Tony Award for best leading actress in a musical in front of a loudly cheering Broadway audience and a national television audience of twelve million. For all its popularity and critical acclaim, her role in *Miss Saigon,* however, also raised controversies. When the popular show headed for Broadway in a hurricane of publicity with advance ticket sales of $39 million and a top ticket price of $100, the Actors' Equity union demanded, because of earlier disagreements, that Salonga be replaced because she was Asian and not American. Although it was eventually decided that she would not be replaced, the event almost triggered of an international incident.

Salonga's musical interests had always been encouraged by both her parents. Her father, who was musically inclined, was instrumental in launching Salonga's career. Her first stage role was in the Manila production of *The King and I,* after which came *Fiddler on the Roof,* and the title role in *Annie.* When she was twelve years old, she hosted a TV musical variety show for kids, "Love, Lea," for two years.

Princess Jasmine, Singer

Salonga's mother Joy has been her social guide, keeping a close watch over Salonga, reportedly chaperoning her daughter's dates until she reached the age of twenty-one. In fact, just prior to rehearsals for the show in 1989, Salonga had never been kissed. Salonga entertains herself by reading Robin Cook mysteries and watching "Charlie Brown" and "Garfield" cartoons. Although she is technically on vacation from medical school, she doubts that she will return. Salonga is also interested in working in television and film. In 1992 she provided the singing voice of Princess Jasmine in the Disney hit movie *Aladdin.* She has also released an album of pop songs simply entitled, "Lea Salonga," while at the same time continues to maintain an active stage career. Salonga hopes that the story of her success can be used as an inspiration to others.

Sources:

Goodman, Mark. "The New Princess Lea." *People Weekly,* June 17 1991, p. 55.

Henry, William. "Last Exit to the Land of Hope." *Time,* April 8, 1991, p. 72.

"Lea Salonga: The Fifty Most Beautiful People in the World." *People Weekly,* July 1991, p. 63.

Sheward, David. "Saigon, Rogers, in Tony Tie with Eleven Nominations Each." *Back Stage,* May 10, 1991, p. 1.

Walsh, Thomas. "Salonga a Go for Saigon, Arbitrator Says." *Back Stage,* January 11, 1992, p. 1.

———. "Salonga Now Has Saigon Partner." *Back Stage,* February 1, 1991, p. 1.

"A Whole New World for Lea Salonga." *Science World,* November 19, 1993, p. 16.

—*Sketch by Visi R. Tilak*

Scott M. Sassa
(1959–)
Broadcasting

At age thirty-five, Scott Sassa is one of the youngest executives in the television business. Ten years ago he was a low-level employee at a public relations firm, and today he is president of Turner Entertainment Group, with the

Scott M. Sassa

start-up of two programming networks to his credit. The most successful of these was Turner Network Television (TNT), the largest launch in cable television history. TNT started with 17 million subscribers and in a short time has grown to its present level of more than 57 million subscribers. Sassa serves on the Turner Broadcasting System (TBS) board of directors, on the TBS executive committee, and as TBS corporate vice-president of the Entertainment Group. He is responsible for all operations and programming for Turner Entertainment Networks, which includes TBS Superstation, TNT, the Cartoon Network, TNT Latin America, the Cartoon Network in Latin America, TNT and Cartoon Network in Europe, and Turner Home Entertainment. He also oversees Hanna-Barbera Productions, Turner Entertainment Company, and Turner Pictures Worldwide.

Scott Sassa was born on February 2, 1959, in Los Angeles and grew up in Hollywood. He attended University of Southern California where he took business courses but never completed his business degree since he did not get credit for a television internship he took during the 1980 election. Rather than contest the university's decision and officially get a diploma. Sassa decided to enter the workforce. He joined Rogers & Cowan, a small public relations firm, as an assistant working basically as a gopher. A year later at a fraternity dinner in Los Angeles Sassa met a colleague who was leaving Turner and offered him his job. Sassa went to a cable show and heard Turner speak. "It was a very exciting time," he said. "Cable was the big idea."

The Journey Begins

Sassa, at only age twenty-three, joined Turner in 1982 as assistant to Gerry Hogan, a Turner executive now with Whittle Communications. Hogan was impressed with the young man's abilities. "He's obviously extraordinarily bright," said Hogan. "He has an engaging personality that lends itself to building teams."

Sassa's work with Hogan exposed him to several opportunities. "I was able to work on a lot of projects, like the initial attempt to buy CBS," said Sassa. "And I worked on a business plan and presented it for a network that would have been called TNT from a combination of Metromedia and TBS." This plan was presented to Jamie Kellner, who later hired Sassa at Fox.

Sassa also took part in production at Turner in addition to his business responsibilities. At age twenty-five, he produced a music video show called "Night Tracks" and developed an idea to launch Turner's Cable Music Channel in late 1984. The program was supposed to rival MTV. Although it only lasted thirty-six days, Sassa learned from the experience what he needed to know for future start-ups. Years later the TNT success and the creation of the new cartoon network established Sassa as a key figure in the broadcasting business. "A lot of it comes down to opportunity," said Sassa. "I think I was lucky in a lot of ways. But I also think that, as in *Dead Poets Society* and in the line 'seize the day' you get those opportunities and you have to make sure they play out."

After his initial experience at Turner, Sassa was offered the position of running *Playboy*'s home video business in Los Angeles. While at *Playboy*, Sassa met Kellner who suggested working on the launch of a fourth network. Sassa joined the start-up team of Fox Broadcasting network but soon quit over "philosophical differences." He then joined Ohlmeyer Communications, and it was there that Hogan contacted him about working on TNT. As the man in charge, Sassa built TNT into a phenomenal success. From a basic movie channel, TNT expanded into made-for-cable and NBA and NFL broadcasts. According to Sassa timing was a crucial factor: "Had we launched it three months earlier or three months later, I think it would have never happened the way it happened," he said. "It's always Ted's vision to start out with, but in terms of the execution, I feel comfortable in taking credit for the original programming we put together."

Back in Atlanta, Sassa married Ellen Griffin on September 22, 1990. Over the years he has grown to like the city and does not miss his native Hollywood too much. One of the things that drew him to Atlanta and Turner was TBS's philosophy that television should enlighten. "It's kind of nice to come to work and know that you can do things that are the right things to do, and you don't always have to do things because they will make money," he said.

The Drive to do Better

Sassa is now preparing for the hundreds of channels that will be competing for viewers in the future. "We are in a very competitive market right now," he said. "The key is to just be able to hold on to your audience." According to Sassa there is not enough quality programming for the number of possible channels. "The market will bear a certain efficiency," he said, "and allow only so many channels to survive because people can't watch all those channels."

The recent purchase of New Line Cinema and Castle Rock Entertainment by Turner has given rise to rumors that Sassa may leave his employer perhaps over differences concerning the $650 million deal. Whatever the outcome, Sassa, known as one of Hollywood's top strategic planners has no shortage of possible opportunities.

Sources:

Periodicals

"Fifth Estater. Scott Sassa: Seizing the Opportunity." *Broadcasting,* July 15, 1991.
"Power Brokers." *A. Magazine,* December 15, 1993, pp. 25–34.

Other

Turner Entertainment Group. "Scott Sassa." Biography, April 1993.

—*Sketch by Natasha Rafi*

Dalip Singh Saund
(1899–1973)
Politician, businessman

From a small village in northern India, Dalip Singh Saund traveled to California where he became a farmer, later a businessman, and ultimately the first Asian to ever serve in the U.S. Congress. Characterized as a unique combination of meditative idealist and shrewd crossroads politician, Saund is considered one of the most effective ambassadors of goodwill that America ever sent to India.

Dalip Singh Saund was born on September 20, 1899, in the village of Chhajalwadi in northern India. His parents, Natha Singh Saund and Jeoni Kaur Saund, were wealthy landowners and government contractors for canals and railroads. They were Sikhs, a sect of Hindus who for centuries have been opposed to the caste system, which rigidly divided people into distinct social classes. Even though his parents were illiterate, they encouraged the young Saund to pursue his studies. He attended schools in the town of Amritsar, India, and earned a bachelor of arts degree with honors from the University of Punjab in 1919. At the time, India was under British rule. Because he was a follower of Mahatma Gandhi's nationalist movement which called for Indian independence from Great Britain, Saund was not permitted to join the civil service. He instead decided to further his education. Inspired by the ideals of Abraham Lincoln and Woodrow Wilson, he came to the United States in 1920 to attend the University of California at Berkeley where he studied the canning industry. He planned to return to India after finishing school and set up his own business. While a student, Saund worked summers at canning factories in California. Apart from studying food preservation he also took courses in mathematics, leading to his master's degree in mathematics in 1922 and to his doctorate in 1924.

From Farmer to Speaker

While in the United States, Saund continued to attend religious services at the Sikh temple in Stockton, California. He became acquainted with many Hindus at the temple who had become successful farmers in the Imperial Valley in southern California. Following their lead, he began his own agricultural ventures in the fall of 1925. He grew a variety of crops from maize to watermelons and experimented with crops that were then new to the valley, such as sugarbeets and Punjab flax. Like other farmers, Saund had his good and bad crops. His deep-rooted Indian values, however, prevented him from filing customary bankruptcy procedures when his harvest failed; instead he spent years paying off his debts to avoid the shame of bills unpaid.

Before he settled down to full-time farming, Saund had written a book, *My Mother India*, in response to a book entitled *Mother India* which Saund felt portrayed an unfair picture of his home country. A man of broad interests, including politics and civic affairs, Saund began to make speeches on topics such as India and Franklin D. Roosevelt. His fame as a speaker grew, and he decided to run for the U.S. Congress. Because Indians were among those denied citizenship rights, however, he was unable to do so. Instead of resigning himself to the fact that Congress was beyond his reach, Saund decided to do something about it. He formed the India Association of America in 1942 and became its president.

One of the first missions for the India Association of America took Saund to Washington, D.C., to urge the adoption of an amendment to the immigration law which would make Indians eligible to become citizens. His efforts led to a bill being passed in 1946, and Saund received his naturalization papers in 1949. He then enrolled as a member of the central committee of the Democratic party in Imperial County, California, and ran for the judgeship in Westmoreland, California, in 1952.

Dalip Singh Saund

Although he won the election, he was not permitted to assume office because he had not yet been a citizen for a whole year.

Saund again ran for the same position the following year and won. His main objective was to clean up prostitution, gambling, and narcotics in Westmoreland. He also started his own business around the same time, becoming the proprietor of D.S. Saund Fertilizers in Westmoreland.

In late 1955, Saund announced that he would run for Congress in California's twenty-ninth congressional district, which traditionally had voted Republican. Saund ran against Republican Jacqueline Cochran Odlum on the platform that America is not prejudiced and that he could help promote better understanding between Asian countries and the United States. He won the election and in 1956 became the first Asian member of the U.S. House of Representatives.

Politics

In January 1957, Saund took his seat in the eighty-fifth Congress and was appointed to the House Foreign Affairs Committee, an honor for a first-term congressman. One of his initial assignments was to survey the U.S. foreign aid program in Asia. This gave Saund the opportunity to fulfill his campaign promise to go back to India and deny Communist propaganda about anti-Asian discrimination in the United States. A highlight of Saund's publicized tour of the Far East and Middle East was the invitation to address a joint session of India's houses of Parliament. The trip reinforced his belief that misunderstandings between Asians and Americans arose from the failure of the United States to make its motives and policies clear. He called for the expansion of the foreign exchange program, especially between Asian and American educators and journalists.

During his tenure as a U.S. representative, Saund supported a number of foreign affairs bills that were in favor of increased communications and programs between Asia and the United States. On the domestic front, he backed bills relating to civil rights and social benefits. In 1957, Saund won an Urban League award for improving race relations and in 1958, he won a Lord and Taylor award for making "perhaps the most effective tour of India by an American on record."

Saund was an active member of the American Mathematics Society, the Mathematics Association of America, Sigma Psi, Toastmasters, and Lions Clubs. While on a visit to Los Angeles in the late 1920s, Saund had met Marian Kosa, a student at the University of California, and on July 21, 1928, Saund and Kosa were married. Their son Dalip Singh Saund, Jr., is a veteran of the Korean War. The Saunds also had two daughters, Julie and Eleanor.

On April 23, 1973, Saund died. He had fulfilled his aspiration to be what he often described as a living example of American Democracy in practice.

Sources:

Books

"Saund, Dalip Singh." *Current Biography.* New York: H.W. Wilson, 1960, pp. 359–360.

Periodicals

"Saund, Dalip Singh." Obituary. *New York Times*, April 24, 1973, p. 44.

—*Sketch by Visi R. Tilak*

Allen Say
(1937–)
Author, illustrator

Allen Say is an award-winning illustrator and author of children's books whose themes explore the nature of the immigrant experience in America. His illustrations for *The Boy of the Three-Year Nap* by Dianne Snyder, which combined vivid colors and strong angles, won several awards, including a 1989 Caldecott Honor award. In his 1993 book *Grandfather's Journey*, Say tells the story of his grandfather's life in Japan and America, weaving moving descriptions of life as an outsider in America with paintings that combine photographic and classical elements. In 1994, *Grandfather's Journey* was awarded the prestigious Randolph Caldecott Medal for most distinguished children's American picture book.

Allen Say was born in Yokohama, Japan, on August 28, 1937, to a Korean father and a Japanese American mother. He began drawing at an early age, but was discouraged in artistic pursuits by his father who was much more interested in fostering Say's capacity for business. Say has many unhappy memories of his childhood and told *Booklist* in October of 1993, "You notice that I hardly ever talk about my father, whom I really hated all my life. I still do to this day, and that's why he just hovers in the background."

His parents were divorced when Say was twelve and he was sent to live in Tokyo with his grandmother, with whom he did not get along. She soon offered to get him his own apartment where he would be free to draw and read as much as he wanted. As he told *Booklist*, "I thought at first she was kidding, but she wasn't." So Say began to live by himself at the age of twelve.

Apprenticeship to a Great Cartoonist

Alone in a large city, Say realized he needed guidance, and one day he showed up at the studio of a highly regarded Japanese cartoonist named Noro Shinpei. In the young man's mind, he was looking for a master in the traditional Japanese sense, but looking back, he said in *Booklist*, "I realized I was effectively trying to replace my father. Noro Shinpei turns out to be my spiritual father to this day. Each time I send him a book of mine to read, he sends me a three-page critique of color, composition, etc. He wrote me about *Tree of Cranes*: 'Not only have you become a master, but poetry has entered your work.' Of course I cried."

When he was sixteen years old, Say left for America. He could speak no English when he arrived at a military academy in southern California. World War II had only been over eight years and Say encountered a lot of anti-Japanese animosity. He describes these years as very difficult and painful, and as soon as he graduated from high school he went back to Japan, hating southern California. He was hoping to experience Japan as a home, but there too he felt out of place and after only a year returned to California.

His Two Careers

In Los Angeles Say met a Jewish woman, and they were forced to elope when the woman's father, outraged that

Allen Say

she was dating an Asian, threatened Say with a pistol. "Then I was drafted and sent to Germany," he said in *Booklist*. When I came out of the army, I was twenty-seven years old, my marriage fell apart, and I was only interested in making lots of money." By this time, Say had virtually stopped drawing and painting. He turned to photography, which had become a hobby while he was in the military. Soon he became one of the most highly paid photographers on the West Coast. It would be more than twenty years before Say returned full time to his art and children's books.

Say continued to dabble in illustrating and writing, however, but with no great critical success at first. In 1968 Say illustrated his first book, *A Canticle of Waterbirds*, written by Brother Antonius. Four years later he wrote and illustrated his own book, *Dr. Smith's Safari*. In 1979, his self-illustrated *The Inn-Keepers Apprentice,* received the American Library Association's Notable Book Award and Best Book for Young Adults. In 1982, Say garnered his most successful reviews for *The Bicycle Man*, which he wrote himself and illustrated with elegant watercolors and pen-and-ink drawings. *The Bicycle Man* told the story of two American soldiers who become friends with a group of Japanese children after World War II. Like many other of Say's works it combined ancient themes with modern settings.

Through the rest of the early 1980s, Say continued to have limited successes, but by the middle of the decade he had grown discouraged and was considering going back to

photography exclusively. He was persuaded to put off that decision, however, by an editor who wanted him to illustrate one last book. Written by Dianne Snyder, *The Boy of the Three-Year Nap* proved very successful and earned for Say his first Caldecott Honor award. But more importantly, the experience of illustrating this book convinced him that, at age fifty, he had found what he wanted to do with his life.

In 1989, Say wrote *The Lost Lake,* in 1990 the critically acclaimed *El Chino,* in 1991 *The Tree of Cranes* and in 1993, *Grandfather's Journey,* which won the 1994 Randolph Caldecott Medal. Say said that writing *El Chino*, which tells the story of the first Chinese bullfighter, took him only two days once the paintings were completed. "I wasn't sure what the message of that book was," he told *Booklist.* "In the middle of the story, I was wondering, 'What is this story? What's the revelation?' Then I came to the frame that shows Billy Wong dressed up like a Spaniard standing in a Spanish field holding a suitcase. And, if you notice, he has no eyeballs. His face is completely obscured by his cap. In other words, he has no identity. And then the low hairs on the back of my neck rose. This is what I wait for. This is the revelation. It came from the art. I said to myself, 'He has no identity.'" The paintings, which look photo-like because of the lighting elements, had taken two years.

In describing his place in America as a non-European immigrant, Say told *Booklist,* "I know that I am categorized as an ethnic, as a multicultural artist, but that's not really where I'm coming from. All I'm trying to do is art. I consider myself a uniquely American artist and author. Because I certainly would not have done this kind of work had I stayed in Japan, or had I been born here. It's like Goethe saying that in order to truly know your own language, you must know another. It gives you perspective."

Say lives in San Francisco with his daughter Yuriko.

Sources:

Books

Olendorf, Donna, ed. *Something About the Author.* Vol. 69. Detroit: Gale, 1992, pp. 181–183.

Periodicals

Roback, Diane. "Houghton Mifflin Sweeps Newberry, Caldecott Awards." *Publisher's Weekly,* February 14, 1994.

Rochman, Hazel. "The *Booklist* Interview: Allen Say." *Booklist,* October 1, 1993, pp. 350–351.

—Sketch by Jim Henry

Tiaina "Junior" Seau
(1969–)
Football player

Junior Seau is one of the finest linebackers in professional football today. He was a first-round draft pick by the San Diego Chargers (fifth overall) in 1990 after his junior year at the University of Southern California, where he was a consensus All-American and the Pac-10 Defensive Player of the Year. He already has played in three Pro-Bowls in his short career, missing out only in his rookie season.

Tiaina Seau was born on January 19, 1969, in San Diego, California, to Tiaina, Sr., and Luisa Seau, native Samoans from the island of Aunuu. They had come to the United States in the mid-sixties seeking medical attention for Seau's older brother David, who was diagnosed with a lung disease at age four. Neither of his parents spoke English and they took menial jobs to support the family and provide the medical help for David. As a child, Seau and his three brothers slept in the garage, which had been converted into a bedroom. The family was poor, but the elder Seau managed to instill a moral sense in his children, combining traditional Samoan values with Christianity. Seau told Jill Lieber of *Sports Illustrated*, "Dad taught us about morals, values, and goals. Having a tight-knit family was important to him. The one question he always asked us was, 'How do we protect the Seau name?'"

Athlete at an Early Age

Seau began lifting weights and working out at a very early age. He played football in high school, leading the Oceanside High Pirates to the city AA championship. He was named the defensive MVP of San Diego County and the offensive MVP of the Avocado League, and, reflecting his versatility as a player, *Parade* magazine named him to their All-American team of high school athletes simply as an athlete, with no specification as to position.

Seau was recruited by the University of Southern California (USC), traditionally one of the great football powerhouses in the country. His first two years at USC, however, were marked by setbacks. In his freshman year he was not allowed to play because he scored ten points below the NCAA-mandated score of 700 on his SATs. Seau told Lieber: "Everything I'd worked for, everything my family had stood for was gone. I was labeled a dumb jock. I went from being a four-sport star to an ordinary student at USC. He added, "I found out who my true friends were. Nobody stuck up for me—not our relatives, best friends or neighbors. There's a lot of jealousy among Samoans, not wanting others to get ahead in life, and my

Tiaina "Junior" Seau

parents got an earful at church: 'We told you he was never going to make it.'"

Seau showed great determination, however, in enduring this letdown. In the spring of his freshman year he defeated the entire team in USC's annual superman contest, an multi-event test of strength, physical endurance, and speed. In his second year at USC, Seau injured his right ankle during preseason practice, and he sat out that season as well. His break came in his junior year when two starters were injured and Seau was put in just weeks before the season began. He had an excellent season and was named a consensus All-American and the Pac-10 Defensive Player of the Year. Seau decided to leave school after his junior year to be eligible for the professional draft, an increasingly common trend among top-rated college players. He was signed by the San Diego Chargers, where he has played ever since.

Becoming a star professional football player has brought Seau notoriety and a large income, which he does not spend lavishly. He lives simply, he told Lieber, "Just give me a shack on the beach and a couple of tuna fish sandwiches and I'm happy." In 1991 he started the Junior Seau Foundation, whose purpose, as quoted in *Sports Illustrated*, is "to promote the protection of children by supporting child-abuse prevention efforts, drug and alcohol awareness and anti-juvenile delinquency programs." Commenting on his community work, Seau said: "Too many athletes are living in a tiny window. They have no vision for themselves—what they can be outside of football and what they can mean to a community. They just don't know any better. My hopes and dreams are unlimited."

Sources:

Lieber, Jill. "Hard Charger." *Sports Illustrated,* September 6, 1993, p. 64.

San Diego Chargers. "Junior Seau." Press release and publicity, San Diego, California, 1994.

—Sketch by Jim Henry

Vikram Seth
(1952–)
Author

Vikram Seth

After six years of a self-imposed exile, Vikram Seth offered the draft of his opus, *A Suitable Boy,* to publishers. And then the bidding began—an unusually frenzied bidding, even if Seth's story was one of the longest English-language novels to be published in the twentieth century. Penguin offered $360,000. Another firm offered more than its previous year's net profit. Orion suggested a half-million. The eventual winner, Harper Collins, offered Seth a $600,000 advance with $200,000 backed up to market the book. In an interview with *Vanity* in June 1993, Seth recalled retreating to his agent's garden and standing under a fig tree. "My goodness," he thought. "My life is changing before my eyes."

Before the novel—all 1,349 pages of it (weighing four pounds in its hard-cover version)—hit the presses, Seth already had won acclaim for his three books of poetry, for a nonfiction work entitled *From Heaven Lake: Travels Through Sinkiang and Tibet,* and for *The Golden Gate,* a story of San Francisco told entirely in verse. Nevertheless, the length of *A Suitable Boy* alone has pushed him to a different literary level. In a May 1993 interview with Richard B. Woodward of the *New York Times Magazine,* Seth expressed a desire to "get a vaguely maverick reputation."

Saga Set in India

A Suitable Boy is the story of an Indian family. Set in a fictitious town, Brahmpur, in 1951 (the year before Seth himself was born), it opens at the scene of an all-Indian family gathering, a wedding. The bride's mother, Mrs. Rupa Mehra, is in a tizzy—not especially because her daughter, Savita, is about to be married, but more out of worry over her younger, livelier daughter, Lata, for whom

she must next seek a suitable boy. The story progresses through Mehra's search for potential husbands for Lata. But, like a great Indian movie, it contains dozens of subplots that wind the reader through family interactions, regional politics, communal and religious violence and, it seems, the quest for romance. The novel's fans compare Seth to Tolstoy and Pushkin. Its harsher critics deride it as little more than a soap opera—a label Seth can appreciate. "I used to be hooked on 'Dynasty,'" he told Woodward, "I used to sit there with my mouth open, wondering what would happen next."

Seth admitted the dozens of characters in *A Suitable Boy* are based on the lives of actual people—family and friends. "Every novelist does [this]," he told Woodward. "But then the characters come into contact with those they would never meet in real life, and they change quite considerably." Nevertheless, bits and pieces of Seth's life can be found scattered throughout the novel.

Vikram Seth was born in 1952 in Calcutta, but spent much of his early childhood in London, where his father, Prem, had been transferred by his Czech employers. Prem Seth, like Haresh Khanna, one of Lata's suitors in *A Suitable Boy,* was in the shoe business. In London, Vikram Seth's mother, Leila, began to study law, much as Lata's sister, Savita, did in the novel. Leila Seth passed the bar in England and eventually became India's first female high court justice.

The family moved back to India in 1957, and Vikram, at age six was sent to the prestigious Welham School in Dehra Dun because he showed strong math and verbal skills. He then was sent to the expensive and exclusive Doon School, which former prime minister Indira Gandhi's two sons also attended, where he was educated among the children of bureaucrats, writers, and scholars.

At Doon, Seth stood out as a star student, the boy who was good at everything and way ahead of everyone else in the class. Nevertheless, Seth's memories of Doon tend to be filled with unhappiness. "I was teased and bullied by my classmates . . . ," he said in a 1992 address to Doon School alumni, according to the *New York Times Magazine* interview. "Because of my interest in studies and reading, because of my lack of interest in games, because of my unwillingness to join gangs and groups, because of my height—and, most importantly of all—because I would get so furious when I was bullied." (Seth is a relatively small man—5 feet, 3 inches tall with a slight frame.)

Despite his unhappiness, emotions that resurface in yet another *Suitable Boy* character caught in a similar boarding school situation, he never complained to his parents. He realized that they didn't have much money and had made large sacrifices to send him to Doon.

After finishing school in India, he attended Oxford, where he studied philosophy, politics, and economics. At Oxford, he also began to write poetry, learn Chinese, and study music. College classmates remember him as serious and withdrawn. But when Seth entered graduate school at Stanford in 1975 to study economics, he said he found bliss.

"For the first time in my life I found that I could enjoy myself," he admitted to Woodward. "Stanford is a very tolerant place. And the thing that I feared—that I would find only thick-headed beach boys—wasn't true at all." This new atmosphere seemed to open him up as well. At Stanford, he met Timothy Steele, a poet, who remains one of his closest friends and a mentor. Steele, in the *New York Times Magazine* article, described Seth as "warm and funny" and said that in *A Suitable Boy,* Seth is "exploiting his talents in newer ways but always drawing on resources that were there at the very beginning."

Seth, the Poet

Seth published his first book of poems, *Mappings,* in 1980 while he was doing research for his dissertation at the University of China in Nanjing. He then hitchhiked to Delhi via Tibet in 1981, keeping a journal, which eventually became *From Heaven Lake.*

Returning to Stanford, Seth procrastinated on the task of assembling the data he had collected in China. Instead he began working on *The Golden Gate,* a story of five friends and lovers. The work was rejected by most poetry editors, until it found its way to Random House and met a favorable editor, Ann Freedgood. When published in 1986, Seth became a literary sensation of sorts. Women threw flowers at him at readings, rumors circulated that he was bisexual and that the story—which includes a bisexual love affair—was actually a self-portrait. He was interviewed by *Playboy* and *People Weekly,* and appeared on television talk shows. Growing weary of the attention, Seth left a low-paying job as an editor at Stanford University Press and moved back to India to begin work on *A Suitable Boy.*

Unlike many well-known writers, Seth began work on the story without any idea as to whether it would be published. One reason for returning to India and his parent's home was to be able to write without worrying about income. Initially, he did not plan to write a novel. Instead, he envisioned several short stories that would cover Indian society from 1950 to the present. What happened, he told Woodward, was that his characters got in the way. He had started writing a scene between Lata and her mother, Mrs. Rupa Mehra, and realized several months later that he didn't know enough about his characters. "I had opened the door partly wide and there were all these people walking into this huge drawing room and I didn't have anything to feed them," he explained. "It took me a long time to familiarize myself with the time, and then with the professions, activities, events—these geographies of the mind."

The book may be a piece of fiction, but it has been carefully researched. Seth spent months reading newspapers from the early 1950s, studying Urdu, visiting tanneries and interviewing people. Birds, trees and flowers are carefully checked to ensure that they appear in the book in accordance with the proper season. He drew much of his information from his father, appearing at dinner with extensive questionnaires, checking and cross-checking multitudes of information that his father gave him.

Writing, at times, consumed Seth, giving him a reputation among Indian journalists as an unfriendly recluse. Sometimes he would write for seventeen hours, other times not at all. He developed hand cramps, repetitive strain injury, and at one point, dictated material to a friend.

Now, with the book completed and a bestseller, he has turned his attention to writing plays. "This book has gouged out my thirties," he told Woodward. "I don't want to spend my forties so isolated. I have a reputation for being hermitlike. I'm not. I'm just obsessed with my work."

Sources:

Periodicals

Hitchens, Christopher. "A Suitable Sensation." *Vanity Fair,* June 1993.

Rachlin, Jill. "Talking with…Vikram Seth." *People Weekly,* May 24, 1993.

Woodward, Richard B. "Vikram Seth's Big Book." *New York Times Magazine,* May 2, 1993.

—Sketch by Himanee Gupta

Bright Sheng

(1954–)

Composer

In 1982, Bright Sheng made a decision that would alter the course of his life. He decided to leave the Shanghai Conservatory of Music, where he already had proven himself to be the school's most talented student, to try making it in music as an unknown in New York. Why the United States? Why New York? "I always considered myself as writing for Western music," said Sheng in an interview with Himanee Gupta. "What better place to study and to learn about music for me than New York?"

His father tried to dissuade him. He and Sheng's mother had emigrated to New York a few years earlier and could see the hardships an artist would face. In a letter to his son, he gently suggested that Sheng take up computer science. But Sheng had worked hard and had thought of nothing but music for many years. He decided to give himself a test: if, after five years, he could get enough work as a composer to live in one room with a piano, he'd stay in the United States. Otherwise, he'd go back to China.

Success on Many Fronts

More than a decade has passed. Sheng is living in a room with a piano. Only the room is in a spacious, comfortable condominium suite in Seattle's trendy Belltown neighborhood, with windows that offer a breathtaking view of the Olympic Mountains and Elliott Bay.

And Sheng, whom some critics consider a Chinese Bartok, has learned to survive as a composer quite well. In his twelve years in the United States, he has served as composer-in-residence for the Lyric Opera of Chicago, where he composed his opera *The Song of Majnun*, the Santa Fe Chamber Music Festival, and La Jolla Chamber Music Summerfest. Sheng also was artistic director for the highly acclaimed "We Ink 93" festival in San Francisco, and he recently completed two years as a composer-in-residence for the Seattle Symphony Orchestra.

His teachers have included Leonard Bernstein, Jack Beeson, Chou Wen-Chung, Mario Davidovsky, George Perle, and Hugo Weisgall. In many ways, his work is so much in demand that he is finding himself stretched almost too thin. "Sometimes I think that I have to slow down," he told Gupta. "I have to have time to think. It's that way when you are composing music. I can spend hours and nothing may happen. But if I have to write something, just to produce, I'm not very happy."

Bright Sheng

Sheng is best known for his orchestral work *H'un*, which tells the story of how Mao Zedong systematically destroyed all free thought and creativity in China during the ten-year cultural revolution that began in 1966. The work, which *Seattle Times* music critic Melinda Bargreen describes as "uncompromising, vividly descriptive, at times frightening," was named as the first runner-up for a Pulitzer Prize in 1989. It propelled Sheng to the forefront of Western composers of the late twentieth century and caused critics to rave about his uncanny ability to fuse Chinese techniques with Western artistry.

Cultures Combine in Music

For Sheng, creativity and art flow from this bicultural fusion. Just as *H'un* is partly about his personal suffering as a musician separated from his instrument, the mix of Chinese and Western culture continually shapes his life and his music. At first, he considered this a schism and often worried about blending two distinct styles. Now, he has learned to reconcile both, and he allows himself to relax and let whatever mix of creativity flows define the music for the moment.

"No matter how well I speak English, I still look Chinese," Sheng told *Seattle Post-Intelligencer* music critic R.M. Campbell in 1991. "And in China I would be regarded as highly Westernized."

Sheng today speaks with a distinct Chinese accent, but in many ways, acts Western. He greets a visitor at the door, dressed in blue jeans and in stocking feet. He prepares a pot of chamomile tea, which he sips as the sky darkens over Puget Sound. The view is nice, he acknowledges, but he often gets so caught up in his work that he forgets it is there.

He was born Liang Sheng, December 6, 1954, in a suburb of Shanghai, to a relatively wealthy family. (Liang is a literal translation for Bright, which is how he began to identify himself after emigrating to the United States.) His grandfather owned nearly five thousand acres of rice fields, and at a time when many Chinese immigrants to the United States worked as laborers, he studied engineering at a U.S. university. Sheng's father worked as a medical radiologist. The family's education and wealth made Western culture and arts a fixture around the household. Sheng began taking piano lessons at age four, first from his mother, then from a tutor.

But in 1966, when he was eleven, the cultural revolution started, and his family's wealth and Western education suddenly came under suspicion. Members of the Communist party came to their flat and took away the piano. "My grandfather, because he once owned land and because he still earned a salary as an engineer, was labeled an enemy of the state," Sheng told Gupta. "They went down three generations—to me. And they took away the piano." His voice rises with incredulity as he adds, "Me, growing up, just a little kid, an enemy of the state."

Consequently Sheng suffered a tortured adolescence. Because of the cultural revolution, the Communists took over many rooms in the family's apartment. Sheng was given no bed; he was forced to sleep on the floor. He was afraid to go to school—as an "enemy" it would be all right for him to be beaten—but he knew that if he rebelled things could become much worse.

Arts and the Revolution

As the cultural revolution deepened, industrial production ground to a standstill. Agriculture was thrown into chaos, and famine set in. Schools were instructed to lower their level of education, because, Sheng wryly observed, if you learn too much, you start to think and ask questions. But soon it became clear that Mao was going to have to provide some sort of job for these poorly educated high school graduates. So, he ordered children to become farmers. The only exceptions were those who possessed musical talent—largely because Mao's wife, Jiang Qing, loved the performing arts. As a result, "every kid said he played the violin," Sheng recalled to Gupta.

Sheng missed his piano desperately, so sometimes he would sneak into high school classrooms to play. Because he had no teacher, he'd try to listen to what was on the radio and try to remember the sound. He'd often be beaten when discovered, but he also found that he could display his artistic talent by performing in "Shuan Chuan,"

a sort of school talent show that promoted Mao's propaganda. At age fifteen, he auditioned to join an orchestra for a music-dance company in Qing Hai province near the Tibetan border.

He stayed in Qing Hai for nearly eight years, until the cultural revolution ended with Mao's death in 1976. During that time, he played timpani, drums, and piano and worked as a conductor. He also started to write music. "It was such a small place that it was great in that respect," he said to Gupta. "You could copy your music, and the orchestra would play it the next day. You learn a great deal that way." Also, during this time, he developed a method of self-teaching which he still uses today. He would listen to music and try to write down the notes. When musicians came through the province, he would talk to them and try to digest the breadth of their music. In the province, which was noted for a large population of exiles and ethnic minorities, he learned to recognize the beats and cadences of different folk music. Sometimes, he would record the folk music sounds for later use. Other times, he would stroll through farm fields and talk with farmers, peasants, and daily market workers about the meaning of music.

"The weather was very bad, so travel was limited," Sheng recalled to Gupta. "There was no form of entertainment except for singing. Every day the people would sing. Each minority would contribute something, and they would all blend. I studied the music, I taped it and collected it. Even today I write music based on that material."

In 1978, after the revolution, Sheng returned to Shanghai and enrolled in the Shanghai Conservatory of Music. It was here that he began to compose, rather than perform, music. He studied a great deal of Western musical forms, ranging from Baroque to Romantic periods. But he also studied classical Chinese musical styles, instrumentations, acrobatics, and dance. Meanwhile, his parents left China to settle in New York in 1980. Two years later, Sheng decided to follow them. The Shanghai Conservatory wasn't pleased. Even though he'd finished his bachelor's degree studies, he was denied a degree. At the same time, his father's letter arrived, suggesting he consider computer science. Sheng felt a bit of a crisis, but nevertheless decided to make the move to New York City.

Life in the United States

Sheng was accepted to Columbia University's master's program, but he couldn't afford the tuition and didn't know enough about American universities to seek financial aid. He wound up at Queens College, where he earned his master's of music. He then attended Columbia to complete his doctorate in musical arts—this time with a full fellowship. While studying, Sheng also began writing and trying to find work as a composer.

During this time, Sheng realized that his training and knowledge of two different cultural traditions were not going to remain separate. He could see he was very Chinese, with a deep understanding of the time-free joy of listening to an Asian musical piece slowly evolve. At the same time, all of his training was Western. The instruments he grew up playing—piano, timpani, percussion—were Western. The pace of Western music was completely different: it emphasized time, dramatic openings, and strong conclusions. "I began to understand that I knew each one of these traditions in-depth," he told Gupta. "In that way, I believe I am unique. At first, it was a problem. But now I see it as an adventure."

H'un, Sheng's piece about the cultural revolution, exemplifies his unique approach to composing. It has no melody. Sheng came up with the theme—social tragedy and the cost a country must pay—and then tried to write a melody. But everything seemed "too beautiful for such a sad piece," he told Gupta. Eventually, he left out the melody and the piece was a thunderous success. Writing in the *Seattle Times,* Bargreen critiqued *H'un* after it was first performed by the Seattle Symphony in 1989: "Through Sheng's brilliant orchestration and his command of instrumental writing, *H'un* emerged as a searing tone poem in which emotional states are vividly shown: Scurrying woodwinds darting for cover, sinister advances from the bass instruments, repeated percussion effects that sound like blows, quick ascending rifts suggesting calls of alarm, a climactic section that is overcome with horror, and a mourning period in which artful dissonances and percussion effects slowly wane away. . . . This is a work that should be regularly performed at political summit meetings, where heads of state discuss warfare and disarmament: *H'un* could certainly influence the peace process."

For Sheng, *H'un* was a learning experience. He realized that he could take nontraditional approaches with music and still write what he wanted. It helped him feel more relaxed with his blending of Chinese and Western traditions. As he told Gupta, "Before, I used to worry, what is Chinese, what is the West? Now I write what to me sounds good. I don't try to solve the problem. If I stop worrying, and just let it flow it will represent me more truthfully."

Sources:

Periodicals

Bargreen, Melinda. "Cultural Fusion." *Seattle Times,* December 1992.

———. "Symphony Serves Up Variety Aplenty," *Seattle Times,* October 31, 1989.

Campbell, R.M. "A Chilling Twenty-Minute Musical Portrait of the Chinese cultural revolution." *Seattle Post-Intelligencer,* October 31, 1989.

———. "East Meets West in the Compositions of Bright Sheng." *Seattle Post-Intelligencer,* March 1, 1992.

Kosman, Joshua. "A Bright Light in American Music." *San Francisco Chronicle,* March 15, 1991.

LaFave, Ken. "Against All Odds, Composer Excels in Western Music." *Phoenix Gazette,* August 3, 1993.

"Quartet Will Premiere 'Chinese Bartok' Work." *Indianapolis Star,* November 7, 1993.

Other

Sheng, Bright, interview with Himanee Gupta, April 6, 1994.

—Sketch by Himanee Gupta

Bapsi Sidhwa
(1938–)
Writer

Bapsi Sidhwa's work was first published in 1978 by the author herself. After receiving numerous rejection slips from publishers over several years, Sidhwa, then a forty-year-old homemaker with no formal training in creative writing, decided to go ahead and self-publish her first book in Pakistan. She is now the award-winning author of short stories and four novels, *An American Brat, Cracking India* (published as *Ice-Candy-Man* in England), *The Bride,* and *The Crow Eaters.* One of the first Pakistani authors writing in English to be published internationally, Sidhwa has had her works translated into German, French, and Russian. The cross-cultural appeal of her writing has won her awards and grants in several countries. She has given lectures and readings in Europe, Canada, Thailand, Pakistan, and the United States, and has taught at Columbia University, Rice University, and the University of Houston.

The Roots of Sidhwa's Success

Born in Karachi, India, on August 1, 1938, to a Parsee family, Sidhwa grew up in Lahore. Her ancestors, the Parsees, are descendants of fourteenth-century Persian immigrants to the Indian subcontinent and are also known as Zoroastrians. When she was two years old Sidhwa contracted polio and consequently received no formal education until the age of fourteen. In an interview with Natasha Rafi, Sidhwa explained, "This left me with a problem until my middle teens, when I had a few operations and it more or less vanished. But it affected my entire life." A lonely childhood and adolescence led to a habit of voracious reading that laid the foundation for her writing career. Sidhwa's inspirations were the classics of English literature that were her companions through her growing years. However it was many years later that she actually had the opportunity to write and publish.

Bapsi Sidhwa

Growing up in the conservative atmosphere of the tiny Parsee community in Lahore, Sidhwa, like other young Parsee women, was expected to adhere to tradition. Following custom, Sidhwa was married at nineteen and had three children shortly thereafter. She lived most of her young adulthood as an upper-class Pakistani housewife with her businessman husband. On one of the family's vacations, Sidhwa heard the story of a young woman who, forced into marriage, tried to escape but was later tracked down and killed. The spirit of this unfortunate girl caught Sidhwa's imagination and compelled her to write the story. Because she was afraid that people might think she was being pretentious, Sidhwa wrote in secret. Painstakingly handwritten and later typed, the novel, entitled *The Bride*, was finally completed. Eventually Sidhwa summoned the courage to show it to some friends who really liked it. One of these friends was an American who helped her place it with an agent in the United States.

The Journey Begins

For the next seven years Sidhwa endured a round of rejection slips. She was told that although her work was good, Pakistan was too remote a country for her writing to be "commercially viable." Undaunted by discouraging publishers and encouraged by her agent, she wrote another book called *The Crow Eaters,* a humorous look at the Parsee community. "I was receiving rejection slips for two books from both sides of the Atlantic," Sidhwa recounted to Rafi. "It was heartbreaking." Eventually, even

her agent gave up and Sidhwa herself, feeling totally dejected, stopped writing for almost eight years. In 1978 a close friend who was also a writer read *The Crow Eaters* and encouraged Sidhwa to publish it privately. The following year it was published in India by Orient Longman who asked Sidhwa to cut out thirty pages to cut costs. The dutifully cropped version of the book was finally published and a friend sent it to an agent in Britain. Jonathan Cape, a prestigious publishing firm in England, decided to publish it and Sidhwa was on her way to becoming a writer of international repute.

The Crow Eaters elicited a strong negative reaction from the Parsee community in India and Pakistan, although it was received favorably in England and the United States. The Junglewalla clan featured in the novel became a source of lively characters for Sidhwa's subsequent novels. Cape's publication of *The Bride* in 1984 and *Ice-Candy-Man* further established Sidhwa's reputation as an international writer. The latter, published in the United States as *Cracking India,* was named a *New York Times* notable book in 1991. (The publishers decided to change the original name because they feared the American public might confuse the name *Ice-Candy-Man* with a drug pusher.)

Like many writers, Sidhwa bases her novels and short stories on the experiences and events that have shaped her life. A prominent theme is that of the partition of British India, one the bloodiest events in world history, as well as growing up in the Parsee community in Pakistan. One of her most recent novels, *An American Brat*, is about a Pakistani girl who leaves her country to study in the United States. Sidhwa herself moved to the United States in the early eighties, settled in Houston, and sent all her children to American colleges. What makes Sidhwa's novels unique is that they are told from the point of view of women who live in a society that is extremely patriarchal. She exposes the helplessness and hopelessness of women living in a system that destroys their individuality and independence.

Sidhwa's writing has earned her international acclaim. In 1986 she was appointed Bunting Fellow at Radcliffe/Harvard and was a visiting scholar at the Rockefeller Foundation Study Center in Bellagio, Italy. She was awarded a National Endowment for the Arts grant in 1987. In 1991 she received the Liberaturepreis in Germany for her novel *Ice-Candy-Man*. That same year the Pakistan government honored her with the Sitara-i-Imtiaz (the star of excellence) in recognition of her literary achievements. More recently, Sidhwa received the Lila Wallace–*Reader's Digest* Writer's Award in 1993 which includes a grant of $105,000.

Besides writing, Sidhwa is active in social causes, particularly women's issues. She represented Pakistan at the Asian Women's Congress in 1975. As part of her *Reader's Digest* award she has chosen to work with the Houston Chapter of The Asia Society to organize a program that would bring Hindus, Muslims, Sikhs, and other religious groups from South Asia together in an effort to create a common ground.

She hopes that getting people together in America will thwart the divisive forces that are destroying the subcontinent along religious and ethnic lines. The program, called The Bangla-Lanka-Indo-Pak Friendship Forum Meeting, is due to start in October 1994. As part of her work Sidhwa hopes to promote and encourage other South Asian writers and professors. She believes that Asian writers in America have a tremendous advantage because they have access to formal training and publishers in a way that she never had. "An impossible miracle occurred with me," she told Rafi.

Sources:

Books

Afzal-Khan, Fawzia. "Bapsi Sidhwa." In *International Literature in English,* 1991.

Periodicals

Ali, Zainab. "Bridging Cultures." *The Nightly Minnesota Daily,* January 20, 1994.
Bernard, April. "Fanfare." *New York Newsday,* January 17, 1993.
Book Review. *Los Angeles Times,* August 9, 1992.
Compton, Robert. "Texas Books Will Surface in the Spring Flood." *Dallas Morning News,* March 22, 1992.
Edwards, Kamala. *Belles Lettres,* Fall 1991.
Harvard Bookstore Author Series, *The Boston Phoenix,* September 3, 1993.
Hower, Edward. "A Loss of Innocence Amid Pakistan's Birth Throes." *New York Newsday,* September 19, 1991.
Hutchinson, Paul E. Book Review. *Library Journal,* May 15 1992.
Kapur, Parul. "Coming to America." Fanfare. *New York Newsday,* November 7, 1993.
Kirkus Reviews, August 1, 1993.
Kopple, David. "Readings: Pick of the Week." *LA Weekly,* March 1992.
"Land of the Free," *The Economist,* December 11, 1993.
Lanham, Fritz. "Write Stuff Gets Houstonian $105,000." *Houston Chronicle,* January 7, 1994.
Lumpkin, Carol Fleming. "A Pakistani's View of America: Cynical, Brazen—and Promising." *Houston Chronicle,* January 7, 1994.
"Nine Writers Get $105,000 Each From RD." *Publishers Weekly,* January 10, 1994.
Ross, Robert. "Revisiting Partition." *Book World Review,* June 1992.
Ryan, Richard. "India in an Evil Hour." *Washington Post,* November 24, 1991.
Tharoor, Shashi. "Life with Electic-aunt and Slavesister." *New York Times Book Review,* October 6, 1991,
Villarreal, Edith. "Feroza Goes Native." *Washington Post,* 1993.
Wright, Carolyne. "The Crow Eaters," *New York Times Book Review,* January 10, 1993.

Other

Sidhwa, Bapsi, telephone interview with Natasha Rafi, February 1994.

—Sketch by Natasha Rafi

Sichan Siv

(1948–)

Investment banker, presidential aide

When Sichan Siv first arrived in the United States in 1976 as a Cambodian refugee, he knew no one—not even the Peace Corps officer who sponsored him. Thirteen years later, Siv became the highest ranking Asian American on the White House staff. He was appointed Deputy Assistant to the President of the United States during the administration of George Bush, a post he held from 1989 to 1992. He served as Deputy Assistant Secretary of State for South Asian Affairs from 1992 to 1993. White House aides describe Siv as "a wily immigrant" who survived the horrors of the brutal Khmer Rouge political regime in Cambodia, escaped via Thailand into the United States, and managed to work his way from picking apples in Connecticut and driving a taxicab in New York, to eventually consulting and negotiating with foreign governments and international organizations. In 1993, Siv became senior vice-president at Commonwealth Associates, a New York-based bank and brokerage firm.

The Roots of Siv's Success

Born in Phnom Penh in 1948, Siv was named Sichan which means "beautiful moon" in Khmer. He was only nine years old when his father, a provincial police chief, died. His mother, a devout Buddhist, was left to raise him, his brother, and two sisters with limited resources. Siv and his brother did all they could to help by fetching water and firewood for the house while the girls helped their mother inside. From his mother he learned to be calm and to endure throughout difficult times. Siv told *Notable Asian Americans* he remembers standing by his mother's side as she cooked, listening to her words. She would say, "Remember Sichan. Whatever happens, never give up hope."

At the age of fifteen Siv was admitted to an exclusive high school in Phnom Penh. After graduating in 1968, he became a flight attendant for Royal Air Cambodge and took this opportunity to improve his English. By 1970, tourism had become a casualty of the continuing war in

Sichan Siv

Vietnam and Cambodia and Siv decided to go to college in Phnom Penh where he studied law briefly after graduation and eventually became an English teacher. In 1974, he went to work for CARE, a U.S. relief agency.

By April 1975, Phnom Penh, the capital of Cambodia, was full of fleeing refugees from the war-ravaged countryside. After years of war, the communist Khmer Rouge were threatening to overrun the city and destroy anti-communist supporters. Twenty-seven-year-old Siv was told about evacuation plans at the U.S. Embassy on April 12. But, wanting to leave with "a clear conscience," he drove that day to meet with a regional governor about delivering more rice and medical supplies to the refugees who needed them. As a result, he missed the last evacuation helicopter by thirty minutes. Five days later, Phnom Penh was taken over. Aware that the Communists hated the country's intellectuals, Siv quickly threw away his eyeglasses, convinced that they would mark him for death.

Siv and his family were relocated to their father's native village and put to hard labor in the fields. Using forged passes and a borrowed bicycle, Siv decided to leave Cambodia once more. He bade his family a heart-breaking farewell and headed toward Thailand. On his way, he saw daily evidence of the bloodbath that was sweeping his country. For three weeks, Siv slept in bushes and escaped notice, showing false papers to Khmer Rouge soldiers. But only a few miles from the Thai border peasants reported

him and he was arrested and sent to a succession of slave labor camps. Siv had to work eighteen hours a day digging ditches and fixing roads, coming back at night to a bowl of rotten soup and exhausted sleep. Through it all he never forgot his mother's words, "Whatever happens, never give up hope," and he continued to seek an opportunity to escape.

One day he was assigned to a lumber crew near the border and managed to escape into the jungle. His second night without food or water, he fell into a deep hole after hearing loudspeakers announcing a Buddhist festival. Siv feared he was still in Cambodia, and it was not until he climbed out of the hole the next morning and discovered fruit cans with Thai labels, saw footprints of sneakers, and observed people wearing colored clothes that he sensed he had made it through the border. Sneakers were banned by the Khmer Rouge in Cambodia, as were colored clothes and free mingling of the sexes.

However, Siv's problems were not completely over. He was arrested by the Thai border police. Only after a friend came to bail him out was he transferred to a refugee camp. Industrious as ever, he proceeded to organize English classes. A U.S. embassy official contacted by CARE eventually found Siv in the camp and made arrangements for his immigration to the United States. Before coming to America, Siv became a Buddhist monk. He remains a Buddhist although he gave up the priesthood when he came to America. Siv later learned that almost all his family—his mother, older brother and sister and their families—were brutally murdered by the Khmer Rouge. Friends say it is his faith in Buddhism that has helped him emerge through the gruesome experiences in Cambodia without an unbearable bitterness tainting his life.

A New Life

Siv started his new life in America picking apples and later making hamburgers at a chain restaurant in Connecticut. Moving to Manhattan, he became a cab driver, was robbed several times, and eventually got a job counseling refugees for a Lutheran organization. In 1979, he wrote passionate letters to deans at several U.S. universities describing his background and goals. Columbia University offered him a full graduate scholarship. In 1982, he became an American citizen and a year later, married Martha Pattillo, a native Texan who works for the World Bank. After earning a master's degree in international relations, Siv worked for a bank, the Episcopal Church, the United Nations, and later the Institute of International Education in New York.

In 1987 Siv volunteered for the Bush campaign which marked a turning point in his career. He worked hard for the campaign in New York and was friendly with a Bush aide who, impressed with Siv's knowledge and personality, recommended him for the job of presidential aide. Soon after the interview, Siv was offered the $65,000-a-year job with the historic distinction of being the first Asian American to become a ranking presidential aide. "It's a tremendous honor," he said, "not just for me, but for all Cambodians, for all Asian Americans, for all refugees."

Siv told *Notable Asian Americans*, "Volunteerism is an important part of a successful life." He urges young people to "have the strength to become somebody who can help." Siv strongly believes Americans are in a privileged position that should not be taken for granted. "Success means being able to help others," he said. "Young people should stay away from drugs and avoid negative forces."

The Drive to Always be Better

Siv made every effort to assume leadership positions. He was the president's principal liaison to key public interest groups and spoke regularly on the president's behalf to explain administration policies. He was also the leader of the White House Communications Task Force on national security issues, the co-chairman of the United States delegation to the Geneva conference on refugees, and the senior adviser to the U.S. delegation to the Paris conference on Cambodia. Bobby Kilberg, another White House deputy assistant said about Siv: "You can trust him with your life. He tells you what he really thinks, and often in politics that's not what happens."

Siv's next appointment was as Deputy Assistant Secretary of State for South Asian Affairs where he was responsible for the formulation and implementation of U.S. policy toward Afghanistan, Bangladesh, Bhutan, India, Maldives, Nepal, Pakistan, and Sri Lanka. In summer 1993, after the Republican party lost the election, he joined Commonwealth Associates, a New York-based investment bank and brokerage firm, as a senior vice-president heading the firm's Asian and Pacific department. About his new job, Siv said, "My international experience and personal history will complement the firm's growth and worldwide reach."

Siv is a recipient of many awards, including the Outstanding Asian American Award by the Asian Pacific American Heritage Council, the Twice the Citizen Award by the Reserve Officers Association of the United States, and the CARE Honor for "Selflessness and Courage in Pursuit of his Lifelong Commitment to Human Freedom, Opportunity, and Dignity." Siv is a lieutenant colonel of the U.S. Air Force Auxiliary Civil Air Patrol, and also serves on the boards of the United States Committee for Immigration and Refugee Services of America, Center for Migration Studies, Smithsonian Institution Arthur M. Sackler Gallery, and the National Council for Christians and Jews. He speaks four languages: English, French, Spanish, and Khmer.

"My success," Siv told *Notable Asian Americans*, "is based on my belief that I had to adapt and to be adopted (that is, accepted) by my new country. My advice to others is adapt and be adopted." According to Siv, America is a nation "where you have the right to dream and the ability and opportunity to make your dream come true."

But Siv's adaptation to his new country did not mean severing ties to Cambodia. Siv has always been involved with events concerning his birthplace. He recently revisited Cambodia during the United Nations-supervised election campaign and wrote in the *International Herald Tribune* that he was happy with Cambodia's progress and believed that the democratic effort would benefit from international help. He also expressed confidence in King Norodom Sihanouk's ability to provide "clean leadership" that would help ensure Cambodia's progress towards peace and democracy.

Remembering His Mother

Through all the difficult moments in his life, Siv recalled his mother's advice to never give up hope, and he never has. "I am a strong believer that dreams do come true. I have every right to be," he said. Siv has managed to maintain a positive outlook despite his past experiences in Cambodia. He explained it this way, "If you let emotions run your life, you'll never get anything done." For now, Siv's plans are to continue doing what makes him happy—"to be in a position to help other people, especially Cambodians," he told *Notable Asian Americans*.

Sources:

Periodicals

McAllister, Bill. "A Cambodian Emigre's Route from the Killing Fields to the White House." *The Washington Post,* March 31, 1989.

Nugent, Tom. "Escape from the Inferno." *People,* March 27, 1989.

Ryan, Michael, "I Survived on Hope." *Parade,* July 8, 1990.

Siv, Sichan, "Help Can Work in Renascent Cambodia." *International Herald Tribune,* April 8, 1994.

Other

Commonwealth Associates, "Sichan Siv," press release, September 27, 1989.

Siv, Sichan, telephone interview with Susan Gall, April 16, 1994.

—Sketch by Natasha Rafi

Pitambar "Peter" Somani
(1937–)
Physician

Pitambar "Peter" Somani

Pitambar Somani is director of health at the Ohio Department of Health, making him the highest-ranking American of Asian Indian descent to serve in state government in the United States and the first to serve in a cabinet-level position. As director of health, Somani oversees an agency of 1500 employees and is responsible for the agency's mission of protecting and maintaining the health of all of Ohio's people. He is also a noted author and researcher and holds four U.S. patents.

Somani was born on October 31, 1937, in Chirawah, India, the youngest of four children. His father, Shri Narendra Kumar Somani, was a well-regarded headmaster of the local high school. When Somani was one year old, his family moved to Gwalior, in central India, where Somani grew up. As a child, he was not much inclined toward academics; his two older brothers excelled in school, however. It had already been decided early on that his oldest brother would be a doctor, so not much was expected of Somani, who was mainly interested in sports. Somani told *Notable Asian Americans* that it was "disappointing to be considered a total failure in comparison to my brothers. Everyone around me, except my sister, always pulled me down due to my interest in sports, and for not spending an appropriate amount of time studying to become somebody important."

Going into Medicine

As a senior in high school, Somani surprised his family and even himself by scoring the second highest marks in the state on a college entrance exam. Also in his senior year, his mother became chronically ill and he decided to pursue medicine. In 1955, he enrolled in the G.R. Medical College of Vikram University in Gwalior, India, and five years later received his M.D. He graduated at the top of his class, earning honors in six subjects in the medical curriculum. He also continued to participate in organized athletics. He played on the university's field hockey team and won the G.R. Medical College table tennis championships five years in a row.

After medical school, Somani enrolled in the All India Institute of Medical Sciences, where he completed his medical training in 1962. In that year he immigrated to the United States with his wife and newborn daughter as a postdoctoral fellow of the Wisconsin Heart Association at Marquette University in Milwaukee, Wisconsin. In 1965, Somani earned a Ph.D. in pharmacology from Marquette. The research he had pursued in the course of his studies led to the development of beta blockers, a class of drugs that are today widely used in the treatment of heart disease throughout the world. In 1966, he became an assistant professor of pharmacology and then in 1969, an associate professor at Marquette.

In addition to his academic and research work at this time, Somani also worked as a consultant for several private pharmaceutical firms. He worked full time for three years at Abbott Laboratories in North Chicago, Illinois, where he served as director of cardiovascular pharmacology and then as director of general pharmacology. In both positions, and in his continued affiliation with Marquette, Somani continued his research on beta blockers and new drugs for heart diseases.

In 1974, Somani took a position as full professor of pharmacology and medicine at the University of Miami, Florida. This was a major accomplishment for someone of Somani's relatively young age, and a greater accomplishment considering the times and his ethnicity. It also indicated that he was recognized by his peers for the important work he had accomplished. At the University of Miami, Somani began groundbreaking research into the application of new drugs for the treatment of various cardiovascular ailments. He was the first researcher to use two new drugs, flecainide and lorcainide, in patients with irregular heart beats. The trials he conducted with these two drugs led to the Food and Drug Administration's approval of flecainide for use in patients.

In 1980, Somani was appointed director of the division of clinical pharmacology and professor of medicine and pharmacology at the Medical College of Ohio at Toledo. His clinical research there concentrated, again, on beta blockers, and other groundbreaking drugs, such as calcium channel blockers, anti-arrhythmic drugs, cholesterol lowering agents, and drugs for congestive heart failure. Somani's research in the area of cardiovascular health brought him funding from the federal government through many grants from the National Institutes of Health, where there is great concern about heart disease, one of the leading causes of death in America today.

Public Health Policy Advocate

In 1989, Somani took a sabbatical from the Medical College of Ohio to serve as a United Nations, technical adviser to the government of Thailand. In this capacity he worked with the Thailand Institute of Scientific and Technical Research in Bangkok to help establish cardiovascular research laboratories that would be used to test traditional Thai medicines for their usefulness in treating high blood pressure and heart failure.

In 1991, Somani was appointed by Ohio's governor, George Voinovich, to be the assistant director of health. And, in 1992, when the director stepped down, Somani was given that position. Since becoming director, Somani has pursued an activist course of leadership, working with the Ohio legislature on issues concerning health care reform and the delivery of health care in the state. Some of Somani's initiatives include providing funding for families of hemophiliacs to help them purchase and maintain adequate private insurance coverage; funding a program to immunize poor and indigent infants against hepatitis-B; creating the Women's Health Initiatives, one of the first offices of its kind nationally, which will serve as an adviser to the Department of Health on a variety of women's health concerns, track funding resources, and act as a clearinghouse for research findings; and establishing the Medicare Balance Billing Program, which protects Medicare patients from being overbilled. Somani has also contributed to the current national debate on the creation of a new health care system. His proposal, called "Managed Choice," blends aspects of Health Maintenance Organizations, traditional fee-for-service plans, and the idea of medical savings accounts.

Personal Experiences

Somani is married to Kamlesh, also a native of Gwalior, India. The couple has three children. Somani told *Notable Asian Americans* that his guiding principle in life has been to never accept defeat. He recalls that his father instilled in all his children his philosophy, which Somani summed up as, "Do your duty, and don't worry about the reward." That philosophy, he said, "has allowed me to carry on with everything I have done in life, to persist even though immediate results were not secured. It has taught me to

have patience, and to not be disappointed if an expected outcome does not materialize."

On being an Asian American, Somani said: "America is a wonderful country where people have come from all over the world, each bringing a unique personal heritage. Being an Asian Indian has helped in my success because as a professional from India, it is expected that I am smart and intelligent; therefore, my expertise is rarely doubted." He added that although he has on occasion noticed "a raised eyebrow when [he is] introduced as director of health . . . being a minority in America at the present time can be an asset because everyone is attempting to balance the composition of the work force, including appointments to leadership positions. While my professional activities were not helped or hindered by my ethnic heritage, appointment to my current position was most likely due to my Asian Indian heritage."

Sources:

The Ohio Department of Health. "Biographical Sketch of Pitambar Somani, M.D., Ph.D." Columbus, Ohio, 1994.
Somani, Pitambar, written interview with Jim Henry, May 5, 1994.

—Sketch by Jim Henry

Cathy-Lynn Song
(1955–)
Poet

Cathy Song was still in her twenties when her first book of poetry, *Picture Bride*, won the Yale Series of Younger Poets Award, the most prestigious national poetry prize for young poets in the United States. In choosing Song's first book for the Yale Series, Richard Hugo wrote that her "poems are flowers: colorful, sensual, and quiet, and they are offered almost shyly as bouquets to those moments in life that seemed minor but in retrospect count the most. She often reminds a loud, indifferent, hard world of what truly matters to the human spirit." This award firmly cemented her at the top of the world of emerging poets, and she has continued to contribute steadily to her award-winning body of work ever since.

Song's work has appeared in numerous literary journals including *American Poetry Review, Michigan Quarterly Review, Ploughshares, Poetry,* and *Shenandoah.* Her work has also been widely anthologized in such collections as *The Open Boat: Poems from Asian America, Breaking Silence: An Anthology of Contemporary Asian American Poets,* the *Morrow*

Cathy-Lynn Song

Anthology of Contemporary Asian American Poets, the *Heath Anthology of American Literature,* and the *Norton Anthology of Modern Poetry.*

Early Life

Born in Honolulu, Hawaii, August 20, 1955, Cathy-Lynn Song was the middle of three children of Andrew and Ella Song. Andrew Song was a second-generation Korean American whose father had come to Hawaii with the first wave of Korean laborers. His wife came later as a "picture bride," a bride whose marriage was arranged through the exchange of photographs. Song's mother, Ella, is Chinese American. "My father was a pilot, so we did a lot of traveling," recalled Song in an interview with Susan Gall. "Our family travels started my writing. I guess I was around nine years old when I decided I wanted to be the family chronicler." Song's parents, older sister Andrea, and younger brother Alan, all provided episodes and anecdotes for this enthusiastic young wordsmith. She wrote constantly, creating so many of her own magazines and books that her father resorted to buying surplus Army target paper, so Song's earliest works are backed by a bull's-eye. In *Poetry,* a reviewer wrote, " . . . Cathy Song shows herself a resourceful historian of her family. . . . she also shows herself aware of the tenuousness of what she is about . . . One values her sensitivity and precision, whether she is remembering childhood play with her brother amid the hanging laundry or conducting an inventory of her mother's button collection. . . . Song renders details with great clarity. . . .

She sees the present moment as potential memory, the latest addition to the palimpsest that is the past."

During her high school and college years, writing became a natural process for Song. "Every experience seemed more complete if I wrote about it," Song explained. And it was while she was a student in Hawaii that her first mentor, noted poet and Hart Crane biographer John Unterecker, encouraged her to pursue and develop her interest in writing. She told David Choo of the *Honolulu Weekly,* "He was someone who encouraged me from very early on. Generosity—I was so lucky to find such generosity." The idea of generosity is a strong impulse in Song's lyric and narrative poetry. Her friend, the poet Naomi Shihab Nye, writes, "The poems of Cathy Song graciously, generously open up the world. They carry us into the deep heart of 'family' and 'place,' guiding with gentle, passionate precision. They are supple as sky, embracing as the largest life."

Song traveled from Hawaii to Boston to attend Wellesley College, where she earned her bachelor's degree in English literature in 1977. She went on to earn a master's in creative writing at Boston University in 1981. It was while in Boston that Song was influenced by her second strong mentor, Kathleen Spivack. As a student in Spivack's advanced writer's workshop, Song considered looking for a publisher for her work. She told Gall, "I remember thinking of first trying to get my poems out and directing my attention toward the ethnic publications. She [Spivack] encouraged me to send my work to mainstream publications, not just Asian American publications." The advice was appropriate, since Song's first volume of poetry, *Picture Bride,* was published in 1983 by Yale University Press, and her second volume, *Frameless Windows, Square of Light* was published in 1988 by W.W. Norton. The University of Pittsburgh Press published her third collection, *School Figures,* in 1994.

Song married Douglas McHarg Davenport while she was living in Boston and he was a medical student at Tufts University. Davenport, originally from Sante Fe, New Mexico, did his residency at Denver General Hospital in Colorado from 1984 to 1987. Song spent those years writing *Frameless Windows, Square of Light* and starting a family. After Davenport completed his training in Denver, the family settled in Honolulu, where they have lived ever since.

Image as a Poet

Song objects to the observations some have made that she's a middle-class poet. She told Choo, "It's very annoying. It's easy for someone to look at me and say, 'She hasn't suffered. . . . Her husband's a doctor; she drives around in a Volvo.' I think it's very unfair. We all suffer in different ways. I don't have to have grown up on the plantation speaking pidgin and having someone beat . . . me to write good poetry." Song currently is focusing on women's issues. She told Gall. "Being a woman and an Asian American has only helped my work as an artist. You have to be on the periphery, on the outside looking in, marginalized in some way, to gain a different perspective, a perspective which only provokes your art because there is no way you can possibly accept the party line. " Song also feels that, as a mother, it is important to continue her work while raising her two sons and a daughter. She continued: "I write a lot of poems about motherhood, and I try to deal with the complexities of the many roles of women. I believe that women can take full possession of their lives by finding ways to articulate through art, or other *meaningful* work, their right to define their own existence without being trapped in the male dominant culture ideal." Song also realizes that, as a mother, it is important to continue her work while raising her two sons and a daughter. "I feel it helps my children—particularly my daughter—to see me working, to watch the process, and to realize how I feel when my work touches people," she told Gall.

Award-winning Poet in the Schools

Hawaii's well-recognized "Poets in the Schools" program enables public school children from kindergarten through high school to work with and learn from working poets. Since 1987, Song has been an active participant in the program, and finds the experience rewarding. "I tell my students that true freedom and power comes from getting a hold of language and your feelings," she told Choo, " . . . Monetarily, you don't get compensated very well [in the Poets in the Schools program]; you'll never get rich. But I get so much back. What these students give to me is so life-enhancing." Song finds inspiration, even when transcribing poems of kindergartners. "I learn so much from the insights of the youngest students," she told Gall.

Song also tries to influence young writers, acknowledging the strong influence her early teachers had on her. She told Choo, "I'm not there to give them [the students] false praise. It's not going to do them any good. . . . Sometimes I tell them to rewrite something over and over, and they do, creating a really good poem. You've got to be willing to dismantle . . . to realize that poetry is something made outside of yourself."

In 1993, Song won the Hawaii Award for Literature, becoming the youngest person ever to capture the award. Adding to her list of recognitions, also in 1993, the Poetry Society of America awarded Song the prestigious Shelley Memorial Award. In the early fall of 1994, she was invited to travel to Korea and Hong Kong under the United States Information Agency's Arts America program.

Song's message for aspiring poets is not to be afraid to start at the top when trying to publish your work, and to take advantage of the help and advice of mentors. Song related her early influences to Gall: "As Kathleen Spivack told me, 'Your voice has just as much importance as any other American writer.' Young poets and writers should remember that ethnic background doesn't make your

voice any less American. Don't limit yourself—when you feel it's ready, send your work to the best publications you know." Song is proof that this strategy works.

Sources:

Periodicals

Choo, David. "Cathy Song." *Honolulu Weekly*, June 15, 1994, pp. 6–8.
Hugo, Richard. Yale Series of Younger Poets Award., 1983.

Other

Lee, Li Young. Correspondence with Cathy Song, August 1994.
Nye, Naomi Shihab. Correspondence with Cathy Song, August 1994.
Song, Cathy, telephone interview with Susan Gall, July 28, 1994.

—Sketch by Susan Gall

Somtow Sucharitkul
(1952–)
Author, composer, conductor

Somtow Sucharitkul is an author (sometimes using the pen name S.P. Somtow) and a composer and conductor of modern, avante garde music who made his international conducting debut at the age of nineteen with the Holland Symphony Orchestra. He has since had his compositions performed by major orchestras around the world. Sucharitkul began writing science fiction in 1979, and in 1981 he published his first novel, *Starship and Haiku*, which was critically well received and won Sucharitkul two awards. He has since written several novels and short story collections, and continues to compose.

Somtow Papinian Sucharitkul was born on December 30, 1952, in Bangkok, Thailand, to Sompong and Thaitow Sucharitkul. Sompong, his father, was a career diplomat with the Thai government. Sucharitkul was educated in private schools and then attended college at Cambridge University where he received both his bachelor's and master's degrees from St. Catherine's College.

Composer

By 1974, Sucharitkul had established himself as an important composer. He represented Thailand at two major international conferences, the Asian Composer's Conference-Festival in Kyoto, Japan, and the International Music Council of UNESCO. In 1977 Sucharitkul was named director of the Bangkok Opera Society. He also began working with other orchestras around the world, including the Cambridge Symphony, the Holland Symphony Orchestra, and the Florida Atlantic University New Music Ensemble. In 1978 he was named artistic director of the Asian Composer's Conference-Festival held that year in Bangkok.

Writer

In 1979, Sucharitkul, who had by this time moved to the United States, turned his attention to writing. His first novel, *Starship and Haiku,* and was a post-apocalyptic story of a society inhabited solely by Japanese. In dealing with the holocaust that had destroyed most of humanity, society had deteriorated into two camps, one which was trying to start a new existence in outer space with the help of whales, while the other advocated suicide.

In the early 1980s Sucharitkul wrote a sequence of related books collectively entitled *Chronicles of the High Inquest.* The series consists of the novels *Light on the Sound* (1982); *The Throne of Madness* (1983); *Utopia Hunters* (1984); and *The Darkling Wind* (1985) and tells the story of a race of mutated humans who try to eradicate a race of whale-like beings. The humans operate under the direction of an astral species known as the Inquestors, who are steadily demonized throughout the series and eventually die in an apocalypse.

Another sequence of novels from the mid-eighties was the *Aqualiad,* a richly imagined play on *The Illiad,* in which the ancient Romans discover America. The series, consisting of *The Aqualiad* (1983); *The Aqualiad #2: Aquilia and the Iron Horse* (1988); and *The Aqualiad #3: Aquilia and the Sphinx* (1988), established Sucharitkul as a master of irony and dark humor. Throughout the series he introduces characters with latinized Indian names, incorporates the names of contemporary science fiction writers, and presents the mythical figure of Bigfoot as the leader of a group of mutated Jews.

In 1985 Sucharitkul began publishing under the name S.P. Somtow, and steadily changed his focus from science fiction to fantasy and horror. In this vein is the *Valentine* series of novels, consisting of *Vampire Junction* (1984) and *Valentine* (1992), both of which are vampire tales. In 1989 he published *Moondance,* a novel about werewolves.

Sucharitkul also writes short stories, many of which have been anthologized in books such as the *World's Best SF, The 1980 Annual.* He has been published in science fiction and fantasy magazines such as *Amazing, Analog Science Fiction-Science Fact, Chrysalis, Isaac Asimov's Science Fiction Magazine,* and *Other Worlds.* He writes book reviews for various magazines and newspapers, including the *Washington Post*

Bookworld, and writes about music for *Tempo* and *Musical Newsletter.* He is a contributing editor and columnist for *Fantasy Newsletter.*

Sucharitkul also writes children's books. He has written novelizations of episodes of the short-lived television series "V," and has written a screenplay. He divides his time between his native Bangkok and Los Angeles.

Sources:

Books

May, Hal, ed. "Somtow Sucharitkul." *Contemporary Authors,* Vol. 118, Detroit: Gale Research, pp. 456–7.

—Sketch by Jim Henry

Anna Sui
(1955–)
Fashion designer

Anna Sui made a name for herself in the highly competitive world of fashion design in an almost word-of-mouth way. Her eccentric, kitschy designs attained a cult-like following among pop culture icons such as Madonna and Lady Miss Kier of Dee-Lite and internationally famous models like Naomi Campbell and Linda Evangelista. She also managed to keep her designer prices well below those of her competitors, reflecting her belief that fashion is essentially for fun. As she told the *New York Times,* with her designs, "you don't have to worry about damaging a $2,000 jacket. What's fun about fashion to me is that it's always changing, and what I try to do is offer a new thing that's affordable." At this Sui has succeeded. She runs a $1.75 million business selling her fashions in more than 200 department stores in the United States, Canada, Japan, and Europe, and has her own retail outlet in Manhattan's SoHo district.

Anna Sui was born in Dearborn, Michigan, to first-generation Chinese American parents. Her father, Paul Sui, is a structural engineer and her mother, Grace Sui, is a homemaker who once studied painting in Paris. Sui became interested in fashion early in life and would create elaborate tissue-paper dresses for her brothers' toy soldiers, pretending they were on their way to her imaginary version of the Academy Awards.

Sui herself became a flamboyant dresser while still young, gaining a reputation as an eccentric in her small town junior high school. She made some of her own

Anna Sui

clothes, beginning in those days what would later become a Sui trademark: outfits with matching shoes, hats, and handbags. She was voted the best-dressed student in her ninth-grade class.

The Genius File

In Sui's teen years she began pouring through fashion magazines, cutting out whatever fashions caught her eye. She began collecting these cut-outs in what she called a "genius file" and dreaming of a life in fashion design. She'd heard about Parson's School of Design in New York City and thought it would be a good place from which to launch her career. Her parents were dismayed by her decision. Her mother especially had wanted her to become a doctor or a nurse, but after graduation from high school Sui moved to New York and began classes at Parsons.

While in school Sui met and befriended Steven Meisel, who was to become one of the world's top fashion photographers. The two became close friends at school and remained so even after Sui left Parsons in her sophomore year to work for a sportswear company as a designer. She also worked as a stylist for Meisel's increasingly prestigious fashion shoots for the Italian magazine *Lei*. This was a fun, experimental time for the young fashion designer and her photographer friend. When they weren't working together on a shoot they would often play with ideas and looks, using friends and even people off the street who they would lure into Meisel's studio for a "makeover."

The Beginnings of Success

Sui continued working for various designers throughout the late seventies and into the early eighties. In her free time she created her own designs as well. In 1980 she showed six original Lycra garments and received an order from Macy's, the giant New York retailer, which used one of these designs in an advertisement in the *New York Times*. This early success encouraged Sui's ambitions and in that same year she started her own business, which she ran out of her apartment. "There were boxes piled up to the ceiling, and we were shipping clothes out of here," she told *Vogue* in 1992.

Sui's business grew steadily but modestly throughout the eighties and she was able to sell through more and more retailers. In 1991 she reached a landmark in the fashion design business: she had her first runway show. Held in part due to the encouragement of her old friends Steven Meisel and Paul Cavaco, a public relations executive, the show created a stir. Writing in the *New York Times* Woody Hochswender quipped, "There was a fashion collision Wednesday evening. It looked as if Sly and the Family Stone crashed into Coco Chanel and then got rear-ended by Christian Lacroix. The show, the first by Anna Sui, was a riot."

The show's success was a major accomplishment for the young designer and marked a turning point in her career. She finally moved her business out of her apartment and rented office space in Manhattan's legendary garment district. She continued showing her designs to rave reviews and in 1992 Macy's gave Sui her own boutique in its Herald Square store. In February of 1993 she was awarded the coveted Perry Ellis Award for New Fashion Talent.

Despite her reputation for creating some of the liveliest, most engagingly original designs in current fashion, Sui has steadfastly refused to allow her prices to skyrocket along with her fame. An Anna Sui jacket still sells for about half the price of those of comparably prominent designers, an indication that Sui does indeed believe that above all else, fashion should be fun.

Sources:

Periodicals

Doppelt, Gabe. "Vogues' View." *Vogue*, February 1992, pp. 90, 92.

Hochswender, Woody. "Anna Sui's Slam-Bang Look: A Wistful Glance at the 60s." *New York Times*, April 12, 1991.

James, Laurie, "Sui Success." *Harper's Bazaar*, September 1992, p. 274.

Schiro, Anne Marie. "Nostalgia with a Look That's Now." *New York Times*, December 1, 1991. p. 68.

—Sketch by Jim Henry

Sara Suleri

(1953–)

Writer, academic

Sara Suleri is an award-winning writer of nonfiction, whose two books, *Meatless Days* and *The Rhetoric of English India* have been well received. She is a professor of English at Yale University and serves as the editor of the *Yale Journal of Criticism.*

Sara Suleri was born on June 12, 1953, in Karachi, Pakistan, the daughter of Ziauddin Ahmed, a political journalist, and the former Mair Jones, a Welsh professor of English. Her father was a fairly prominent journalist who wrote often on Pakistani independence. Her mother taught English at Kinnaird College. Suleri recalled in her memoir, *Meatless Days,* that her childhood was full of reading. "Afternoons were reading time. . . ," she wrote. "My mother's children would retire to their various beds with books: each afternoon the house was quiet with reading."

Suleri was educated at Kinnaird College, where she earned a bachelor's degree in 1974. From there she went on to Punjab University, where she earned a master's degree in 1976, and then she came to the United States where she earned a Ph.D. at Indiana University in 1980. In 1981 she was offered a position as a professor of English at Yale. She also served briefly as a special correspondent to the United Nations from Pakistan.

Reflections of a Muslim Woman

Suleri wrote *Meatless Days,* her first book, in 1989. It is a collection of nine autobiographical meditations on her family history and her own experiences as a woman who grew up in a biracial, highly educated, and fairly prominent family in a Muslim, third-world country. The book received good reviews. Writing in the *New York Times Book Review,* Daniel Wolfe called it a "parallel exercise in post-colonial partition. Ms. Suleri's territory, though, is the self. In [these] tales that move back and forth among Pakistan, Britain, and the United States, Ms. Suleri examines the names that describe her: Pakistani, sister, teacher . . . narrator of two mother tongues." Wolfe goes on to say that "readers looking for pat exoticism should look elsewhere. . . . Ms. Suleri is at home with cultural and linguistic differences and well able to steer clear of subcontinental clichés." He added that the "writing is beautifully constructed."

Writing in *Publisher's Weekly,* Laura Mathews said, "With gaiety, sadness and an exquisite feeling for language

[Suleri] straddles two worlds, the 'meatless days' of her youth (when the rich blithely ignored government rationing), and her more recent 'cast out of paradise' as an American university professor. Suleri's vivid remembering becomes an act of mourning for all her lost ones."

In 1991 Suleri published *The Rhetoric of English India,* a critical look at English misconceptions, misunderstandings, and obfuscations of Indian and Pakistani culture and history, especially as it existed in colonial times. She includes in this work essays on such Anglo-Indian writers as Rudyard Kipling, E.M. Forster, Salman Rushdie, and V.S. Naipaul. She also examines the work of a variety of lesser-known nineteenth-century female diarists and Anglo-Indian women writers and painters who, according to *Publishers Weekly,* Suleri accuses of, "veil[ing] the colonizers' rape of the Indian subcontinent in picturesque images." *Publisher's Weekly* went on to say "Suleri subtly decodes Anglo-English novels, political speeches and nonfiction to expose self deception and brutality at the heart of Britain's colonial operation in India."

Writing in *Library Journal,* T.L. Cooksey said, "While many theorists focus on the theme of an impenetrable 'Otherness' in [the experience of Indian culture], Suleri is concerned with a sense of identity and self-recognition in the Other. . . . [H]er insights are compelling, providing a valuable theoretical model for discussing the confrontation of diverse cultures."

In 1989 Suleri received a Pushcart Prize for *Meatless Days,* and that year she was also recognized by Yale University as an outstanding teacher. As of early 1994, Suleri was at work on a novel.

Sources:

Books

Suleri, Sara. *Meatless Days.* Chicago: University of Chicago Press, 1989.

Periodicals

Cooksey, T.L. Review of *The Rhetoric of English. Library Journal,* November 15, 1991, p. 82.

Mathews, Laura. Review of *The Rhetoric of English India. Publishers Weekly,* November 15, 1991, p. 44.

Wolfe, Daniel. "Talking Two Mother Tongues." *New York Times Book Review,* June 4, 1989, p. 30.

—Sketch by Jim Henry

Betty Lee Sung

(1924–)

Academic, author

Betty Lee Sung

Betty Lee Sung is a highly regarded scholar of Asian American studies and the author of *Mountain of Gold,* an account of the Chinese immigrant experience in America. Published in 1967, the book was heralded as a landmark work in the field of ethnic studies and received excellent reviews across the country, one of which was read into the *Congressional Record* by Senator Hiram Fong on the floor of the U.S. Senate. Sung has written eight other books and contributes extensively to magazines, journals, and anthologies. In 1970 she was hired as an assistant professor of Asian American studies at the City College of New York, then the only such degree granting program in the country. By the time of her retirement in 1992, she chaired the department.

Betty Lee Sung was born in Baltimore, Maryland, on October 3, 1924, to Chinese parents. She spent her early childhood in the United States before moving back to China at the age of nine. She stayed in China for the next four years, during which time her mother would die and her father would be forced to flee the country, having no choice but to leave behind three of his four children. This was in 1935, and World War II was beginning in Asia. The children were left with enough money to make it to the United States to join their father, and, after a long, dangerous journey, the family was reunited in Washington, D.C.

Breaking Tradition

After graduating high school in 1944, Sung enrolled in the University of Illinois. Her father, who had worked all his life as a laundry man, was opposed to his daughter getting an education because it ran contrary to centuries of Chinese tradition. Undaunted, Sung earned money on her own to attend college, mostly through scholarships. She was elected to the Phi Beta Kappa society in her junior year and was awarded a Phi Beta Kappa scholarship in her senior year. She was also a member of Alpha Kappa Delta, the sociology honors society. She graduated in 1948 with a double degree in economics and sociology.

Sung's first job was with the "Voice of America" as a radio script writer from 1949 to 1954. The "Voice of America" is a radio service funded by the U.S. government that broadcasts news and information into countries of the world cut off from the international community by authoritarian regimes. It was used almost exclusively during the Cold War to broadcast into communist countries such as China and the Soviet Union. Sung's job was to research and write scripts about the lives of the Chinese in

America. It was while doing research for these scripts that Sung noticed that there was very little accurate, non-racist information on the Chinese American experience. As she told the City College *Clarion* in 1990, "I found the same stereotyped labels ascribed to the Chinese; things like opium dens, coolie labor, yellow peril. It set my hair on end." She worked for the "Voice of America" until 1954 when she quit her job to devote herself full time to raising her children. In 1948 she'd married Hsi Yuan Sung, with whom she would have four children. Sung considers the work she did raising her children—there would be four more step-children in a future marriage—to be far more important than any academic work she's done or any books she's published.

Sung returned to the workforce in the 1960s. She worked in the publishing industry as a copy editor and a free-lance editor for such publishers as Doubleday and McGraw Hill. In 1965 she got a job as a librarian in the Queens Borough Public Library and soon after began working on a master's degree in library science at Queens College in New York, which she completed in 1968.

Mountain of Gold

In 1967, Sung published her first book, *Mountain of Gold.* Written in response to her experience doing research for the "Voice of America," the book was Sung's attempt at correcting the historical record of Chinese contributions to the building of America (especially in the west) and a record of how Chinese immigrants lived in contemporary America. The book was very successful, both critically and commercially. The book review journal *Best Sellers* reported, "*Mountain of Gold* is a history of the Chinese in America from Gold Rush days to the present. Any American who professes a humane interest in Civil Rights has an obligation to read it."

In 1970 Sung quit her job at the Queens Borough Library to become an assistant professor at the City College of New York, which had just gone through a difficult student strike in which minority students had demanded freer access to the college, better representation on the faculty, and the establishment of ethnic studies programs. Sung was sympathetic to all of these demands and actively worked to help Asian students get the assistance to which they were entitled, often directing them to government and private resources.

As an assistant professor, Sung continued to publish, and in 1971 Collier's released *The Story of the Chinese in America,* culled from the text of *Mountain of Gold.* Among the other books she has published are *The Chinese in America* (1973), a children's book, and *Survey of Chinese American Manpower and Employment* (1976), a book intended for academic audiences that, like her first book, earned excellent reviews for the quality of its research and the uniqueness of its content. In the journal *Sociology and Social Research,* Charles Choy Wong called it a "valuable contribution to contemporary Chinese American studies." The book was named an Outstanding Book of the Year by *Choice* magazine, the foremost reviewing magazine for academic libraries.

Sung continued to write throughout the seventies and eighties. Her works include *Album of Chinese Americans* (1977); *Transplanted Chinese Children* (1979); *Adjustment Experience of Chinese Immigrant Children in New York City* (1987); and *Chinese Intermarriage* (1990). In 1994, she worked with a National Endowment for the Humanities grant to transfer early immigration records of Chinese Americans to a computer database. While researching a book on the history of New York's Chinatown, Sung came across 581 boxes of previously unstudied immigration documents dating from the mid-1800s through the mid-1900s. She immediately put her history of Chinatown on hold to devote herself to documenting this important find.

In 1983, while teaching at City College, Sung earned a Ph.D. in sociology from the Graduate Center of The City University of New York. In her career she has been awarded many honors. These include the "Champion of Excellence" award in 1986 from the Organization of Chinese American Women; the "Honoree of the Year" award in 1987 from the Chinese American Alumni Association of City College; and the "Distinguished Service Award" in 1990 from the Asian Pacific American Librarians Association at their tenth annual conference in Chicago. She has

successfully raised eight children from two marriages and is the grandmother of two. She divorced her first husband in 1966 and married Charles C.M. Chung in 1972.

Sources:

Periodicals

McAlee, John J. "Mountain of Gold," *Best Sellers,* December 1, 1967, p. 357.
Towle, Lisa H. "Setting the Record Straight," The City College of New York *Clarion,* December 1990, pp. 7, 9.
Wong, Charles Choy. Review of *Survey of Chinese American Manpower and Employment. Sociology and Social Research,* vol. 66, no. 4.

—Sketch by Jim Henry

Bob Suzuki

(1936–)

University administrator

Bob Suzuki was named president of California State Polytechnic University at Pomona, in September 1991. Like many distinguished Japanese Americans, he came with impressive credentials: bachelor's and master's degrees in mechanical engineering; a Ph.D. in aeronautics; a solid background in administration, teaching and community service; and a lengthy list of published materials.

And, like many distinguished Japanese Americans, Suzuki's resume includes a strong background in political and civil rights work. This stems, in many ways, from some of his earliest and most painful childhood memories: World War II and years spent in relocation camps.

Childhood Internment

Bob Suzuki was born January 2, 1936, in Portland, Oregon, to Japanese immigrants. When World War II started, he and his family were forced under armed guards to board a train bound for a relocation camp in southern Idaho. Suzuki was only six years old. For three years, the family lived in the Idaho desert behind a fence of barbed wire and guard towers. Some of the time was spent living in stalls used to exhibit farm animals. Suzuki received his first three years of schooling in the internment camps.

Years later, the experience lingers. It helped shape Suzuki into a man with a deep commitment to civil rights, diversity, and the need to address the issues that would shape his desire to examine the role of multiculturism in modern U.S. society. "More than anything else, that experience [in the camps] developed my commitment to civil rights," Suzuki told the *Los Angeles Times* shortly after his appointment to California Polytechnic University at Pomona in 1991.

After World War II ended, Suzuki's family left the relocation camps and settled in Spokane, Washington, where they raised cucumbers, lettuce and strawberries. When the crops failed, the family didn't eat. Although Suzuki's mother had only an eighth-grade education she taught Suzuki the value of a good education. He was student body president in high school and graduated as class valedictorian. He then went on to the University of California at Berkeley where he received a bachelor of science degree in 1960 in mechanical engineering, and a master's degree in 1962. He worked for two years as a research engineer for Boeing Aircraft in Seattle before returning to graduate school at the California Institute of Technology in Pasadena, where he completed his doctorate in aeronautics. He then went on to teach aerospace engineering at the University of Southern California (USC).

Suzuki attended USC between 1967 and 1971, a time of great turmoil on U.S. college campuses. Students and faculty were protesting the lack of U.S. civil rights and the nation's ongoing involvement in the Vietnam War. This mood couldn't help but affect him, and he became deeply involved in civil rights and public and community affairs.

Among other things, Suzuki helped lead a nationwide campaign to get Congress to repeal the Emergency Detention Act of 1950. He also served as chair of the national education commission of the Japanese American Citizens League (JACL), and as vice-governor of the Pacific Southwest Division of the JACL. In this position, he initiated action that eventually led to the inclusion of Asian Americans as a protected group in federally-mandated affirmative action and equal opportunity programs. He joined a community advisory committee, seeking desegregation of Pasadena's public schools. He was also a campus activist, serving on a number of equal-opportunity program advisory committees.

Activism and Academia

All of this involvement in civil rights prompted him in 1971 to change careers. He decided that he wanted to devote himself full time to work that would directly address societal problems. He took a job in the School of Education at the University of Massachusetts in Amherst teaching science/math education, Asian American studies, and urban education. Two months after his arrival, he was asked to fill the position of assistant dean for administration in the School of Education. He remained in the position for three and a half years before he decided to return full time to teaching and research. By this point, his teaching and research work lay mostly in multicultural

Bob Suzuki

and international education, sociological and cultural foundations of education, and Asian American studies. He began presenting papers and lectures that addressed the issues of Asian Americans in education.

Since the early 1980s, Suzuki has become a nationally recognized expert on multicultural education. He was, for instance, among the first scholars to break down the "model minority" myth, which portrayed Asian Americans as ideal immigrants, often pitting their ability to blend into mainstream culture, against African Americans, who for centuries have been unable to do so. His knowledge makes him a frequent keynote speaker at conferences and symposiums, as well as a seminar leader and multicultural consultant to numerous school and community groups throughout the United States.

Suzuki remained at the University of Massachusetts at Amherst until January 1981, when he decided to return to academic administration. He served as dean of graduate studies and research at California State University in Los Angeles from 1981 to July 1985. He then became vice-president for academic affairs at California State University in Northridge, where he supervised academic and instructional support areas of the university and oversaw an annual budget of more than $100 million.

In some ways, his position as president of California State Polytechnic University might seem an odd fit. The school was traditionally known for agriculture, science, and engineering rather than for multicultural education. Nevertheless, the job has, in many ways, brought Suzuki back into touch with his old roots. He did, after all, study engineering before he shifted his focus to multicultural education. And the campus he inherited was very much one in transition, filled with simmering discontent among students and a need to upgrade the college's curriculum with more international, high-tech agribusiness, liberal arts, and business administration courses.

The university was founded in 1938 as an agricultural polytechnic institute geared toward serving a largely rural community. Over the years, as California grew more populous, the campus became hemmed in by development. At the same time, its student body grew increasingly ethnic— 45 percent white, 30.5 percent Asian Pacific, 16 percent Latino, 3 percent African American and 5 percent other races when Suzuki took over. The administration was struggling to meet new student body needs. In the year before Suzuki became president, the campus was rocked by a demonstration in which minority students accused the administration of being insensitive to their complaints of harassment.

Before joining California Polytechnic University, Suzuki spent months reading about campus issues and formulating ideas. He immediately pledged to step up programs to recruit and retain minority students and to help organize workshops and seminars on multicultural issues. "I'm not the type of administrator who's satisfied with the *status quo*," he told the *Los Angeles Times* in 1991. "I will push the campus toward change."

Sources:

Periodicals

Hamilton, Denise. "New President of Cal Poly Pomona Will Seek Change." *Los Angeles Times,* July 1, 1991.

Other

California Polytechnic Institute. "Bob Suzuki." Biographical materials, 1994.

—Sketch by Himanee Gupta

T

Shirin R. Tahir-Kheli

(1944–)

Ambassador, academic

Dr. Shirin Tahir-Kheli is currently working on her autobiography *Ambassador from Where?*—a question she was often asked when serving as an ambassador at the United States Mission to the United Nations. "It took some of the staff a year to realize that I worked there and was not visiting from some other embassy," Tahir-Kheli told Shazia Rafi in an interview. Tahir-Kheli's career is marked by many "firsts"—the first Asian ambassador to represent the United States at the United Nations; the first Muslim ambassador to represent the United States at the United Nations; the first Muslim senior government official appointed by the President and confirmed by the Senate, to name a few. She is also one of the few women in the field of national security, which is usually dominated by men with a military background.

Shirin Tahir-Kheli was born in Hyderabad, India, in 1944. Her grandfather was the premier minister to the nizam of Hyderabad. The family moved to Pakistan when Hyderabad lost its independence during the partition of India. Her father, who had always encouraged Tahir-Kheli to pursue her interests, became the vice-chancellor of Peshawar University—one of Pakistan's premier academic institutions. "Many foreign delegations would visit the university," she told Rafi. "I had met Chou En-Lai by the time I was nine years old!"

Tahir-Kheli's initial career choice was textile design. "I knew I wanted to do something, not become a *begum* (housewife), and it wasn't to become a doctor. I fainted at the medical school." Since cotton textiles were the upcoming industry in Pakistan, she initially completed a bachelor of arts in textile design, at Ohio Wesleyan University in 1961 at the age of seventeen. The dire predictions of family and friends that sending a young girl to study in the United States would lead to disaster turned out to be untrue when Tahir-Kheli returned to Pakistan and married Dr. Reza Tahir-Kheli, a nuclear physicist. Following her husband back to the United States, Tahir-Kheli

Shirin R. Tahir-Kheli

switched careers to study international relations at the University of Pennsylvania where her husband taught.

"Ambassador Robert Strauss-Hupe was then head of the Foreign Policy Institute at University of Pennsylvania and he got me admission for my master's which I completed in one year," she said. Tahir-Kheli went on to complete her doctorate, her dissertation being "Pakistani Elites and Foreign Policy towards the Soviet Union, Iran, and Afghanistan."

The first phase of Tahir-Kheli's career was in academics. She taught at Temple University as an assistant and then associate professor from 1973 to 1985. She was given tenure in 1979 but had to resign from tenure to take up the second phase of her career in government. She has published extensively on Pakistan's foreign policy, U.S. policy in South and Southwest Asia, and the former Soviet Union's policy in Afghanistan.

In 1982 she was asked to join the Office of the Secretary of State as a member of the policy planning staff. She was later made director of political-military affairs (1984 to 1986) and subsequently director of Near East and South Asian affairs (1986–89). Her tenure in government culminated in her appointment as ambassador and alternate U.S. representative for special political affairs to the United Nations (1990–93).

Of her years as a South Asian in the Reagan and Bush administrations, Tahir-Kheli remembered: "There were many who were uneasy about my ability to be comfortable in both worlds. . . . [They would wonder] Not only does she know the president here but she knows the president there (Pakistan)." It is a dilemma that all immigrants face but in the field of national security and political affairs, it gathers greater urgency over the issues of loyalty and to which nation. Tahir-Kheli also felt pressure from people in both Pakistan and India on her role as representing the interests and goals of the United States. Nevertheless Tahir-Kheli was able to perform her job successfully, she said, "because Larry Eagleburger and George Bush believed in me. . . . My goal with regard to United States policy in South Asia was to show that it did not need to be a zero-sum game between India and Pakistan; it was possible to improve U.S. relations with both."

Tahir-Kheli definitely sees her experience as a role model for other Asian Americans, particularly women. "Parents are trying to recreate South Asia in America and the girls particularly are suffering from the dichotomy between the two cultures," she said. Tahir-Kheli lectures at colleges, schools, and to South Asian groups. Her message is simple: "We must decide where our loyalties are. . . . My own preference is to be part of the U.S. political system." She became a U.S. citizen as soon as she was eligible in 1971 and credits her clarity of purpose as the key to her success in government.

When Bush lost the 1992 presidential election to Bill Clinton, Tahir-Kheli returned to academia and policy analysis. She is currently a fellow at the Center of International Studies at Princeton University, and she cochairs a study group on "The Future of United States Policy in India and Pakistan." She is also working on an initiative on technical cooperation between India and Pakistan on energy/environment issues, while working on her autobiography. "There was life before the White House, you know," Tahir-Kheli said with a smile.

Sources:

Tahir-Kheli, Shirin R., interview with Shazia Rafi, July 1994.

United States Mission to the United Nations. "Shirin Tahir-Kheli." New York, NY, July 1990.

—Sketch by Shazia Z. Rafi

Ron Takaki
(1939–)
Academician, historian, writer

Ronald Takaki began college with the intention of becoming an Episcopalian priest. Between his junior and senior years, however, he became involved in a summer-long debate with an atheist over the existence of God. "At the end of the summer," recalled Takaki in an interview with Terry Hong, "I lost the debate. I couldn't prove that God existed. So after my senior year, I decided instead to go to Berkeley and get a Ph.D. in history. And that's how I became an historian."

Takaki's first professorial post took him to the University of California at Los Angeles where he taught the school's first African American history course. During his five years at UCLA, he helped found its centers for African American, Asian American, Chicano, and Native American studies. In 1972, Takaki returned to Berkeley where he served as chairperson of the ethnic studies department and where he helped found the first Ph.D. program in ethnic studies in the United States.

In 1979, Takaki published the critically acclaimed study, *Iron Cages: Race and Culture in Nineteenth Century America.* His fifth book, *Strangers from a Different Shore: A History of Asian Americans,* received numerous awards, including a 1989 Pulitzer Prize nomination for nonfiction, the Gold Medal for nonfiction by the Commonwealth Club of California, and Notable Book of 1989 by the *New York Times Book Review.* His latest work, *A Different Mirror: A History of Multicultural America,* published in 1993, has been lauded by various publications.

Island Son

Born on April 12, 1939, Ronald Takaki grew up in a working class, multiethnic neighborhood in Honolulu, Hawaii. His mother was second-generation Japanese American and his father was first-generation. "I can remember when I was young going to friends' houses and hearing the parents speaking in Portuguese, Japanese, Chinese, etc. As kids, we thought that was normal. But at school, we were not taught why we were so diverse. It was a very Eurocentric education that we were exposed to and, ironically, it was being taught mostly by Japanese American teachers," recalled Takaki.

At the youthful age of five, Takaki failed the entry exam to the local English standard school, a school system he would need to attend for future college entry. "I was one of the kids who flunked because my English was so bad. I spoke mostly Pidgin English." In the fifth grade, Takaki's parents transferred him to a private school so he "could be on the college-track." In spite of his parents' encouragement, Takaki recalled, "As a teenager, I wasn't much of an academic. I have to confess this. I was more interested in surfing. My parents owned a hot-plate lunch restaurant on Waikiki Beach and I would help out, cutting onions and peeling shrimp. Then when I was done, I would just surf. I used to be a pretty good surfer."

During his senior year in high school, a teacher recommended that Takaki go to a small liberal arts college on the mainland. So convinced was the teacher of Takaki's academic promise that he wrote to the dean of the College of Wooster in Ohio. "The dean wrote a letter back that said 'You've been accepted, but please fill out an application,'" laughed Takaki. "I guess it was an early version of affirmative action."

As the first person in his family to go to college, Takaki arrived at the College of Wooster where the student body totaled approximately one thousand, including five Asians. "Of the five, only two were Asian Americans. I can remember whites asking me how long had I been in the United States, where did I learn to speak English, etc.," Takaki recalled. He added, "Today, I've been visiting campuses all over and Asian American students are still being asked the same kinds of questions. Not much has changed in the last thirty years."

At Wooster, Takaki studied history at the recommendation of his bishop, to whom he had expressed a desire to enter the ministry. After the failed debate with his coworker about the existence of God, Takaki chose graduate school instead. "I entered Berkeley in the 1960s and got swept up in the civil rights movement. The students wanted to organize and protest against racism. But the regents prohibited rallies of any kind. So it all exploded into the free speech movement. I was a T.A. [teaching assistant] at the time and I went out on strike. That really politicized me. That's when I decided to focus my dissertation on the study of slavery in the 1850s. It became my first book, *A Pro-Slavery Crusade.*" Published in 1970, the book was a study of the Southern ideological defense of slavery.

A Professor's Life

In the fall of 1967, Takaki joined the faculty at UCLA where he offered the school's first African American history course. "At first I was met with skepticism," he recalled. "There were four hundred students enrolled and when the black and white students first saw me, their first reaction was, 'Gee, he doesn't look black.' I had to prove that I had something to teach." He became very involved in organizing the Black Students Union, and acted as the group's faculty adviser. He was also actively involved with the Chicano and Asian American students. After two years of teaching African American history, Takaki developed another ground-breaking course, "The History of Racial Inequality," a comparative study of inequality across various minority groups.

Ron Takaki

In spite of—or perhaps because of—the multicultural legacy Takaki helped establish at UCLA, including the development of ethnic studies curricula and the establishment of the centers for African American, Asian American, Chicano, and Native American studies, he was not granted tenure. "I became involved in an intense, bitter controversy with the senior faculty and to this day, I believe I was denied tenure due to political reasons," he stated simply.

Takaki returned in 1972 to his alma mater, the University of California at Berkeley, after accepting an invitation to join the ethnic studies department there. "I had a chance to help strengthen an autonomous ethnic studies department that had the power to hire faculty and offer courses." Today, Berkeley is recognized as the center of the country's most elaborate ethnic studies department.

Although Berkeley is home base, Takaki has also been invited to lecture at universities throughout the United States, including Cornell University. In 1988, he was awarded the Goldwin Smith University Lectureship at Cornell and, in 1993, he was the Distinguished Messenger Lecturer, which is Cornell's most prestigious lecturer appointment.

In addition to receiving kudos as a teacher, Takaki is also a noted writer. "Writing is inherently political," he emphasized. "Writing is a chance to challenge orthodox scholarship. It's a chance to redefine America, what

America means to different people, to make sure that African Americans, Asian Americans, Chicanos and Native Americans all get included in the definition of America. Scholarship is a contested terrain, so it's very important for scholars of color to publish in a world that is otherwise dominated by Eurocentric scholars. It's not enough to be only teachers."

Author, Author

"My books are all related to my teaching and to my politics," Takaki explained. "My scholarship was initially influenced by my involvement in the 1964 free speech movement and my horror at the murder of the three civil rights workers in Mississippi and the bombing of churches in Alabama. So I wrote *A Pro-Slavery Crusade* and *Violence in the Black Imagination* [a study of nineteenth century African American novelists, published 1971]." In 1979, Takaki broadened his study of race in *Iron Cages,* a comparative analysis of African Americans, Asian Americans, Chicanos, and Native Americans. "I was writing in the wake of the Watts riots, but I realized that race was not just black and white, that others—Chicanos and Asian Americans—must also be included."

While writing *Iron Cages,* Takaki returned to his native Hawaii. "I had three young kids at the time and I wanted to teach them Pidgin English and how to surf." When Takaki described his current project to his favorite maternal uncle, the uncle replied, "Why you no go write a book about us, huh? Why you just write books about mainland folks? Your history is here on Hawaii's plantations." Takaki recalled, "He was asking me to write a book about the plantation laborers of Hawaii. We were drinking beer together at the time, so I took a swig and said, 'why not?'"

Published in 1983, *Pau Hana: Plantation Life and Labor in Hawaii* was a different kind of history book than Takaki had previously written. "Before *Pau Hana,* I had used a very academic style, very philosophical language. But now I was writing a book for my uncle and people like him in Hawaii, and so I decided to use a narrative storytelling style with the voices of the people telling their own stories. By letting people tell their own stories, they thereby reclaimed their own history."

"*Pau Hana* taught me a new way to challenge traditional scholarship. It showed me how to contribute to the community. After it, I was finally ready to write *Strangers from a Different Shore,* a study of Asian Americans in the islands and on the mainland. Again, it was a book filled with the stories of people with minds, wills, and voices."

Takaki's latest book, *A Different Mirror: A History of Multicultural America,* covers the years from the founding of Jamestown in 1607 to the end of the Cold War in the 1990s. "It developed out of *Strangers,* in the wake of the L.A. riots. As I was writing *A Different Mirror,* I kept asking myself how can we get along unless we learn about one another. I realized that *Strangers* did not contribute to cross-cultural understanding. With *Mirror,* I wanted to write something between two covers that tried to include many different groups—African Americans, Asian Americans, Chicanos, and American Indians, as well as the Irish and Jews. I wanted Americans of each group to learn about themselves and each other. In the sharing of their varied stories, Americans from different shores create a community of a larger memory."

A Scholar Abroad

For the past decade, Takaki has traveled extensively to share his revisionist historical expertise with many universities and organizations. In addition to his travels, Takaki has made numerous television appearances, including NBC's "Today Show," ABC's "Good Morning America," CNN's "International Hour," PBS's "McNeil/Lehrer Report" and many others.

"Multiculturalism is on everyone's front burner," Takaki explained. "Students and educators recognize the need to create a more inclusive curriculum because a more inclusive curriculum means a more accurate curriculum. Many colleges and universities are saying 'Yes, we need multiculturalism, but how do we do it?' And that's where they find my scholarship is helpful."

Takaki continued, "I enjoy the lecturing and traveling, for it means learning from other cultures. And I also enjoy sharing what I know about U.S. society and culture. Ethnic conflict, after all, is a global issue." In past years, Takaki has lectured in Japan and the former Soviet Union. His latest travel destination includes a U.S. State Department-sponsored trip to South Africa to talk on multiculturalism in the United States.

With his many international visits, it is not surprising that the focus of Takaki's next book reaches beyond U.S. borders. His new book will be a study of multiculturalism in relation to World War II, a topic Takaki touched upon in chapter 14 of *A Different Mirror.* Although Takaki said the book will not be ready for publication "for at least several years," he laid out a clear plan for its contents: "I want to show that World War II represented the first multicultural defense of America. African Americans described the war as a 'double victory'—victory over Nazism abroad and victory over racism at home. I believe historical scholarship has overlooked the multicultural dimension of World War II—it was the first time that many ethnic groups went to war for the U.S. They included Navajos from the reservations, Chicanos from the barrios, African Americans from the ghettos and even Japanese Americans from the internment camps. All of them wanted to claim America in the struggle for what President Franklin Roosevelt called the 'Four Freedoms.' Yes, America was victorious, but I ask the question, 'What didn't we win?' What happened in Hiroshima reveals something about us Americans that is especially frightening. Then there's the

Holocaust. What did American policy makers really know? What did the media know? When did they know and what did they do? Both events represent the greatest moral issues of human history—they unshrouded a certain darkness of the heart."

"History is memory," Takaki concluded. "The question for me is what do we remember. I think we need to remember the Holocaust and remember Hiroshima."

Sources

Takaki, Ronald, telephone interview with Terry Hong, June 10, 1994.

—Sketch by Terry Hong

Jokichi Takamine

Jokichi Takamine
(1854–1922)
Chemist

Jokichi Takamine isolated epinephrine (adrenaline), the first of the gland hormones to be discovered in pure form, from the suprarenal gland in 1901. His discovery, made while he was a researcher at Johns Hopkins University, benefited the advancement of medicine and surgery in incalculable ways.

Jokichi Takamine was born in Takakao, Japan, in 1854. His father was a physician, as had been many of his relatives for several generations. He spent his young life immersed in science and learning, and at the age of twelve his father sent him to Osaka to learn English.

In 1879, Takamine graduated from the University of Tokyo's College of Engineering and Science and was selected as one of twelve students to be sent by the Japanese government for postgraduate study at Glasgow University and Anderson's College in Great Britain. He was a very curious student and spent much of his free time visiting industrial plants, paying close attention to the methods used, especially in the creation of fertilizers and other products that could benefit Japan's agricultural output.

When he returned to Japan in 1883 he joined the Department of Agriculture and Commerce. It was Takamine's belief chemistry and industry should be used primarily to develop Japan's agricultural system, not to compete with other nations.

In 1884 he first visited the United States as one of Japan's commissioners to the International Cotton Centennial Exposition in New Orleans. It was here that Takamine met his future wife, Caroline Field Hitch, the daughter of an American colonel. Upon returning to Japan Takamine was made chief of the Division of Chemistry in the Department of Agriculture and Commerce. He left government service in 1887 to develop the first superphosphate works in Japan, the Tokyo Artificial Fertilizer Company. At the same time he was working independently in his private lab on the development of Takadiastase, a powerful starch-digesting enzyme.

America's Commercial Opportunities

In 1890 he moved to America to attempt to find commercial applications Takadiastase. He first tried the distilling industry, but found little success. Then in 1894, the production of his enzyme was taken over by the pharmaceutical manufacturer Parke-Davis and Company of Detroit, which used it for medicinal purposes. Takamine remained closely allied with Parke-Davis for the remainder of his career.

Toward the turn of the century, as Takamine grew prosperous, his interests widened. He aided in the development of several industries in Japan, including aluminum fabrication, Bakelite production, development of the electric furnace, and nitrogen fixation. One of his top priorities in life became furthering relations between the United States and Japan, his two countries. His private research laboratory in Clifton, New Jersey, became a mecca for young chemists. Takamine took pride and delight in helping young people in any way he could. But his interest was not limited to science—he also helped to finance young artists' and musicians' studies in France and Italy. His home on Riverside Drive in New York City became a sort of cultural center, and ambassadors, industrialists, royalty, and other powerful and colorful figures were frequent guests.

Takamine was cofounder and president of the Japanese Association of New York and the Nippon Club. He declined "honorary" U.S. citizenship until the laws were changed to allow people of Japanese descent to become naturalized citizens. He was honored by the Imperial University of Japan in 1899, 1906, and 1912; became a member of the Royal Academy of Science in 1913; received the Fourth Order of the Rising Sun in 1915, and the Senior Degree of the Fourth Rank (Sho Shii) and the Third Merit (Kum Santo) in 1922.

He was also influential in the creation of the Imperial Research Institute in Japan in 1913. At his death in 1922 he was survived by his wife and their two sons.

Sources:

Americans of Japanese Ancestry and the United States Constitution, 1787–1987. San Francisco: National Japanese American Historical Society, 1987.
"Jokichi Takamine." *Dictionary of American Biography.* New York: Charles Scribners Sons, 1964.

—*Sketch by Jim Henry*

George Takei

(1940–)

Actor

George Takei is a television, theatre, and film actor who is best known for his portrayal of Sulu in the "Star Trek" television series of the late 1960s and the Star Trek films of the 1970s and 1980s. He is also politically active in the Democratic party in California, where he ran for office on two occasions. Takei is also the author of a juvenile fantasy novel, *Mirror Friend, Mirror Foe.*

George Hosato Takei was born on April 20, 1940, in Los Angeles to second-generation Japanese Americans. When he was one year old the United States entered into war with Japan. In a blatantly unconstitutional move, the U. S. government imprisoned American citizens of Japanese descent on the West Coast in remote camps. The Takeis

were sent to a camp in Arkansas. Takei said in an interview for *Starlog* magazine in June of 1981 that he has few memories of his family's imprisonment, and that the ones that he has are mostly pleasant. "You have to remember though," he qualified, "that I was just a very little boy. For my parents it was a terrible time. My mother felt the whole idea of being kept behind barbed wire at gunpoint and not knowing if you were committing your children to a lifetime of such treatment was abysmal."

Takei's mother believed the internment was contrary to her country's promises of justice and liberty for all citizens, so she joined with many other imprisoned Japanese Americans and renounced her American citizenship. Takei explained, "It was a symbolic gesture, but for my mother, being a citizen of a country that was doing this to her family was intolerable." In retaliation for her mother's outspokenness, the family was transferred to a hard-core prison camp in California, where they remained for the remainder of the war.

After the war ended and the Takeis were allowed to return to a normal life, Takei proved to be an excellent student with an outgoing personality. He attended Mount Vernon Junior High and Los Angeles High School. He was active in extracurricular activities—including the drama club—and was elected student body president at both schools. After graduation he enrolled in the University of California at Berkeley where he intended to study architecture, in deference to his parents who persuaded him that acting was not a substantial enough career.

His First Roles

While at Berkeley Takei met an importer of low-budget Japanese science fiction films who needed actors to dub voices in English over the Japanese soundtrack. Takei explained to *Starlog,* "I needed a summer job, so I did it. The movie turned out to be *Rodan!* . . . Later on I did a few other films including *Rodan Meets Godzilla, The Jelly Monsters,* and *Retreat from Amchitka.*"

After his second year of college, Takei transferred to the University of California at Los Angeles (UCLA) and switched his major to acting. Shortly thereafter he was contacted by an agent he had met while dubbing the Japanese films. The agent landed him a role in a "Playhouse 90" episode called "Made in Japan." Takei later was signed by another agent, Hoyt Bowers, who had seen him perform in a college production. He was soon being cast in small parts in television shows like "Hawaiian Eye" and "77 Sunset Strip."

In addition to his studies at UCLA and his television work, Takei was also studying acting at the Desilu Workshop, a school for television and film studies. There he studied under Joe Seargent, who would go on to a successful career directing films and television shows, including an episode of "Star Trek." At UCLA Takei also starred in

George Takei

classmate Francis Ford Coppola's student film *Christopher.* Coppola later would become a prominent film director.

After graduating from UCLA in 1960, Takei lived briefly in New York where he starred in a small production of the play *Fly Blackbird.* Afterward he spent a summer in Europe, where he studied Shakespearean drama at the Shakespeare Institute at Village of Stratford-upon-Avon in England. He then returned to the United States and UCLA where he enrolled in the master's program in theatre arts. It was then that his agent called him to say that the producer Gene Rodenberry wanted to interview him for a role in a potential series called "Star Trek."

Star Trek

Takei met with Rodenberry about playing the part of the astrophysicist, Sulu. Recalling the meeting for *Starlog,* Takei said, "My feeling was that [it] wasn't successful because of the way it was carried on. Gene didn't ask me a thing about my experience. We just discussed current events and the movies we had recently seen. I figured Gene was being polite, but that he wasn't interested in me." As it turned out, though, Rodenberry was interested and Takei was offered the part. Early into "Star Trek"'s first season his role was changed, however, from that of an astrophysicist to helmsman. This was done in part to get Takei's character, whom the producers found intriguing, into the thick of the action on the bridge with the other main characters.

The story of "Star Trek"'s initial life on network television was not one of harmony between the producers and the network that broadcast it, NBC. In 1968, at the end of its first two seasons, the network announced it would cancel the show, only to be deluged with letters from the show's devoted fans imploring them to keep it on the air, which they did, almost grudgingly. After the second season, NBC scheduled the show in a time slot sure to bring about its demise, Friday nights at ten o'clock, when few of its fans would be home to watch it. Rodenberry, the show's creator, essentially took leave of the production of the show in protest and it was cancelled in 1969 after the third season.

"Star Trek" had a tremendous cult following, however, that would not accept the show's demise. Conventions of "Trekkies," as devoted fans came to be known, were held around the country for years after the show was cancelled—and continue to be held today. Appearing at these conventions became a lucrative business, Takei told *Starlog* in August of 1981: "The conventions grew to be big, big business, so the actors began to feel that we should participate. . . . Our speaking fees wound up supplementing our incomes in a very nice way."

Politics

Also after the cancellation of "Star Trek" Takei became involved in civic and community affairs in a more visible way. He began hosting a local talk show on the Los Angeles PBS station called "Expressions: East/West." He also became active in local Democratic politics and served as a delegate to the 1972 Democratic National Convention in Miami Beach. In 1973 Takei ran for the Los Angeles city council seat vacated by Tom Bradley when he was elected mayor. In an interview for *Starlog,* Takei recalled: "My campaign for public office held a *lot* of surprises. I had always known that there were a lot of people who would stoop to any level to win an election, but I really saw them in action for the first time. . . . Someone in the opposition even accused my father of having been a communist—which of course he was not—so therefore *I* must be a communist as well." Takei lost the bitterly fought election by three percentage points.

For the remainder of the seventies, Takei worked in a variety of television shows including "Kung Fu," "Ironside," "The Six Million Dollar Man," "Chico and the Man," "Hallmark Hall of Fame," and "The Blacksheep Squadron." He also continued his interest in public service. He organized and served as the founding chairman of the Friends of Far Eastern Arts at the Los Angeles County Museum of Art, as National Cultural Affairs Chairman of the Japanese American Citizens League and on the Academy of Television Arts and Sciences' Blue Ribbon Committee for the Emmy Awards. He also served as vice-president of the board and chairman of the personnel committee of the Southern California Rapid Transit District. During this time Takei also wrote a book, *Mirror*

Friend, Mirror Foe, with science fiction writer Robert Asprin. Published by Playboy Press in 1980, it did remarkably well. Also in 1980, he ran for a seat in the California assembly, although he abandoned his campaign in midstride among allegations that the newly released Star Trek film in which he played his old role gave him an unfair advantage.

The Star Trek Films

With a huge body of dedicated fans—some might call them obsessed—it was only a matter of time before another Star Trek project was put together. In 1979 Paramount released *Star Trek—The Motion Picture,* in which Takei revived his role of Sulu.

The film's reviews, however, were less than favorable; it was ridiculed by critics when it was released. There had been many problems during production with script revisions and character development. Takei explained in *Starlog,* "Some of the earlier screenplays were more interesting for the secondary characters . . . but what we wound up doing wasn't at all fulfilling. It was like reading a fancy restaurant's menu with tantalizing descriptions of the meals that you could order and then discovering that what you have placed in front of you is a plain hamburger patty with french fries."

Despite the bad reviews the film did well at the box office and Paramount released a series of sequels including: *Star Trek II: The Wrath of Khan* in 1982; *Star Trek III: The Search for Spock* in 1984; and *Star Trek IV: The Voyage Home* in 1986.

Other Work

Aside from his work in the Star Trek films, Takei has acted in several foreign film productions and in the theatre in New York. In 1991 he starred in *The Wash,* a play written by Philip Kan Gotanda, a prominent Asian American playwright. In an article published in *Drama-Logue* in January of 1991, Takei discussed two recent foreign roles and the difficulty of finding non-stereotypical roles as an Asian in America: "I have to go abroad to get producers to cast me in challenging, dimensional roles. *Return to the River Kwai* is British, and *Blood Oath* is Australian. There's an interesting message there."

Sources:

Burns, James H. "George Takei: Part I." *Starlog,* June 1981, pp. 37–39, 62.

———. "George Takei: Part II." *Starlog,* August 1981, pp. 44–47.

Scaffadi, Richard. "This Star Is Still Trekkin'." *Drama-Logue,* January 24–30, 1991, p. 30.

—Sketch by Jim Henry

Amy Tan
(1952–)
Author

Amy Tan is one of the most successful new writers of serious fiction to emerge in the last several years. Her first book, *The Joy Luck Club,* was a phenomenal bestseller, remaining on the *New York Times* best-seller list from April of 1989 through November. It was a finalist for the National Book Award and the National Book Critics Circle Award and won the Bay Area Book Reviewers Award. Tan became an instant celebrity, earning a huge readership and a seven-figure deal with Vintage for the book's paperback publication rights. She has since written a second novel and a children's book, both of which have been very well received. That Tan's second novel was successful, both commercially and critically, established her as a noteworthy presence on the literary scene, less easily dismissed as a genre writer, or an ethnic writer, or just a lucky beginner.

Amy Tan was born in Oakland, California, in 1952 to John and Daisy Tan, both first-generation Chinese Americans who met and married in the United States. John was an electrical engineer who had worked for the U.S. Information Service during World War II, before immigrating to the United States. Tan's family moved around the Bay Area sporadically through much of her childhood, eventually settling in Santa Clara, California. They remained there until Tan's father and her older brother died of brain tumors within eight months of each other in 1968. The family was devastated and decided to move, thinking there might be something toxic in the house. Tan's mother took her and her surviving brother to live in Montreaux, Switzerland, where Tan finished high school. She became rather wild and rebellious, becoming involved with some unsavory characters with connections to drug dealing.

The Tans left Europe in 1969, after having spent just one year, and returned to the Bay Area. Tan enrolled in a small Baptist college in Oregon called Linfield College. Her mother had chosen both the school and her course of study, which was to be pre-med. Tan spent only a year at Linfield, and in 1970 moved with her boyfriend to San Jose, California, and enrolled in San Jose City College, changing her major to English and linguistics. She earned a bachelor's degree from San Jose City College in English in 1972 and then went on to earn a master's in linguistics from that same institution in 1974. She intended to go on to earn a doctorate at the University of California at Santa Cruz, but she dropped out in 1976, when she took a job with the Alameda County Association for Retarded Citizens as a language development consultant.

Amy Tan

Beginning to Write

Beginning in the early 1980s, Tan began working freelance as a business writer, a field in which she became very successful. Also at this time she began trying to distract herself from becoming consumed by her work by reading contemporary fiction. In 1985 she joined a writer's workshop that was run by a professor at the University of California at Irvine. The first story she finished in the workshop was published by *FM* magazine and reprinted in *Seventeen*. Buoyed by her success, Tan continued writing, and in 1986 she signed with the literary agent Sandra Djikstra.

In 1987 Tan took a trip to China with her mother to visit relatives she had never met before. In taking this trip she was trying to connect with her Chinese roots, something that had never been discussed in the Tan house. When she returned to the United States, she found that her agent had sold a collection of her stories to G.P. Putnam for a $50,000 advance, a very high price for an unknown writer. Tan finished a series of stories to complete the collection and then wove them together in such a way that they became more of a novel than a collection of unrelated stories.

The Joy Luck Club and Beyond

The Joy Luck Club was published in 1989. Writing in the *New York Times Book Review,* Orville Schell described the

young writer as having "a wonderful eye for what is telling, a fine ear for dialogue, a deep empathy for her subject matter, and a guilelessly straightforward way of writing." He went on to say that the stories and vignettes that make up the novel, "sing with a rare fidelity and beauty." Most other critics were as unqualified in their praise, and the book made Tan a national celebrity.

Tan agonized over her second novel, fearing the wrath of envious critics who seemed at times to be salivating at the opportunity to discredit her status as a serious writer. In an interview with the *New York Times* in 1991, Tan described the painful process of beginning her second novel with, essentially, the whole world watching. She said that she tried to write something completely different, so as not to be "pegged as a mother-daughter expert." Her attempts to be different, however, proved fruitless, with Tan "realiz[ing] that rebellion was not a good reason to write what I was writing."

Tan finally decided on telling a story much like that of her mother's who had come of age during World War II, a particularly brutal time in Chinese history when the mainland was under near-constant assault from the Japanese. Her mother had hardly spoken about what she had endured in those years, and as Tan pushed her for information, she had her inspiration for her book. In 1991 Tan published *The Kitchen God's Wife*. It was a much-anticipated event in the publishing world, and one that many people had predicted would be a disappointment. The reviews, however, were generally quite good, although many critics faulted the novel's laborious structure, which switches back and forth between the narrative action of the story and scenes of the storyteller in the fictional present.

Writing in the *New York Times Book Review,* Robb Forman Dew judged, "Amy Tan's second novel is a harrowing, compelling and at times bitterly humorous tale in which an entire world unfolds in a Tolstoyan tide of event and detail. No doubt it was daunting to attempt a second book in the wake of the enormous success of *The Joy Luck Club,* but none of Ms. Tan's fans will be disappointed. *The Kitchen God's Wife* is a more ambitious effort and, in the end, greatly satisfying."

Writing in the *Wall Street Journal,* Julie Just said, "Where *The Joy Luck Club* was a group portrait, *The Kitchen God's Wife* above all tells the story of [one person] . . . the most richly imagined character Ms. Tan has yet created. The story—which describes a brutal first marriage set against turbulent times—is closely based on her mother's life in China before, during and after World War II, and the wartime scenes, especially, have the force of a compelling oral history. But this is fundamentally a novel: its power lies in the author's impressive ability to create a world."

In 1992, Tan published a children's book called *The Moon Lady.* Writing in the *New York Times Book Review,* Ellen

Schechter described the book as "an invitation to . . . attend a long-ago autumn moon festival in China . . . with 7-year-old Ying-ying, spending a wide-eyed day of pleasure waiting to encounter Lady Chang-o, who lives on the moon and who once a year fulfills the secret, unspoken wishes of the heart. This is a story with deep, satisfying meanings, a tale of a lost child who for a prolonged and terrifying moment risks losing even her sense of self."

Amy Tan described herself for a *New York Times* interview with Mervyn Rothstein as having created a second personality she puts on when playing the role of celebrity, a role with which she is decidedly uneasy. "I have a different personality in public than I have in private. I put on the public personality. I ironed these clothes for you this morning," she told Rothstein, "Otherwise what I would be wearing would be really grungy." She went on to describe her private personality as "sillier . . . and a lot bitchier" than her public persona and said she is most comfortable "walking around back home with my husband, or when I'm having a conversation with him and he's sort of drifting off trying to read the paper, and I say, 'Well, this is good; I'm as boring as I ever was.'"

Sources:

Dew, Robb Forman. "Pangs of an Abandoned Child." Review of *The Kitchen God's Wife, New York Times Book Review,* June 16, 1991, p. 9.

Just, Julie. "A Mother's Lifetime of Secrets Revealed." Review of *The Kitchen God's Wife, Wall Street Journal,* June 17, 1991, p. A8.

Rothstein, Mervyn. "A New Novel by Amy Tan, Who's Still Trying to Adapt to Success." *New York Times,* June 11, 1991 p. C13.

Schechter, Ellen. "Girl Overboard." Review of *The Moon Lady, New York Times Book Review,* November 8, 1992, p. 31.

Schell, Orville. Review of *The Joy Luck Club, New York Times Book Review,* March 9, 1989.

—Sketch by Jim Henry

Thomas Tang

(1922–)

Judge

Thomas Tang is an appellate court judge serving the Ninth Circuit, a position he has held since 1977. The highest ranking Chinese American federal judge, Tang is currently fourth in seniority among the twenty-eight active judges on the Ninth Circuit Court of Appeals, the jurisdiction of which covers nine western states.

Thomas Tang was born on January 11, 1922, in Phoenix, Arizona, to second-generation Chinese immigrants. His father was a wholesale grocer. Tang was educated in Catholic schools until high school, when he switched to the public school system. He was an excellent student and was a member of the National Honor Society. Upon graduation in 1939, Thomas entered the University of Santa Clara, in Santa Clara, California, where in his second year his studies were interrupted by the outbreak of World War II. Tang entered the army in 1942 through the ROTC enlisted reserve and was trained at the army language school in Monterey, California. He served as a 1st Lieutenant in the China-Burma-India theater of operations, where he trained Chinese artillery units. At the end of the war in the Pacific, in August of 1945, Tang was transferred to Shanghai, China, where he served out the remainder of his duty. He returned to the United States and finished his education, receiving a bachelor's degree from the University of Santa Clara in 1947.

A Career in Law

In 1950, Tang received his J.D. from the University of Arizona and then spent the following year as a clerk for Justice Evo DeConcini of the Arizona Supreme Court. In this position, Tang researched case law and prepared memorandum and drafts of opinions for DeConcini. With the outbreak of the Korean War, Tang, who had remained in the military reserves, was recalled into action. He served mostly in Tokyo as a military intelligence officer, but also served time on the Korean peninsula interrogating prisoners in Pusan, among other duties.

Upon his discharge in 1953, Tang returned to public service when he was appointed the deputy county attorney for Maricopa County. In this position, he prosecuted criminal cases on behalf of the state. Tang served in this position until 1957 when he was appointed assistant attorney general of the state of Arizona, where he represented the state in appeals and was legal counsel to a variety of state agencies.

In 1960, Tang left the attorney general's office to go into private practice. He set up a solo general law practice where he worked for the following three years. During this time he was elected to the Phoenix city council, where he served two terms. In his second term he was elected by his fellow councilmen to the position of vice-mayor, which he held until leaving the council in 1963.

His First Position on the Bench

In 1963, Tang was elected to the superior court of Arizona for Maricopa County, where he heard both civil and criminal cases on the state level. He served on the trial

Thomas Tang

bench for eight years, leaving in 1970 to return to private practice. Also at this time, he sat on the Arizona State Bar Board of Governors and in 1977, he was elected that organization's president.

Tang was appointed to the U.S. Court of Appeals for the Ninth Circuit in October of 1977. He was appointed under President Jimmy Carter's merit selection system for the nomination of federal judges. Carter was the first president to institute such a system for the nomination of judges to the appellate court. All other presidents had left it to U.S. Senators to recommend appointees, which often resulted in cronyism. The merit system allowed the local legal community—lawyers, judges, law professor—to nominate persons they felt were the most qualified for judicial appointments. Tang was one of five persons recommended for the Ninth Circuit appointment, and from those he was chosen by the president. In this position, Tang hears cases on appeal from all over the western United States. In an interview with Jim Henry, Judge Tang recalled three examples of the types of cases he normally hears.

The first was a widely publicized case in which Vietnamese American fishermen were being prohibited from fishing off the coast of Monterey, California, by a 150-year-old statute that was clearly not intended to be so blatantly discriminatory. Ultimately, the case was not decided by the court—although it was brought in the Ninth Circuit, which recommended arbitration—because Congress intervened to exempt the Vietnamese from this statute.

The second case the judge recounted was *Zobrest* v. *Catalina Unified School District.* This case dealt with the First Amendment separation of church and state in a dispute over whether public school money could be used to pay a sign language interpreter for a deaf child at a parochial school. The court ruled that it could not, that to do so was a violation of the First Amendment. Tang disagreed and wrote the dissenting opinion. When the case was heard on appeal by the Supreme Court of the United States, they overturned the lower court's decision, essentially taking Tang's position.

The last case the judge mentioned was *Atonio* v. *Ward's Cove,* a class action worker's discrimination suit brought against an Alaskan cannery by the predominantly Asian workers, almost none of whom ever were promoted to management positions. Tang found in favor of the workers, but the Supreme Court overturned his decision. This case, Tang told Henry, especially exemplifies the ongoing discrimination faced by Asians and other minorities in this country.

In speaking about racism in America against Asians, Tang said that the outright racism of the past is largely gone, but that it remains today in more isolated and insidious forms. He said that as a young lawyer he could not get an interview with a law firm in San Francisco, although in Phoenix he could. He attributed this to the fact that there was not a large Asian presence in Phoenix as there was in San Francisco, and so Asians were not seen as a threat to the established order. Tang added that although he recognizes there is a substantial amount of racism in America, it generally has not played a large role in his career. He remarked, "You feel different, but you ignore it."

In 1947, Tang married Pearl Mao Tang, a physician who served as director of the Maricopa County Maternal and Child Health Bureau.

In addition to his judicial duties, Tang has served on several committees, including the Committee for Administration of the United States Bankruptcy System. He has also served on the American Bar Association's Commission on Increasing Opportunities for Minorities in the Legal Profession, and on the Commission on Legal Problems of the Elderly.

Sources:

The Ninth Circuit Court of Appeals. "Judge Thomas Tang: Biographical Information." Press release. Phoenix, Arizona.

Tang, Thomas, telephone interview with Jim Henry, May 11, 1994.

—Sketch by Jim Henry

Shashi Tharoor
(1956–)
Novelist, political satirist, international diplomat

Add Indian patriot to the labels novelist, political satirist, and international diplomat, and perhaps you have Shashi Tharoor in a nutshell.

At age eleven, Tharoor had his first work of fiction published—a six-part series on the adventures of a fighter pilot. Three years later, nearly every English-language publication in India had carried his stories. Now he works as a career diplomat with the United Nations and has served as part of the U.N.'s peacekeeping operations team in the former Yugoslavia. But he continues to write on the side, and rave reviews of his first two novels, *The Great Indian Novel* and *Show Business*, give him a secure spot among a growing cadre of U.S.-based Indian writers.

For Tharoor, writing fiction is a means of self-expression. It is also a vehicle for him, as a career diplomat expected to remain relatively apolitical, to express his opinions on world issues. And, in many ways, it's a means of conveying to the rest of the world that, despite centuries of a foreign rules, Indians do have a distinct and unique cultural identity. "I've found fiction a more practical means of expressing my concerns about the world than scholarship," he said in a 1992 interview with *New York Times Book Review* writer Alison MacFarlane, shortly after his second novel, *Show Business* was published. "In my fiction, I've always been inspired by Moliere's credo; that is, you've got to entertain in order to edify."

Tharoor achieves that goal in both of his novels. In *The Great Indian Novel*, he explores Indian identity by retelling *The Mahabharatha*, an ancient Hindu epic, in a twentieth-century setting. The book's characters, plots, and descriptions show Indians that they do indeed have a long and richly varied heritage—a crucial issue in a nation that has spent nearly fifty years learning to acclimate itself to the idea of independence following centuries of first Moghul, then British colonial rule.

Show Business takes on a lighter subject: India's wacky and comical film industry, which produces even more films each year than Hollywood. But the social message is just as significant. In the novel, Tharoor tells the story of the rise, fall, and rebirth of a fictitious Indian movie star, Ashok Banjara, (whose initials and life resemble the career of Amitabh Bachchan, a real Indian film superstar who took a misguided and corrupt turn into politics). But the story is really about Indian society, its fascination with cultural icons, and the damage that such worship can ultimately produce. It also comments on the lingering traces

Shashi Tharoor

of British domination. In one scene, for instance, Ashok is talking as a makeup artist applies blush to his face. "Nearly thirty years since Independence," he remarks, "and we still associate pink skin with healthiness."

Shashi Tharoor was born in 1956 in London but grew up in India. A child prodigy, he had a reputation for devouring Enid Blyton children's stories and later British classics. He raced through school, attending St. Xavier's School in Calcultta, studying history at Delhi University, and receiving a doctorate from the Fletcher School of Law and Diplomacy at Tufts University in the United States by age twenty-two.

Shortly after completing school, he began working for the U.N. High Commissioner for Refugees in Geneva in 1978, where he stayed for eleven years. During this time, he spent three years in Singapore dealing with Vietnamese boat people. "You could put your head to the pillow at night feeling you had made a difference in people's lives," he recalled in a 1992 *New York Times Book Review* interview.

He began writing in 1989, when the U.N. posted him in New York. His earlier experiences in India had taught him how to write for an audience, he told the *Economic Times*, and he had reached a point where he wanted to get in touch with a wider audience. "Many people write well, but it is basically for themselves," Tharoor said. "To me, a book is important only if it means something to others."

After the release of *The Great Indian Novel* in 1991, Tharoor became highly sought-after. His book was included in several university English literature courses, and he was pressed to give readings in several different countries.

However, his job as a U.N. diplomat continues to be his first priority. He relegates writing to nights and weekends, when demands of the job are not pressing. Shortly after completing *Show Business,* he admitted ruefully to the *New York Times Book Review* that he had started work on a third novel. Unfortunately, crisis in the former Yugoslavia put a brake on those efforts.

Though his work is international, Tharoor writes from a strongly Indian perspective, returning to India frequently for inspiration. And, in addition to fiction, he occasionally writes commentaries for the opinion pages of both U.S. and Indian newspapers, usually on Indian political issues. In late 1992, for instance, he spoke out against communal violence in an essay for the *New York Times* after a Muslim mosque in Ayodhya was destroyed by Hindu fundamentalists.

In the essay, he explains that he and his wife have taught their eight-year-old twin sons not to identify themselves as "Hindu," "Calcuttan," or "Malayali" but as Indian. A true India, he asserts, is more a "smorgasbord" of different cultures, rather than the "melting pot" concept used in America. He calls on Indians to quiet discord by learning to respect all differences.

"The raging battle is for India's soul," he concludes in the essay. "For my sons, the only possible idea of India is the one their parents grew up with, that of a nation greater than the sum of its parts. That is the only India that will allow themselves to continue to call themselves Indian."

Sources:

Alfred, Rajesh. "Bollywood Follies." *The World and I,* August 1992.

Amirthanayagam, Indran. "Entertaining and Edifying." *India Currents,* October 1992.

Boyd, William. "Hooray for Bollywood." *New York Times Book Review,* September 27, 1992.

Lee, Kyu-Young. "The Writer As Modern-day Developmentalist." *Earth Summit Times,* September 14, 1992.

MacFarlane, Alison. "The More War, the Less Writing." *New York Times Book Review,* September 27, 1992.

Shankar, Lekha J. "Riding on 'Show Business.'" *Economic Times,* August 7, 1991.

Tharoor, Shashi. "The Revenge of History." *New York Times,* December 11, 1992.

———. "Rajiv Gandhi and the Politics of Fear." *New York Times,* May 22, 1991.

—Sketch by Himanee Gupta

Chang-Lin Tien
(1935–)
Educator

The fall of 1990 was a tumultuous one for University of California students in Berkeley. A fraternity house fire killed three students; a gunman held thirty people hostage at a popular hotel pub, killing one and injuring seven others before being shot himself by police. Not the best welcome for a new chancellor perhaps, but Chang-Lin Tien took it in stride. Tien, the first Asian American to head a major U.S. university, arrived on campus July 2, 1990, with a pledge to transform Berkeley from a huge, uncaring institution into a warm, personal university that cares deeply about its students, particularly its undergraduates. Tien draws his inner strength from Buddhism, the philosophy of Confucius, and an unwaveringly optimistic belief that "all obstacles or challenges are opportunities." It didn't take him long to turn the challenges of fall 1990 into opportunities.

Rather than holing up in his office, Tien spent an entire day at the fire-ravaged fraternity house, comforting students and talking to parents. When the hostage crisis erupted a few weeks later, he stayed in the police command center and was among the first to embrace students after their release. Later, he wrote letters to all the students' parents, reassuring them that the campus was safe. When the pub reopened, he went to its welcoming party.

Tien's appointment was hailed—and criticized—as a response to the growing diversity of the university's student population. An influx of students of color had produced a racially mixed and increasingly fractious student body. Whites, who in the 1980s had accounted for two-thirds of all undergraduates, now made up less than 40 percent of all undergraduates and were outnumbered by Asians in the freshman class for the first time in Berkeley's history. In an effort to maintain a racially and ethnically diverse student body, administrators had imposed admissions quotas on white and Asian applicants. From the beginning, many predicted Tien, who came in with a credo of "Excellence Through Diversity," would face his biggest challenge in unifying the polarized student body.

Frequent Moves

An appreciation for diversity was something Tien understood well. Born July 24, 1935, in Wuhan, China, Chang-Lin Tien was the son of a wealthy government banking official. During World War II his family fled to Shanghai to escape the invading Japanese. After the war, the family fled again to Taiwan following the Communist revolution in 1949. His life changed drastically after each

Chang-Lin Tien

move. In Shanghai, Tien recalls having chauffeur-driven cars, maids, butlers, and servants. In Taiwan, he and his parents lived in cramped conditions. Though his father re-established himself in the government and Tien's sweetheart (later his wife), Liu Di-Hwa, was the daughter of a top army general, Tien's family fell into poverty when his father died in 1952.

Living as a refugee in Taiwan, Tien learned the value of education. He did well academically and graduated from National Taiwan University in 1955, with a degree in mechanical engineering. Though only 5-foot-6, he achieved a bit of notoriety shortly after graduation playing basketball for a military academy. Later, he realized his height was an impediment, and he decided to pursue a career in academia. He borrowed $4,000 from relatives and came to the United States to attend the University of Louisville and ultimately Princeton, where he earned his Ph.D. in mechanical engineering.

He took a teaching position at Berkeley in 1959, and began working in what became his field of specialization, thermal radiation. As a teacher and researcher, Tien collected numerous awards, fellowships, and honorary positions. He had never planned to go into administration, but he found that he enjoyed the work. Over the years, he held several administrative positions, serving as chairman of the university's thermal systems division and later of the department of mechanical engineering. In 1983, Tien joined the campus's central administrative staff as vice-

chancellor of research, but resigned the job in 1985 because he wanted to return to research and teaching. When the University of California at Irvine offered him the position of vice-chancellor in 1988, he initially expressed reluctance; he had received an endowed chair at Berkeley and was quite happy. However, he was in what he described as a "mid-life kind of situation" and a visit to the Irvine campus helped him decide to take the job. He stayed for two years, until he was offered the position of chancellor at Berkeley. He returned to Berkeley with his wife and four children, all of whom graduated from the University of California.

New Land, New Problems

Tien's firm commitment to diversity can be traced to the experiences he had as a newly arrived immigrant in a new land. When he came to the United States in the late 1950s, the country was considered the land of hope and prosperity. He quickly learned it also was a land of racial discrimination. On a bus to Louisville, he noticed washroom signs at bus stop stations marked "Colored" and "White." Barely able to speak English, he felt confused. Which washroom should he use? he wondered. He was told to use the "White" washroom, but later he learned that American prejudice didn't stop at that point. A college professor insisted upon calling him "Chinaman." When Tien learned it was a derogatory term, he asked the professor to call him by his name, Chang-Lin Tien. "The professor came right back and said, 'How can I remember all those strange names, Ching, Chong, Tong, Cong,'" recalled Tien in an interview with *Asia Inc.* in 1993. "I got so mad, I said, 'If you can't call me by my name, don't call me.'" The professor didn't call him by any name for the next nine months.

The memories linger. Tien wants no student to suffer the indignities he did, and he talks of eliminating racism by selecting nearly half of each incoming freshman class at Berkeley on the basis of diversity rather than academic merit. However, Tien's idea of diversity extends beyond ethnicity. It includes people of different political and sexual persuasions, for example. At times, this open-mindedness has drawn criticism from some conservative Californians who have dubbed the Berkeley campus "Beserkley."

Not the type to shut himself inside an office, Tien frequently strolls around campus, greeting students and working the crowds, some say, like a seasoned politician. He stops, chats, and moves on after admonishing students to say hello to their parents. Tien considers this interaction essential to making Berkeley more student-friendly. "When I first became chancellor and started walking around, nobody said anything to me," Tien said in an interview with *World Monitor* magazine. "They'd never seen a chancellor."

But some question whether this sunny mode of operation offers up too much style and not enough substance. When the administration made harsh cuts in Berkeley education programs and raised undergraduate fees, angry students often lobbed hard-ball questions at Tien and got, they complained, evasive responses at best.

Dedication to Quality

Tien, however, is showing that despite his optimistic demeanor, he can talk tough and straight. He recently threatened to resign when chancellors at other University of California campuses supported a faculty retirement program that he feared would drain Berkeley of its best teachers. Since then, he's worked to protect the quality of education at Berkeley in other ways.

Shortly after his appointment as chancellor, the Tang Foundation in San Francisco welcomed Tien back to Berkeley with a $1 million grant, which has since been increased to more than $4 million. Tien also travels frequently to Asia to organize alumni and build relationships with Asian governments and corporations, which has resulted in numerous additional grants to the university. Still, Berkeley, which lost $32 million in state support in the early 1990s, faces deeper budget cuts. While working to offset this loss by cutting administrative costs and raising student fees, Tien warns that further cuts could hurt the fine programs Berkeley is noted for. "When you tear apart a great university program, you cannot rebuild it overnight," he was widely quoted as saying in 1993. Although his words won him praise, the strength of his legacy rests, in the long run, on maintaining Berkeley's sterling reputation amid an era of diminished resources.

Sources:

Periodicals

"Berkeley's Not-So-Secret Weapon." *Sacramento Bee,* May 23, 1993.
Curtis, Diane. "New Chancellor Takes Command at UC." *San Francisco Chronicle,* July 2, 1990.
DePalma, Anthony. "For Chief at Berkeley, a Time for Perspective." *New York Times,* June 17, 1991.
DeVoss, David. "Berkeley's Asian Connection." *Asia Inc.,* September 1993.
"Facing 4th Year of Cuts, Berkeley Chancellor Leads Budget Revolt." *New York Times,* May 12, 1993.
Gordon, Larry. "Berkeley Battles the Blues." *Los Angeles Times,* June 13, 1993.
———. "Chang-Lin Tien: Maintaining Berkeley's Excellence at a Time of Stiff Budget Cutbacks." *Los Angeles Times,* September 13, 1992.
Hallanan, Blake. "Excellence in Ethnic Diversity." *Time,* April 1, 1991.
Magner, Denise K. "The First Asian American to Head a Major U.S. Research University." *Chronicle of Higher Education,* October 24, 1990.
Morain, Dan. "Chancellor Says Funding Research Is Best Economic Cure." *Los Angeles Times,* February 25, 1992.
Schoch, Russell. "A Conversation with Chang-Lin Tien." *California Monthly,* September, 1990.
Shao, Mario. "He's Seen our Future, And . . ." *World Monitor,* July 1992.
Wood, Daniel B. "Preaching Excellence in Diversity." *Christian Science Monitor,* October 24, 1990.

—Sketch by Himanee Gupta.

Samuel C.C. Ting
(1936–)
Nuclear physicist

When he returned to the United States in 1956, Samuel Chao Chung Ting had a hundred dollars in his pocket, very little knowledge of English, and the determination to study. Twenty years later, in 1976, he shared the Nobel Prize for physics with Burton Richter for discovering the existence of a new particle called j/psi.

Nuclear physicist Samuel Chao Chung Ting was born on January 27, 1936, in Ann Arbor, Michigan. He was the eldest of the three children of Kuan Hai Ting, an engineering professor, and Tsun Ying Wang, a psychology professor. Two months after his birth, the family decided to return to mainland China, which was where Ting spent his childhood years. His teenage years were spent in Taiwan, where his father taught at the National Taiwan University.

In 1956 Ting returned to the United States to study at the University of Michigan. Even though he had only $100 with him, his determination and quest for knowledge helped him get support in the way of scholarships and grants. He got his bachelor's in mathematics and physics in 1959, a master's in physics in 1960, and a Ph.D. in physics in 1962, all within a remarkably short period of time. In 1960 Ting married Kay Louise Kuhne, an architect. They have two daughters.

Particle Acceleration

In 1963 Ting joined CERN (the European Organization for Nuclear Research) in Geneva, Switzerland, where he worked closely with the Italian physicist Guisseppe Cocconi on a type of particle accelerator, the proton synchrotron. After two years at CERN, he then went to Columbia University in New York where he became involved in an experiment conducted at Harvard University's electron accelerator. The results of the experiment involving "pair

Samuel C.C. Ting

production" seemed to violate certain predictions of quantum electrodynamics (which describes the interaction of matter with electromagnetic radiation).

At this point, in 1966, Ting took a leave of absence from Columbia University and went to Hamburg, Germany, to duplicate the Harvard experiment at the DESY facility, named for the Deutsches Elektronen-Synchrotron (German electron synchrotron). Ting's team built an instrument called the double-arm spectrometer, which helped them determine that the quantum electrodynamics description of pair-production was correct to distances as small as one hundred-trillionth of a centimeter.

Ting's pair production study continued, as did his search for new particles whose decay products were electron-positron pairs (electrons and positrons are similar but for the fact that electrons are negatively charged particles and positrons are positively charged). He also accepted a faculty position in physics at the Massachusetts Institute of Technology (MIT) in 1967, where he became a full professor two years later.

In 1971, Ting and his group began a particle search at the Brookhaven National Laboratory in Upton, Long Island, New York. To find what they were looking for, Ting and his team decided to build a very sophisticated version of the double-arm spectrometer. This extremely complicated and painstakingly built apparatus, the brainchild of

Ting, worked almost the first time it was turned on. With this, the reputation Ting had earned grew even more.

J Particle

In August 1974, Ting thought he observed a new and unpredicted particle. Since Ting wanted to investigate the nature of this particle further he did not submit a report and publish his results. Instead he reported his finding to Giorgio Bellettini, director of the Frascati Laboratory in Italy. The Frascati physicists confirmed Ting's discovery within two days. Papers by Ting and the Frascati group appeared in *Physical Review Letters*. Since his work had involved electromagnetic currents which bore the symbol "j" he decided to name this particle "j."

At a routine meeting at the Stanford Linear Accelerator Center (SLAC) in California, SLAC's director, Wolfgang Panofsky, informed Ting that only a few days earlier a SLAC physicist, Burton Richter, had reported similar findings. Ting and Richter compared notes and found that they had discovered the same particle after all, but Richter had named the particle "psi." The particle was thus named "j/psi," in recognition of their independent and almost simultaneous discoveries. Many physics labs started researching j/psi, and nuclear theorists started to incorporate it into their concepts.

Nobel Prize

For this pioneering work in the discovery of a heavy elementary particle of a new kind, Ting and Richter were awarded the Nobel Prize for physics in 1976. Ting continued his search for new particles and also continued his faculty duties at MIT, where he was appointed as the first Thomas Dudley Cabot Institute Professor in 1977.

A member of the American Academy for Arts and Sciences and the National Academy of Sciences, as well as the American, European, and Italian Physical Societies, he received the Ernest Orlando Lawrence Memorial Award for Physics from the United States Energy Research and Development Agency in 1976. He also holds an honorary degree from the University of Michigan.

Known as a quiet, intense man and a meticulous scientific experimentalist, Ting more than proved himself with his determination and thirst to find out more about the unknown in the world of physics.

Sources:

Wasson, Tyler, ed. "Ting, Samuel C.C." *Nobel Prize Winners: An H.W. Wilson Biographical Dictionary,* New York: H.W. Wilson, 1987.

—Sketch by Visi R. Tilak

Tamlyn Tomita
(1966–)
Actress

Tamlyn Tomita is one of the most recognized Asian American faces on the big screen. She played Ralph Macchio's love interest in *The Karate Kid, Part II* (1986), Dennis Quaid's wife in *Come See the Paradise* (1990), and the adult Waverly, the chess prodigy, in the film adaptation of *The Joy Luck Club* (1993). Although Tomita has built a reputation around a considerable list of dramatic roles for film, television, and on stage, she confesses a penchant for doing comedy. "With a dramatic character, there's a set process. You go through ups and downs, you build, peak and experience as sense of retribution," she told Terry Hong in an interview. "Comedy is much more of a challenge and I'm scared to death of that. You have to go out of yourself. It's timing and listening to the audience. There's an internal dialogue going on between your own self and the character you play, the other characters and the audience. You have to always be aware of all that."

Born in 1966 in Okinawa, Japan, to a second-generation Japanese American father and a Japanese-Filipino mother, Tamlyn Tomita arrived in the United States at age three months with her parents. Growing up as what she described as "an all-American girl" in San Fernando Valley in southern California, Tomita went to the University of California at Los Angeles (UCLA) to study history. "A lot of research is needed in such a discipline, research that I've been able to apply to much of my acting. The acting has brought to life that research, what I've seen and read about historical events," she said.

While a student at UCLA, Tomita attended a Japanese American festival in Los Angeles where she met a woman, Helen Funai, who suggested that Tomita audition for a role in the upcoming *The Karate Kid, Part II*. Funai later became Tomita's manager and she got the part as the luminary beauty that captivates Ralph Macchio's heart. She refers to the film as her "favorite role . . . because it was the first, it was brand new."

The Work Begins

After her first role, Tomita began taking acting lessons seriously, practicing her craft on what she refers to as "episodic television," including a regular stint on the soap opera, "Santa Barbara," as well as guest appearances on series such as "Quantum Leap," "The Trials of Rosie O'Neill," "Raven" and "Tour of Duty." Tomita also had starring roles in *Vietnam, Texas* with Dr. Haing Ngor and *Hawaiian Dream,* the first Japanese-produced film shot entirely in the United States.

In 1990, Tomita starred opposite Dennis Quaid in Alan Parker's *Come See the Paradise,* the story of Kawamuras, a Japanese American family interned during World War II. Although the film has been widely criticized because of the story's focus on a non-Asian American (a working-class white man played by Quaid) in one of the first major mainstream films about a historical landmark of Asian American history, Tomita is quick to defend the film. "Not everyone is going to be pleased," she said. "People have to take it with a grain of salt. They have to understand that the studio thought they needed a star with recognition to pull in audiences. . . . It's not the perfect film, but it does say something and it's out there for posterity's sake. The film is a beginning point to legitimizing the arguments that will make sure that something like this can never happen again." Regardless of who the star is, emphasized Tomita, the film itself "tells a story that needs to be told." Many Americans, she said, even "Dennis [who] had never heard of the camps of the 1940s," are still unfamiliar with what happened to the Americans of Japanese descent during the war.

Filming *Come See the Paradise* was also a personal journey for Tomita. "My father and father's family were interned at Manzanar, California, during the war years, so it's always been a part of my legacy," she told *American Film* magazine in 1991. "I recall when I was a little girl in elementary school reading about World War II and seeing a very small paragraph saying, 'On the West Coast, in Hawaii, and in portions of Canada, 110,000 Japanese Americans were evacuated under Executive Order 9066.' And there were no details furthering the story. So I went home and asked my father, 'Did this really happen? Were you guys interned?' And he goes, 'Yes,' and it shocked . . . me."

Two years later in 1993, Tomita portrayed the adult Waverly, a child chess prodigy who aspires to be the best she can at everything, letting nothing stand in her way, in the adaptation of Amy Tan's blockbuster bestseller, *The Joy Luck Club.* The film, directed by veteran Chinese American Wayne Wang and produced by Oliver Stone and Janet Yang, was the first mainstream Hollywood film with a virtually all-Asian cast. In general, the film received outstanding reviews, although loud grumblings could be heard in the Asian American community over the negative portrayals of Asian men and the chronic exotification of Asian/Asian American cultures with stunning Asian women and exotic, mystical tales of the inscrutable Orient.

Again Tomita patiently explained: "The film is not the definitive picture about Asian Americans. . . . Is *Joy Luck* going to be the apex of Asian American films? Of course not. It's just a blip on the screen; maybe a big blip, bigger than most thus far. It's a great point in the history of Asian American filmmaking, but it's certainly not going to be the greatest. There's still a lot of work to be done. . . . The film is a step, a point toward some kind of enlightenment. It's an opportunity to see people of different color, with different facial characteristics as people first. Of course our people are not going to be represented by one story. Sadly, there's a part of the population who thinks that when they see an Asian face on film, there must not be a real person behind it. You have to be either really patient with people like that, or you have be constantly up in their faces about it.

"It might be that we will have to wait until our kids are our age in order to gain a realistic viewpoint of how people of color really are . . . it won't be until the higher echelons of the WASP, upper class become the minority. While that might not happen in the near future, it will happen."

Other Stages

When Tomita is not in front of the camera, she continues to learn new roles for the theatre. Most recently, she appeared in the January 1994 world premiere of Philip Kan Gotanda's *Day Standing on Its Head* at the Manhattan Theatre Club in New York. In the story of a law professor who, on the verge of middle-age, embarks on a dreamscape/nightmare journey toward his true self, Tomita played the beautiful/ugly Nina, a role that was "both physically and emotionally demanding because it was not bordered by the paradigm of a normal person's world; the character existed in someone's head."

Other theatre credits include the world premiere of *Nagasaki Dust* for the Philadelphia Theatre Company, *Don Juan: A Meditation* for the Mark Taper Forum's Taper Too and the title role in *Winter Crane* at the Fountain Theatre, for which Tomita received a Drama-Logue Award. Tomita is a charter member of the Antaeus Project, an actor-run classical repertory company assisted by the Mark Taper Forum/Center Theatre Group.

The Future to Come

One of Tomita's greatest concerns as an actress echoes those of the majority of people of color in the media: the need for more substantial roles. "We need to push for more Asian Americans to be seen in roles. Just because people see one Asian face, that face isn't the face for all Asians. It's the face of one individual." she stated. "We need to break the notion that we are all children of long-suffering parents who gave up everything for us. We need to break the notion of the heroic Asian. We need to counter the myth of Asian Americans as the model minority."

"The future is going to be tough," she continued. "With the advent of so many new Asian American and Asian films, people are getting confused. They're thinking that people with these faces are all the same. But we have to be careful to say that I'm American first. My culture, heritage, race are all American. My experience has nothing to do with Peking Opera, my wedding has nothing to do with the processions in *The Wedding Banquet*. . . . Yes, as a group we have to emphasize we're Asian Americans, but we have to emphasize more that we're Americans first."

Sources:

Periodicals

Seidenberg, Robert. "Come See the Paradise: Tamlyn Tomita Relives Her Family's History." *American Film*, vol. 16, January 1991. pp. 48–49.

Other

Tomita, Tamlyn, telephone interview with Terry Hong, January 3, 1994.

—Sketch by Terry Hong

Charles D. Toy
(1955–)
Attorney

On a journey from a tenement on New York City's lower east side to the heady world of Washington, D.C., politics, Charles D. Toy has done his best never to forget his roots. Appointed by President Bill Clinton in 1993 as vice-president and general counsel of the Overseas Private Investment Corporation, Toy also has served on the board of trustees and development committee of the Lower East Side Tenement Museum in New York. The museum was added to the National Register of Historic Places in 1992 and serves as a realistic tribute to America's melting pot. "I serve, proudly, as proof and witness to the deep and enduring value of the hopes and dreams held by all those who passed through the immigrant and tenement experience before I did, including my parents, as well as those who are part of that experience today," Toy said in a June 1994 statement before the U.S. House's Subcommittee on National Parks, Forests, and Public Lands.

Charles D. Toy was born in New York City's Chinatown on June 29, 1955, to Chinese immigrant parents. His father, Frank H. F., had come to the United States from China in 1928 at the age of fourteen. He met and married Louise Sook Kin Louie in Hong Kong in 1954, and she returned with him to New York. Frank worked in Chinese restaurants throughout his life, even though he was educated as an engineer. "He never did anything but work in a restaurant because he knew it would be a struggle [as a Chinese man] to go into a profession like engineering," Toy said in an interview with Mary Anne Klasen. Louise worked in New York's garment district, and in the mid-1990s she continued that work, while serving as her shop's union representative. Toy and his younger brother and sister were guided from a young age in their mother's principles. "The most resonant lesson she taught all of us was to be modest about our achievements and not to count chickens before they hatched," Toy told Klasen. "Even today, that's a guiding principle in how I act."

Educational Opportunities

Toy's parents also taught him the value of a good education. Believing that New York's Catholic schools offered a better education and more opportunities than public schools, they sent Toy to Transfiguration School in Chinatown through grade five. Then came what Toy described as the "seminal event of [his] life." During his fifth grade year, Toy was accepted into the Monsignor William R. Kelly School, which had been established by the Catholic church in 1965 to educate talented, disadvantaged students from around the city in a preparatory school environment. "Kelly opened my eyes and my parents' eyes to the opportunities offered by a prep school education," Toy told Klasen. "I was the only Asian in my class, so it was a good introduction to bigger changes in the future." The biggest change came when Toy was accepted into the prestigious Phillips Academy in Andover, Massachusetts, for secondary school. "That transition required an extraordinary adjustment," Toy said. "I was one of three or four Asians at Kelly, and at Andover there were thirty or forty in a school of nine hundred. Both Kelly and Andover pushed me to look beyond what I knew and was familiar with and gave me the ability and credibility to advance further."

After graduating *cum laude* from Andover in 1973, Toy enrolled at Harvard College, where he majored in social studies with a concentration in economics and East Asian studies. After graduating *cum laude* in 1977, he continued his studies at Harvard's law school, where he received his J.D. in 1980. Soon thereafter, he accepted the first position in his professional career as an associate at the Wall Street law firm Milbank, Tweed, Hadley & McCloy. Back in New York, he worked in the firm's corporate department, negotiating, drafting, and reviewing financial contracts and agreements. International law became one of his specialties, and, in 1984, he accepted a position with another major international firm, Kaye, Scholer, Fierman, Hays & Handler, which at the time had offices in New York and Washington. Toy's new employers took advantage of his language proficiency—he speaks three Chinese dialects plus Spanish and German—by giving him the responsibility of opening new firm offices in Hong Kong and Beijing in 1984. Toy lived in Hong Kong from 1984 to 1991 before returning to New York. "Hong Kong opened my eyes as well," Toy said. "Despite being Chinese, I had never really traveled. In fact, until I moved to Hong Kong, I had never been west of Chicago."

Elected a partner in the firm in 1988, Toy maintained an international flavor in his practice even in New York. He represented clients from the United States, Europe, and Japan in their investment, commercial, and trade

Charles D. Toy

activities throughout Asia. Joint ventures, copyright and licensing rights, and foreign investment all were part of the job. Toy has written and spoken extensively on foreign trade and business and is a member of special sections and committees on those subjects for the American Bar Association, the American Arbitration Association, the New York State Bar Association, and the Association of the Bar of the City of New York.

Overseas Private Investment Corporation

In 1993, Toy was appointed vice-president and general counsel of the Overseas Private Investment Corporation (OPIC), an executive branch agency of the U.S. government that provides project financing, investment insurance, and a variety of investor services to American businesses in more than 140 developing countries and emerging markets throughout the world. OPIC's purpose is to strengthen the U.S. economy by generating exports, thus creating jobs for Americans both in the United States and abroad. It also tries to encourage economic reform and democratization in developing and formerly communist countries. Toy's experience both professionally and personally are uniquely suited to his OPIC role. His career as a private attorney has given him close ties both to American businesses and the foreign marketplace. His personal perspective as the successful son of immigrants has provided him with the motivation to encourage others to seek economic and personal success with the same vigor.

Toy's sense of obligation to his family and ancestors prompted his leadership role in the development of the Lower East Side Tenement Museum on Orchard Street in Lower Manhattan. He has been a board member since 1992, and served as the first chairman of the museum's development committee. The museum was listed on the National Register of Historic Places in 1992. In his June 1994 congressional testimony, Toy urged that it be affiliated with the National Park Service so it will continue to receive government support and additional resources: "Its listing on the National Register of Historic Places . . . confirmed it as a representative marker of the beginning of American life for many Americans, and, as the school motto for Phillips Academy at Andover, in whose dormitories I first experienced living beyond the tenement I was born into, succinctly and accurately says: '*Finis origine pendet*'—the end depends on the beginning. We should all remember our beginnings."

Toy responded to criticism that the Tenement Museum building has no architectural distinction by comparing tenements to other long remembered and sometimes romanticized American dwellings: "That place of ordinary urban dwellers deserves the same preservation and honor as the uptown homes of famous people, the log cabins of rural people, and the grand mansions of rich people, because, in one way or another, they all have a tenement in their past. . . . It was a first place to live, to die, to keep house, to keep boarders, to keep Christmas, to keep the Sabbath, to celebrate Thanksgiving. The museum that will save, restore, and reinvigorate that building will also restate and clarify the meaning of the immigrant experience and relate it to today's Americans and today's immigrants."

Toy has made another major community commitment, this one to De La Salle Academy, a middle-school for gifted inner city children in New York. He serves as a member of the strategic planning committee and development subcommittee for the academy, whose goal is to provide students from low-income families a top-quality education and opportunities similar to those at the finest private institutions. De La Salle is the successor to the Monsignor William R. Kelly School, which Toy credits with much of his success.

In his congressional testimony, Toy expressed the hope that places like the Tenement Museum will foster the philosophy upon which he has based his life and work: "Understanding and acceptance of the different backgrounds and hence unique contributions brought to this country by all immigrants, and tolerance for the infinite variety yet ultimate similarity of immigrant life in America and the different kinds of Americans that make up America." Toy told Klasen that if he and his wife Sandra L. Youla had children, he would give them this advice: "Asians have made great strides and you should work to continue that progress. You should be proud and not ashamed of what you are."

Sources:

Overseas Private Investment Corporation. "Charles D. Toy." Washington, D.C., July 1994.

Toy, Charles D., telephone interview with Mary Anne Klasen, July 14, 1994.

U.S. Congress. House. Statement of Charles D. Toy before the Subcommittee on National Parks, Forests, and Public Lands of the Committee on Natural Resources, June 21, 1994.

—Sketch by Mary Anne Klasen

Tritia Toyota

Television journalist

Tritia Toyota is a pioneering Asian American broadcast journalist in the Southern California area, having worked in both radio and television since 1970. Today she is one the area's best-known television news anchors and reporters. She is also a co-founder of the Asian American Journalists Association (AAJA), and has served as the president of the southern California chapter of the AAJA.

A fourth-generation Japanese American, Tritia Toyota was born and raised in the Pacific Northwest. She was educated in the public school system before enrolling in Oregon State University, where she received a bachelor's degree in communications and home economics. As an undergraduate she was elected to Theta Sigma Phi, the national journalism society for women. After graduating from Oregon State, Toyota continued her education at the University of California at Los Angeles, from which she received a master's degree in electronic journalism.

Toyota's first job in broadcasting was with KNX-CBS radio in Los Angeles, a local news station. She served in a variety of positions, beginning as a copy person and eventually working as an on-air reporter. She also worked as a writer, producer, and ombudswoman.

In 1972 Toyota joined KNBC television in Los Angeles, where she worked as a general assignment reporter. In 1975 she was elevated to weekend anchor and in 1977 she was named anchor of the daily 5:00 P.M. news broadcast. In 1978 she took on the additional duty of anchoring the 11:00 P.M. broadcast. In addition to her anchoring duties, Toyota served as KNBC's head reporter in coverage of elections, special events, and investigative series. She reported and produced "Asian America," a one-hour documentary focusing on the Asian Pacific American community in southern California. This ground-breaking

Tritia Toyota

television broadcast was the first serious journalistic examination of the huge Asian American community in Los Angeles.

Asian American Journalists Association

In 1981 Toyota and Bill Sing, a reporter with the *Los Angeles Times,* founded the Asian American Journalists Association. She was inspired to found the AAJA by the success of the California Chicano News Media Association, many of whose members were friends of Toyota's. The AAJA has grown from the original Los Angeles chapter to an organization with more than fifteen chapters across the country. Toyota served the organization loyally for more than ten years, in a variety of positions, and in 1991 stepped down as president of the board of directors, although she still retains unofficial contacts and advisory positions. She also continues to speak on behalf of the organization and is deeply committed to its ideals, which are to advance Asian Americans in all areas of both broadcast and print journalism.

In 1985 Toyota left KNBC to assume new anchoring and reporting duties at KCBS-TV in Los Angeles. As of the summer of 1994, Toyota was the anchor of both the 6:00 P.M. and 11:00 P.M. news broadcasts. She is KCBS's principal reporter for major political events, and she recently filed reports from the besieged city of Sarajevo, Bosnia-Herzegovina, and from Seoul, South Korea.

Respected Celebrity and Mentor

Toyota is a well-known member of southern California's large and ethnically diverse Asian Pacific Islander community. She is a frequent speaker at community and professional events and has earned a reputation as a dignified, professional representative of Asian American interests and concerns. She speaks at colleges whenever she can and makes herself as available as possible to young journalists looking for advice or inspiration. Many Asian American journalists point to their contact with Toyota as an important influence in their career.

Throughout her career, Toyota has received Emmy Awards for her work as a journalist, and has garnered many other honors, including the Golden Mike for best news broadcasts, Outstanding Young Woman of America, the Los Angeles Human Relations Commission Achievement Award, the Greater Los Angeles YWCA Communicator of the Year Award, the Los Angeles City Asian American Association Person of the Year Award, Asian American Journalists Association Lifetime Achievement Award, and the U.S.-Asia Institute Achievement Award.

Toyota and her husband, an Asian American criminal defense attorney, are active in many community and civic organizations. In addition to her professional and community commmitments, she is at work on a doctorate in cultural anthropology.

Sources:

Asian American Journalists Association. "Tritia Toyota."
Toyota, Tritia, telephone interview with Helen Zia, August 22, 1994.

—Sketch by Jim Henry

Eugene Huu-Chau Trinh
(1950–)
Physicist, astronaut

Physicist and astronaut Eugene Trinh was a payload specialist aboard NASA's first long-duration space shuttle flight in June of 1992. As a member of STS-50, the first microgravity laboratory mission, Trinh spent fourteen days aboard the shuttle and circled the earth 350 times. As a payload specialist, Trinh was responsible for conducting more than thirty experiments in fluid dynamics and space manufacturing. In addition to his work for NASA, Trinh is a highly regarded physicist in the field of fluid dynamics. He holds three patents and has been widely published.

Eugene Huu-Chau Trinh

Eugene Huu-Chau Trinh was born in Saigon, Vietnam, on September 14, 1950. His father, a civil engineer with the United Nations sent his family to live in Paris, when Trinh was only two years old. Vietnam at the time was involved in an increasingly violent anticolonial war, and the elder Trinh wanted to spare his family the violence.

Education in Science

Trinh was educated in Paris in the French public school system and then came to the United States in 1968 to attend Columbia University in New York City, to which he had won a full academic scholarship. Columbia University at that time was the site of some of the country's most virulent anti-Vietnam War protests. In an interview with Jim Henry, Trinh recalled the protests as tame compared to the student strikes of Paris in 1968, and said that he was very sympathetic to the American students who did not want to go fight in his homeland. He said that having grown up in Paris he had "been pretty much won over by the Western perspective of things."

Trinh graduated from Columbia in 1972 with a bachelor of science degree in mechanical engineering and applied physics. He then went to Yale University in New Haven, Connecticut, for graduate work. In 1974 he earned a master of science degree in applied physics, a master of philosophy in 1975, and a Ph.D., also in applied physics in 1977. Following completion of his doctoral dissertation, Trinh remained at Yale where he worked as a

postdoctoral fellow for one year. He then moved to the Jet Propulsion Laboratory (JPL) at Cal-Tech, where he worked in laboratory-based experimental research in fluid mechanics. Trinh told Henry that fluid mechanics is the study of the motion of fluids (fluids can refer to either liquids or gases) and the laws of physics that govern the motion of such bodies. In application, fluid mechanics can describe, for example, the effect of the motion of the atmosphere or the ocean on the earth. On a smaller scale, fluid dynamics can describe the motion of aerosols and other small particles of liquids and gases.

In this area of scientific inquiry, weightlessness is often required to perform experiments on the behavior of gases and liquids in a containerless state. To this end, Trinh established experiments to be conducted aboard NASA KC-135 airplanes flying in what is referred to as "low-G" parabolas, in which weightlessness is achieved for short periods of time in the cargo bays of airplanes that are essentially free-falling from great altitudes. Of course, experiments of this type are extremely limited and the ideal conditions for experiments in weightlessness occur naturally in outer space. With the introduction of the space shuttle program, NASA began doing scientific research beyond the reach of the earth's gravity.

Applying to the Space Program

Trinh first applied to work aboard the space shuttle in 1983 as one of a group of physicists headed by Taylor Wang that was preparing the Drop Dynamics Module experiment for Spacelab 3. Wang was selected as the payload specialist for the 1985 flight and Trinh as his backup. The next NASA mission in which Trinh was involved was the United States Microgravity Laboratory 1 (USML-1), scheduled to be launched in June of 1992. He applied to be a part of the crew and was accepted as a payload specialist.

Trinh told Henry that the experiments he performed in space had to do with fluid dynamics generally, and with the surface tension of liquids in low gravity specifically. Trinh described surface tension as the forces that dictate the shape of a liquid in low gravity. These experiments allow scientists to probe the magnitude of surface tension and to test its strength in a liquid that is dominated by its force—a condition that does not occur on earth—and to observe the dynamics of oscillating liquid globes or bubbles. The science of surface tension is used in the production of surfactants which allow for the production of such diverse products as mayonnaise, pharmaceuticals, cosmetics, detergents, and a wide array of industrial products. Another practical application of Trinh's work performed is in environmental science. This type of information is useful in understanding the motion of the ocean and the way it transfers gases to the atmosphere—and the atmosphere to the ocean—which sheds light on the dynamics of climate.

Trinh said that his time in space was very enjoyable, although the workload was very hard. Payload specialists conduct experiments in twelve-hour shifts, during which time they are almost constantly busy. Despite this, Trinh said, he did take a lot of time to look out the window, which he said was "the best thing one can do . . . going around the earth, being able to look down at the ocean and the earth." The most surprising thing about his flight, he added, was how well he got along with his fellow astronauts, considering that they didn't know each other very well and were confined to such a small area for an extended period of time. "It's surprising how humans can interact so easily," he commented, "so there's hope for most of the interaction we have on this planet as it gets more crowded."

Although there are continuing opportunities for Trinh to fly again, he is careful to balance his desires in this area with his family commitments. Trinh and his wife Yvette have a daughter, Claire, who celebrated her first birthday while Trinh was in space.

Trinh believes strongly that one should keep open to opportunities. He told Henry that he never imagined that someday he would be able to fly in outer space as an American astronaut, but the fact that he did is proof that there really are no limits to what one can achieve, unless those limits are self-imposed. He also emphasized the importance of work and education. Although he believes that schooling is vital, he contends it's possible to have a good time along the way.

Sources:

Trinh, Eugene Huu-Chau, telephone interview with Jim Henry, June 1, 1994.
NASA. "Eugene Trinh." Biographical materials and press releases, 1993.

—Sketch by Jim Henry

Gerald Tsai

(1928–)

Businessperson

Gerald Tsai is a Wall Street investment strategist who first came to prominence in the late 1950s as a stock analyst with an aggressive style of quick, profit-taking trading that shook up the rather conservative mainstream of institutional traders then dominant on Wall Street. Since that time, Tsai has regularly achieved high-status, high-profit positions in asset management concerns, many of which were largely of his own making.

Gerald Tsai

Gerald Tsai was born in Shanghai, China, on March 10, 1928. He was educated at Boston University, where he received a bachelor's and a master's degree. Following his graduation in 1951, Tsai went to work for Bache & Company, a brokerage firm, as a securities analyst. He stayed with Bache until 1952 when he was offered a job with Fidelity Investments in Boston as a junior stock analyst. It was with Fidelity that Tsai first began to make his presence in the financial markets known. In a profile in *Business Week* Ron Stodghill II wrote, "Tsai wowed Wall Street with an unprecedented method of picking speculative stocks for short-term appreciation and selling them the moment their growth slowed. The method shook up the conservative money-management establishment and inspired a whole new breed of portfolio manager."

Investment Manager to Investor

Tsai was named vice-president of Fidelity in 1960, director in 1961, and executive vice-president in 1965. In 1966 he left Fidelity to form his own investment management firm. Using his reputation as a keen trader Tsai was able to raise $247 million in initial investments for the Manhattan Fund, which he managed for the next two years. It was during this period of Tsai's career that he earned a reputation as one of the key players in what was to become known as the "go-go sixties" in the stock market, a time of high profit-taking, an expanding economy, and international domination of American industry.

In 1968, Tsai sold the Manhattan Fund to a giant insurance company, CNA Financial Corporation, for $27 million in CNA stock. Tsai then took a seat on the board of CNA and essentially took control of the company as one of its largest stockholders. Writing in *Forbes*, Tatiana Pouschine and Carolyn T. Geer described this series of transactions as "a brilliant deal, superbly timed. Tsai had parlayed control of a hot but untested mutual fund [the Manhattan Fund] into virtual control of a giant insurance company." In 1973 Tsai sold his CNA stock when it was valued in the twenties, reaping a huge profit. (Within the year CNA stock had plummeted to under four dollars a share.)

G. Tsai & Company is Born

Tsai took his profits and bought a seat on the New York Stock Exchange, trading under the auspices of G. Tsai & Company. In 1978 he bought a small insurance company called Associated Madison for $2.2 million, with the idea that he could sell insurance through the mail and save huge amounts of money on seller's commissions. He was able to persuade investors that this idea would take off and investment in Associated Madison, largely on Tsai's assurances of profit and his history of providing them, surged. He once again began investing the company's assets shrewdly and also began acquiring other companies. Four years later he sold the company to American Can Company for $162 million. American Can's chairman had wanted to get into financial services and saw the deal with Tsai and Associated Madison as his ticket. Tsai, for his part, saw a subsidiary mail order business of American Can's as a way to expand his mail order insurance business. As part of the deal, Tsai took a position as executive vice-president and, as their largest stockholder, a member of American Can's board. A few years later, Tsai sold to American Can his brokerage business, G. Tsai & Company, for another $3.8 million in stock and a controlling interest in American Can. In 1986, he was named chief executive officer.

Tsai renamed the company Primerica and began building its assets. In 1987 he acquired Smith, Barney, Harris, & Upham, a moderate-sized investment house. Tsai paid nearly double the firm's assets for control, a move that might have proved successful had the stock market not crashed in October of 1987, when brokerage firms throughout Wall Street were devastated by steep losses. In 1988, Tsai sold Primerica for $1.5 billion, or roughly $30 a share—down from the 1987 high of $54.

In March of 1992 Tsai launched his latest investment strategy. He led a group of investors in purchasing a closely held insurance company in Memphis, Tennessee, Delta Life Corporation. *Business Week* reported that Tsai believes that "financial woes and bankruptcies among larger insurers will cause flight toward safer, untainted companies such as Delta Life. About 75% of its $751 million in assets is invested in U.S. government securities and it has few bad loans." They go on to quote Tsai as saying that in the present cautious investment climate, Delta Life assets "will grow at least 20 percent a year."

Sources:

Pouschine, Tatiana, and Carolyn T. Geer. "Be Careful When You Buy From Gerry Tsai." *Forbes,* April 15, 1991, pp. 84–88.

Stodghill, Ron II. "You Thought Gerry Tsai Was Retired? So Did He." *Business Week,* May 11, 1992, pp. 102–105.

—Sketch by Jim Henry

U

Yoshiko Uchida
(1922–1992)
Children's author

When American-born Yoshiko Uchida first journeyed to Japan at age twelve she delighted in blending in for the first time in her life. Yet, when she was unable to read a Japanese street sign for an elderly woman, she knew that in many ways she was still an outsider. Recalling this experience in her 1991 memoir, *The Invisible Thread,* she wrote, "I wasn't really totally American, and I wasn't totally Japanese. I was a mixture of the two, and I could never be anything else." This image of herself as both Japanese and American intensified as she grew older, and her experiences in U.S. internment camps with thousands of other Japanese Americans during World War II formed the basis for many of her stories. After her release, she began writing children's books to relay these experiences and her sense of Japanese values to future generations. Between 1948 and 1991 she wrote twenty-nine books, all but two of them for children. Today she is considered the foremost author of books for young people about the Japanese American experience.

Love and Magic

Born in Alameda, California, in 1922, Uchida lived much of her life in the nearby city of Berkeley. Her mother, a poet, instilled a love of all literature and Japanese traditions in Uchida and her older sister, Keiko. Her father, a gregarious businessman, brought home a parade of diverse visitors, many of whom provided the basis for characters in Uchida's books. While keeping a diary as a child she first discovered the power of writing. She wrote in *The Invisible Thread* that after recording the death of a beloved family dog, she realized "that writing was a means not only of holding on to magic, but of finding comfort and solace from pain as well. It was a means of creating a better ending than was sometimes possible in real life."

Uprooted

At the predominantly white, affluent University High School in Oakland, Uchida experienced her first real taste

Yoshiko Uchida

of prejudice. Despite her American birthright, she was seen as Japanese because of her physical features. She graduated at age sixteen and entered the University of California at Berkeley to study English. Here she developed strong friendships with other Japanese Americans and found a sense of belonging. In December of 1941, during her senior year at Berkeley, Japan bombed Pearl Harbor. Her sense of integration was challenged again. She was forcibly evicted along with 120,000 other West Coast Japanese and Japanese Americans who were assigned to internment camps throughout the nation.

The first stop for Uchida and her family was in San Mateo, California, at Tanforan race track which had been converted and renamed an "assembly center." It was there that she received her diploma from Berkeley, rolled in a cardboard tube and delivered to Stall Number 40, her new home. The internees organized and staffed essential functions within the camp including hospitals, churches, and schools. Although Uchida had been interested in a teaching career, she hadn't majored in education at Berkeley because she knew that few teaching opportunities existed for Japanese Americans. At Tanforan there were plenty of opportunities. She was quickly given a class of second-graders and a salary of sixteen dollars a month.

After five months her family was again uprooted and moved to Topaz, a dilapidated stretch of barracks in Utah's Sevier Desert. Here the internees endured isolation, unreliable water and heat sources, endless dust storms, and cramped living conditions. Uchida and her family lived in an eighteen-by-twenty foot room with four cots. Of this time she wrote in *The Invisible Thread*, "The Japanese endured with dignity and grace and it is that spirit which has made me especially proud of my heritage." That spirit also led her to tell the stories of her people through her books.

Starting Anew

In May of 1943 she was awarded government clearance to leave Topaz. She had taught throughout her internment and with the help of the Quaker-backed National Japanese Student Relocation Council, she had secured a full graduate fellowship in the Department of Education at Smith College. In 1944 she received her master's degree. Her first teaching position was at the Frankford Friends School, a Quaker school near Philadelphia where she taught a class of first and second graders.

Uchida lived in the eastern United States until 1952 when she returned to Japan for a year on a Ford Foundation Fellowship. There she was reintroduced to her Japanese roots and explored the culture, art, and spiritualism with enthusiasm. When she returned to the United States she relocated to Berkeley, California, where she had lived as a child. She brought with her a deep desire to share with third-generation Japanese Americans the same sense of pride and self-esteem she felt about their cultural history. Folk tales she collected in Japan eventually became parts of two books, *The Magic Listening Cap* and *The Sea of Gold*.

In her Rinko trilogy, which includes *A Jar of Dreams, The Best Bad Thing*, and *The Happiest Ending*, Uchida tells the story of an early Japanese immigrant family. Through their story, she hoped to convey the sense of purpose, hope, and affirmation that sustained her own and other early immigrant families. In all her works she tells the stories not only of her characters but of people who inspired them.

Leaving a Legacy

Uchida created a profoundly integrated whole from the many pieces of culture she experienced, both Japanese and American. She conveyed not only what the first-generation Japanese brought to America from their homeland but how it expressed itself here. She wrote of what they and their children experienced in their new nation during World War II and of how their Japanese values helped them to endure it. She was proud of the way they emerged from it, with their values and grace still intact.

In June of 1992, Uchida, age seventy, died of a stroke in her Berkeley home. In *The Invisible Thread*, she wrote in the epilogue, "I hope the young people who read these books ... will learn to see Japanese Americans not in the usual stereotypic way, but as fellow human beings. For although it is important for each of us to cherish our own special heritage, I believe, above everything else, we must all celebrate our common humanity."

Sources:

Books

Uchida, Yoshiko. *The Invisible Thread, A Memoir.* New York: Julian Messner, 1991.

Periodicals

"Author, Yoshiko Uchida, 70, related Japanese-American life," *Chicago Tribune*, June 28, 1992, p. 6.
The Regents of the University of California, "Nisei Author and Philanthropist, Yoshiko Uchida, Evokes the Traditions of the Past to Promote Cross-Cultural Understanding." *Cal Futures*, vol. 1, no. 4, pp. 2–4.

—*Sketch by Cindy Washabaugh*

Huynh Cong Ut
(1951–)
Photojournalist

Huynh Cong "Nick" Ut is an award-winning photojournalist, known best for his work with the Associated Press during the Vietnam War. During that time he distinguished himself as a reliable combat photographer, unafraid of work in hostile areas. In 1972 he took a photograph of a nine-year-old Vietnamese girl running down a dirt road near Trang Bang, Vietnam, after her family home had been hit by napalm—the chemical defoliant developed in the United States to destroy the thick jungle foliage the North Vietnamese used so effectively in their guerrilla war. The photo, so clearly documenting the horror that the war was indiscriminately inflicting on the impoverished civilian population of Vietnam, was widely reproduced all around the world, won nearly every major photojournalism award including the Pulitzer Prize, and helped the antiwar movement prove its case to the American public.

Huynh Cong Ut was born on March 29, 1951, to a family of rice farmers in rural Long An Province, southwest of Saigon in the Mekong Delta. Vietnam had been divided after World War II, with the Chinese occupying the north prior to the ascension of the Maoist guerrilla leader Ho Chi Minh, and the British and the French occupying the south. The European colonial powers initiated many attempts to unify the country, but these ultimately deteriorated into wars fought by the French, the pro-Western regimes of the south, and, beginning with the French withdrawal in 1954, the United States. As a young man, Huynh moved to Saigon where he lived with his brother.

One of Huynh's nine brothers (he also had six sisters), Huynh Thanh My, was a photographer for the Associated Press (AP) and was killed in 1965 covering combat in the Mekong Delta. The younger Huynh was only fourteen at the time, but he persuaded some of his brother's friends to give him a job working in the darkroom. He was a good worker and showed interest in all aspects of photography, expressing especially a desire to follow in his brother's footsteps as a combat photographer. His boss, Horst Faas, the AP photo editor in Saigon, was reluctant to let the young man do such dangerous work. By 1966 though, he relented, and assigned Huynh as a combat photographer.

While covering the Vietnam War, Huynh traveled all over Indochina to Laos, Cambodia, Thailand, and both Vietnams. He was wounded twice while covering the American invasion of Cambodia, and on several occasions worked alongside veteran AP war correspondent Peter Arnett, whose texts his photos often accompanied.

The photograph that made Huynh's reputation came in June of 1972. The South Vietnamese air force was dropping napalm near the village of Trang Bang, and some villagers' homes were inadvertently hit, as was often the case in such bombings. After the raid, Huynh photographed a nine-year-old girl named Kim Phuc running down Route 1, her naked body seared and nearly smoldering from the incendiary defoliant dropped on her home. The photograph was reproduced all over the world and stood as a symbol for the random brutality of the war. After taking the picture, Huynh rushed the girl to the hospital and the Saigon bureau of the Associated Press opened a bank account to help pay for her medical expenses.

Huynh's photograph earned him an international reputation, and several prestigious awards. Among them are the Pulitzer Prize for photography, the World Press Photo Award, the George Polk Memorial Award, and recognition from the Overseas Press Club, the National Press Club, and Sigma Delta Chi. Huynh continued to cover the war for the Associated Press until the fall of Saigon in 1975. In that chaotic time, the photographer was airlifted out of Vietnam and ended up living for a time in a refugee camp set up in Camp Pendleton Marine Corps base in Southern California. He lived there for a month before being reassigned by the Associated Press to their Tokyo bureau as a general assignment photographer.

Huynh Cong Ut

In 1977 he was transferred to Los Angeles, again as a general assignment photographer. In 1993, Huynh was sent to Hanoi to open the AP's new bureau. While there he met with the family of Kim Phuc, the young girl whose photograph had made his reputation. They still lived in Trang Bang, although the young girl no longer did. She had left the country to study in Cuba and had very recently married and defected to Canada. Huynh stayed at this temporary assignment for several months, and told Jim Henry in an interview that he found the people very friendly and was thrilled to be back in his home country. He added that when his children are old enough (Huynh married in Tokyo and has two teenage children), he intends to return to work in the Hanoi bureau permanently.

Huynh told *Notable Asian Americans* that he feels very gratified to have worked in a field in which he was able to show the world the horror of the Vietnam War, which he described as "probably one of the largest and most unforgotten wars of this century." His advice for aspiring photojournalists is to study the art of photojournalism and specifically the work of those photojournalists you admire.

Sources:

Associated Press. "Bio of Nick Ut." Press release. Los Angeles, California, 1994.

Ut, Huynh Cong, telephone interview with Jim Henry, June 30, 1994.

—Sketch by Jim Henry

V

Urvashi Vaid

(1958–)

Attorney, community activist

Urvashi Vaid is a community organizer whose involvement in the gay/lesbian and feminist movement spans more than fifteen years. Vaid served as the executive director of the National Gay and Lesbian Task Force (NGLTF) for three years and as that organization's director of public information for an additional three years. She is a former staff attorney with the American Civil Liberties Union (ACLU), where she worked on behalf of prisoners in the ACLU's National Prison Project. She has written widely in the gay and mainstream press and in 1995 will publish a book on the politics of the gay and lesbian civil rights movement.

Urvashi Vaid was born on October 8, 1958, in New Dehli, India. In 1966 the family moved to the United States when her father, a novelist, was offered a teaching position at the State University of New York at Potsdam, where Vaid spent her childhood. She was politically and intellectually precocious as a child, and at the age of eleven she participated in an antiwar march. She graduated from high school in three years and went on to Vassar College on an academic scholarship. The climate at Vassar was politically charged at the time and Vaid was very affected by it, especially by the more militant strains of feminism. Vaid told Liz Galst of the *Boston Phoenix:* "I've gotten criticized throughout my political life for having a multi-issue agenda. All I can say is that that agenda derives from the oppression I experience. As a woman who is a lesbian, who's out, and who's a woman of color—it's not possible for me to divorce the prejudice I experience one from the other."

In 1979 she received her bachelor's degree in English and political science. After graduation she worked as a legal secretary and administrative assistant for a small criminal and business law firm in Boston. In 1980 she enrolled in law school at the Northeastern University School of Law in Boston, from which she graduated in 1983.

Urvashi Vaid

Vaid began political organizing in college, and has continued it since. In 1979, she served for three months as a volunteer intern with the Women's Prison Project. In 1980 she co-founded and served on the steering committee of the Allston-Brighton Greenlight Safehouse Network, an anti-violence neighborhood organizing project which worked on community education, empowerment, and intervention to respond to violence against women. And in 1982 she co-founded the Boston Lesbian/Gay Political Alliance, a nonpartisan political organization that interviews and endorses candidates for political office and acts as an advocate for Boston's gay community. Vaid continued to be politically active in a variety of organizations throughout the eighties. Explaining her commitment to a broad perspective when it comes to her activism, she told Galst "I have a 'big picture' view of lesbian and gay liberation. . . . It's important as a radical to keep a broader perspective. In my opinion, the people who criticize multi-issue work are the ostriches who are quickly being left behind by the pace of the movement."

In 1983, after completing law school, she worked as a staff attorney with the ACLU on the National Prison Project in Washington, D.C. In this position, she conducted class action civil rights litigation to improve conditions in the prison system. In 1984 she initiated the National Prison Project's work with prisoners with AIDS and HIV.

National Gay and Lesbian Task Force

Vaid became involved with the NGLTF in 1985 when she served on the organizations board of directors. In 1986, she became NGLTF's director of public information. Using her prior experience in media relations, she professionalized NGLTF's dealings with both the mainstream and gay and lesbian media, and computerized all media communications systems to make contact with the media more efficient. In doing so she increased coverage of NGLTF's activities and established the organization as a principal source of information on issues concerning gay and lesbian rights. Vaid told Galst, "We concentrated on making sure that gay issues were going to be . . . in the media's face, and hatched a lot of plots to do that."

In 1989, Vaid became the executive director of NGLTF's Policy Institute in Washington, D.C., the national center for gay and lesbian organizing, education, and research. In this position, Vaid tripled the operating budget from $700,000 to $2 million as she solidified the group's work in a variety of areas. She increased staff, launched major fund-raising and public outreach programs, co-founded the NGLTF Creating Change conference (which remains the only national gay and lesbian political conference). Through the conference, Vaid helped guide the gay and lesbian movement's political strategy during the 1988 and 1992 presidential campaigns, and dramatically increased the visibility and viablility of NGLTF.

In 1992 Vaid left the NGLTF and moved to Provincetown, Massachusetts, to work on a book. She described her outlook at the time to Luisita Lopez Torregrosa of *Vanity Fair:* "To me my mission is about ending sexism, about ending racism, and about ending homophobia. . . . As a lesbian of color, I can't help but bring more than one identity and more than one issue to the table, and try to lead our movement not just on this narrow issue called homosexuality but on this larger thing called oppression."

Vaid is seen in the gay community as a fiery orator. She strongly supports the kind of direct-action politics advocated by groups like ACT-UP and Queer Nation, which use radical public confrontations and heavily symbolic acts of civil disobediance to draw media attention to their causes. Vaid has directly organized scores of national and local protests, and has been in the forefront personally in a number of them. In 1990 she disrupted President George Bush's first policy address on AIDS by holding up a sign that read "Talk Is Cheap, AIDS Funding Is Not" and was removed from the audience by police. And in 1991 she was arrested in front of the White House along with sixteen other feminists protesting the Supreme Court's *Webster* decision granting states the right to enact laws limiting abortion in certain prescribed ways.

In addition, Vaid has frequently articulated her views in the mainstream and the gay and lesbian press. Her articles have appeared in the *Nation,* the *Advocate,* and the *New Republic.* Her forthcoming book is tentatively titled *Margin to Center: The Mainstreaming of Gay and Lesbian Liberation,* and is scheduled to be published in the fall of 1995 by Anchor/Doubleday.

Vaid is encouraged about the increased attention being given to lesbian and gay issues, but she acknowledges there's still a lot to be done. As she told Surina Khan in *Metroline:* "We've made huge progress. I don't mean to put a negative spin on all this—there's been a tremendous momentum that's been built up today—but we really have a long way to go."

Sources:

Periodicals

Galst, Liz. "Homo Beat: On Guard." *Boston Phoenix,* January 9, 1993, p. 16+.
Khan, Surina A. "Still Out Front." *Metroline,* June 10, 1993, pp. 22-24.
Torregrosa, Luisita Lopez. "The Gay Nineties." *Vanity Fair,* May 1993, pp. 124–29.

Other

Vaid, Urvashi. Resume, provided by Vaid, August 1994.
———, telephone interview with Jim Henry, August 8, 1994.

—Sketch by Jim Henry

David Valderrama
(1933–)
Politician, lawyer

David M. Valderrama, a naturalized American, is the first probate judge in the United States of Filipino ancestry and a well-known civil and human rights activist. As a delegate to the Assembly of Maryland, he is also the first high-ranking Filipino elected official and until recently, the only Filipino state assemblyman in mainland United States.

David Valderrama

In describing his path to politics, Valderrama told Visi R. Tilak in an interview: "Some people—friends and well-wishers—came to me and said 'Run.' I said no. Then they came back again and again and said that there needed to be a voice and they thought I would be very capable and diligent. I finally told them that if my wife agreed I would. Initially she was very adamant and against my entering the political scene. But they managed to convince my wife. I was shocked and dumbfounded that she had agreed. Then I said 'Fine, you've got me, I will run if that is what everyone wants.'"

His Youth and Family Life

Born in Manila, Philippines, David Valderrama was twenty-seven when he came to the United States to study for a masters' degree in law. He was always looked at as a precocious child because he started tap-dancing at age five, playing the violin when he was seven, and was a member of a symphony orchestra at age thirteen. His father was a lawyer and a role model for Valderrama, who described his father as a man of principles. His mother always told him that he should follow in the footsteps of his father and study law, and he did just that. Valderrama's mother was a strict disciplinarian and brought up her nine children in a disciplined environment.

When the Japanese invaded the Philippines during World War II, Valderrama's father refused to serve the occupying Japanese government. As punishment, his

hands and legs were cut off and he was brutally executed. Thereafter, Valderrama's mother refused to speak to any person of Japanese heritage. Valderrama, however, said, After the war I went to Japan and I thought they were the nicest, courteous, and most industrious people. In fact I have the privilege of being one of the guests of President Clinton to receive the emperor and empress of Japan."

Aside from his father and mother, Valderrama acknowledged that his older brother, Nick, has been very important to him. The Philippines' ambassador to Pakistan, Nick "has always been a big influence in my life," Valderrama admitted. "I learned to play the violin because he did, and to this day he accepts that I am better at it than he." He added, "I used to be my brother's tail. I literally worshipped him. I was anti-Marcos, but since he was serving the Philippine government, he was with them. It was quite difficult and our family is glad that it is all over and part of history now."

Valderrama received his bachelor of law degree from Far Eastern University in Manila. After practicing law in the Philippines, Valderrama emigrated to the United States in 1961. He obtained his master of comparative law degree from George Washington University, Washington, D.C. "When I did not top the bar exam like I was expected to, my mother was absolutely disappointed. My parents kept pushing me and had total faith in me. I consider this an important part of my Asian heritage," Valderrama told Tilak.

Political and Social Activist

During Valderrama's student and early career years in the Philippines, he had worked as an anti-Marcos activist and was deeply involved with the "Free Philippine Movement." Later, he expanded his interest to the fight against apartheid in South Africa. "I was one of those people who demonstrated in front of the South African embassy at the height of the apartheid movement. I was a judge, yet I was thrown in jail," said Valderrama, whom the media described as the Asian symbol of civil rights. he also served as chairman of the Southeast Asian Refugee Task Force.

Career and Professional Life

Valderrama's first foray into politics was his election as a member of the Democratic Central Committee, a non-paying party position. In 1982, he began his upward climb in politics when he was elected by the membership to serve as vice-chairman of the central committee. His first political task was to manage the campaigns for Maryland Democratic candidates running for both houses of the U.S. Congress.

In 1985, three years into his term as vice-chairman, Valderrama was appointed by Governor Harry Hughes of Maryland to serve an unexpired term as judge of the Orphans' Court, and elected office. In 1986, as his term was running out, he stood for election in his own right and won overwhelmingly in an unusually crowded field of eleven candidates. "This was my second election.... Let me tell you this: the first time I ran, people told me I was not going to win, especially non-Asians. Again, the second time I ran, they told me the same thing. I won both times!" exclaimed Valderrama. Following his election, he became the Maryland State representative to the National College of Probate Judges and the Orphans' Court liaison judge from Prince George's County to the Maryland General Assembly.

"Three and a half years into my second term I took a gamble and resigned my position as judge to run for the [Maryland] House. Being a judge is nice, [but] what you are doing in that position is limited to interpreting the law.... The impact for change is greater when you are in the legislature," asserted Valderrama. On July 5, 1990, he resigned from the Orphans' Court to run for delegate of the Maryland General Assembly. When he won, he became the first and highest ranking Filipino American elected official in the United States.

Valderrama serves on a number of boards, including the Board of Directors of the Southern Christian Leadership Conference (Prince George's Chapter). He is a member of National Association for the Advancement of Colored People, Common Cause, MD Network Against Domestic Violence, and a number of Asian cultural, business, and professional organizations. His legislative committees include Constitutional and Administrative Law, Environmental Matters, and Law Enforcement. He was also a part of the 1992 presidential campaign as a National Surrogate Speaker for Democratic candidate Bill Clinton. In 1993 Valderrama was appointed to represent the Maryland General Assembly in the board of directors of the Council of Governments, an organization composed of local and state officials in the Metropolitan Washington, D.C., area. He is also the recipient of numerous awards including the Most Outstanding Filipino and Honored American Award.

To his job as assemblyman, Valderrama has brought a wealth of experience. He has been a band leader, sales executive, bank executive, television correspondent, author, small businessman, publisher, and editor. His published works include *Law and Legal Literature of Peru*, and *Law and Legal Literature of Mexico*, which he co-authored.

Despite his many accomplishments, Valderrama has felt the sting of being judged by his ethnicity. "When I became a judge I was going to my court room. As I was walking along the passageway meant for judges the guards stopped me thinking I was a tourist. I introduced myself and they were most apologetic. however they became close friends of mine," recollected Valderrama. he believes that the dominant culture in the United States sees ethnicity in terms of black and white only, and that Asians are viewed as having no legitimate claim to citizenship. "When I was

entering the legislature for the first time the same thing happened. I was stopped by the state troopers and asked for identification," he recounted.

Marriage and Family

Valderrama married his high school sweetheart, Nellie; they have two daughters. His wife, who comes from a political Philippines family, has been very influential in his life and is a strong moral support in all his endeavors. Recollecting their storybook romance, Valderrama said: "I completely forgot about her when I came to the United States and I had my share of girlfriends here. So did she [forget about me], she had her share of boyfriends. One fine day her sister, who I was in touch with, called me from Canada and asked me to give her away in marriage. At this wedding in Canada, I met Nellie again after several years. She had flown in from the Philippines to attend her sister's wedding. We started going out again and in a few months we were married." Their daughter Kriselda, born in 1971, is studying respiratory therapy in Salisbury, Maryland. Vida, born in 1973, as a graduate of American University (with high honors), where she majored in economics and political science.

Guiding Philosophy

Valderrama said that his role model is Martin Luther King, who followed the steps of an Asian, Mahatma Gandhi, and echoed the thoughts of a white man, Thomas Jefferson. He admires all three people. He believes in Confucius' philosophy that "hard work equals success," and says he has always striven to realize his goal through hard work. A Catholic, Valderrama was disappointed when he was reprimanded by the church for taking a pro-choice stance on the abortion issue. "I have always been a lector, reading scriptures in my local parish. I had to take a position on abortion. I am personally against abortion. However, I believe that a woman should do what she feels is right for her own body and therefore I am pro-choice. When my church found out they called me over immediately. I was shown my literature and told that the church did not want me to continue as a lector. I was totally devastated," he said.

As a nine-year-old child, Valderrama learned the high price of idealism. He remarked, "The lesson I learned from my father's execution was that you stick to your beliefs no matter what." After such terrible loss during his childhood and a long steady climb up the ladder, that is exactly what Valderrama is attempting to do: stick to his beliefs and help bring about change for the betterment of the Asian and American communities.

Sources:

Periodicals

Greenberg, Rick. "Ambition: Here Comes De Judge." *Regardie's: The Business of Washington*, February 1988.

Other

"David Valderrama." Maryland House of Delegates. Biographical information and press releases, 1994.

Valderrama, David. Telephone interview with Visi Tilak, June 9, 1994.

—*Sketch by Visi R. Tilak*

Doan Van Toai

(1946–)

Political dissident, scholar

Doan Van Toai is a Vietnamese exile who came to national prominence in the mid-1980s as the author of three books chronicling the oppression of the communist regime in Vietnam that took power after the United States withdrawal from the Vietnam War. His books, *Portrait of the Enemy, A Vietcong Memoir,* and *The Vietnamese Gulag,* had a major impact on international recognition of human rights abuses in postwar Vietnam, something many people, especially on the left, were reluctant to admit after having supported the victory of the communists over the United States and the South Vietnamese forces. In the years since coming to the United States from France, Toai has become a respected scholar and writer, publishing widely in both popular and academic publications.

Doan Van Toai was born in a small village in the Mekong Delta called Cai Von on September 14, 1946. Vietnam at this time was involved in a series of civil wars with the colonial armies of France and Japan, as well as internal ethnic conflicts between villages and tribes. The Mekong Delta was a place of particular violence. There were ethnic battles between the Khmer people (ethnic Cambodians) and the Vietnamese who shared the delta, and there was a war between the Vietminh—a loose confederation of anticolonial fighters, not all of whom were communists—and a militarized Buddhist sect known as the Hoa Hoa. At the time of his birth, Toai's father and older brother were both fighters with the Vietminh.

Toai grew up in a Vietminh controlled village, called Rach Ranh in Vin Long province, about eighty miles from Saigon. Writing about his childhood in *The Vietnamese Gulag* Toai said: "For the children of Rach Ranh, the war was a periodic, natural catastrophe—a little like a bad thunderstorm. There were long stretches when life was normal. Then suddenly there would be war. Afterward things would go back to normal, but the thunderstorms could break out at any moment. That was life."

Early Politics

As a young man Toai became increasingly politicized and began to work intermittently with the Vietminh underground in the south, helping to undermine the republican regime of Ngo Dinh Diem. After the 1963 coup that deposed Diem, Toai spoke at a rally in celebration of the event at his high school. He was well known among his fellow students as an articulate critic of the republican South, and many of them encouraged him to become more involved in the underground. Although his sympathies were certainly with their cause, his father, a teacher, cautioned him not to become too embroiled in politics at such a young age. Toai continued his studies and in 1964 he took the national university entrance examinations, which he passed.

Toai began studies at Saigon University in 1964, studying in the school of pharmacy. While a student he formed a newspaper for pharmacy students called *Hoa Sung.* In 1965 the U.S. military presence in Vietnam increased dramatically. Toai observed in *The Vietnamese Gulag:* "Then came the invasion of GIs. Tens of thousands at first, then hundreds of thousands. They urinated from the tops of their tanks and littered the streets with Coca-Cola cans. Overnight there was an epidemic of bars. Prostitutes appeared in amazing numbers. The country was flooded with consumer goods. . . ." He was disgusted with the Americans' commercialism and their total disregard for the people of Vietnam.

In 1966 he worked for an aide of Senator Edward Kennedy interviewing refugees in central Vietnam. Toai's newspaper was becoming more interested in politics than pharmacy as the war intensified, along with the American presence. Toai began to read about and admire the communist leader of the north, Ho Chi Minh. All this activity led Toai to drop out of pharmacy school and enroll in law school, where his political activism found a better outlet.

Opposition Leader

In 1969 Toai founded an opposition magazine called *Tu Quyet* (self-determination). The magazine became a leading voice of the opposition parties, who were allied under an umbrella organization called the National Liberation Front, or just the Front. Toai himself resisted joining the Front, but he continued as a student activist and contributed to each issue of *Tu Quyet.* The magazine also published articles by international critics of the South Vietnamese regime and American support of it. Among these were several Americans, including the eminent linguist and political critic Noam Chomsky.

Toai's political activities of this period include a brief occupation of the National Assembly, a month-long student strike, and an occupation of the Cambodian embassy to protest recent Cambodian massacres of ethnic Vietnamese in Cambodian border villages. The student movement had become a loud voice in Vietnamese affairs, one

Doan Van Toai

that had wide popular support so that the regime found it difficult to suppress it. In 1970 Toai left Vietnam to speak in Hong Kong, Paris, and the United States. He found himself fascinated by the United States, by the bigness of it, the strange customs, and the state of the antiwar movement. Writing in *The Vietnamese Gulag* he said, "When I got out to California for my first antiwar speaking engagement, my impression of Americans as people of strange personal habits was intensified. At Redlands University the audience seemed full of young people with long and wildly unkempt hair, many of them wearing raggedy clothes, often with the sleeves cut out of their shirts. . . . It was as if I had landed on another planet, full of creatures who found it impossible to take themselves seriously."

In 1971 Toai got married and took a job with the Nam Do bank as a manager. He worked in various branches around the country. He used his position to discreetly aid the Front in the subversion of the government. Other than these small forays into politics, Toai's involvement in the war and the antigovernment forces was minimal over the next few years. In 1975, the government of the south fell to the armies of the north as the United States left the country. Toai and his family decided to stay in the country, although they had the opportunity to leave with Toai's brother. There was great uncertainty about what life would be like under the communist government of the north, but Toai reasoned that with his long history of opposing the American puppet regime is Saigon, he would be in no danger.

Imprisonment and Release

In 1975 Toai accepted a job with the Provisional Revolutionary Government in the finance committee. He quickly became disillusioned with their severe plan to nationalize the economy of the south, however, and was considering resigning his post in protest of their hard-line policies when he was arrested in what at first appeared to be a case of mistaken identity. Toai was held in a series of prisons in abhorrent conditions for slightly over two years. In the prison system he met many people he knew from his student resistance days and came to the conclusion that the occupying armies of the north were systematically purging the south of an entire generation of activists, intellectuals, and artists. Toai was never charged with a crime, was never put on trial, and then on November 1, 1977, without explanation, he was released and told to go to France, where his wife and children had already gone.

In France, Toai was reunited with his family and also with Vietnamese political leaders in Paris' large expatriate community. He arranged a press conference to publicize the story of what he called the Vietnamese gulag, and it was largely successful. He then came to America where he further criticized the Hanoi regime, this time with the backing of dozens of former antiwar activists, including folk singer Joan Baez and writer Henry Miller, both of whom Toai met and became friends with. In 1979, Toai moved permanently to the United States when he enrolled in the Fletcher School of Law and Diplomacy at Tufts University outside of Boston.

Toai remained at Tufts for three years. In 1983 he became a research associate for the Institute of East Asian Affairs at the University of California at Berkeley. In 1987 he served for one year as the program analyst at the Institute for Foreign Policy Analysis in Cambridge, Massachusetts. That year he also became executive director of the Institute for Democracy in Vietnam, a post he holds still. As of mid-1994, Toai was serving as director of the International Program at the Southern California University for Professional Studies.

Toai has written prolifically on the topic of his experience in Vietnam and in the area of international relations in general. He has written three books, all with David Chanoff: *A Vietcong Memoir* (1986); *The Vietnamese Gulag* (1986); and *Portrait of the Enemy* (1987). He is also editor and publisher of *Vietnam Update,* an English-language journal covering events in Vietnam. He has written widely in both the academic and popular media. In his book *The Vietnamese Gulag,* Toai wrote about his experiences in America and his impressions of American society and political awareness: "I have found [the United States] a blessed land, a place where one can work freely and give one's children a decent life, a place where one can be oneself and go about the business of life unafraid and unintimidated. I have also found that Americans are largely unimpressed by the peculiar beauties of their culture—the rights they enjoy. Perhaps it is the immigrants' function from generation to generation to remind them of what a treasure it is they own."

Sources:

Toai, Doan Van. *The Vietnamese Gulag.* New York: Simon and Schuster, 1986.

—Sketch by Jim Henry

Phillip Villamin Vera Cruz
(1904–1994)
Labor leader

Phillip Villamin Vera Cruz was a longtime leader of the movement, begun in the 1960s, to unionize the nation's farmworkers, especially the immigrant, itinerant workers who do much of the back-breaking, extremely low-paying work on the majority of America's large non-grain farms. Vera Cruz was a leader of the successful Filipino-led sit-down strike in the vineyards of Coachella, California, in 1965. It was this galvanizing event that led to the creation of the United Farmworkers of America.

Early Life

Phillip Villamin Vera Cruz was born on December 25, 1904, in Ilacos Sur province in the Philippines. He immigrated to the United States in 1926 in the wave of Filipino immigration that followed the U.S. government ban of Chinese and Japanese workers. This wave of immigrant labor was used largely in menial jobs, perhaps the most prominent of which was agricultural labor. From the time of his arrival in the United States until the mid-sixties when Vera Cruz began organizing farmworkers, he worked on these farms throughout California and the country. Writing in *Asian Week,* Sam Cacas quoted Kent Wong, president of the Asian Pacific American Labor Alliance, and director of the University of California at Los Angeles's Center for Labor Education and Research, as saying, "[Vera Cruz's] experiences were very much related to the 'manong,' the first-generation Filipino immigrants who were treated and worked like dogs throughout their lives and most died poor and lonely, yet Phil chose to organize unions and dedicated his life to that work."

Labor Activism

In 1965, Vera Cruz began his work as a labor activist when he joined the Agricultural Workers Organizing Committee (AWOC) of the AFL-CIO. He was very active in this union and later that year helped organize a strike against vineyard owners in Coachella, California. The strike was successful and the tactic spread, with the union organizing a similar action later that year in Delano, California. This strike brought together labor leaders from various organizations and with its successful resolution the United Farmworkers of America (UFW) was born.

The UFW was headed by the great labor leader Cesar Chavez, who would become a nationally recognized leader in later years for his work on behalf of migrant workers. That the new union was led by Chavez caused some dissention among the early members of the AWOC, who were uncertain about Chavez's goals and politics. Vera Cruz, however, sided with the new leader, believing the goals of the union as a whole far outweighed any one personality. With Chavez heading the union, however, Vera Cruz's role became less prominent, although he continued to work as a spokesman and activist for the union.

In the 1970s Vera Cruz began another sort of campaign. He began working to build a retirement village for single, family-less farmworkers. Like Vera Cruz himself, many of the early immigrants were unable to marry outside of their nationality due to anti-miscegenation laws, and so after a lifetime of back-breaking work in the fields had no one to support them. The site Vera Cruz chose for the facility was the grounds of the United Farmworkers' headquarters in Delano. The complex was opened in 1975, having been built almost entirely by volunteer labor, and was called Agabayani Village, after Paul Agabayani, a farmworker who was shot to death during a strike.

Vera Cruz resigned from the UFW in 1977 and moved to Bakersfield, California, two years later, where he stayed until his death in 1994. In 1989 the government of the Philippines awarded Vera Cruz the first Ninoy M. Aquino award for lifelong service to the Filipino community in America. When he went to the Philippines to accept the award, it was the first time he had been to his home country in more than sixty years. In 1992 Vera Cruz published an oral history of his life, *Phillip Vera Cruz: A Personal History of Philippine Immigrants and the Farmworkers Movement.* He continued to speak at universities around the country and was a well-respected voice for the concerns of migrant workers well into his eighties.

Vera Cruz grew increasingly ill in later years due to emphysema. He died after complications resulting from surgery on June 11, 1994, at the age of eighty-nine. In recognition of his long career of service, the University of California at Los Angeles established a scholarship in his name for undergraduates pursuing study in Asian American labor history.

Sources:

Cacas, Sam. "Filipino American Labor Leader Dies." *Asian Week,* June 17, 1994, p. 14.

—Sketch by Jim Henry

W

John D. Waihee
(1946–)
Governor

John D. Waihee dreams of Hawaii—his birthplace and home for most of his life—as a state filled with thousands of trees, where lands once used to raise sugar cane are restored to native forest. He dreams of state environmental plans that preserve watersheds, and of beaches that are free for all people to walk on, without having to maneuver through crowded hotels to get to his state's spectacular coasts. He dreams of promenades, superior education, Pacific Rim trade; a time when engineers from Hawaii are helping to develop China and other burgeoning Asian economies. Ten years from now, "I hope the Hawaiian people are happy in Hawaii," he said in a recent interview with *Honolulu* magazine. "I really do."

Waihee is Hawaii's fourth elected governor, the first of Hawaiian ancestry. And in many ways, it is appropriate for him to dream. His second term as governor ends in 1994, and state term limit laws prohibit him from running for re-election again. Despite much speculation about his future ambitions, his plans remain up in the air. Perhaps he will run for U.S. Senate, or take a job elsewhere in government. Or go into publishing. Or work for a television station. He is forty-seven years old; life remains wide open.

When Waihee was first elected in 1986, after edging out a favored Democrat in the state's primary, he was widely regarded as a rising political star. He came into office touting a new generation of political leadership that offered tax breaks, innovative traffic solutions, a diversified economy, and an educational system that would be second to none. Although supporters herald him as an able reformer, critics point to charges of scandals and Democratic party corruption during his tenure as governor.

Mainland Education

Waihee was born May 19, 1946, in Honokaa, on the island of Hawaii. His father worked as a telephone company line worker. His mother, born Mary Parker Purdy, was a descendant of a Massachusetts sailor who eventually

John D. Waihee

became an adviser to King Kamehameha I. After earning his bachelor's degree in history and business from Andrews University in Michigan, Waihee didn't stay on the mainland as many talented Hawaiians do, but returned to the state to become a member of the first graduating class of the William S. Richardson School of Law. His classmates included a number of future prominent state lawmakers. He practiced law at a Hawaiian firm for four years, before starting his own law practice in 1979.

Hawaii voters tend to vote Democratic, and politicians typically rise through the ranks to the governorship. Waihee, however, quickly acquired a reputation for bucking the establishment. In 1972, at age twenty-six, he joined a renegade political force called "Coalition 72" which attempted to challenge the Democratic party leadership at the party's state convention. The challenge failed and placed Waihee firmly outside the political establishment. He was labeled an idealist and an activist, which he says still applies to him today. Six years later, at the state's 1978

Constitutional Convention, he shrewdly brought together the old-time political establishment with young activists and emerged from the convention as a clear leader. During that time, he began to identify with a political movement known as "Palaka Power" which argued that the power of government rests with local activists. Even as Waihee rose to the spot of governor, he continued to oppose any statewide initiatives on the belief that they would dilute the strength of a locally-based system.

Triumph as the Underdog

Waihee was elected to the state House of Representatives in 1980, and two years later, jumped into a race for lieutenant governor, challenging a front-runner, then-state senator Dennis O'Connor. Though an underdog, Waihee built up a grass-roots political following throughout many of the state's smaller islands and wound up winning the race. Four years later, he entered the gubernatorial race. Once again, he faced a political favorite and despite being outspent won the race narrowly.

His mother, who passed away in early 1994, recalled the governor's race in a 1990 interview with the *Honolulu Advertiser*. All of her relatives were Republicans, but when her son's campaign held rallies in Waimea, the relatives came. When the votes were tabulated, she realized they'd sacrificed their party allegiance to vote for Waihee.

In his eight years as governor, Waihee takes credit for promoting a tax-reduction program that resulted in the return of $700 million to taxpayers. He also has worked to reform education so that schools are managed at the local level. A $200 million program championed by Waihee resulted in increased levels of affordable housing. And during Waihee's tenure, Hawaii grew rapidly and boasted one of the lowest unemployment rates in the nation. Though he will not be governor when a rapid-transit system is built in Honolulu, he can take credit for helping to champion the idea as well as pressing for increasing development of alternative energy.

Like most political leaders, however, Waihee has experienced his share of controversy. He drew angry headlines when he nominated a politically well-connected candidate to the state supreme court. After Hawaii's state senate refused to confirm the candidate, Waihee's standing dropped in the polls. Later, controversy surfaced again when one of his aides admitted to sidestepping government procurement procedures to buy a computer system and when Waihee's office ordered a $10,784 koa desk at a time when the state was approaching a massive budget crisis. Waihee, often described as affable, defends himself, and says that in some ways it was his willingness to make government more open (before 1987, many now-public records were confidential) that brought on the scandals.

Before his final term as governor ends, he hopes to complete some unfinished business and spend time with his wife, Lynne Kobashigawa Waihee, and their two children, Jennifer and John. His future, however, remains open.

Sources:

Periodicals

Honolulu Advertiser, November 15, 1990; January 13, 1993; January 19, 1994.
Honolulu Magazine, January 20, 1993.

—*Sketch by Himanee Gupta*

An Wang
(1920–1990)
Inventor, entrepreneur, philanthropist

From an initial investment of $600, An Wang, inventor of the magnetic core memory (an instrumental component of early computers), built a one-person electrical fixtures store into one of the most rapidly-growing, successful businesses in American history. From its inception in 1951 through the late 1980s, Wang Laboratories grew at an astonishing annual rate of 42 percent, becoming one of the giants in the computer business. In 1984 Wang and his family owned approximately 55 percent of the company stock and his personal wealth was estimated to be $1.6 billion by *Forbes* magazine, making him at the time the fifth richest person in America.

Wang gave generously from this wealth. He donated $4 million to fix the roof of the Boston Performing Arts Center, more than $4 million to Harvard, $1 million to Wellesley, $6 million to create the Wang Institute of Graduate Studies for software engineers and China scholars, and he constructed at a cost of $15 million a factory in Boston's Chinatown that provided jobs for 300 impoverished city residents. Citing these gifts and the fact that Wang Laboratories' headquarters was in the previously economically depressed town of Lowell, Massachusetts, the former governor of that state, Michael Dukakis, said of Wang, "I don't know how many countless thousands and thousands of people owe a debt of gratitude for what he did."

An Wang was born on February 7, 1920, in Shanghai, China, to Yin Lu and Zen Wan (Chien) Wang. His father taught English at a private elementary school in Kun San, about thirty miles from Shanghai. He also practiced traditional Chinese medicine using herbs and other organic substances to treat common illnesses. This was at the time the only form of medicine available to ordinary Chinese. Because of his father's education and status, the Wang family lived a relatively middle-class existence. Until the time he was twenty-one, Wang lived in either Shanghai or Kun San, where his father's ancestors had lived for six hundred years. China is one of the world's oldest civilizations, and one of the traditions of its families is to keep a written family history that is continuously updated every few generations. The Wang family had such a book that, remarkably, claimed to be accurate for twenty-three generations, back to the time of Marco Polo's journeys from Europe to China. In writing about these books in his 1986 autobiography, *Lessons,* Wang said, "[They] gave our families a sense of continuity and permanence that I don't see in the more mobile West.

Wang's father was a strict disciplinarian who preached the value of a good education. The young Wang heeded this advice and became a good student, especially in math and science, at which he excelled. He graduated from high school at age sixteen and was accepted into the Chiao Tung University in Shanghai, a highly regarded institution comparable in prestige to the Massachusetts Institute of Technology, where he studied electrical engineering and communications.

The Age of Confusion

While Wang studied, China was going through one of the most tumultuous periods of recent history, sometimes referred to as the Age of Confusion. There was civil war between feudal warlords and the Nationalist forces of Chiang kai-Shek, between the Nationalists and the Communists under Mao Zedong, and, most disturbingly, there was the brutal invasion of the militarily superior Japanese army. During these various battles Wang lost both his parents and one sister but remained safe at the university, which was inside a French-held district of Shanghai.

Upon his graduation in 1940 Wang spent a year as a teaching assistant in electrical engineering, but then, thinking the Japanese would soon control all of Shanghai, he volunteered along with eight of his classmates to secretly penetrate the interior of the Japanese-held countryside to design and build transmitters and radios for Nationalist troops. He worked at the Central Radio Works in Kweillin from 1941 until 1945. The Japanese bombed the area throughout the time Wang spent there.

Immigrant to Inventor

After the war, Wang applied to a program set up by the Nationalist government to send highly-trained engineers to the United States for training that would help rebuild war-ravaged China. Wang was accepted into the program, and in June 1945, he arrived in Newport News, Virginia. Six years later he would found Wang Laboratories.

The idea behind the program that brought Wang to America was that the participants apprentice themselves to a large American corporation such as Westinghouse or RCA as a technical observers, but it occurred to Wang that he might learn a lot more and be of more service to his country if he continued his studies at a prestigious

An Wang

American university. He chose Harvard and was accepted. He earned a master's degree in 1946 and then a doctorate in 1947 in applied physics.

From 1948 until 1951 Wang worked as a research fellow in the Harvard Computation Laboratory under Howard Aiken, one of the pioneers of modern computer science. In 1944 the Computation Lab had designed the first binary computer in the United States, a mammoth, noisy machine fifty-one feet long and eight feet high, riddled with thousands of mechanical relays. Wang was given the task of designing a method by which the machine could record and access large amounts of information without mechanical motion. It was a problem Aiken and his colleagues had been struggling with for some time. Wang's solution, the magnetic memory core, revolutionized computing and served as the standard method for memory retrieval and storage until the invention of the microchip in the 1960s.

The Beginning of Wang Labs

In 1951 Wang left the Harvard Lab to begin Wang Laboratories. His first office was a 200 square foot unfurnished loft in Boston from which Wang directed his efforts toward small-scale commercial uses for his memory cores. One of his first jobs was to build the new scoreboard at New York's Shea Stadium. From there he moved into the desktop calculator market in which his company prevailed.

Wang worked tirelessly during this period and gained a reputation as a brilliant strategist, always able to anticipate where the market in electronic computing was going next. His company continued to gain market shares and grow at the phenomenal rate of 42 percent annually. In the 1970s Wang showed tremendous daring in taking on IBM in the office typewriter market. He developed a typewriter with electronic memory that was priced below the standard IBM of the time, and then introduced what has become a mainstay in home and office computing: the television-like monitor attached to a keyboard on which text could be manipulated, or processed. Wang Labs became known in the media as "the word processing company."

Wang Laboratories continued its incredible growth, developing such systems as the Office Information System (OIS) that integrated word and data processing and allowed for specialized upgrades to fit the specific needs of its user. By 1981 the company had earned $100 million on revenues approaching $1 billion after five years of 55 percent annual growth. But competition was intensifying in the computer business as such giants as Hewlett Packard, AT&T, IBM, and the Digital Equipment Corporation began seriously pursuing market shares. In 1983 Wang went into semi-retirement and named John F. Cunningham president and chief operating officer. By 1985, amidst a growing depression in the computer market, revenues and earnings dropped and Wang Labs was forced to lay off 1,600 workers. In June of 1985 Cunningham retired, and Wang returned to running the day-to-day operations of the company. He retired again in 1986, this time relinquishing control to his son, Frederick, who ran the company until being removed by his father in 1988.

By the end of the eighties, Wang Labs was hit with a series of setbacks, steep losses, product delays, and the loss of key executives to competitors. In August of 1989 the company announced losses of $374.7 million. In response, a series of drastic restructuring moves were initiated, which has led to the partial comeback of Wang Labs today.

Wang died on March 24, 1990, of cancer of the esophagus, with which he had battled for more than a year.

Sources:

Books

Wang, An, with Eugene Linden. *Lessons: An Autobiography,* Reading, Mass.: Addison Wesley, 1986.

Periodicals

"An Wang." Obituary, *New York Times,* March 25, 1990.

—Sketch by Jim Henry

Charles B. Wang
(1944–)
Business executive, entrepreneur

With three associates, a single software product, no venture money and a modest dream, Charles B. Wang (pronounced Wong) built the world's leading business software company while having fun in the process. In 1976, the newly established Computer Associates International, Inc. (CA) was so short on cash that Wang initially provided business consulting services to his landlord in exchange for rent. Wang's three associates, too, bartered their consulting services as systems programmers in lieu of computer time in order to develop new products for CA. Despite such humble beginnings, in 1989 CA became the first independent software company to exceed $1 billion in revenues. The company quickly earned the title of the world's largest software company until Microsoft Corporation eclipsed that position. CA remains a close second. Today, Wang is not only chairman and CEO of a company with more than 7,000 employees, over 300 products, offices in twenty-seven countries and calendar year revenues in 1993 in excess of $2 billion, but he is still managing to have fun. According to company lore he once pushed a borrowed cart through the CA offices, distributing frozen treats to each of his overheated employees after the air conditioning failed.

The Roots of Wang's Success

Born in Shanghai in 1944, Wang was eight years old when he immigrated to the United States with his parents and two brothers. Forced to flee their homeland following the Communist takeover of China, the family settled in Queens, New York, and began a new life with almost nothing, having abandoned most of their possessions. Part of Wang's drive to succeed is rooted in his early childhood experiences in a refugee family struggling to survive in a new country.

Wang's father, a former Supreme Court justice in China, advised his three sons to pursue careers in math and science, areas where language would be less of an obstacle to success. Only Charles followed the advice, attending Brooklyn Technical High School, then graduating from City University of New York's Queens College in 1967 with a B.S. in mathematics. He began his computer career as a programming trainee at Columbia University's Riverside Research Institute. Eventually he became the vice president of sales for Standard Data Corporation, a small data processing services company in New York City. Wang had just finished successfully launching the company's software division when a Swiss firm called Computer Associates

International, Ltd. offered a contract to Wang's boss to sell its software in the United States. The boss's refusal proved to be Wang's opportunity.

The Journey Begins

In 1976, together with three associates and an exclusive contract to distribute one CAI-developed software program—*CA-SORT*—Wang started his own company, a subsidiary of CA International. Not only was he the "marketing department" and the "sales force," Wang also made most of the furniture for the small CA office. The other three associates divided the responsibilities of finance, administration, personnel, product development, and customer support.

The inaugural product proved to be an easy sell. The program was a more efficient and faster version of an IBM product that provided a means of organizing computer files. By the end of the first year, Wang's company had a client base of 200 users. CA was growing quickly and began hiring more development, support, and sales personnel throughout the United States. As the company was not yet able to purchase office space, the first non–New York–based employees worked out of their homes.

In spite of economically strained beginnings, by the middle of 1977 CA founded its first data center in Danbury, Connecticut. In the same year, the company released its first CA-developed product, CA-DYNAM/D, used to save and catalog disk space. CA-DYNAM/D was the first of more than 300 products to implement the CA product philosophy—create greater product efficiency through integrating new products with the old.

Growth continued exponentially for CA, so much so that Wang asked his brother, Anthony, to quit his Manhattan corporate law firm and join the company. Anthony's level-headed, rational approach complemented his brother's impulsiveness and enthusiasm. As chairman and CEO, Charles focused on company strategy, markets, and technology, while Anthony was president and chief operating officer in charge of CA legal and financial business until he retired in 1992.

In 1980, CA bought out the Swiss parent company that had given Wang's company its start. The acquisition allowed CA to expand into Europe, as the Swiss company came with established operations in most European countries. Year to year, CA continued to grow at a phenomenal rate, in both domestic and foreign markets. Their software products continued to focus predominantly on the IBM mainframe. Over the years, CA aggressively acquired more than fifty software companies, the largest being a $780 million buyout of archrival Uccel Corporation in 1987. By 1989, CA became the first independent software company to reach $1 billion in sales. Five years later, revenue for the

Charles B. Wang

fiscal year ending March 1993 reached $1.84 billion, up 22 percent from $1.51 billion a year earlier.

The Drive to Always be Better

Wang could never be accused of complacency. He continues to explore new paths and search for greater challenges. His latest goal for CA is to carefully diversify with more products for desktop and midrange computers. Currently, mainframe software accounts for almost 75 percent of CA's sales revenues, with 10 percent from PCs and 15 percent from midrange computer packages. Wang intends to create a more equal distribution in CA's products.

Amid criticism that Wang grew CA through rapacious acquisitions, tumbling troubled competitors and stripping them of overhead while downsizing staff, Wang's admirers tout him as the entrepreneurial buccaneer who shuns bureaucracy and rewards creativity. One such admirer is Hesh Kestin, a former contributing editor to *Forbes* magazine. In his book *Twenty-first Century Management: The Revolutionary Strategies that Have Made Computer Associates a Multibillion Dollar Software Giant,* Kestin refers to Wang's achievement as "nothing short of a modern business phenomenon." He lauds Wang for his lean, unpretentious management style that runs counter to the models taught in business school. At CA, there are no rules, no positional perks, no memos, no fixed roles. When Kestin first asked Wang to explain his success, Wang answered "It's just good people."

To Wang, CA employees are an extended family, figuratively and literally. While other business environments avoid practicing nepotism, Wang does not think twice about aggressively recruiting family and friends, people he already knows and trusts. While most family businesses fail, CA's family has remained intact because "the trust is always tempered with fairness." The bottom line is always performance, and the company rewards achievement richly. Wang believes star performers should receive star salaries regardless of age—an especially talented engineer in his or her twenties could be paid as much as $200,000 a year. In addition, Wang believes in challenging each employee to the fullest by regularly moving people into new and different roles. For example, to prevent burnout or job stagnancy, a programmer might be moved to the product marketing department. As unorthodox as it sounds, this constant company reorganization—personally administered by Wang each year—may be the best explanation of CA's amazing success.

Heeding His Father's Advice

Considering CA's new sixty-three-acre corporate headquarters in Islandia, New York—complete with employee perks that include a health club, high-tech security, free breakfast, and a huge day-care center—to say Charles Wang is successful seems almost an understatement. Wang did well to listen to his father's advice to pursue a math or science career. Ironically, when Wang is asked by Asian American high school students what the most important course to take in college is, Wang's answer is always English. "You have the greatest idea in history—a computer model, a cure for cancer, or a single square-inch solar cell that could power the entire state of Arkansas. However, if you do not know how to communicate your idea clearly, it dies with you." Like many children of immigrant parents, Wang was raised to believe that "if you specialize in something technical, somebody has to hire you." That was certainly true for him. However, he argues that "unfortunately for Asians, our emphasis on electronic specialization has led to our being stereotyped as technicians. We rarely are viewed as administrators, marketers, salespeople, or CEOs."

This is why Wang sees language as the most indispensable tool in gaining success. "Language can lift an idea beyond itself. It can move a business into the international market, elevate a worker form technician to administrator, and break the walls that keep a person from accomplishment," he advises all young Asian Americans. "Why shouldn't Asian Americans start their own corporations? How come so few of us are politicians?" Wang asks. He concludes, "There is no reason that Asian American students should not succeed in any branch of business that excites them. The important thing, however, is to be able to communicate with fluency to colleagues and clients. Hear me clearly: If you master language your possibilities are unlimited."

Sources:

Books

Kestin, Hesh. "Twenty-first Century Management: The Revolutionary Strategies that Have Made Computer Associates a Multibillion Dollar Software Giant." Excerpted by Vision Business Book Summaries from the book by the same name, New York: Atlantic Monthly Press, 1992.

Periodicals

Associated Press, "Little-known Firm Seeks Bigger Image." *Twin Falls* (Idaho) *Times-News,* November 7, 1993, pp. E1-E2.
Bunker, Ted, "Computer Associates' Wang: 'You've Got to Feel That What You Do Has a Value,'" *Investors Business Daily,* December 22, 1992.
Krushensky, Cindy, "Computer Associates International Inc.: Acquiring Success in Software," *PC Novice,* December 1992, pp. 18–22.
Schwartz, Evan I., "Charles Wang" from "25 Executives to Watch." *The 1993 Business Week 1000,* 1993, p. 98.
"Software Pragmatist: An Interview with Charles B. Wang," *Leaders.* October–December 1993, pp. 104–105.
Wang, Charles B., "Communication Skills Can Open Up Your Entire World.," *Tzhe College Digest.* Fall 1993, pp. 62–64.
———, "Reconnecting Technologist with Business Professionals," *Computer Reseller News,* December 6, 1993, pp. 231–233.

—Sketch by Terry Hong

Charles Pei Wang
(1940–)
Social worker, political appointee

As head of the Chinese American Planning Council (CPC) in New York City for more than twenty years, Charles Pei Wang was instrumental in making the CPC one of the largest and most prominent social service agencies for the Chinese American community. He has worked tirelessly on behalf of Chinese Americans on the local, state, and national level, and in 1990 was appointed by former President George Bush to a five-year term as vice-chairman of the U.S. Commission on Civil Rights.

Charles Pei Wang was born in 1940 in the small town of Baipei in China during World War II. His father added the middle name "Pei" to his name because he wanted his son to remember where he was born. Wang's family traveled from place to place until the war was over and eventually settled in Taiwan where they finally were free from the dangers and worries of war.

As the ninth in a family of eleven children—five boys and six girls—Wang received a lot of help from his siblings. Following Asian traditions, his older brothers and sisters, who were all educated and working, supported him both emotionally and financially throughout his schooling. His eldest brother and sister especially exerted a lot of positive influence. "Nevertheless, my parents were the most influential and supportive," he said in an interview with Visi R. Tilak.

Early Career Decision

Wang attended Cheng Chi University in Taiwan where he studied Chinese language and literature. He received a bachelor's degree in 1964. He left for the United States one year later to attend graduate school at St. Johns University in New York, where he got his masters in Asian history. He also did some postgraduate work at New York University and Columbia University. Wang told Tilak that he discovered early that he was suited for a career in public service. "I have always been interested in public service. Through my high school and college years I was outspoken and in the political sense ahead of everybody. I was constantly sending out different tones, and was not so easily upset by status quo. This was not common with the rest of the people. Looking at these qualities, my teachers and professors indicated to me that I should probably be in public service. They had more or less decided on that career for me," he recalled.

It was after finishing graduate school, however, that he firmly decided on his career. "New York has a massive recruitment of social workers to work for city government. I saw that as an interesting opportunity for me to help the underprivileged in our society," he told Tilak. Wang responded to the call of these recruitment efforts, eventually landing a job in a private children's organization rather than in city government because, he said, "private agencies have better salary scales."

The job opened his eyes and got him interested in social work. "I answered a *New York Times* advertisement to work for the Chinese American Planning Council and eventually landed the job. That changed the whole dimension of my work from general social work to helping new Chinese immigrants. This allowed me to utilize my language skills, cultural background, and education to help my compatriots. I considered this as a very rewarding experience."

Soon after joining the CPC, however, Wang realized that he had his work cut out for him. He was confronted by the local traditional conservative leadership who, he said, "maintained a posture that they were a model minority, they had no problems, no crime, no need for any services. In the sixties it was a relatively small community with

Charles Pei Wang

only approximately 20,000 Chinese in a city of eight million." He added, "They weren't so sure what I was doing. They thought I was a revolutionary and a communist and I was trying to stir up trouble in the community. The social structure was very tight and was controlled by a strong leadership. When I tried to break in and make a difference they were very suspicious. This on one hand merely indicated to me that my job was not going to be an easy one, but on the other it hand made it more challenging as well." Wang eventually persevered, breaking these barriers and winning the support of the people.

Accomplishments

Wang remained at the CPC from 1968 until 1989. He held various positions there including that of managing director and executive director. During his tenure the CPC grew to be an important social service agency for the Chinese American Community. Wang's efforts there and his affiliation with several other organizations helped to bring the concerns of Chinese Americans before New York City government.

Some of Wang's most notable accomplishments include arranging the first public hearing on New York–Asian American affairs sponsored by the U.S. Commission on Civil Rights in 1974, the opening of a social security administration branch office in Chinatown in 1976, and a Chinatown post office in 1978. He has also served on the Asian American panel of the President's Commission on

Mental Health and on the New York State Crime Prevention Task Force on Bias Related Violence. He was a member of the New York State Advisory Committee to the U.S. Commission on Civil Rights for several years in the 1970s. He was also chairman of the Pacific Asian Coalition-Mid Atlantic Region, co-chairman of the Asian American Council of Greater New York, vice-chairman of New York City Health System Agency, secretary of the Private Industry Council and chairman of the U.S. Bureau of the Census 1990 Asian and Pacific Islanders Committee. Wang currently is secretary on the board of directors of United Way of New York City, co-chairman of the New York City Human Services, treasurer of the Federation of Asian American Social Service organization, and a member of the New York City Partnership.

Wang told Tilak that he is philosophically aligned with the teachings of Shung Tse, one of the major disciples of Confucius. Unlike the official descendant of Confucius, Mencius, who holds that human nature is pure and virtuous until society corrupts it, Shung Tse teaches that human nature is intrinsically evil and people must strive to overcome it through good acts.

Role Models

For examples of great leaders, Wang looks to Mahatma Gandhi and Winston Churchill. He told Tilak that he considers Gandhi "a true leader who led a very humble life." He said he admires Churchill for graciously stepping down when the people did not re-elect him even after he won the war. "I think he set an example of how democracy really works. He did not use his political power to manipulate the situation and gladly accepted the mandate of the people and paved the way for democracy," explained Wang, adding, "Not only Churchill's leadership during the war but also his postwar actions were very noble." Wang also respects a leader from his own homeland: "Chou En Lai, the prime minister who was under the total domination of Mao, is another of my role models from the contemporary Chinese aspect. He presented a moderate and a very democratic kind of approach and helped Mao move China to a more modern and humane society." Wang told Tilak that he believes all of China's problems today are due to Mao's mistakes, and China's accomplishments are because of Chou En Lai.

Wang's guiding motto is that if there were no poor people there would be no need for him to exist. He added, "They need my services and I owe it to the people. It is not because I am smarter or more capable than any other person, it is because they have a need for me." Wang, a Baptist, is a longtime and active member of the church. He told Tilak: "I believe that we all have our purposes, given to us by God to serve the world. We have to do our best to serve mankind, be it a small or big favor. I never look down on people, I have a lot of friends among the underprivileged, they are comfortable talking to me because I don't believe in upper or lower class. I find myself less comfortable working with upper class people," he

laughed. "People are people and they all ought to be treated with respect and kindness."

Wang feels that his Asian Pacific Islander heritage has been a very large part of his success and to some extent a part of his failure. "Asians are less assertive, aggressive, and more willing to compromise," he maintained. "These are Asian characteristics that are very deep-rooted. Living in the American society we have to be otherwise. Maybe I could have accomplished more if I was more assertive or aggressive." Yet Wang's contributions to the Chinese American community are undeniable. As he told Tilak, "Now I have become one of the better-known people in the [Chinese American] community, my actions impact the lives of our community members. All this is quite a challenge on one end and on the other it is also very gratifying."

Sources:

Wang, Charles Pei, telephone interview with Visi R. Tilak, March 1994.

—Sketch by Visi R. Tilak

Taylor G. Wang
(1940–)
Astronaut, scientist

Taylor G. Wang is the Centennial Professor of Applied Physics and the director of the Center for Microgravity Research and Applications at Vanderbilt University. He is also an astronaut with NASA who flew aboard the space shuttle *Challenger* as a payload specialist during the STS-51 mission from April 29 to May 5, 1985.

Taylor Gangjung Wang was born on June 16, 1940, in Shanghai, China. The family fled their homeland for Taiwan, however, in the civil war that led to the Communist victory in 1949. At the age of twelve, Wang decided to become a physicist, a difficult decision for the young boy considering his father was a wealthy businessman who had expected Wang to take over the family business.

As a child, Wang had two role models. The first was his mother, whom he described as a "very intelligent woman [who has] the wisdom of focusing on big pictures and just causes, establishing in me, early on, the proper responsibilities and duties of an individual." His other role model was the great Chinese general, Yua Fay, who believed that each individual had responsibilities to live up to that came from a higher calling.

Taylor G. Wang

An Eye-Opening Experience

After high school all students in Taiwan must take a college entrance exam before being admitted to a university. Wang had always done well in school, but rarely devoted himself to his studies. He found most classes fairly easy and assumed he would do very well on the entrance examination. When he failed the exams, however, he realized that he would have to devote himself seriously to achieving what he wanted to accomplish in life.

Wang ended up coming to America for his education and in 1971 he finished work for his Ph.D. at the University of California at Los Angeles. In 1972 Wang accepted a position at the Jet Propulsion Laboratory (JLP) at the California Institute of Technology in Pasadena, California, where he worked in applied physics. In 1974 NASA accepted a proposal he had made for an experiment to be conducted in space at some point in the future. Wang's particular field of interest—fluid dynamics and containerless experiments—was one that was especially suited to the zero gravity conditions of outer space. By 1980 his team at JPL finished designing the mechanical hardware required to conduct the proposed experiments. Two years later NASA had started thinking about who they would need to conduct these complicated experiments in space. As Wang wrote in the journal *Engineering and Science* in January of 1986: "NASA . . . asked the question: 'Is it better to train a career astronaut as a scientist or to train a career scientist as an astronaut?' NASA headquarters finally

opted for the latter, since this mission would be primarily science oriented." NASA announced an open selection for astronauts and, from a huge pool of applicants, Wang was chosen.

Payload Specialist/Astronaut Scientist

Wang was trained in all aspects of space flight before being fully accepted as a payload specialist. He described for *Engineering and Science* the wide range of activities he was trained in: "The third component [of training] involved space shuttle training—familiarizing ourselves with the whole spacecraft. There are about 4,000 switches and six computers on the spacecraft. We are supposed to know what all the switches are for—so in case the five career astronauts all die on me, I can bring the spacecraft back."

The experiments Wang conducted on the shuttle involved investigating the equilibrium shapes of a rotating spheroid and a large amplitude oscillation experiment on a droplet which is stimulated with sound waves to go into various oscillation modes. Both experiments were to test hypotheses that had been around for a long time—since Isaac Newton in the case of the former—but which could never be accurately tested due to the physical impossibility of sustaining zero gravity conditions on earth. The second experiment, dealing with the behavior of a compound water droplet in a containerless cell of zero gravity displayed properties that theoreticians had never anticipated, and so turned out to be quite important to the field of biophysics.

Wang holds more than twenty U.S. patents and is the author of approximately 160 articles published in scientific journals. He is the recipient of many awards, including the NASA Exceptional Scientific Achievement Medal (1987), the NASA Space Flight Medal (1985), and the Chinese Institute of Engineering Outstanding Accomplishment Award. He was honored by the government of the United States with "Taylor G. Wang Recognition Day" in Washington, D.C., celebrated on October 11, 1985. Another of Wang's experiments was chosen to be conducted aboard a space shuttle mission, this one during the summer of 1993.

Wang married his high school sweetheart, Beverly, in 1965, and the couple has two children, Kenneth and Eric. Wang told *Notable Asian Americans* he believes that to succeed in life it is necessary to "do your best, but never accept failure as a conclusion." He added that life is very short and should not be wasted on frivolity.

Sources:

Periodicals

Wang, Taylor G. "A Scientist in Space," *Engineering and Science,* January 1986, pp. 17–23.

Other

Wang, Taylor G, written interview with Jim Henry, April 7, 1994.

—Sketch by Jim Henry

Vera Wang
(1949–)
Fashion designer

Vera Wang is perhaps the most prominent designer of bridal wear in America today. She went into bridal design in 1989 after searching for a wedding dress for her own wedding and finding the market slim and lacking in taste and creativity. She opened the Vera Wang Bridal House on New York City's Madison Avenue in 1990. She also started a separate couture business called Vera Wang Made to Order, which designs both bridal and evening wear. Today she has a thriving business through her own shop and sells through the New York–based Barneys department store. In 1994, she added a line of evening clothes, which is sold through upscale retailers such as Saks Fifth Avenue, I. Magnin, and Neiman Marcus.

Vera Wang was born in June of 1949 in Manhattan. Her father, Cheng Ching Wang, is chairman of the U.S. Summit Company, a pharmaceuticals distribution and trading concern, and her mother is a former United Nations translator, and is the daughter of one of the last feudal warlords in China. As a child, Vera studied ballet at New York's School of American Ballet and was a competitive ice skater. She was educated in private schools and went to college at Sarah Lawrence in New York and spent her junior year at the Sorbonne in Paris. She earned a bachelor's degree in art history, and later did graduate work at Columbia University in New York.

Wang's first job after college was as a senior editor at *Vogue*, where, at age twenty-three, she was made an editor, one of the youngest in the magazine's history. That she chose to pursue a career instead of starting a family was a sore point with Wang's mother. Wang told the *New York Times Magazine:* "When I was made a *Vogue* editor my mother was very sad. 'Why work so hard?' she wanted to know, 'Why don't you want to make a family?' And I didn't. I was the Beatles generation, the 1960s, S.D.S. . . . I was driven in my career, afraid of what marriage and children might really mean to me." Her job at *Vogue* was as a sittings editor, and as such she was responsible for creating the photographs that in fashion publishing essentially *are* the magazine. Wang worked at *Vogue* for sixteen years

Vera Wang

and then moved into fashion design, which she had always wanted to do.

Ralph Lauren as Mentor

She found a job with Ralph Lauren, where she was creative director, involved in ten of the designer's lines. She was in charge of the production of women's accessories and furs. Discussing her introduction to the design world in *Asian Week*, Wang said that "Lauren was my mentor." She stayed with Lauren for two years, leaving in 1990 to form her own venture.

Wang opened her business, as she told Beulah Ku in *Asian Week*, because "I was trying to find a wedding gown in 1989 when I was planning my wedding. I couldn't find anything that I really liked, and that inspired me to open my bridal shop in September 1990." The new business was financed by her father, who remains her major investor. And, although Wang's businesses have yet to show a profit, she expects 1995 to be her turnaround year. She does a brisk and high-profile business. She has created wedding gowns for a couple of the Kennedys, pop singer Mariah Carey (with a twenty-seven-foot train), and for Nancy Davis. She is also well-respected among celebrities for her couture designs. She designed dresses for actresses Sharon Stone, Marisa Tomei, Penelope Ann Miller, and Holly Hunter for the Academy Awards. In 1992 and 1994, Wang designed figure skater Nancy Kerrigan's Olympic costumes.

Bridalwear Success

One often-stated reason for Wang's success in the bridal market is the tendency among those in fashion to stay away from this highly formalized, tradition-bound market. It usually is considered an area in which there is little room for creativity. But Wang, defying conventional wisdom, followed her instincts on this matter. She commented in the *New York Times Magazine:* "If I were to listen to many other voices I would have done a safe product. Would anyone believe that a sheer illusion low-cut-back slinky dress would ever have sold in the bridal market? Ten out of ten people would say you are out of your mind. I said there've got to be girls like me who are not twenty-three and want to look sophisticated and sexy."

According to Beulah Ku of *Asian Week,* "Wang has established a style for women with understated, modern tastes and who are body conscious without being obvious. Wang's bridal collections for the spring and summer represent a tour de force of draping, detailing, silhouette and sophistication. It is the most comprehensive collection of wedding dresses to be found anywhere. Her dresses have the tradition of white as well as touches of color, but are known for their sexy cuts, exquisite gown trimmings and bows, illusion sleeves and bareback simplicity with style."

In the late spring and early summer of 1994, Vera Wang introduced her much-anticipated line of ready-to-wear evening clothes to generally positive reviews in the fashion press. Her clientele is still very much the well-to-do, with basic black dresses priced from nine hundred to three thousand dollars. The pressure she felt was tremendous, waiting for the critical response to her creations. She told the *New York Times,* "I see myself as a madwoman scrambling to keep 100 marbles on the table before they fall off." In spite of this pressure, however, Wang counts herself lucky to have gotten to where she is in the incredibly competitive, world of fashion design.

Vera Wang has been honored with a number of awards for her achievements. In 1993, she was the Chinese American Planning Council's Honoree of the Year. In 1994, the Girl Scout Council of Greater New York awarded her the Women of Distinction. Also in 1994, Vera Wang was elected to membership in the elite Council of Fashion Designers of America.

Sources:

Periodicals

Ku, Beulah. "Designs of Elegance and Style from Vera Wang." *Asian Week,* January 21, 1994, pp. 12–13.

Witchel, Alex. "From Aisle to Runway: Vera Wang." *New York Times Magazine,* June 19, 1994, pp. 22–25.

—Sketch by Jim Henry

Wayne Wang
(1949–)
Filmmaker

When Wayne Wang was approached to direct the film version of Amy Tan's phenomenal debut novel, *The Joy Luck Club,* he was at first reluctant. "I didn't want to do another Chinese movie," Wang told the *New York Times* in 1993. "I said for years that I was being stereotyped. Yet I loved the book. The stories reminded me so much of the stories I heard from my parents, and I felt the book transcended just being Chinese.

"Made under the auspices of Walt Disney Studios for a relatively low budget of $10.5 million with a screenplay written by author Tan and Ronald Bass (*Black Widow, Rain Man, Sleeping with the Enemy*) and executive-produced by Oliver Stone and Janet Yang, *The Joy Luck Club* proved to be a bonafide blockbuster hit, grossing some $32 million before its release on home video. The success of the film has most likely made Wang the most powerful Asian American director in Hollywood.

In spite of Wang's ambivalence about Chinese-focused films, his career is founded on critically acclaimed, low-budget features dealing with Chinese American life, including *Chan is Missing,* about two Chinatown taxi drivers in search of a shady entrepreneur to whom they entrusted money, *Dim Sum,* about the relationship between a Chinese mother and her American-born daughter, *Eat a Bowl of Tea,* about newlyweds in 1949, and *Life Is Cheap . . . but Toilet Paper Is Expensive,* about a Japanese/Chinese American cowboy getting into trouble in Hong Kong, which Wang called "a really down-and-dirty offbeat film."

Not Another Starving Painter

Wayne Wang was born in 1949 in Hong Kong, six days after his family arrived in the city after fleeing the Communist Revolution in their homeland of China. Wang's father, an engineer and businessman fluent in English, was so enthralled with American movies that he named his second son after a Hollywood star. "My father named me after seeing John Wayne in *Red River,*" Wang told the *New York Times.* "What appealed to him, I think, was the freedom and righteousness, the whole American mentality. My father loved to play football. He loved anything American."

Growing up in Hong Kong, Wang was educated by Jesuits while attending Roman Catholic schools and learned English as a child. At age eighteen, he arrived in the United States, having been urged by his mother to escape the political upheaval in Hong Kong at the time. He enrolled at Foothill College near Palo Alto, California, to study painting. Wang recalled his first college experience to Tony Chiu of the *New York Times*: "It was a very lily-white, suburban, country-club type of junior college. I developed a lot of insecurity about being Chinese there. There was no direct prejudice—people didn't call me 'Chink' or look down at me. But indirectly, I felt that out of fear, out of not knowing the Chinese, out of media stereotypes, a lot of them were locking me in as this or that."

After two years at Foothill, Wang attended the California College of Arts and Crafts in Oakland, eventually earning an MFA in film and television. "My parents wanted me to go into medicine or become an engineer. My parents said, 'Oh, no!' when I went into art. I lived mostly on scholarships. When I got into film, my dad was actually glad because he loved movies so much, and he said at least I wasn't going to be a painter starving in the streets," recalled Wang in an interview with Bernard Weinraub of the *New York Times*.

With his new degree, Wang returned to his native Hong Kong. His first jobs came quickly, directing segments on small films and television series, but left him creatively frustrated. He returned to the United States, settling in San Francisco's Chinatown where he immersed himself in making films for community activism. "I really immersed myself in the problems immigrants face, in racism," Wang told Chiu, "and that's where Chan really started—I knew I was going to make a film about my experiences."

The resulting work, *Chan is Missing*, completed in 1982, was Wang's first feature and his first success. Made for just $22,000, which Wang received in grants from the American Film Institute and the National Endowment for the Arts, the black-and-white film was shot over ten consecutive weekends. The work featured two Chinese American cab drivers searching for a man named Chan, to whom they had entrusted $4,000, and who has apparently disappeared with their hard-earned cash. Chan was a surprise hit, quickly earning some fifty times its initial investment.

Establishing a Film Career

In 1984, Wang completed the acclaimed *Dim Sum* with a budget twenty times that of Chan. Ironically, *Dim Sum* originally focused on four Chinese mothers who met weekly for mah-jongg—the exact focus of Tan's later *The Joy Luck Club*. "Just a coincidence," Wang assured *New York Newsday* in 1990. Somewhere in the middle of filming, Wang decided to narrow the story to the relationship of one Chinese-born mother to her American-born daughter. Gentle and poignant, the film flowed easily between the Cantonese and English languages, moving from one world to another with an almost languid fluidity in spite of the cultural differences experienced by both mother and daughter.

Three years later, Wang directed his first film with a non-Asian cast. *Slamdance*, a mystery thriller starring Tom Hulce and Mary Elizabeth Mastrantonio, was well received at the Cannes Film Festival, but it was not a commercial success. Bypassing the big screen, the film quickly disappeared and was released on video.

Wang returned to the world of Chinese America in his 1989 film, *Eat a Bowl of Tea*, based on the novel of the same name by Louis Chu, about a newly wed couple in 1949. He cast as the young bride from China his own wife, Cora Miao, a popular Hong Kong actress he had met in 1983 and hired for a small role in *Dim Sum*. Leading man Russell Wong played the American-born groom who was one of the first Chinese American men after World War II to bring his bride to New York's Chinatown. (Due to Chinese anti-immigration laws, women were not allowed to immigrate before the war.) Although backed by Columbia Pictures, the budget was tight and most of the period sets of New York were built in Hong Kong.

Back in his hometown, Wang was inspired to create *Life Is Cheap . . . but Toilet Paper Is Expensive*, in which he explored for the first time the cultural clash he himself had been experiencing. Released in 1990, the black, almost hallucinatory thriller/comedy follows the adventures of a half-Japanese, half-Chinese American cowboy sent to Hong Kong handcuffed to a briefcase that is to be delivered to the The Big Boss. The film captures the jarring, sometimes violent cultural clash that occurs when the two worlds of an Asian American collide. Slapped with an X-rating from the Motion Picture Association of America, *Life Is Cheap* opened in New York with a rating of its own: "A" for Adult. Although a departure from his previous films, *Life Is Cheap* was, nonetheless, critically acclaimed.

Making History

Wang was the only director that *The Joy Luck Club*'s author ever considered. Ironically, Wang and the film's executive producer, Oliver Stone, already had a not-so-flattering history together. Years before, Wang had denounced Stone's screenplay for *Year of the Dragon*, a film considered by most Asian Americans to be one of the most racist insults to come out of Hollywood. Not to be outdone, Stone responded to Wang's criticism by referring to *Dim Sum*'s characters as "boring." A decade later, the two collaborated to create the most commercially successful Asian American film made thus far.

In spite of the rave reviews garnered from mainstream critics, this 1993 film about four Chinese-born mothers and their American-born daughters has remained controversial in the Asian American community. On the surface, the film has been criticized for its unflattering, two-dimensional portrayals of Asian American men. On a deeper level, both the novel and the film have been accused of distorting Chinese traditions and myth, led by the angry voice of writer and critic Frank Chin.

Regardless of the controversy, with its mainstream praise and big-dollar studio backing, *The Joy Luck Club* is already paving the way for a more accepting climate for future Asian American-focused films. Wang expressed to the *Washington Post* in 1993 that he hoped his celluloid representations of Asian America will reach "the heart of America." He added, "I don't think most of America knows that Chinese Americans are just as American as they are."

For the time being, Wang is moving away from Asian American projects. His next project is a film adaptation of stories by Brooklyn author Paul Auster. Entitled *Smoke*, the film has a single Asian character. "I definitely want to step away from the Chinese thing for a while," he told Weinraub. "I'll eventually get back to it—I'm sure I will—but at the same time, I feel I'm just as American as anyone else. There are stories and characters about America that I want to tell."

Sources:

Periodicals

Chiu, Tony. "Wayne Wang—He Made the Year's Unlikeliest Hit." *New York Times*, May 30, 1982, pp. 17, 35.

Hsiao, Andy. "The Man on a 'Joy Luck' Ride." *Washington Post*, September 27, 1993, pp. B1, B3.

Kasindorf, Martin. "Wayne Wang's Subtle Film Punch." *New York Newsday*, August 3, 1989, pp. 3, 13.

Mandell, Jonathan. "Culture Clash." *New York Newsday*, August 20, 1990. pp. 8-9, 16.

Weinraub, Bernard. "'I Didn't Want to Do Another Chinese Movie.'" *New York Times*, September 5, 1993, Sec. 2, pp. 7, 15.

—Sketch by Terry Hong

Sadao Watanabe

Sadao Watanabe
(1933–)
Jazz saxophonist

He averages at least one major concert in Tokyo every two months, and tickets are always sold out weeks in advance. Sadao Watanabe has achieved many firsts in jazz and continues to take jazz to higher elevations of recognition in Japan.

Sadao Watanabe was born on February 1, 1933, in Utsunomiya, a Japanese city with a population of about 150,000, located ninety miles north of Tokyo. He was one in a family of four brothers and one sister. His father was a professional musician and singer specializing in the "Biwa," a four-stringed guitar-sized instrument.

Birth of a Musician

At the age of fifteen he was inspired to learn the clarinet by the movie *Birth of the Blues* in which Bing Crosby plays the role of a clarinetist. After paying five cents each for three lessons from an old man who played at the local silent movie theatre, Watanabe decided to teach himself to play.

In 1949 he formed a combo with some high school friends and a traveling street band player. They planned to play at one of the many United States Occupation Force clubs in Utsunomiya. Reminiscing about playing at the Hotel Kanaya in Nikko, Watanabe told Max Lash of *Down Beat*, "About 90 percent of the hotel guests were GI's from an infantry division. During the evening most of them were too drunk to take notice of the frequent squeaks and bad notes that dominated my playing then." During these first few professional gigs, he would put down his clarinet to play the alto-saxophone, the instrument that later brought him success.

In 1953 he started the rhythm and blues band Jafro, a name reflecting a combination of jazz and Afro music. At one of his regular sessions he met Toshiko Akiyoshi, leader of the Cozy Quartet. Akiyoshi invited Watanabe and Akira Miyazawa, then Japan's top tenor sax player and

Watanabe's friend to join the quartet. The Cozy Quartet began to tour the U.S. military bases, bringing them recognition among fellow musicians.

To earn a living, Watanabe supplemented his quartet performances by playing in dance bands and doing radio shows. In 1956 when Akiyoshi left for the United States, Watanabe became the leader of the Cozy Quartet.

On September 29, 1957, Watanabe married Mitsuko Itoh. Their daughter, Mako, was born in October of 1958. By this time, Watanabe's popularity had grown steadily and the Tokyo-based jazz monthly *Swing Journal* named him best alto saxophonist in its 1959 "Readers' Popularity Poll." He recorded his first solo album, *Sadao Watanabe*, in 1961.

Education in the United States

In 1962, at the urging of Akiyoshi, Sadao Watanabe left on his first trip to the United States to study at the prestigious Berklee College of Music in Boston. There he added theory and technique to his natural aptitude for music. During his three years abroad, he had the opportunity to play with many well-known musicians, including Gary McFarland and Chico Hamilton. With his soft samba beat, McFarland had the greatest influence on Watanabe's music. It was after this experience of playing with other musicians that Watanabe's world of jazz expanded and he started blending his rhythms to a bossanova jazz style.

On November 15, 1965, he finished three and a half years of study at Berklee and returned to Tokyo. Immediately after his return he recorded his second album *Sadao Watanabe Plays*. Excited by what he had learned abroad, he formed his own group and started a small jazz school to teach young musicians theory and technique. At the same time he also formed a regular quartet that frequented clubs and radio shows. In the mid 1960s he recorded a number of albums and also did a Japan tour with guitarist Laurindo Almeida.

At the age of thirty-two, he began seven years of classical flute study with Ririko Hayashi, a renowned Tokyo teacher and lead flutist with the Tokyo Philharmonic. The late 1960s was a period of firsts for Watanabe. He became the first ever to win six "Bests" in the *Swing Journal's* "Readers' Popularity Poll." In January of 1969 he started a weekly Saturday midnight AM radio program, the first of its kind, called "Nabesada and Jazz." (Nabesada was Watanabe's nickname in Japan.) In 1968, he made his first international jazz festival appearance at the Newport Jazz Festival, followed by the Montreux Jazz Festival in 1970.

In the 1970s Watanabe began making yearly trips to America, Africa, Europe, and South America. He blended the melodies and rhythms from the countries he visited with hiw own style to create a unique fusion sound that his audiences found very appealing. He received the

Japan Jazz Award in the Jazz Disc Awards for his album *Sadao Watanabe*. In 1977 he won the Art Festival Grand Prix Award (the Japanese equivalent of the Grammy) for *Sadao Watanabe Recital,* a composition that was influenced by African ethnic music. His album *California Shower* also received the Victor Golden Disc Award for sales exceeding 100,000.

Watanabe's recital "Live at Budohkan," with a full orchestra for a crowd of 30,000, was an history-making event in the history of Japanese jazz. Following this recital Watanabe signed a two-year contract with the United States recording company CBS. His one-year coast-to-coast U.S. tour in 1980 brought him international recognition. *Fill up the Night* was a best-selling jazz album in Japan, and in the United States it topped the jazz chart of radio and records. The album *Rendezvous* was number two on the U.S. Billboard Jazz chart.

Maisha, with special guest Herbie Hancock, was Watanabe's first self-produced album and his first music video. Released in April 1985, the video was shot in the Sahara desert in Africa. He also published his photographs of Africa in his book, *Maisha.* After a long interval, Watanabe did a tour of Japan with Japanese musicians in 1986.

Watanabe had always invited other artists he met during his travels to perform in Japan so that the Japanese people would get the opportunity to hear musicians from all over the world. In 1985, he initiated and promoted *Bravas Club 85* and one year later, *Bravas Club 86,* an international jazz event that has since become an annual happening in Japan. He received the Japanese Ministry of Education Award for his work on *Bravas Club 85* as well as for *Maisha.*

In the mid-1990s, Watanabe is considered a father figure in Japanese jazz. He has won eleven Jazz Man of the Year Awards since 1968, and every year since 1959 he has won the Best Alto Saxophonist Award. Both awards are presented by *Swing Journal.* Jazz in Japan achieved a new peak of acceptance, thanks mainly to the efforts of Sadao Watanabe.

Sources:

Periodicals

Lash, Max E. "Japan's First Jazz School." *Down Beat,* May 15, 1969.

Other

Elektra Asylum Records. "Sadao Watanabe." Biographical information, 1994.

—Sketch by Visi R. Tilak

Michiko Nishiura Weglyn
(1926–)
Costume designer, writer, activist

Michi Weglyn's first career, which she began at the age of twenty-one, catapulted her to fame as the first nationally prominent Japanese American costume designer in the United States. By the 1950s, Weglyn was a regular fixture behind-the-television-scenes, best known for her flattering, successful creations for "The Perry Como Show," a weekly musical variety hour for which she designed costumes from 1956 to 1965. As a designer, she was lauded for her ability to hide the figure flaws of some of Hollywood's most famous celebrities at the time, including Ginger Rogers, Dinah Shore, Betty Grable, Anne Bancroft, and Jane Powell. Weglyn's designing career, which lasted nearly two decades, took her onto the sets of many of the most popular television musical variety series of the late 1950s and 1960s, including "The Jackie Gleason Show," "The Patti Page Show," "The Tony Bennett Show," and "The Dinah Shore Show." She eventually established her own manufacturing and design studio.

In 1967 after the "The Perry Como Show" commitment ended, Weglyn's life changed dramatically. In a 1976 article in *Pacific Citizen,* a childhood friend referred to the change as "the radicalization of Michi Weglyn." From glamorous designer, Weglyn metamorphosed into an acclaimed historical writer. It was the height of the civil rights movement of the late 1960s. Then-U.S. attorney general Ramsey Clark appeared on a television show and stated that there had never been, and never would be, concentration camps in America. Having spent more than two years of her life at the camp in Gila (pronounced heel-ah) River, Arizona, Weglyn justly referred to Clark's words as "an outright lie." She recalled to *Rafu Shimpo* in 1993, "I decided they were not going to get away with that. That was the catalyst for my book." That landmark work, *Years of Infamy: The Untold Story of America's Concentration Camps,* exposed the horror and suffering of some 110,000 Japanese Americans imprisoned in U.S. concentration camps during World War II. Writer and activist Frank Chin called *Years of Infamy* "the only Asian American book to change Asian American history," referring to its unparalleled contribution to the success of the Japanese American redress campaign of the late 1980s and early 1990s.

Farm Life

Born in Stockton, California, on November 29, 1926, Michiko Nishiura was one of the two daughters of Tomojiro and Misao (Yuasa) Nishiura. The family lived in a large, run-down house on a 500-acre farm in Brentwood, a small village in Contra Costa County, California,

Michiko Nishiura Weglyn

approximately fifty miles east of San Francisco. Growing up, Weglyn worked on the farm for a few hours before she went to school, feeding the chickens and horses. She wanted to prove to her father that she was just as valuable as the son he never had. "In Japanese culture," Weglyn explained in a 1976 interview with Harriet Shapiro, "it's disastrous if a family doesn't have an heir, a male offspring to carry on the family name and help in the fields."

At grade school, Weglyn found friends among the Mexican American and Filipino children. "Even when I was a little child my parents instilled in me *enryo,* a backing away, a shyness, especially with white people. I knew my place. Later, in high school, I was very self-conscious and terribly concerned about what people would think of me. My parents had taught me that I must not offend. They used to talk often about *haiseki,* or discrimination," she told Shapiro.

The day after Japanese bombers attacked Pearl Harbor on December 7, 1941, Weglyn felt very anxious about going to school. When she arrived, she recalled the teacher telling the other students, "It's not the fault of the Japanese Americans. You are not to mistreat them." Unfortunately, the general public was not as fair-minded. "I recall my parents going out in the middle of the night and burning books and burying things—anything that might show their attachment to Japan, such as photographs of relatives, letters, even some of their beloved art treasures," Weglyn told Shapiro.

On February 19, 1942, President Franklin Roosevelt signed Executive Order 9066, which called for the evacuation of all persons of Japanese descent (two-thirds of whom were American citizens) on the West Coast to ten "relocation camps" where the internees couldn't pose a threat to the U.S. military efforts against Japan. Families were given six to ten days to dispose of their property and businesses. Weglyn told Shapiro with great insight: "The Japanese Americans very obediently turned themselves in. Although they thought it dreadfully unfair to have to leave their homes, they felt powerless. The Issei [first generation], as enemy aliens, had no political voice, and neither did the Nisei [second generation] since most were not yet of voting age." When the evacuation order reached the Nishiuras, they were in the midst of packing. Weglyn recalled to Shapiro: "People wanted to buy our bicycles and automobiles for next to nothing, and the chickens for a quarter apiece. At that price Mom decided it would be better to eat as many chickens as we could before we left. To this day, when my sister and I talk about that period, the hurried killing and eating of our pet chickens was one of the most traumatic aspects of the evacuation. Our father and mother were losing everything they had worked for, but my sister and I had little realization of that. For us it was parting with our animals: our cats, dogs, chickens, our possum, and our parrot. Most were left abandoned. I guess that's what war is like. But these are the things that are not written up in history books."

On May 12, 1942, the Nishiuras were loaded on buses that carried them to a so-called assembly center where they found guard towers, guns, and barbed wire awaiting them. Young Weglyn was not yet sixteen years old. After several months, the family boarded another train which shuttled hundreds of families to the relocation camp in Gila River, Arizona. After two days and nights of traveling, the evacuees arrived in a barren desert, the site of their new home for several years.

Camp Life

In spite of the often inhumane conditions of camp life—the 130-degree heat, the unrelenting sand storms, the inedible food, the overcrowded housing, the communal bathrooms without even partitions for the toilets—the teenaged Weglyn thrived. Ironically, she told Shapiro that she felt a sense of relief and liberation in her new home. "Suddenly I was with my peers. I didn't have to feel inferior. I didn't have to feel small. Or to face the humiliation I had begun to feel more intensely in school. I was liked for what I was, not because of what my parents did or didn't do. I had finally gained a feeling of respect, and I was managing to do the kinds of things that had been denied me, back at home, as a person who was of Asian descent." Weglyn emerged as a true leader and achiever among her peers. She became president of the Girl Scout troop that she organized. She held a day-long Girls League Convention which brought in some 500 high school girls from various Arizona cities to the camp where

they participated in a talent show, were given a tour of the camp, ate together in the mess halls, and discussed timely issues. "They took back to their homes the news that we were as American as anybody else. It helped turn the feelings of distrust," Weglyn told Shapiro.

In 1944, Weglyn went to Phoenix to take entrance examinations for Mount Holyoke College in Massachusetts. Just before her exam, she stopped at a nearby drug store for a soda, but was asked to leave. The storekeeper would not serve her, because she looked Japanese. For the previous two years, Weglyn had been shielded from such racism and abuse, living among only Japanese Americans at camp. In spite of the racist reception outside of camp, Weglyn eventually traveled to the East Coast and entered college. Although she does not remember the details of her arrival at Gila, she clearly remembered leaving: "I was full of the spirit of forgiveness and love and very grateful to the many dedicated fellow Americans who had made it possible for me to attend Mount Holyoke College on a full scholarship," she said to Shapiro.

Weglyn discovered her design aptitude in college, although her interest went back to her childhood. She recalled that at a young age, she had made sweaters for some genetically mutant pet chickens that were born without feathers. At Mount Holyoke, she won a campuswide design contest—for costumes, sets, and scenery for a college production. Unfortunately, her college career did not last long. In 1945, Weglyn was forced to leave Mount Holyoke and was placed in a sanatorium for tuberculosis which she had contracted at Gila. In 1947, she returned to school, this time to Barnard College in New York City, but again was forced to leave for health reasons. Weglyn later studied costume design at New York's Fashion Academy between 1948 and 1949. One year later, on March 5, 1950, she married Walter Matthys Weglyn, a perfume chemist, who came to the United States in 1947 after having survived the Holocaust. "Walter is my most exacting critic and mentor," Weglyn said of her husband in a brochure from California State Polytechnic University.

In the 1950s, under the name Michi, Weglyn began designing theatrical costumes for ice shows, night clubs, Broadway and television, including the Roxy Theatre (1952–53), "The Jackie Gleason Show" (1953), "Kraft Television Theater" (1954), *Hit the Trail* (a Broadway musical, 1954), "The Patti Page Show" (1958), "The Tony Bennett Show" (1959), "The Dinah Shore Show" (1961), "The Jimmy Dean Show" (1964), and, of course, "The Perry Como Show" from 1956 to 1965. From 1964 to 1967, Weglyn was also the founder and head of costume manufacturing and the design studio for Michi Associates Limited.

War

By the time Weglyn retired from designing in the late 1960s, war was a very controversial topic in the United States and beyond. The Vietnam War was raging abroad while the civil rights movement gained momentum at home. Weglyn explained in 1993 during her commencement address at California State Polytechnic University in Pomona, California, "As I look back, I would first have to credit both the Vietnam War (when the use of technological savagery on the lives, habitats, and ecosystem of a small Asian nation was shocking the entire civilized world), and the civil rights movement (when each day was filled with rage and racial violence) for the transition that took place within me. From an apolitical innocent I became a traumatized citizen. I was enraged by a democracy's flagrant disregard for elemental human rights, especially as they related to ethnicity and skin color, and by America's shocking disregard for a reverence for life which we had been taught to hold sacred.

"What startled me into disbelief during the heat of the antiwar and civil rights agitation was the preposterous lie spewed forth by the then-attorney general Ramsey Clark when asked on television if the protesters would be put in concentration camps. His astonished reply, that 'we have never had, do not now have, and will not ever have concentration camps here' was the catalyst. His blatant untruth convinced me that uncovering the probable lies of our long-revered wartime president Franklin Delano Roosevelt would surely lead me to the truth as to why we innocents had been consigned to prison camps.

"Indeed in the FDR Library, later at the National Archives and other repositories, a treasure trove was there for the digging. For an untrained researcher it was agonizing to decide how to proceed, when certain of my suspicions proved true: that textbooks, for example, were perpetuating a myth in scapegoating the fear hysteria of the West Coast, when the hysteria was actually in the White House."

Weglyn spent eight years in search of the truth. In 1976, the result of her passionate labors, *Years of Infamy: The Untold Story of America's Concentration Camps*, was published by William Morrow and Company. For the first time in history, Weglyn was able to break the paralyzing guilt that had bound Japanese Americans in silence. With careful research and documentation, Weglyn shed light on the abuses of power in the highest reaches of the U.S. government that failed to protect the basic rights of Americans of Japanese descent. Her work helped release a new social activism among Japanese Americans, to become more involved in promoting civil and human rights, which eventually led to the redress movement of the late 1980s and early 1990s.

Both the book and Weglyn have been lauded for changing the face of Asian American history. Weglyn has been given much of the credit for the success of the Japanese American redress campaign. Bert Nakano, national spokesperson for the National Coalition for Redress and Reparations (NCRR), was quoted by *Rafu Shimpo* in 1993,

referring to *Years of Infamy* as the significant element in the redress campaign, adding "Her book was the primer that people referred to in order to get familiar with the [Japanese American internment] issue."

The Fighting Spirit Continues

Since 1976, Weglyn has remained actively involved in the Asian American community and beyond. She has been an adviser and consultant on countless projects, including the Japanese American National Museum in Los Angeles (1988–90), The Japanese American Library in San Francisco (1987–present), Loni Ding's award-winning film, *Color of Honor* (1987), the Congressional Study on the Commission on Wartime Relocation and Internment of Civilians (1981–82), and the Smithsonian Institution's exhibit, "A More Perfect Union: The Japanese Americans and the U.S. Constitution" (1975–76).

The honors and awards Weglyn has received also seem limitless. They include the "Justice in Action" Award from the Asian American Legal Defense and Education Fund (1987); the Anisfield-Wolf Award in Race Relations for *Years of Infamy* (1977), and the Japanese American of the Biennium Award "in recognition of outstanding service by a Japanese American in making America a better place for all people" from the Japanese American Citizens League (1976). In addition, Weglyn has been bestowed honorary doctorates from Hunter College in 1992 and from California State Polytechnic University in 1993. Also in 1993, California State Polytechnic University established the Michi Nishiura and Walter Weglyn Endowed Chair for Multicultural Studies. And in June 1994, almost five decades after she was forced to leave due to health problems, Weglyn received an honorary doctor of letters from Mount Holyoke College.

"By reading the life histories of individuals who have excelled in bettering the human condition, you will find their tragedies and triumphs to be a constant source of empowerment," Weglyn advised *Notable Asian Americans*, writing from her own experiences. While she cites such luminaries as Albert Schweitzer, Mother Theresa, and Maya Angelou as her role models, indeed, Weglyn herself has become a laudable example for all those who seek truth and justice with unwavering dedication and compassion.

Sources:

Books

Chan, Jeffery Paul, Frank Chin, Lawson Fusao Inada and Shawn Wong. "Michi Weglyn." In *The Big Aiiieeeee*, New York: Meridian, 1991.

Shapiro, Harriet. "Michi."

"Weglyn, Michiko Nishiura." *The International Register of Profiles*, 1260.

Periodicals

Christy, George. "So You Have a Figure Problem." *TV Guide,* November 11, 1961, pp. 18–21.

Nakayama, Takeshi. "Nisei Author Honored by Cal Poly Pomona," *Rafu Shimpo,* June 14, 1993.

Perkins, Robert. "U.S. 'Infamy' Recalled." *The Springfield Union,* March 11, 1977.

Seko, Sachi. "Digging for Roots." *Pacific Citizen,* February 27, 1976, p. 4.

Other

Weglyn, Michi Nishiura. Biographical information, July 1994.

—Sketch by Terry Hong

Anna May Wong

(1907–1961)

Actress

Anna May Wong became America's first Asian American movie star before films could even talk. She maintained her popularity for more than a quarter of a century, and remained one of the highest-salaried stars of her time. She built a career around being the mysterious evil villainess, repeatedly playing the roles created by Hollywood's stereotypical fantasies of the Oriental woman. She was the exotic slave girl, the powerful dragon lady, the mysterious siren of the Orient with deadly charms.

In spite of her international fame, Wong spoke out vehemently against the racist Hollywood regime. Disgusted with the American motion picture industry, Wong fled two times to Europe. In a 1933 interview entitled "I Protest" which appeared in a London magazine and was reprinted without specific source citiations in a document at the Lincoln Center Performing Arts Library, Wong told interviewer Doris Mackie: "When I left Hollywood I vowed I would never act for the film again! . . . I was so tired of the parts I had to play. Why is it that the screen Chinese is always the villain of the piece? And so crude a villain— murderous, treacherous, a snake in the grass! We are not like that. How should we be, with a civilization that is so many times older than that of the West? . . . We have our rigid codes of behavior, of honor. Why do they never show these on screen? Why should we always scheme, rob, kill? I got so weary of it all—all the scenarists' conception of the Chinese character. You remember *Fu Manchu? Daughter of the Dragon?* So wicked!"

Hollywood Beckons

Born on Flower Street in Los Angeles, California in 1907, Anna May Wong was named Wong Liu Tsong, which in Cantonese means "frosted yellow willow." Wong was third-generation Chinese American; her father was born in Sacramento and his father had emigrated to California during the Gold Rush.

Growing up, Wong and her six brothers and sisters lived in a flat over the family's ramshackle laundry. Her first memories were of constant steam and the pungent odor of hot-ironed linen. As a young child, Wong became fascinated with the the brand-new movie world. She began skipping Chinese school in the evenings to watch such movies as *The Perils of Pauline* (1914) at the local nickelodeon. By the age of eleven, Wong decided she was going to be a movie actress. In spite of the enormous improbability of such a goal, she got her first part at age twelve. James Wang, an agent who cast Asian talent for movies, was hiring three hundred Chinese girls as extras in the 1919 film *The Red Lantern.* Hardly visible in the final release version of the film, the small part nevertheless led to a few minor roles, including one in *First Born,* with Sessue Hayakawa, the only Asian leading man in the 1920s.

For two years, Wong thanklessly worked after school as an extra. Knowing her parents would not approve, she kept her extracurricular career a secret. At age fourteen, her father found her a job as a secretary, but Wong was fired one week later for her poor shorthand. When she returned home, fearing her father's anger, she found a letter from a director's office offering her a role in the film *Bits of Life* (1921), which would bring Wong her first screen credit. Although Wong's father strongly objected to his daughter's chosen career, he eventually relented on the condition that an adult escort, often he himself, would chaperone the young Wong on the film sets at all times. When she was not in front of the cameras, her father locked her into her room on the set.

At age seventeen, Wong had one of the few romantic lead roles she would ever play in *Toll of the Sea* (1923), the first Technicolor feature ever made. As a young village girl who marries an American sailor, Wong captured the media's attention for the first time. Reporters began to appear at the laundry in the hopes of catching Wong for an interview or a photo.

International acclaim came in 1924 with *The Thief of Bagdad,* in which Wong played an exotic Mongol slave girl opposite Douglas Fairbanks, Sr. By then, she was five feet, seven inches—an inch taller than Fairbanks. Although the film was the greatest success of the year, it scandalized Wong's family. Although Wong would continue to support her family for many years, from the time of *Bagdad's* release, an irreparable rift developed. Wong would only remain close to her brother, Richard.

Anna May Wong

The Movie Star's Life

The success of *Bagdad* led to countless new offers. She appeared as an Eskimo in *The Alaskan* and a Native American girl in *Peter Pan*. In addition to film roles, Wong also worked as a model. She made a few more films, including *Old San Francisco* with Warner Oland and *Mr. Wu* opposite Lon Chaney. In 1928, she took a supporting role in *The Crimson City,* which starred a made-up-to-look-Asian Myrna Loy.

Disillusioned with her own roles that seemed to lack any honest credibility, as well Hollywood's practice of casting non-Asians in the few leading Asian roles, Wong finally fled to Europe in a flurry of disgust. In London, she co-starred with the emerging Charles Laughton in E.A. Dupont's *Piccadilly*. After the film, director Basil Dean bought the rights to and adapted a Chinese play, *A Circle of Chalk,* specifically for Wong. She successfully played opposite the rising new talent, Laurence Olivier, in London's New Theatre.

Wong remained in Europe for three years, where she was fêted both in Britain and the Continent for her film and stage appearances. In Germany and France, she made foreign versions of her British films, including Germany's first sound picture. So convincing was her mastery of both German and French that critics could hardly believe that her voice had not been dubbed. "Although I had little or no schooling in my youth, I managed to educate myself, and learned to speak English, Chinese, French, German and Italian," she said with modesty in a 1957 interview with *New York Enquirer.* Later in Vienna, Wong sang and danced for ten months in a musical show, *Tchin Tchi* (Springtime).

In 1931, the leading role in the Broadway version of the Edgar Wallace thriller *On the Spot* beckoned Wong back to the United States. The play ran successfully for thirty weeks, until Wong was called back to Los Angeles when her mother died in an automobile accident.

Wong's next screen role, *Daughter of the Dragon,* cast her in yet another stereotypical role as the daughter of the infamous Dr. Fu Manchu. Wong then appeared as the mistress of the Chinese warlord she finally kills in the Joseph von Sternberg thriller *Shanghai Express,* starring Marlene Dietrich. Often considered her most memorable role, Wong's portrayal of the bad girl turned good, a prostitute trying to reform, was lauded by the press over Dietrich's overrated performance. Years later, Dietrich would complain that Wong had upstaged her.

Wong then made one independent Sherlock Holmes picture and quickly returned to England where she felt her true audiences were. Like many ex-patriot minority artists at the time, such as Josephine Baker, Wong felt Europe had less racism to contend with. There she enjoyed the company of royalty and the social elite. Wong remained in England for almost three years, during which time she appeared in films such as *Tiger Baby, Chu Chu Chow,* and *Java Head.* She also toured throughout England, Scotland and Ireland with a vaudeville act.

An Early Retirement

In 1936, Wong weathered what was most likely her greatest career disappointment. The film version of Pearl S. Buck's award-winning novel, *The Good Earth,* was being cast by MGM. The studio asked Wong to test for the part of the concubine Lotus—again the villainess. Wong, who was familiar with the book, felt the role of the older O-lan was the role for which she had been preparing her whole life. She told the studio she would be glad to test for the film but only for the part of O-lan. She made it clear she would not play Lotus. The studio was not interested in Wong's demands and the German actress Luise Rainer, who never looked Asian in spite of heavy make-up, was cast as O-lan, a role which won her the Academy Award.

Furious and frustrated, Wong again left Hollywood. She had long talked about a trip to the Far East, including China, the home of her ancestors. In spite of an extravagant initial welcome, Wong was heavily criticized for her degrading portrayals of Chinese women and was told that many of her films were banned in China. In her defense, Wong pleaded that she had only played those degrading roles to get a start in a heavily competitive business, and pointed to her later European work as examples of good she had done. She also made the case that in coming to China, she could learn to better portray its people to the West. Many of her harsher critics later retracted their judgments.

Wong remained in China for ten months, studied Mandarin Chinese, purchased costumes for films and plays and wrote articles on her travels. She learned to her chagrin that she was too westernized for the Chinese stage, and, perhaps more tragically, that she would never be considered American enough for Hollywood's uncompromising, racist views of the celluloid world.

Upon her return to the United States, Wong starred in one sympathetic role before World War II. In *Daughter of Shanghai,* she played a detective in search of traffickers of illegal immigrants. With the advent of the war, she then appeared in two war epics, *Bombs Over Burma* and *The Lady from Chungking.* Ironically, as more war movies were being cast, she was not hired as an actress, but as a scene coach to teach Caucasian actors how to be more believable as Asians.

In 1942, finally fed up with the Hollywood system, Wong retired from films at the age of thirty-five. "I had to go into retirement for the sake of my soul. I suddenly found no more pleasure in acting. My screen work became a weary and meaningless chore—and Hollywood life a bore!" Wong told *New York Enquirer* in 1957. Throughout the war, she contributed to the war efforts by working for the United China Relief Fund and touring with the USO. During the 1940s and 1950s, Wong took occasional small parts on television, even starring in her own series, "Mme. Liu Tsong," in which she played the owner of an international chain of art galleries who was also a sleuth.

Seventeen years after retirement, Wong attempted a film comeback. She returned as Lana Turner's mysterious housekeeper in the 1950 film, *Portrait in Black.* In 1961, while she was preparing for the role of the mother in *Flower Drum Song,* Wong died of a heart attack in her sleep.

With more than eighty film credits to her name, Wong is recognizably the leading Asian American presence on celluloid. However, in the six decades since the height of her career, the roles available to Asian American actors have, unfortunately, not greatly improved. These actors continue to struggle as Wong did, against stereotypical representations of Asians as witnessed in such recent films as *Rising Sun* and *The Year of the Dragon,* as well as fighting against the casting of non-Asians in major Asian roles as exemplified by Jonathan Pryce's performance as the Engineer in the controversial blockbuster play *Miss Saigon.*

In spite of Wong's disappointed resignation, Asian American actors today continue her battle for accurate, fair and equal representation on film.

Sources:

Periodicals

"Anna May Wong: Combination of East and West," *New York Herald Tribune,* November 9, 1930.

Davis, Mac. "Fled from Fame for 5 Years," *New York Enquirer,* February 18, 1957.

Mok, Michel. "Anna May Wong, with Chinese Courtesy, Makes Newspaper Photographer Blush," *New York Post,* April 26, 1939.

Sakamoto, Edward. "Anna May Wong and the Dragon-Lady Syndrome," *Los Angeles Times,* Calendar section, July 12, 1987, pp. 40–41.

Other

Unsourced and undated short biography of Anna May Wong found at the Lincoln Center Performing Arts Library in New York in Wong's clippings file.

—*Sketch by Terry Hong*

B.D. Wong
(1962–)
Actor

Only twenty-something when he won theater's highest accolade—a Tony Award as best featured actor in 1988 for his performance in *M. Butterfly,* B. D. Wong could have rested on his many laurels. He is the first Asian American actor to receive awards from Actors' Equity, Theatre World, Outer Critics Circle, and Drama Desk—in addition to his Tony. But Wong is not the kind of person to focus on his own career without regard for his community. B.D. Wong has become a well-known name among Asian Americans for his dedication to fair portrayals of Asians as much as for his famed acting ability.

Early Life

Born in San Francisco on October 24, 1962, Bradley Darryl Wong is the second of Roberta and Bill Wong's three sons. Second-generation Chinese Americans, his parents lived in San Francisco's North Beach area bordering Chinatown when B.D. was born. When he was a toddler, they moved to the city's Sunset district, now a popular area for Chinese families. But back then, they were isolated. "We were the second Chinese family on the block," Roberta Wong, a retired telephone company supervisor, told the *San Francisco Examiner*; it was hard for her sons to do things that made them seem Chinese. The Wong boys went to a Chinatown youth group every Saturday and Chinese American camp each summer, but B.D. never quite fit in—he wasn't good at sports, and the other Chinese kids taunted him. Older brother Brian became a doctor, young brother Barry a firefighter—but the youthful B.D. dreamed of becoming an actor.

"I chose this profession because I knew at an early age that I had to be creative," said Wong in an interview with Helen Zia. "I just took to this medium. It was so liberating." As a child he loved drawing and art and considered becoming an architect, but he was terrible at math and technical design. At Lincoln High School, Wong performed in a number of school productions, each succeeding role feeding his passion for acting. His parents supported his efforts at community theatre, but were uncertain about his future. "Being Chinese, we were a little apprehensive because we knew there were very few roles for Asians," father Bill Wong, a retired postal worker, told the *San Francisco Examiner*. "Even in our jobs, there were very few opportunities for promotion."

In high school, Wong felt he could play any role, in part because he didn't think of himself as *Asian* American. "Growing up and never seeing any positive images of Asians, I couldn't look in the mirror and acknowledge that I was Asian American just like anyone in Chinatown," Wong recalled to Zia. "I didn't have a strong sense of self-image as an Asian American." But when he auditioned for the role of a sailor in *Anything Goes* in a community theatre production and instead was selected to play a coolie, he found he couldn't bring himself to play the part. "I was so ashamed of that role," he confessed. "Probably not unlike a lot of young Asians, I wished that I was white."

After graduating from high school, Wong attended San Francisco State University for a year, but spent so much time in the drama department he received "Incompletes" in all his courses. Once he had saved enough money, he moved to New York in 1981. There he became one of thousands of aspiring young actors, working at odd jobs while performing in summer stock and dinner theatres. After a role in the chorus with national touring company of *La Cage Aux Folles* took him to Los Angeles in 1985, he decided to stay and study with Donald Hotton, a student of Lee Grant and Mira Rastova. While in Los Angeles, he was asked to audition for *M. Butterfly*, written by David Henry Hwang.

M. Butterfly and Beyond

Ever since his acclaimed performance as Song Lingling, a man who fooled a French diplomat into believing he was a woman while maintaining an intimate relationship for several years, Wong has acted in many challenging roles. He has played the lead in *Peter Pan,* a student in *Crash Course,* a Chinese gang lord in *Mystery Date,* an assistant wedding coordinator in *Father of the Bride,* a gay artist in

B.D. Wong

And the Band Played On, the nerdy geneticist in Steven Spielberg's *Jurassic Park,* and the brother of comedian Margaret Cho in "All American Girl," the first television sitcom featuring an Asian American family. Wong insists on performances that are true to the character and not one-dimensional stereotypes of Asians. "In my own small way, I want to try to share the essence of the character I'm playing," he told Zia.

Wong took a very public stand on his principles when the play *Miss Saigon* first opened on Broadway—featuring a white actor in "yellow face" playing the role of the Eurasian Engineer. No Asian male actors had been auditioned for the part, and Asian American actor and activists were outraged. In spite of possible recriminations for his own career, Wong spoke up against the casting for the play. Drama critics across the country from the *New York Times* to *Variety* attacked him, saying he wanted the part. "There was a lot of B.D. bashing," he remarked to Zia, "but I got a great deal of respect for my stand. No matter what people said about me, they had to acknowledge that we were raising some real issues about racial stereotypes and images and how casting decision are made." Wong has received numerous awards from Asian American community groups for his courageous stand.

Living in New York City with his manager Richard Jackson, Wong is modest about his achievements. "I'm just an actor, not a Nobel Prize winner," he told Zia. But he is committed to seeing roles for Asian Americans continue to evolve. "The representation of Asian Americans in the media means being able to bring a little kid to the theatre and having him or her see that Asian people have full human characteristics that are special and derive from a specific kind of culture. It's about affirmation as people, not stereotypes."

Sources:

Periodicals

Chin, Steven. "The World of B.D. Wong." *San Francisco Examiner,* September 5, 1993.

Lin, Sam Chu. "B.D. Wong. Flashing Dino-Sized Talent." *Asian Week,* June 18, 1993.

Other

Wong, B.D., telephone interview with Helen Zia, July 1994.

—Sketch by Helen Zia

Flossie Wong-Staal
(1947–)
Medical researcher

Flossie Wong-Staal is considered one of the nation's top AIDS researchers. She was the first researcher to clone an AIDS (Acquired Immune Deficiency Syndrome) virus and work out its anatomy in 1984. An internationally recognized leader in virology, Wong-Staal is a professor of medicine and biology and Florence Seeley Riford Chair in AIDS Research at the University of California, San Diego (UCSD). In the May 28, 1990, issue of the *Scientist,* she was named "one of the ten superstars of science."

Early Life

Wong-Staal has had a meteoric rise to the top of the scientific world. She was born Yee Ching Wong in China in 1947. At age five in 1952 her father took her and her brothers and sisters to Hong Kong to escape communist China.

The nuns at the Catholic school Wong was enrolled in insisted little Yee Ching Wong should have an English name. Although her family's first language was Cantonese, Wong's father spoke and read English fluently. He chose her English name from a newspaper report about a typhoon named "Flossie" which had hit Hong Kong the previous week. "I used to be embarrassed by it. Now, I'm

trying to change the image of the name," Wong-Staal told Yvonne Baskin in *Discovery.*

In high school she excelled in her studies and her teachers insisted she become a scientist. She told *National Geographic World:* "At first my teachers made the decision. High school students with good grades were steered into science." In 1965 Wong-Staal went to the University of California, Los Angeles (UCLA), and decided on her own to major in molecular biology. She did postgraduate work in the same area, she told *National Geographic World,* "because there were so many exciting discoveries being made."

Wong-Staal attended graduate school at UCLA, becoming a research assistant in bacteriology. Along the way she married a physician, whom she later divorced, though she has kept her married name. In 1972 she became a postdoctoral researcher at UCSD. Two years later, she joined Robert Gallo's team in the laboratory of the National Cancer Institute and began research into retroviruses.

Prominence in AIDS Research

Wong-Staal worked at the institute for more than a decade, during which time her reputation as an AIDS researcher grew. In 1990, she became chair of AIDS research at the UCSD, where she is focusing her efforts on the development of an AIDS vaccine and therapy. She is concentrating on understanding how HIV reproduces itself and causes disease, and on finding novel approaches for vaccine development and therapy. In the mid-1990s, she embarked on the exciting project of using gene therapy for treating AIDS.

To understand her work, it is important to understand how viruses infect organisms. The virus that causes AIDS is called HIV. HIV's genes are composed of ribonucleic acid (RNA), which is converted to deoxyribonucleic acid (DNA) after infection. (Most virus genes are composed of DNA.) When a virus infects an organism, it penetrates the cell and integrates its genes. The HIV virus destroys patients' T-cells (also known as white cells), an important component of the immune system. Normally, when a virus or bacterium enters the human body, the T-cells trigger manufacture of antibodies, or they directly kill the infected cells. Since HIV infects and destroys T-cells, the immune systems fails to fight off these invaders. Eventually persons infected with HIV die from infections and viruses which would be repelled by a normally functioning immune system.

Wong-Staal's goal is to introduce a gene that represses HIV in T-cells or "stem" cells (cells that give rise to all cells of the immune system), so they can no longer be infected. She and her colleagues have demonstrated that this strategy works well in the laboratory. Their protocol, which calls for the use of a ribozyme "molecular knife" to inactive HIVRNA, has received a lot of attention from the scientific community. It was the second such protocol to

Flossie Wong-Staal

receive government approval to be tested in AIDS patients. The first AIDS patients may be tested with this procedure in early 1995.

Wong-Staal told *Notable Asian Americans*: "I did not really have a role model in my family when I was growing up. All the women in the family were full-time housewives. Most of the men were in business, and rarely pursued post-college education. However, my parents did take pride in me when I did well in school and encouraged me to pursue an academic career. Surprisingly my being female was not an issue with them. I have a feeling that my mother, who was—and still is—very intelligent but did not have a chance to realize her professional aspirations was happy that I had more doors open to me."

Wong-Staal lives in San Diego and is the single parent of two daughters. Her eldest daughter Stephanie was born in 1972. Caroline was born in 1983. She told *Notable Asian Americans* that she is proud of her daughters' achievements and hopes they adopt her personal motto for success, "One should enjoy and find pride in what one does."

Sources:

Periodicals

Alvarez, Emilio, and Ann Crystal Angeles. "Science Superstar." *National Geographic World*, June 1993, pp. 25-27.
Baskin, Yvonne. "Intimate Enemies." *Discover*, December 1991, pp. 16–17.

Clark, Cheryl. "Researcher Stays Hot on the Trail of Deadly Virus." *San Diego Union-Tribune*, November 11, 1992, p. C-1.
Fikes, Bradley J. "In Fight Against AIDS, She Tries to Win One for Humanity." *San Diego Union-Tribune*, November 11, 1992, pp. C-1 to C-5.
Garrett, Laurie. "On the Front Line." *Sunday Newsday*, November 17, 1991, pp. 4-5.
International Journal of Oncology. 1991, vol. 3, no. 547, cover.
Johnson, Greg. "Sharpening the Attack on AIDS Virus." *Los Angeles Times.* November 11, 1992.
Pendlebury, David. "Science Leaders: Researchers to Watch In the Next Decade." *Scientist*, May 28, 1990, pp. 18-24.

Other

Wong-Staal, Flossie, written interview with Helen Zia, June 14, 1994.

—Sketch by Douglas Wu

S.B. Woo
(1937–)
Physicist, politician

For most of his adult life, S.B. Woo has devoted his efforts to research and teaching in physics. In 1984, however, he was elected lieutenant governor of Delaware. As such, he held the highest elected office at the state level ever achieved by an Asian American in the continental United States. He has also been involved at the local and national levels in efforts to help Asian Americans, specifically Chinese Americans, to understand and appreciate their heritage while living in and contributing to American society.

Shien-Biau (S.B.) Woo was born in Shanghai, China, on August 13, 1937, to Koo-ing Chang Woo, a homemaker, and C. K. Woo, a wool merchant. The family, including a brother and two sisters, moved to Taiwan in 1949, then to Hong Kong a few months later. His parents believed the United States offered a brighter future for S.B., especially offering more opportunities for college scholarships and better job prospects. So at eighteen, Woo traveled to the United States to study physics and math.

Woo received his bachelor of science, summa cum laude, in mathematics and physics from Georgetown College in Kentucky. He continued his studies at Washington University in St. Louis, earning his Ph.D. in physics in 1964. He then did postdoctoral study at the Joint Institute

S.B. Woo

for Laboratory Astrophysics (JILA), in Boulder, Colorado, from 1964 to 1966.

Physics Professor to Public Servant

For the next twenty years, Woo taught physics at the University of Delaware. During this time, he observed that the United States was lagging behind other countries in technology and education, especially in the sciences. He believed what was needed was for more scientists to be involved in government, in order to develop more educational and technological advances. With this as his motivation, and after becoming a U.S. citizen at the age of thirty-five, Woo chose a new career path and sought public office.

In 1984, Woo was elected to the office of lieutenant governor of Delaware, serving under a Republican governor. During his term, he was responsible for a report to the state on developing high tech industry. This led to the start of state investment in high tech areas. At the same time, Woo was disappointed in being unable to have much influence on education at the state level, due to the governor's decision. He told Susan Ketchum, "I was more involved in education outside of politics." He stepped down from office in order to run for the U.S. Senate, winning the primary but losing the general election. He later ran for a seat in the U.S. House of Representatives, with the same results.

Woo's role model during his years of public service was Abraham Lincoln. He was also influenced by his own brother, C.H. Woo, who, Woo told Ketchum, was "so willing to give of himself to help others." Other Asian Americans encouraged and helped him in his political aspirations, among them Anna Chennault, the wife of General Chennault; Congressman Norman Minata of California; An Wang, CEO of Weng Laboratories; Harvard professor Larry Ho; and David Lee and David Lam of Silicon Valley, California.

Woo did not limit his public involvement to elected office, but served his community in many other areas. He founded both the Chinese School of St. Louis in 1963 and the Chinese School of Delaware in 1967. Children of Chinese American families attended classes on weekends to learn about their culture. The schools never asked for federal aid, but were completely funded by the parents.

While at the University of Delaware, Woo was a member of a college steering committee and founded a faculty bargaining unit. He was president, chief negotiator and chief spokesman for the American Association of University Professors, University of Delaware Chapter, from 1971 until 1973. From 1976 to 1982 he served as trustee for the university. He also helped found a Chinese Community Center and co-chaired a citizen's committee to mediate a dispute between the editors and owners of the only statewide newspaper in Delaware.

Woo believes success is achieved through integrity and hard work, which he says were imbued in him by his Asian heritage. He also tries to help the people he works with to achieve their maximum potential. He carried this philosophy with him while an Institute Fellow at the Kennedy School of Government at Harvard University in 1989, and as president of the Organization of Chinese Americans (OCA) from 1990 to 1991. At OCA, he was guided by a simple vision—to help make the Asian American an equal partner in the making of the American dream.

Woo married Katy K.N. in 1963. They have a son, Chih-I, and a daughter, Chih-lan. They live in Newark, Delaware. Woo is currently professor of physics at the University of Delaware.

Sources:

The Office of S.B. Woo. Professional resume, 1994.

Woo, S.B., telephone interview with Susan Ketchum, June 22, 1994.

———, written interview with Susan Ketchum, June 1994.

—Sketch by Susan Ketchum

Chien-Shiung Wu
(1912–)
Physicist

Chien-Shiung Wu was born on May 31, 1912, in Liuhe, a small town near Shanghai, China. Her father, Wu Zhongyi, a participant in the revolution of 1911 that toppled the Manchu dynasty, was the founder and principal of a private girls school—one of very few in China, where educating girls has never been a high priority. Wu attended this school until the age of nine at which time she was sent to the Soochow Girls School. The school's curriculum was Western and often professors from major American universities lectured there. Wu received an excellent education there and in 1930 graduated at the top of her class.

Wu went on to college at Nanjing University where she studied physics and, again, became a top student. After graduating in 1934, she spent one year teaching in a provincial university and another year doing research in the field of X-ray crystallography at the National Academy of Sciences in Shanghai. Here she met a woman scientist who encouraged her to continue her studies in the United States because China did not have a physics program at the postdoctoral level. With the encouragement of her family and the help of a rich uncle, Wu sailed for America in 1936.

Higher Education

Her original intention was to study at the University of Michigan, where her friend at the National Academy had earned her Ph.D., but once Wu had arrived in America she stayed in San Francisco for a number of reasons. The University of California at Berkeley was an exciting place to be in the 1930s for a student of physics. Wu had also learned that at the University of Michigan, women were not allowed to use the student union building, a segregationist policy Wu found appalling. She also decided to stay in San Francisco to be with a man she had met upon arriving in the United States, Luke Yuan, who would later become her husband.

Wu began her work at Berkeley in the area of nuclear physics, which at the time was headed by the renowned particle physicist Ernest Livermore. She worked as an assistant to Emilio Segre, a future Nobel laureate. After her first year she was recommended by the physics department for a fellowship, which was turned down in a thinly shrouded racial slight. This was in 1937, the year of Japan's invasion of China. With that event, she was completely cut off from her family, whom, even after the war, she would never see again.

Chien-Shiung Wu

For her thesis work, Wu studied the electromagnetic energy given off when a particle passing through matter slows down, and the radioactive inert gases emitted when uranium nuclei split. She received her Ph.D. in 1940, staying on at Berkeley for two years as a research assistant. During this time she became well known in the scientific community as a reliable expert on fission. Despite her renown, Berkeley still refused to hire her; the only conceivable reason was racism and sexism. In 1942, she married Yuan and the couple moved to the East Coast. Yuan found a job working at the RCA Laboratories in Princeton, New Jersey, and Wu took a position teaching at Smith College in Northampton, Massachusetts. Smith did not have a research department, however, and research is what primarily interested Wu. She soon left Smith for a position at Princeton, which didn't have a research department either, but did allow her to live with her husband.

In 1944, Wu was recruited by the Division of War Research at Columbia University. She worked at a secret facility in New York in the development of sensitive radiation detectors for the atomic bomb project. After the war, she was one of the few physicists hired for war research retained by the university. Also after the war, Wu finally heard from her family. All had survived the war and she and her husband considered returning to China. The peace, though, was not long-standing and a civil war between the nationalist Chinese and communist insurgents persuaded them to stay in America.

Monumental Work

In the late 1940s and early 1950s Wu studied problems in the area of beta decay as theorized by the eminent physicist Enrico Fermi. As explained in *Nobel Prize Women in Science* by Sharon Bertsch McGrayne,

Experimentalists were confused because Fermi's theory predicted unequivocally the number of electrons that would come out at particular speeds [during beta decay]. According to Fermi, most of the electrons would burst out of the nucleus at very high speeds. Yet all the experiments produced enormous numbers of slow electrons.

In a series of careful experiments, Wu discovered that previous researchers had used radioactive materials of uneven thickness. Electrons traveling through thick sections had simply ricocheted off more atoms and lost more energy. When they emerged into the open air, they were traveling at slower speeds than electrons from thin sections containing fewer atom. Wu used a uniformly thin radiative material and got exactly the electron speeds predicted by Fermi.

This work was widely regarded as monumental within the scientific community and many people considered it worthy of recognition by the Swedish Academy, but it technically did not fit the requirements for a Nobel prize in that it wasn't a discovery or invention. As quoted in *Nobel Prize Women in Science,* a former graduate student of Wu's said of this work, "She had straightened up a big mess in physics quite elegantly, but it wasn't quite a discovery."

After her work with beta decay, Wu began work with Tsung Dao Lee of Columbia University and Chen Ning Yang of the Institute for Advanced Study at Princeton on the problem of the irregularity of K-meson decay in particle accelerators, a problem that called into question a long-held belief among physicists that the laws of parity and symmetry applied to subatomic particles as they did to all others. The K-meson appeared to behave inconsistently—in some particle collisions it decayed into two particles, and in others it decayed into three. This suggested to Wu, Lee, and Yang that the K-meson violated parity, which would make it unique in the subatomic world and would radically amend an unquestioned, accepted law of nature.

Wu began studying this phenomena at the National Bureau of Standards. She worked independently of Lee and Yang, but her experiments were based on their observations. Her laboratory was underfunded and much of the equipment was below standard. Nevertheless, in January of 1957, Wu's team had sufficient experimental corroboration to publicize their findings, which were that K-mesons did indeed violate parity. The announcement took the scientific world by storm. Physicists from around the world were stunned by the result. Similar work was begun by physicists throughout the country, who began finding other particles that violated this once sacred law of nature. Wu, Yang, and Lee became national celebrities, their findings reported on the front page of the *New York Times* and in *Time* and *Newsweek.* Later that year, Yang and Lee won the Nobel prize for physics. Wu was not included for her work because the idea behind her experimental research was not original to her.

More Research

Wu continued her research in other areas of physics. In 1963 she experimentally confirmed a difficult hypothesis involving beta decay hypothesized by Richard Feynman and Murray Gell-Mann, two world-renowned American theoretical physicists. Their theory had been widely tested for years by scientists around the world, but none had been able to confirm or disprove it. In confirming this theory, Wu contributed to the unified theory of fundamental forces.

Wu was given an endowed professorship by Columbia University in 1972. She has through the years received many honors for her groundbreaking work. She was the first woman to receive the Comstock Award from the National Academy of Sciences, the first woman to receive the Research Corporation Award, the first woman to serve as president of the American Physical Society, and the seventh woman selected into the National Academy of Science. Wu has received honorary degrees from more than a dozen universities, including Harvard, Yale, and Princeton, where she was the first woman ever to receive an honorary doctorate of science degree. She is also the first living scientist with an asteroid named after her.

Wu retired in 1981 and has since traveled extensively. She has lectured and taught at universities around the world, including in China and Taiwan. Wu has been an outspoken critic of the dismissive attitude institutional science has toward women. She encourages girls to break the imposed barriers and study science regardless of their teachers' attitudes.

Sources:

McGrayne, Sharon Bertsch. *Nobel Prize Women in Science: Their Lives, Struggles, and Momentous Discoveries.* New York: Carol Publishing Group, 1993.

—Sketch by Jim Henry

Y

Kristi Yamaguchi
(1971–)
Figure skater

Kristi Yamaguchi

Despite carrying the title of reigning world figure skating champion into the 1992 Winter Olympics in Albertville, France, Kristi Yamaguchi was not the favorite to win the gold medal. Japan's Midori Ito, the powerhouse skater who had been the first woman to perform a triple axel jump in competition, was favored to finish first, with Yamaguchi second.

When Ito first arrived in Albertville, she was in the best shape of her life, having recovered from an earlier injury that plagued her in the World Championships. During practice sessions, rival coaches were literally covering their eyes, so fearless and awe-inspiring were her famous jumps. But the pressure from her home country and the near-constant attention from the relentless media finally took their toll on Ito; she fell while attempting a triple Lutz—a jump that neither coach nor athlete could ever remember her missing—and ruined any hopes of winning the gold.

The modest Yamaguchi, on the other hand, did not arrive burdened with high expectations. Instead, she set her sights on enjoying the Games. She marched in the opening ceremonies, at the insistence of her parents, although her competition did not start for another eleven days. She stayed at the Olympic Village, went dancing with other athletes, and when it was time, went into her practice sessions clearly focused, her young mind untrammeled by the media pressure machines.

Yamaguchi's unburdened attitude translated well onto the ice. She received the highest scores from all nine judges for her short program. Although she fell on a triple loop—her easiest jump—during the long program, she made fewer errors than her rivals and captured the gold. Ito came in second, with Nancy Kerrigan trailing third.

California Golden Girl

Born on July 12, 1971 in Hayward, California, and raised predominantly in nearby Fremont (both cities in the San Francisco Bay area), Kristi Tsuya Yamaguchi is one of three children of Jim Yamaguchi, a dentist, and Carole Yamaguchi, a medical secretary. Ironically, the infant Yamaguchi who would become renowned for her elegant footwork on ice, was clubfooted at birth. Fortunately, the deformity was easily treated with corrective shoes and she did not suffer any long-term damage.

Although Yamaguchi's parents and grandparents were interned during World War II, along with 120,000 other Americans of Japanese descent, they rarely discussed that period of their lives with Yamaguchi and her two siblings. Instead, they encouraged the children to appreciate American values and work hard. "My grandfather didn't talk much about World War II, but he let me know how proud he was to see me make it as an Asian American representing the United States," Yamaguchi told the *Chicago Tribune* in 1991. "My parents let us know how fortunate we are now. Otherwise, they really don't look back on it too much."

In 1976, when Dorothy Hamill captured gold at the Winter Games, Yamaguchi's desire to someday compete in the Olympics was born. At age five, she began skating lessons and quickly showed natural talent. She entered her first competition at age eight, and by age nine she was getting up at four o'clock in the morning to practice at the local skating rink for several hours before going to school. She began training with Christy Kjarsgaard-Ness, her singles coach with whom she would train throughout her skating career.

In addition to singles training, Yamaguchi embarked on pairs skating in 1983. She found partner Rudi Galindo and under the direction of their coach, Jim Hulick, the two young athletes began to gain national attention in 1985 when they finished fifth in the National Junior Championships. By 1986, they won that competition. In the same year, Yamaguchi, who was also developing into a strong singles skater, became the Central Pacific junior champion and placed fourth in the national junior medal event. In 1988, she took gold in both the singles and pairs categories at the World Junior Championships. That year, the Women's Sports Foundation named her the Up-and-Coming Artistic Athlete of the Year.

Skating into the Spotlight

In 1989, Yamaguchi won her first senior title—the gold medal in the pairs competition at the National Championships in Baltimore, Maryland. She also placed second in the singles division and became the first woman in thirty-five years to win two medals at the nationals. Although Yamaguchi's overall scores were higher in the pairs competition, she caught the attention of both the audience and the media with her first-place performance during the free-skate segment of the ladies' singles contest in which she performed what was generally regarded as among the most technically difficult routines in the competition, if not the world. In spite of her unparalleled performance, what placed Yamaguchi second behind Jill Trenary, the then-U.S. champion, had been Yamaguchi's weakest event—the compulsory figures. The compulsories, or school figures, are specific exercises in which skaters must trace patterns on the ice, first with one foot and then the other; judges then come out to the ice to judge the etched patterns.

While Yamaguchi was commended for her outstanding athletic prowess, she was also heralded for elegance. In March of 1989, Yamaguchi competed for the first time in the World Championships, held in Paris that year. She placed sixth in the world in singles, and she and Galindo finished fifth in pairs.

The next three years leading up to Yamaguchi's dream of entering the 1992 Olympics proved personally difficult and professionally challenging. In the spring of 1989, her singles coach, Kjarsgaard-Ness, married a Canadian and moved to Edmonton, Alberta. Yamaguchi left California for Edmonton the day after her high school graduation. Her partner, Galindo, too, relocated to Edmonton, and the pair commuted between Canada and San Francisco to continue training with pairs coach, Hulick. In December of 1989, Hulick died of colon cancer. About the same time, Yamaguchi's maternal grandfather passed away.

Yamaguchi and Galindo could not find a pairs coach to succeed Hulick. That loss, together with their inability to better their fifth-place finish during the 1990 World Championships, led Yamaguchi to withdraw from pairs competition in May 1990 and devote herself fully to singles.

The Singles Sensation

With the elimination of the tedious compulsory figures from all major competitions after July 1990 and the end of her pairs training, Yamaguchi swiftly emerged in the second half of 1990 as one of the top three or four female singles skaters in the world. At the 1990 national and world competitions, she finished second and fourth, respectively.

At the 1991 nationals, Yamaguchi placed second to a new challenger, Tonya Harding, who became the second woman in history to land the triple axel in competition. Yamaguchi did not dwell on the defeat and immediately focused her full attention on the upcoming world competition in Munich. There she skated a near-perfect short program, then gave the best free-skate performance of her career. She garnered eight 5.9s (out of a possible 6.0) for technical merit, and seven 5.9s and one 6.0 for artistic impression to win first place.

The following year, as a precursor to the Olympics in Albertville, France, Yamaguchi captured gold again at the World Championships. In February 1992, Yamaguchi had not only achieved her dream of skating in the Winter Games, but she entered the games as both the reigning national and world champion.

Going into the competition as the seeming underdog, Yamaguchi somehow was able to escape most of the frenzied media-generated pressure that eventually overwhelmed the other competitors. While her rivals tumbled on the ice one after the other throughout opening night on February 19, Yamaguchi glided through the short program "as if all that mattered was making people smile," reported the *New York Times* in 1992. "With Strauss' 'Blue Danube Waltz' setting a soft, romantic mood, she fairly floated from one required element of her program to the next and won the highest scores from all nine judges." Two days later, she skated to "Malagueña," and although she fell on her easiest jump—the triple loop—which caused her to downscale an intended triple salchow to a double, she made far fewer errors than the other skaters and won gold. "I'm a little surprised everything happened so fast," she told the *New York Times* after her victory. "I've dreamed about this since I was a little girl and I first put on a pair of skates. To think about how far I've come, it's all still sinking in."

Ironically, Yamaguchi's most vivid memory from the Games was not having the gold medal placed around her neck; instead, it came moments after she finished her long program. Coming off the ice, waving to the crowd, the pressure was finally off. But rather than relief, Yamaguchi felt a sharp sense of loss. She told *Sports Illustrated,* "I knew I'd done well, and I was happy for that. But I remember thinking, Is this it? This is the Olympics. You've always dreamed of it, always, your whole life, I didn't want it to be over yet."

The following month, Yamaguchi successfully defended her world championship. She was the first American skater to defend the world title since Peggy Fleming did so in 1968. Although that accomplishment put her in the company of such skating luminaries as Sonja Henie and Carol Heiss, Yamaguchi modestly told the *Los Angeles Times* in 1992, "I've never thought of myself as a Henie or a Heiss. They are legends. But it's an honor that people are talking about me and those things."

After The Gold

In September 1992, Yamaguchi decided to turn professional, which meant she could no longer compete in amateur competitions such as the World Championships and the Olympic Games.

Since her Olympic victory, Yamaguchi has been busy, not only with professional skating performances throughout the country, but also with her numerous endorsement contracts. Although many business media experts predicted that she would never be offered the endorsement opportunities of previous U.S. figure skating gold medalists due to her Japanese American ancestry, Yamaguchi's many commercial appearances have proved otherwise.

Hours after her gold medal win in Albertville, the cereal giant Kellogg began printing Special K cereal boxes on which Yamaguchi appeared wearing the costume she skated in during the final round of competition. She became the only athlete to grace a Special K box.

Although post-Olympic endorsements were down in general for all athletes in 1992, most likely due to the sluggish economy, Yamaguchi nevertheless fared well. She signed lucrative contracts with Hoechst Celanese Corporation, makers of acetate fabrics for fabric designers, Dura-Soft contact lenses and Wendy's restaurants. She had glamorous four-page spreads in *Elle, Seventeen,* and *Vogue,* made television commercials for Dura-Soft and Wendy's and did the national talk-show circuit. She even had a walk-on next to famed Olympic diver, Greg Louganis, in Disney's family movie, *D2: The Mighty Ducks,* with Emilio Estevez. Yamaguchi is currently appearing in major cities throughout North America as part of the Discover Card Stars on Ice tour, joined by fellow Olympic medalists Paul Wylie and Scott Hamilton.

At times, Yamaguchi's new professional career seemed almost as grueling as her intensive training days: "I was pretty overwhelmed by the number of decisions I immediately had to make after the Olympics. Before, there'd been only one way: to reach my skating goals. Now there were all these different ways I could go," she told *Sports Illustrated* in 1992.

"I'm just an athlete. I don't think I've changed," added Yamaguchi. "It's still funny to have other people fussing over your hair, pretending you're a model for a day. I still feel I'm the same old kid, and someone who still wants to be one."

Sources:

Book

"Yamaguchi, Kristi." *Current Biography Yearbook,* New York: H.W. Wilson, 1992, p. 56.

Periodicals

Hersh, Phil. *Chicago Tribune,* February 15, 1991, section IV, p. 1+.
Janofsky, Michael. *New York Times,* February 20, 1992.
Miller, Cyndee. "Special K Loves Kristi, But Will Asian Heritage Hinder Other Endorsements?" *Marketing News,* March 30, 1992, pp. 1–2.
Swift, E.M. " A Golden Snub?" *Sports Illustrated,* March 23, 1992, p. 7.
———. "All that Glitters," *Sports Illustrated.* December 14, 1992, pp. 70–79.

—Sketch by Terry Hong

Hisaye Yamamoto
(1921–)
Writer

Hisaye Yamamoto began writing fiction at the age of fourteen and received her first acceptance from a literary magazine at the age of twenty-seven. In between, "I got a whole slew of rejection slips," she recalled with a laugh during an interview with Terry Hong. Throughout her long career, she has written dozens of short stories, many of which were published in journals and short story collections. In 1988, her best known short stories were collected in a much-acclaimed slim volume, *Seventeen Syllables and Other Stories.*

Despite the length of Yamamoto's career, she cannot be described as a prolific writer; however, she has consistently produced some of the most anthologized stories in the Asian American literary canon. According to the editors of the seminal Asian American compilations, *Aiiieeeee: An Anthology of Asian American Writers,* and *The Big Aiiieeeee: An Anthology of Chinese American and Japanese American Literature,* Yamamoto's "modest body of work is remarkable for its range and gut understanding of Japanese America. . . . Technically and stylistically, hers is among the most highly developed of Asian American writing." As well, Yamamoto's early stories "form the only portrait of pre-war rural Japanese America in existence."

Yamamoto was one of the first Asian American writers to gain national literary recognition after World War II. In spite of the rampant anti-Japanese sentiment throughout the United States immediately after the war, Yamamoto's stories prevailed. The story, "Yoneko's Earthquake," was chosen for inclusion as one of the Best American Short Stories of 1952. Three other works—"Seventeen Syllables" (1949), "The Brown House" (1951), and "Epithalamium" (1960)—were also chosen for the yearly lists of "Distinctive Short Stories" included in the *Best American Short Stories* collections. Since 1948 when Yamamoto wrote "The High-Heeled Shoes," her first story accepted by a major publication, she has emerged as one of the clearest, most resilient voices of Asian America.

A Working Woman

Hisaye Yamamoto was born on April 27, 1921, in Redondo Beach, California, to immigrant parents from the Kumamoto region of Japan. She remembered that the family "moved around a lot because in those days, California state law forbade aliens from owning property and becoming citizens. We would lease land for two or three years and then move on again." Although the family moved from various locations throughout southern California, Yamamoto was able to attend Compton Junior College, where she majored in French, Spanish, German, and Latin.

At the age of twenty, Yamamoto and her family were living in Oceanside, California, when they were relocated to Poston, Arizona, soon after the bombing of Pearl Harbor by Japan. At the internment camp, Yamamoto served as a reporter and columnist for the camp newspaper, the *Poston Chronicle,* and published "Death Rides the Rails to Poston," a serialized mystery. In addition to being a writer, Yamamoto was also an avid reader during her camp years. She told Hong, "There were a bunch of old *New Yorkers* in the camp library. I would sit on a plank on top of piled-up crates and read all the small print and practically fall off laughing. It would really make my day. It really hit my funny bone." At the Poston camp, Yamamoto developed a lasting friendship with Wakako Yamauchi, who would later become a noted writer and playwright.

Yamamoto left the Poston camp with one of her brothers for a month and a half to work in Springfield, Massachusetts. "I was supposed to be a cook and my brother a valet to a wealthy widow. We had wanted to go [to Massachusetts], but after we learned of the death of another brother fighting in Italy, we went back to camp as our father requested. I guess he wanted to keep the family together," she recalled.

When the war was finally over, Yamamoto returned with her family to the Los Angeles area. From 1945 to 1948, she worked for the *Los Angeles Tribune,* an African American weekly. "It was a very educational experience. I learned the extent of racism, besides what happened to us during the war. In those days, there were lynchings going on in the South," she told Hong. For three years, Yamamoto was, as she said, "the extra arm who did a little of this and that," predominantly proofreading articles and writing a column of her own. "The column was something very personal. It was on anything I wanted to write about at the time." Occasionally, Yamamoto was sent out of the office to do "man-on-the-street interviews" and gather the "world-news roundup."

In 1948, Yamamoto began to publish her writing in well-known literary journals, including *Partisan Review, Kenyon Review, Harper's Bazaar, Carleton Miscellany, Arizona Quarterly,* and *Furioso.* Awarded one of the first John Hay Whitney Foundation Opportunity Fellowships, Yamamoto was able to write full time beginning in 1950. Between 1953 and 1955, she lived on a rehabilitation farm on Staten Island, New York, with her adopted son, Paul, and worked as a volunteer for the Catholic Workers of New York. She married Anthony DeSoto and returned to Los Angeles. Eventually, she became the mother of four more children.

Because she was both a writer and a mother, she told Hong, "shorter pieces were more viable since I always had kids to bring up which meant little time in front of a typewriter. So I never thought about writing a novel." Although Yamamoto describes herself simply as a housewife, she has been lauded by numerous scholars, Asian American and non-Asian American alike, as one of the finest short story writers of the postwar era. "[H]er stories are equal to the masterpieces of Katherine Mansfield, Toshio Mori, Flannery O'Connor, Grace Paley, and Ann Petry," wrote King-Kok Cheung, professor of English and Asian American Studies at the University of California at Los Angeles, in her introduction to the compilation, *Seventeen Syllables and Other Stories.*

Yamamoto, the Storyteller

According to Cheung, three themes recur in Yamamoto's work: "The interaction among various ethnic groups in the American West, the relationship between Japanese immigrants and their children and the uneasy adjustment of the Issei in the New World, especially the constrictions experienced by Japanese American women."

The interaction of diverse ethnic backgrounds in Yamamoto's stories varies from outright racism and bigotry as in "Wilshire Bus," in which a drunk white man demands that a Chinese couple go back to where they came from, to inter-ethnic bonding as in "Epithalamium," in which a Japanese American volunteer falls in love with an alcoholic Italian American. Yamamoto portrays intergenerational relationships in stories such as "Las Vegas Charley," about the uneasy bond between a drinking gambler and his exasperated son, or "Morning Rain," about a visiting father and his daughter who becomes newly aware of her father's loss of hearing. In a number of stories, Yamamoto also focuses on the difficulties of first-generation Japanese American women as in "Yoneko's Earthquake," in which a lonely woman begins an affair with her husband's worker, is forced to have an abortion by her husband and soon thereafter, loses her only son. In "Seventeen Syllables," the immigrant mother who finds solace in writing seventeen-syllabled haiku is misunderstood by her modern American-born daughter and punished by her indifferent husband when she wins a haiku contest sponsored by a Japanese American newspaper.

Although Yamamoto's writing is not exactly autobiographical, she does draw on her own experiences. "I can only write about what I know. I can't write science fiction or great dynasty novels or things like that," she chuckled. "I write when something sticks in my craw and I think it might be worth writing down. Writing is a compulsion or an itch. I love to read, so writing is a pretty wonderful thing to be doing."

Year after year, Yamamoto continues to both read and write. She is currently engrossed with Asian American literature: "I'm really impressed by Maxine Hong Kingston, Gus Lee, David Wong Louie, Amy Tan, and Gish Jen." She continues to write short stories, which are published in anthologies and literary journals. When asked if she would ever consider teaching, Yamamoto answered with her usual modesty, "Oh, no. The farthest I've gone is junior college. You need more degrees to teach." Then she added with a laugh, "Besides, it's time I retired anyway. At seventy-two, you don't begin a new career."

Sources:

Books

Chin, Frank, Jeffery Chan, Lawson Inada, and Shawn Wong. "Hisaye Yamamoto." In *Aiiieeeee! An Anthology of Asian American Writers.* New York: Mentor, 1974.

———. "Hisaye Yamamoto." In *The Big Aiiieeeee! An Anthology of Chinese American and Japanese American Literature.* New York: Meridian, 1991.

Yamamoto, Hisaye. *Seventeen Syllables and Other Stories.* Introduction by King-Kok Cheung. Latham, New York: Kitchen Table: Women of Color Press, 1988.

Other

Yamamoto, Hisaye, telephone interview with Terry Hong, April 27, 1994.

—Sketch by Terry Hong

Minoru Yamasaki
(1912–1987)
Architect

Minoru Yamasaki was a self-made architect who distinguished himself in the 1950s with a series of graceful textile-like buildings, and then gained worldwide fame as the architect of the twin towers of New York's World Trade Center. The two identical 110-story buildings standing side-by-side at the southern tip of Manhattan are arguably the world's most recognizable modern skyscrapers.

Minoru Yamasaki was born in Seattle, Washington, on December 1, 1912, to first-generation Japanese immigrant parents. His father had owned much land in Japan, but in America the family lived in near poverty. Their first home was a tenement in the Yesler Hill section of Seattle that had no hot water and no indoor bathrooms. They did not live there long, however, for Yamasaki's father was a very hard worker and he often held two or three jobs in his determination to improve the living standard of his family.

In high school, Yamasaki did very well, as was expected of him. He especially excelled in math and science courses. It was during his high school years that he had an experience that altered the course of his life. As he recalled in his autobiography, *A Life in Architecture*, "My Uncle Koken had just graduated in architecture from the University of California. After graduation he had been promised a job in Chicago, and he stopped to visit us on the way there. He unrolled the drawings he had made at the university and I almost exploded with excitement when I saw them. Right then and there I decided to become an architect."

After graduation Yamasaki enrolled in the University of Washington to study architecture. He initially had a very difficult time, especially in the creative classes such as sculpture, drawing, and art, but he overcame his hardships with devotion and diligence. He became an excellent engineer and routinely headed his classes in subjects dealing with straight sciences. When he again had trouble in his later years with building design, he considered abandoning his dream of becoming an architect and settling for the more mundane life of an engineer. A professor in whom he confided, however, encouraged him to stick it out, surprising Yamasaki by saying he thought Yamasaki would go on to become one of the best architects the school had ever graduated.

The Yamasaki family at this time, like many American families, was experiencing financial difficulties. The Great

Minoru Yamasaki

Depression was three years old and work was scarce. Yamasaki supported himself through college working in the canneries of Alaska. It was grueling work with long hours and poor pay, about fifty dollars a month, plus twenty-five cents for overtime. The workers lived miserable lives in bunkhouses equipped with little more than straw mats.

New York in the Depression

Yamasaki graduated from college in 1934 and headed for New York with very little money and a few letters of reference. There was almost no work in New York for architects, so he was forced to take a job wrapping dishes for a Japanese company that distributed Noritake china in the United States. He also enrolled in night classes at New York University to get his master's in architecture.

His first architectural job in New York came in 1935 when he was hired by Githens and Keally. One year later he went to Shreve, Lamb and Harmon, architects of the Empire State Building. He stayed there until 1943, working primarily in the production and checking of shop drawings, the drawings that detail the actual construction of a building. His next move was to Harrison, Fouilhoux and Abramowitz, architects of Rockefeller Center. From there he went to Raymond Loewy Associates, a firm that specialized in industrial design, which Yamasaki hated.

Leaving New York

In 1945 Yamasaki went to Detroit to become the head of design at Smith, Hynchman and Grylls. Four years later he began his own firm of Yamasaki, Hellmuth and Leinweber, consisting mainly of people from the offices of Smith, Hynchman. The firm's first major job was the St. Louis Airport, built in 1953. Writing about the airport in the International Directory of Architects, John Winter described it as consisting of "three great shells, separated from one another by glazing.....By placing service functions below the main concourse level, the architects achieved a simple, breathtaking space uncluttered by baggage handling and the mundane functions which clutter up so many airports."

Major works of Yamasaki's in the 1950s include three buildings in Detroit—the American Concrete Institute, the Reynolds Metals Company offices, and McGregor Memorial Building for Wayne State University—and one in Japan, the American consulate in Kobe. In the 1960s, as his international reputation grew, Yamasaki designed the Dharhan Air Terminal in Dharhan, Saudi Arabia; the United States Pavilion at the World Agricultural Fair in New Delhi, India; and the Queen Emma Gardens in Honolulu, Hawaii. He also designed the Woodrow Wilson School of International Affairs at Princeton, New Jersey.

The World Trade Center

In 1962, the Port Authority of New York and New Jersey asked Yamasaki Associates, as the firm was then called, if they would be interested in the architectural development of a project with an estimated cost of $280 million. Yamasaki was shocked by the offer, since his office had only fifty-five people at the time. He assumed that a mistake had been made, but when he went to meet with the men in charge of the project, he found out that they were looking for a chief architect who would put together and head a design group of the best architects in the country. There were more than forty architectural firms considered, but Yamasaki Associates was chosen for the job, in conjunction with Emory Roth and Sons.

The buildings took fourteen years to complete, and were at the time of their construction, the tallest buildings in the world. Aside from formulating the design, Yamasaki was confronted with all sorts of logistical problems, including digging the foundation, the choice of construction materials light enough to be supported at such heights but strong enough to withstand the wind, and many other such considerations. Writing about the Trade Center, Yamasaki said, "I believe the Trade Center will come to be seen and experienced as one of the really exciting places in New York, which I am confident will continue to be the most marvelous, stimulating, contemporary city in the world.

Chen Ning Yang

Notable works Yamasaki designed after the World Trade Center include the Century Plaza Towers in Century City, California; the Ranier Bank Tower in his home town of Seattle, Washington; and the Eastern Province International Airport in Saudi Arabia.

Minoru Yamasaki died of cancer on February 6, 1987, at the age of seventy-three. He married Teruko Hereshiki in 1941, and they had three children: two sons, Taro (who won a Pulitzer Prize for photography while with the *Detroit Free Press*) and Kim, and a daughter, Carol Yamasaki Chakrin.

Sources:

Books

Winter, John. "Yamasaki, Minoru." *The International Dictionary of Architects*. Detroit: St. James Press, 1993.
Yamasaki, Minoru. *A Life in Architecture*. New York: Weatherhill, 1979.

Periodicals

Rimer, Sars. "Minoru Yamasaki," Obituary. *New York Times*, February 9, 1987.

—Sketch by Jim Henry

Chen Ning Yang
(1922–)
Physicist

Chen Ning Yang shared the Nobel Prize for physics with Tsung Dao Lee in 1957 for their extensive work in particle physics. Hailed by the Royal Swedish Academy of Sciences for their success in unlocking "a most puzzling deadlock in the field of elementary particle physics where now experimental and theoretical work is pouring forth." The Nobel laureates were cited for their penetrating investigations into the law of the conservation of parity, which has led to important discoveries regarding elementary particles.

Early Life

Born in Ho-Fei in the province of Anhwei in northern China, on September 22, 1922, Yang was the oldest of five children born to Ko-Chuan Yang, a mathematics professor. In 1929 the Yang family moved to Peking where Yang's father taught at Tsinghua University. Yang attended the Chung Te Middle School.

When China was invaded by Japan in 1937, the location of Tsinghua University was moved to another town, K'unming, and consolidated with the National Southwest Associated University. In 1942 Yang earned a bachelor of science in physics for which he had to write a thesis on group theory and molecular spectra. He then went on to get a master of science in 1944, also from the National Southwest Associated University, and he wrote his thesis on contributions to the statistical theory of order-disorder transformations.

In 1945 Yang received a fellowship from the National Southwest Associated University to study under Enrico Fermi at the University of Chicago. He accepted the offer and in 1948 he completed his Ph.D. thesis, titled "On the Angular Distribution in Nuclear Reactions and Coincidence Measurements," under the supervision of Edward Teller. Yang spent another year at the University of Chicago as an instructor in physics.

Yang joined the Institute for Advanced Study in Princeton, New Jersey in 1949. In 1953 he spent the academic year as a senior physicist at Brookhaven National Laboratory in Long Island, New York. Yang returned to the Institute for Advanced Study in 1955 as a professor of physics, where he spent eleven years. He then joined the State University of New York (SUNY) at Stony Brook, Long Island, as Albert Einstein Professor of Physics and director of the Institute of Theoretical Physics.

During Yang's course of study at the National Southwest Associated University in K'un-ming, and at the University of Chicago, Tsung Dao Lee was his fellow student. When Yang was at Stony Brook, he started meeting regularly with Lee, who was at Columbia University, to continue a discussion of physics which they had begun while at the University of Chicago. In May 1956, they started working on a puzzle concerning the law of conservation of parity.

Nobel Prize Work

The conservation of parity, among other things, means that nature is symmetrical and that experimental trials should bear this out. First formulated in 1925 the law of conservation of parity had been universally accepted because it had led to useful theoretical and experimental results. Studying this law in great detail, Yang and Lee found that the total parity of elementary particles could not always be the same before and after an interaction. This was something that defied the law of conservation of parity. Considering this unresolvable dilemma, Yang and Lee investigated the experimental support for this law. Being theorists, they had outside help to get all the experimental evidence they needed to explain the failure of the law of conservation of parity. This stimulated a surge of theoretical and experimental research, thereby giving rise to new avenues of thought. This resultant discovery earned Yang and Lee the Nobel Prize in physics in 1957.

Yang's interest was in the areas of theory of fields and particles, statistical mechanics, and symmetry principles. A new principle he established in 1954 with another scientist, Robert Mills, gave birth to the Gauge Theory, which is believed to underlie all the basic interactions in nature.

When Yang came to the United States in 1945, he had decided he would like an American name that would be easier for Americans to pronounce. Out of admiration for Benjamin Franklin whose biography he had read, he changed his first name to Franklin and was called Frank by his American friends. In 1950 Yang wed Chih Li Tu. They have two sons and a daughter. Yang became an American citizen in 1964.

To help promote mutual understanding and friendship between his native country and the United States, Yang has visited the Peoples Republic of China annually since 1971.

Yang has received honorary doctorates from Princeton University, the University of Minnesota, the University of Durham, and several other institutions. Two of his most prestigious awards are the Albert Einstein Commemorative Award from Yeshiva University (1957), and the Rumford Medal of the American Academy of Arts and Sciences (1980). He is a member of the National Academy of Sciences, the American Philosophical Society, the Brazilian Academy of Sciences, the Venezuelan Academy of Sciences, as well as a fellow of the American Physical Society.

At the Nobel Prize Awards ceremony, O.B. Klein of the Royal Swedish Academy of Sciences said, "The result of their investigation was unexpected, namely that the validity of the symmetry assumption, even in the best known process, had no experimental support whatsoever. The reason being that all experiments had been so arranged as to give the same result whether the assumption was valid or not."

Sources:

Wasson, Tyler, ed. "Yang, Chen Ning," *Nobel Prize Winners: An H.W. Wilson Biographical Dictionary,* New York: H.W. Wilson, 1987.

—Sketch by Visi R. Tilak

Janet Yang
(1956–)
Producer/filmmaker

Yin and yang, the ancient Chinese concept of complementary attributes which together form the whole, is one of the primary leitmotifs in the life of Janet Yang, president of Ixtlan, the film production company of Academy Award-winning director Oliver Stone. "Janet has thousand-year-old patience and ten thousand years of virtue; she is my 'yang' to my 'yin'," her partner, Stone, was quoted as saying in *AsianWeek.* Yang, one of the most influential Asian American film executives in Hollywood, was recently recognized for her work as executive producer of *The Joy Luck Club,* a film based on Amy Tan's best-selling novel. It is the story of the conflict and tragedy endured by four Chinese women who fled their country in the 1940s and the influence of that experience on the generational relationships between the women and their American-born daughters. The film, which grossed $35 million, was the first movie from a major Hollywood studio to break the stereotypical Chinese image on the screen created by such characters as Charlie Chan and Susie Wong (*Flower Drum Song*). It is also a story which vividly echoes the personal memories and experiences of Janet Yang.

Early Life

Yang was born July 13, 1956, in New York City to mainland Chinese parents who had fled their country in 1945 after the Communist takeover. Her mother, Anna, came to the United States from Hunan to study and eventually established a career at the United Nations. Her father, T.Y., an engineer from Shanghai, emigrated in 1947. Yang was raised on Long Island in the only Chinese family in a predominantly Jewish community. As an American-born Chinese or second-generation immigrant, Yang had difficulty as a child reconciling family values of modesty, duty, and familial piety with those of others around her, but at the time it never occurred to her to explore her heritage or question the differences between herself and her peers.

"I was somewhat in denial of the fact that I was Chinese. I didn't ask my parents . . . what it was like being Chinese. I was, I think, more interested in trying to be a chameleon . . . not be Chinese . . . blend in with the rest of the crowd," she reflected in *Asian-American Players.*

However, a trip to China in 1972 when Yang was fifteen changed all that. Following President Richard Nixon's landmark trip to China, Yang and her mother capitalized on the opening up of relations between the countries and returned to Hunan. She developed a consuming interest in Chinese culture, traditions, and values and began to pour through Chinese classics. Upon her return to the United States, she submerged herself in the study of the Chinese language for a summer term at Middlebury College. After graduating from Phillips Exeter Academy, Yang pursued Chinese studies for two years each at Brown and Harvard, where she learned of a position available in Beijing with the Foreign Language Press (FLP). She took the job and spent a year and a half in China. When not polishing the English in books and magazines designed for export by the FLP, Yang plunged into the underground culture of the prolific Chinese film industry. Inspired by a desire to market Chinese films in the United States, Yang returned to New York and earned a master's in business administration at Columbia University. She then moved to San Francisco where she took a job with World Entertainment, running the company and traveling regularly to China to develop and buy films by Chinese filmmakers for American audiences. A few years later, her talent and unique background evident, she was lured by MCA/Universal Studios to be their Far Eastern director. There Yang broke the film trade barrier, bringing the distribution of American films to China. Before leaving Universal, Yang also persuaded the studio to produce *Dragon: The Bruce Lee Story,* a movie biography about the Asian movie star who crossed many barriers to become one of the world's most reknowned martial artists.

A Start in the Film Industry

Fluent in Mandarin and competent in both Shanghaineze and Cantonese, Yang, now considered a China expert, was asked by Steven Spielberg's Amblin Entertainment to serve as a consultant with the Chinese government on the film *Empire of the Sun,* one of the first big-budget American films to provide a glimpse into China. This job also opened the door for Yang into film production. However, she soon became frustrated with the politics of the film industry and the cynicism and lack of passion that were the earmarks of Hollywood decision-making. Yang sought

a new alliance with Oliver Stone at Ixtlan Production Company as vice-president of production.

"It was actually my idea that I planted in his ear to hire someone," she said in an article in *Sunday Morning Post Magazine.* "I knew that he needed help—that he would get distracted from his directing work . . . and I managed to convince him. . . . He goes by instinct. . . . He just did it."

Yang, now president of Ixtlan, works with Stone in a complementary and harmonious relationship echoing the concept of yin and yang. He is the artist and she is the voice of reason; he creates while she manages. Pouring through hundreds of scripts, ideas, books, and magazines each month, Yang and her staff select ideas that appeal on a gut level and, together with Stone, develop those "that say something about humanity, empowerment, transformation, and the human spirit," related Yang in *AsianWeek.* Among the films co-produced by Yang and Stone are *The Joy Luck Club, The Doors, JFK, South Central, Zebrahead, The Mayor of Castro Street,* and *Johnny Spain.*

Nineties and Beyond

"In the eighties, I felt we were working against the grain. I think the nineties are going to be a good time for us," Yang said in *San Francisco Weekly,* referring to the social and political consciousness that permeates much of what Ixtlan produces. "I sense a change in people. We don't have to be victims; we can find the strength and conviction to work for what we believe in."

As for the future, Yang is not sure what lies ahead in terms of her career. But she knows exactly who she is and her sense of mission is clear. "I know being Asian and a woman has propelled me," she admitted in *AsianWeek.* "I thought I was going against the grain somehow, and I think it did drive me in a lot of ways. I really believe that you have to know what you want. I followed my instincts, my guts, my heart. Along the way there were different choices. It's not a matter of what you should do, but what you want to do."

Sources:

Periodicals

Cohen, Karen. "'Joy Luck' Producer's Parents Tell Story of her Career." *Rossmoor News,* October 6, 1993.

Fox, Michael. "Ten Who Mattered." *San Francisco Weekly,* December 29, 1993.

'Ixtlan's Janet Yang." *Asian American Players,* 1993.

Klapwald, Thea. "Yin and Yang." *Sunday Morning Post Magazine,* October 10, 1993.

Lin, Sam Chu. "Janet Yang Makes Waves in Hollywood." *AsianWeek,* December 19, 1993.

—Sketch by Nancy Moore

Linda Tsao Yang
(1926–)
Businesswoman

Linda Tsao Yang

"**I** was very young, maybe about nine or ten years old. I had been to downtown Shanghai with my mother, and there I saw a beautiful building with a shiny brass plaque which said 'Shanghai Women's Bank.' I then asked my mother, 'Why is there a women's bank?' She said that it is because women often don't feel comfortable going to a bank, because banks are always run by men. Then another interesting thought flashed through my mind—maybe I should be a banker," laughed Linda Tsao Yang in an interview with Visi R. Tilak. This thought became a reality for Yang, who is now the U.S. representative to the prestigious Asia Development Bank.

Linda Tsao was born in Shanghai, China, on September 5, 1926, where she grew up with her two brothers and two sisters. As a child she always enjoyed reading, especially history and biographies, and cooking. Ever since she was young she has felt very strongly about issues of social justice regarding women. "When I was young I heard a lot of stories about young girls being abused. Even as I was being driven to school in Shanghai, I could see other girls of my age working very hard as maids, getting up early and going to bed late, some of them not even being treated well by their masters. I always wondered, 'Why?'" recalled Yang.

Education

Yang was educated in Shanghai and attended St. Johns University, where she received her bachelor's degree in economics. In 1946, Yang arrived in the United States to attend the Graduate School of Business at Columbia University in New York, where she majored in banking and international economics.

Yang's family was always very supportive of her, particularly her older brother, who had always encouraged her to go as far as she could. "Being a minority and a woman in the United States, especially in those days, he told me that I need to work at least three times harder than the others to prove myself," Yang remembered. She had learned from both her brother and mother that it was very important never to lose hope or be discouraged and to always be self-confident. "I have learned to believe in who I am. Possessing self-dignity and self-esteem will help you believe in yourself," she asserted.

Yang grew up believing that she could do what she wanted to if she put her heart into it. She said that her mother was her role model: "My mother who is ninety years old now, never really worked outside the house. Nevertheless, she always told me and my sisters that it is very important for a young woman to be educated and have skills and to be able to manage her own affairs so she can be independent," she recalled. She was influenced very much by her upbringing, as were her sisters, one of whom is a business executive and the other a medical doctor.

"I know that I am not a super woman," said Yang, laughing. "People's lives go through different stages. At some points in life, some things are more important than others. After my children were born, I took a twelve-year sabbatical from work to be a full-time mother till my children were grown up enough to take care of themselves. My career certainly did take a back seat. My friends were moving on and new people were moving in. However it was a choice I had made." Yang said she is thankful that she had the luxury to make this choice, unlike many women today who are unable to, because of economic or personal reasons.

During her twelve years as a homemaker she maintained steady contact with her network of professional colleagues. She continued to keep pace with the developments in her profession and attended seminars and conferences to continually update her knowledge as best she could. When she went back to work, she was able to draw upon her professional network as well as the knowledge she had accumulated.

From Homemaker to Banker

In the late 1970s Yang began a new venture, perhaps sparked by the memory of the Shanghai Women's Bank. "I got together with a group of friends and decided to establish a bank. It was a savings bank but we wanted to pay special attention to women customers. It was a tremendous experience," said Yang who was the organizer and founder of Mother Lode Savings Bank in Sacramento which was subsequently acquired by the U.S. Bancorp at a premium.

In March 1980, she was appointed commissioner of the California Savings and Loan, becoming the first minority and the first woman named to that position. She was confirmed by the state Senate, and she headed a department with a hundred-member professional team of lawyers, examiners, and appraisers, and a support staff of sixty. She regulated the then $80 billion chartered savings and loan industry from early 1980 to the end of 1982.

In 1983 Yang decided to establish her own business. She founded Linda Tsao Yang and Associates, a modest financial consulting practice. Her clientele grew steadily, thanks to her wide professional network. Yang also became the first Asian Pacific American to be appointed to the board of administration of the Public Employees' Retirement System, State of California (CALPERS). As vice-chair of the CALPERS investment committee, she took an active role in formulating investment strategies for the system's then-$13 billion portfolio. Yang refers to this period as "a wonderful period of public service."

Yang was also the director of the 1990 Institute, a California-based non-profit think tank. She chaired the Research Management Committee of the institute which has launched, with the cosponsorship of the Federal Reserve Bank of San Francisco, major policy-oriented studies on China's economic reforms. She also served on the board of directors of the Blue Cross of California, and its Budget and Finance Committee. During her service on the board, the organization undertook substantial asset restructuring to strengthen its capital reserves and to improve service to its policyholders.

Yang has also served on the Advisory Committee on Real Estate and Urban Economics for the School of Business at the University of California in Berkeley, and on the Dean's Advisory Committee of the College of Agricultural and Environmental Sciences at the University of California in Davis. She was a member of the California Commission on the Teaching Profession (Commons Commission) funded by the Hewlett Packard Foundation. Major recommendations of the commission to improve K-12 education have been made into law in California.

Yang was a delegate to the Democratic National Convention in 1984, 1988, and 1992. After the 1984 convention, she was appointed to serve on the Fairness Commission and the Compliance Assistance Commission of the Democratic National Committee. She also wrote for the *Hong Kong Economic Journal,* a Chinese language newspaper widely read by business, academic, and governmental leaders in Hong Kong.

Yang's deep beliefs have helped her define her values. "An individual's choice in what she wants to do must be in harmony with the interests of the people around her, whether it is her community or her family," she asserted. She firmly believes in the saying, "Don't do to others what you don't want others to do to you," she explained, "This is also the one common teaching of all religions and an extremely powerful guide by which to live life."

Yang has been married for forty-one years. Her husband, An Tzu Yang, is currently Professor Emeritus in the department of mechanical engineering at the University of California, Davis. They have two sons aged thirty-two and twenty-seven. Her older son, an international lawyer and the younger son, a mortgage loan officer, both live in California.

"My Asian Pacific heritage and the essence of the Chinese culture really strengthens my backbone," Yang said. Although she left China when she was very young, she has always carried with her the culture and tradition of China which taught her that an individual never exists alone. "Being a part of a community, what I do not only affects myself, but also the community as a whole. Thus there is always a sense of mutual responsibility and obligation within me." She added, "Whether I am successful or not, at least I can tell myself I have done the very best."

Sources:

Yang, Linda Tsao. Biographical material provided by Yang, June 1994.
———, telephone interview with Visi R. Tilak, June 1994.

—Sketch by Visi R. Tilak

Melinda Yee
(1963–)
Public policy activist

Melinda Yee has spent her career in government working on behalf of Asian Americans from all sectors of society. A 1985 graduate of the University of California with a bachelor's degree in communications, Yee received her master's degree in public administration from the University of Southern California. In 1988 she was named

Melinda Yee

executive director of the Organization of Chinese Americans (OCA), a national, nonpartisan advocacy organization headquartered in Washington, D.C. There she was exposed to civil rights, human rights, and other issues concerning the Asian community in the United States. Yee also testified extensively before Congress on pro-family immigration policies.

After leaving the OCA in 1990, Yee served as the director of constituencies for the Democratic National Committee. She also began working for the Democratic party in preparation for the 1992 presidential elections. In 1991 she coordinated the first national Asian Pacific American Democratic Summit, and in 1992 she organized the political program and gala reception for the Democratic National Convention. During the 1992 Clinton/Gore campaign, Yee was named national director of Asian Pacific American Political Affairs. She organized many political and fund raising events across the country and designed programs to maximize voter participation in the election. Yee also served as the chief adviser to President Clinton on issues that impacted the Asian Pacific Community.

Political Appointee

After Clinton won the election, Yee was appointed special assistant in the Office of Presidential Personnel in the White House. In this capacity she processed thousands of applications and made personnel recommendations for White House appointments to agencies, boards, and commissions. With her assistance in the personnel office, Clinton appointed many Asian Americans to government positions during his first year in office. He named Doris Matsui, wife of U.S. House representative Robert Matsui, as the deputy assistant of the president for public liaison. Maria Haley, a Filipino American, was appointed deputy director for personnel of Clinton's transition team. Clinton named Barbara Chow as a special assistant of domestic policy, Shirley Sagawa as a special assistant of legislative affairs, and Brant Lee as a special assistant in the Office of the Staff Secretary. In addition, Clinton offered the position of secretary of transportation to House representative Norman Mineta, but he declined.

After the appointments were completed, Yee wrote in the *Houston Chronicle* that, "It is important to note that despite the Asian American appointments made by former President Bush, he never made an offer to, nor had an Asian Pacific-American in his Cabinet."

In March 1993 Clinton asked Secretary of Commerce Ron Brown to study the effects of Clinton's economic policies on the economic problems of California. Yee was appointed Northern California liaison. Her job was to coordinate the interagency task force with business, community, and labor leaders in designing a plan to stimulate economic growth in the region. In May of 1993 she was appointed special assistant to the Secretary of Commerce and senior adviser on the Pacific Rim.

Yee is a founding member of the National Network Against Anti-Asian Violence. She is also founding member of the Conference on Asian Pacific American Leadership, an organization designed to encourage young Asian Americans to enter public service.

Sources:

Department of Commerce. "Melinda Yee." Official resume and press releases, 1994.

—Sketch by Douglas Wu

Laurence Yep
(1948–)
Writer

Laurence Yep is a multi-faceted writer. His best-known works include two children's books, *Dragonwings* and *Dragon's Gate,* both of which were named Newbery Honor books. His audiences include children and adults of all ages. Although he is best known as a science fiction writer, he doesn't limit himself to one genre. He has written mythology and historical fiction, picture books and short stories, novellas as well as full-length novels. And, in the last ten years, Yep has added play writing to his growing repertoire.

Born in San Francisco, California, on June 14, 1948, Laurence Yep was named by his then-ten-year-old brother who later admitted that, being unsure about gaining a sibling, he had named his younger brother after a saint who had died an especially brutal death.

A third-generation Chinese American, Yep lived in an apartment above his parents' grocery store in the Western Edition District, a predominantly black neighborhood of San Francisco. He rode the bus into Chinatown for school, he told Terry Hong in an interview. "Going back and forth between those two ghetto areas is why I got interested science fiction," he explained. "In the 1950s when I was growing up, there were no books on being Chinese American. And I couldn't identify with the standard children's books because in all of them, the kids lived in houses where the front door was always unlocked and they all had bikes. I didn't know anyone like that. I really liked science fiction because kids from the everyday world were taken to another world, and had to learn another language, another culture. Science fiction was about adapting and that's what I was doing every time I got off the bus traveling between my two worlds."

The Writer and the Academic

High school brought new changes to Yep's life. "That was the first time I was around so many whites," he recalled about the preparatory school run by Jesuits. "It was also in high school that I got involved with writing for the first time. I was going to be a chemist which is what my father wanted to be before he had to drop out of college during the Depression. In my senior year, I had an English teacher who told me that if I wanted an A in the course, I had to get something accepted by a national magazine. So I started sending in stories, and started getting rejections. The teacher eventually retracted the demand, but I had already gotten into the habit of sending in my stories."

At age eighteen, as a freshman at Marquette University in Milwaukee, Wisconsin, Yep had his first story accepted by *Worlds of If*, a science fiction magazine no longer in publication. "A few years later, the story was anthologized in *The World's Best Science Fiction of 1969*," said Yep. He did not last long away from California and quickly returned home. "I couldn't stand the winters out there," he chuckled. In 1970, Yep graduated from the University of California at Santa Cruz (UCSC) with a degree in literature. He continued to write and publish science fiction, both short stories and novellas, while pursuing his academic degree.

"A friend of mine had gone to work for Harper and Row [now HarperCollins] in the children's section and

Laurence Yep

asked me to write science fiction for children. So I did and my first novel, *Sweetwater*, was published in 1973. I didn't realize it at the time, but the aliens in the book are based on the bachelor society in Chinatown," explained Yep, referring to the large numbers of unmarried Chinese immigrant men who were unable to marry because miscegenation (intermarriage) was illegal and strict Chinese anti-immigration laws barred Chinese women from entering the United States. These Chinese men, these "aliens," were therefore forced into lives of lonely bachelorhood.

Yep would also realize later that as he wrote his first-person narratives about strangers and aliens from a faraway world facing a totally foreign culture, he was actually exploring his own feelings of being caught between his two worlds, China and America. "I look at the stories that I published during those years and they're all about either alienated heroes or science fiction aliens. That sense of isolation and not belonging is still predominant in my writing today—in stories about outsiders and survivors. And, I think that's a theme that really appeals to both children and adults today. For example, the very pace of technology in our society tends to alienate us from society and from one another."

As Yep continued his fiction writing, he earned his Ph.D. in English literature from the State University of New York at Buffalo. "Other English departments used to call it 'the Buffalo zoo' because any new theory of literature was on display there," Yep recalled with a laugh. Not surprisingly, his dissertation topic also explored the alienated, isolated hero—*Psycholinguistic Strategies of William Faulkner's Early Heroes* was Yep's academic version of a familiar theme.

In the same year that Yep finished his doctorate, he published *Dragonwings*. The 1975 young adult novel told the story of an actual Chinese American aviator who built and flew a flying machine in 1909. *Dragonwings* enjoyed wide success; in addition to being chosen a 1976 Newbery Honor Book, it received numerous awards, including the 1976 IRA Children's Book Award, Notable Children's Books of 1971–1975, the Best of Children's books for 1966–1978, and the 1976 Carter G. Woodson Award. In promotional material for *Dragonwings*, a 1975 review from the *New York Times Book Review* is quoted: "[*Dragonwings* is] an exquisitely written poem of praise to the Chinese American people, it is a triumph."

Choosing the Writer

From Buffalo, Yep returned to California with the intention of teaching. However, due to a broad cut in state educational funds, teaching jobs became extremely scarce. "So I decided to concentrate on writing," he said. With years of academic literary training behind him, Yep returned to basic storytelling skills in his writing. "Instead of just telling the story, I had been taught to be very aware of the act of storywriting . . . layers of narrative, etc. It took me awhile to get back to just basic storytelling."

Although Yep often writes of alien worlds and futuristic landscapes, he ironically draws much of his material from his own experiences. The impetus for writing a work like *Sweetwater*, about the first colonists sent from Earth to the star Harmony, is the same for such historical works as *Dragon's Gate*, a story of immigration and the construction of the transcontinental railroad during the mid-1800s. "When I write a Chinese piece that I haven't completely explored, I begin by first writing science fiction. I use the science fiction as testing and experimenting ground to explore the psychology and dynamics of a potential subject before I actually write it," Yep explained.

Yep's own family stories, too, are a special source of inspiration for his writing. "My father never talked about his own growing up, so I grew up with the stories my mother and grandmother shared with me about West Virginia. Those stories were so close to me, that I consider West Virginia, not necessarily China, my homeland. My mother's family was, for some unknown reason, completely accepted there. I heard stories about searching for Indian arrowheads in the creek, about sledding in the winter, and about how my grandmother's apple pies were always the first to sell out at the church socials." Those inherited memories were memorialized in Yep's 1991 novel, *The Star Fisher*.

In addition to his family's memories, Yep has also relied on his Chinese heritage for such works as the 1989 award-winning *The Rainbow People*, which features twenty folk tales told by Chinese immigrants and retold by Yep. Two years later, he followed the work with *Tongues of Jade*, which contains an additional seventeen tales.

Yep also uses his writing to preserve and celebrate Asian American literary traditions. In 1993, he edited and published the award-winning *American Dragons*, a compilation of stories, poems and essays by twenty-five noted Asian American authors, including Maxine Hong Kingston, Toshio Mori, and Jeanne Wakatsuki Houston.

The Writer as Teacher

As Yep continued to publish and grow as an author, he eventually began to teach creative writing, first as a part-time instructor at San Francisco Bay Area junior colleges and later at the University of California at Berkeley. "Writing is definitely a craft that you can teach someone," insisted Yep. "It's like building a well-made cabinet. I saw a hunger in many students who were going to be computer programmers and physicists and scientists—a real hunger to express themselves. That's the part of teaching that I enjoy most. I especially enjoy the interaction—arguing with students who are so passionate about things, for whom everything is so black and white."

Ten years ago, due to time restraints, Yep stopped teaching when he began writing plays. "I was part of a play writing experiment which brought together three science fiction writers and three playwrights to create a science fiction stage work that did not require special effects. I was one of the science fiction writers," he recalled. "Writing for the theatre was a real revelation to me. I can't watch someone reading my books, but I can watch an audience watching my plays."

One of Yep's most successful play writing endeavors was the adaptation of his novel, *Dragonwings*, for the stage. A collaborative effort between Yep and Asian American director Phyllis S.K. Look, *Dragonwings* was produced in such noteworthy venues as New York's Lincoln Center and Washington, D.C.'s Kennedy Center. "It was most interesting to meet a certain group of actors who ended up doing about three hundred performances of the show. They knew the characters much better than even I did. Toward the end of rehearsals, the actors even began to talk about the characters as 'I,' as if all the lines between their real selves and their characters had blurred and even disappeared."

Currently, Yep is at work on a number of projects, including two children's works, *Dream Soul* and *Thief of Hearts*, both sequels to *The Star Fisher* and *Child of the Owl*, respectively. He is also at work on picture books based on

Shirley Young

Chinese folk tales, as well as an adult novel derived from one of his one-act plays, *Fairy Bones.* "This one's an ongoing project," he added specifically. "It's a real labor of love. It might be another twenty years before I actually finished this one."

Amidst writing the seemingly endless short stories, novels, and plays about real and imagined people, places, and events, Yep professes that he does not have a preference for a certain kind of writing. "Every one of the different styles brings new interesting challenges," he said and paused, before continuing, "I think doing plays, though, is the most challenging because by now, I know whether a written story is good or not by the time I've finished writing it. But with a play, I don't know until I've actually gone into the theatre with the actors and heard the lines. And it's a strange sensation sharing my fantasy with a dozen others."

Sources:

HarperCollins, promotional material for *Dragonwings,* April 1994.

Yep, Lawrence, telephone interview with Terry Hong, August 1, 1994.

—*Sketch by Terry Hong*

Shirley Young
(1935–)
Businessperson

Shirley Young is the vice-president for consumer market development with General Motors Corporation, a post she has held since June 1, 1988. General Motors (GM) hired Young in hopes that her expertise as a strategic marketing planner would help regain its share of the domestic auto market, which had been sliding throughout the 1980s as the giant automaker retooled and reshaped its management to more effectively compete with the burgeoning import market. Prior to her work at GM, Young worked for more than twenty-five years at the New York-based Grey Advertising, where she had held a variety of positions, including executive vice-president and a member of the Agency Policy Council, before being named president of Grey Strategic Marketing in 1983.

Shirley Young was born in Shanghai, China, on May 25, 1935. Her father was a career diplomat with the Nationalist Chinese government then in power. This was a tumultuous time for China. Japan had been occupying Manchuria for some time and was fighting the Chinese government for control of the huge country. In 1942 her father was stationed in the Philippines, a country Japan had also invaded, and as a representative of the government of China, Young's father was executed by the Japanese. Following the war, Young and the remainder of her family fled to the United States where she has lived ever since.

Young was educated at Wellesley College in Massachusetts, from which she graduated in 1955 with a bachelor's degree in economics. After graduation, her first job was as a project director with the Alfred Politz Research Organization, where she worked for three years before joining the Hudson Paper Corporation as a market research manager. In 1959, she was hired as a researcher by the prestigious Madison Avenue agency, Grey Advertising.

It was in her first position at Grey that she helped pioneer what is referred to in the advertising field as attitudinal studies. As described in a *Business Week* profile of Young, "her method, Market Target Buying Incentive Studies, helps packaged goods companies such as Proctor & Gamble Company and General Foods Corporation understand how consumers go from thinking about a product to actually buying it." Young continued her market research at Grey, assuming various marketing positions before being named executive vice-president. In 1983 she became president of Grey Strategic Marketing; five years later she was elevated to chairperson.

A GM Relationship is Born

Young began working with General Motors in 1983 on a consulting basis. One of her first accomplishments was the initiation of a roadside assistance program and a toll-free hotline for Cadillac owners, two programs meant to restore the air of exclusivity to Cadillac buyers as the historic quality of the cars diminished along with their size and distinctiveness of design. In 1988 Young was hired full-time by GM chairman Roger Smith. Since then Young has concentrated her efforts on enhancing the giant company's responsiveness to consumers, an acknowledged flaw in the past.

In 1990 Young initiated a marketing campaign with the tagline "Putting Quality on the Road," her first corporation-wide campaign, and it was a risky one. As *Business Week* said, "The new ads have an unmistakable implication: That for years GM's cars fell short of its customers' expectations." In addition to convincing consumers that GM was back from the crisis days of the late 1970s and early 1980s when by anyone's standards the entire American auto industry fell far behind its foreign competitors, Young's campaign was meant to reinvigorate the GM workforce. She told *Business Week*, "A lot of this job is what I call persistent evangelism."

Another project of Young's at GM has been to establish distinctiveness among the automaker's five divisions, working less on selling than on creating brand recognition and loyalty with consumers, Young's specialty. The marketing image she laid out for each of the divisions, as reported in *Business Week*, attempts to lock in the mind of the car-buying consumer specific images or ideas with each of the division's names. A Buick, for example, is the "Premium American motorcar": a Cadillac, "The standard of luxury worldwide"; a Chevrolet, "More than the customer expects"; an Oldsmobile, "Innovative technology"; and Pontiac, "Performance-oriented [automobiles] for young people."

Corporate and Community Leadership

Young has earned a reputation at GM as a furious and demanding worker. Although she has a powerful position, she works out of a fairly small and simple office a few doors from that of the chairman and employs only one assistant. In addition to her work at GM, Young sits on the board of directors of Bell Atlantic and the Promus Companies. She also served for twelve years as a consultant director for the Dayton Hudson Corporation and in 1980 served as a vice-chairman of the nominating committee for the New York Stock Exchange.

Young is also involved in several community service and cultural organizations. She is chairman of the Committee of 100, a national Chinese American leadership resource and is a founding member of the Committee of 200, an international organization of leading businesswomen. She also serves on the national board of directors of Junior Achievement and is trustee of Wellesley College and

member of the board of directors of the associates of the Harvard Business School, Wellesley's brother school. She was awarded an honorary doctorate of letters from Russell Sage College and in 1986 was given the Wellesley College Alumna Achievement Award.

Sources:

Periodicals

Lander, Mark. "Shirley Young: Pushing GM's Humble Pie Strategy." *Business Week,* June 11, 1990, pp. 52–53.

Other

General Motors. "Shirley Young." Press release, resume. Detroit, Michigan.

—Sketch by Jim Henry

Connie Young Yu
(1941–)
Writer

"**O**ne of the best introductions I have been given was at a meeting at the Chinese Historical Society. The person said, 'Connie only writes for a purpose,'" explained Connie Young Yu to Terry Hong. "Boy, did he get that right. I write when I feel there is a cause. . . . And sometimes I feel guilty because writers are always supposed to keep writing, . . . but unless I feel the need, the commitment, it doesn't happen."

The author of countless articles and two books *(Profiles in Excellence: Peninsula Chinese Americans* and *Chinatown San Jose, U.S.A.)* that focus predominantly on Chinese Americans, Yu has established herself as a writer with a historical cause. "When I started writing," she continued, "it was for a purpose. I needed to establish Chinese America, to put our history back in its place in American history." Through articles, essays, lectures, and community activities, Yu has devoted her energies for more than a quarter of a century in rediscovering a history of Chinese and Asian America that has, for the most part, been forgotten, overlooked, and even hidden.

Born on June 19, 1941, in Los Angeles, California, Connie Young Yu lived in nearby Whittier for the first six years of her life. When she was six months old, her father left the family to fight in World War II for three and a half years. "Even though I was too young to remember my father's actual leaving, I still have a very strong sense of

World War II. I was about four when he came back. During the time he was gone, I always felt a sense of patriotism, of pride in being American," she recalled.

In 1947, Yu's family moved to San Francisco's Chinatown where her father became a soy sauce manufacturer. "Most of the people who lived in Chinatown were involved professionally with Chinatown," she explained. The family later moved to the Richmond district of San Francisco: "We were one of the first Chinese families there and we were the very first on our block. There was lots of prejudice in those days and because of the discrimination, my father had to have an army buddy buy our house and then he bought it from the friend. It was that way for a lot of Chinese American families," Yu remembered.

The Extended Family

Yu grew up surrounded by Chinese Americans of various generations. In addition to grandparents who lived with the family for many years, the Young house also provided a home base for many older Chinese American bachelors who did not have families of their own as a direct result of the limits against Chinese immigration into the United States. "So many old men were always coming to the house," explained Yu. "I was always aware of the several generations and I felt very fortunate to have experienced that. . . . I thought that's the way it was supposed to be, to always have all those generations living together."

Through the influence of Yu's grandparents and the "adopted" old-timers, Yu grew up "with a very strong sense of being Chinese." Both her grandparents and parents were active in the Chinatown community's reform movements of the 1940s and 1950s, especially in improving the quality of life in Chinatown and the creation of low-cost housing. "My father and mother were always going to different kinds of meetings in Chinatown," she recalled.

Yu attended public schools in San Francisco, then enrolled at Mills College in 1959. During her senior year in a seminar about Mark Twain, she was encouraged by the professor to write the final paper on Mark Twain and his dealings with the Chinese. "Very few people were writing about Chinese Americans in 1963," Yu recalled. "I didn't know if I would find much material. I've learned since then that there are a lot of available sources about the Chinese on the West Coast. . . . The hard part is to know where to look. You really have to just ask around."

After graduating with a degree in English, Yu married Dr. John Kou-Ping Yu (currently chief of oncology at Kaiser Permanente in Santa Clara, California) almost immediately out of college, spent three years in New York City, and had three children close together. "I was so busy raising children that I had no time to write," she said. When Yu returned in 1967 to the San Francisco Bay area with her growing family, she became more involved in researching Chinese American history. "In California, there is more interest in Chinese America. There was a

Connie Young Yu

historical society where I could start my work," she explained. Yu began to write short articles for Asian American publications and eventually received local recognition when her full-page article, "The Unsung Heroes of the Golden Spikes," appeared in the May 10, 1969 Sunday edition of the *San Francisco Examiner*. The focus of the article was about the Chinese railroad workers, a subject familiar to Yu because her own great-grandfather had worked on the transcontinental railroad. Yu had found her niche giving new voice to the Chinese American history that had too long been omitted from America's history books. "That's when it all started," Yu recalled. "That's how I became a historical writer. I never had any formal training. It was all my own work."

Activism

During the 1960s and 1970s, Yu became heavily involved with the anti-war movement, the social change movement, and the ethnic studies movement. "All the movements were related. If you belonged to one, you would eventually meet the people involved with the others," she remarked. In 1973, Yu helped found Asian Americans for Community Involvement (AACI), an organization whose purpose was "to make social changes and social justices for Asian Pacific Americans a reality." From a group of twelve community leaders, AACI today has a staff of more than fifty professionals, a budget of almost $5 million and a 100,000-square foot facility in San Jose. In October 1993, in celebration of AACI's Twentieth anniversary, the group honored Yu, together with Congressman Norman Mineta (a Democrat from California), with the Freedom Award.

Yu did not limit her community activism to only Chinese American causes, but joined peace groups and women's groups as well. "I got very side tracked from writing with my activism for awhile," she recalled. It was that activism, however, that fueled Yu's writing. "From the activism, I saw the need for Asian American resources, the need to write about Asian American history and issues." From her foundation of Chinese American historical works, Yu began to branch out to write about Japanese Americans interned during World War II, about new waves of Vietnamese refugees, and the latest issues of Asian immigration into the United States. "It's not a contest of who suffered more," Yu remarked. "What is most important is that the injustices, travails, and hardships experienced by all Asian Americans helped define who we are today. That's our history, the history that defines us as America and Americans. That history is what helps us define ourselves."

In order to preserve Chinese American history, Yu has written two books. Published in 1986 by the Stanford Area Chinese Club, is *Profiles in Excellence: Peninsula Chinese Americans,* a collection of biographies of thirty-seven notable Chinese Americans who are role models for the Asian American community. "When I was writing these short biographies, I learned a lot from each of these people about their direct experiences with immigration laws, discrimination, etc.," Yu said. Her second book, *Chinatown San Jose, U.S.A.,* published in 1991, was commissioned by the San Jose Historical Museum Association to tell the story of a little-remembered Chinatown that was once located in San Jose, California. "My father was born in San Jose's Chinatown . . . and my grandfather was a Chinatown shopkeeper, so I heard many stories when I was growing up," said Yu. Following the 1887 arson fire that drove Chinese Americans away from the original San Jose Chinatown, a new Chinatown was established on a plot of land leased from a John Heinlen, a German American willing to allow Chinese Americans to settle on his land. The area came to be known as Heinlenville and would remain San Jose's Chinatown until the 1930s. The first structure to be built on the site was the Ng Shing Gung Temple which was recently restored and today houses the San Jose Historical Museum. Understandably, Yu feels a unique affinity with the museum: "So many of the artifacts in the museum are from my family, especially from my grandparents and parents," she explained.

The Sporting Life

In addition to Yu's growing historical credits, she is also recognized as a teacher, not only of Chinese American history, but of the art of fencing. Yu recalled: "I started fencing after the antiwar movement. It was a time to do some deep thinking, to regroup. I decided I needed exercise, tried fencing and really liked it. I got my children inter-

ested in it and they proved to be very good at it, with all three of them going on to national championships. So I got more involved, did some competing myself and now I teach several days a week. . . . Fencing is more than just a sport. It's really an attitude. I think sports can teach you a lot about life."

For four years, Yu taught fencing in San Francisco's Chinatown. "It was very exciting to go into the Chinatown 'Y' each week and teach." Currently, Yu is teaching locally in San Jose and Palo Alto and manages The Fencing Center at San Jose as a volunteer. "That's my community service."

While Yu continues to write, she admitted, "It's the fencing that keeps me in contact with people. Writing can be so isolating." Although she is better known as a historical writer, Yu has also returned to her first writing interest—fiction. In addition to short pieces and poetry, Yu has two works in progress: one, a historical novel about four generations of Chinese Americans, and the other a coming-of-age novel about a young ethnic-Chinese girl originally from Vietnam now living in the United States. She admits that writing fiction is very different from writing historical pieces: "With research, you've found something that adds to the pool of resources and people always need that. You always know that someone will publish that research, whether it's a museum or a community group. Writing about history is a community service, whereas writing fiction is a money-making thing. . . . Writing about history fills a need; with fiction, it's a business and . . . often it's difficult to get published." In spite of any difficulties Yu might be facing, she remains determined to keep writing both historical articles as well as fiction. "In writing fiction," she continued, "I hope that I can convey a sense of humanity in a non-dogmatic way."

History, however, remains Yu's focus for writing. "It's very, very exciting how, in the span of just three decades, the concept of an Asian American consciousness has gone from zero to the American lexicon. That shows how history changes. People need to realize and understand what is happening. That's why history is so important," she emphasized.

Sources:

Periodicals

Lee, Bobbie. "Mighty with Both the Pen and the Sword." *AsianWeek,* September 24, 1993, p. 17.

———. "Mineta and Connie Young Yu Honored with Freedom Award." *AsianWeek,* October 22, 1993.

Other

Yu, Connie Young, telephone interview with Terry Hong, April 25, 1994.

—Sketch by Terry Hong

Diane C. Yu
(1951–)
Attorney

Diane Yu should be used to "firsts" by now. In 1983, at the age of thirty-one, Yu was the first minority, the first woman, and youngest person ever to be appointed superior court commissioner for the Alameda County Superior Court in Oakland, California. Three years later, she was the first White House fellow ever appointed from the judicial branch of government to serve as special assistant to the U.S. trade representative. And in 1987, at age thirty-six, she was the first minority, woman, and youngest person ever appointed as general counsel of the State Bar of California. In addition to being named one of Ten Outstanding Young Women of America in 1985 for professional achievement and community service, Yu was also featured as one of Twenty Young Lawyers Whose Work Makes a Difference by *Barrister*, a publication of the American Bar Association's Young Lawyers Division in 1986. Her name and career are cited in *Who's Who in American Law, Who's Who of American Women, Who's Who in the West, Who's Who in California,* and the *International Directory of Distinguished Leadership.* She also argued and won a case in the U.S. Supreme Court in 1989.

Despite the success of her relatively short but outstanding career in law, Yu is surprisingly self-effacing and humble. She casually tosses off humorous anecdotes as endnotes to the story of each accomplishment, like the time when Yu's mother came to Alameda County Superior Court to watch her daughter, the youngest superior court commissioner ever appointed in the state of California. Observing her mother's serious, almost grim expression during the proceedings, Yu asked her during the recess what was wrong. "You're the most indecisive of my daughters, and they pay you to make decisions!" she exclaimed, according to an article published in the *California Lawyer.*

Yu credits her parents as her primary role models. Both her father, now deceased, and her mother were medical doctors born and raised in China. They immigrated to the United States in the 1940s when the Communists came to power. Yu was born December 25, 1951, and grew up in Rochester, New York, where she lived until she left for college. Her father was a cardiologist and the first minority and foreign-born person to ever serve as president of the American Heart Association. Her mother was also a pioneer—a woman pediatrician in the 1950s, a time when two-career families and women professionals were the exception rather than the rule. Since the Yus had no extended family in the States because all their relatives (except for one uncle) had remained in China, they had

Diane C. Yu

to rely on each other for support and entertainment. They took trips throughout the northeastern United States and Canada. Growing up the second-oldest of four daughters, Yu told *Notable Asian Americans* she remembers a "fair share of sibling rivalry," but credits it as "good practice for dealing with constant competition and limited resources in later life." Her sisters' intelligence and talent set high standards for her, but most importantly they were good sounding boards and critics—people on whom she could count "for honest opinions, solicited or not," she added.

Throughout her life, Yu had strong and deep mentoring relationships with teachers, bosses, judges, and staffers which she believes gave her insight into different worlds and experiences and helped her to develop self-confidence and perspective, especially in the area of career choice. After spending her senior year at Oberlin College as an Asian studies major in the overseas program in Taiwan, Yu decided to extend her stay as an instructor in English at Tunghai University. In a quandary over future career choices, she wrote to five of her favorite professors to seek their opinions on a possible career. Four out of the five suggested law school, citing her interest in politics and policy issues and strong verbal abilities. What clinched the decision, she quipped, was her discovery that the LSAT (Law School Admission Test) had no math portion and her erroneous conviction that "lawyers didn't work as hard as doctors!" In 1977, she received her law degree from Boalt Hall at the University of California at Berkeley.

Formative Experience in Eighth Grade

Professionals at the pinnacle of their careers might credit any number of people or experiences as having influenced their success. Yu humbly suggests that an eighth grade election did it for her. "I was elected president of the student council in eighth grade, and had the time of my life," Yu told *Notable Asian Americans*. "I found out that I had a flair for chairing meetings, setting up a plan of action, hearing all sides of various issues, learning how to deal with controversy in non-confrontational ways, collaborating with my peers and motivating them to accomplish all of our goals and objectives. To this day, the management and social skills I acquired through that experience are still in regular use."

Strongest among the core beliefs that have guided Yu both in her life and her career is her commitment to help others, especially those less fortunate. Since high school, she has given much time to what she describes as "good causes," serving on the board of directors of University YWCA, the advisory committee of the University of San Francisco Center for the Pacific Rim, the board of directors of the Chinese Cultural Foundation of San Francisco, the Commonwealth Club of California, the Ad Hoc Study Committee for Professional Education in Law at the University of California, the California Consortium to Prevent Child Abuse, the Attorney General's Asian/Pacific Advisory Committee and Commission on Racial, Ethnic, Religious and Minority Violence, and the San Francisco Regional Panel of the President's Commission on White House Fellowships.

Yu's pride in her Asian heritage has been a constant in her life. Although her ethnic consciousness as a child was limited to taking Chinese lessons, which she disliked because they were mandatory, and enjoying terrific Chinese food every day, because her father preferred it, Yu also encountered the downside of being a minority in America. "When I was growing up, I was constantly amazed how many people made decisions about others based on race or ethnicity," Yu explained to *Notable Asian Americans*. "I was very lucky, because bias and discrimination, while present in my childhood years in Rochester, were not day-to-day occurrences. Only when I got out in the world did I begin to experience the less benign side of being a minority in America. People would ask me where I was from, and shake their heads when I replied, 'Rochester' because they regarded me as a foreigner. Others would compliment me on my English, and then be astonished or upset to learn I was born and raised in the States. There were the taunting children who called me 'slant eyes,' 'Chink,' or 'Jap,' or 'Ching chong Chinaman.' I eventually got the message that at least some people did not welcome minorities of Asian extraction here."

Advocate for Women and Minorities

Since becoming a lawyer, Yu has continuously devoted a significant portion of her time toward efforts to eradicate bias and discrimination in the legal profession and judiciary, and to promote better relationships between different racial and cultural groups. As a member of the American Bar Association (ABA), she has served on numerous commissions and committees. Yu is the first Asian American woman to serve on the ABA commission on minorities, commission on women, and its accreditation committee.

"I think there's been a lot of progress for women and minorities," Yu added in a profile on her in *California Lawyer* magazine, but it still may be more difficult in some areas to feel we're accorded the same chances and opportunities. Over time, I would hope a person's success would depend on merit rather than gender or ethnic background."

Sources:

Periodicals

"Perry Mason, Mistaken Notion Help Carve Trail for State Bar's First Woman General Counsel-Diane Yu." State Bar Report: *California Lawyer,* April 1992.

Other

Yu, Diane C., Resume, 1994.
———, written interview with Helen Zia, June 17, 1994.

–Sketch by Nancy Moore

Eleanor Yu

(1959–)

Advertising executive, entrepreneur

Eleanor Yu is the founder and president of the San Francisco-based advertising agency Adland, the largest advertising agency in North America targeted to Asian Americans. She formed the agency in 1984 with an investment of $3,000; billings in 1993 exceeded $16 million. Yu is also the founder and publisher of *Asian Marketing Focus,* a newsmagazine covering the demographics of the Asian American community. Her agency also keeps the country's largest computer database on Asian American demographics.

Eleanor Yu was born in Hong Kong in 1959 to a British father and a Chinese mother. Her father is a barrister, an international businessman who sits on the boards of several of the world's largest corporations, and was a member of Britain's parliament. Her mother comes from a wealthy Hong Kong family. As a young girl, Eleanor liked ballet, but, as she told Lee Kerry in *Adweek,* "I enjoyed perform-ing and I enjoyed the limelight, but I knew my dad would never permit a daughter of his to be in show business. He was a barrister, as were others in my family. That trend, which continued with my brother, stopped with me."

At the age of eleven Eleanor was sent to England where she went to the Headington Aristocratic Ladies College in Oxford, a school for the children of members of parlia-ment and members of the diplomatic corps. From there she went to Oxford where she majored in philosophy, psy-chology, and economics, a liberal arts degree referred to in England as a PPE. After graduation, she wanted to live in the United States, but her parents were against it. As a compromise, she went to Canada and enrolled in the Uni-versity of Ottawa where she got a second undergraduate degree, this one in communications.

Introduction to Advertising

In 1979, Yu left Ottawa for New York City and a job in the renowned advertising agency of Ogilvy and Mather, which hired her into its trainee program. She described her time with Ogilvy and Mather for *Connections,* the alumni magazine of Golden Gate University: "I advanced from trainee to junior copywriter pretty fast. . . . They needed a writer who knew a bit of Chow Mein—and I hap-pened to be available." After three months with Ogilvy and Mather, her husband, Kenneth Yu, a telecommunica-tions expert with Bell Labs, was transferred to Philadel-phia.

In Philadelphia, Yu worked as an account executive trainee for the J. Walter Thompson Agency and took classes at the Wharton School of Business at the University of Pennsylvania. She worked her way up at J. Walter Thompson, becoming a very successful account executive, in charge of high-profile accounts, such as Burger King. After five years her husband was offered a position teach-ing at the University of California at Berkeley, and the Yus decided to give the Bay area a two-year trial.

Yu was offered several jobs in San Francisco, but, as she told Kerry: "The corporate environment wasn't suited to my personality. I didn't like conformity, I felt stifled. I guess I was more of an entrepreneur than a follower. I wanted to start an agency that would inspire creativity, one with a more relaxing atmosphere."

In 1984, Yu created just such an agency—Yu Interna-tional. Her first client was signed on her first day of busi-ness when Yu walked into a neighboring business called Techline, a furniture manufacturer and distributor in San Mateo, California, and sold them on a direct mail cam-paign. Techline grew considerably over time and they are still an account with Yu's company. After Techline, Yu International signed several retail accounts and a small family-owned company called Peking Handicrafts, importers of handicrafts from China. Yu helped Peking

Eleanor Yu

Handicrafts with their entire marketing strategy. The company grew dramatically and now owns a four-story building that covers an entire city block.

Tapping the Asian Market

In 1987, Yu moved her agency to Union Square in downtown San Francisco. She changed its name to Adland and opened an Asian American division. She had for some time been interested in what she perceived to be a fast-growing, virtually untouched market of consumers, many of whom were better off and better educated than their Anglo-American counterparts: the Asian Americans. Adland became the only full service agency with a division devoted solely to Asian American advertising. She devel-oped an expertise in reaching this vast segment of the American population and drew major clients who relied on her to help them avoid embarrassing advertising errors, such as picturing Japanese models in print ads tar-geted at Chinese, printing pictograms upside down, or translating slogans literally into meaningless gibberish. Adland has on staff copywriters who are fluent in the many different languages and dialects that comprise the Asian American community.

In the late eighties and early nineties, Adland expanded into an international agency with offices in Hong Kong, Sydney, and Toronto, with affiliate offices in London, Sin-gapore, and Tokyo, broadcast production facilities in Sacramento and Toronto, and a print shop in Hong Kong.

Its American client list includes American Express, Pacific Bell, Acura, DHL Worldwide, Ford, and many others.

Adland is set up much as Yu envisioned her agency would be when she first started thinking about it. She described it for *San Francisco Business Magazine* in March of 1994: "We are positioned for the 21st century as a virtual corporation. We have little hierarchy and a mission statement written by the staff. . . . There is no power structure within the [project] circles. Everyone defines the goals and is responsible for work in progress and completion of the project. They feel empowered. Our work environment is designed to keep the stress level down to encourage creativity."

Because of her renowned expertise in the field of ethnically targeted advertising, Yu frequently hosts seminars on the topic. She has received numerous awards and recognition for leadership including Outstanding Asian American Woman of the Year 1991, and Top Twenty-five Women and Minority Owned Businesses, 1989 to 1992. She is listed in *Who's Who in America* and has received a Marketplace Salute from ABC's business program "Marketplace" for her outstanding success as a women entrepreneur and visionary.

Becoming so successful has proven draining on Yu, and she now makes it a point to spend more time with her family than was possible when she was building her business up. She told *San Francisco Business Magazine*, "I work 35-1/2 hours a week, and I don't work weekends. I keep my mind clear of distractions, concentrating on what is at hand, so when I close the office door, I leave work behind me."

Sources:

Periodicals

Christensen, Pat. "Passion to Excel." *San Francisco Business Magazine*, March, 1994. p. 4.

Kerry, Lee. "A Young Lady with a Big Idea." *Adweek*, July 24, 1989.

Steinberg, David. "Yu Knows Who, and What." *Connections*, Fall 1992.

Other

Adland. "Biography: Eleanor N. Yu." Promotional packet. San Francisco, California, May 1994.

—Sketch by Jim Henry

Z

Teddy Zee
(1957–)
Entertainment executive

Teddy Zee is among the power elite in Hollywood, combining business acumen and creative instinct to produce winning entertainment products. In 1994 he was executive vice-president of movie production at Columbia Pictures, with projects such as *First Knight* starring Sean Connery and Richard Gere, and *Blankman* starring Damon Wayans and David Alan Grier underway. With major successes such as *Indecent Proposal* starring Robert Redford, Demi Moore, and Woody Harrelson and *My Girl* starring Macauley Culkin and Anna Chumsky, Zee has proven his ability to combine a keen business sense with a strong instinct for finding and shaping an idea that will capture the imagination (and admission dollars) of the movie-going public.

Teddy Zee was born May 15, 1957, in Liberty, New York, where his father, Charles A. Zee, was a restaurant worker at the well-known Catskills resort, Grossingers. With two older brothers and an older sister, Teddy was the youngest in the family. His father had immigrated to the United States from China in the 1940s and enlisted in the U.S. Navy after gaining experience in the merchant marine in China. After leaving the Navy, Zee's father worked in the vacation communities on the New Jersey shore and at the famous Algonquin in New York City as a busboy, and was eventually able to save enough money to send for Zee's mother, Chu Yue, and oldest brother, Richard, who had stayed behind in China. Two more children were born in New York City before the Zee family moved to Liberty for the more promising employment opportunity at Grossingers Hotel. Grossingers is one of the best-known and oldest of the resorts that loosely form what is referred to as the "borscht belt." These resorts were frequented by middle-class New Yorkers—many Jewish of Eastern European and Russian descent—and featured stand-up comedians and middle-of-the-road singers.

"It was very strange growing up in Liberty. I was the all-American boy who fit in everywhere, but didn't fit in anywhere—not even at home, because Chinese was spoken

Teddy Zee

there. In fact, as I grew older a real language barrier developed between my mother and me. My Chinese deteriorated because I only spoke it at home, and when I communicated at home, everything had to be spelled out very carefully, to be sure we all understood," Zee told Susan Gall. "We didn't belong to a church, we weren't part of the community except through the school."

Expanding Horizons

The Zee family was poor, but all four children wanted to go to college, so the whole family worked and saved for college educations. As soon as Teddy was old enough to work, he joined the staff at Grossingers as a bellhop. The Hotel and Restaurant Workers and Bartenders Union, to which Zee's father belonged, offered a college scholarship to a student planning to study labor relations. Zee was selected from all the applicants nationwide, and in 1975, entered Cornell University on a full scholarship to study industrial and labor relations. "Before I went to Cornell, I had never traveled—never been south of the Jersey Shore or west of Buffalo, New York. While I was at Cornell, I felt my horizons expanding," Zee recounted.

After college graduation in 1979, Zee took a position as management associate with NBC-TV in New York. The management associates spent about six months rotating through various departments, and Zee's experience included preparation for broadcast of the 1980 Summer Olympic Games from Moscow, then the capital of the Soviet Union. In the end, the United States, in a decision by President Jimmy Carter, led a boycott of the Olympic Games to protest the Soviet Union's invasion of Afghanistan in late 1979, so the planned broadcast by NBC never developed.

Zee then was transferred to NBC's Los Angeles base of operations in Burbank, California. He became director of compensation there and also directed NBC's experiment with "teletext," a technology that would broadcast periodicals and newspapers to homes via television. In the early 1980s, the concept of teletext was viewed as very futuristic—but, in fact, the widespread application of personal computers has simply changed the viewing screen from television to computer monitor. The experiment Zee led in the 1980s is reality in the 1990s in a modified form.

Feeling ready for a career change and challenge, Zee applied to the Harvard Business School and was accepted. After completing his master's of business administration, Zee moved back to Los Angeles hoping to land a job with a motion picture production company. After an unsuccessful job search, Zee became a management consultant with Touche Ross and "was miserable." He then stepped up his efforts to land a job in the entertainment industry, and had interviews at Disney and Paramount. Paramount gave Zee the opportunity he was seeking. In 1985, Dawn Steel, the highest ranking woman in Hollywood at the time, was intrigued by Zee's unique combination of attributes. "She liked my 'borscht belt' background, and she gave me a shot," Zee related. He started as a creative executive at Paramount, advancing in five years to become senior vice-president for production. In 1990, he left Paramount for Columbia Pictures, where he is executive vice-president for production.

When asked what it was like to make such a dramatic career change—from management consultant to movie mogul—Zee replied, "We should all do what we love doing. I didn't want to do what was expected of me: I wanted work to meet *my* expectations. I didn't want to deal with life and death situations—I wanted to bring joy and happiness—to help people enjoy themselves."

Zee is as devoted to his family as he is passionate about his work. His wife, Elizabeth, was a classmate at the Harvard Business School. They were married in 1986, and have two daughters.

"Growing up Asian American, I always felt special—which is a nice way of saying I always felt different. It made me aware of who I was, and how I was different from others. I see this as an advantage, not a disadvantage."

Sources:

Periodicals

"Power Brokers," *A. Magazine,* vol. 2., no. 3, December 15, 1993, p. 25–34.

Other

Zee, Teddy, telephone interview with Susan Gall, July 21, 1994.

—Sketch by Susan Gall

Hoyt Zia
(1953–)
Attorney

When Hoyt Zia was in junior high, he was rounded up with the other Asian American males in the school and placed in a lineup after a white student reported that an "Oriental-looking" boy had stolen something from him. But instead of becoming embittered by this and other early encounters with racism, Zia transformed his anger into a force for improving the lot of other Asian Americans. Ultimately, it was the fuel that helped create the National Asian Pacific American Bar Association, the first national organization for Asian American attorneys.

"The experiences that served to motivate me when I was young and which have lasted even until now are negative ones involving racism and prejudice that I encountered growing up," Zia told *Notable Asian Americans.* "The feelings of inferiority and self-hate from these experiences engendered and motivated me to overcome them."

Hoyt Zia was born in Newark, New Jersey, on April 24, 1953. When he was five years old, the family moved to the planned suburban community of Levittown (now Willingboro), one of the first one hundred families to buy a house in one of the country's earliest postwar subdivisions. It was there that he grew up, attending the same school system from kindergarten through high school.

But for Zia, who was in one of the few Asian families in the subdivision, the years growing up in that community were no suburban idyll. "There was discrimination and prejudice and racial slurs . . . enough to make me not like what I was," he told the *San Francisco Banner Daily Journal* in 1988.

Family Support

He found support in his close-knit family. Zia's father, a Chinese scholar who had settled in the United States after serving as a diplomat representing the Nationalist government of Taiwan, stressed the importance of education. Zia said he also drew strength from his older brother, Henry, and his older sister Helen, who guided him through college and helped him to understand his identity as an Asian American. Zia also turned to tae kwon do (karate), in which he eventually earned a black belt while in high school, as a source of self-knowledge and self-confidence. "Being an Asian American has probably been the greatest influence in my life," he told *Notable Asian Americans*.

After graduating from high school, Zia studied at Dartmouth College, where he majored in Asian studies. While in school, Zia became active in protests against the Vietnam War, and was even arrested for blocking the entrance to the federal government's Cold Region Research Lab, which was targeted by antiwar activists because it conducted military research.

He spent his junior year studying in Hong Kong and Taiwan. While he was in Taiwan, Zia ran out of money and his siblings, who had little cash themselves and needed funds for their own schooling, each sent him money so he could stay longer. "It's difficult to describe the importance of my siblings to me," he told *Notable Asian Americans*. "But their real support goes well beyond that, from sharing their experiences in life and sharing the experience of growing up in a very strict Chinese household."

As he was preparing to graduate from college, a friend of his older brother suggested to Zia that he join the military. "I didn't know anything about the military," he said in an interview with the *Banner*. "But the idea of learning leadership, the physical challenge, and the chance for overseas duty intrigued me." When he first applied to the Marines he was questioned about his arrest for protesting the war, but he was accepted nevertheless. For three years he served as a marine officer posted in Okinawa and then was sent to the California desert at Twenty Nine Palms. Zia later said it was the military that gave him direction.

Legal Activism

After serving in the Marines, Zia decided to study law, the arena through which he thought he could best contribute to society. He was accepted into law school at the University of California at Los Angeles (UCLA). In his freshman year he took honors in a moot court competition and was later a member of the school's Jessup International Law Moot Court Competition Team. When he graduated from UCLA in 1981, he moved north and settled in the Bay Area, becoming a litigation associate for the San Francisco law firm of Bronson, Bronson & McKinnon.

He quickly gained a reputation as a doer. He was active in various Asian American organizations and pushed the American Bar Association to increase minority influence in the legal profession. He was president of the Asian Pacific Bar of California, an Asian American lawyer's group, and was also a board member and president of the Asian American Bar Association of the Greater Bay Area, chair of the state bar's ethnic minority relations committee, and a member of the board of managers of the San Francisco Chinatown Youth Center. "He was always trying to organize things," said fellow Asian American attorney Dale Minami. "I remember when he first came out from New Jersey, he was trying to organize an ice hockey team. We West Coast Asians looked at this guy like he was crazy."

After two years at Bronson and a short stint at another San Francisco firm, Zia decided he didn't want to specialize in litigation and discovered he was more interested in counseling people or businesses about the law. He was hired by Motorola Corporation in 1984 to join its legal department. He rose steadily through the corporate ranks to later head the company's legal staff in the Bay Area.

In 1989, Zia was one of California's representatives at the American Bar Association Convention in Honolulu. That year also saw the formation of the National Asian Pacific American Bar Association, a goal that Asian American attorneys had been pursuing for a decade. Zia, who was instrumental in the creation of the organization, became its first president. "It took someone with the stature and vision of Hoyt to make this dream a reality," said Michael G.W. Lee, a fellow attorney, in a 1989 interview with the *San Francisco Banner Daily Journal.* "He is an unusual blend of sensitivity, hard work, and an impossible sense of humor."

After the group's first convention, Zia said that the creation of a national organization of Asian American attorneys would offer a way to press for change on legal issues of interest to the Asian American community. It also offered another kind of support. "Willingboro seems like a million miles away," Zia said in the 1989 *Banner* article. "But in a sense, what we are doing here is coming full circle, going back to places like Willingboro to find Asian and Pacific American attorneys who are working in isolation, and showing them that they are not the only ones."

Zia is married to Leigh-Ann Miyasato, who is also an attorney. The couple has two children, Emily and Rory. In 1991, they moved to Hawaii, Miyasato's home state, so the children could grow up in an extended family. There Zia became the vice-president and associate general counsel for Amfac/JMB Hawaii.

"Serving the Asian American community has been my reason for being and the driving force behind my achieving what success I have achieved," Zia said. "I want to be part of changing the environment for Asians so that there are no more hate crime victims like Vincent Chin, and so that my kids can seek positive motivation from being who they are to propel them forward, instead of having to overcome negative motivating factors like I did."

Sources:

Periodicals

Hall-Michael J. "Asian-American Leader Varied His Experiences on Way to Law." *San Francisco Banner Daily Journal,* August 25, 1988.

———. "Zia's Role as Leader Brings Him Full Circle." *San Franscisco Banner Daily Journal,* November 14, 1989.

Other

Zia, Hoyt. Biographical statement and resume supplied by Zia, May 9, 1994.

———, written interview with Helen Zia, May 9, 1994.

–Sketch by Ferdinand deLeon

Subject Index